ATLAS OF HAWAI'I

ATLAS
OF HAWAI'I

THIRD EDITION

DEPARTMENT OF GEOGRAPHY, UNIVERSITY OF HAWAI'I AT HILO

EDITED BY SONIA P. JUVIK AND JAMES O. JUVIK

CHIEF CARTOGRAPHER THOMAS R. PARADISE

 UNIVERSITY OF HAWAI'I PRESS, HONOLULU

Copyright © 1973, 1983, 1998 University of Hawaiʻi Press

All rights reserved

Printed in China

02 01 00 99 98   5 4 3 2 1

Library of Congress Cataloging-in-Publication Data

University of Hawaiʻi at Hilo. Dept. of Geography.

    Atlas of Hawaiʻi / Department of Geography, University of Hawaiʻi,
at Hilo; edited by Sonia P. Juvik and James O. Juvik; chief cartographer,
Thomas R. Paradise. — 3d ed.

       p.   cm.

    Includes bibliographical references and index.

    Contents: Reference maps—The physical environment—The biotic
environment—The cultural environment—The social environment.

    ISBN 0–8248–1745–1.—ISBN 0–8248–2125–4 (pbk.)

    1. Hawaii—Maps.   I. Juvik, Sonia P.   II. Juvik, James O.
III. Paradise, Thomas R. IV. Title.

    G1534.20 .U51998   <G&M>

      912ʹ.969—DC21   97–49817

                                      CIP

                                 MAPS

The Cover: The 3-D image depicts the main Hawaiian Islands viewed from above
at a point in the southeast. The image was constructed by converting the U.S
Geological Survey 1:250,000 scale DEM (Digital Elevation Models) database into
a greyscale map that was then rendered in KPT Bryce software on a Macintosh
computer. The final image was edited and enhanced in Adobe Photoshop. The
vertical exaggeration is 2.5 times the horizontal scale to show prominently the
landforms of the islands.

Book design by Ken Miyamoto

Co-editor and Project Director: Sonia P. Juvik,
    Professor of Geography, University of Hawaiʻi at Hilo

Co-editor and Deputy Project Director: James O. Juvik,
    Professor of Geography, University of Hawaiʻi at Hilo

Chief Cartographer: Thomas R. Paradise,
    Assistant Professor, Department of Geography, University of Hawaiʻi at Hilo

ATLAS STAFF

Project Coordinator: Noreen M. Parks

Cartographer/Geographic Information Systems Specialist: Julsun Pacheco

Cartographer Assistants: Drew Kapp, MaryAnne Maigret

Research/Technical Assistants: Nancy Elmer, Raynell Uchida, Catherine Tignac

UNIVERSITY OF HAWAIʻI PRESS ATLAS TEAM

Director: William H. Hamilton

Computer Specialist: Wanda T. China

Designer: Kenneth A. Miyamoto

Design Assistant: Jennifer R. O. Lum

Editor: Keith K. Leber

Manufacturing Manager: Paul D. Herr

Design and Production Manager: JoAnn M. Tenorio

CONTRIBUTING AUTHORS

Isabella A. Abbott
Department of Botany, University of Hawai'i at Mānoa

George H. Balazs
National Marine Fisheries Service, Southwest Fisheries Center,
Honolulu Laboratory

Glenn Bauer
Division of Water Resource Management, Department of Land and
Natural Resources, State of Hawai'i, Honolulu

Andrea Gill Beck
Hawai'i Energy Extension Service, Department of Business, Economic
Development and Tourism, State of Hawai'i, Hilo

David Bess
College of Business Administration, University of Hawai'i at Mānoa

Paul H. Brewbaker
Bank of Hawai'i, Honolulu

Leon Bruno
Formerly Lyman House Memorial Museum, Hilo

Nina Buchanan
Department of Education, University of Hawai'i at Hilo

David L. Callies
The William S. Richardson School of Law, University of Hawai'i
at Mānoa

Ronald Cannarella
Department of Land and Natural Resources, State of Hawai'i, Honolulu

Hampton L. Carson
Department of Genetics and Molecular Biology, University of Hawai'i
at Mānoa

A. Didrick Castberg
Department of Political Science, University of Hawai'i at Mānoa

David A. Clague
Monterey Bay Aquarium Research Institute, Moss Landing, California

Sheila Conant
Department of Zoology, University of Hawai'i at Mānoa

John S. Corbin
Aquaculture Program, Department of Land and Natural Resources,
State of Hawai'i, Honolulu

George Curtis
Department of Natural Sciences, University of Hawai'i at Hilo

Thom Curtis
Department of Sociology, University of Hawai'i at Hilo, West Hawai'i

Kathleen Delate
Sustainable Agriculture, Department of Horticulture,
Iowa State University

Cliff Eblen
President Emeritus, Hawaii Public Radio

Pierre Flament
Department of Oceanography, University of Hawai'i at Mānoa

Charles H. Fletcher III
Hawai'i Institute of Geophysics, School of Ocean and Earth Sciences,
University of Hawai'i at Mānoa

James H. Furstenberg
Formerly Honolulu Academy of Arts

Robert Gavenda
Natural Resources Conservation Service, U.S. Department of Agriculture,
Kealakekua, Hawai'i.

Thomas W. Giambelluca
Department of Geography, University of Hawai'i at Mānoa

William G. Gilmartin
Hawai'i Wildlife Fund, Lā'ie, Hawai'i

Samuel M. Gon III
The Nature Conservancy of Hawai'i, Honolulu

Jon Goss
Department of Geography, University of Hawai'i at Mānoa

Michael G. Hadfield
Kewalo Marine Laboratory, Pacific Biomedical Research Center,
University of Hawai'i at Mānoa

Donald N. B. Hall
Institute for Astronomy, University of Hawai'i at Mānoa

Christina Heliker
Hawaiian Volcano Observatory, U.S. Geological Survey

Don J. Hibbard
Historic Preservation Office, Department of Land and Natural Resources,
State of Hawai'i, Honolulu

Shelia Hollowell
Department of Sociology, University of Hawai'i at Hilo, West Hawai'i

Sara Hotchkiss
Department of Ecology, Evolution and Behavior, University of Minnesota

Francis G. Howarth
Bishop Museum, Honolulu

James O. Juvik
Department of Geography, University of Hawai'i at Hilo

Sonia P. Juvik
Department of Geography, University of Hawai'i at Hilo

Lilikalā Kame'eleihiwa
Center for Hawaiian Studies, University of Hawai'i at Mānoa

Edward Kanahele
Department of History, Hawai'i Community College

Pualani Kanehele
Department of Hawaiian Studies, Hawai'i Community College

Eric M. Kapono
Department of Hawaiian Studies, University of Hawai'i at Hilo

Drew Kapp
Department of Geography, University of Hawai'i at Mānoa

James L. Kelly
   Department of Geography, University of Hawai'i at Hilo

Sean Kennan
   Department of Oceanography, University of Hawai'i at Mānoa

Larry L. Kimura
   Department of Hawaiian Studies, University of Hawai'i at Hilo

Patrick V. Kirch
   Department of Anthropology, University of California at Berkeley.

Mary Lou Kobayashi
   Office of Planning, Department of Business, Economic Development,
   and Tourism, State of Hawai'i, Honolulu

Lydia Kualapai
   University of Nebraska, Lincoln

Ramdas Lamb
   Department of Religion, University of Hawai'i at Mānoa

Charles M. Langlas
   Department of Anthropology, University of Hawai'i at Hilo

Charles H. Lamoureux
   Lyon Arboretum, Honolulu

Lloyd L. Loope
   USGS, Biological Resources Division, Haleakalā National Park, Maui

Claude Lumpkin
   Department of Oceanography, University of Hawai'i at Mānoa

Barrie Macdonald
   Department of History, Massey University, New Zealand

James E. Maragos
   Program on Environment, East-West Center, Honolulu

Henry Marcus
   Massachusetts Institute of Technology

Matthew McGranaghan
   Department of Geography, University of Hawai'i at Mānoa

Loyal A. Mehrhoff
   U.S. Fish and Wildlife Service, Portland, Oregon

Mark Merlin
   Biology Program, University of Hawai'i at Mānoa

Sara Millman
   Department of Sociology, University of Hawai'i at Hilo

John Mink
   Mink & Yuen, Inc., Honolulu

Darryl Mleynek
   Small Business Development Center, University of Hawai'i at Hilo

Steven L. Montgomery
   Biological Consultant, Waipahu, Hawai'i

Joseph R. Morgan
   Department of Geography, University of Hawai'i at Mānoa

William P. Mull
   Associate, Bishop Museum, Honolulu

Junko Ida Nowaki
   Librarian, University of Hawai'i at Hilo

Dennis Nullet
   Department of Geography, University of Hawai'i at Hilo

Michael Ogden
   Department of Communication, University of Hawai'i at Mānoa

Paul Okubo
   Hawaiian Volcano Observatory, U.S. Geological Survey

Thomas R. Paradise
   Department of Geography, University of Hawai'i at Hilo

Noreen M. Parks
   Monterey Bay Aquarium Research Institute, Moss Landing, California

Gordon Pi'ianaia
   Hawaiian Studies, Kamehameha Schools, Honolulu

Samuel G. Pooley
   National Marine Fisheries Service, Honolulu

Linda W. Pratt
   USGS, Biological Resources Division, Pacific Island Ecosystems
   Research Center, Hawai'i Volcanoes National Park

Marcia Sakai
   Department of Economics, University of Hawai'i at Hilo

Michael Sawyer
   Department of Oceanography, University of Hawai'i at Mānoa

Robert C. Schmitt
   Hawai'i State Statistician (Retired)

Russell Schnell
   Mauna Loa Observatory, National Oceanic and Atmospheric
   Administration, Hilo

Thomas A. Schroeder
   Department of Meteorology, University of Hawai'i at Mānoa

Albert J. Schütz
   Department of Linguistics, University of Hawai'i at Mānoa

Christopher Smith
   Natural Resources Conservation Service, U.S. Department of Agriculture,
   Honolulu

Edward D. Stroup
   Department of Oceanography, University of Hawai'i at Mānoa

Ron Terry
   Geometrician Associates, Kea'au, Hawai'i

Donald M. Thomas
   Hawai'i Institute of Geophysics, University of Hawai'i at Mānoa

Nicole Vollrath
   Natural Resources Conservation Service, U.S. Department of Agriculture,
   Washington, D.C.

James C. F. Wang
   Department of Political Science, University of Hawai'i at Hilo

F. R. Warshauer
   USGS, Biological Resources Division, Hawai'i Volcanoes National Park

Everett A. Wingert
   Department of Geography, University of Hawai'i at Mānoa

CONTENTS

PREFACE

One of our first tasks when we began work on the third edition of the *Atlas of Hawai'i* in late 1994 was to solicit suggestions from users of earlier editions of the *Atlas* and from prospective users. Over seven hundred survey forms were sent to teachers, librarians, consultants, governmental agency personnel, and others. Suggestions from the respondents about what to include are reflected in the contents of the *Atlas*.

This version of the *Atlas of Hawai'i* is entirely new. The content, design, style, and technology are substantially different from previous editions. While the prior editions served as models, most of the text and all the graphics were replaced, and several new topics were added.

The table of contents of the *Atlas* presents an exciting array of topics grouped into five sections. The introduction to the state and to each of the main islands is followed by four sections on the major themes of the Hawai'i environment: physical, biotic, cultural, and social. Fifty-four separate chapters, plus sidebar features, provide a comprehensive description of the geography of Hawai'i. The volume also offers a list of references for further reading, a list of sources for the graphics, a set of statistical tables, and a gazetteer.

The list of contributors boasts some of Hawai'i's most distinguished scholars. For the most part they were selected because of their previous contributions to knowledge in their fields. The photographs were chosen to illustrate essential features of the natural, cultural, and social milieux. The reader should note that statistical information in various sections of the *Atlas* may not always agree because different assumptions or time periods are involved. Likewise, racial designations in some sections of the *Atlas* differ from those used in the U.S. census.

The technology used to produce this edition is much different from that used in previous editions. The production of maps and other graphics epitomizes the transformation of cartography by computer technology. A variety of computer software and mapmaking methods were employed. Likewise, the rich colors that enhance the *Atlas* are an example of the possiblities available with an electronic (computerized) palette. The use of computer technology enabled the cartographers to mix a four-color palette in an endless selection of recipes. An additional advantage of modern cartographic technology is that the digital files for the contents will be archived for future retrieval and updating. This will greatly reduce the cost and time required to update the contents for future editions.

Another departure from the first two editions is the shape of the book. This change was made to avoid the difficulties of shelving an oversized volume. Although the new shape necessitated a change in page layout of the Island chain, a significant benefit is that each island is presented at a slightly larger size than before, providing better resolution of the patterns displayed.

Hawaiian words and place names in the *Atlas* conform mostly to spellings in the *Hawaiian Dictionary* by Mary Kawena Pukui and Samuel H. Elbert and *Place Names of Hawaii* by Mary Kawena Pukui, Samuel H. Elbert, and Esther T. Mookini. As a rule Hawaiian words are italicized, while Hawaiian place names are not.

The *Atlas of Hawai'i* is a rich source of information offered in a style that should satisfy a variety of interests. It can be used as a textbook, a general reference, or for pleasure reading. We hope it will reveal the features that make Hawai'i a special place.

ACKNOWLEDGMENTS

Over eighty individuals from the university community, government agencies, and the private sector contributed text and data for the maps, diagrams, and tables that appear in this edition of the *Atlas.* Through all of our dealings with them—from soliciting their participation to discussing the data—what stood out as remarkable was their enthusiasm for the project and their spirit of cooperation and understanding even when page limitations meant we had to eliminate text over which they had labored.

Similarly, we were not denied a single request to a federal, state, or county agency for data or verification of data. Many of the graphics in the *Atlas* could not have been prepared without the statistical tables compiled by the Department of Business, Economic Development and Tourism. The support of the Office of State Planning, likewise, has been indispensable. They provided numerous land use digital files, maps, and generous amounts of consultation time. For the outstanding help and support of these and numerous other agencies of the state, county, and federal government, we are appreciative.

Dozens of individuals and private firms also helped us in major ways. For land ownership data we gratefully acknowledge the Hawai'i Board of Realtors. The generosity of professional artists and photographers whose work enlivens our presentation is also celebrated. Each of their contributions is acknowledged throughout the *Atlas.*

The administrators, faculty, and staff of the University of Hawai'i at Hilo rightly share in our accomplishments. This project could not have been undertaken or completed without their unfaltering support and constant encouragement. Our colleague Professor James Kelly worked full time with us in the final months, assisting with editing, research, and generally serving as a source of calm. We gratefully acknowledge former chancellor Edward Kormondy for the trust he showed in our ability to complete the task. Special recognition is due former University of Hawai'i at Hilo chancellor Kenneth Perrin, who assured us institutional support and constantly gave his moral support. Our colleagues on the faculty have been supportive as well. The list is long of those who have helped us reach the finish. We honor them for their many forms of outreach.

Noreen Parks served from August 1994 to June 1996 as *Atlas* project coordinator, enthusiastically and expertly performing a range of tasks, from soliciting and editing manuscripts to general administration.

Julsun Pacheco, project cartographer and geographic information systems specialist, suspended graduate studies in geography at University of Hawai'i at Mānoa to work on the *Atlas* from July 1995 to June 1996. We thank the Mānoa Geography Department for its cooperation and for allowing us access to its cartography lab. Significant contributions to planning for suitable cartographic procedures were made by Mary-Anne Maigret, who was employed by the project briefly before giving birth to twins. Drew Kapp and Nancy Elmer were volunteer staff who joined us toward the end of the project, bringing new energy and diligence to executing demanding tasks. Drew also spent weeks laboriously checking place names and other information on the reference maps. Lee Motteler's knowledge of geography, cartography, and Hawaiiana proved invaluable to his careful and thorough reading and checking of the proofs.

Professor Craig Severance assisted with advice on fisheries, and soil conservationist Steve Skipper helped with a model of a sustainable agriculture farm. Catherine Tignac volunteered many hours as research assistant; Raynell Uchida, a fine arts major, impressed us with her cheerfulness and accuracy. Her knowledge of the Hawaiian language spared us hours of turning to the Hawaiian dictionary. John Schinnerer was a good friend of the project whose computer expertise was often needed and willingly given. Special recognition is also due Nicole Anakalea for developing enough competency in her introductory cartography course to volunteer her digitizing skills.

We acknowledge the huge commitment that the director of University of Hawai'i Press, William H. Hamilton, has made to this *Atlas,* and we have strived to live up to the trust he placed in us. We extend a sincere *mahalo* to him and to other members of the University of Hawai'i Press Atlas team, whose diverse talents were indispensable in taking this project to completion.

Finally, the entire project benefited from the virtuosity of Iris Wiley, former University of Hawai'i Press executive editor, whose guidance in logistical matters and whose mastery of editing were invaluable. It was she who encouraged us to undertake the project and we thank her for the opportunity.

For the contributions of these and dozens of individuals who have not been mentioned by name, we are deeply grateful.

INTRODUCTION

Eō e ku'u lei mokupuni o nā kai 'ewalu
I call to you, acknowledge O my lei islands of the eight seas

Located between 19 and 22 degrees north latitude, Hawai'i is the southernmost state in the United States and has the same general latitude as Hong Kong and Mexico City. It is situated almost in the center of the Pacific Ocean and is one of the most isolated yet populous places on Earth. The west coast of North America, for example, is 2,400 miles (3,900 kilometers) from Honolulu, and Japan is 3,800 miles (6,100 kilometers) away. Six time zones separate Hawai'i from the eastern United States. This means that 9:00 A.M. (eastern standard time) in Washington, D.C. and New York City is 6:00 A.M. in Los Angeles and 4:00 A.M. in Hawai'i.

Hawai'i is one of the smallest states in the United States—it ranks forty-seventh in size—larger in land area only than Rhode Island, Connecticut, and Delaware. The 6,425 square miles (16,640 square kilometers) of land consist of 8

Hawai'i, the fiftieth state. The map emphasizes the isolation of the islands near the center of the Pacific Ocean. Small and remote though it may be, Hawai'i is one of the best-known places on the globe.

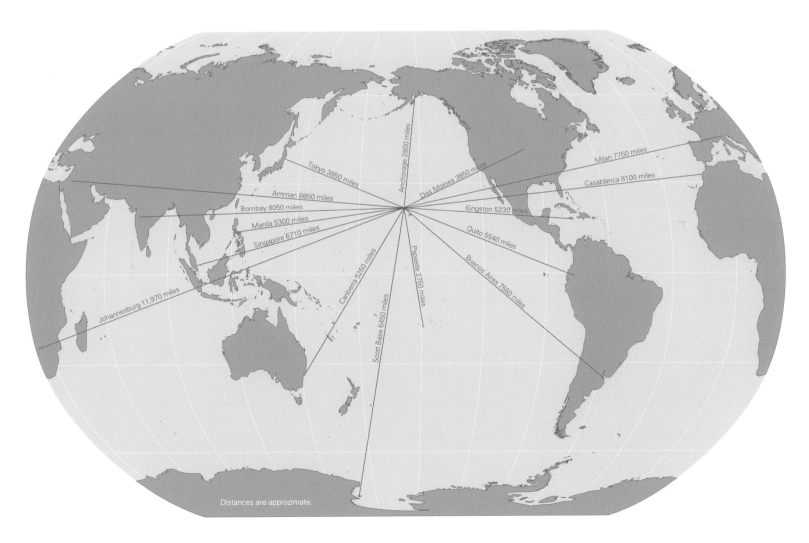

Distances are approximate.

large islands and 124 small islands, reefs, and shoals. The 8 large islands—Hawai'i, Maui, Lāna'i, Moloka'i, O'ahu, Kaho-'olawe, Kaua'i, and Ni'ihau—are recognized in the Hawai'i state flag by 8 horizontal stripes, alternately white, red, and blue. The British Union Jack in the upper left corner of the flag represents the years that the Islands were under British protection. Each of the major islands has its unique features and its own official color and emblem.

Hawai'i is divided into four counties: Hawai'i, Maui (which includes the islands of Maui, Moloka'i, Lāna'i, and Kaho'olawe), O'ahu, and Kaua'i (Kaua'i and Ni'ihau). The county is the lowest civil subdivision in the state. As a result, counties in Hawai'i provide some services, such as fire and police protection and street maintenance, that in other states are performed by cities or towns. Counties also elect a mayor and a council. Likewise, the state government often takes on functions usually performed by counties or cities on the U.S. mainland. Hawai'i is the only state, for example, with a single, unified public school system.

Because Hawai'i is an archipelago, transportation within the state has always been expensive. Land transportation is limited to intraisland travel, and, because of the mountainous nature of the islands, road networks have been sparse and, in some places, limited to a single highway near the coast. Inter-island cargo moves by ship and by air. Interisland passenger travel is entirely by air. Air flights are frequent and convenient, but comparatively expensive. Three of the ten most expensive airfares per mile in the United States are the connections between Honolulu and Maui, Honolulu and Kona, and Hono-lulu and Kaua'i. Hawai'i has no rapid transit facilities. The plantation railroads of the past are gone, and no railroads exist in the Islands today, except for short lines serving tourists.

The Hawaiian Islands were formed by volcanic eruptions, and these eruptions continue today on Hawai'i Island. Related to this volcanic activity are earthquakes, which are not infrequent. Hawai'i generally has a tropical climate, although changes in elevation generate variations. Because of the effect of mountains on wind patterns, most islands have distinct windward and leeward systems of rainfall. In addition, coastal areas are generally drier than the interior uplands. Fortunately, the warm tropical temperatures are usually ameliorated by persistent trade winds. Moreover, the surrounding ocean keeps temperatures from becoming extremely warm. Sweltering summer temperatures typical of many parts of the South and Midwest of the United States are unknown in Hawai'i. The

The State Bird of Hawai'i: the *nēnē,* or Hawaiian goose, *Branta sandvicensis.* [R. J. Shallenberger]

State of Hawai'i

Settled by Polynesians:	A.D. 300–700
Statehood:	1959, 50th State
Nickname:	The Aloha State
Capital:	Honolulu
State flower:	*pua ma'o hau hele,* yellow hibiscus, *Hibiscus brackenridgei*
State fish:	*humuhumunukunukuapua'a,* triggerfish, *Rhinecanthus aculeatus*
State bird:	*nēnē,* Hawaiian goose, *Branta sandvicensis*
State tree:	*kukui,* candlenut, *Aleurites moluccana*
Land area of archipelago:	6,423.4 square miles (16,636.5 square kilometers)
Resident population (1996):	1,183,700 (includes 103,300 military and their dependents)
Defacto population (1996):	1,342,600 residents and average daily visitors
Median age (1993):	33.7
Life expectancy (1990):	75.90 years (males), 80.06 years (females)
Visitors (estimated total arrivals 1997):	6,877,500
Economic mainstays:	Tourism, federal defense spending, and agriculture
Energy resources (1993):	90 percent imported petroleum
Motor vehicle registration (1993):	880,152
Per capita personal income (1996):	$25,159
Median price of single-family house (1995):	$281,000
Gross State Product (1996):	$33.5 billion

Urban Honolulu. [J. Juvik]

The State Flower, *Hibiscus brackenridgei,* a native yellow hibiscus known as *ma'o hau hele.* [R. Hobdy]

State Flag of Hawai'i. [State Archives]

highest temperature recorded in the Islands, for example, was 100°F in 1931.

One of the major attributes of the State of Hawai'i is its natural environment, which provides pleasant living conditions for residents and attracts tourists to the Islands. How to maintain an economy that provides jobs and income for the state's residents while at the same time protecting this natural environment remains a constant problem. Many indigenous plants and animals are already extinct or endangered, mostly because of habitat destruction and the introduction of plant and animal species from outside Hawai'i.

One of the major characteristics of population distribution in Hawai'i is the high concentration of people in or near Honolulu. An overwhelming 75 percent of the resident population lives on O'ahu, concentrated in the Honolulu metropolitan area. A highly centralized government and economy on O'ahu, and the high cost of transporting goods to the neighbor islands, seems to have impeded the spread of Honolulu's urban and industrial activities.

Plantations dominated the state's economy for more than a hundred years. However, beginning with World War II and continuing during the Cold War and the wars in Korea and Vietnam, military expenditures, concentrated on O'ahu, increased. At one time the military employed more people than any other industry in Hawai'i. With the proliferation of jet travel beginning in the late 1950s the number of visitors to Hawai'i expanded tremendously, along with the number of hotels and tourism-related jobs. Today tourism is the state's leading industry. The military is still of major importance, but plantation agriculture continues to decline. Increasingly important to the economy and society of Hawai'i are the agencies of the state, county, and federal governments. Business and the manufacturing industry have been curtailed by several factors often acting collectively. Fossil fuels and major mineral resources are absent, prices of usable land remain high, the long distance to large markets increases transportation costs, and labor costs are much higher than in many newly industrialized countries of Asia.

Per capita income in Hawai'i is above the national average, but the cost of living is much greater than in most other states. Hawai'i's per capita tax burden is also one of the highest in the United States. In spite of these disadvantages Hawai'i's image as a Pacific paradise remains mostly intact, and the state continues to be attractive as a place to live or visit. More than 6 million visitors a year vacation in the state. Most people who live in Hawai'i continue to prefer it over all other places. With the state's prolonged economic slowdown in the mid-1990s, for the first time the number of people who leave Hawai'i to live elsewhere in a given year exceeded the number of new arrivals.

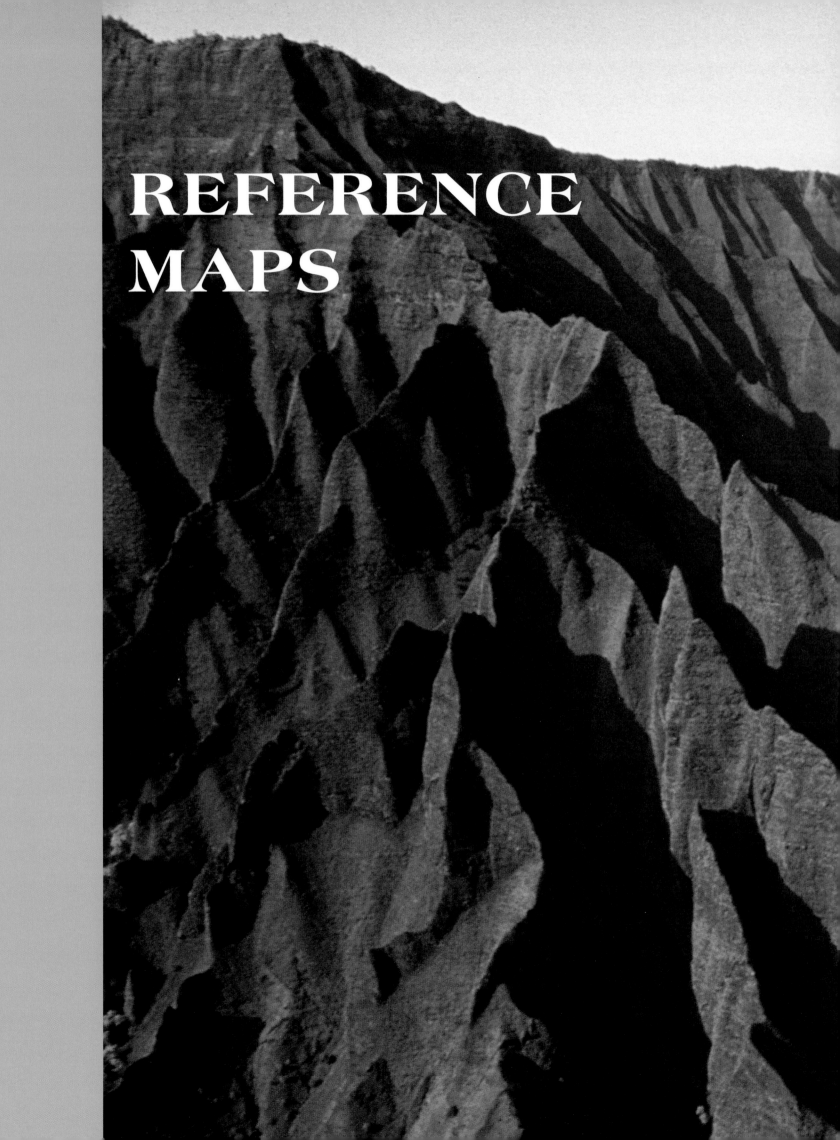

REFERENCE MAPS

All place names on the reference maps are listed alphabetically
in the Gazetteer at the end of the *Atlas.*

KAUA'I AND NI'IHAU

KAUA'I

Maika'i Kaua'i, hemolele i ka mālie, Kaua'i o Manokalanipō
So fine is Kaua'i, tranquil in the calm, Kaua'i of the chief
　　Manokalanipō

Riding northwestward on the Pacific lithospheric plate, Kaua'i long ago vacated the volcanic "hotspot" over which the island of Hawai'i is now positioned. The 5 million year old volcanic shield that formed the island of Kaua'i has therefore had ample time to be sculpted by the action of wind, rain, and waves. The plateau of Kaua'i reaches elevations of 5,148 feet (1,569 m) at Wai'ale'ale and 5,243 feet (1,598 m) at Kawaikini and is directly exposed to trade winds ascending abruptly over precipitous *pali* (cliffs). As a consequence, the mountain summit of Kaua'i is one of the wettest spots on Earth. Average annual rainfall at Wai'ale'ale is 444 inches (11,278 mm). The interior mountains of Kaua'i have been eroded by running water to produce the spectacular topography of Waimea Canyon and Nā Pali Coast. The transported alluvium formed broad coastal plains with deep soil and extensive beaches. This landscape is the foundation for Kaua'i's economy: agriculture and tourism.

Kaua'i has been severely impacted by hurricanes three times in the past 40 years. The greatest destruction was caused by Hurricane Iniki in September 1992. With 145 mph winds, it was the most devastating hurricane in the recorded history of Hawai'i. Property damage totaled more than $3 billion and much of the economy was left in ruin. As a result, the number of hotel and condominium units on Kaua'i decreased by 40 percent the first year after the hurricane. As of 1997, visitor totals for Kaua'i (992,780) had not yet recovered to pre-Iniki levels of 1.27 million visitors annually.

In the first half of the 1990s sugar plantation acreage declined on the northern and eastern coasts of Kaua'i because of the closing of Kīlauea and McBryde plantations. The plantations on the southern and western coastal plains, extending from Kōloa to Mānā, however, contain some of the highest yielding sugarcane acreage in the state. Total acreage in sugarcane on Kaua'i in 1994 was 34,500 acres (14,000 ha), down by 34 percent from 52,300 acres (21,000 ha) in 1969. Declining revenues from sugar production have been partially offset by the planting of more than 2,000 acres (800 ha) of coffee in the area between 'Ōma'o and 'Ele'ele.

Nickname:	The Garden Isle
Color and emblem:	purple; *pua mokihana,* the fruit of *Pelea anisata*
Land area:	552.3 square miles (1,430.5 square kilometers)
Largest perennial stream:	Hanalei River, 140 million gallons (530,000 cubic meters) per day
Resident population (1996):	56,435
Visitors (estimated total arrivals 1997):	992,780
Per capita personal income (1993):	$19,887
Median price of single-family house (1995):	$250,000

Nā Pali Coast, Kaua'i. [B. Gagné]

NI'IHAU/KA'ULA

KA'ULA

160°32'30"

21°40'

Kaho'omoa Channel

Kahalauaola
(Shark Cave)

Hewa Channel

548

Manohua

Rock Shoal

22°15'

0   0.5 mi

0   1 km

160°30'

Kapa'a, Kaua'i inset

Moalepe Str.

Kapa'a Str.

Kawaihau

Kawaihau Rd.

Kumukumu

Ka'apuni Rd.

Pōhāki'iki'i
880

Kapa'a, Kaua'i

St. Catherine's
School

Keālia

Kapa'a Elem,
Int. & High
School

Konohiki Str.

'Olohena Rd.

Kapa'a

Kūhiō Hwy.

Kalana Str.

Kapa'a New
Park

Kapa'a Beach Park

'Opaeka'a Str.

Post Office

Waipouli
Park

Nounou
Mountain
(Sleeping
Giant) 1241

Waiānuenue

Waipouli
Town Center

Waipouli

Wailua Homesteads

Hale'ilio Rd.

Koholālele Falls

Waipouli
Beach Park

'Opaeka'a
Falls

Post Office

Alakukui Pt.

Holoholokū Heiau

Wailua

160°15'

160°

0   0.4 mi

0   0.6 km

REFERENCE MAPS

scale

0 ——————— 10 miles

0 ——————— 10 kilometers

Reference Maps INDEX

NI'IHAU   KAUA'I

Ka'ula

O'AHU

MOLOKA'I

LĀNA'I

MAUI

KAHO'OLAWE

NORTHWESTERN HAWAIIAN ISLANDS

Kure Atoll
Midway Atoll
Pearl and Hermes
Atoll
Lisianski Is
Laysan Is
Maro Reef
Gardner Pinnacles
French Frigate
Shoals
Necker Is
(Mokumanamana)
Nihoa

HAWAI'I

Legend

☐ Urbanized area	**Roads**	— Stream (perenial or intermittent)
Population	══ Divided, controlled access	
⊛ More than 300,000	━ Principal through	┼ Waterfall
◉ 20,000–40,000	━ Secondary through	⌒ Dam and reservoir
● 12,000–20,000	━ Other (paved, gravel, graded dirt)	
● 7,000–12,000	Primitive (4-wheel)	+ Point elevation in feet
● 3,000–7,000	Foot trail	⌣ Mountain pass
● 1,000–3,000	⌗ Tunnel	
○ less than 1,000	H2 Freeway	▆ High school/college
× locality or site		■ Point of interest
⊛ State capital	✚ Airfields	
⬠ County seat	✈ Scheduled airlines	A¹⌐ Gazetteer location grid
┈ District boundary	✦ Military	
▨ Military land		

NI'IHAU (main island map)

Kaulakahi Channel

Kahauna Pt.

Naupaka Pt.

Lehua Island

Kaunuakalā
699

Pu'u Kole

Kamakalepo Pt.

Keapahe'ehe'e

Keamano Bay

Kīkepa Pt.

Kahiowaho Channel

Ka'aku'u Bay (Lehua Landing)

22°

Kaunuokahaha Pt.

Palikoa'e Pt.

Papa'ki'u'u

Ki'i

Kaunu o Pou Pt.

Keawanui

Pu'u
'Alalā
210

Nānaiko'olau Ridge
Ka'alipua'a
Pōleho

Kapaka Valley

Kaunupu Pt.

Keawanui Bay

Kanalo Valley

Pāni'au 1281 (highest elev. on Ni'ihau)

Kauwaha Bay

Kanunali'i Valley

Keanauhi Val.

Ko'olaukani Valley

Kalanaei

Kalehu Pt.

1228

Pākilehua Gulch

Kaluahonu Pt.

Kaumuhonu Val.

Puni a Kapo Val.

Kamaluki'i Gulch

Kūakamoku Reef

Pu'uwai

Ha'ao Val.

Ka'eo
1018

Kealahula Valley

Kamahakahaka

Ki'eki'e

Apana Val.

Pu'u Lua
1130

Kōnouli Val.

Kāwā Point

Halawela

Ka'ailana Val.

Pueo Point

Kanahā Pt.

Halulu
Lake

Kalaumaki Val.

Namu Val.

Nonopapa

Kalaheo'au Val.

Kalaoa Bay

Paia (cliff)

WAIMEA

Makahū'ena

Kalaeloa Ridge

Halali'i
Lake

Keolea Pt.

Kawa'ewa'e 290

Po'ooneone Pt.

Kiloi'a Bay

Kamalino

Aliaki Lake

'Ō'iamoi Point

NI'IHAU

Mau'uloa
198

Pāhau Pt.

Kaha'ino

Kōwahi Point

Ke'elināwi Pt.

Kolea

Lē'ahi Pt.

178

Kealea Bay

Kaunuakalā 548

Kaumuhonu Bay

Kawaihoa Point

21°45'

Kaho'omoa Channel

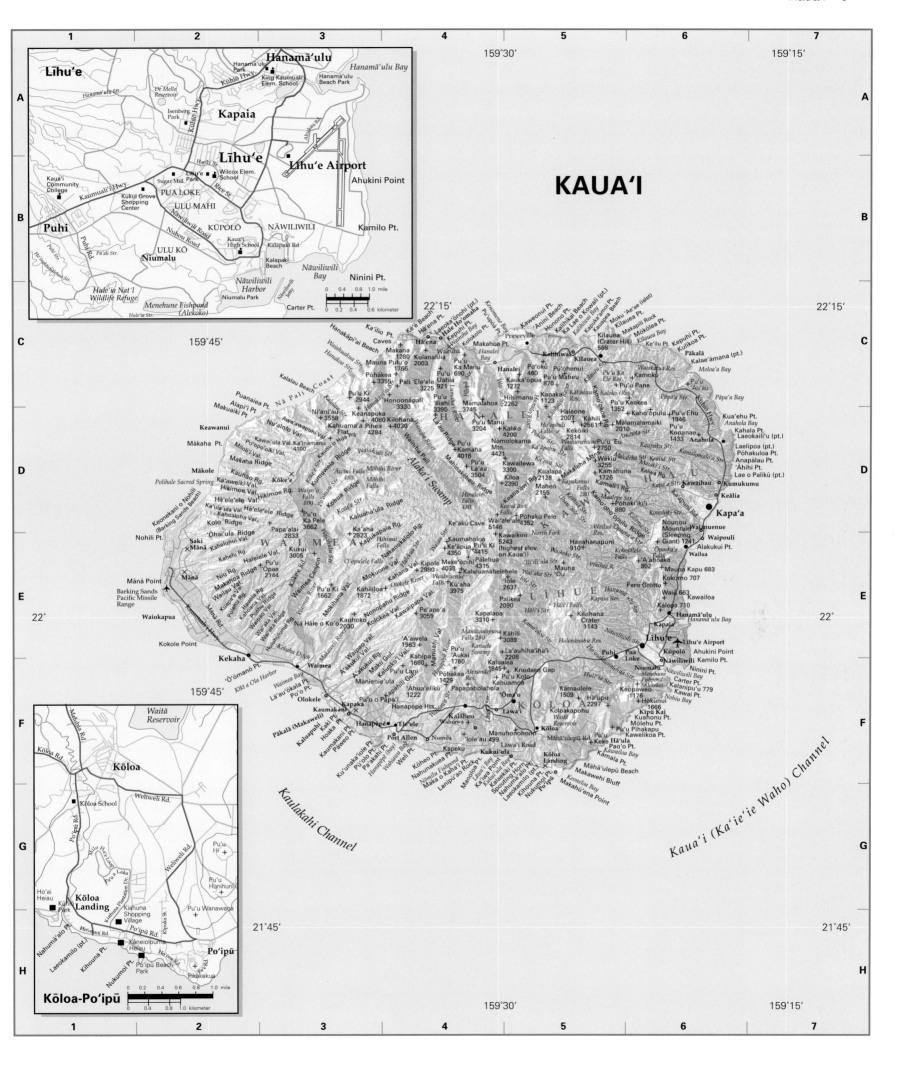

NI'IHAU

'O Ni'ihau o Kahelelani, 'o Ni'ihau i ke kīkū
Ni'ihau of the chief Kahelelani, Ni'ihau of self-reliance

Ni'ihau is formed from a single volcanic shield slightly younger (at 4.9 million years) than adjacent Kaua'i. Unique geomorphic features of the island include several intermittent lakes. These are the rough equivalent of desert "playa," or ephemeral saline lakes. Shallow Halulu Lake covers approximately 182 acres (74 ha), while Halāli'i Lake is several times larger. Although the island rises to only 1,281 feet (390 m) at Pānī'au, there are precipitous sea cliffs along the eastern coast.

Lying in the rain shadow of Kaua'i, only 17.2 miles (27.7 km) across the Kaulakahi Channel, this semiarid island has been owned by members of the Robinson family since 1864. The Native Hawaiians there numbered 230 in 1990 and are mostly employed in sheep ranching on the island.

Nickname:	The Forbidden Isle
Color and emblem:	white; *pua Ni'ihau,* the Ni'ihau shell *Columbella*
Land area:	69.5 square miles (179.9 square kilometers)
Resident population (1996):	230

O'AHU

'O O'ahu, ka 'ōnohi o ke kai, O'ahu o Kākuhihewa
O'ahu, the gem of the sea, O'ahu of the chief Kakuhihewa

The parallel ranges formed by the Ko'olau and Wai'anae Mountains are the eroded remnants of two shield volcanoes that erupted 1.3 and 2.2 million years ago. Aligned perpendicular to the prevailing northeast trade winds, the mountains produce distinctive windward and leeward climate regimes. Annual rainfall exceeds 250 inches (6,350 mm) per year on the crest of the Ko'olau Range. Leeward coastal areas, however,

from Nānākuli to Mākaha receive less than 20 inches (500 mm) of rainfall annually. A distinctive feature of O'ahu's geomorphology is the broad plain that extends from Diamond Head across Pearl Harbor to 'Ewa and Barbers Point. Composed of raised coralline limestone, this emergent coastal plain is partly the result of upward seafloor warping or tilting, in response to the weight of the larger islands of Maui and Hawai'i.

Possessing superb natural harbors, a dry leeward climate, and abundant freshwater streams descending from the Ko'olau Range, Honolulu and the surrounding hinterlands of O'ahu were destined quickly to become the commercial and urban center in the archipelago. In 1994, 74 percent of the state's population of 1,178,600 resided on O'ahu, and more than 80 percent of the 1995 Gross State Product of $32.8 billion was generated there.

Central O'ahu's Leilehua Plateau was long cherished by state and county planners as an agricultural greenbelt on the urban fringe. This vision, however, could not survive the pressures of urbanization in the 1990s. In 1996, sugarcane production ceased on O'ahu after more than 150 years. Both governmental agencies and the private sector are now fully

Diamond Head, skyline, O'ahu. [Hawai'i Visitors Bureau]

Urbanization of former sugarcane lands at Kapolei on the 'Ewa Plain, O'ahu. [J. Juvik]

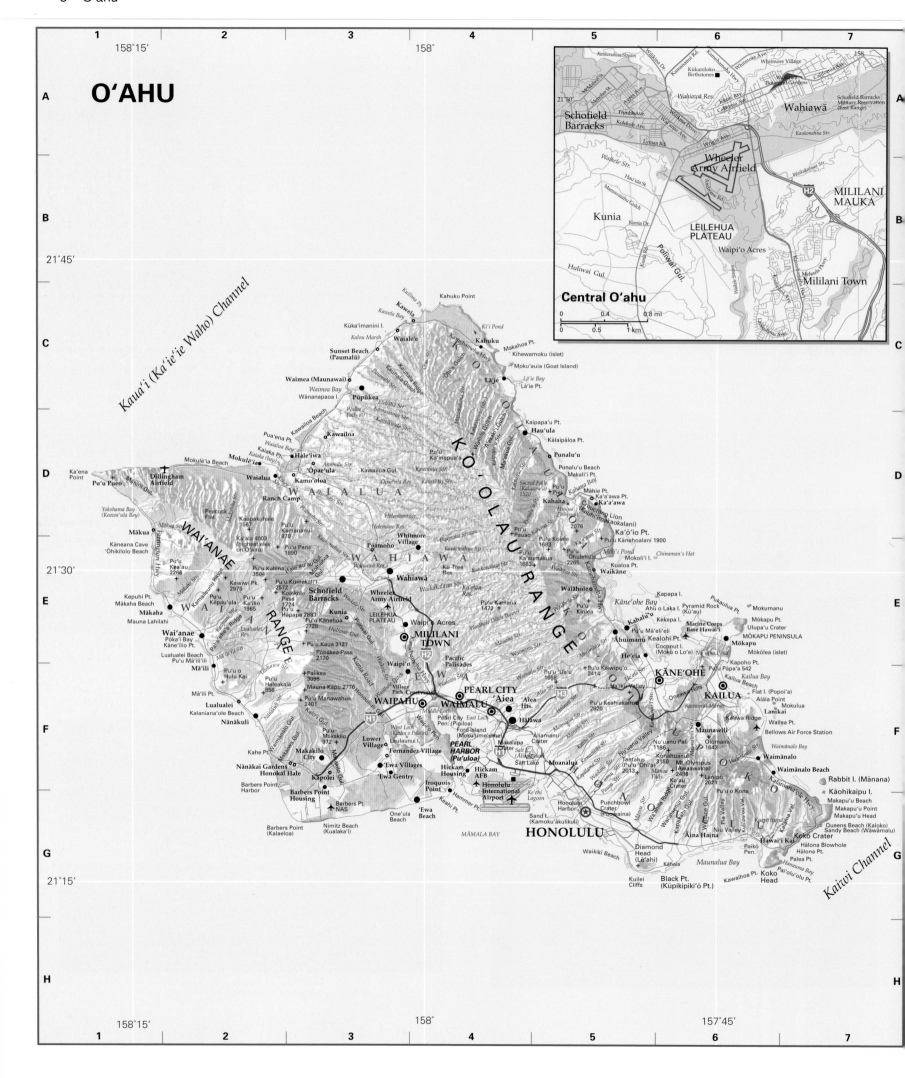

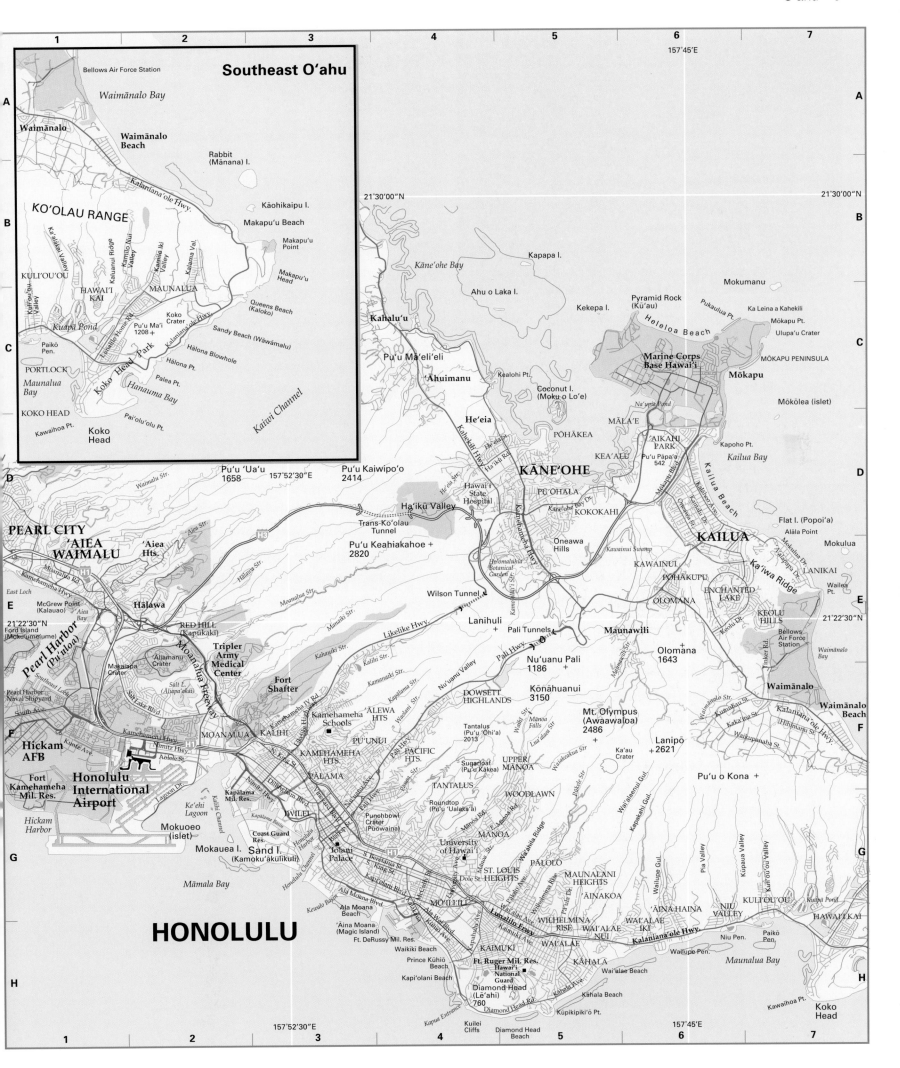

Southeast O'ahu

Bellows Air Force Station

Waimānalo Bay

Waimānalo

Waimānalo Beach

Rabbit (Mānana) I.

KO'OLAU RANGE

Kalaniana'ole Hwy.

Kāohikaipu I.

Makapu'u Beach

Makapu'u Point

Ko'olikai Valley   Kaluanui Ridge   Kamilo Nui Valley   Kamilo Iki Valley   Kalama Val.

Makapu'u Head

KULI'OU'OU

HAWAI'I KAI   MAUNALUA

Kuli'ou'ou Valley

Queens Beach (Kaloko)

Kuapa Pond   Pu'u Ma'i 1208 +   Koko Crater   *Kalaniana'ole Hwy.*   Sandy Beach (Wāwāmalu)

Paikō Pen.

Koko Head Park   Hālona Blowhole

PORTLOCK   Hālona Pt.

Maunalua Bay   Palea Pt.   *Hanauma Bay*

KOKO HEAD   Pai'olu'olu Pt.

Kawaihoa Pt.   Koko Head   *Ka Iwi Channel*

21°30'00"N ——————————— 21°30'00"N

157°45'E

Kāne'ohe Bay

Kapapa I.

Mokumanu

Ahu o Laka I.   Kekepa I.   Pyramid Rock (Ku'au)   Pukaulua Pt.   Ka Leina a Kahekili

Kahalu'u   *Heleloa Beach*   Mōkapu Pt.   Ulupa'u Crater

Pu'u Ma'eli'eli   **Marine Corps Base Hawai'i**   MŌKAPU PENINSULA

'Āhuimanu   Kealohi Pt.   **Mōkapu**

Coconut I. (Moku o Lo'e)   Mōkōlea (islet)

He'eia   Na'upia Pond

PŌHĀKEA   MĀLA'E

He'eia St.   'AIKAHI PARK

Pu'u 'Ua'u 1658   Pu'u Kaiwipo'o 2414   **KĀNE'OHE**   Pu'u Pāpa'a 542   *Kailua Bay*

157°52'30"E   He'eia Str.   Hā'ikū Rd.   PU'OHALA   Kapoho Pt.

Hawai'i State Hospital   Kāne'ohe Bay Dr.   KOKOKAHI   Kailua Beach

Ha'ikū Valley   KEA'ALU

Trans-Ko'olau Tunnel   Ho'omaluhia Botanical Garden   Oneawa Hills   Flat I. (Popoi'a)   Alāla Point

PEARL CITY   Pu'u Keahiakahoe + 2820   **KAILUA**   Mokulua

'AIEA WAIMALU   'Aiea Hts.   KAWAINUI   *Kawainui Swamp*   PŌHĀKUPU   LANIKAI

'Aiea Str.   Hālawa Str.   Wilson Tunnel   ENCHANTED LAKE   Wailea Pt.

McGrew Point (Kalauao)   Hālawa   OLOMANA   KEOLU HILLS

East Loch   *'Aiea Bay*   Moanalua Str.   Lanihuli +   Pali Tunnels   **Maunawili**   21°22'30"N

21°22'30"N   Ford Island (Moku'ume'ume)   RED HILL (Kapūkaki)   Likelike Hwy.   Olomana 1643   Bellows Air Force Station

Pearl Harbor (Pu'uloa)   Tripler Army Medical Center   Nu'uanu Pali 1186 +   *Waimānalo Bay*

'Āliamanu Crater   Makalapa Crater   Nu'uanu Valley   **Waimānalo**

Pearl Harbor Naval Shipyard   Salt L. ('Āliapa'a'akai)   Fort Shafter   DOWSETT HIGHLANDS   Kōnāhuanui 3150   **Waimānalo Beach**

South Ave.   Kahauiki Str.   Kalihi Str.   Mt. Olympus (Awaawaloa) 2486

Hickam AFB   Kamehameha Hwy.   Kalihi IV Rd.   Kamanaiki Str.   'ĀLEWA HTS.   Tantalus (Pu'u 'Ōhi'a) 2013   *Mānoa Falls*   Lanipō + 2621

Kuntz Ave.   MOANALUA   KALIHI   Kamehameha Schools   PU'UNUI   Sugarloaf (Pu'u Kākea)   UPPER MĀNOA   Ka'au Crater

Fort Kamehameha Mil. Res.   Nimitz Hwy.   KAMEHAMEHA HTS.   PACIFIC HTS.   Roundtop (Pu'u 'Ualaka'a)   Pu'u o Kona +

Aolele St.   PĀLAMA   TANTALUS   WOODLAWN

Honolulu International Airport   Lagoon Dr.   Kapālama Mil. Res.   Dillingham Blvd.   IWILEI   Punchbowl Crater (Pūowaina)   MĀNOA   MAUNALANI HEIGHTS

Hickam Harbor   Ke'ehi Lagoon   Coast Guard Res.   Honolulu Harbor   'Iolani Palace   University of Hawai'i   ST. LOUIS HEIGHTS   PĀLOLO   'ĀINA HAINA   KULI'OU'OU

Mokuoeo (islet)   Mokauea I.   Sand I. (Kamoku'ākulikuli)   S. Beretania St.   S. King St.   Dole St.   PĀLOLO

Niu Valley   HAWAI'I KAI

Māmala Bay   Ala Moana Blvd.   MŌ'ILI'ILI   MAUNALANI HEIGHTS   'ĀINAKOA   Kuapua Pond

HONOLULU   Ala Moana Beach   WILHELMINA RISE   WAI'ALAE NUI   WAI'ALAE IKI   Niu Pen.   Paikō Pen.

'Āina Moana (Magic Island)   Lunalilo Fwy.   KAIMUKI   WAI'ALAE   *Maunalua Bay*

Ft. DeRussy Mil. Res.   KĀHALĀ   Wai'alae Beach

Waikīkī Beach   Kapi'olani Blvd.   Ft. Ruger Mil. Res.   Wailupe Pen.

Prince Kūhiō Beach   Hawai'i National Guard   Kāhala Beach

Kapi'olani Beach   Diamond Head (Lē'ahi) 760   Diamond Head Rd.   Kawaihoa Pt.   Koko Head

Kapua Entrance   Kuilei Cliffs   Diamond Head Beach   Kupikipiki'ō Pt.

157°52'30"E   157°45'E

Magic Island, O'ahu. [Hawai'i Visitors Bureau]

Nickname:	The Gathering Place
Color and emblem:	yellow; *pua 'ilima,* the flower of *Sida fallax*
Land area:	597.1 square miles (1,546.5 square kilometers)
Largest perennial stream:	Waikele Stream, 27 million gallons (102,000 cubic meters) per day
Resident population (1996):	871,800
Visitors (estimated total arrivals 1997):	5,002,530
Per capita personal income (1993):	$24,929
Median price of single-family house (1995):	$349,000

committed to urban development of the 'Ewa Plain, centered on a "second city" hub at Kapolei. In addition, after several decades of planning and construction, the opening of the H-3 Freeway in 1997 (America's most expensive highway on a cost per mile basis) can be expected to facilitate additional urbanization on the windward side of the island. The limited potential for additional freshwater resources on O'ahu, however, and tensions over the allocation of existing water resources may, more than land scarcity, slow the rapid pace of future urban expansion.

Artificial lagoons at Ko Olina Resort and Barbers Point deep draft harbor, leeward coast, O'ahu. [J. Juvik]

MOLOKA'I AND LĀNA'I

MOLOKA'I

'O Moloka'i nui a Hina, lei ana i ke kukui
Great Moloka'i of the goddess Hina, adorned with the lei
of kukui

Fifth in size of the Hawaiian Islands, Moloka'i has remained isolated from the dramatic changes that have transformed the archipelago over recent decades. The population (6,717 in 1990) is predominantly rural and of Native Hawaiian ancestry. The island retains a local lifestyle and ambiance that, with the exception of inaccessible Ni'ihau, is disappearing elsewhere in the state.

Moloka'i was formed from the coalescence of three separate volcanoes. Like the other high, rugged islands of Hawai'i, considerable environmental diversity is compressed within its small land area. The eroded mountains of East Moloka'i (1.8 million years old) are dominated on the north coast by precipitous sea cliffs that rise to more than 3,000 feet (900 m). Also opening to the windward coast are the spectacular amphitheater-like valleys of Pelekunu, Wailau, and Hālawa. The ridges of these valleys converge on the island's summit at Kamakou (4,970 feet, 1,514 m). The gulch-scored leeward slopes of East

Moloka'i descend to a narrow coastal plain fronting the 'Au'au and Pailolo Channels that face Lāna'i and Maui.

Although Hawaiians constructed intricately terraced, irrigated taro fields in the windward valleys of all islands, the most extensive and elaborate aquaculture complexes to be found anywhere in Oceania were developed on the protected south coast of Moloka'i. Rock-lined ponds were constructed on shallow offshore reef flats along much of the south coast. In recent decades, soil erosion and the invasion of alien mangrove trees along the shoreline have greatly altered the ecology of this coastal zone.

The terrain of West Moloka'i differs markedly from that in the east. Here a slightly older (1.9 million years) but lower volcanic dome rises to 1,381 feet (421 m) at Pu'u Nānā. This elevation is insufficient to check the blustery trade winds or induce significant orographic rainfall. As a result, dry and windy conditions prevail and extensive coastal and inland sand dunes occupy the area known as Mo'omomi. The Department of Hawaiian Homelands, as well as the island's major private landowner, Moloka'i Ranch, have large landholdings in central and West Moloka'i.

The third distinctive volcanic component of Moloka'i is the small Kalaupapa Peninsula on the north-central coast.

Kalaupapa Peninsula, Moloka'i. [D. A. Clague]

North coast sea cliffs, Moloka'i. [J. E. Maragos]

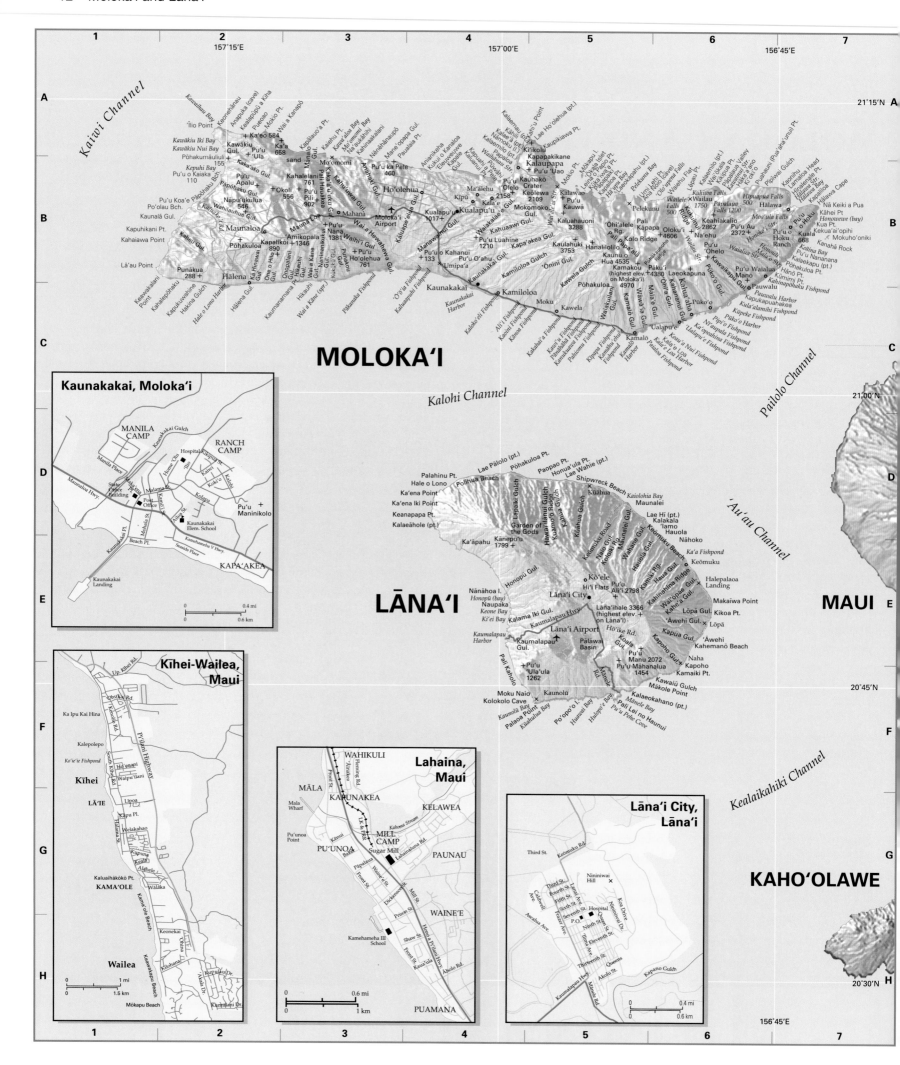

Hawaiian fishpond, Puhaloa, Moloka'i. [J. E. Maragos]

Kalaupapa is effectively isolated from the rest of Moloka'i by steep, windward cliffs that rise to 1,600 feet (500 m) and are negotiable only on foot or by mule. This remote area was chosen as the site for a Hansen's disease (leper) colony in 1865. A National Historical Park has been created at Kalaupapa to honor the memory of the ostracized disease patients and the Belgian priest Father Damien de Veuster and others who worked there in the late nineteenth century. A total of 68 residents remained at the facility in July 1996.

Pineapple, produced on central and West Moloka'i, was the island's economic mainstay for decades but gradually declined and was ultimately abandoned by the early 1980s. High unemployment and limited economic opportunities are reflected in the low rate of population growth (from 5,280 in 1950 to 6,717 in 1990). Young people in particular leave the island to pursue education and job opportunities elsewhere. Tourism has remained relatively low-key, with the number of hotel rooms static at 245 over 20 years. In addition to tourism, cattle ranching, irrigated fruit and vegetable farming, and coffee remain the most significant components of the rural economy.

Nickname:	The Friendly Isle
Color and emblem:	green; *pua kukui,* the flower of *Aleurites moluccana*
Land area:	260.0 square miles (673.5 square kilometers)
Resident population (1990):	6,717
Visitors (estimated total arrivals 1997):	78,230
Per capita personal income (1993):	$10,175
Median price of a single-family house (1995):	$160,000

LĀNA'I

'O Lāna'i a Kaululā'au, hiehie iā Lāna'ihale
Lāna'i domain of the chief Kaululā'au, distinguished with its peak of Lāna'ihale

The island of Lāna'i was formed from a single volcano that last erupted about 1.3 million years ago. The Pālāwai Basin, now an alluvium-filled depression on the central plateau, is all that remains of the volcano's caldera.

Small Lāna'i lies hidden from the trade winds in the lee or rain shadow of the more massive West Maui Mountains that rise to an elevation of 5,788 feet (1,764 m) across the 'Au'au Channel. Annual rainfall on the summit of Lāna'ihale at 3,370 feet (1,030 m) is 30–40 inches (760–1,015 mm), but considerably less, 10–20 inches (250–500 mm), over much of the rest of the island. This aridity has shaped and constrained human use of Lāna'i since the first settlement.

Beginning in the late nineteenth century, overgrazing by domestic cattle, feral goats, and axis deer led to excessive soil erosion over most of the island. As a consequence some of the most devastated areas near Kānepu'u have taken on a desert "badlands" appearance. This boulder-strewn terrain is marketed to tourists in the 1990s as the "Garden of the Gods."

Evidence suggests that the island was never heavily populated. The first official census of Lāna'i in 1838 counted 1,200 resident Hawaiians, and this number declined to 616 within 8 years. Missionaries arrived in 1837, and in 1855 Mormon immigrants launched an ill-fated agricultural colony on the central plateau. By the early 1920s Castle & Cooke had acquired more than 98 percent of the island and established a 16,000-acre (6,500 ha) pineapple plantation surrounding its company town, Lāna'i City.

Largely populated by immigrant Filipino labor, the island remained, for most of the twentieth century, one of the most pervasive examples of plantation culture in Hawai'i. New corporate ownership, the lure of tourism, and declining profitability of pineapple forced major changes on Lāna'i in the early 1990s. The pineapple plantation closed and the loss of hundreds of plantation jobs was partially offset by employment in tourism. New luxury hotels opened at Kō'ele (102 rooms) and Mānele Bay (250 rooms).

Nickname:	The Private Isle
Color and emblem:	orange; *pua kauna'oa,* the native dodder *Cuscuta sandwichiana*
Land area:	140.6 square miles (364.0 square kilometers)
Resident population (1994):	2,426
Visitors (estimated total arrivals 1997):	105,260
Per capita personal income:	$13,584
Median price of a single-family house (1995):	$140,000

MAUI AND KAHO'OLAWE

MAUI

'O Maui o nā hono a'o Pi'ilani, Maui no ka 'oi
O Maui of the many bays of Pi'ilani, Maui excels

Maui is the second largest island in Hawai'i, but it has less than 30 percent of the area of Hawai'i Island. The central Maui isthmus bridges two separate volcanoes that form the island. The older West Maui Mountains (1.3 million years) are dramatically eroded and rise to an elevation of 5,788 feet (1,764 m) at Pu'u Kukui, a spot that vies with Wai'ale'ale on Kaua'i as one of the rainiest places on Earth. By contrast, East Maui is dominated by the much larger volcano of Haleakalā (750,000 years), which is considered volcanically active although its last summit eruption was 800 to 1,500 years ago. The most recent flank eruption occurred above La Pérouse Bay in 1790.

Maui has beautiful beaches and scenic vistas that make it a favored tourist destination. The rapid expansion of the island's tourism sector, beginning in the late 1960s, is reflected in the number of hotel rooms, condominiums, and other vacation rental units, which increased almost sevenfold, from 2,641 in 1970 to 17,442 in 1996. Resort development is concentrated in the leeward areas, especially the West Maui Coast extending from Lahaina through Kā'anapali to Kapalua, and sheltered East Maui from Kīhei to Mākena. Maui's resident population has grown faster than that of any other island in the state, increasing from 38,691 to 91,361 between 1970 and 1990.

Kapalua Resort, West Maui. [J. Juvik]

Olowalu Gulch, West Maui. [J. Juvik]

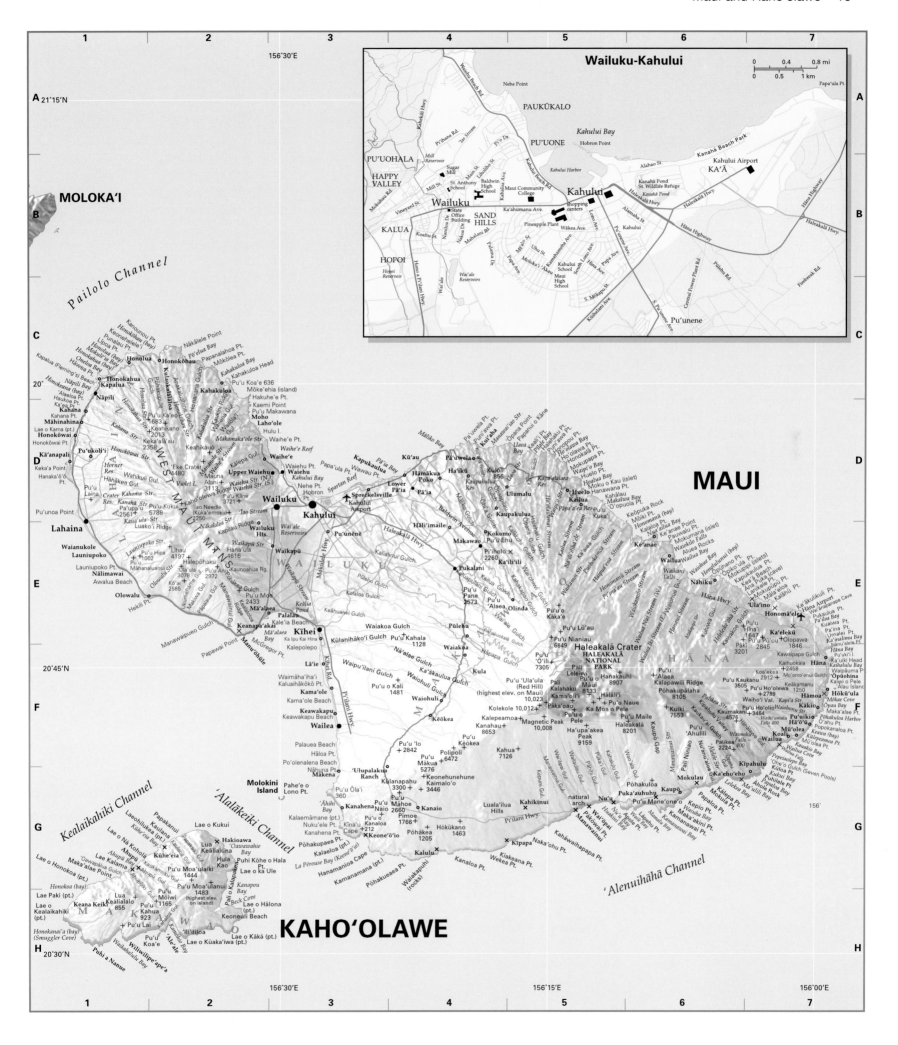

MOLOKA‘I

Pailolo Channel

Wailuku-Kahului

0   0.4   0.8 mi
0   0.5   1 km

Tao Stream
Waiehu Beach Rd.
Nehe Point
Kahekili Hwy.
PAUKŪKALO
Kahului Bay
PU‘UOHALA
Pi‘ihana Rd.
Pi‘o Dr.
PU‘UONE
Hobron Point
Mill Reservoir
Kahana Beach Park
Kahului Harbor
Alahao St.
Kahului Airport
Sugar Mill
Main St.
Lākāhī Ave.
KA‘Ā
HAPPY VALLEY
Mill St.
St. Anthony School
Baldwin High School
Maui Community College
Kanahā Pond St. Wildlife Refuge
Kanahā Pond
Ka‘ahakana Hwy.
Mokuhau Rd.
Wailuku
State Office Building
Kahului
Ka‘ahumanu Ave.
Lono Ave.
Ahimeha St.
Haleakalā Hwy.
KALUA
Vineyard St.
SAND HILLS
Pineapple Plant
Wākea Ave.
Puʻunene Ave.
Kahului
Hāna Highway
HOPOI
Koahu St.
Mahalani St.
Maui High School
Kahului School
South Lono Ave.
Hina Ave.
Papa Ave.
Central Power Plant Rd.
Hopoi Reservoir
Wai‘ale Reservoirs
Molokaʻi ‘Ākau
Maui High School
S. Mōkapu St.
Kaʻelahoni Ave.
Pu‘unene
Firebreak Rd.

Pailolo Channel

Honolua Honokōhau
Nākālele Point
Pā‘elua Bay
Papanalahoa Pt.
Mōkōlea Pt.
Kahakuloa Bay
Kahakuloa Head
Honokahua Kapalua
Pu‘u Koa‘e 636
Mōke‘ehia (island)
Hakuhe‘e Pt.
Nāpili Kahakuloa
Keahikano
Kaemi Point
Pu‘u Makawana
Kahana Mōkō
Māhinahina
Keahikauō
Laho‘ole
Hulu I.
Lae o Kama (pt.)
Honoköwai
Keka‘alā‘au
Waihe‘e Pt.
Kapukaulua
Māliko Bay
Pa‘uwela Pt.
Pu‘u o Kāne
‘Opana Point
Honokōwai Pt.
Pu‘ukoli‘i
Waihe‘e Reef
Ku‘au
Papanu o Kāne
Mananan‘ian Str.
Ka‘anapali
Waihe‘e
Pā‘ula Pt.
Kuilī
Ho‘olua Pt.
Ho‘okipa Pt.
Kā‘anapali
Mauna Kahālāwai 4480
Upper Waiehu
Waiehu
Kahului Bay
Pa‘uwela
Kuiaha
Huelo
Mokupapa Pt.
Keka‘alā‘au
‘Eke Crater
Mauna Alani 3113
Waihe‘e
Hobron Pt.
Ha‘ikū
Hāmākua Poko
Kaupakulua Res.
Kapa‘a‘alaea
Waipi‘o Bay
Hoalua Bay
Keka‘ala‘au
Kā‘eleku Res.
Kahakuloa
Huelo Hanawana
Ho‘olawa Pt.
Ke'anae
Violet L. 1683
2013
Wailuku
Spreckelsville
Lower Pā‘ia
Pā‘ia
Nāilima Str.
Ka‘uo Point
Moku o Kau (islet)
MAUI
Horner Res.
Wahikuli Gul.
Hāhākea Gul.
Pu‘u Kāne 3721
Tao Needle (Kūka‘emoku)
Kahului Airport
Baldwin Avenue
Naliko Gulch
‘Opana Str.
Kaupakulua
Kailiili Str.
Keōpuka Rock
Honomanu (bay)
Keōpuka Rock
Ka‘uiki Head
Kahanu Gul.
Pu‘u o Kila
Moku‘ula
Kū‘au
Ke‘anae
Honomanu Bay
Ko‘olau Gulch
Nua‘ailua Bay
Ka‘uiki
Lahaina
Tao Stream
Tao Needle 2250
Nākaola Ridge
Kaupakulua
Kokomo
Kuka‘alaea
Ulumalu
Pauwalu Pt.
Mokumana (islet)
Waiohue Bay
Wailua Wailua Bay
Waianu
Waikani Falls
Pu‘u ‘Ehu
Waiakoa
Pu‘u Kāne
Kūlanihāko‘i Gulch
Waikapū Hts.
Wai‘ale Reservoir
Pu‘unene
Haleakalā Hwy.
Hāli‘imaile
Kailua
Makawao
Kahili Str.
Nāhiku
Waikani Falls
Ke‘anae Arboretum
Lae o Pele
Waianu Str.
Nāhiku
Kea Point
Lanikele (cave)
Lahaina
Kahoma Str.
Pa‘upa‘u 2561
5788
Pu‘u Kukui 5788
Kaua‘ula Str.
Luako‘i Ridge
Kapilau Ridge
Pu‘u ‘Ōpūlaha
Olinda
Pi‘iholo
Ka‘ili‘ili
2260
Pi‘ina‘au Stream
Makapipi St.
Mokupapa (islet)
Mokupapa (cave)
Mu‘oloa Pt.
Kalani Pt.
Launiupoko
Waianukole
2585
Kaua‘ula Str.
Lihau 4197
Pu‘u Hipa 1002
‘Ula‘ula 3078
Kalua 2972
Halepōhaku
Waikapū
Pūlehu Gulch
Kolaloa Gulch
Pukalani
Pu‘u Nianiau 6849
Waimoku Falls
‘Ula‘ino
Ko‘olau Gap
Wailuaiki
Pu‘u Pane 2573
Pu‘u ‘Alaea
Wailua Nui Stream
E. Wailuaiki Stream
Ka‘ākūlikuli Pt.
Hāna Airport
Kawaipapa Cave
‘Alaea Point
Kuakua Pt.
Pu‘uki‘i Head
Kuiawa
Hāna Bay
Olowalu
Hekili Pt.
Ka‘i‘ili Str.
Mā‘alaea
Pu‘u Moe 2433
Palalau
Kale‘ia Beach
Keālia Pond
Keāhuawai Gulch
Kofaloa Gulch
Nā‘alae Gulch
Pūlehu
Waiakoa
Ka‘ō‘ehe
Kula
Pu‘u ‘Ula‘ula (Red Hill) (highest elev. on Maui) 10,023
Pu‘u ‘Ōlili 7305
Pu‘u Lū‘au
Leleiwi
Pali Kalahaku
HALEAKALĀ CRATER
HALEAKALĀ NATIONAL PARK
Pu‘u Maile
Ko‘olau Gap
Kaupō Gap
Pu‘u Kaukau 2845
3201
Pu‘u Pu‘u
Pu‘ulii Head
Hāna
Ka‘eleku
Kakio
Ha‘o‘u
Kawaipapa
Ko‘a‘ekea 2458
Mo‘omo‘onui Onui Pt.
Waianapanapa Cave
Keanapa‘akai
Mā‘alaea Bay
McGregor Pt.
Kīhei
Ka Ipu Kai Hina
Kalepolepo
La‘ie
Waipu‘ilani Gulch
Waiohuli Gulch
Ka‘ākaulua Gulch
Hanakauhi 8907
Māui 8133
Kama‘oli‘i
Hanakauhi
Kapalaoa
Kalapawili Ridge
Pōhakupālaha 8105
Paliku
Kuhiwa Valley
Kaumakani 4576
3464
Pu‘uki‘o
Mū‘olea
Haneo‘o
Waio‘nohonu Str.
Opua Bay
Pōpokalaoa Pt.
Kama‘ole
Kama‘ole Beach
Pi‘ilani Hwy.
Waiohuli
Pu‘u ‘O‘ili 7305
Kolekole 10,012
Magnetic Peak 10,008
Pu‘u o Pele
Pu‘u Naue
Ka Moa o Pele
Kō‘eleka
Kalepeamoa 8653
Kanahau
Ha‘upa‘akea Peak 9159
Haleakalā 8201
Pu‘u Nīnau
Maka‘akini Pt.
Kailua Gul.
Ho‘āu
Koali
Wailua
Mū‘olea Pt.
Kīpahulu
Kawakapu Beach
Wailea
Palauea Beach
Po‘olenalena Beach
Nāhuna Pt.
Mākena
Pu‘u ‘Io 2842
Pu‘u Kō‘eka
Polipoli
Pu‘u Mākua 5276
Kahua 7126
Pu‘u Māile
Kaupō
Mokulau
Ka‘eho‘eho
Kukui Bay
Pāpā‘au Bay
Kīpahulu
‘Ohe‘o Gulch (Seven Pools)
Kuloa Pt.
Puhilele Pt.
Lelekea Bay
Mū‘olili Bay
Ahole Rock
Molokini Island
Pahe‘e o Lono Pt.
‘Ulupalakua Ranch
Keonehunehune
Kaimalo‘o 3446
Kahua 7126
Kanaio
Luala‘ilua Hills
Kahikinui
natural arch
Nu‘u
Pu‘u Mane‘one‘o
Pūhā‘auhuhu
Lelekea
Kepio St.
Mokalā Pt.
Kipapa Pt.
Manawainui
Kamanawai Pt.
Kaupō
Maka‘akini Pt.
Naka‘ohu Pt.
Kahāwaihapapa Pt.
‘Āhihi Cove
Kalaemāmane (pt.)
Kalaeloa (pt.)
Mākena
Pu‘u Naio
Pu‘u Mōhoe 2660
Pu‘u ‘Ōla‘i 360
Pimoe
Pōhākea 1205
Pu‘u ‘Ili 1766
Kanahena
Kanahena Pt.
Nuku‘ele Pt.
Keone‘ō‘io
La Pérouse Bay
Hanamanioa Cape
Kanahena Pt.
Pu‘u ‘Ili 212
1463
Pōhākea
Hōkūkano
Kanaio
Kamanamana Pt.
Pōhakueaea Pt.
Kalulu
Wekea Pt.
Kahikinui
Pi‘ilani Hwy.
Naka‘ohu Pt.
Kīpapa
Naka‘ohu Pt.
Waiakapuhi Pt.
Waiakapuhi (rocks)
Kanaloa Pt.
‘Alenuihāhā Channel

Kealaikahiki Channel
‘Alalākeiki Channel
Papakanui
Laeohilukea Gul.
Kūhe‘ia Bay
Lae o Nā Kohola
Lae o Kukui
Hakioawa
Lua Keālialua
‘Oawawahie Bay
Kūhe‘eia
Papakanui
Kaulana
Ahupū
‘Oawapālua Gulch
Kaukamoku Gul.
Puhi Kōhe o Hala
Lae o Kā Ule
Ahupū Gul.
Lua Makika
Ahupū
Maka‘alae Point
Puhi Kōhe o Hala
Honokoa (bay)
KAHO‘OLAWE
Lae Paki (pt.)
Pu‘u Moa‘ulaiki 1444
Pu‘u Moa‘ulanui 1483 (highest elev. on island)
Kanapou Bay
Beck Cove
Lae o Hālona (pt.)
Keana Keiki
Lua Keālialalo 855
Kahua 923
MAKA Pu‘u Lai
WAI Pu‘u Mōiwi 1165
‘Ili‘ilika Bay
Lae o Kākā (pt.)
Lae o Kūaka‘iwa (pt.)
Honokanai‘a (bay) (Smuggler Cove)
Lae o Honokoa (pt.)
Lae o Kealaikahiki (pt.)
Wiliwilipe‘ape‘a
Ale‘ale
Kumuhoa Bay
Kuheta
Waikahalulu Bay
Keoneuli Beach
Puhi a Nanue
Waikahalulu Bay

MOLOKA‘I
21°15'N
20°
20°45'N
20°30'N
156°30'E
156°15'E
156°00'E

Wailuku-Kahului, Maui. [J. Juvik]

Maui's agricultural sector also remains vibrant, since the island has so far escaped most of the contractions and closures that have characterized sugar and pineapple operations across the state since 1970. There also has been a rapid expansion of high value, diversified agriculture on the cooler, upland slopes of Haleakalā around Kula, where temperate vegetables and fruits, including the sweet "Maui onion," are grown. Extensive cattle ranches occupy more marginal *mauka* (upland) areas on the slopes of Haleakalā.

Nickname:	The Valley Isle
Color and emblem:	pink; *pua lokelani,* the small pink rose of *Rosa* sp.
Land area:	727.3 square miles (1,883.7 square kilometers)
Resident population (1994):	91,361
Largest perennial stream:	'Īao Stream, 43 million gallons (163,000 cubic meters) per day
Visitors (estimated total arrivals 1997):	2,271,330
Per capita personal income (1993):	$21,354
Median price of a single-family house (1995):	$273,000

KAHO'OLAWE

'O Kaho'olawe o Kanaloa me Kealaikahiki
Kaho'olawe of the god Kanaloa and the seaway Kealaikahiki

The small island of Kaho'olawe lies 6.7 miles (11 km) across the 'Alalākeiki Channel from Nuku'ele Point on East Maui. Located in the lee of towering Haleakalā, and with low relief, reaching only to 1,477 feet (450 m) elevation, Kaho'olawe is an arid island. Its sparse native dry forest was, perhaps, reduced by anthropogenic fires in past centuries. What vegetative cover remained was further ravaged by feral and domestic ungulates beginning in the mid-nineteenth century. During World War II the U.S. military assumed control of Kaho'olawe and for decades used it as a target island for naval and aerial bombardment training.

In 1993 the island of Kaho'olawe was transferred to Native Hawaiian control. The Kaho'olawe Island Reserve Commission was established to oversee cleanup of the island, including the removal of unexploded ordnance and the restoration of native ecosystems and traditional cultural uses.

Nickname:	None
Color and emblem:	gray, *pua hinahina,* the plant *Heliotropium anomalum*
Land area:	44.6 square miles (115.5 square kilometers)
Resident population:	uninhabited

HAWAI'I

'O Hawai'i nui kuauli, Hawai'i o Keawe
The great island of Hawai'i with vistas of green, Hawai'i of
  the chief Keawe

The island of Hawai'i was formed from the coalescence of five volcanoes—Kohala, Mauna Kea, Hualālai, Mauna Loa, and Kīlauea. Each mountain has distinctive features and occupies a different position on the geologic continuum from active shield building to erosion and subsidence. The oldest mountain, Kohala, was formed only 430,000 years ago, but already its windward slopes are deeply incised with large erosional valleys such as spectacular Waipi'o Valley.

Dormant Mauna Kea rises to an elevation of 13,796 feet (4,205 m) and is typically snowcapped in winter. The summit area of Mauna Kea in the past supported a small alpine glacier that expanded, retreated, and disappeared in synchrony with the major continental ice ages of the last several hundred thousand years. The shield-building lavas of Mauna Kea are now largely buried under a veneer of cinder and ash deposits, the product of late phase explosive eruptions that ceased about 3,600 years ago.

Rising high above Kailua-Kona is Hualālai volcano, which is still active, having last erupted in 1801. Like Mauna Kea it bears a mantle of cinder and ash. Mauna Loa has the classic profile of an active shield volcano—a smooth dome with gently sloping flanks and a large summit caldera (Moku-'āweoweo). While it has a slightly lower summit elevation than Mauna Kea, it is a much more massive mountain. Kīlauea, the youngest and most active of the island's five volcanoes, is embedded in the eastern flanks of the much larger Mauna Loa and thus lacks a distinctive "stand alone" mountain profile.

Island of Hawai'i, computer simulation from satellite image, view from southeast. [NASA Jet Propulsion Laboratory]

Hilo, Hawai'i. [J. Juvik]

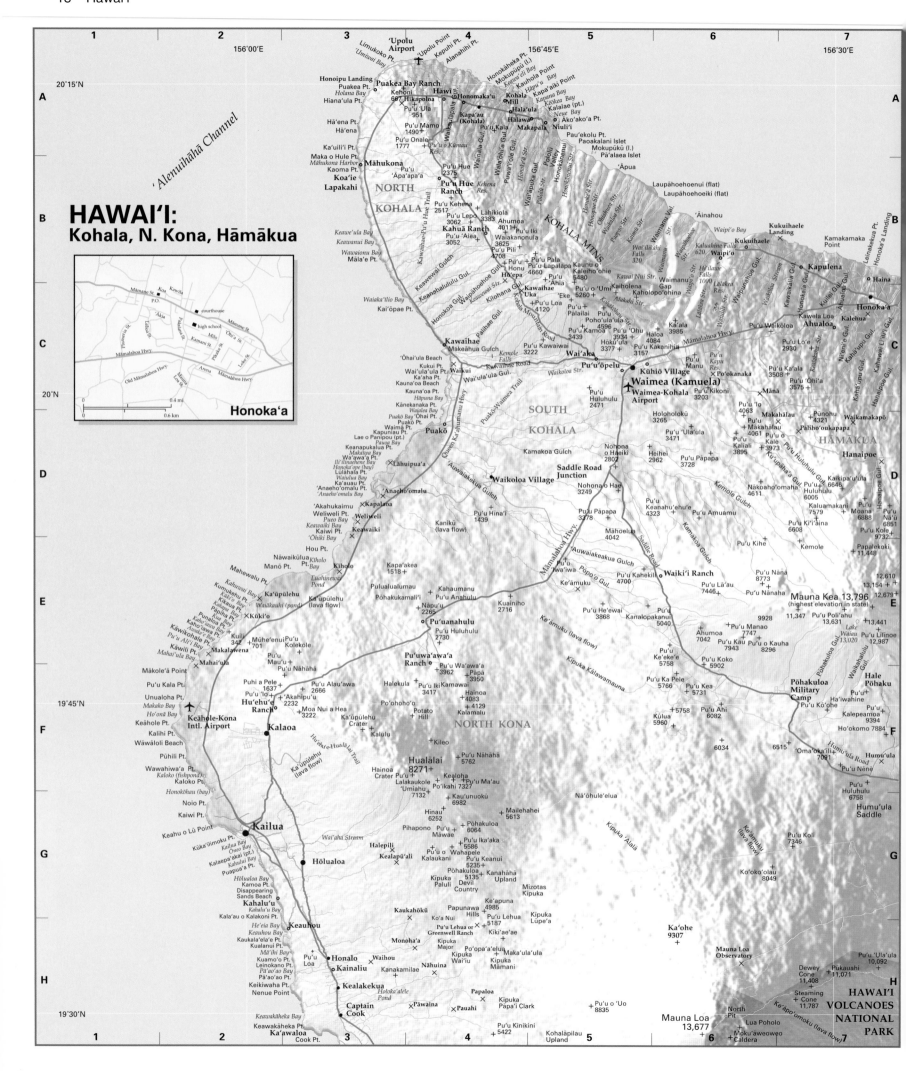

HAWAI'I:
Kohala, N. Kona, Hāmākua

'Alenuihāhā Channel

Honoka'a

NORTH KOHALA

SOUTH KOHALA

HĀMĀKUA

KOHALA MTNS

NORTH KONA

Mauna Kea 13,796
(highest elevation in state)

Hualālai
8271

Mauna Loa
13,677

HAWAI'I VOLCANOES NATIONAL PARK

'Upolu Airport

Keāhole-Kona Intl. Airport

Waimea-Kohala Airport

Kailua

Waimea (Kamuela)

Honoka'a

Captain Cook

20°15'N

20°N

19°45'N

19°30'N

156°00'E

156°45'E

156°30'E

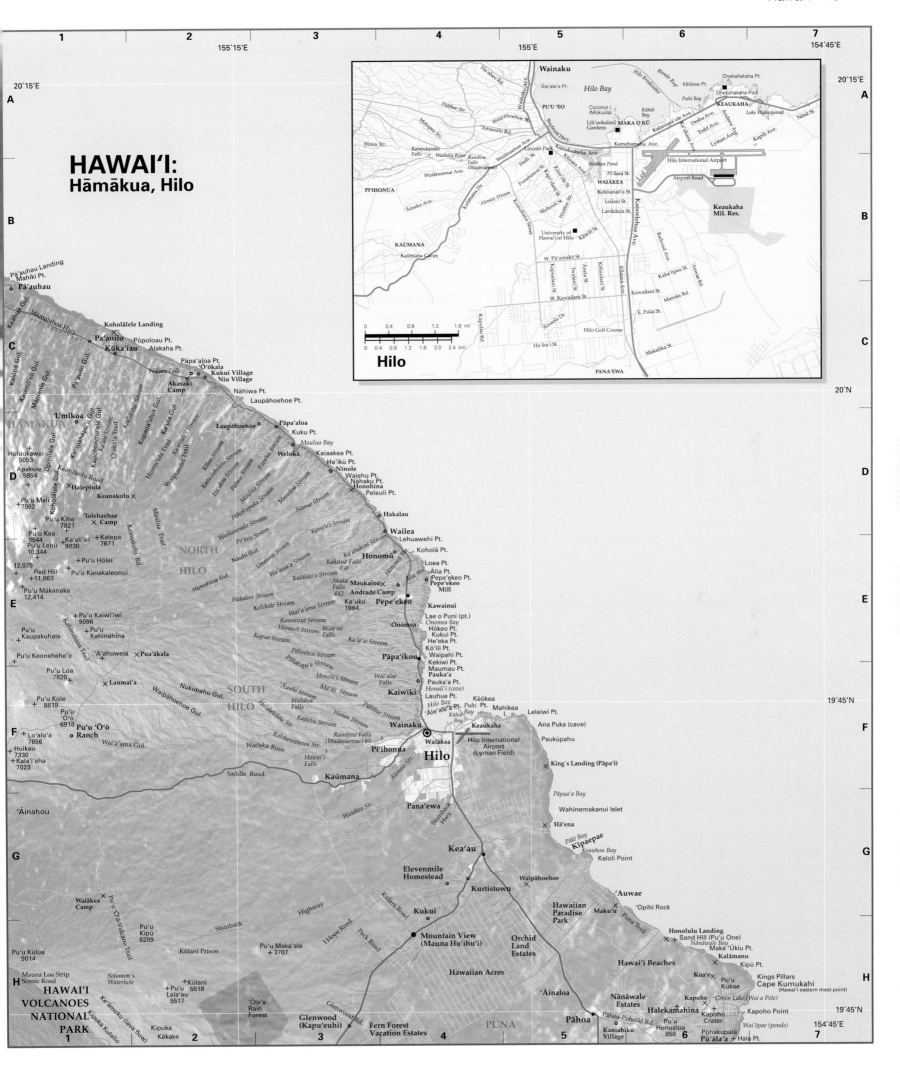

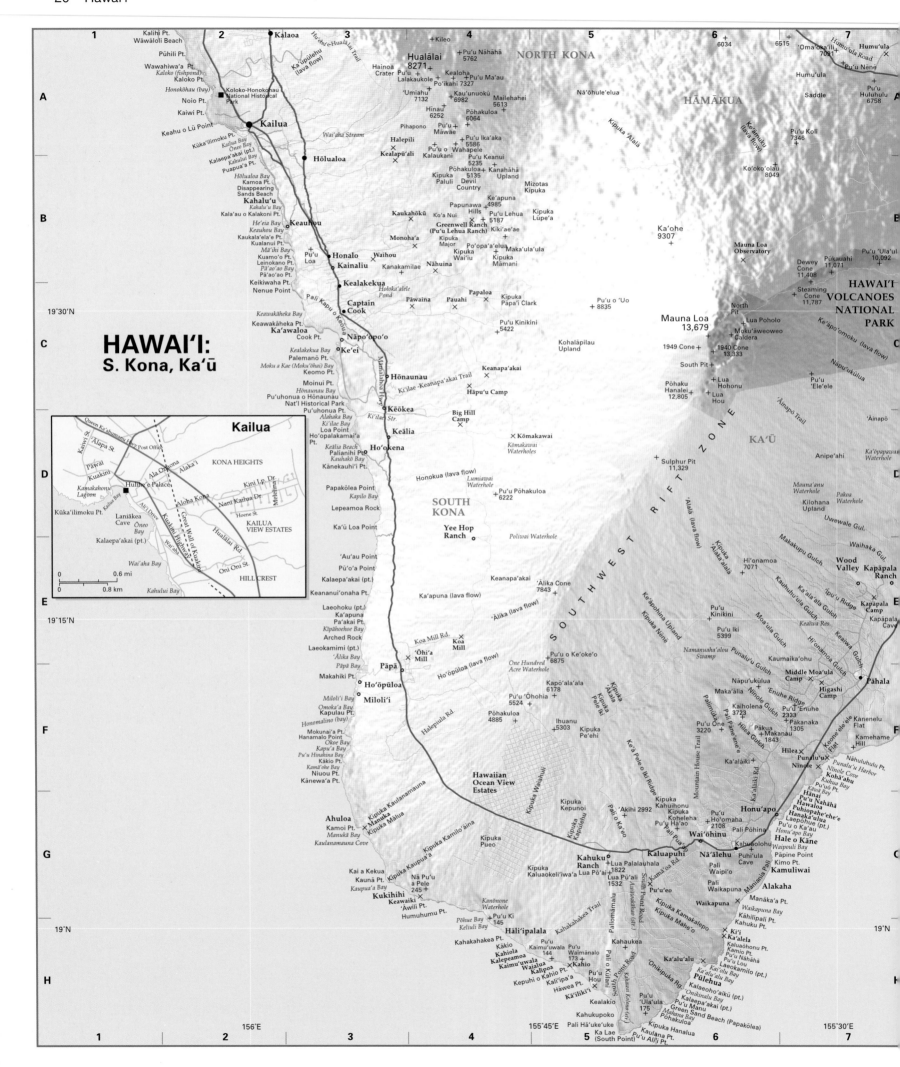

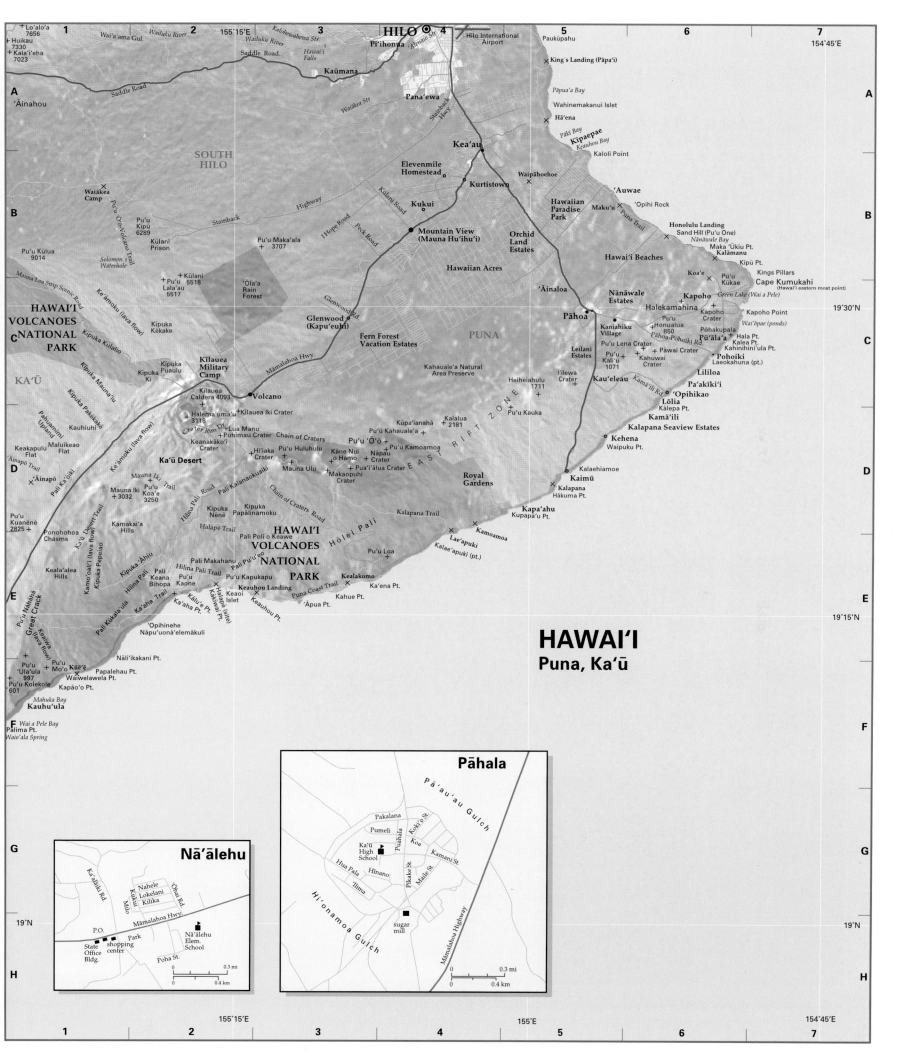

Hawai'i Island is larger than all the other islands of the archipelago combined, and with its greater mass and higher elevations it has more distinctive climatic zones and ecosystem types than can be found elsewhere in the state.

Sugarcane was the consistent mainstay of the island's economy for more than 120 years, and as late as 1969 plantations located throughout the Hāmākua, Kohala, and Ka'ū Districts contributed more than 37 percent of the state's sugar production of 1.18 million tons. The process of downsizing and closing plantations began in the 1970s and culminated in the abandonment of sugarcane production on the island in the spring of 1996. Throughout the years of decline of the sugar industry, there has been growth in the island's tourism sector that is based largely in the Kona and South Kohala Districts where over 90 percent of the island's 9,100 hotel rooms are located. This change in the island's economic base has led to a gradual shift of economic and political power away from East Hawai'i (Hilo) to West Hawai'i. There has also been rapid population growth in the poorly serviced rural subdivisions, especially in Puna District. Puna is nearly as large as O'ahu and, perhaps, is the last place in the state where comparatively affordable, fee simple land is available, volcanic hazards notwithstanding.

Mauna Loa summit from Mauna Kea, Hawai'i. [J. Juvik]

Diversified agriculture on Hawai'i Island is dominated by macadamia nuts, papaya, flowers, tropical and temperate vegetables, and specialty coffee that is grown in the unique summer rainfall belt on the middle slopes of the Kona District. Cattle ranching also makes use of extensive areas of the island. The Parker Ranch, located on leeward Mauna Kea above Waimea town, is the state's second largest private landowner with 139,000 acres (56,000 ha). The combined value of diversified agriculture on the island was $133 million in 1995, down from $150 million in 1989.

Nickname:	The Orchid Isle
Color and emblem:	red; *pua lehua,* the red blossom of *Metrosideros polymorpha*
Land area:	4,028.2 square miles (10,433.1 square kilometers)
Largest perennial stream:	Wailuku River, 250 million gallons (950,000 cubic meters) per day
Resident population (1996):	138,400
Visitors (estimated total arrivals 1997):	1,255,480
Per capita personal income (1993):	$17,519
Median price of single-family house (1995):	$155,000

Kahauale'a eruption, East Rift, Kīlauea, Hawai'i, 1977. [J. Juvik]

NORTHWESTERN HAWAIIAN ISLANDS

Mai ka pi'ina a ka lā i Ha'eha'e a i ka lā welowelo i Kānemiloha'i
From where the sun rises at Ha'eha'e (Kumukahi, Hawai'i
    Island) to its setting at Kānemiloha'i (Kure)

Dotting the North Pacific along a linear path extending slightly more than 1,000 miles (1,600 km) beyond Kaua'i and Ni'ihau, the Northwestern Hawaiian Islands provide mute testimony to the relatively short geologic life span of these basaltic islands. Nīhoa (130 miles [209 km] from Ni'ihau) and Necker (a further 180 miles [290 km] beyond Nīhoa) are nearest the main islands. Both are small, residual fragments of volcanoes that formed 7.2 and 10.3 million years ago respectively. Although both of these islands were uninhabited at the time of their modern discovery in the late eighteenth century, there is an extensive *heiau* complex on Necker, and agricultural terraces and other Hawaiian archaeological features can be found on Nīhoa. Despite this evidence of earlier human use, the islands continue to support an assemblage of endemic plants and animals not found elsewhere in the archipelago.

As the age of the islands increases toward the northwest, volcanic rocks disappear completely and are replaced by coralline atolls and reefs built on submerged volcanic foundations. The basaltic rocks underlying Midway Atoll have been dated at 27.7 million years. This age, in addition to the known distance (1,580 miles, 2,540 km) separating Midway from Hawai'i Island (which is now positioned over the geologic "hotspot" where Midway earlier formed) enables a rough calculation of the speed at which the Pacific crustal plate has been moving northwestward. The result suggests crustal plate movement of approximately 3.4 inches (8.6 cm) per year.

La Pérouse Pinnacle. [G. H. Balazs]

Lisianski Island. [G. H. Balazs]

Necker Island. [G. H. Balazs]

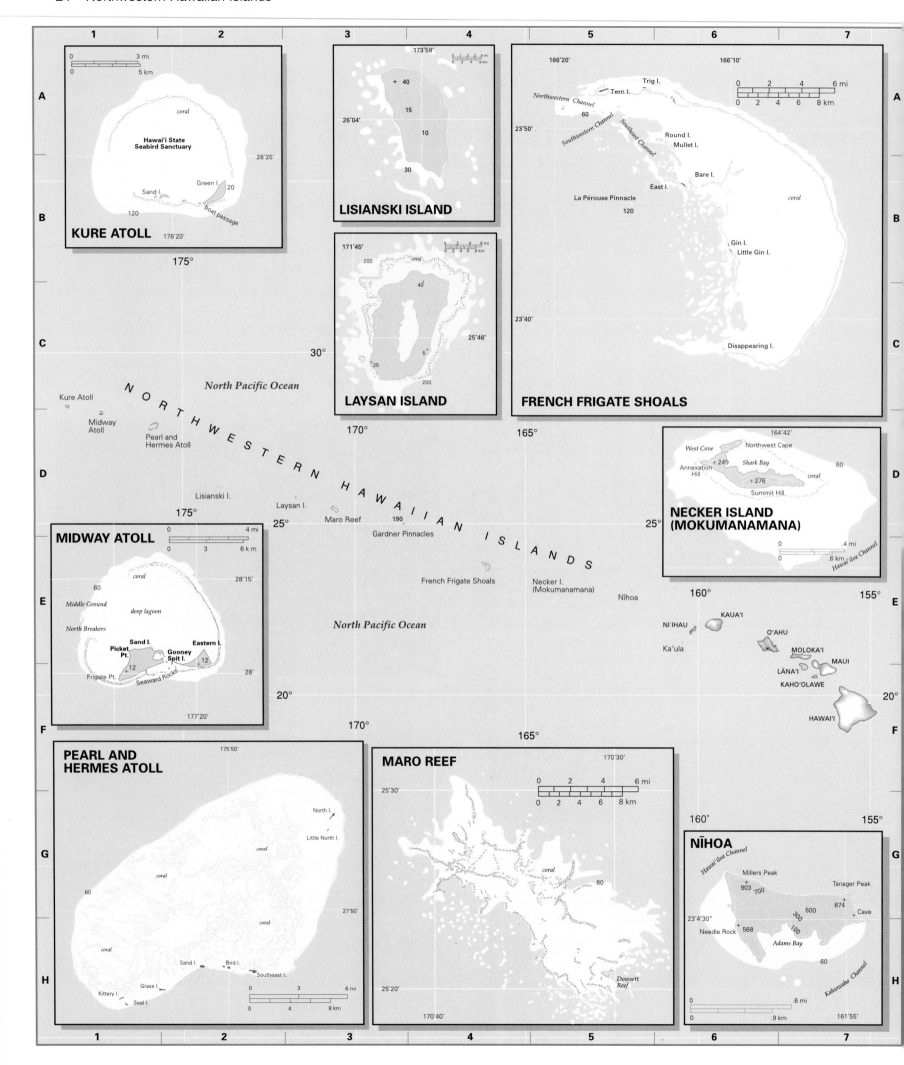

KURE ATOLL

0   3 mi
0   5 km

coral

**Hawai'i State
Seabird Sanctuary**

Sand I.   Green I.   20

120   boat passage

28°25'
178°20'
175°

LISIANSKI ISLAND

173°58'

+ 40
26°04'
15
10
30

LAYSAN ISLAND

171°45'
200   coral
40
5
25   200
25°46'
30°
170°

FRENCH FRIGATE SHOALS

166°20'   166°10'

0   2   4   6 mi
0   2   4   6   8 km

Northwestern Channel   Trig I.
Tern I.
60
23°50'   Southwestern Channel   Round I.
Southeast Channel   Mullet I.

Bare I.

East I.   coral

La Pérouse Pinnacle   Gin I.
120   Little Gin I.

23°40'

Disappearing I.
165°

NECKER ISLAND (MOKUMANAMANA)

164°42'
West Cove   Northwest Cape
+ 249   Shark Bay
Annexation   60
Hill   + 276   coral
Summit Hill

0   .4 mi
0   .6 km
Hawai'iloa Channel

North Pacific Ocean

NORTHWESTERN HAWAIIAN ISLANDS

Kure Atoll
Midway
Atoll
Pearl and
Hermes Atoll

Lisianski I.
Laysan I.   25°
Maro Reef   190
Gardner Pinnacles

French Frigate Shoals   Necker I.
(Mokumanamana)   Nīhoa

North Pacific Ocean   25°

160°   155°

NI'IHAU   KAUA'I
Ka'ula   O'AHU
MOLOKA'I
LĀNA'I   MAUI
KAHO'OLAWE

20°

HAWAI'I   20°

175°

MIDWAY ATOLL

0   4 mi
0   3   6 km

coral   28°15'
60
Middle Ground
deep lagoon
North Breakers

Sand I.   **Eastern I.**
Picket   Gooney   12
Pt.   Spit I.   12
+ 12
Frigate Pt.   Seaward Rocks
28'
177°20'

160°   155°

PEARL AND HERMES ATOLL

175°50'

North I.

Little North I.

coral

coral

60   27°50'

coral

coral

Sand I.   Bird I.
Grass I.   Southeast I.
Kittery I.   Seal I.

0   3   6 mi
0   4   8 km

MARO REEF

170°30'

0   2   4   6 mi
25°30'   0   2   4   6   8 km

coral

60

coral

Dowsett
Reef
25°20'

170°40'

NĪHOA

Hawai'iloa Channel
Millers Peak   Tanager Peak
+   +
903   700   874
500   + Cave
23°4'30"   300
Needle Rock   568   100
Adams Bay
60   Kahiqwaho Channel

0   .6 mi
0   .9 km   161°55'

170°   165°   160°

Hawaiian monk seal and green sea turtle at French Frigate Shoals.
[G. H. Balazs]

The Northwestern Hawaiian Islands are all within a federal wildlife refuge established in 1909 to protect the large colonies of seabirds and a variety of marine organisms, including sea turtles and the critically endangered Hawaiian monk seal. The recent withdrawal of the military from bases at Midway has left the U.S. Fish and Wildlife Service with the difficult task of managing this far-flung refuge. In 1996 the U.S. Fish and Wildlife Service established a cooperative agreement with a private aviation contractor that allows limited public access to Midway via commercial flights from Līhu'e, Kaua'i.

SONIA P. JUVIK
AND JAMES O. JUVIK

HAWAIIAN PLACE NAMES

The spelling of place names on the reference maps and in the gazetteer of this *Atlas* differs from that used on the U.S. Geological Survey maps in its inclusion of the glottal stop, or *'okina,* and the macron, or *kahakō.* The glottal stop, which is indicated by the single open quote mark ('), represents a whole letter in the Hawaiian alphabet; thus, it takes up one letter space. The macron, a horizontal line over a vowel, indicates the vowel is longer than a vowel without a macron. Without the 'okina letter and the macron, one would not know that the Moloka'i town, Kāla'e, and the southernmost point of Hawai'i Island, Ka Lae, are not pronounced the same. Or that 'Ala'ē, a place on Hawai'i Island, ends in a long *e,* thus differing in pronunciation from 'Alae, a crater on the same island. As the number of Hawaiian-language users has increased, and the importance of these symbols has become more widely known, they are now recognized as part of official Hawaiian orthography.

Hawaiian linguist Larry L. Kimura of the University of Hawai'i at Hilo has served as the authority on traditional place names for this edition of the *Atlas.* Kimura maintains that numerous inconsistencies remain in the officially recognized spelling of Hawaiian place names. For example, certain names are sometimes spelled as a single word, and sometimes as two words, as in Mauna Loa (Hawai'i Island) and Maunaloa (Moloka'i). Other examples are Ala Moana and Alapali (O'ahu); Haleakalā (Maui) and Hale o Lono (Moloka'i); and Pu'u 'Ōhi'a and Pu'unui (O'ahu). Another inconsistency shows up in the names of sea promontories; for example, sometimes the English *point* is used, and sometimes the Hawaiian *kalae,* such as Hou Point and Kalaehou (Hawai'i Island) and 'Au'au Point and Kalae'oka'au'au (Hawai'i Island).

Because Hawaiian has a low number of distinctive sounds, it has a correspondingly high number of homonyms. *Hau,* for example, means 'dew' in Honokōhau (bay-draining dew), 'strike' in Hauko'i (strike adze), and the tree *Hibiscus tiliaceus* in Hau'ula (red *hau* tree). *Mo'o* is 'lizard' in Kamo'oali'i (the royal lizard) and 'mountain range' in Kamo'oho'opulu (the wet range). *Lua* is 'pit' in Kalua o Pele (the pit of Pele), a type of free-for-all fighting in Kalua 'Ōlohe (the skilled fighter), and 'two' in Kailua (two seas).

Incorrect word divisions, too, cause difficulties. The name commonly spelled Honuapo is not *honua-pō* 'night land' but *Honu-'apo* 'catch turtle'. The black sand beach—now covered with lava—spelled Kaimū is not *ka-imu* 'the oven', but *kaimū* 'sea crowded' (with surf watchers).

Although most mainland place names are single words (Illinois, Chicago, Miami), about half of all Hawaiian place names are composed of two or more words. Many of them contain grammatical articles—for example, the articles *ka* and *ke,* as in Ka'a'awa (the *'a'awa* fish) and Kekaha (the place), and the possessive prepositions *a* and *o,* as in Haleakalā (house of the sun) and Pu'u o Pele (hill of Pele). The most common prefixes are *hana-* and *hono-,* both meaning 'bay', as in Hanalei (lei bay) and Honolulu (sheltered bay).

Topographic terms commonly used in the place names are:

> *kai* 'sea', as in Kailua (two seas)
> *lae* 'cape, point, forehead', as in Ka Lae (the point)
> *lua* 'pit, crater', as in Kaluako'i (the adze pit)
> *mauna* 'mountain, peak', as in Mauna Kea (white
>   mountain) and Mauna Loa (long mountain)
> *moku* 'island, district', as in Mokumanu (bird island)
> *pu'u* 'hill, mound', as in Pu'unēnē (goose hill)
> *wai* 'stream, river, pond, fresh water', as in Waikīkī
>   (spouting water)

A few adjectives occur frequently: *loa* 'long', *nui* 'large', *iki* 'small', and *'ula* 'red' (by far the most common color found in the place names, red was the Polynesian sacred color and a symbol of royalty).

In terms of their origin, Hawaiian place names may be classified as descriptive, legendary, cultural, Polynesian cognate, and newly coined. Descriptive names include the previously mentioned Honolulu, Mauna Kea, Mauna Loa, and Nu'uanu (cool heights), as well as Kawailoa (the long stream), Pu'u 'Ula'ula (red hill), and many more.

Names with legendary associations include the names of gods and demigods of old, as Nā Iwi o Pele (the bones of Pele) and Waia Kāne (water of Kāne). On each island was a *heiau* called Hale o Lono, dedicated to worship of Lono, god of clouds, the sea, agriculture, and fertility. The island of Maui was named for the culture hero, Māui, who snared the sun in the crater of Haleakalā to lengthen the day so that his mother, Hina, would have time to dry her tapa. The name of the island

Hawaiian Names for the Northwestern Hawaiian Islands

An important aspect of the Hawaiian cultural rebound is the awareness that in numerous instances traditional place names either were replaced with foreign ones or the Hawaiian names were misspelled to the degree that their meanings were changed. The Hawaiian Lexicon Committee has identified the following names for some places in the Northwestern Hawaiian Islands:

Mokumanamana (Necker Island) The original name. A small basaltic islet with numerous *heiau*.

Mokupāpapa (French Frigate Shoals) An atoll of reefs, low sand islets, and the 120-foot-high La Pérouse Pinnacle. *Moku* 'islet' combined with *pāpapa* 'low, flat, expansive reef' means 'islets with low-lying reefs'. Recorded in chants, the name Mokupāpapa refers to an island, or islands, of the name's description located northwest of Niʻihau. The nearest shoal-like place is French Frigate Shoals.

Pūhāhonu (Gardner Pinnacles) means 'surfacing of a turtle for air'. These two isolated islands and various rock outcroppings seem to appear unexpectedly to voyagers at sea, like a turtle coming up for air, its back and head emerging above the surface. Although turtles are rarely sighted on land in the main islands, often they can be seen resting on crevices and rock ledges at Pūhāhonu.

Nalukakala (Maro Reef) Because this atoll is generally covered by breakers, it is given a Hawaiian name that translates as 'surf that arrives in combers'.

Kauō (Laysan Island) This flat island, bordered by sand and surf and harboring a pond, resembles a bird's egg, cracked open, with the yolk surrounded by egg white. *Kauō* can be either the yolk or the egg white, its meaning specified with the modifier *melemele* 'yellow' or *keʻokeʻo* 'white'. Denoting the contents of an egg, the name Kauō also signifies the thousands of birds that inhabit the island.

Papaʻāpoho (Lisianski Island) The literal translation describes the physical appearance of Papaʻāpoho, a flat (island) with a depression.

Holoikauaua (Pearl and Hermes Atoll) This atoll is named for the endangered Hawaiian monk seal—described in Hawaiian as a 'dog-like animal that swims in the rough'—which frequents local waters and hauls out on the beaches of several of the northwestern islands of Hawaiʻi.

Pihemanu (Midway Atoll) Along with many of the northwestern islands, Pihemanu is a refuge for birds. Its name means 'the loud din of birds'.

Kānemilohaʻi (Kure Atoll) The northwesternmost island in the Hawaiian archipelago is thought to have been the place where one of Pele's brothers was left as a guard during the voyage to Hawaiʻi from Kahiki. And so its name commemorates Kānemilohaʻi.

Now that the Hawaiian names of these northwestern islands have been identified, Hawaiian speakers may be tempted to amend the traditional saying, "From where the sun rises at Haʻehaʻe [Kumukahi, Hawaiʻi Island] to its setting at Lehua [a small island north of Niʻihau]," to *Mai ka piʻina a ka lā i Haʻehaʻe a i ka lā welowelo i Kānemilohaʻi:* "From where the sun rises at Haʻehaʻe to its setting at Kānemilohaʻi."

LARRY L. KIMURA

must once have been Māui, but during the centuries it has shortened to present-day ʻMaui'.

Kohelepelepe (fringed vagina) is an old name for Koko Crater. Kamapuaʻa, the pig god, attempted to ravish Pele at Kapoho, Hawaiʻi Island. Pele's sister Kapo had a flying vagina that she could send where she willed. She sent it to entice Kamapuaʻa, who immediately forgot Pele and followed the flying vagina to Koko Crater, Oʻahu, where it landed, left an imprint, and then flew away to Kalihi.

Places are also named for plants, animals, and objects of material culture. Therefore, *hale* 'house', *pā* 'fence or enclosure', *waʻa* 'canoe', *lei* 'garland', *lama* 'torch', and *koʻi* 'adze' are names or parts thereof. Plant names, especially *kukui* 'candlenut' and *hau* 'hibiscus', are common: on each of the major islands is a place called Kukui. The *kukui* is the state tree, a symbol of enlightenment and wisdom because its nuts were used to provide oil for lamps. Other plant names frequently used are *niu* 'coconut', *hala* 'pandanus', the *maile* vine, and the *lehua* flower. At least 153 plant names have been noted in place names.

Names of fish and other sea life are less common. They include *manō* 'shark', *puhi* 'eel', and familiar fish such as *ʻahi, ʻamaʻama, ʻanae, ʻawa, kala, kūmū, uhu,* and *ulua*. Land animals such as *puaʻa* 'pig', *ʻīlio* 'dog', *ʻiole* 'rat', and the birds *pueo* 'owl', *ʻalae* 'mudhen', *ʻalalā* 'crow', and *ʻelepaio* 'flycatcher', as well as *manu* 'bird', are also included in place names.

Names transferred from Polynesia in the original migrations to Hawaiʻi may once have been numerous, but only a few survive that are definitely known as place names elsewhere. Hawaiʻi, Kaʻū, ʻUpolu, and Manuʻa are derived from Savaiʻi, Taʻū, ʻUpolu, and Manuʻa—all of them islands or island groups in Samoa. Cognates—that is, words derived from the same source—of *koʻolau* 'windward' and *kona* 'leeward' occur in most parts of Polynesia (for example, the Tokelau Islands north of Samoa and the Kingdom of Tonga, far to the south). Kahikinui on Maui is cognate with Tahitinui in Tahiti and Tawhitinui in New Zealand. Except for Koʻolau and Kona, these names have no meanings in Hawaiian. Other important names without meaning, and for which cognates have not been found in the South Pacific islands, include Kauaʻi and Molokaʻi.

Malihini (newcomers) soon realize that part of adjusting to life in the Islands is learning to properly pronounce the names of streets and public places that are typically in Hawaiian, one of the state's two official languages. All four counties require that all such names be Hawaiian, correctly spelled with *ʻokina* and *kahakō*. However, exceptions to this policy can be found on all islands where non-Hawaiian names are of long-standing, common usage, and associated with the local history of a place. Names of public personalities and former sugarcane plantation villages are examples.

Place names are continually being coined, especially by developers who, in seeking names for their projects and new streets, unfortunately do not search for the old Hawaiian names or endeavor to consult with the original landowners. Thus the area once known as Kaʻelepulu (the wet blackness) is now Enchanted Lake. Kokokahi (one blood) was the name given by Theodore Richards for an interracial camp. The name Lanikai is probably a mistake for Kailani (heavenly sea).

Hawaiian place names, then, hold other attractions beyond their pleasant and mellifluous sounds, for they describe the Islands, the deeds of Hawaiian heroes, the links between Hawaiians and their Polynesian kin to the south, and the intimacy Hawaiians have always felt with the natural forces that surround them, physically and spiritually.

—ADAPTED FROM SAMUEL H. ELBERT
Atlas of Hawaiʻi, SECOND EDITION

MAPPING AND GEODESY

Historical Mapping Techniques

The earliest maps of the Hawaiian Islands were nautical charts produced by the British expedition commanded by Captain James Cook. On his third and last voyage he constructed a chart of Kealakekua Bay and a general coastal chart of the main islands with considerable accuracy and detail, considering the instruments available. In the years following Cook's visit Jean François de Galaup de La Pérouse, George Vancouver, Iurii Lisianskii, and Charles Malden made additional contributions to nautical charts and produced more detailed maps of coastlines, as did Charles Wilkes, who led the U.S. Exploring Expedition to Hawai'i in 1841.

Topographic mapping of the islands came with the division of lands under the *Māhele* of 1848, which required the survey of small land parcels (*kuleana*) for distribution and grant of title to former tenants of the king and chiefs. These parcels were usually irregular in shape, following natural features such as gulches, streams, ridges, and in some cases actual area in use. It soon became apparent that an accurate and coordinated effort was needed to replace the many individual land surveys being performed, and in 1870 the Hawaiian Government Survey was established under the direction of W. D. Alexander.

The first survey of the islands began in 1871 with measurement of a four-mile baseline on Maui, and triangulation was extended from there across central Maui. In 1872 a second baseline was measured on O'ahu. Triangulation of all the individual islands was substantially complete by 1900, when the Territory of Hawai'i came under the charting jurisdiction of the U.S. Coast and Geodetic Survey. Hydrographic surveys of important harbors and roadsteads were initiated, followed by work in the deeper interisland and ocean waters. After numerous unsuccessful attempts dating from 1910, the triangulation schemes of O'ahu and Kaua'i were joined in 1928, tying the islands together geodetically.

Under the Hawaiian Government Survey there were six different standards of latitude and four of longitude. The hydrographic adjusted latitude was later calculated from the six original standards, and 13 additional latitude determinations made at various points in the islands. In 1927 a single datum for all the islands, subsequently referred to as the Old Hawaiian Datum, was defined in terms of the coordinates of the O'ahu west base. These were determined as 21° 18′ 13.89″

north latitude and 157° 50′ 55.79″ west longitude, with an east-to-west base azimuth of 291° 29′ 36.0″.

At the time of the Hawaiian Government Survey, uniform standards had not been adopted, and thus the accuracy of older surveys cannot be determined. By today's standards, however, they were almost certainly inaccurate. Modern equipment and improved procedures have greatly increased the accuracy of land surveys. The latest horizontal control survey of O'ahu, completed during 1969 by the U.S. Coast and Geodetic Survey (now the National Ocean Survey) and the State of Hawai'i, consists of first-order triangulation and second-order traverse. On the accompanying map, locations of first-, second-, and third-order stations are shown. In the early 1980s all U.S. Geological Survey topographic maps of the Hawaiian Islands were revised utilizing new aeronautical photography. However, the maps are still on the Old Hawaiian Datum and are based on surveys done in 1969.

JOSEPH R. MORGAN

Contemporary Mapping Techniques

In recent years advances in mapping science have altered the frame of reference (latitude and longitude coordinates) underlying the data from which the maps in this *Atlas* were compiled. Since the late 1950s scientists have been studying the orbits of artificial satellites to learn more about the shape of Earth. In the 1980s the U.S. Department of Defense began launching navigational satellites that orbit in several planes some 11,000 miles (17,200 km) above Earth. Known as the Navigation Satellite Timing and Ranging Global Positioning System—usually abbreviated GPS—these satellites transmit precise identification and timing information that can be detected by terrestrial receivers. The data accumulated by the early 1980s allowed a redefinition of the shape and size of Earth such that subsequent mapping could proceed on a single base. Previously, mapping throughout the world had been based on many different geodetic models of Earth, which caused considerable difficulty when one mapping system abutted or overlapped another.

In the United States the new mapping model was named the North American Datum of 1983 (NAD83). It replaced

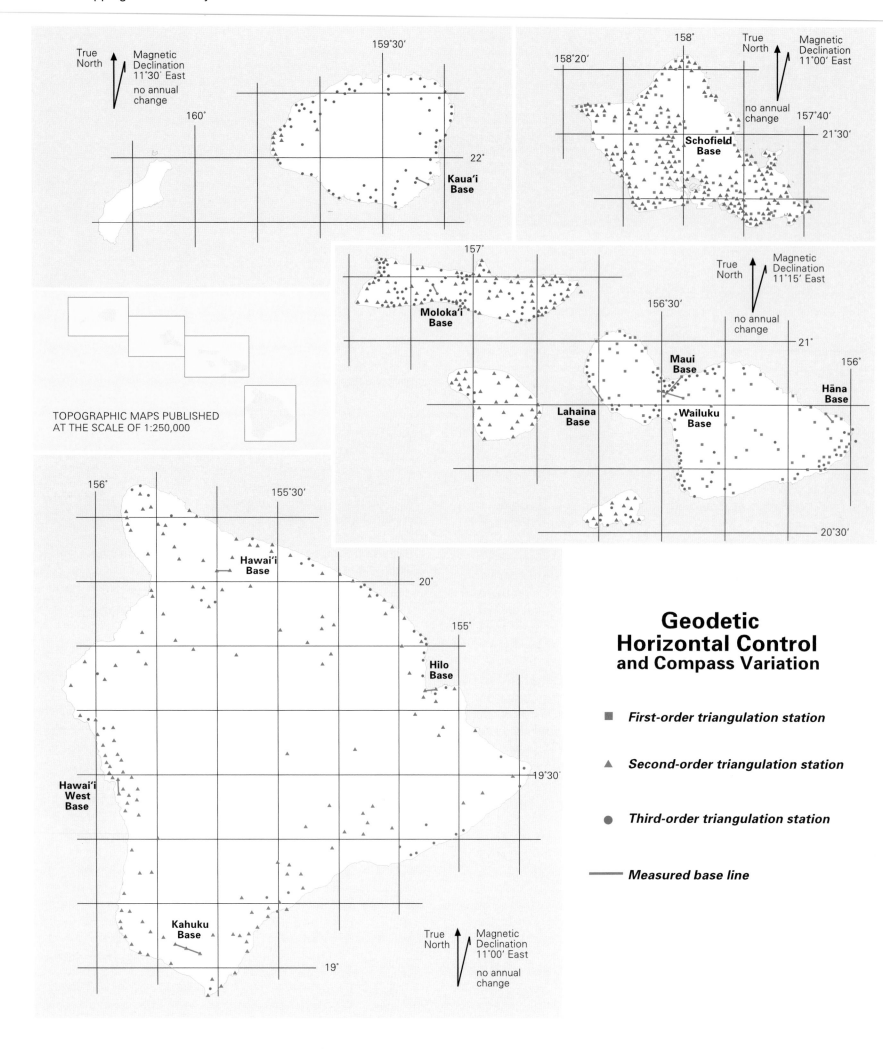

True North
Magnetic Declination 11°30' East
no annual change

160°

159°30'

22°

Kaua'i Base

158°20'

158°

True North

Magnetic Declination 11°00' East

no annual change

157°40'

21°30'

Schofield Base

157°

Moloka'i Base

True North

Magnetic Declination 11°15' East

no annual change

156°30'

21°

156°

Maui Base

Hāna Base

Lahaina Base

Wailuku Base

20°30'

TOPOGRAPHIC MAPS PUBLISHED
AT THE SCALE OF 1:250,000

156°

155°30'

Hawai'i Base

20°

155°

Hilo Base

19°30'

Hawai'i West Base

Geodetic Horizontal Control and Compass Variation

■   *First-order triangulation station*

▲   *Second-order triangulation station*

●   *Third-order triangulation station*

─   *Measured base line*

Kahuku Base

19°

True North

Magnetic Declination 11°00' East

no annual change

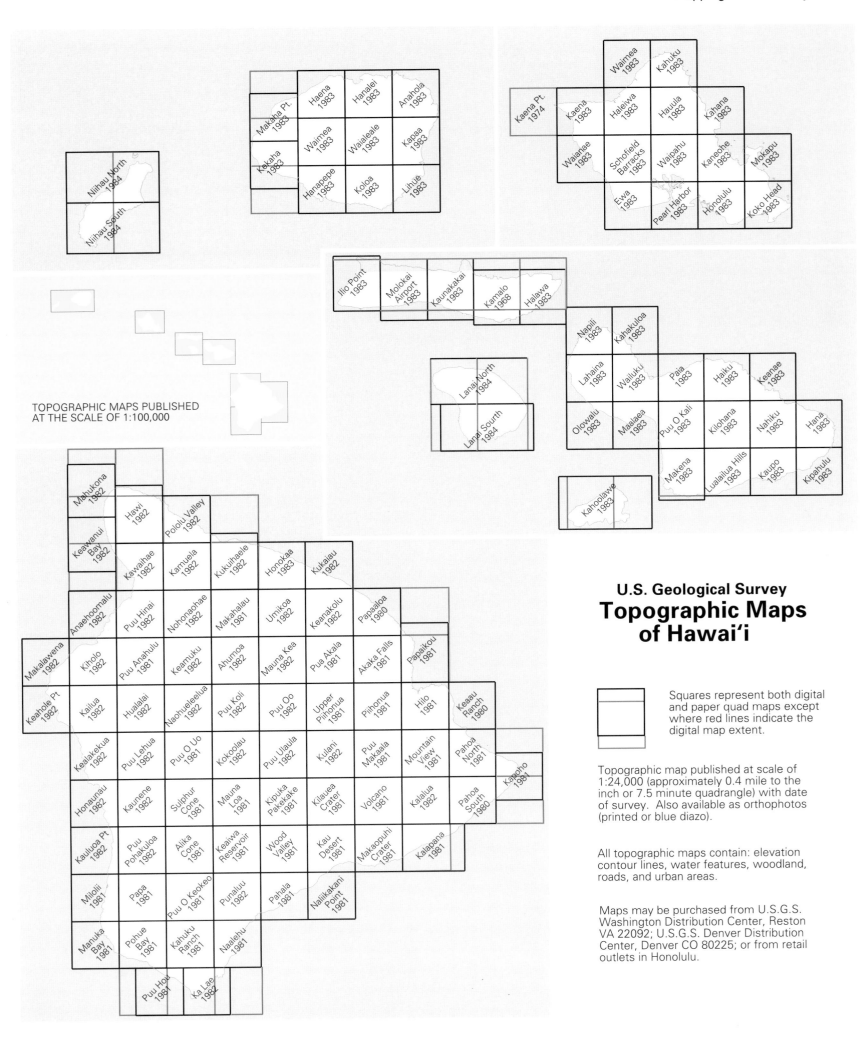

TOPOGRAPHIC MAPS PUBLISHED
AT THE SCALE OF 1:100,000

U.S. Geological Survey
Topographic Maps
of Hawai'i

Squares represent both digital and paper quad maps except where red lines indicate the digital map extent.

Topographic map published at scale of 1:24,000 (approximately 0.4 mile to the inch or 7.5 minute quadrangle) with date of survey. Also available as orthophotos (printed or blue diazo).

All topographic maps contain: elevation contour lines, water features, woodland, roads, and urban areas.

Maps may be purchased from U.S.G.S. Washington Distribution Center, Reston VA 22092; U.S.G.S. Denver Distribution Center, Denver CO 80225; or from retail outlets in Honolulu.

Remote Sensing in Hawai'i

Remote sensing is the operation of instruments, such as cameras, multispectral scanners, and radar from airplanes and satellites, to gain a bird's-eye view of Earth. These instruments "look" not only in the visible light portion of the electromagnetic spectrum, but also in the ultraviolet, infrared, and microwave portions.

Surveyors, scientists, planners, historians, illustrators, and others utilize air photos in their work. The University of Hawai'i, the Bishop Museum, the State of Hawai'i Archives, and several private firms collect and preserve historical and contemporary air photos.

Remote sensing by satellite came of age in Hawai'i with the state's LANDSAT project in 1978. The program demonstrated that

(continued on the next page)

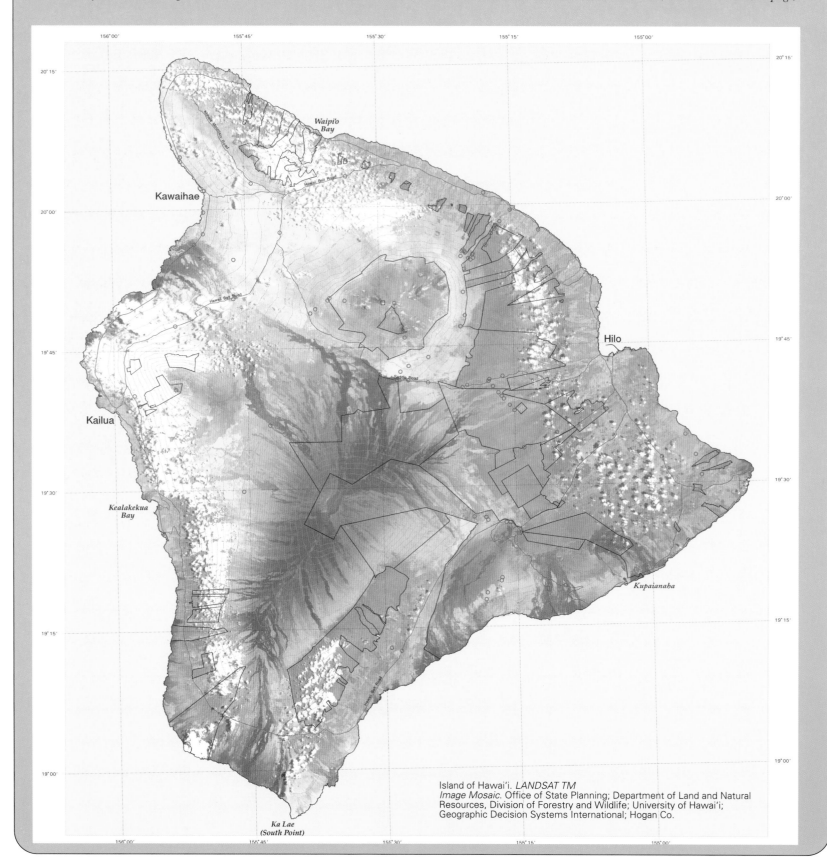

Island of Hawai'i. *LANDSAT TM*
Image Mosaic. Office of State Planning; Department of Land and Natural Resources, Division of Forestry and Wildlife; University of Hawai'i; Geographic Decision Systems International; Hogan Co.

satellite data held great promise for planning and resource management. In 1995, with support from NASA, the state carried out a similar project using Thematic Mapper data of Hawai'i Island. In the accompanying image, satellite data from two mid-infrared bands are displayed in red and green, while data from the red band of visible light are shown in blue. Vegetation stands out sharply from lava and bare soil in this "false-color" composite image, and Kīlauea's active lava flows appear orange.

Evidence of the growing demand for high-resolution, multispectral satellite data is reflected by the unprecedented cooperation of some two dozen government agencies and private firms in 1996 to purchase SPOT (Système Pour L'Observation de la Terre) imagery of the entire state. The data will be used for purposes such as vegetation classification, range and crop management, coastal research, and urban planning.

Highly advanced remote sensing is carried out at the University of Hawai'i at Mānoa. The Satellite Oceanography Laboratory pro-

vides real-time satellite images, including output from the Advanced Very High Resoultion Radiometer (AVHRR) and meteorological and oceanographic data on the World Wide Web. The Institute of Geophysics and Planetology uses Synthetic Aperture Radar (SAR) to study the inflation of Hawaiian volcanoes from space.

An exciting development in remote sensing is the availability of hyperspectral imagery collected by airborne sensors. This technology can resolve images as small as a shrub, a road sign, or a sea turtle, and it uses dozens of narrow spectral bands to discriminate between images that appear identical to the human eye.

The number of regular users of remotely sensed images is rapidly increasing. Anyone with access to a personal computer and modem can download satellite imagery of Hawai'i from the Internet and process it with readily available software.

RON TERRY

NAD27, which had long served as the basis of most mapping in the United States. While the adoption of NAD83 made little difference in mainland maps, in Hawai'i it shifted latitude and longitude 1,161 feet (354 m) north and 932 feet (284 m) west on the Universal Transverse Mercator (UTM) and State Plane Coordinates used in large-scale mapping.

This change may seem rather small considering the state's size; however, the fact that not all mapping systems adopted the change at the same time, or at all in some cases, can cause considerable confusion when maps are compiled from many different large-scale sources. Much of this *Atlas* is based on digital forms of topographic maps at different scales. These data are mostly recorded in Universal Transverse Mercator coordinates based upon the Old Hawaiian Datum. When these data were used as a frame of reference for the State Geographic Information Systems (GIS), they were not converted to NAD83. The State Plane Coordinate System, the basis of most

surveying records that define land ownership, have also not been changed to NAD83.

The U.S. Geological Survey has not yet changed the standard 7.5 minute quadrangles for Hawai'i. However, the Defense Mapping Agency adopted NAD83 when they converted the 7.5 minute quadrangles to a 1:50,000 scale series of topographic maps in 1991, and the National Oceanic and Atmospheric Administration (NOAA) began using the new system for air traffic control and aeronautical charts in 1992.

It will be some time before all maps, data, and surveys in the state are converted to the single NAD83 system. Readers of this *Atlas* should appreciate the extra effort taken in analyzing and converting the data to assure that all classes of geographic information fit each other correctly in the variety of map displays contained here.

EVERETT A. WINGERT

THE PHYSICAL ENVIRONMENT

Overleaf: Hawaiian beach with terns. [V. McCormick]

GEOLOGY

The Hawaiian Islands belong to a linear chain of volcanoes that stretches for approximately 3,800 miles (6,100 km) from the central to the northern Pacific, almost to the Aleutian Islands. About halfway up its length, the chain bends, dividing the older Emperor Seamounts (guyots)—now sunken to great depths—from the younger Hawaiian Ridge. From northwest to southeast, each volcano is progressively younger. The oldest dated seamount, near the northern end of the chain, was formed about 80 million years ago, while dinosaurs still roamed Earth.

What forces formed these islands, the farthest archipelago from any continent, over such a long span of time? Why are they lined up across the Pacific? Earth scientists believe that the Hawaiian Islands owe their existence to two geological phenomena: a "hot-

spot" and plate tectonics. Beneath the active volcanoes of Hawai'i Island, a plume of hot rock anchored hundreds of miles deep in Earth upwells to form a hotspot beneath the Pacific Plate, one of several dozen tectonic plates that comprise the planet's crust. Most of the world's active volcanoes are located at the edges of these tectonic plates, as exemplified by the Pacific "ring of fire." But the Hawaiian hotspot, like many of the other hundred or so hotspots around the globe, is positioned within the plate, where it has apparently remained fixed over the past 40 million years. As the hotspot has continuously fed magma through the crust to fuel countless volcanic eruptions, the Pacific Plate has drifted west-northwestward about 3.5 inches (9 cm) a year. Like a conveyor belt, the plate has rafted each new volcano (about 129 in all, including the 15 volca-

Volcanic Island Growth Cycles

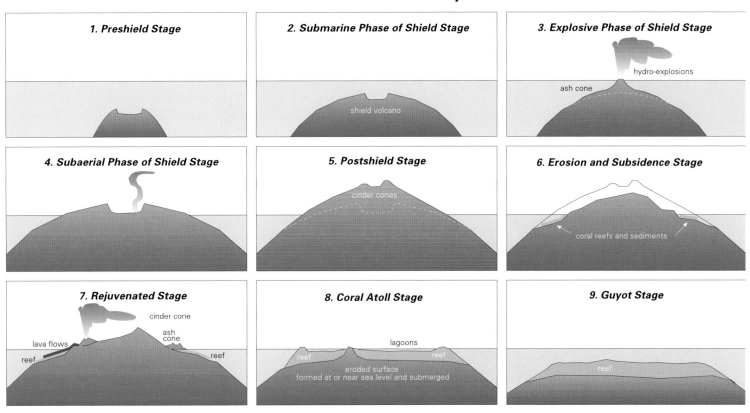

1. Preshield Stage

2. Submarine Phase of Shield Stage

3. Explosive Phase of Shield Stage

4. Subaerial Phase of Shield Stage

5. Postshield Stage

6. Erosion and Subsidence Stage

7. Rejuvenated Stage

8. Coral Atoll Stage

9. Guyot Stage

Age Progression of Hawaiian Islands

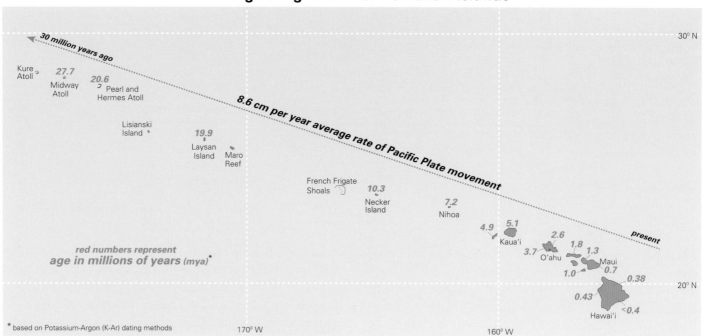

30 million years ago

Kure Atoll

27.7
Midway Atoll

20.6
Pearl and Hermes Atoll

Lisianski Island

19.9
Laysan Island   Maro Reef

8.6 cm per year average rate of Pacific Plate movement

French Frigate Shoals

10.3
Necker Island

7.2
Nihoa

4.9   5.1
Kaua'i

3.7   2.6   1.8   1.3
O'ahu   Maui

1.0   0.7   0.38

0.43   <0.4
Hawai'i

present

30° N

20° N

red numbers represent
age in millions of years (mya)*

* based on Potassium-Argon (K-Ar) dating methods

170° W   160° W

Pillow lava. [J. P. Lockwood]

noes making up the major islands of Hawai'i) away from its place of origin, across the Pacific Ocean. Thus the age and orientation of the volcanic chain records the direction and rate of the plate's movement. The pronounced bend between the Hawaiian Ridge and the Emperor Seamounts marks a dramatic change in the plate's direction, probably caused by the collision between the Eurasian and Australian-Indian Plates that ultimately created the Himalaya Mountains.

The Evolution of a Hawaiian Volcano

Each volcano in the chain has evolved, or is evolving, through essentially the same sequence of life stages. When a new volcano forms, the rates of lava eruption gradually increase over several hundred thousand years, attain their peak for perhaps 500,000 years, and then decline rapidly. As eruption rates change, so does the composition of the lavas. Also, the position of the vol-

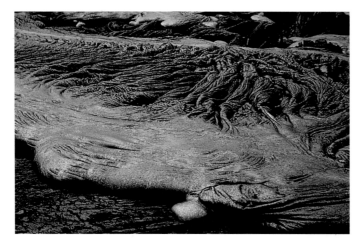

Pāhoehoe lava. [D. W. Peterson]

'A'ā lava. [J. J. Dovork]

cano's summit relative to sea level determines the style of eruptive activity. Several million years may pass before activity at a volcano ends and the volcano becomes extinct.

A volcano's life starts deep underwater, with occasional eruptions of relatively small volumes of alkalic basalt lavas, rich in sodium and potassium, beginning at the seafloor. What is known about this *submarine preshield stage* comes from recent research on Lōʻihi Seamount, the only volcano whose preshield lavas have not been buried beneath later lavas. The Hawaiian chain's youngest volcano, Lōʻihi lies about 3,200 feet (975 m) below sea level off the southeast coast of Hawaiʻi Island. Samples of lava from the young volcano are the "pillow" lavas typical of deep underwater eruptions. Submarine eruptions are building a steep-sided volcanic edifice with a shallow caldera, or basin-shaped depression, at the summit. Two rift zones radiate from Lōʻihi's summit and will remain prominent features of the volcano during all but the final eruptive stage. As a young volcano grows, small landslides cut into the steep slopes, scarring its flanks. The submarine preshield stage lasts for perhaps 200,000 years yet produces only a fraction of the volcano's final mass.

An increase in the frequency and volume of eruptions and a change in lava composition to tholeiitic basalt with higher concentrations of silica and lower concentrations of sodium and potassium signal the transition to the next stage of formation. During this transition, which Lōʻihi seems to be currently undergoing, tholeiitic and alkalic lavas erupt alternately over long periods, forming interbedded layers. At the end of the transition, the volcano enters the *submarine phase of the shield stage.* During this phase continued eruptions of pillow basalt build up the volcanic edifice almost to sea level. When the volcano's summit has grown to the point that it is only shallowly submerged, magma and seawater mix to produce explosive eruptions, and the *explosive phase of the shield stage* begins. These ash-generating eruptions persist until the volcano has grown to perhaps 4,000 feet (1,200 m) above sea level, occurring intermittently for up to several hundred thousand years.

When the volcano attains a sufficient height above sea level, explosive eruptions cease, signaling the onset of the *subaerial phase of the shield stage.* Subaerial (above sea level) eruptions form flows of either ropy *pāhoehoe* or blocky *ʻaʻā. Pāhoehoe* lavas are generally produced by low-volume, sustained eruptions, while *ʻaʻā* flows are produced by high-volume eruptions that are usually limited in duration. Other factors that partly determine the type of flow are the slope of the ground and the physical properties of the erupted lava, such as its temperature, composition, amount of suspended crystals, and quantity of bubbles. Lava that flows into the ocean shatters into sand- and gravel-sized fragments that blanket the submarine slopes.

Submarine Landslides of Hawaiʻi

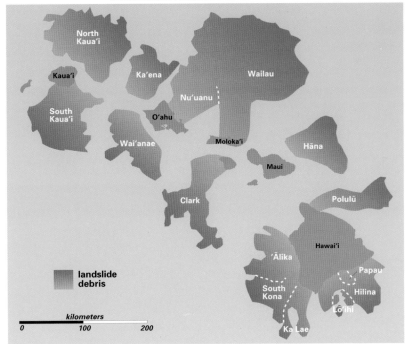

Flexure of the Lithosphere below Hawaiʻi

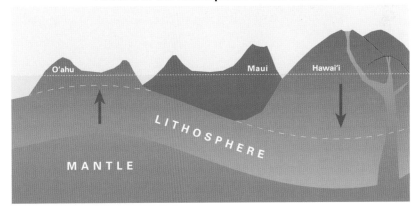

During all three phases of the shield stage the summit caldera repeatedly collapses, fills up with thick, ponded flows, and then collapses again. The frequency and rates of eruption peak during the shield stage. Over a period of roughly 500,000 years, the volcano accumulates about 95 percent of its mass, taking on the "shield" shape (named for its resemblance to a warrior's shield) characteristic of Hawaiian volcanoes. But the volcano also loses mass as weathering and erosion relentlessly wear it down. Its seaward, unsupported flanks are unstable and slip toward the ocean, creating large faults and causing major earthquakes and, infrequently, catastrophic landslides.

Such landslides can be enormous, as evidenced by the vast fields of blocky debris recently discovered and mapped on the seafloor around the major Hawaiian islands. These submarine deposits indicate the past occurrences of at least 17 major landslides and suggest that such events happen roughly every 100,000–200,000 years. In some cases, "slumps"—slow-moving landslides—can be distinguished from "debris avalanches," sudden, catastrophic landslides.

Not all Hawaiian volcanoes undergo the *postshield stage,* during which a cap of alkalic basalt overlays the shield. High fountains spew out cinders, and the volcano's slopes become steepened as short, pasty *'a'ā* flows pile up near vents around the summit and along the previously active rift zones. Spatter cones, cinder cones and, sometimes, pumice cones are typical vents. Over perhaps 250,000 years the eruptions taper off and then cease. The final caldera of a volcano that undergoes the postshield stage is inundated by alkalic lavas and eventually buried beneath the cap.

Following the postshield stage the forces of weathering and erosion gain the upper hand on the volcano. During this *erosional stage* deep canyons incise the flanks, often along faults previously created by landslides. Pressed down by the volcano's enormous weight, the underlying lithosphere (Earth's outer layer) flexes downward, and the volcano and the island to which it belongs subside or sink. As this occurs, fringing coral reefs grow at the shoreline, and sediments from the reef accumulate in lagoons. In some places around Hawai'i, ancient reefs are preserved offshore, in series like stairsteps. Each reef originally grew at an old shoreline during an era of global climate cooling, when the polar ice caps enlarged, pulling sea level down. The dual process of island subsidence and falling sea level kept the shoreline relatively stable, allowing the reef to grow. When global temperatures increased, the polar ice caps shrank and sea level rose again, drowning the reef, which could not grow fast enough to keep pace with the rising sea and the still-sinking island. Thus, on the slopes of rapidly subsiding young volcanoes, the deepest reef is the oldest, and each shallower reef is progressively younger.

After this period of weathering and erosion, a volcano may undergo the *rejuvenated stage,* a final eruptive stage during which strongly alkalic lavas are discharged—often through previously formed reefs—creating ash cones or rings. Lava flows are funneled down stream valleys carved out during the previous erosional stage. Lavas characteristic of this stage exist not only on several of the major Hawaiian islands, but also on their underwater flanks and the surrounding seafloor. Eruptions during this stage are infrequent and volcanic output minimal, but activity may occur over several million years.

The long duration of the rejuvenated stage on Kaua'i and Ni'ihau suggests that lavas of this stage

Hawaiian Lavas

Hawaiian lavas contain relatively few minerals. The most common is olivine, a greenish yellow, iron-magnesium silicate. Pyroxene ranks second in abundance and appears as two types: a dark-green-to-black, calcium-magnesium-iron silicate and a dark brown, iron-magnesium silicate, similar in composition to olivine, but containing more silica. The third most common mineral is plagioclase feldspar, a white-to-colorless, calcium-sodium-aluminum silicate. These are virtually the only crystals found in common Hawaiian lavas. Some rarer, strongly alkalic lavas are named after other minerals that crystallize when lava does not contain enough silica to form the more common minerals. For example, nephelinite is named for the mineral nepheline, which resembles feldspar in composition but contains less silica. Likewise, melilitite is named for melilite, which is similar in content to pyroxene but also contains significantly less silica.

Although most Hawaiian lavas appear quite similar, they vary broadly in composition. The most common type, tholeiitic basalt, makes up about 95 percent of the mass of a Hawaiian volcano. It usually contains rare-to-abundant olivine crystals and, more rarely, some crystals of plagioclase feldspar and pyroxene. It is high in silica and low in sodium and potassium.

The next most abundant lava type, alkalic basalt, also contains rare-to-abundant olivine crystals and, usually, feldspar and pyroxene crystals. However, it is low in silica and high in sodium and potassium. Alkalic basalt makes up most of Lō'ihi Seamount and the postshield stage lavas, such as those on Hualālai volcano. To discriminate reliably between tholeiitic and alkalic basalt usually requires a chemical analysis.

Other Hawaiian lavas of the postshield stage include hawaiite, mugearite, benmoreite, and trachyte. These less dense lavas are derived from alkalic basalt by the crystallization and settling out of more dense minerals (olivine, pyroxene, and feldspar) as the magma cools inside, or beneath, the volcano. Gray, pasty, and relatively low in temperature, they form thick, stubby *'a'ā* flows.

The final type is strongly alkalic lava, which is very high in sodium and potassium content and low in silica and appears only in the rejuvenated stage. In addition to alkalic basalt, these lavas consist of basanite (which also occurs in the preshield stage), nephelinite, and melilitite. They tend to be rich in volatiles, particularly water and carbon dioxide, that make their eruptions more explosive. Strongly alkalic lavas form dense flows that contain small crystals of olivine and pyroxene.

Many lavas, particularly the alkalic and strongly alkalic lavas, bring fragments of coarse, crystalline material to the surface. Most of these rocks, called xenoliths (foreign rocks), are fragments of solidified magma chambers and consist largely of olivine or a combination of olivine and pyroxene. Other xenoliths also contain plagioclase feldspar and are called gabbro. They are the slowly cooled equivalents of lava, which is why their individual crystals are larger. Yet other xenoliths are pieces of the mantle (the layer of Earth beneath the crust) through which the lavas passed. These fragments consist mostly of olivine and pyroxenes, but rare ones also contain garnet.

DAVID A. CLAGUE

Geology of Ni'ihau, Kaua'i, O'ahu

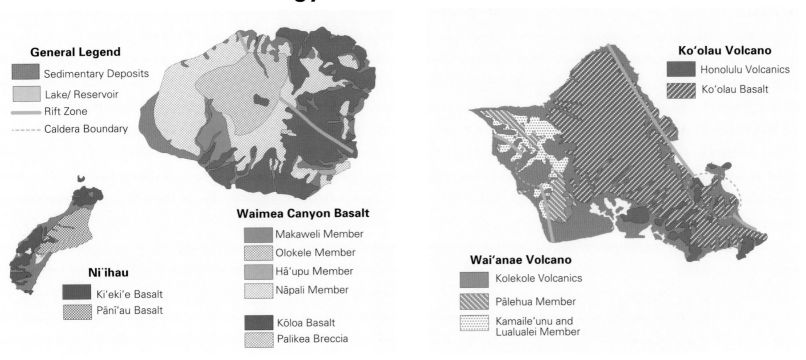

General Legend
- Sedimentary Deposits
- Lake/ Reservoir
- Rift Zone
- Caldera Boundary

Ni'ihau
- Ki'eki'e Basalt
- Pānī'au Basalt

Waimea Canyon Basalt
- Makaweli Member
- Olokele Member
- Hā'upu Member
- Nāpali Member
- Kōloa Basalt
- Palikea Breccia

Ko'olau Volcano
- Honolulu Volcanics
- Ko'olau Basalt

Wai'anae Volcano
- Kolekole Volcanics
- Pālehua Member
- Kamaile'unu and Lualualei Member

could erupt again on West Maui, East Moloka'i, and the Ko'olau Range on O'ahu, or could begin to erupt on West Moloka'i, Lāna'i, Kaho'olawe, or even Kohala on Hawai'i Island.

As the rejuvenated stage wanes, erosion and subsidence predominate once again, eventually reducing an extinct volcano, or volcanic island, to sea level. With continued subsidence, a volcanic island is transformed to an atoll: a ring of coral surrounding a lagoon, such as those that lie west of La Pérouse Pinnacle, the westernmost and oldest subaerial volcanic remnant of a former Hawaiian island. If the water becomes too cold for active growth because of northward drift of an extinct volcano, or if sea level fluctuates, as discussed above, the reefs that make up the atoll die. A volcano continues to subside after its reef dies. Once below sea level, a flat-topped, coral-capped volcano is called a guyot. Although a few volcanoes apparently never grew above sea level, nearly all the volcanoes in the Hawaiian-Emperor volcanic chain older than 30 million years are guyots.

Kaua'i, Ni'ihau, and O'ahu

Kaua'i consists of at least one extinct volcano, with lavas from the shield (5.6–5.0 Ma, or million years ago) and postshield stages (4.9 Ma), as well as abundant rejuvenated-stage lavas (3.65 Ma to 500,000 years ago). Kaua'i is unique among Hawaiian volcanoes for its lack of obvious rift zones, and the presence of an enormous caldera complex with a graben, or down-dropped block, on the caldera's south side. Rejuvenated-stage lavas of alkalic basalt, basanite, nephelinite, and melilitite have covered much of the eastern

half of the island and erupted on its east and southeast submarine flanks. In some instances lava flows filled canyons and diverted rivers and were later carved into river beds again.

Shield-stage lavas filled the caldera and the graben with thick, ponded flows. The Makaweli graben was probably formed by a large landslide off Kaua'i's southern coast. Other landslides modified Kaua'i's north, northeast, and possibly east flanks. The caldera complex of a second, smaller volcano may be represented by ponded lavas in the southeast part of the island. Deep erosion, weathering of the flows, and voluminous rejuvenated-stage lavas make unraveling Kaua'i's early history difficult.

Ni'ihau, an extinct volcano with lavas of the shield (4.9 Ma) and rejuvented (2.5 Ma to 400,000 years ago) stages, has no exposed summit caldera complex; it was apparently removed during a large landslide to the east. The postshield stage consists of a single dike (an intrusive magma body) and the erosional remnant of a cone, both alkalic basalt. Rejuvenated-stage lava, all alkalic basalt, covers about a third of Ni'ihau and forms Lehua Island, a small tuff (ash) cone off the north shore. Numerous cones and flows of rejuvenated-stage lava also dot the seafloor west of Ni'ihau.

O'ahu consists of two extinct volcanoes: Ko'olau on the east and Wai'anae on the west. Wai'anae volcano consists of shield lavas (3.9–3.5 Ma) overlain by a thick sequence of postshield-stage alkalic basalt (3.2–2.5 Ma). A posterosional sequence of lava, once thought to be of the rejuvenated stage, is 2.5 Ma and has been reinterpreted as postshield. The erosional unconformity that separates these lavas from the earlier part of the postshield stage has been attributed to a large landslide to the southwest, named the Waiʻanae slump.

Koʻolau consists of the eruptive products of the shield (2.5–1.7 Ma) and rejuvenated stages; no post-shield-stage lavas are known. A caldera complex in the Kailua region on the northeast shore of the island was bisected by the catastrophic Nuʻuanu landslide. Rejuvenated-stage lavas mainly erupted in the Honolulu area, hence their name: the Honolulu Volcanics. Although some of the lavas could be considerably younger, most lavas, which include flows of alkalic

Haleakalā summit area, Maui. [D. A. Clague]

basalt, basanite, nephelinite, and melilitite, appear to be older than 100,000 years. The most reliably dated vent, Black Point, is 410,000 years old. Many of the vents erupted through a coral reef that grew along Oʻahu's south side. These eruptions tended to be explosive, and most vents along the coast produced tuff cones, such as Diamond Head, Salt Lake Crater, and Hanauma Bay (now a breached cone). Flows from inland eruptions were funneled down valleys such as Mānoa and Nuʻuanu, creating flat valley floors.

Maui, Molokaʻi, Lānaʻi, Kahoʻolawe

Kahoʻolawe, whose eastern half slid away during a catastrophic landslide, is an extinct volcano that has undergone the shield and postshield stages. A few vents and flows represent the postshield stage, and a west-southwest rift zone is identifiable by aligned vents.

Lānaʻi is a single extinct volcano with only shield-stage lavas exposed, dated at 1.28 million years old—an age that seems too young, based on those of nearby volcanoes. The Clark landslide, the remnants of which form a large deposit on the seafloor south of the island, was derived from Lānaʻi, or possibly from Penguin Bank. Basalt and coral cobbles and finer material have been found on the southeast flank of Lānaʻi up to heights of 1,000 feet (330 m) above sea level. These have been interpreted as the deposits of a tsunami triggered when Mauna Loa's west flank failed about 110,000 years ago and caused the ʻĀlika landslide.

West Molokaʻi, an extinct volcano with lavas erupted during the shield (1.9 Ma) and postshield

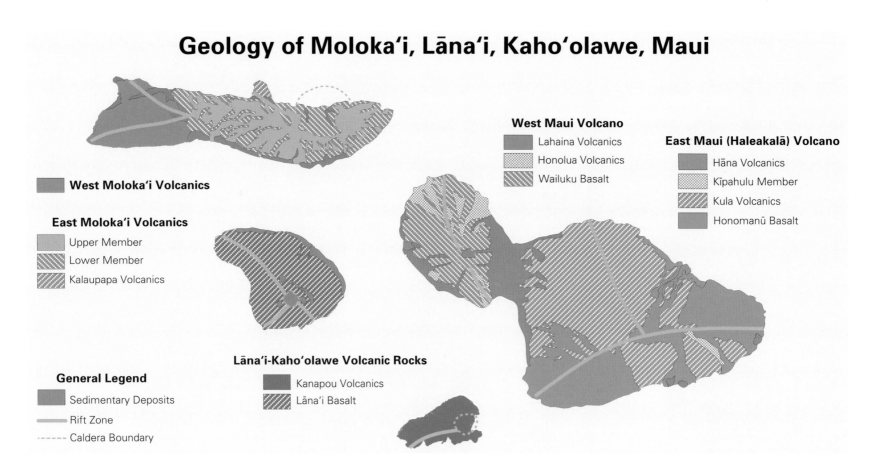

Geology of Molokaʻi, Lānaʻi, Kahoʻolawe, Maui

West Molokaʻi Volcanics

East Molokaʻi Volcanics
- Upper Member
- Lower Member
- Kalaupapa Volcanics

General Legend
- Sedimentary Deposits
- Rift Zone
- Caldera Boundary

Lānaʻi-Kahoʻolawe Volcanic Rocks
- Kanapou Volcanics
- Lānaʻi Basalt

West Maui Volcano
- Lahaina Volcanics
- Honolua Volcanics
- Wailuku Basalt

East Maui (Haleakalā) Volcano
- Hāna Volcanics
- Kīpahulu Member
- Kula Volcanics
- Honomanū Basalt

(1.8–1.75 Ma) stages, has no exposed caldera complex. A series of normal faults that steps down to the east probably marks the headwall of a landslide that down-dropped the summit and eastern half of the volcano. This presumably occurred before East Moloka'i had grown and buttressed the eastern flank of West Molo-ka'i.

West of Moloka'i, a broad shoal called Penguin Bank appears to be a separate volcano that has now subsided below sea level and is covered with a carbonate bank deposit of unknown thickness. Lavas recovered from the southern flank of Penguin Bank are all of the shield stage, distinct in composition from those of adjacent West Moloka'i. Much of the original caldera complex may be strewn across the seafloor as landslide blocks.

East Moloka'i is an extinct volcano with lavas erupted during the shield (1.5 Ma), postshield (1.5–1.35 Ma), and rejuvenated stages (570,000–350,000 years ago). Probably late in the shield stage its summit caldera was bisected by the enormous Wailau land-slide, which slid northward and thrust kilometer-sized blocks onto the seafloor up to 100 miles (166 km) off-shore. The high, steep sea cliff on the north side of the volcano, which marks the landslide's headwall, exposes about 4,900 feet (1,490 m) of shield- and postshield-stage lava flows. The postshield stage consists of flows

and vents of alkalic basalt, hawaiite, mugearite, and trachyte. The rejuvenated stage is represented only by the lavas that formed the Kalaupapa Peninsula.

An extinct volcano whose evolution includes shield (1.6–2.0 Ma), postshield (1.5–1.2 Ma), and rejuvenated stages forms West Maui. Numerous cones, domes, dikes, flows, and pyroclastic deposits of mugearite, hawaiite, and trachyte represent the postshield stage, while the only evidence of its rejuvenated stage is a few vents and flows located mainly near Lahaina. Erosion has exposed nearly 4,900 vertical feet (1,490 m) of volcanic layers on West Maui.

Haleakalā, an active volcano in its rejuvenated stage, last erupted about 1790. Its frequency of activity is not well established, but eruptions probably occur every several hundred years. The volcano's three rift zones extend to the northwest, east, and southwest. A large summit depression, originally interpreted as a caldera and later as an erosional feature (the merged headwalls of two river canyons), may have been formed by the coalescence of the headwalls of two landslides to the north and south of the summit. The volcano consists of shield-stage lava (1.1 Ma–900,000 years ago), postshield-stage lava (860,000–410,000 years ago), and rejuvenated-stage lava less than 400,000 years old. Its rejuvenated-stage eruptions have created a unique alignment of vents along the rift zones. Haleakalā is a

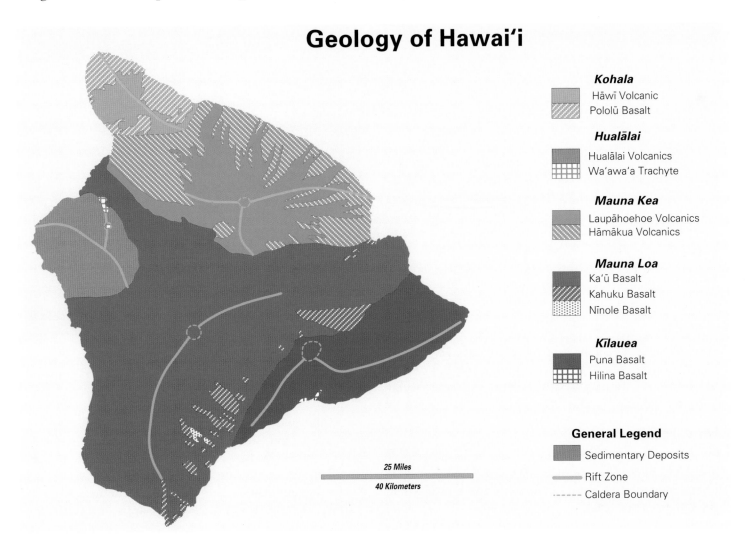

Geology of Hawai'i

Kohala
Hāwī Volcanic
Pololū Basalt

Hualālai
Hualālai Volcanics
Wa'awa'a Trachyte

Mauna Kea
Laupāhoehoe Volcanics
Hāmākua Volcanics

Mauna Loa
Ka'ū Basalt
Kahuku Basalt
Nīnole Basalt

Kīlauea
Puna Basalt
Hilina Basalt

General Legend
Sedimentary Deposits
Rift Zone
Caldera Boundary

25 Miles
40 Kilometers

Moku'āweoweo Caldera, Mauna Loa, Hawai'i. [D. W. Peterson]

Kīlauea spatter cone, Hawai'i. [T. T. English]

Kīlauea fault blocks, Pu'u Kapukapu, Hawai'i. [D. A. Swanson]

Pu'u Ka Pele, Mauna Kea cinder cone, Hawai'i.
[J. P. Lockwood]

potentially dangerous volcano that is likely to erupt in the next hundred years.

The large ancient island of Maui Nui included West Maui, Haleakalā, Kaho'olawe, Lāna'i, East Moloka'i, West Moloka'i, and Penguin Bank, which coalesced, or grew together. Maui Nui's maximum size was probably about 6,200 square miles (16,062 square km), more than 2,000 square miles (5,180 square km) larger than present-day Hawai'i Island. About 300,000–400,000 years ago, Maui Nui subsided to form two islands, the first consisting of Penguin Bank, Moloka'i, and Lāna'i, and the other composed of Maui and Kaho'olawe. Within the last 100,000–200,000 years Kaho'olawe separated from Maui, and Lāna'i separated from Moloka'i, while Penguin Bank has probably become submerged only within the last several hundred thousand years.

Hawai'i Island

Hawai'i consists of five coalescent, subaerial (above sea level) volcanoes, an extinct submarine volcano, and Lō'ihi Seamount, a young active volcano that has not yet grown to sea level.

Pu'u Wa'awa'a pumice cone, North Kona, Hawai'i.
[D. A. Clague]

Mahukona, the first volcano to form part of Hawai'i Island, lies submerged off the island's northwest shore. It has a prominent west rift zone, but its summit and any other rift zones are now buried beneath coral deposits and flows from the adjacent volcanoes Kohala and Hualālai. It apparently became extinct about 410,000 years ago, at the transition between the shield and postshield stages. A stairstep series of drowned coral reefs occurs on the northwest- and southwest-facing slopes of the volcano. These reefs record the subsidence of the island from about 465,000 years ago to the present. At its zenith, Mahukona apparently stood no more than 820 feet (270 m) above sea level; it became submerged about 435,000 years ago.

Kohala volcano is extinct. Its shield lavas include the island's oldest known lavas, dated at about 460,000 years old, and its postshield lavas as recent as 60,000 years old. Kohala's northwest rift zone extends through a summit depression, apparently a basin at the head-wall of the Pololū landslide, which occurred off the island's northeast shore before the postshield stage began about 260,000 years ago. Waipiʻo and Pololū Valleys have formed along the faults that bound this landslide. The thick ash cover on Kohala is probably derived mostly from Mauna Kea eruptions, although some is probably of local origin.

Mauna Kea, a dormant volcano in its postshield stage, last erupted about 4,500 years ago. Alkalic lavas have buried the final summit caldera. A few flows funneled down streambeds and reached the coast, but most recent lavas are short flows and large cinder cones. The oldest exposed lavas are about 250,000 years old. Many of Mauna Kea's eruptions were explosive and produced widespread ash deposits. Such eruptions may have been triggered by the interaction of lava with glacial water during periods of glaciation at the summit. Most of the thick ash covering its flanks came from its own eruptions, although up to 3 feet (0.9 m) of ash may be from explosive eruptions on Kīlauea about 50,000 years ago. Mauna Kea could erupt again, although it is unlikely because postshield-stage eruptions become less and less frequent before they cease altogether.

Hualālai is an active volcano in the postshield stage whose most recent eruptions occurred 200 years ago, about 700 years ago, and three times between 900 and 1,200 years ago. It erupts alkalic basalt every few hundred years; past flows of ʻaʻā and pāhoehoe advanced quickly due to its steep slopes. The final summit caldera is buried, and spatter and cinder cones are aligned along two well-developed rift zones. The volcano's oldest exposed lavas are at Puʻu Waʻawaʻa, a post-shield-stage pumice cone, and the related 825-foot (275 m)-thick flow at Puʻu Anahulu; both erupted about 105,000 years ago. The youngest shield lavas are roughly 128,000 years old. Hualālai is a potentially dangerous volcano that is likely to erupt in the next 100 years.

Mauna Loa is nearing the end of the shield stage, so the volcano's frequency and rate of eruption are declining, although it still discharges lavas of tholei-itic basalt. Between 1843 and 1995 Mauna Loa

Kīlauea volcano, Hawaiʻi, computer simulation from satellite image, view from northeast. [NASA Jet Propulsion Laboratory]

erupted 36 times, but only three eruptions (1950, 1975, and 1984) have occurred over the past 50 years. Besides eruptions along two prominent rift zones, repeated fissure eruptions have occurred on the volcano's north and northwest flanks. To attain its present estimated volume of roughly 10,000 cubic miles (41,650 cubic km), Mauna Loa must have erupted at four-to-five times its historic rates for much of its life span. As with Kīlauea, the southeastern flank of Mauna Loa is slipping slowly toward the ocean on a flat-lying fault that generates large earthquakes. The west flank also slips during large earthquakes. Mauna Loa has spawned at least six catastrophic landslides. The ʻĀlika slide off the volcano's west flank, which probably occurred about 110,000 years ago, is thought to be the most recent landslide in the Hawaiian Islands.

Kīlauea, the most active volcano on Earth, has erupted 60 times since 1840. It has erupted frequently since 1952 and almost continuously since January 1983. Currently in the explosive phase of the shield stage, the volcano primarily discharges lava, but ash deposits from infrequent explosive eruptions (the most recent ones in 1790 and 1924) are interbedded with past lava flows. Eruptions can occur anywhere at the summit or along the two rift zones. Kīlauea's south flank, bounded by the two rift zones, slips toward the ocean at rates of up to 4 inches (10 cm) per year on a flat-lying fault about 6 miles (10 km) deep. Large earthquakes, such as those that occurred in 1975 and 1989, are associated with large-scale movement along this fault.

Lōʻihi Seamount lies about 3,200 feet (975 m) below sea level, 18 miles (29 km) off Hawaiʻi Island's southeast coast. In transition between preshield and

Kohala Coast of Hawai'i, simulation. [NASA Jet Propulsion Laboratory]

shield stages, Lōʻihi has infrequent, small eruptions of alkalic and tholeiitic basalt and has experienced small earthquake swarms (groups of earthquakes occurring close together in time) nearly every year since 1980. A major earthquake swarm in 1996 accompanied a collapse at the summit that formed a new pit crater similar in size to Halemaʻumaʻu. Hot water escapes from vents near its summit and along the upper stretch of its south rift zone. These observations, and the recovery of glassy lava fragments, indicate that Lōʻihi is an active volcano destined to emerge as an island within the next 200,000 years and eventually coalesce with Hawaiʻi.

DAVID A. CLAGUE

GEOTHERMAL RESOURCES

Hawaiian volcanoes grow by two processes: eruption, or discharge of lava from vents on the volcano's surface, and intrusion of magma (molten rock) into underground voids in the existing rock. Recent studies have revealed that intrusive magma bodies, called dikes, may compose as much as half the volume of a Hawaiian volcano. Dikes are usually concentrated beneath the volcano's summit caldera, near the shallow magma chamber that feeds eruptions on the summit and flanks, and along the one or more long, narrow rift zones radiating from the magma chamber. Rift zones act as underground conduits that carry magma as far as 72 miles (116 km) from the central magma chamber, where it may then erupt or be deposited as an intrusive body.

The complexes of dikes that form beneath calderas and within rift zones are responsible for Hawai'i's geothermal, or hydrothermal, systems. In surface eruptions heat dissipates rapidly; but, when magma is intruded underground, the overlaying dense rock insulates the magma, allowing it to cool much more slowly. If the dikes form below the water table, their heat is taken up by the groundwater, which then may be discharged at ground level as steam, or at the top of the water table as steam or hot water. Because Hawai'i's surface rocks are so permeable, the steam is diffused, and the hot springs and geysers that typically mark an active hydrothermal zone do not develop, despite the sub-

Drilling for geothermal energy, Puna District, Hawai'i. [D. Thomas]

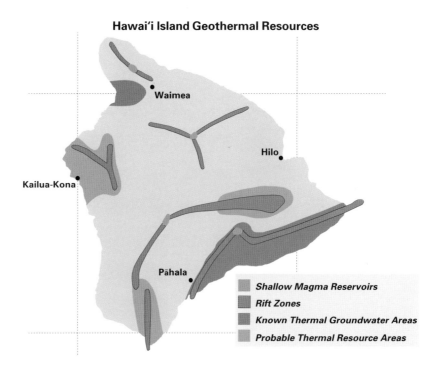

Hawai'i Island Geothermal Resources

Waimea

Hilo

Kailua-Kona

Pāhala

Shallow Magma Reservoirs
Rift Zones
Known Thermal Groundwater Areas
Probable Thermal Resource Areas

Hawai'i Island Geothermal Power Plant Diagram

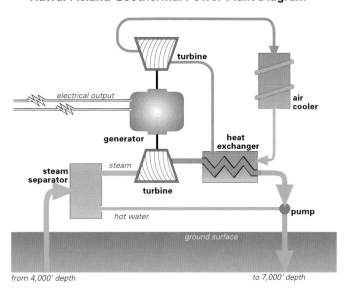

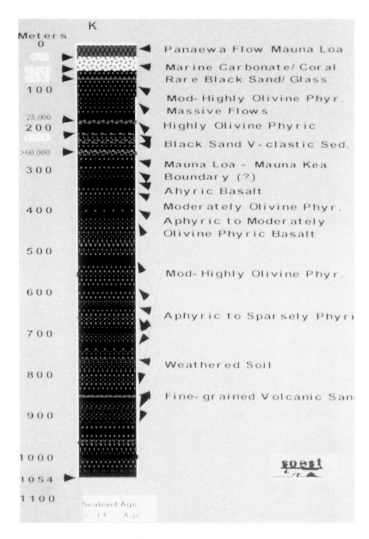

Geothermal well log. [D. Thomas]

stantial amounts of hot water and steam discharged underground. In time the magma body cools and, unless more intrusions occur in the vicinity, geothermal activity wanes and dies out, leaving little evidence of former activity.

Because geothermal systems depend on recent magma intrusions, the younger, more active volcanoes demonstrate the strongest evidence of high-temperature geothermal systems. On Kīlauea, the youngest subaerial (above-water) volcano in Hawai'i, a geothermal system with temperatures exceeding 570°F (300°C) at depths of 1.2 miles (2 km) extends the entire length of its east rift zone. Active geothermal systems where fumarole surface temperatures exceed 620°F (325°C) also exist at the summits of Kīlauea and Mauna Loa. Although researchers have not yet determined the presence of geothermal systems at Mauna Loa's lower elevations, the relative youth of this volcano suggests geothermal activity could still exist within its east or southwest rift zones. Geothermal exploration surveys also have revealed the presence of lower-temperature systems on West Maui volcano and on O'ahu's Wai'anae volcano, as well as evidence of moderate- to low-temperature activity on Mauna Kea, Hualālai, Haleakalā, and Lāna'i volcanoes.

Geothermal systems may play an important role in the state's future energy supply. In 1960 exploration for commercially viable geothermal resources began on Kīlauea's east rift zone. The earliest drilling efforts failed to yield commercial quantities of steam. However, in 1976 the Hawai'i Geothermal Project Well-A (HGP-A) demonstrated the presence of a deep geothermal reservoir with temperatures exceeding 660°F (350°C), capable of producing substantial volumes of steam. Rapidly escalating oil prices during the 1970s and the installation and operation of a pilot power plant on the HGP-A well led to more sustained geothermal exploration during the 1980s. The state's first commercial geothermal power plant was constructed by Puna Geothermal Venture in 1991. Two high-pressure steam wells produced 35 megawatts of electricity, which satisfied about 25 percent of Hawai'i Island's electrical demand in 1997. Geologic data for Kīlauea's east rift zone suggest that the Puna Geothermal Venture plant currently utilizes only a small fraction of the heat resource available.

DONALD M. THOMAS

CLIMATE

Hawai'i's climate may be regarded as one of the state's most important natural resources. Visitors are attracted to the Islands by equable temperatures, moderate humidity, persistent breezes, and abundant sunshine; and residents are loath to leave the state for destinations certain to have less pleasant weather.

The climate of a place can be defined as the composite of its weather, including not just the average conditions, but also the variability. Hawai'i's climate is indeed notable for its low day-to-day and month-to-month variability. The annual variation in mean monthly temperatures is only about 9°F (5°C) for areas at sea level—smaller than the typical diurnal (daily) range of 10–15°F (5.6°–8.3°C) experienced locally.

We generally recognize only two seasons in Hawai'i, as did the early Hawaiians who named them *kau,* the warm season when the sun is almost directly overhead and winds are reliably from the northeast; and *ho'oilo,* the season of cooler temperatures, a lower sun, more variable winds, and extensive rains. Summer is usually defined as the period from May through September and winter from October through April.

While Hawai'i's climate is equable, the mountainous topography makes it one of the most spatially diverse on Earth. Rainfall, solar radiation, temperature, humidity, and wind exhibit spectacular changes over short distances. Sitting on the beach at Waikīkī, where annual rainfall averages 20 inches (500 mm),

Air temperature in Hawai'i has a muted annual cycle because of the small season-to-season changes in solar radiation and the ocean's moderating influence. Differences in temperature from place to place are mainly due to elevation. Small differences in average temperature occur between cloudier, wetter, windward locations and sunny, dry, leeward areas at similar elevations. The rate of temperature decrease with elevation, called the lapse rate, is fairly constant at about 3.6°F per 1,000 feet (6.5°C per 1,000 m) below about 4,100 feet (1,250 m) and 2.2°F per 1,000 feet (4°C per 1,000 m) at higher elevations. (The trade wind inversion is not apparent in the figure because it varies in height and strength and thus becomes "averaged-out.")

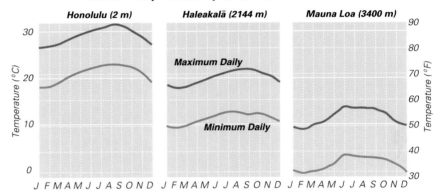

Annual Temperature Cycle at Different Elevations

Monthly maximum and minimum temperatures at Honolulu, Haleakalā, and Mauna Loa have similar annual patterns. The temperature differences are due mainly to elevation.

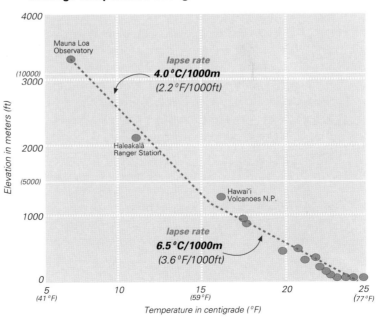

Average Temperature Change with Elevation in Hawai'i

49

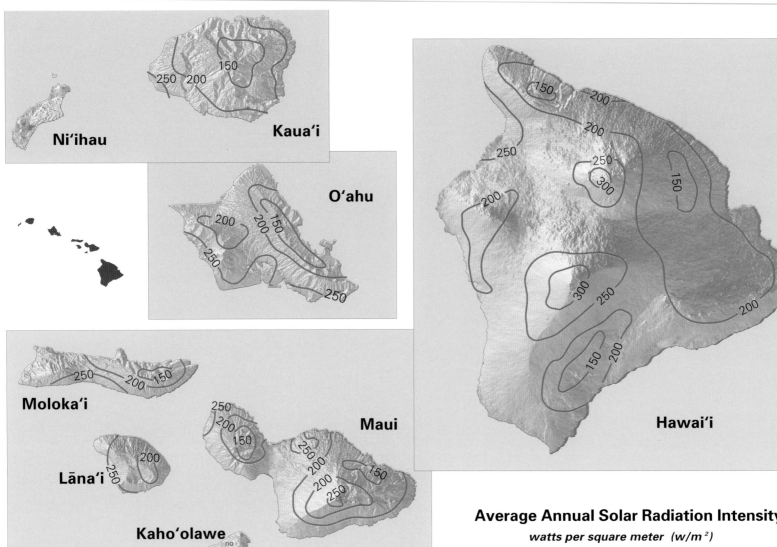

Average Annual Solar Radiation Intensity
watts per square meter (w/m²)

one can gaze at the nearby peak of Tantalus, where 160 inches (4,000 mm) of rain fall each year. Changes in climate are especially noticeable along mountain slopes, where air cools as elevation increases. With the highest mountains reaching nearly 14,000 feet (over 4,000 m), the state experiences a wide temperature range, including freezing conditions. Because of this spatial variation of climate and the consequent diversity of plant and animal life, Hawai'i resembles a continent in miniature, with ecosystems ranging from deserts to tropical rain forest and even frozen alpine tundra, all in close proximity.

Climate Controls

Latitude The character of Hawai'i's climate can be explained largely by its geographic location. Ranging from approximately 19 to 22 degrees north latitude, the inhabited islands lie at the margin of the tropics and inside a belt of persistent trade winds and accompanying downwelling of upper-level air.

In this region both tropical and temperate mid-latitude storms affect the climate. Twice during the

Average annual solar radiation received in Hawai'i differs substantially from place to place. Highest solar radiation occurs along leeward coasts and atop the highest mountain peaks. The coastal areas of high radiation have attracted major resort development. The patterns on the map result from spatial differences in the amount of solar radiation absorbed and reflected before reaching the ground. Air pollutants, naturally occurring aerosols, and gases absorb solar radiation; thus the amount of solar radiation reaching the ground can be reduced by urban pollution, fires, volcanic emissions, and suspended particles of sea salt, as well as by increased stratospheric ozone concentration and humidity. Distance above sea level is also a factor, since at higher elevations radiation traverses shorter paths through the atmosphere to reach the ground. But by far the most important cause of variation in solar radiation received at the ground is clouds. The orographic process that produces clouds, and the extreme spatial variations in rainfall, are also responsible for the radiation pattern.

year, in May and July, the sun's rays are directly overhead. At its lowest position, during December, the noon sun reaches an elevation of about 45 degrees in the southern sky. The length of the daylight period changes little throughout the year in the tropics. The longest and shortest days of the year in Hawai'i differ by only 2 hours and 34 minutes, while in Montreal, Canada, at 45 degrees north, the difference is 6 hours and 52 minutes. As a result, the amount of solar radiation reaching the ground varies much less through the year in Hawai'i than at higher latitudes. Montreal in December, for example, receives less than 20 percent of the sunlight it gets in July. In contrast, Honolulu's December sunshine is 60 percent of the July amount.

Pacific Ocean Situated in the middle of Earth's largest ocean, the Hawaiian Islands rank among the most oceanic land areas on the globe—that is, the most distant from the effects of continents. Hence, the atmosphere over the Islands is strongly influenced by the ocean, which supplies moisture to the air and regulates its temperature. Because of ocean water's transparency, high heat storage capacity, and abilities to diffuse heat by mixing and to dissipate heat through evaporation, ocean temperatures fluctuate much less than those of land surfaces. This fundamental difference between land and water strongly affects the atmosphere, producing continental and maritime climates, which are distinguished principally by their annual temperature range. Hawai'i has one of the planet's most pronounced maritime climates. The ocean acts as a "thermal flywheel," damping the seasonal day-to-day and day-night swings in temperature. A good example of a location with a continental climate is Chicago, where the difference in average January and July temperatures is more than 45°F (25°C), compared with 9°F (5°C) for Honolulu.

Atmospheric Circulation The large-scale features of motion in the atmosphere, known as the general

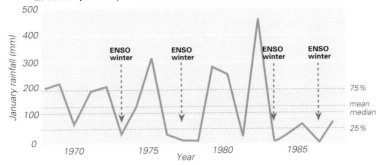

El Niño (ENSO) Influence on Honolulu Winter Rainfall

Cool season rainfall varies substantially from year to year. In some years Kona storms are absent and cold fronts are weak. A prominent cause of this year-to-year variability is the El Niño Southern Oscillation (ENSO).

The Pacific-wide ENSO consists of two phases: a period of warm sea surface temperatures in the central and eastern equatorial Pacific (called El Niño after the annual warm current that arrives off coastal Peru around Christmas), followed by a period of cool sea-surface temperatures (sometimes called La Niña).

Warming phases generally occur every four to seven years. Shifts in oceanic temperature patterns coincide with atmospheric changes, the most important to Hawai'i being the development of thunderstorms over the equator near the International Dateline. These clouds cause heating of the atmosphere, creating high pressure at 35,000 feet (10,600 m), which in turn alters the winds north of the equator. Under these conditions, winter winds subside over the Islands, suppressing Kona storms and weakening fronts. The trade winds fail, and along with them, the rains.

The warm phase of an ENSO also brings the development of westerly winds along the equator, which favors the formation of tropical cyclones south of the Islands. ENSO warm-phase years generally, but not always, correspond with a greater number of tropical cyclones.

A reversal of warm-year patterns occurs during cold-phase years. The effects of ENSO events are stronger in Hawai'i than at higher latitudes because of the state's location nearer to the source of the actual disturbance at the equator.

Relative Humidity

Average relative humidity depends on ambient air temperature and moisture content. Since the Hawaiian Islands are surrounded by ocean waters, in theory variability should be small. Annual ranges shown in the table are 3.5 percentage points at Līhu'e, a windward coastal site; 12.4 percentage points at Honolulu Airport, a leeward coastal location; and 4 percentage points at Hilo, a very rainy, windward coastal site. Annual relative humidity minima correspond to summer high temperatures. At least 40 years of humidity data have been recorded at all three sites.

	Līhu'e	Honolulu	Hilo
January	77.5%	77.2%	78.0%
February	76.2	74.5	77.5
March	75.8	69.0	78.8
April	75.5	67.8	79.8
May	74.8	66.0	77.0
June	74.0	64.8	77.8
July	74.0	65.0	79.8
August	74.5	66.0	80.2
September	74.5	65.5	77.2
October	76.5	67.0	77.8
November	77.5	71.0	81.0
December	77.0	73.5	79.5

Diurnal Variation in Relative Humidity on Hawai'i Island

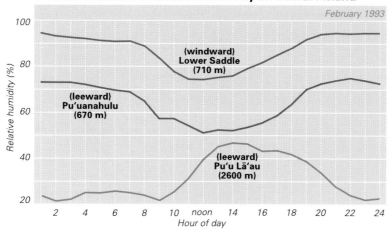

In Kona, clouds produce afternoon rain on the slopes, then dissipate at night, resulting in a diurnal rain cycle unique in Hawai'i. The role of slope circulation is evident in a comparison of relative humidity at varying elevations. Stations below the trade wind inversion have minimum relative humidity measurements at midday, the expected result where moisture content is steady but air temperature rises due to insolation. Above the inversion (at Pu'u Lā'au) relative humidity is low. The midday rise in relative humidity indicates that air from below the inversion has been carried aloft by upslope winds.

Global Atmospheric Circulation

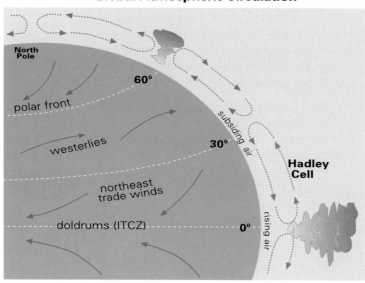

The Hadley Cell circulation, named after the seventeenth-century English scientist who first proposed it, is driven by warm air rising near the equator. At the rising limb of the Hadley Cell, towering thunderstorm clouds are frequent and rainfall is copious. At the descending limb, cloud development is suppressed and rainfall is low.

circulation, also profoundly influence climate. A major component of the atmospheric general circulation is initiated by the rising of air heated near the equator. This warm air drives a system in each hemisphere called the Hadley Cell, whereby air moves poleward at high altitudes, sinks back to the surface over a broad area centered at around 30 degrees north, and then returns to the equator at the surface. In the Northern Hemisphere, air moving back to the equator along the surface is deflected by Earth's rotation to flow from northeast to southwest. Widely known as the trade winds because their reliability made this zone a favorite route of seagoing merchant ships in the days of sail, these northeasterly surface winds are a dominant feature of tropical climate outside of the monsoon regions of Asia and Africa.

Hawai'i lies within the Northern Hemisphere Hadley Cell, where persistent northeast winds and descending air from above have pronounced effects on climate. Sinking air in the Hadley Cell warms as it is compressed. In contrast, air heated at the planet's surface rises, expands, and cools. Where rising and sinking air meet, a layer forms in which air gets warmer as altitude increases; this is generally known as a temperature inversion. In Hawai'i this layer is called the trade wind inversion. It occurs most frequently during summer and varies in altitude between about 5,000 and 10,000 feet (1,500 and 3,000 m).

Rising air is of particular importance to weather because it is responsible for most cloud formation and precipitation. Persistent conditions promoting or inhibiting rising air are responsible for many of the differences in climate from place to place. The trade wind inversion inhibits rising air, creating a ceiling through which warm, moist, buoyant surface air cannot penetrate. Thus clouds that form are capped at the level of the trade wind inversion. Being shallow, they are much less effective than deeper clouds at producing rain, making the region around Hawai'i one of relatively low

Tree deformed by persistent northeast trade winds near Ka Lae (South Point) Hawai'i. [J. Juvik]

rainfall. Because the inversion acts to keep humid marine air from reaching high altitudes, the upper slopes of the state's highest mountains usually experience clear skies, low humidity, and minimal precipitation.

Descending air from the Hadley Cell also creates a globe-girdling belt of high pressure at the surface in each hemisphere. Within these belts, quasicircular high-pressure systems known as subtropical anticyclones are nearly permanent features of surface weather patterns. The trade winds reaching Hawai'i originate from the North Pacific anticyclone, located northeast of the Islands.

Poleward of the subtropical anticyclones, systems of low and high pressure (cyclones and anticyclones) follow regular paths as they migrate from west to east across the midlatitudes. Subtropical anticyclones shift with the seasons, moving closer to the equator during winter. The North Pacific anticyclone moves farther north and, on average, is stronger and more persistent in summer. During winter, with the anticyclone farther south, weaker, or sometimes absent, storms (midlatitude cyclones) move closer to the Hawaiian Islands, often disrupting the trade winds and related weather conditions. Typically, cold fronts associated with midlatitude cyclones bring clouds and rain with winds from the northeast through the northwest. However, when cold fronts pass directly over the Islands, heavy rains accompanied by southwest winds may occur. The frequency of the passage of fronts varies from year to year and is responsible for wet and dry years in leeward regions, which receive much of their rainfall from fronts.

Kona (Hawaiian for leeward) storms are another type of low-pressure system that develop in the subtropics at high altitudes and gradually extend toward the surface. Occasionally a Kona storm will form west of Hawai'i, bringing moist, southerly winds and rain, which may persist for a week or more.

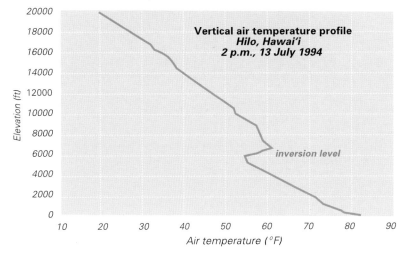

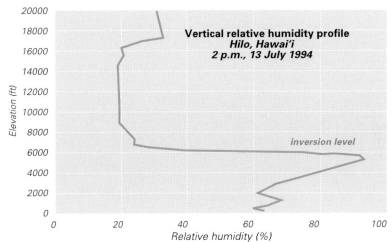

The trade wind inversion can be seen in measurements transmitted from balloon-borne instruments launched twice daily by the National Weather Service from Hilo and Līhu'e airports. The inversion itself is a relatively shallow layer in which temperature increases rather than decreases with elevation. The graph shows the trade wind inversion at 6,000 feet (1,800 m) elevation on 13 July 1994 above Hilo. This seemingly minor fluctuation in the temperature profile has enormous consequences for the atmosphere. Air rising for any reason at the level of the inversion will be cooler than the air above, and therefore too heavy to ascend farther. Vertical motion below the inversion creates a well-mixed marine air layer with abundant water vapor and suspended particles of sea salt, as well as smoke from automobile exhaust and particulates from Hawai'i Island's volcanic eruptions. The lower graph shows the humidity profile measured at the same time as the temperatures on the upper graph. The abrupt change in humidity at 6,000 feet (1,800 m) is evidence of the effectiveness of the inversion in containing surface air. The photo shows the effect on cloud development. Rising air reaches saturation and begins to condense water at around 2,000 feet (610 m), but cloud development is halted at the inversion. Consequently rainfall in Hawai'i is limited, except when the large-scale atmospheric pattern displaces the inversion, or where orographic lifting produces rainfall on windward slopes.

Vertical cloud development blocked by upper level temperature inversion, windward, Mauna Kea. [J. Juvik]

Seasonal High Pressure Systems and Wind Patterns

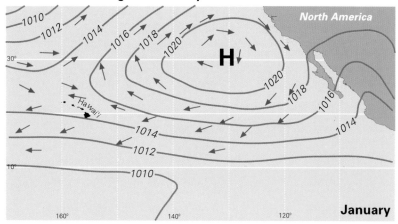

January

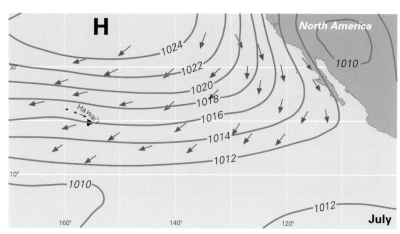

July

Tropical cyclones develop over warm ocean surfaces and initially move from east to west. They are smaller than midlatitude storms and sometimes become very powerful hurricanes, delivering rain, high surf, devastating winds, and elevated sea level if they reach land areas. (See section on Hurricanes.)

Terrain The varying terrain of the Hawaiian Islands also significantly affects climate patterns. The islands are almost continuously buffeted by wind, usually northeast trades. The mountainous relief changes the wind's direction and speed—slowing it in some areas, accelerating it in others. Moist air blowing against steep slopes is forced to rise, cooling and saturating the air and creating clouds. Rain produced by this process, called orographic rainfall, is very consistent in windward areas, leading to exceptionally high

Left: Average January and July positions of the North Pacific anticyclone (H) are shown along with the pattern of air pressure at the surface. Units of pressure are millibars (mb). Arrows show the approximate wind patterns. Anticyclones are centers of high pressure and produce winds that spiral outward in a clockwise fashion in the Northern Hemisphere. The anticyclone is larger, stronger, and centered farther north in July, as compared with January. Trade winds are frequent in summer, whereas winds are more variable in winter.

Kona Storms and Cold Fronts

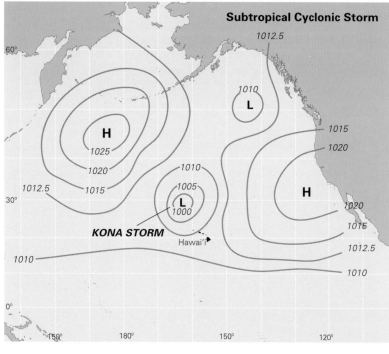

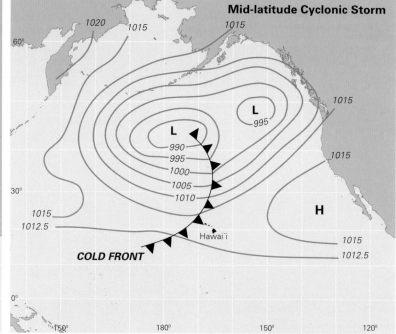

Kona storms are low-pressure areas (cyclones) of subtropical origin that usually develop northwest of Hawai'i in winter and move slowly eastward, accompanied by southerly winds, from whose direction the storm derives its name, and by the clouds and rain that have made these storms synonymous with bad weather in Hawai'i. Kona storms vary in number from year to year. Some winters have had none, others five or more. **Cold fronts**, common

between October and April, mark the leading edges of cold air masses associated with low-pressure systems moving north of the Islands in the prevailing westerlies. They bring widespread clouds, heavy rain, and occasional thunderstorms. Vigorous fronts may be preceded by strong southwest winds and followed by gusty northerly winds. Kaua'i experiences as many as 20 cold fronts per year, but generally only about half of them reach Hawai'i Island.

Diurnal Variation in Wind Direction and Speeds on Hawai'i Island

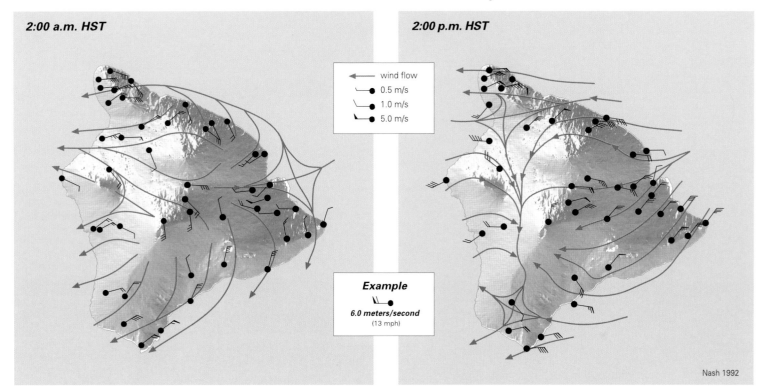

2:00 a.m. HST

2:00 p.m. HST

wind flow
0.5 m/s
1.0 m/s
5.0 m/s

Example
6.0 meters/second
(13 mph)

Nash 1992

The winds during the day on Hawai'i Island vary in a consistent fashion. These examples show mean wind flows at 2:00 A.M. and 2:00 P.M., based upon a 42-day sample from 50 portable automated weather stations. The results comply with meteorological predictions for the behavior of air above a heated island in a trade wind flow.

Surface Wind Flow. The prevailing trade winds interact with the mountainous islands. In a study that mapped wind-deformed trees to determine mean winds on O'ahu and Maui, the results match theory and previous meteorological measurements.

average rainfall totals. In contrast, leeward areas are influenced by descending, warming air from which some moisture has been removed as it passes over the mountain. Consequently, leeward areas are usually clearer and drier than windward areas. Where mountains reach heights above the inversion layer, such as on Mauna Loa, Mauna Kea, and Haleakalā, air is forced to flow around, rather than over, the mountain. As a result, orographic rainfall usually does not reach the upper slopes, and they remain quite dry. Cloud formation and rainfall associated with the interaction of trade winds, the inversion, and island topography are responsible for the incredible climatic diversity found in Hawai'i.

Prevailing Wind Patterns on Maui and O'ahu

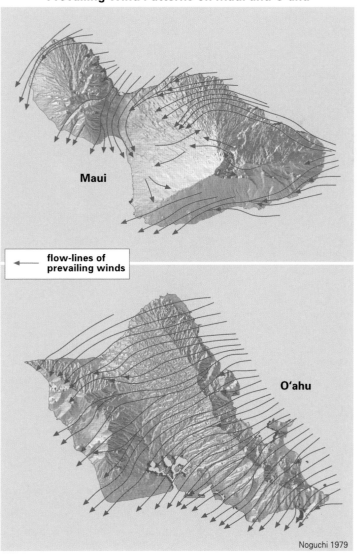

Maui

flow-lines of prevailing winds

O'ahu

Noguchi 1979

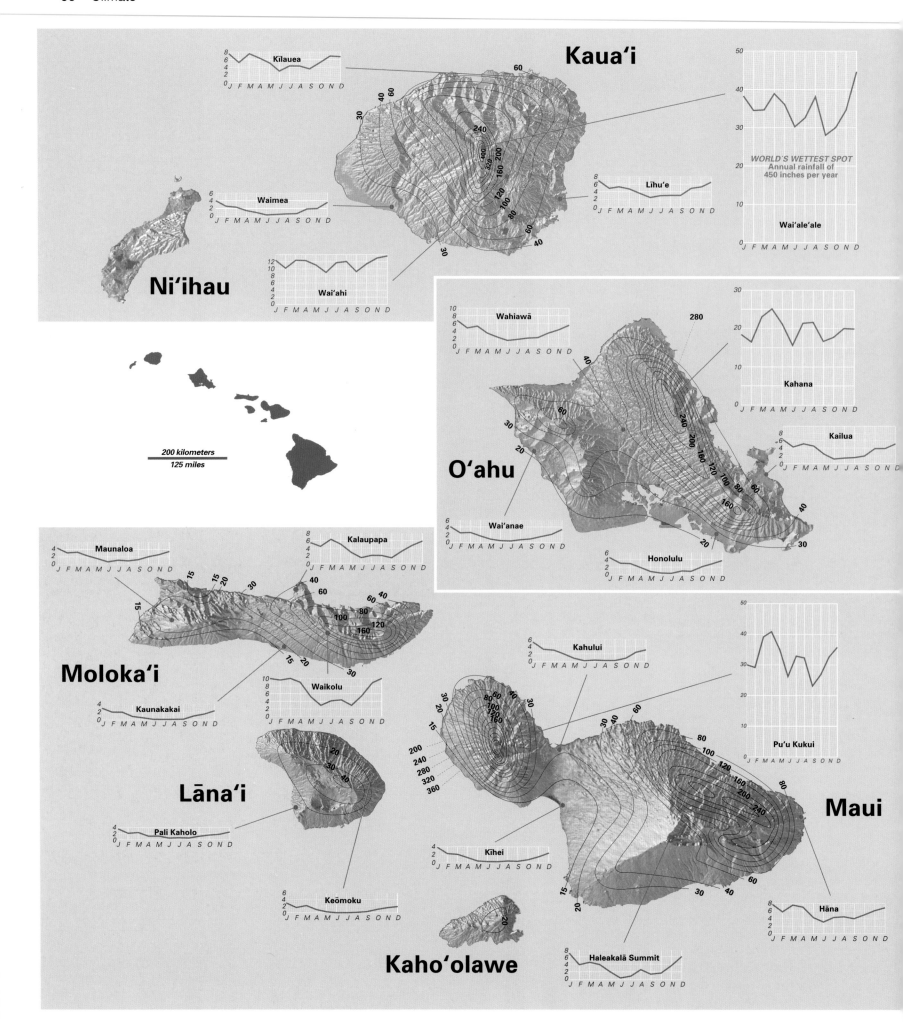

Kaua'i

Kīlauea

Waimea

Līhu'e

WORLD'S WETTEST SPOT
Annual rainfall of
450 inches per year

Wai'ale'ale

Ni'ihau

Wai'ahi

O'ahu

Wahiawā

Kahana

Kailua

Wai'anae

Honolulu

Moloka'i

Maunaloa

Kalaupapa

Waikolu

Kaunakakai

Lāna'i

Pali Kaholo

Keōmoku

Kaho'olawe

Maui

Kahului

Pu'u Kukui

Kīhei

Hāna

Haleakalā Summit

200 kilometers
125 miles

Hawai'i

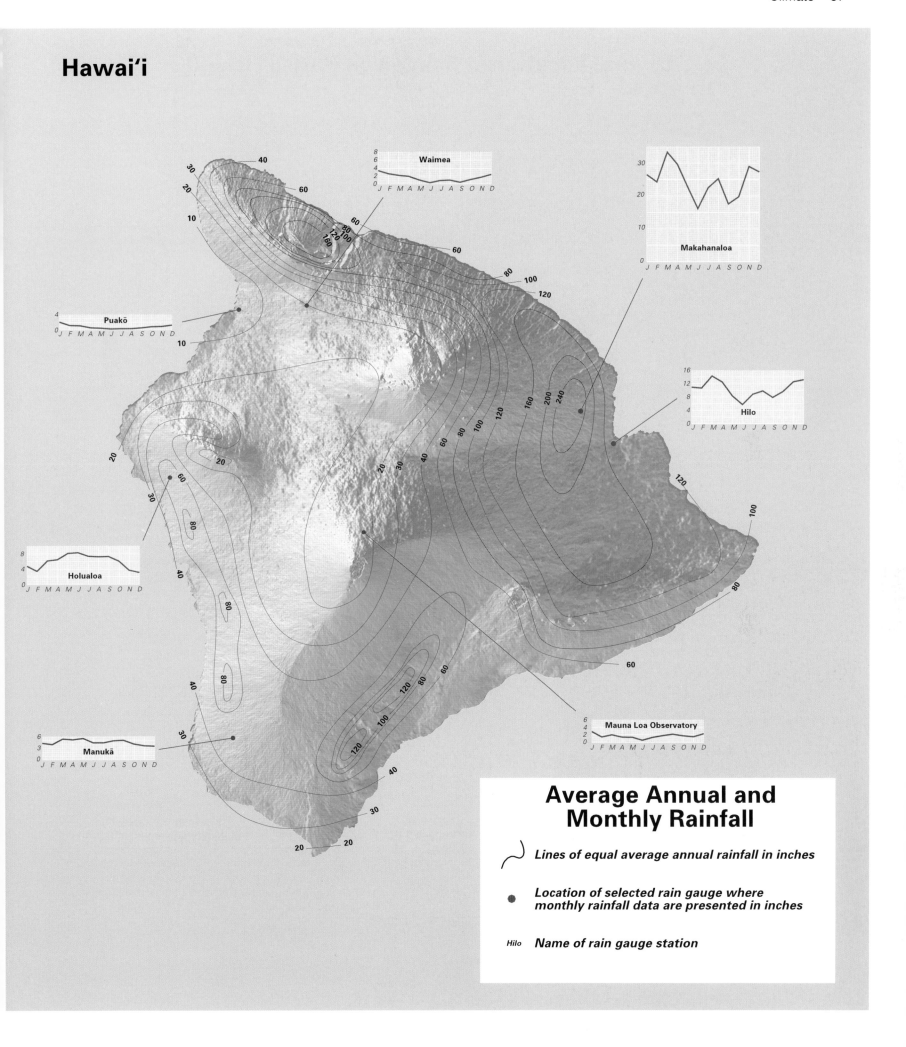

Waimea

Makahanaloa

Puakō

Hilo

Holualoa

Manukā

Mauna Loa Observatory

Average Annual and Monthly Rainfall

Lines of equal average annual rainfall in inches

Location of selected rain gauge where monthly rainfall data are presented in inches

Hilo   Name of rain gauge station

Diurnal Variation in Rainfall on Hawai'i Island

The combination of large islands, intense daytime sunshine, and steady winds creates a climate characterized by distinct diurnal weather patterns. While all the major islands exhibit diurnal patterns, the most well defined ones appear on Hawai'i Island, where during the day breezes blow from the sea and upslope from valley bottoms, while at night breezes blow from the land, down the mountain slopes. In Hilo, at the foot of Mauna Loa, maximum precipitation occurs at night as downslope winds converge with oceanic trade winds to form clouds that drift over Hilo and deposit rain. Thus, although Hilo is often cloudy and annual rainfall ranges from 133 inches (3,400 mm) at the airport to more than 300 inches (7,700 mm) at higher elevations above the city, Hilo residences are able to utilize solar water heaters, because cloudiness and rainfall are minimal at midday during peak sunlight hours.

Rainfall

Hawai'i is located in a region where descending air inhibits the formation of deep clouds. Were the islands without steeply sloped high mountains, rainfall would range between 22 and 28 inches (560 and 700 mm) per year. The importance of the orographic effect in Hawai'i is revealed clearly by the pattern of average annual rainfall, which ranges from 10 inches (250 mm) to 445 inches (11,300 mm). Other rain-producing mechanisms—frontal passages, Kona storms, tropical cyclones, and convection of air heated over the islands —either enhance the orographic pattern, or produce widespread, uniform rainfall.

Statewide, the areas of highest average rainfall are near Pu'u Kukui at the summit of the West Maui Mountains and at the summit of Wai'ale'ale on Kaua'i, one of the wettest spots on Earth. Lower mountains, such as the Ko'olau Range on O'ahu or Kohala on Hawai'i Island, receive substantially less rainfall. Higher mountains—Mauna Kea and Mauna Loa on Hawai'i Island and Haleakalā on Maui—also experience less rainfall than Pu'u Kukui and Wai'ale'ale; on these mountains maximum rainfall occurs on windward slopes at elevations of around 2,100 to 3,000 feet (650 to 900 m).

Orographic rainfall is effective throughout the year and supplies the bulk of Hawai'i's water resources. Areas away from windward slopes depend on storms for rainfall and show a distinct annual pattern. Leeward coastal areas, such as Puakō on Hawai'i Island and Wai'anae on O'ahu, and summits of high mountains have clearly defined summer (dry) and winter (wet) seasons. In high-rainfall areas such as Pu'u Kukui on Maui and Wai'ale'ale on Kaua'i, however, rainfall is more uniform throughout the year.

On the Kona Coast of Hawai'i Island, a unique summer maximum rainfall pattern occurs. There the prevailing winds are effectively blocked by two large mountains, Mauna Loa and Hualālai. In the absence of strong trades, ocean-land temperature and pressure differences generate local diurnal variations in wind. Surface heating causes upslope winds during the day that give rise to convectional rainfall at middle elevations (the "coffee belt") in the afternoon. Wind direction reverses at night, as cooled mountain air moves downslope. Increased surface heating in summer intensifies this process, resulting in the only summer rainfall maximum in the state.

THOMAS W. GIAMBELLUCA AND
THOMAS A. SCHROEDER

Airflow and Orographic Rainfall

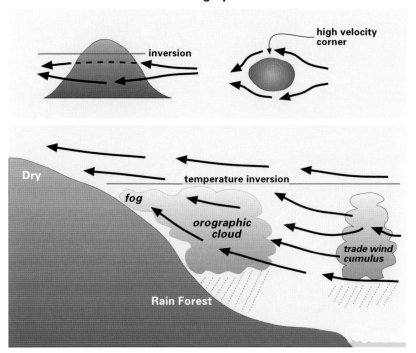

Generalized weather along the windward slope of a high mountain such as Mauna Loa.

HAWAI'I AND ATMOSPHERIC CHANGE

Global Air Pollution

Humans are altering the composition of the atmosphere on a massive scale. As the world population grows and economic development accelerates, rising levels of urbanization, industrialization, and deforestation release ever-increasing quantities of gases and particles into the atmosphere. Many pollutants persist for up to a hundred years, degrading the air we breathe and drifting into the upper atmosphere where they interfere with the balance of radiation entering and leaving Earth and contribute to the thinning of the ozone layer.

Atmospheric Monitoring at Mauna Loa Observatory

The remoteness of the Hawaiian Islands from any large sources of industrial pollution serves to keep the composition of the surrounding air relatively pure. Because of this, Hawai'i's regional atmosphere represents a standard of air quality against which air in other regions can be measured. To monitor the atmospheric concentrations of various gases, in 1956 the National

Oceanic and Atmospheric Administration (NOAA) established the Mauna Loa Observatory (MLO) on Hawai'i Island.

Siting this "clean air" sampling facility on the active volcano Mauna Loa may seem paradoxical. But at 11,500 feet (3,500 m), MLO is well above an atmospheric temperature inversion layer, which serves as a barrier that prevents the mixing of locally polluted air from below with the purer air above. Thus MLO is perfectly situated to sample the composition of dry, well-mixed, global "background" air from the upper atmosphere. With an unbroken record of measurements of solar radiation, particulates, and atmospheric gases, MLO is the oldest facility in a worldwide network of atmospheric monitoring stations. It has served

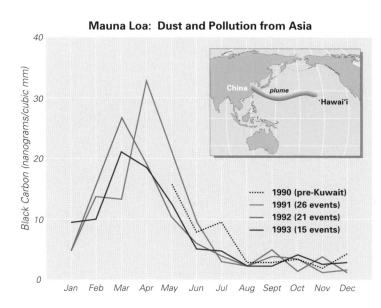

Mauna Loa: Dust and Pollution from Asia

- 1990 (pre-Kuwait)
- 1991 (26 events)
- 1992 (21 events)
- 1993 (15 events)

At Mauna Loa Observatory, a stratospheric aerosol LIDAR (laser radar) measures particulates in the stratosphere from volcanic eruptions. A remote-sensing instrument similar to radar, LIDAR utilizes a laser as an energy beam, while radar uses radiowaves. [P. Buklarewicz]

Dust and Air Pollution from Asia. Each spring, wind storms in northwest China stir up large amounts of dust that is carried 3,600 miles (6,000 km) across the Pacific Ocean to Hawai'i. These winds also bring air pollution in the form of black carbon produced by fossil fuel combustion (best visualized as the exhaust from diesel powered vehicles) to Hawai'i in concentrations ten times greater than normal.

Global Atmospheric Climate Monitoring Sites,1997

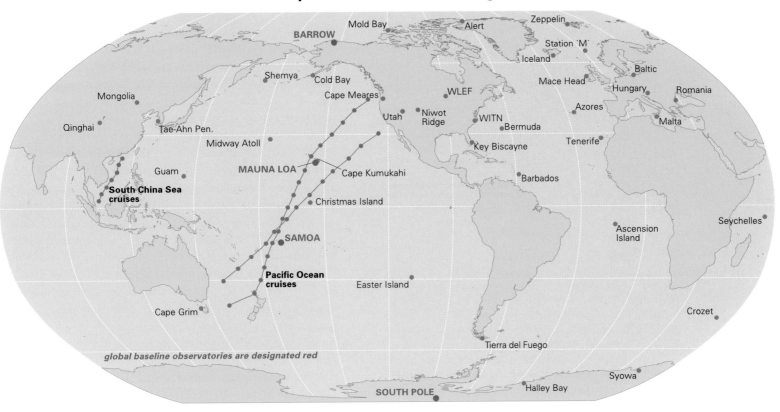

global baseline observatories are designated red

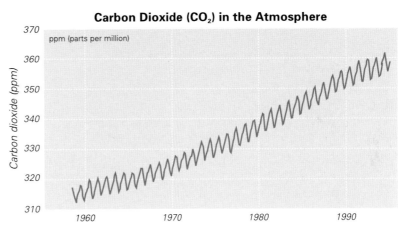

Carbon Dioxide (CO$_2$) in the Atmosphere

ppm (parts per million)

Mauna Loa: Atmospheric Carbon Dioxide Concentration. The spurt of plant growth each spring in the Northern Hemisphere lowers atmospheric concentrations of carbon dioxide and produces annual fluctuations in the ever-increasing levels of carbon dioxide generated by fossil-fuel combustion.

Aerial view of NOAA Mauna Loa Observatory with upslope lava flow diversion berm. [G. Brad Lewis]

as a model for many other stations and as a training ground for atmospheric scientists.

Greenhouse Gases

Among the scores of atmospheric gases measured regularly at MLO and other monitoring stations, carbon dioxide, methane, and nitrous oxide are particularly important because of the role they play in regulating Earth's temperature in a process known as the "greenhouse effect." As sunlight strikes Earth's surface, some

Chlorofluorocarbons (CFCs) in the Atmosphere

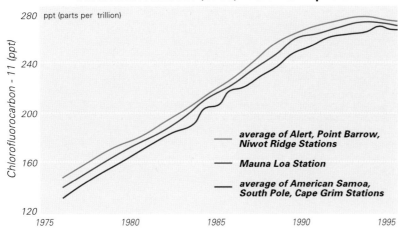

average of Alert, Point Barrow, Niwot Ridge Stations

Mauna Loa Station

average of American Samoa, South Pole, Cape Grim Stations

CFC F-11 and Stratospheric Ozone. In 1984 and subsequent years, a significant thinning of the ozone layer was observed to occur in the springtime over Antarctica. This "ozone hole" is now known to be caused by CFCs released by humans into the atmosphere. For certain types of CFCs, one molecule is capable of destroying thousands of ozone molecules. The production of one of these (CFC F-11) has declined substantially in most nations under the terms of the international Montreal Protocol, implemented in 1989. The effects of this agreement are apparent in the figure, which shows a leveling in the global CFC-11 concentrations beginning in the late 1980s.

Mauna Loa Stratospheric Transparency - LIDAR

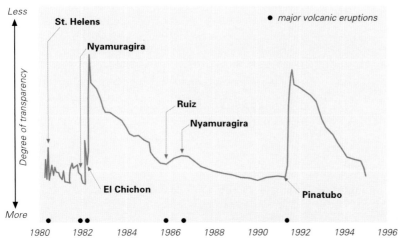

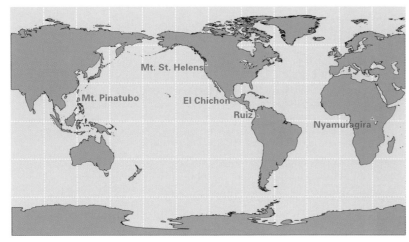

of the energy is absorbed, and some is reradiated back to the atmosphere or space as longwave infrared radiation (heat). In a manner similar to the heat-conserving glass of a greenhouse, gases such as carbon dioxide and methane are transparent to light but trap some of Earth's radiated heat energy, which continues to warm the lower atmosphere. Although some greenhouse gases are released by natural processes, many scientists believe the growing share of human-generated greenhouse gases is initiating global climate change. The amount of carbon dioxide has risen by 15 percent since 1958, when scientists at MLO began measuring it in the atmosphere. This marked increase is attributed to deforestation and the combustion of fossil fuels, which by the mid-1990s were emitting 6 billion tons of carbon dioxide into the atmosphere worldwide each year.

Increased heating of the atmosphere may already be altering wind-flow patterns as the atmosphere adjusts to new energy balances. This may have immediate local consequences, because even small changes in average wind speed and direction produce substantial climate effects in the Hawaiian Islands. For example, when the normal northeast trade winds weaken—especially during El Niño events in the eastern Pacific off South America—rainfall on the east side of Hawai'i Island, normally an almost daily occurrence, is drastically reduced. El Niño events also induce westerly wind flows, producing Kona winds and triggering rainfall over the normally dry west side of Hawai'i Island. Global climate change could similarly alter the weather of Hawai'i and other Pacific islands and modify the normal pattern of hurricane tracks across the Pacific Ocean.

Ozone Destruction

Industrial chemicals have depleted another gas vital to life: stratospheric ozone, a form of oxygen created by a chemical reaction in the presence of sunlight about 10–38 miles (16–64 km) above Earth's surface. For billions of years a thin layer of ozone molecules has acted as a shield by reducing the amount of potentially harmful ultraviolet radiation that reaches the planet and its life forms. Over the past few decades chlorofluorocarbons (CFCs) have been used in refrigerators, air conditioners, and aerosol containers, and since the late 1970s atmospheric concentrations of CFCs have more than doubled. Ultimately these highly stable compounds mix upward into the stratosphere, where they act as catalysts to drive a reaction that destroys ozone. The most dramatic manifestation of this process is the ozone "hole" produced by widespread depletion of

Volcanic Dust in the Stratosphere. The El Chichon and Pinatubo volcanoes injected ash and sulfur dioxide into the stratosphere that circled Earth for many years.

ozone over Antarctica each austral spring. Locally, stratospheric ozone above Hawai'i has steadily decreased for five or so years. A particularly severe depletion persisted during the winter of 1994–1995. Although not completely understood, this event is thought to have resulted from a combination of chemical destruction, transport of ozone-poor air from the tropics, and residual effects in the stratosphere from the 1992 Mt. Pinatubo eruption in the Philippines.

Volcanic Ash in the Stratosphere

Occasionally, explosive volcanoes eject enormous quantities of ash and sulphur dioxide high into the stratosphere, where the materials slowly orbit Earth and settle out over a few years. The presence of particulates reduces the amount of solar radiation reaching Earth's surface, often with measurable climatic effects such as surface cooling. (Volcanic ash provides surfaces upon which stratospheric ozone destruction may occur, and it also reduces ozone formation by blocking sunlight.) So voluminous was the outpouring of volcanic material from the 1982 eruption of El Chichon in Central America that it was still detectable in the atmosphere in 1990. Traces of the Pinatubo ash cloud, formed in 1992, were still being measured at MLO in 1995. The El Chichon eruption diminished solar radiation to a larger degree than did that of Mt. Pinatubo, due to the greater size and height of its ash cloud. In contrast, the Mount St. Helens eruption, in Washington State, although dramatic, had no effect on solar radiation because its ash did not reach sufficient height to be widely transported in the stratosphere.

RUSSELL SCHNELL

PALEOCLIMATE AND GEOGRAPHY

Current concerns over the potential for global climate change focus largely on the role of human impact. Earth, however, has undergone a long history of climate fluctuations due to natural causes. As the Hawaiian Islands adjusted to global change over the past several million years, local climate variations markedly altered many geographic features. During and between the great glacial ages, sea level changes accompanied the rise and fall of global temperatures as water shifted between continental ice sheets and the oceans. On average, during the past 2 million years global temperatures and sea levels were lower than at present, as the record in the graph indicates.

Perhaps the most intriguing geographic effect of past lower sea level was the reemergence of Maui Nui—the landmass composed of Maui, Moloka'i, Lāna'i, and Kaho'olawe—as the ocean withdrew from the shal-

low basin between the islands. (This area is well known today as a breeding area for humpback whales.) The aerial perspective shows Maui Nui as it would have appeared 21,000 years ago. While Maui Nui existed, the exposed land bridges connecting the islands allowed easier dispersal and migration of plants and animals—a past that left today's remnants of Maui Nui with a lower density of endemic species (those unique to a given location) than is found on O'ahu or Kaua'i, which remained isolated. A dramatic increase in land area also occurred during glacial epochs on the atolls of the Northwestern Hawaiian Islands, where now-submerged reefs may have once stood as much as 300 feet (100 m) above sea level.

Past sea levels have also occasionally stood higher than at present, as evidenced by ancient reefs underlying coastal plains such as 'Ewa and Kāne'ohe peninsula

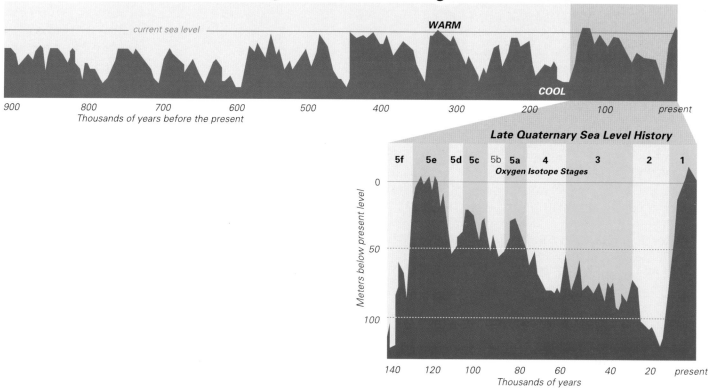

Global Sea Level Change — *900,000 Years Ago to the Present*

current sea level

WARM

COOL

| 900 | 800 | 700 | 600 | 500 | 400 | 300 | 200 | 100 | present |

Thousands of years before the present

Late Quaternary Sea Level History

| 5f | 5e | 5d | 5c | 5b | 5a | 4 | 3 | 2 | 1 |

Oxygen Isotope Stages

Meters below present level

0

50

100

| 140 | 120 | 100 | 80 | 60 | 40 | 20 | present |

Thousands of years

Reemergence of Maui Nui, 21,000 Years Ago

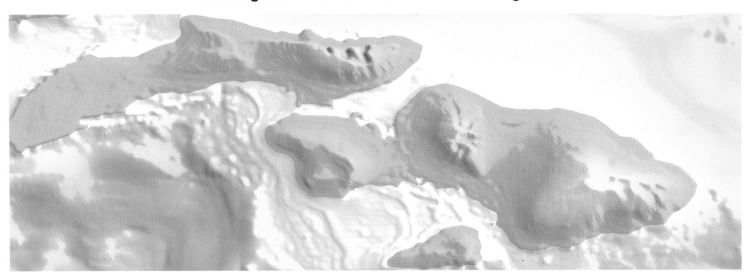

V-shaped terminal glacial moraine, Pōhakuloa Gulch, Mauna Kea, Hawai'i. [J. Juvik]

History of Mauna Kea Glaciation

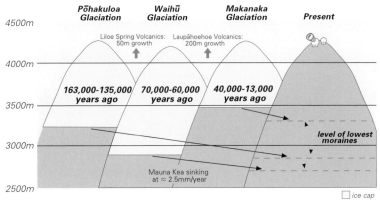

on Oʻahu, and terraces and notches cut by wave action inland from today's shorelines. For example, 126,000 years ago, Oʻahu's shorelines stood approximately 33 feet (10 m) higher than at present. This shoreline elevation probably resulted from the combined effects of absolute sea level rise and island uplift in response to the flexing of Earth's crust under the weight of geologically younger Hawaiʻi Island to the southeast.

Cooler temperatures in recent geologic time caused another phenomenon unexpected on tropical islands: glaciers. Scattered around the summit of Mauna Kea on Hawaiʻi Island are glacial features—including moraines, rock striations, and erratics (isolated boulders)—that testify to its ice-capped past.

These relict features, as well as buried fossil ice, are preserved in the Mauna Kea Ice Age Natural Area Reserve. The reserve also includes one of the highest lakes in the world, Lake Waiʻau, which, at an elevation of 13,020 feet (3,968 m), occupies a shallow depression once filled with ice. Major glacial episodes on Mauna Kea over the past 200,000 years flowed and ebbed in synchrony with the advances and retreats of continental glaciers.

Other clues pointing to local climate variations during geologic time come from a range of sources. For example, the alignment of ancient sand dunes and the asymmetrical shape of cinder cones, both of which depend on prevailing wind direction, indicate that the northeast trade winds apparently persisted throughout the cooler glacial periods. Yet the larger size of ancient dust particles from Asia—carried to Hawaiʻi by upper-level westerly winds—implies a higher average wind velocity than that of today.

Evidence from pollen analysis, soils, and erosional features, such as the deeply incised valleys of some leeward slopes, suggests that past rainfall patterns were altered with the changing climate. During cooler epochs in the past, wetter conditions than at present

Mountain Ecozone Response to Climatic Change

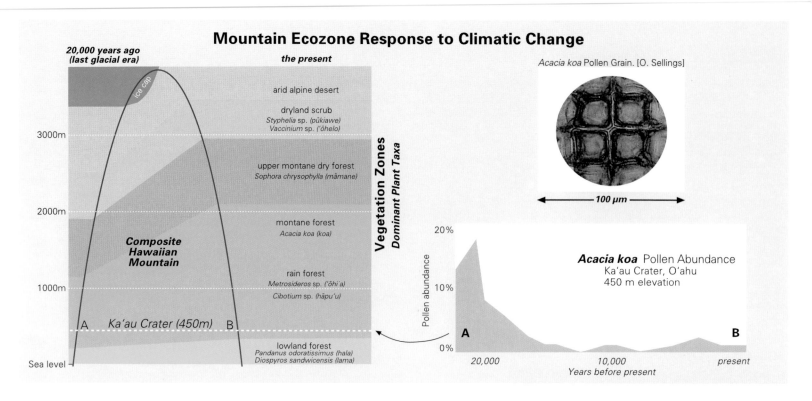

Stone stripes created by freeze-thaw cycles on Mauna Kea summit, Hawai'i. [J. Juvik]

Lake Waiau, Mauna Kea, Hawai'i, elevation 13,020 ft. (3,968 m). [J. Juvik]

apparently prevailed at lower elevations, helping carve leeward O'ahu's Mākaha Valley, for example. Higher mountain slopes, however, between 3,000 feet and 6,000 feet (1,000 m and 2,000 m), seem to have experienced drier conditions. The drier climate was probably caused by a lower average altitude of the trade wind inversion, which would limit the penetration of clouds into this elevation range. During warmer periods the reverse situation appears to have predominated, with drier conditions in coastal areas and wetter conditions at high elevation locations. Partial evidence for these conclusions comes from sequences of plant pollen in mountain bogs on Maui, Moloka'i, and Kaua'i. The pollen record from bogs at 4,000–6,000 feet (1,200–1,800 m) documents the dominance of xerophytes (dry-tolerant plants) and mesophytes (plants tolerant

of average moisture and dryness) at the end of the last glacial period, 10,000 years ago. In contrast, during the postglacial temperature maximum 4,000–6,000 years ago, hydrophytes (plants requiring very wet conditions) abounded at middle elevations. The pollen record also indicates that vegetation zones occupy different elevations in response to temperature and rainfall changes. Based on the current distribution of plants and the pollen record, during past cooler periods vegetation zones probably occupied a narrower range of elevation lower on the mountain slope.

Dennis Nullet,
Charles H. Fletcher III,
Sara Hotchkiss, and
James O. Juvik

NATURAL HAZARDS

Natural hazards are extreme environmental phenomena that can cause human injuries and deaths, severe damage and destruction to property, and other economic losses. Hawai'i may be one of the most hazard-prone areas on Earth, subject to climatic events such as hurricanes, droughts, rainstorms, and flooding; geologic threats that include volcanic eruptions, earthquakes, and shoreline retreat; oceanographic disturbances such as tsunamis and storm surges; and long-term hazards such as erosion and sea level change.

For an area to be considered hazardous, the historical record of past hazardous events must be reconstructed and the risk of their recurrence estimated. People often confuse hazard with risk. A hazard is a potentially perilous event, while a risk is the probability that a hazard will occur repeatedly and affect a specified population. Risk has two components: the probable frequency of hazard occurrence and its magnitude, based on the degree of danger inflicted and the number of people exposed. Thus, a "high-risk" zone can be either a place of moderate-sized population exposed to a severe hazard with a high probability of recurrence, or an area where a large population is subject to a moderately frequent but less dangerous hazard. Risk therefore includes the notion of cumulative impacts in an area.

To lessen the risks from natural hazards, we must answer a number of critical questions: How often have hazardous events occurred in the past in specific locations? How damaging were the impacts of these events? Has the population at risk increased in size and location since the last events? If so, how might these changes intensify the consequences, or increase the risk, of another disaster?

The relative infrequency of disasters—that is, extremely hazardous events—makes assessment of risk difficult when no reliable historical record of such occurrences exists even though other evidence indicates a potential for disaster. Scientists often rely on landscape features, as well as written and oral records, to estimate a hazard's frequency and magnitude. For example, the southern slopes of Hawai'i Island show evidence of large landslides in the past, but the historical record offers scant detail about such events. By using sophisticated techniques to examine landscape and stratigraphy (rock layers), researchers have found evidence that such a catastrophic landslide may have triggered a tsunami so large that it transported debris nearly a thousand feet upslope on Lāna'i about 105,000 years ago. If a tsunami of this size struck a populated section of Hawai'i's coastline today, it would be devastating in terms of deaths and property damage. The reconstruction of the history of past disasters and their effects underscores the need for scientific studies to evaluate natural hazard risks adequately.

Since we cannot prevent natural hazards, we must attempt to mitigate them—that is, to reduce the risks

Cautions on the Use of Natural Hazard Maps

Hazard and risk maps have become important tools in land use planning and risk mitigation. However, there are distinct differences between a hazard map and a risk map that should be appreciated by map users. The purpose of a hazard map is to provide a record of hazardous events that have occurred at various locations. Risk maps have a different purpose. They reflect an attempt to establish the degree of harm to a population that can result from a hazardous event. For example, an earthquake risk map for a large city would delineate areas with varying degrees of risk based on evaluation of a combination of factors such as soil type, quality of construction, and distance of a neighborhood from fire or ambulance services. Any number of mitigating factors could be included in the creation of a natural hazard risk surface for the city. As such, no true risk map appears in this *Atlas*. Instead, the maps portray a historical record of hazardous events that have occurred in the Islands.

to populations and property by minimizing damaging effects. Hazard mitigation includes engineering, physical, and social policy measures. Structural engineering mitigation, such as reinforcing buildings and constructing dams for flood control, can decrease the consequences of certain hazards. Physical mitigation involves the collection of data that allow us to understand the causes of disasters better, to forecast the likelihood of hazardous events, and to set up disaster prevention programs. Social aspects of mitigation include the evaluation of losses incurred by hazards and the implementation of policies that could reduce risk (for example, the limitation of residential development in past tsunami inundation zones).

Past hazard research has focused on the physical aspects of disaster assessment. However, recent experience indicates the need for more effective land use planning and more extensive education of at-risk populations. A community that is well informed about local hazards will generally be more attuned to the actual risks and better prepared to avoid or cope with a disaster. Historically, communities that have accurately appraised the risk of a natural hazard have avoided the repeat of a disaster or suffered lesser consequences from a hazardous event. A case in point is the creation of Moʻoheau and Bayfront Beach Parks in downtown Hilo following the area's inundation by a tsunami in 1946. When a tsunami hit the Hilo bayfront again in 1960, damage there was minimized because of this change in land use.

Near-total destruction of a church on Kauaʻi by Hurricane ʻIniki. Although there is no way to escape recurrent natural hazards, risks to life and property can be mitigated by rigorous engineering standards, building codes, and public education. [U.S. Army Corps of Engineers, Pacific Ocean Division]

In the following sections on hurricanes, earthquakes, volcanic hazards, tsunamis, and other coastal hazards, the authors discuss the identification and location of Hawaiʻi's most common natural hazards, their causes and history of occurrence, and possible mitigation measures. Although we have no control over the recurrence of these catastrophic events, expanded understanding of natural hazards and improved technology for mitigation can decrease the destructive—and sometimes tragic—consequences.

THOMAS R. PARADISE

EARTHQUAKES

Earthquakes are fundamental to the processes that have built and shaped the Hawaiian Islands. Unlike many other areas where seismic activity accompanies movement along tectonic (crustal) plate boundaries, in Hawai'i most earthquakes are linked to volcanic activity. Such earthquakes can occur before and during eruptions, or when magma (molten rock) migrates underground without actually erupting on the surface. Each year thousands of earthquakes occur in Hawai'i, the vast majority of them so small they are detectable only with highly sensitive instruments. However, moderate earthquakes that can be felt occur periodically and catastrophic ones occasionally rock the Islands.

As the map of past seismic events shows, the island of Hawai'i has experienced numerous earthquakes of magnitude 5 or greater; the first to be recorded occurred in 1823. During historical times seismic activity has been concentrated beneath the island of Hawai'i and the surrounding seafloor south of the island, in the vicinity of the "hotspot" that has

Major Earthquakes on Hawai'i Island, 1929–1993

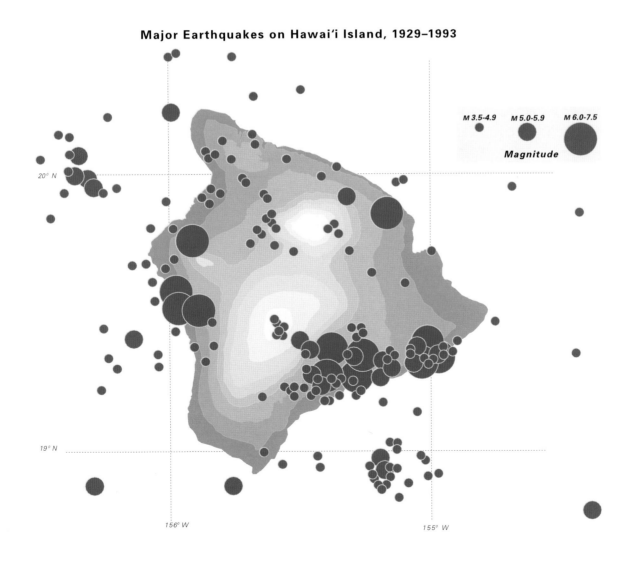

Earthquake-induced fissures and landslides, Crater Rim Road, Kīlauea volcano, Hawai'i, November 1983. [J. D. Griggs]

MODIFIED MERCALLI INTENSITY SCALE

I: Not felt.
II: Felt by person at rest.
III: Felt indoors. Hanging objects swing.
IV: WIndows, dishes, and doors rattle.
V: Felt outdoors. Doors swing, close, open.
VI: Felt by all. Windows and dishes broken.

VII: Difficult to stand. Weak chimneys broken.
VIII: Damage to masonry. Chimneys topple.
IX: General panic. Masonry is destroyed.
X: Masonry, framed structures destroyed.
XI: Railroad tracks bent easily.
XII: Damage nearly total. Objects airborne.

30 times more energy than a magnitude 4 event and roughly 900 times more energy than a magnitude 3 quake. Events of magnitude greater than 3 generally are felt by people in the region of the epicenter (the earthquake's source), and those of magnitude greater than 6 can cause widespread damage.

Closely associated with magnitude is earthquake intensity, which is typically expressed according to the Modified Mercalli Intensity Scale (MMI). Based on reports of damage and the physical sensations of those experiencing the event, the MMI is a subjective measurement scale. It ranges from Intensity I (an event not felt, or only faintly registered by instruments) to Intensity XII (an event causing nearly total destruction). MMI ratings decrease with increasing distance away from an earthquake's source.

As Lyman's account so vividly conveyed, groundshaking during a strong earthquake can damage or destroy buildings and other structures, as well as trigger landslides and mudslides. Such eyewitness accounts and reports of damage and casualties suggest that groundshaking reached the Intensity XII level near the source region of the 1868 event. Its magnitude has been estimated at 7.9. Seismic events also can produce ground cracks and settling, and those centered in coastal regions can create tsunamis (large ocean waves),

fueled Hawaiian volcanoes for millions of years. In April 1868, the area's largest known earthquake struck Hawai'i Island and wrought widespread damage. It was centered in the Ka'ū District, at the southeastern coast of the island. Frederick Lyman, who resided there at the time, described the disaster in his diary:

> We moved forward and backward, two or three feet each time, for several seconds—it made the small children seasick . . . the stone walls were all thrown down. . . . Our house was shaken off its foundations and tilted . . . when the shake came, a storm of mud and a great bank of earth twenty feet high came flying all about, mixed with rocks, logs, and ferns.

The size of an earthquake is commonly expressed in terms of magnitude. This is an instrumental measurement based on the amplitude, or size, of recorded seismic waves, which varies according to the energy released from groundshaking and the distance at which the signal is recorded. Derived from the original Richter scale, magnitude rankings are logarithmic; that is, each whole number increase represents a tenfold jump in seismic wave amplitude, or approximately a thirty-fold gain in energy released. For example, earth movements associated with a magnitude 5 quake discharge

Hawai'i Earthquakes, M6 and Greater, 1918–Present

Year	Origin Date	Time	Mag	Source description
1918	Nov 02	2333	6.2	Ka'ōiki, between Mauna Loa and Kīlauea
1919	Sep 14	1750	6.1	Ka'u District, Mauna Loa south flank
1926	Mar 19	2230	>6.0	NW of Hawai'i Island
1927	Mar 20	0452	6.0	NE of Hawai'i Island
1929	Sep 25	1820	6.1	Hualālai
1929	Oct 5	2122	6.5	Hualālai
1938	Jan 22	2203	6.9	N of Maui
1940	Jun 16	2357	6.0	N of Hawai'i Island
1941	Sep 25	0718	6.0	Ka'ōiki
1950	May 29	1516	6.4	Kona
1951	Apr 22	1452	6.3	lithospheric
	Aug 21	0057	6.9	Kona
1952	May 23	1213	6.0	Kona
1954	Mar 30	0841	6.5	Kīlauea south flank
1955	Aug 14	0228	6.0	lithospheric
1962	Jun 27	1827	6.1	Ka'ōiki
1973	Apr 26	1026	6.3	lithospheric
1975	Nov 29	0447	7.2	Kīlauea south flank
1983	Nov 16	0613	6.6	Ka'ōiki
1989	Jun 25	1727	6.1	Kīlauea south flank

whose impacts can be more devastating than the quake itself. The 1868 earthquake generated a tsunami whose estimated maximum height along the Ka'ū coast was at least 60 feet (18 m).

Research suggests that many of the significant earthquakes on Hawai'i Island have resulted from the seaward sliding of the south flanks of Kīlauea and Mauna Loa along a nearly horizontal fault. This fault is thought to be the buried boundary between the ancient oceanic crust and the volcanic edifice, approximately 6 miles (10 km) deep. Earthquakes along this fault include the November 1975 magnitude 7.2 Kalapana earthquake, which resulted in the loss of two lives, caused considerable damage on Hawai'i Island, and generated a tsunami that inundated the Ka'ū and Puna coastlines. This event was the largest earthquake in the Hawaiian Islands since 1868, and it was felt as far away as O'ahu. Slippage and seismic activity apparently increase along this fault during periods of greater volcanic activity.

Other, less frequent major earthquakes that are not directly related to the active volcanic flanks originate at greater depths (10–35 miles [about 16–56 km]). These events signal adjustments of the lithosphere (Earth's outermost region) to the weight of the islands. The most recent damaging earthquake of this type, in 1973, registered a magnitude of 6.3 and occurred about 24 miles (39 km) beneath Honomū on Hawai'i Island.

PAUL OKUBO

VOLCANIC HAZARDS ON THE ISLAND OF HAWAI'I

Residents of Hawai'i Island, and to a lesser degree Maui, face a unique array of environmental hazards that go along with living on the slopes of an active volcano. Hawai'i Island consists of five volcanoes, two of which —Kīlauea and Mauna Loa—are expected to erupt frequently throughout the foreseeable future. A third volcano, Hualālai, which erupts at about 250-year inter-

Kalapana house destroyed by Kīlauea eruption, Hawai'i, 1990. [J. D. Griggs]

Puna roadway engulfed by Kīlauea eruption, Hawai'i. [J. D. Griggs]

vals, last erupted in 1801. Similarly, Haleakalā volcano on Maui last erupted in 1790 and has roughly the same eruption recurrence interval as Hualālai.

Most Hawaiian eruptions produce fluid lava flows that can travel many miles from their source. For this reason, lava flows are the volcanic hazard most likely to seriously affect island residents and their property.

Other hazards include volcanic gases, explosive eruptions, and ground cracks and settling. Explosive eruptions occur infrequently at Hawaiian volcanoes but can have devastating consequences. The last large explosive outburst from Kīlauea in 1790 killed a band of Hawaiian warriors, who were caught by a pyroclastic surge—a hot, turbulent gas-and-ash flow. Thick deposits of ash exposed on many parts of the island indicate that much larger explosive eruptions at

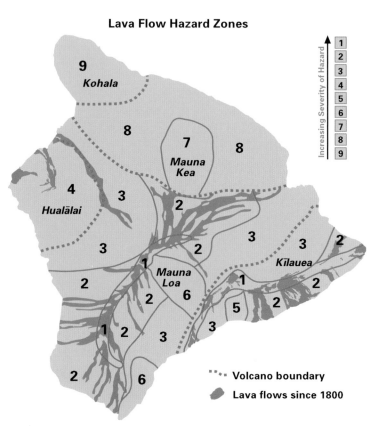

Lava Flow Hazard Zones

Increasing Severity of Hazard

1
2
3
4
5
6
7
8
9

9
Kohala

8

7
Mauna Kea

8

4
Hualālai

3

2

3

2

3

2

1
Mauna Loa

6

1

5

2

3

Kīlauea

3

2

2

2

3

3

1
2
3

2
6

···· **Volcano boundary**

🬭 **Lava flows since 1800**

72

Volcanic Emission

Volcanic gases are emitted during all types of eruptions. The main components of the gas plume rising from an active vent on Kīlauea or Mauna Loa are water vapor, carbon dioxide, and sulfur dioxide. Of these, sulfur dioxide is the main cause for concern, because it reacts with oxygen, dust particles, and atmospheric moisture to form sulfuric acid droplets and sulfate particles that result in volcanic smog, or "vog," and acid rain.

The continuous emission of volcanic fumes during long-lived eruptions, such as the Pu'u 'Ō'ō–Kūpaianaha eruption of Kīlauea, has resulted in persistent vog in areas downwind of the active vents. The west side of the island has suffered the greatest impact, because prevailing trade winds cause the vog to accumulate along the Kona coast. The health effects of vog on island residents are still under study, but it is known that vog can aggravate preexisting respiratory problems.

Acid rain also creates a public health hazard by leaching lead from roofing and plumbing materials in houses with water catchment systems. This has resulted in unsafe levels of lead in the drinking water of many houses, most of which were built before 1988, when new restrictions on lead-bearing building materials were imposed. Acid rain also can corrode metal and retard plant growth.

Another type of gas release, volcanic haze, or "laze," occurs when lava flows enter the ocean. Seawater boils and vaporizes, producing a plume that contains a mixture of hydrochloric acid and concentrated seawater. The acidity of this plume decreases rapidly away from its source and thus is a hazard primarily to people who visit the coastal area to view the lava flows.

CHRISTINA HELIKER

Kīlauea and Mauna Kea occurred in prehistoric times. Ground cracks and settling occur along the rift zones and summits of active volcanoes as the result of shallow underground movement of magma. Roads, utility lines, and buildings that encroach on these high-hazard areas are vulnerable to rapidly forming ground cracks and settling.

Maps showing volcanic hazard zones for Hawai'i Island were first prepared in 1974 by the U.S. Geological Survey. These were revised in 1987 and 1992, and a new map was published that dealt specifically with the hazard from lava flows. The lava flow hazard zones are based on the location of eruptive vents, past lava flow coverage, and the topography of the volcanoes. Hazard zone boundaries are approximate, and the change in degree of hazard from one zone to the next is generally gradual rather than abrupt.

The island is divided into nine zones based on past coverage by lava flows. Zone 1, the most hazardous, includes the summits and rift zones of Kīlauea and Mauna Loa, where vents have been repeatedly active in the last two centuries and lava flows will likely originate in the future. Areas adjacent to, and downslope of, active rift zones make up Zone 2. All of the 181 houses destroyed as of 1997 by the Pu'u 'Ō'ō–Kūpaianaha eruption of Kīlauea were located in Zone 2, about 8 miles from the active vents. Zone 3 includes areas less hazardous than Zone 2 because of greater distance from recently active vents or because the topography makes it less likely that flows will cover these areas.

Greater than 25 percent of the areas designated Zone 1 have been covered by lava in the last 200 years, compared with 15 to 25 percent of Zone 2 and 1 to 5 percent of Zone 3. In the last 750 years, lava flows have covered more than 65 percent of Zone 1, 25 to 75 percent of Zone 2, and 15 to 75 percent of Zone 3.

Zone 4 comprises all of Hualālai volcano, where the frequency of eruptions is lower than on Kīlauea and Mauna Loa. Hualālai is in a single zone because its slopes are steep, and flows could rapidly cover the distance between potential vent sites and the coast. Therefore, the hazard is considered to be essentially equal anywhere on the volcano.

Zones 5 and 6 are areas on Kīlauea and Mauna Loa currently protected from lava flows by the topography of the volcano. Zones 7 to 9 include the dormant and extinct volcanoes of Mauna Kea and Kohala, respectively. The younger part of Mauna Kea, which last erupted about 4,500 years ago, makes up Zone 7; the rest of the volcano is included in Zone 8. Zone 9 consists of Kohala volcano, which last erupted more than 60,000 years ago.

Volcanic hazards will always be present on Hawai'i Island, with the potential to disrupt more and more lives as the population increases. Our best defense against these hazards is education. Residents and public officials should study the available information before deciding where to build houses, develop commercial property, or locate public facilities. A well-informed public will neither overreact to the hazards nor ignore them.

CHRISTINA HELIKER

HURRICANES

Storm systems originating in the tropics, known as tropical cyclones, are classified according to the speed of their sustained winds. A tropical depression is characterized by wind speeds measuring up to 38 miles (61 km) per hour. A tropical storm sustains winds ranging between 39 and 73 miles (63 and 118 km) per hour. Hurricane winds exceed 73 miles per hour. Most storms enter Hawaiian waters from the eastern Pacific, the second most active tropical cyclone region on Earth. Only storms exceeding tropical depression strength are named. Those originating in the central North Pacific hurricane region—a zone bounded by the equator and west longitude lines 140° and 180°—are now given Hawaiian names.

Hurricane and Tropical Storm Tracks, 1950–1992

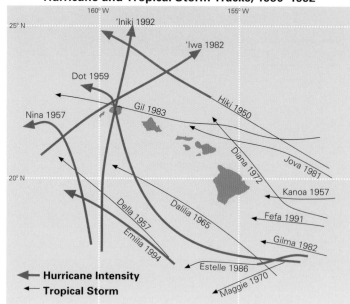

Pacific Hurricane Origins
Summer Sea Surface Temperatures

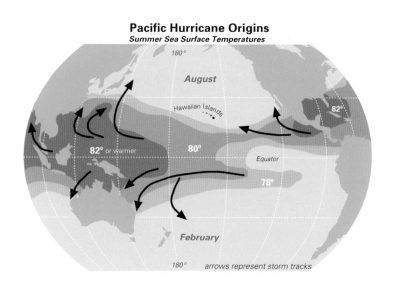

arrows represent storm tracks

Major Historic Hurricanes

Date	Name	Affected Islands	Damages (unadjusted $)
August 9, 1871	unnamed	Hawaiʻi, Maui, Molokaʻi	10,000*
November 30, 1957	Nina	Kauaʻi, Oʻahu	100,000
August 6, 1959	Dot	Kauaʻi, Oʻahu	6,000,000
November 23, 1982	ʻIwa	Kauaʻi, Oʻahu	239,000,000
July 23, 1986	Estelle	Hawaiʻi, Maui, Oʻahu	2,000,000
September 11, 1992	ʻIniki	Kauaʻi, Oʻahu	2,400,000,000**

* unofficial estimate from news account
** estimate still growing, $1.6 billion in insured losses

The first hurricane officially recorded in Hawaiʻi was named Hiki and occurred in 1950. Research indicates that storms of unknown intensity occurred in the nineteenth century. Newspaper accounts document a strong storm that struck Hawaiʻi, Maui, and probably Molokaʻi on August 9, 1871. Since 1960, meteorological data collected by satellites have revealed that storm systems occur more frequently in Hawaiian waters than was previously thought. The islands are small targets and landfalls are rare. Nevertheless, the tremendous damage caused by ʻIwa (1982) and ʻIniki (1992) has highlighted the vulnerability of Hawaiʻi to hurricane risk.

From 1961 to 1995 a total of 44 depressions, 68 tropical storms, and 42 hurricanes have either entered, or formed in, the central North Pacific. Hurricane strength storms typically develop in late summer or fall, when ocean surface temperatures are at a maximum, leading to increased atmospheric instability. The annual average of all tropical cyclones is four to

Satellite pictures of tropical storm Keoni (southwest of the Islands) and Hurricane Fernanda (east of the Islands), August 1993. [NOAA]

Inland debris line at Poʻipū, Kauaʻi, illustrates limits of coastal inundation from storm surge during Hurricane ʻIniki, 1992. [C. Fletcher]

Hurricane Conditions

Hurricanes (known as typhoons west of 180° longitude) form over tropical ocean waters when the following conditions are met:

- Sea surface temperatures must exceed about 80°F (27°C). The heat provided by the ocean must balance the expansional cooling of the air spiraling into the low-pressure storm center. (The pressure difference between a strong hurricane and the surrounding air is equivalent to that encountered by a person climbing from sea level to the top of a 2,000-foot [610 m] mountain.)
- The layer of warm surface water must be sufficiently deep that wind-induced stirring does not upwell cold water from the depths.
- The vertical distribution of temperature and moisture in the atmosphere must support the development of cumulonimbus (thunderstorm) clouds.
- The vertical shear (variation of wind speed and direction with height) of the horizontal winds must be small.
- The weather system must occur about 5 degrees of lat-

itude away from the equator so that cyclonic spin is possible.
- An initial atmospheric disturbance must be present.

Vertical Cross Section of a Hurricane

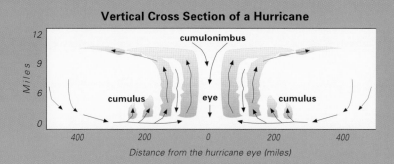

Distance from the hurricane eye (miles)

Generally these conditions are met well east of Hawaiʻi, accounting for the prevalence of storms of eastern Pacific origin. However, during warming events of the El Niño Southern Oscillation (ENSO), wind patterns and sea surface temperatures change, favoring the formation of storms in the central Pacific. Hurricanes Nina (1957) and ʻIwa (1982), for example, occurred during El Niño years.

five, one of which generally forms in the central Pacific. Year-to-year variability, however is significant. For example, in 1979 there were no tropical cyclones in the central Pacific, whereas in 1982 ten named tropical cyclones occurred. The record for hurricanes was set in 1994, when five occurred in central Pacific waters near Hawaiʻi.

Hurricanes cause damage in several ways. Heavy rains and tornadoes can accompany strong winds and storm surges. Surges, intrusions of wind- and pressure-

driven coastal waters above the tideline, are restricted to the first few hundred meters of the coastal zone, while winds impact entire islands. Worldwide the most devastating loss of life wrought by hurricanes has been caused by surges amplified by stream flooding from heavy rains. Hawaiʻi has suffered primarily from winds and storm surges.

THOMAS A. SCHROEDER

TSUNAMIS

The first tsunami recorded in Hawai'i occurred in 1819, and since then 85 others have been observed, 15 of which resulted in significant damage. A tsunami is a series of very long waves triggered by a disturbance at the seafloor that displaces water—usually an earthquake, but sometimes an underwater landslide or a volcanic eruption. These waves move across the ocean at about the speed of a jet airplane and can deliver devastating energy to the coasts they strike.

The Hawaiian Islands are exposed to tsunamis generated at the fault zones bordering the Pacific Ocean, the "Rim of Fire." Pacific-wide tsunamis are attenuated, or weakened, only moderately as they travel

Observed Major Tsunami Runups in Hawai'i, 1819–1994

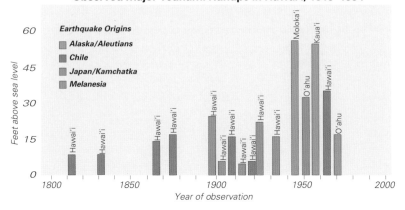

All tsunamis reliably recorded for Hawai'i that had runups greater than 3 feet (1 m) with their source area. Runups shown are the maximum recorded for each island.

How Tsunamis Form

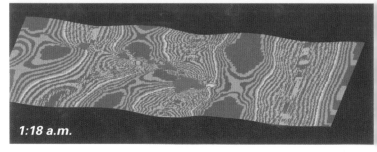

Tsunami Movement Across the State on May 22–23, 1960

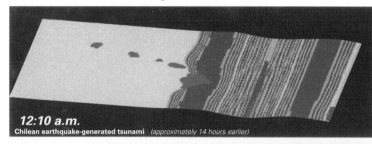

12:10 a.m.
Chilean earthquake-generated tsunami *(approximately 14 hours earlier)*

12:52 a.m.

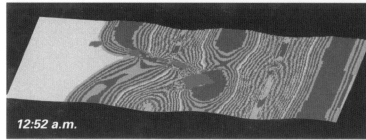

1:18 a.m.

across the ocean. For example, the 1960 event, caused by a massive earthquake in Chile, devastated the Hilo bayfront and caused considerable damage to coastal areas in Japan. Occasionally tsunamis triggered by earthquakes also have originated near Hawai'i Island. Fortunately these local tsunamis do not travel far, although they may severely impact coastal areas for tens of miles from their point of origin.

Tsunami waves are imperceptible in the open ocean. In very deep water a large tsunami wave may measure less than 1 foot (0.3 m) high, but it may span 50–100 miles (80–160 km). As the wave reaches shal-

Lā'ie, O'ahu, tsunami sequence, 1957. [H. Helbush]

Tsunami Travel Time to Hawai'i

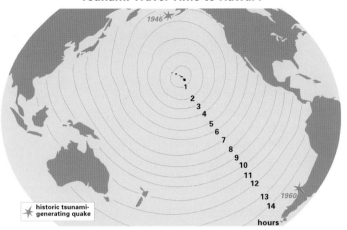

The dates and source locations of the two major tsunamis affecting Hawai'i in the last 100 years, and the time required for the waves from any area to reach the Islands.

1946 Tsunami Wave Runups in Hawai'i

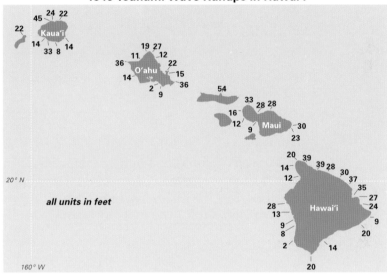

Variation in runup heights in the Islands for the April 1, 1946, tsunami from the Aleutians, 2,200 miles (3,540 km) north of Hawai'i. Similar but more detailed maps have been compiled for all islands for each tsunami since 1946 and are used in hazard mitigation.

low water and slows down drastically, the tremendous energy it contains raises it up to heights as great as 30 feet (9 m). (The "sloshing" action of the wave, or run-up, may measure significantly higher, however). Varying ocean depths and underwater topography cause the waves to change direction as they "wrap" around the islands. Thus large, damaging waves can strike even coasts that do not face the source of a tsunami.

When the waves hit the shore, they generally appear as a series of fast-rising tides spaced about 5–15 minutes apart, rather than as breaking waves. Typically, the third or fourth wave is the highest, with ten or more significant waves arriving over a period of several hours. Waves with such an enormous volume of water, moving onshore at speeds close to 30 miles (50 km) per hour, sweep far inland with great force. In Hilo, tsunami waves have been known to transport heavy equipment and boulders hundreds of feet and to demolish portions of the Hilo Bay breakwater, which is composed of 8-ton rocks. The 1946 tsunami—probably the most destructive in Hawai'i's history—badly damaged the railroads in Hilo and along the Hāmākua coast and the north shore of O'ahu, leading to their abandonment. The community of Shinmachi in Hilo

Hilo, Hawai'i, bayfront before and after the 1960 tsunami.
[Hawaii Tribune-Herald]

was almost destroyed, and the Hawaiian settlement at Cape Hālawa on Moloka'i had to be abandoned.

In addition to extensive damage to property and infrastructure, 234 lives have been lost in the twentieth century alone due to tsunamis in Hawai'i. Sadly, most of these lives could have been saved by a warning and evacuation system. Such a system was developed after World War II, utilizing communication technology that became available at that time. Now based at 'Ewa Beach, O'ahu, the Pacific Tsunami Warning Center of the National Oceanic and Atmospheric Administration serves Hawai'i and 25 countries around the Pacific Rim. When seismographs detect an earthquake that could possibly trigger a tsunami, the speed of wave travel is calculated (based on the ocean depths beneath the projected path of the waves), and arrival times are estimated. Tsunami warnings are issued three or more hours before the arrival of the first wave (except for areas closer to the source), and Civil Defense agencies, police, and fire departments on each island oversee the evacuation of areas at risk for tsunami inundation. Maps of these potentially hazardous coastal areas are included in the county telephone directories.

It is almost impossible to provide warnings against local tsunamis. Fortunately, they are rare and only two have inflicted death tolls. The 1868 tsunami left 46 dead and brought widespread property damage, and the 1975 tsunami killed 2 and caused moderate damage. Both events were linked to strong earthquakes beneath the southern part of Hawai'i Island.

Since 1946, stricter building codes, permit requirements, and insurance regulations have somewhat reduced the risk to property and infrastructure, but the desire to live and the need to work near the ocean continue to exert pressure for development in areas exposed to tsunamis.

GEORGE CURTIS

COASTAL HAZARDS

Island shores are both the traditional setting of work and play and the contemporary focus of Hawai'i's all-important tourist industry. The state constitution guarantees public access to the coast and entrusts the state with the obligation to conserve coastal lands for the people of Hawai'i. Yet shorelines are subject to powerful meteorologic, geologic, and oceanographic forces that can threaten life and property. The use and development of coastal resources must be tempered with the knowledge that natural hazards are a fact of life on Hawai'i's coasts.

The state government's Coastal Zone Management Program has identified the prevention of threats from coastal hazards as a planning priority. In addition, the Department of Land and Natural Resources, the lead agency responsible for resource conservation, incorporates coastal erosion patterns into its efforts to protect and preserve our beaches for future generations of Hawai'i's citizens. Other than shoreline setbacks and the general requirements of the National Flood Insurance Program, however, Hawai'i lacks specific policies regulating the rebuilding of storm-damaged structures away from high-hazard areas; and no restrictions exist regarding the use of public funds for development in such areas. The limited land base and high price of coastal property complicate addressing this planning deficit. Yet, without such policies further development and rebuilding will continue in hazardous coastal areas, and recurrent disasters are likely to generate considerable public costs.

In this section we discuss hazards that specifically impact coastal areas, including stream flooding, seasonal high waves, storm surge, coastal erosion, and sea level rise. Other hazards that can affect the coasts, such as earthquakes, volcanism, and tsunamis, are discussed elsewhere.

Coastal Stream Flooding

Floods caused by heavy rainfall normally occur during winter, and January is typically the month of highest flooding frequency, although tropical storms from June through October can also deliver flood-generat-

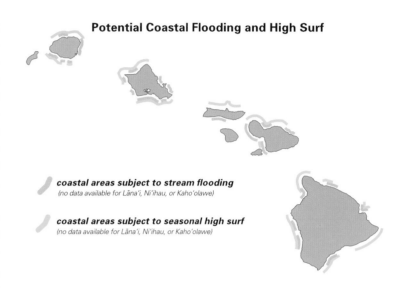

Potential Coastal Flooding and High Surf

coastal areas subject to stream flooding
(no data available for Lāna'i, Ni'ihau, or Kaho'olawe)

coastal areas subject to seasonal high surf
(no data available for Lāna'i, Ni'ihau, or Kaho'olawe)

ing rainstorms. Coastal stream flooding depends on several factors. The greatest danger exists where mountain streams emerge onto low-lying coastal areas, monthly rainfall in the surrounding watershed exceeds 8 inches (200 mm), and adequate flood control structures are lacking to channel excessive runoff.

In Hawai'i streams originate in steep mountains and flow relatively short distances to the ocean. Consequently a downpour swiftly produces runoff, and rainfall in the mountains—often unseen by coastal occupants—can trigger unpredictable flash floods. Coastal plains and stream floodplains on Maui, Kaua'i, and O'ahu are vulnerable to recurrent rainstorm floods, especially where urban development prevents infiltration of water into the ground. Flooding tends to be less intense on Moloka'i and Lāna'i, where annual rainfall often amounts to less than 40 inches (about 1,000 mm). On Hawai'i Island, many regions of high precipitation are incised by deep valleys that effectively channel flood waters. Elsewhere, the high permeability of geologically young lavas deters flooding. However, low-lying areas in Hilo, despite being underlain by young lavas, have a history of serious flooding because of urbanization and inadequate flood-control structures.

Residents throughout the state should know the history of stream flooding in their area and heed flood warnings.

Seasonal High Waves

Sudden high waves and the strong currents they generate are perhaps the most consistent and predictable coastal hazards in Hawai'i. They account for more reported injuries and rescues annually than any other hazard.

"High surf" is a condition of dangerous waves nominally 10–20 feet (3–6 m) high or more. Resulting from ocean swells associated with North Pacific storms, such waves typically occur on the north shores of Hawaiian islands for a few days at a time, most commonly from October through March. On south shores high surf usually forms during summer, when storms in the Southern Hemisphere generate waves of 4–10 feet (1–3 m).

Sets of large waves can develop suddenly, often doubling in size within a few seconds and threatening shoreline occupants. The coastal water level increases under these conditions, and the seaward surge of excess water generates extremely dangerous rip currents.

High Winds and Storm Surge

The severe damage and economic loss brought by hurricanes 'Iwa (1982) and 'Iniki (1992) have raised public awareness of the threat from tropical cyclones. Such storms spawn high winds and waves, heavy rains, marine storm surge and tornadoes, and other small-scale, intense winds. Impacts from these hazards can be considerable even when a hurricane does not pass directly over an island. For example, O'ahu's Wai'anae Coast incurred significant damage from 'Iwa and 'Iniki, neither of which directly "hit" the island.

Studies of Hurricane 'Iniki show that rising water levels forced by waves and low atmospheric pressure at the storm's center are typically the greatest storm-surge threat during hurricanes in the Hawaiian Islands. This contrasts with the flooding caused by hurricanes on the mainland, in which wind acts as the major force driving water against the coast.

Other variables that influence the severity of storm-surge flooding are coastal topography, the tidal stage and height at the time of the storm, and location relative to the eye of the hurricane. Unfortunately, these factors cannot be predicted, and thus storm-surge mitigation measures must be implemented before a hurricane's arrival. Ideally, such measures should include adequate building setbacks to deter development in high-hazard areas, elevation of existing structures to levels recommended by the Federal Emergency Management Agency, and specialized construction techniques that reduce flood damage.

Coastal Erosion and Rocky Shoreline Collapse

Coastal erosion presently plagues more than 70 percent of the world's sandy beaches, and along coastal areas of the mainland United States erosion averages nearly 1.5 feet (0.4 m) annually. On Maui, O'ahu, and Kaua'i, recent studies reveal erosion rates of 0.3–3.5 feet (0.09–1.1 m) per year along some sections of coastline. However, coastlines change in highly variable patterns, and a length of beach may undergo both erosion and accretion in places over the long term.

Among the many factors contributing to coastal erosion, rising sea level plays a major role by causing long-term shoreline retreat or the inshore migration of a beach. While the coastal land erodes, a moving beach with a sufficient supply of sand remains wide and healthy. Hence, there is a distinction between coastal land erosion and beach erosion. Coastal dunes and fossil beaches from past higher sea levels naturally supply many Hawaiian beaches with sand, counteracting beach erosion. However, in many areas seawalls and revetments (sloping seawalls) prevent sand from coastal lands from replenishing beaches, which leads to recurrent beach erosion and, eventually, beach loss.

From 1928 to 1995, approximately 6.4 miles (10.4 km) of beach on O'ahu were lost, and another 11 miles (17.3 km) were narrowed partially as a result of the construction of seawalls and revetments. On Maui, seawalls have been built on about 8 miles (13.5 km) of recreational beaches. In many such areas the beach either disappears at high tide or is altogether absent. Portions of Maui's sandy coastline suffer chronic erosion on the order of 1.25 feet (0.4 m) per year.

Although armoring a coast undergoing long-term retreat with seawalls and revetments temporarily alleviates the threat to buildings, it ultimately leads to beach loss. While seawalls are a response to coastal erosion resulting from a number of factors, they are responsible for causing beach erosion. This trend not

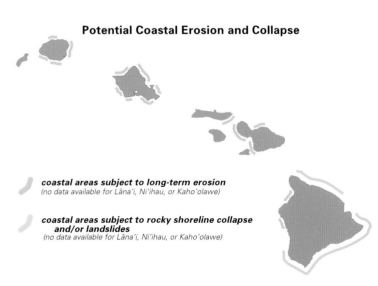

Potential Coastal Erosion and Collapse

coastal areas subject to long-term erosion
(no data available for Lāna'i, Ni'ihau, or Kaho'olawe)

coastal areas subject to rocky shoreline collapse and/or landslides
(no data available for Lāna'i, Ni'ihau, or Kaho'olawe)

Coastal collapse, Puna District, Hawai'i. [J. Juvik]

Sea Level Rise and Island Subsidence

The National Ocean Service maintains and operates a system of tidal gauges that chart fluctuations in sea level, allowing scientists to track long-term rates of sea level change around the state. This historical record reveals that for each island in the chain the rate of sea level change depends partly on how rapidly the island is subsiding, or sinking.

Because of its massive load of geologically young volcanic rock, Hawai'i Island weighs heavily on the underlying crust and flexes it. Hawai'i is subsiding faster than the other islands and thus experiences a relatively rapid rate of sea level rise—about 1.6 inches (4 cm) per decade. Around neighboring Maui, which is also affected by this flexing, the sea is rising almost 1 inch (2.5 cm) per decade. O'ahu and Kaua'i lie farther from Hawai'i and, as older, substantially eroded islands, they are not adding to their mass. The sea surrounding these islands is rising by approximately 0.6 inch (1.5 cm) per decade, which is consistent with satellite measurements of rates of global sea level rise (about 2.1 cm/decade or 2.1 mm/year). Rising sea level associated with subsidence is not presently a reason for alarm. Its most significant impact is to cause shoreline retreat, and hence coastal erosion, as mentioned above.

Scientists note that recent trends in global warming—whether natural or from human impact—may also contribute to changes in sea level worldwide. If Earth's climate is undergoing a long-term warming, the melting of alpine ice and the increase in sea surface temperatures could accelerate rising sea levels. Erodable coasts and low-lying shores would be the most vulnerable to sea level hazards. To date, the capability for predicting future rates of sea level change is inexact, and little scientific consensus exists regarding how high or how fast sea level will rise. Coastal zone managers should pay special attention to coastlines already experiencing rapid erosion rates.

CHARLES H. FLETCHER III

only limits recreational opportunities for state residents but may eventually affect tourism. The solution to this dilemma lies partly in adopting a comprehensive coastal management plan that emphasizes sand-management techniques, variable setbacks based on accurate shoreline change data, cessation of development in rapidly eroding coastal areas, and engineering solutions such as beach and dune restoration to augment deficient coastal sand volumes.

On Hawai'i Island sections of rocky shoreline can suddenly collapse when coastal rock formations and steep slopes are destabilized by landslides and undercutting by waves. This potentially dangerous process is especially prevalent on the island's south coast, where newly cooled lava forms fragile coastal benches that may collapse abruptly after appearing stable for weeks. Along the Hāmākua and North Hilo coasts, steep coastal cliffs show evidence of frequent slumping and landsliding.

THE OCEAN

Water motions occur over a wide range of time and space scales. At the largest scales are seasonal variations, basinwide average ocean circulation, and slow interannual changes such as the El Niño-Southern Oscillation (ENSO). At intermediate scales (weeks to months and tens to hundreds of kilometers) are ocean eddies and fronts. At shorter scales, tides have periods of a few hours, and surface waves of a few seconds. Finally, at the smallest scales of centimeters and seconds, is ocean turbulence—small eddies that eventually mix water properties, much like stirring coffee in a cup.

Tides are caused by the moon's and the sun's gravity. All other water motions (with the exception of tsunamis) result directly or indirectly from interactions with the atmosphere at the surface, through the horizontal force of the wind, heating or cooling by the air, and by radiation, precipitation, and evaporation. Global variations of these processes determine large-scale ocean circulation; local variations shape regional characteristics.

Northeasterly trade winds dominate the Hawaiian Island chain and the region farther south, while westerlies are found farther north. This circulation follows the North Pacific anticyclone, which shifts northward in summer, when trade winds intensify and extend on average to 35° N, and southward in winter, when westerlies reach as far south as 28° N. The annual average trade wind speed is 13.5 mph (6 m/s) at 20° N.

Surface Water, Temperature, and Salinity

Surface water temperatures have a strong north-to-south gradient and a small annual cycle. The average surface water temperature around Oʻahu is coldest from February to April (75°F [24°C]) and warmest from August to October (81°F [27°C]). The variations of temperature tend to parallel the Island chain; that is, surface waters are in general warmer to the west at a given latitude. Surface salinities reflect the balance between evaporation and precipitation. Evaporation exceeds precipitation between 15° N and 36° N, result-

Average Surface Water Temperature (°C)

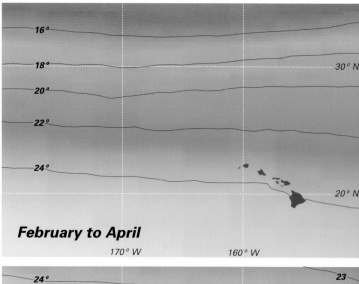

February to April

August to October

ing in a salinity maximum of 35.2 parts per thousand (ppt) at 26° N. Salinities decrease northward and southward of this latitude, reaching a minimum of 34.3 ppt at 10° N in the vicinity of the Intertropical Convergence Zone, where rainfall exceeds evaporation.

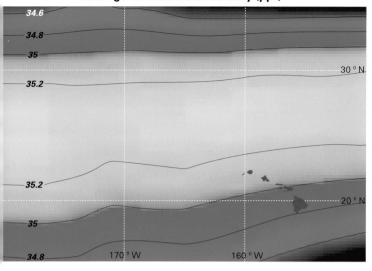

Average Surface Water Salinity (ppt)

Vertical Profiles of Water Properties

The average vertical profiles of temperature, salinity, and nutrients (nitrates and nitrites) in the graphic were computed from a series of monthly surface-to-bottom measurements at 22°45' N 158° W. Near the surface the water column is mixed by the wind and has uniform properties; the depth of this turbulent layer varies from nearly 400 feet (120 m) in winter to less than 100 feet (30 m) in summer. Below the mixed layer there is a sharp decrease in temperature (called a thermocline), from 77°F (25°C) at the surface to 41°F (5°C) at 2,300 feet (700 m) deep, then a gradual decrease to 36°F (1.5°C) at the bottom.

The salinity profile reflects the sinking of water from the north: higher salinity water of 35.2 ppt at 500 feet (150 m) deep, traceable to high-salinity surface water north of Hawai'i; low-salinity water of 34.1 ppt at 1,670 feet (500 m) deep, traceable to low-salinity surface water farther to the northwest. Below this depth salinity increases gradually to 34.7 ppt for abyssal waters. The concentration of nutrients is small at the surface (less than 1 μmole/kg), but it increases steadily reaching 40 μmole/kg at the bottom of the thermocline, then remains relatively constant to the bottom. Similar vertical distributions are found for phosphate and silicate.

The distribution of nutrients illustrates how small vertical motions generally are in the ocean. The upper

330 feet (100 m) or so—the euphotic layer—is illuminated by sunlight, but the lack of nutrients limits growth of phytoplankton (microscopic plants), much as the lack of fertilizers would limit growth of vegetation on land. Deeper in the water, nutrients are abundant, but there is no light to support photosynthesis. Where and when upward vertical motions exist, nutrients are brought into the euphotic layer, resulting in increased biological productivity. Upward nutrient transport occurs when strong winds deepen the mixed layer (for example, in winter or during storms), or when surface currents diverge, causing upwelling of deeper water.

Large-Scale Currents

The depth of the thermocline, by convention the depth at which the temperature is 50°F (10°C), varies markedly, from more than 1,500 feet (450 m) northwest of the Islands to less than 800 feet (240 m) to the northeast and southeast. Variations of temperature result in variations of water density and, therefore, of weight and pressure of water columns. Ocean currents are set up by such variations of pressure. Owing to Earth's rotation, these so-called geostrophic currents follow lines of constant thermocline depth. The average geostrophic currents form a large, basin-scale, clockwise circulation called a gyre, centered at about 28° N. At the latitude of Hawai'i, circulation is roughly from east to west and intensifies southward. The strength of geostrophic currents decreases with depth by a factor of two every few hundred meters; below 3,300 feet (1,000 m) their average is generally less than 0.1 knot (5 cm/s), and their patterns are not entirely known. In the surface layer, however, currents driven by the wind combine with geostrophic currents to yield more complicated flow patterns. Surface currents must be measured directly or estimated from the drift of oceanographic buoys.

South of Hawai'i, the surface North Equatorial Current (NEC) reaches an average westward speed of 0.35 knots (17 cm/s) at 13° N and gradually decreases toward the islands. Between 18° N and 22° N, the currents are strongly influenced by the islands. The NEC forks at Hawai'i Island; the northern branch becomes the North Hawaiian Ridge Current (NHRC) and intensifies near the islands with a typical width of 65 miles (100 km) and speed of 0.5 knots (25 cm/s). West of the islands, two elongated circulations appear. A clockwise circulation is centered at 19° N, merging to the south with the southern branch of the NEC. A counterclockwise circulation is centered at 20°30' N. Between them is the narrow Hawaiian Lee Counter-Current (HLCC), extending in longitude from 170° W to 158° W. Surface currents over the western islands and northeast of the NHRC are variable, and their average is smaller than can be estimated from existing data.

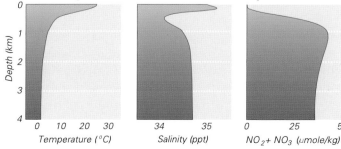

Average Vertical Profiles of Water Properties

Average Depth of Thermocline (in meters)

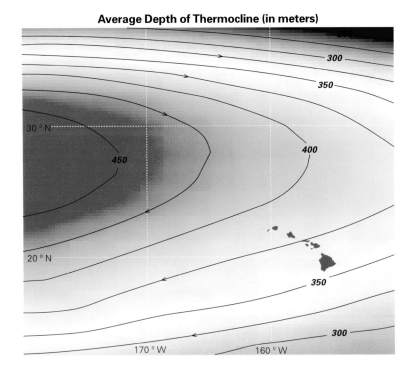

Average Surface Currents and Variability

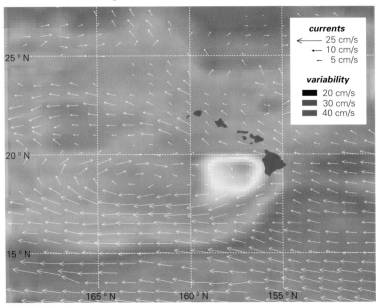

Each grid point shows the most probable current that one would experience. However, because ocean currents vary in time, freely drifting objects never follow exactly the flow patterns illustrated. The map of current variability, a measure of how much actual currents depart from the average, indicates that the lee of the islands is characterized by vigorous eddies, or swirls, which mask the slower average circulation.

Regional Currents

The Island chain affects the ocean by two important mechanisms: interactions with large-scale ocean currents and wind speed variations in the lee of the islands, as shown in the conceptual diagram. At the northern and southern boundaries of each island, trade winds

with speeds of 22–44 mph (10–20 m/s) are separated from the calmer lee by narrow wind shear lines. The northern shear line of Hawai'i Island, bordering rough seas in the 'Alenuihāhā Channel, is a spectacular sight for passengers flying to Kona. The depth of the surface mixed layer depends on wind speed: in the channels deep mixed layers are observed; in the lee stirring by the wind is not sufficient to mix down solar heating, and intense daytime warming of the ocean surface results. Sharp surface temperature changes, called fronts, as great as 7°F (4°C), are often associated with the wind shear lines.

Variations in wind have subtle effects on current patterns. In the Northern Hemisphere, when wind blows for many days over a surface mixed layer, the water moves to the right of the wind, due to the earth's rotation. Therefore, water moves away from the northern shear line. To compensate for this divergent surface motion, water moves up (upwells) from greater depths, appearing as a cold spot at the surface. Similarly, water moves toward the southern shear line, resulting in a deepening of the thermocline there. From these variations of thermocline depth, geostrophic currents result in the form of intense counterclockwise (cyclonic) eddies under northern shear lines and somewhat less intense clockwise (anticyclonic) eddies under southern shear lines. This process is quite dramatic: the depth of the mixed layer in the lee of Hawai'i Island can vary from more than 400 feet (120 m) in the clockwise eddy to less than 65 feet (20 m) in the counterclockwise eddy, where satellite images of surface temperature often show upwelling of cold water. The large counterclockwise average circulation seen in the surface current map is believed to result from the recurrent counterclockwise eddies spun up by the shear lines of Maui and Hawai'i.

Eddies can also be generated by intense currents such as the NEC impinging on the islands, much like swirls found in a swift river downstream of a bridge pile. The large clockwise circulation southwest of Hawai'i Island appears to be caused by many such clockwise eddies repeatedly formed near South Point.

Tides

Forced like clockwork by the moon and the sun, the tides are the most predictable oceanic motions. The gravitational pull of the moon, and to a lesser extent of the sun, creates bulges of water on opposite sides of Earth. A point on Earth passes through these bulges twice a day, resulting in semidiurnal (half-daily) components to the tide. Because the moon and the sun do not lie over the equator, one of the bulges is larger than the other, leading to diurnal (daily) components to the tides. A modulation of the tidal range results from the relative positions of the moon and the sun: when the moon is new or full, the moon and the sun act together to produce larger spring tides; when the moon is in its

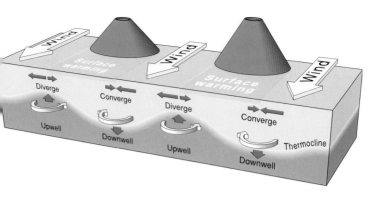

nent (12-hour 25-minute period, called M2) are shown for several coastal sea level stations.

Tidal currents result from tidal variations in sea level, and nearshore they are often stronger than the large-scale flow. The semidiurnal and diurnal tidal currents measured off Oʻahu, Maui, and Hawaiʻi Island tend to be aligned with shorelines. However, due to the variability of tidal currents around the islands and

first or last quarter, smaller neap tides occur. The cycle of spring to neap tides and back is half the 29-day period of the moon's revolution around Earth, and is called the fortnightly cycle. The combination of diurnal, semidiurnal, and fortnightly cycles dominates variations in sea level throughout the Islands, as illustrated by a tidal curve for Hilo.

On oceanic basin scales, tides exist as very long waves propagating in patterns determined by their period and the geometry of the basin. For example, the response of the North Pacific to the tidal period of the largest diurnal component (23 hours 56 minutes, called K1) shows that lines along which high tides occur at the same time (phase lines) converge to a point west of Hawaiʻi where the tidal range is zero (amphidrome). Phase lines rotate counterclockwise around the amphidrome, so that the offshore diurnal tide reaches Hawaiʻi Island first, then sweeps across Maui, Oʻahu, and finally Kauaʻi.

Local bathymetry affects the ranges and phases of tides along the shore as the tidal waves wrap around the islands. For example, high tide at Haleʻiwa on the north shore of Oʻahu occurs more than an hour before high tide at Honolulu Harbor. The ranges and phases of the diurnal component and the semidiurnal compo-

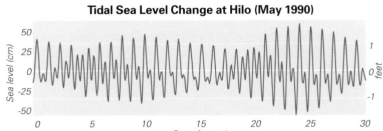

Tidal Sea Level Change at Hilo (May 1990)

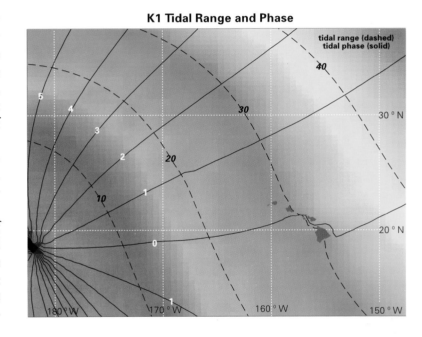

K1 Tidal Range and Phase

tidal range (dashed)
tidal phase (solid)

Observed Tidal Currents and Ranges

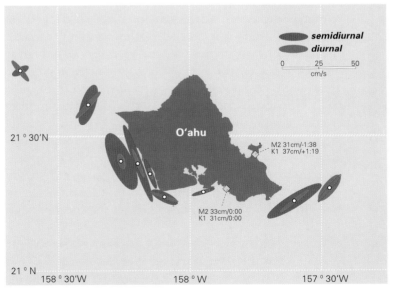

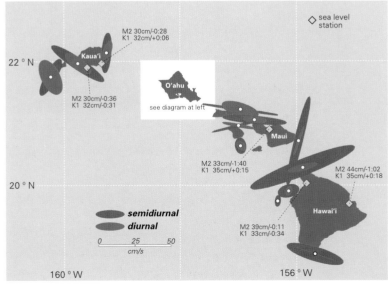

to other processes such as internal waves, this statistical picture may not correspond to the flow at a particular time: tidal currents cannot be predicted as precisely as sea level. Strong swirls often result from tidal currents flowing around points and headlands and can present hazards to divers.

Surface Waves

Waves are the most familiar water motion. The surface of the ocean is constantly moving in response to local seas and to swells from distant storms. Seas result from winds pushing the water into random patterns of rip-

ples and bumps of many wave periods and heights, interacting and breaking. The stronger the wind and the longer it blows, the greater the height of the sea formed. As waves move away, they are sorted into regularly progressing swells traveling in the same direction, with the longest and fastest in front. Offshore of the Hawaiian Islands, the seas are moderately rough, with significant wave heights of 3–14 ft (1–4 m), varying seasonally with trade wind intensity. Between the islands, where the winds are funneled, the seas are intensified. The lee, shielded from the winds, is generally calmer. During winter, however, the wind can shift to the northwest or to the southwest, creating unusual sea conditions.

Along the shores waves become steeper and break as they enter shallow water; both seas and swells can form breakers. The northeast shores of the islands are exposed to moderate trade wind seas. The northwest shores receive some of these waves, but they are primarily exposed to large swells from storms in the northwest Pacific in winter and are calmer in summer. The North Shore of Oʻahu, directly facing winter swells, is famous for its large surf. Breaking waves with faces over 50 feet (15 m) high have occasionally been observed.

The south shores, shielded from northwesterly swells, are usually calm in winter. In summer, swells arrive from storms in the Southern Hemisphere. They take 6–8 days to reach Hawaiʻi and have lost much energy from spreading. They are well sorted and are commonly 3–9 feet (1–3 m) high, rarely approaching the heights seen on the northwest shores in winter. The largest southern waves on record had some faces over 20 feet (6 m) high in June 1995.

Breaking waves transport water toward shore. This water escapes first alongshore and then returns to sea as narrow rip currents generally located where the bottom is deepest. Rip currents shorten and steepen incoming waves, causing a confused sea no swimmer can overcome. Standing on a rocky shoreline can also be dangerous, as one can get washed away by occasional large waves. Although forecasts about general wave conditions can be made, the size or timing of individual waves cannot be predicted. Coastal areas may be threatened by breaking waves large enough to flood roads and houses.

Hurricanes passing close to the Islands are another source of large waves and flooding in Hawaiʻi, occurring a few times a year, usually from July to September. Other surface waves that may cause flooding are tsunamis, which are generated not by the wind but by sudden changes in the seafloor during earthquakes or landslides that can occur anywhere in the Pacific basin.

PIERRE FLAMENT, SEAN KENNAN,
RICK LUMPKIN, MICHAEL SAWYER,
AND EDWARD STROUP

Significant Wave Height (meters)

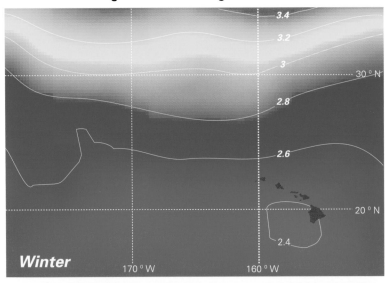

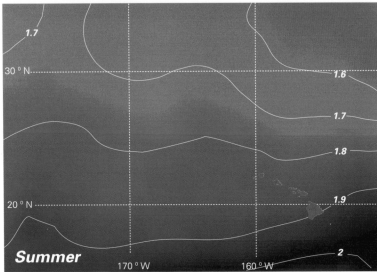

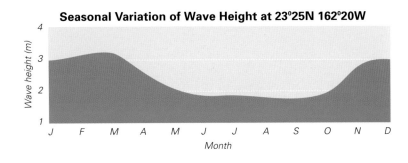

Seasonal Variation of Wave Height at 23°25N 162°20W

WATER

The Hawaiian Islands experience the full range of constraints and advantages associated with the availability of freshwater resources. Areas of each of the major islands are blessed with rainfall adequate for human needs, yet other areas, including all of Kahoʻolawe, are virtual deserts. Even in arid regions, however, a supply of water derived from surplus rainfall in wet regions may be available for development. Such water resources include perennial streams, springs, and groundwater.

The success of traditional Hawaiian civilization depended significantly on the orderly allocation of the water supply, especially for cultivation of taro. This staple of the Hawaiian diet requires large volumes of cool, running water for efficient production. Perennial streams originating in rugged mountains and springs that inundated wetlands were the primary sources for taro irrigation. The Hawaiians built elaborate hydrau-

Exposed dike rock, Haleakalā Crater, Maui. [J. Juvik]

Upper Hāmākua Ditch, Alakahi, Kohala Mountains, Hawaiʻi. [J. Juvik]

Inclined shaft, Hālawa Well, Oʻahu. [J. Juvik]

87

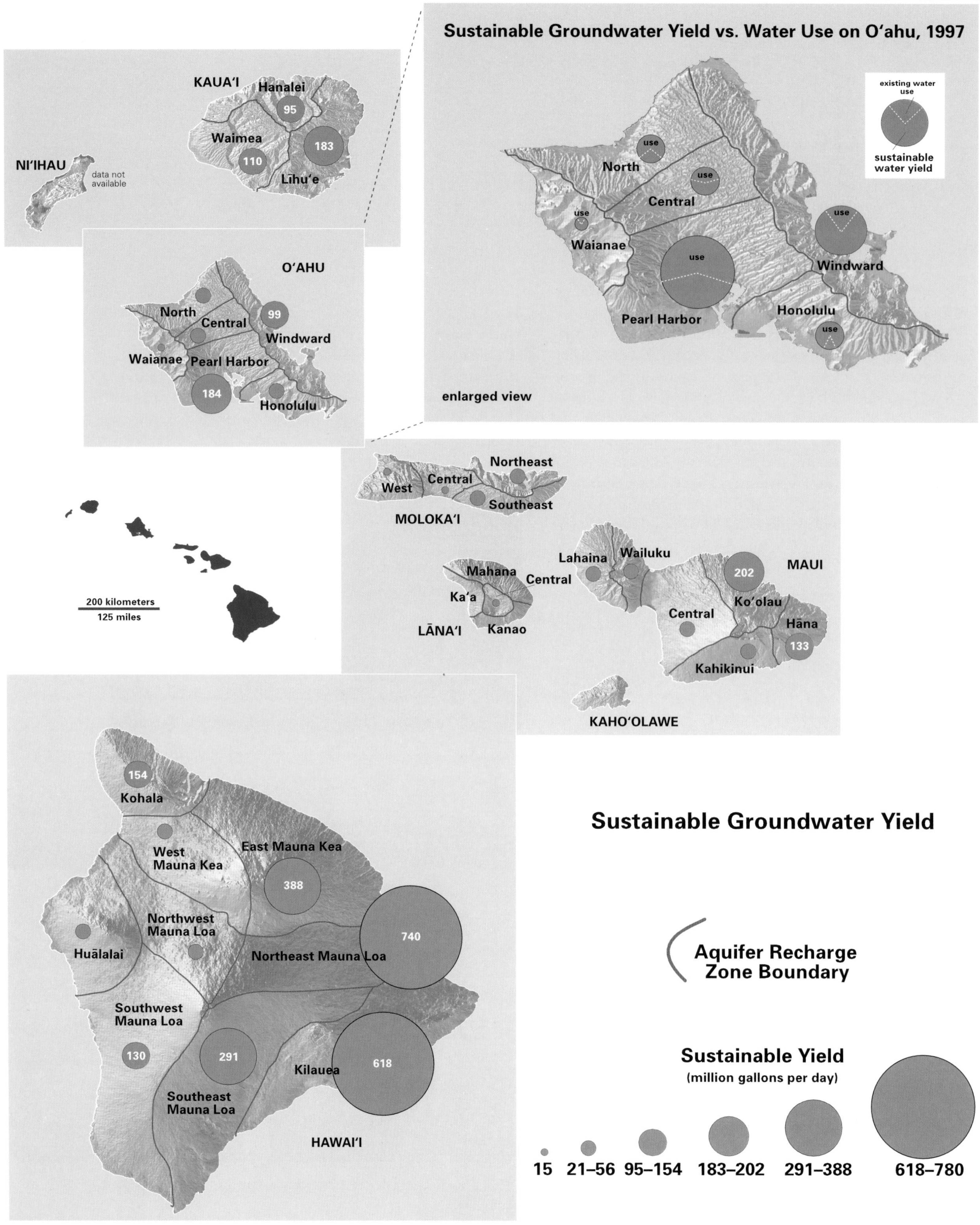

Sustainable Groundwater Yield vs. Water Use on O'ahu, 1997

existing water use

sustainable water yield

North

use

Central

use

use

Waianae

use

Windward

use

Pearl Harbor

Honolulu

use

enlarged view

KAUA'I

Hanalei

95

Waimea

183

NI'IHAU

data not available

110

Līhu'e

O'AHU

North

Central

99

Windward

Waianae

Pearl Harbor

184

Honolulu

200 kilometers

125 miles

Northeast

Central

West

Southeast

MOLOKA'I

Lahaina

Wailuku

Mahana

Central

202

MAUI

Ka'a

Ko'olau

LĀNA'I

Kanao

Central

Hāna

133

Kahikinui

KAHO'OLAWE

Sustainable Groundwater Yield

154

Kohala

West Mauna Kea

East Mauna Kea

388

Northwest Mauna Loa

Huālalai

740

Northeast Mauna Loa

Southwest Mauna Loa

130

291

Kilauea

618

Southeast Mauna Loa

HAWAI'I

Aquifer Recharge Zone Boundary

Sustainable Yield
(million gallons per day)

15   21–56   95–154   183–202   291–388   618–780

lic works, and the rules governing their use evolved as society progressed and prospered.

The traditional system of supplying water prevailed for a century after Captain James Cook's visit in 1778. In 1879 a well drilled through the sediments of the 'Ewa coastal plain in southwestern O'ahu released artesian water from the underlying volcanic rock aquifer. The ground elevation at the drill site was 15 feet (4.8 m) above sea level, yet the artesian water gushed another 15 feet higher. Thus was discovered O'ahu's most voluminous source of controllable water, which initiated a new era of water resource development in Hawai'i. By the 1930s drilling had verified the availability of exploitable groundwater on all the major islands. Kaho'olawe is the only island lacking a significant source of groundwater usable for drinking and agriculture.

Hydrogeology

The principal volcanic feature of hydrologic importance is the presence of thousands of thin-bedded (10 feet [3.2 m] or less), gently sloping (3–10 degrees), extrusive basaltic lava flows that comprise the bulk of the islands. The structural features associated with these flows, such as an abundance of clinker sections, voids between flow surfaces, shrinkage joints, fractures, lava tubes, and gas vesicles, make these rocks porous and highly permeable, and thus ideal aquifers.

In the volcanic rift zones, molten lava intrudes into the fissures and hardens as dikes. Unlike surface lava flows, the dikes are dense, poorly permeable, and nearly vertical sheets of basaltic rock. Measuring a few feet in thickness, these dikes are very important hydrogeologically because they restrict the flow of groundwater. Where dikes make up 10 percent or more of the total rock volume and cut into the permeable basalt flows to form water storage compartments, they are called dike complexes. These are generally located at high elevations and impound rain-fed, percolating water. Natural discharges from the compartments are via high-level springs and streams.

Groundwater

The dominant water resource on each of the islands is groundwater saturating volcanic rock formations. Perennial streams fed by groundwater springs are common on the larger islands, especially Kaua'i, but these flows are only a small fraction of the total groundwater that discharges along coasts from underground aquifers to the ocean.

Groundwater occurs chiefly as either *basal water,* a lens of fresh to brackish water that floats on seawater, or *high-level water,* freshwater that does not rest on seawater.

Basal water occurs principally in the thin, bedded lava layers of the volcanic flanks. Because the flanks are the most regionally extensive volcanic formations, basal water is the most abundant form of groundwater.

The height of the basal water table above sea level is called the head. Because of the density difference between fresh and salt water, about 40 feet (13 m) of freshwater is present below sea level for every foot of freshwater above; that is, the lens thickness below sea level is equal to 40 times the head. A high basal head (more than 5 feet [1.6 m]) within a mile of a coast results from the impedance of coastal discharge by a wedge of low-permeability sediments called caprock. Caprock and coral formations are especially effective in restricting discharge in western Kaua'i, southern and northern O'ahu, and the eastern half of West Maui. In all of these regions basal heads exceed 10 feet (3.2 m). The maximum head of basal water in Hawai'i was measured at 42 feet (13.5 m) at the site of the first artesian well drilled in Honolulu more than a century ago. Nowadays, because of excessive water use the head at that location is about half the original measurement.

High-level groundwater saturates dike complexes in the rift zones. Groundwater accumulates between dikes until it either escapes through fractures or reaches the surface, where it discharges in springs. High-level groundwater also occurs as local zones of saturation in permeable rock underlain by less permeable formations, such as buried ash or soil layers. Called perched water, such resources are generally of much smaller volume than high-level water impounded by dikes, but they may be adequate for limited local needs.

Groundwater also saturates sediments on coastal plains, particularly layers of limestone. This water is not usually fresh enough for drinking, but it may be acceptable for irrigation. Alluvium in stream valleys also carries small amounts of groundwater.

Streams

All Hawaiian streams respond rapidly to storm rainfall because drainage basins are small and the distance of overland flow is short. The intensity and volume of rainfall during severe storms cause very high flow rates. Following a rainfall event, it takes no more than a few hours for the stream to reach maximum flow, and the return to normal flow is also comparatively rapid. The stream flows transport large sediment loads that turn coastal waters from clear green and blue to muddy red and brown.

Perennial streams are sustained by groundwater from high-level aquifers. On a coastal plain, perennial flow may originate from basal groundwater springs. Where groundwater is not accessible in a drainage basin, streams exhibit intermittent flow because they respond only to rainfall and runoff. This is the case in most leeward sectors of the islands. On Kaua'i, the oldest major island in the chain, high-level dike water resources in the interior give rise to perennial streams throughout the island, except on the far-western leeward slope.

On Oʻahu, Maui, Molokaʻi, and Hawaiʻi Island, perennial streams persist to the coast on windward sides where rift zones extend to the sea. In leeward and windward areas where rift zones terminate far inland, the perennial flow is lost during passage of the stream over porous lavas near the coast. Neither Niʻihau nor Kahoʻolawe have perennial streams.

Among the major streams is the Wailuku River, which rises on the volcanic slopes of Mauna Kea, inland of Hilo, and has an average flow of about 275 million gallons per day (mgd) or 12 cubic meters per second (cms). During droughts, however, its flow decreases to a few mgd. On Maui, Waiheʻe Stream has an average flow of nearly 60 mgd (2.6 cms) and a base flow of about 15 mgd (0.7 cms), fed by high-level springs. Kahana Stream on Oʻahu averages 35 mgd (1.5 cms) with a base flow of 11 mgd (0.5 cms). Numerous very large streams drain Kauaʻi, the largest of which, the Wailua River, yields an average flow of more than 200 mgd (8.8 cms). In northeast Molokaʻi, Pelekunu and Wailau Streams carry average flows exceeding 25 mgd (1.1 cms). Most large streams in the Islands have been affected by diversions for irrigation water.

Aquifer Classification

Topographic drainage areas control the occurrence of surface water. The continuous flow of groundwater, on the other hand, does not correspond with land surface features. An aquifer may underlie numerous surface drainage basins. Accurate information about the extent and behavior of groundwater in aquifers throughout most of Hawaiʻi is fragmentary. Only those aquifers where groundwater has been exploited for many years are reasonably well known.

An Aquifer Classification Code has been created for each island as a guide to aquifer location and potential productivity. The basic unit is the Aquifer Sector, a large region with similar hydrogeological features that includes one or more Aquifer Systems where groundwater may occur in different but hydraulically continuous aquifers. The system is further divided into Aquifer Types, defined by the specific hydrogeological environment in which the groundwater exists.

Surface Water Development

Perennial streams and springs, the chief sources of water in traditional Hawaiʻi, continue to serve as important water supplies for large-scale plantation agriculture. Most large streams were diverted for irrigation of sugarcane by way of ditches and tunnels. In some instances the tunnels also acted as drains for high-level groundwater.

Tunnel-and-ditch systems were constructed to transport water on every island except Kahoʻolawe and Niʻihau. Major systems include the Wailua network on Kauaʻi, which carries an average of 150 mgd (6.6 cms); the Waiāhole system on Oʻahu, which transports an average of 30 mgd (1.3 cms); the Waikolu Tunnel on Molokaʻi, which diverts an average of about 5 mgd (0.2 cms) from the Waikolu drainage basin in the northeast to the island's dry central plains; the East Maui system, which transports an average of 164 mgd (7.2 cms) to irrigate arid central Maui; and the Lower Hāmākua Ditch system, which collects an average of 32 mgd (1.4 cms) of drainage in the Kohala Mountains of Hawaiʻi Island.

Groundwater Development

Drilled wells, infiltration galleries, and drainage tunnels are the most common ways to develop, or access, groundwater. More than a thousand deep wells have been drilled on Oʻahu alone. Most drilled wells, ranging between 1 and 2 feet in diameter, are typically equipped with pumps rated at 1–2 mgd (0.04–0.08 cms), but pumps with capacities as large as 5 mgd (0.2 cms) have been successful. The 4,000-foot (1,212 m) deep Waikiʻi Well, located on the slope of Mauna Kea, is one of the deepest water wells in the world. Most production wells in Hawaiʻi, however, are 250 to 750 feet (75–230 m) deep.

Infiltration galleries are horizontal skimming tunnels excavated at the top of the freshwater lens, typically in leeward areas. A well consisting of an inclined or vertical shaft dug to the water table connects with one or more infiltration galleries. First constructed on Maui nearly a century ago to access basal groundwater in the central isthmus, infiltration galleries are important sources of water for both irrigation and municipal use, especially on Oʻahu and Maui. Oʻahu's most famous one is the Hālawa Shaft, which yields an average of about 15 mgd (0.6 cms) to southeastern Oʻahu—enough water for the daily needs of more than 100,000 people. Equally large is the U.S. Navy's Waiawa Shaft, the main source of water for the Pearl Harbor military complex.

Drainage tunnels are horizontal shafts driven into mountain areas to tap high-level perched or dike-confined water. They have been attempted on every island

Oʻahu Water Resources

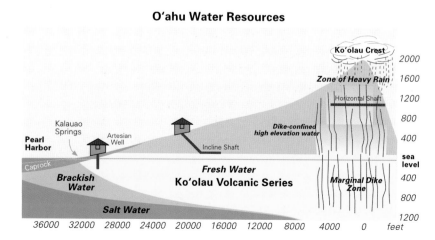

except Ni'ihau and Kaho'olawe, but not all have been successful. On Kaua'i these tunnels mainly develop high-level perched water. On O'ahu several tunnels in Ko'olaupoko exploit the high-level groundwater of the windward Ko'olau Range. The largest of these belong to the Waiāhole system, which includes a main transmission tunnel that enters the mountains at Waiāhole and emerges in Waiawa Valley about 3 miles (5 km) away. The leeward side of O'ahu's Wai'anae Range is also punctured with tunnels, but because of low rainfall and groundwater discharge, their yields are small compared to those of the Ko'olau tunnels.

The longest transmission tunnel in Hawai'i is 5 miles (8.3 km) long and was constructed on Moloka'i to carry water from Waikolu Valley westward to central Moloka'i. In West Maui drainage tunnels were driven at high elevations in many valleys. On Hawai'i Island extensive ditch-and-tunnel systems (Kohala Ditch and Upper and Lower Hāmākua Ditches) exploit high-level surface water in the Kohala Mountains.

Water Production and Sustainable Yield

Because of its innate purity, groundwater is preferred for domestic (municipal) use, while both surface water and groundwater are diverted for agricultural irrigation. On O'ahu and Kaua'i virtually the entire domestic supply is derived from groundwater, while on Maui and Hawai'i Island both surface water and groundwater supply domestic needs. Ni'ihau and Lāna'i depend soley on groundwater, and the presently unpopulated island of Kaho'olawe has no reliable source of potable water.

The term *sustainable yield* is generally applied to groundwater development, although it can be extended to surface water. For groundwater, sustainable yield is defined as the quantity of water that can be extracted from an aquifer indefinitely without diminishing the quantity or quality of the water withdrawn. Groundwater sustainable yields for aquifer systems are approximations, the accuracy of which depends on the hydro-

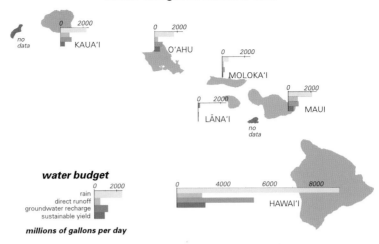

Water Budget of Hawai'i, 1995

water budget
rain
direct runoff
groundwater recharge
sustainable yield

millions of gallons per day

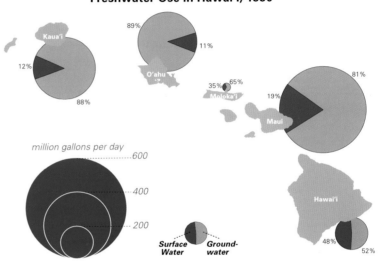

Freshwater Use in Hawai'i, 1990

million gallons per day

Surface Water   Groundwater

geological information available and the record of water withdrawal. The reliability of sustainable yield estimates varies greatly among and within the islands. Estimates for O'ahu are the most reliable because of the long record of use.

Although sustainable yield is hypothetical in that it is based on optimal methods of extraction, estimated yields are useful in making decisions regarding water resource development. Sustainable yields for each of the main islands include groundwater that discharges into streams, and thus full development without consideration of sustainable yield may result in unacceptable changes to stream environments.

As of the mid-1990s, groundwater extraction remained below sustainable yields on all the main islands, as shown by the estimated figures for water production (withdrawals and diversions) listed in the table.

JOHN MINK AND GLENN BAUER

Groundwater: Sustainable Yield and Extraction

	Groundwater Yield (mgd)	Groundwater Withdrawals	Surface Water Diversions
Kaua'i	390	50	350
O'ahu*	465	375	75
Maui	475	200	270
Lāna'i	6	3	0
Moloka'i	80	5	5
Hawai'i	2,500	50	150

* Figures for O'ahu represent the period prior to 1994–1995, when 13,000 acres of sugarcane taken out of production, and not yet replaced with other crops, resulted in a decrease of 60 mgd. O'ahu's 1995 pumpage was 325 mgd. Note: 1 million gallons = 3,785 m³.

SOILS

The success of both traditional subsistence and modern commercial agriculture in Hawai'i has been based on the exploitation of bountiful arable soils. Across the state a range of soil types has evolved through the weathering, or physical and chemical decomposition, of basaltic lavas and volcanic ash. Soils differ from place to place because of variations in the parent material from which they are derived, local climate, slope and drainage conditions, the nature of organic debris added to the developing soil, and the length of time the soil is exposed to weathering processes. The amount and seasonality of rainfall particularly influence soil formation, and water movement on the surface and underground modifies weathering processes. Nonethe-

less, soils of roughly the same age, derived from similar parent material, and developed under like climatic conditions possess similar properties and, therefore, require comparable management techniques.

While similar soil formation processes operate worldwide, consistently warm temperatures accelerate weathering in Hawai'i. The basic processes that convert parent material into soil are alterations in minerals or chemistry, additions and losses, and changes in the location of soil components. For example, organic matter and sediments can be added to the soil, but they can also be removed through erosion. Chemical alterations include the leaching of silica and other elements,

(continued on page 96)

Caption for the following two pages:

Soil orders on the major islands. *Histosols* are organic soils that develop when trees, other plants, and decomposing forest litter alter geologically young lava flows. In Hawai'i, these soils generally form a well-drained, thin (2–8 inches [5–20 cm]) layer on the lava rock. Histosols also often develop in poorly drained areas such as bogs and marshes. Soils found on very young geologic deposits, such as beach sand, alluvial deposits, and volcanic cinders near Kīlauea Crater are *Entisols.* Acid, infertile soils with a bleached subsurface and a subsoil concentration of iron compounds are known as *Spodosols.* These soils, which often form as a result of a fluctuating water table, occur in the Alaka'i Swamp of Kaua'i.

Other weakly to moderately developed soils, called *Inceptisols,* occur on unstable and/or relatively young landscapes on all islands. Inceptisols are exemplified by the soils of Kaua'i's steep, eroded uplands and the floodplain of the Hanalei River valley. Many volcanic-ash-based soils may evolve into *Andisols;* these occur mainly on lava flows older than 3,000 years on Hawai'i and Maui and are characterized by the capacity to take up large amounts of phosphorus. Andisols cover more land than any other soil type in the state and may persist for more than a million years in very moist environments. Other soils derived from volcanic ash in dry leeward areas of Hawai'i, Maui, Moloka'i, and Lāna'i are termed *Aridisols* and *Mollisols.* Both types possess high fertility, but the availability of precipitation limits the agricultural produc-

tivity of Aridisols unless they are irrigated. Mollisols, on the other hand, are normally well-drained, relatively young soils that develop on coral, lava, or alluvium. The fertile topsoil of Maui's central plain, for example, is composed mainly of Mollisols.

In dry areas, expandable clays may become dominant in the soil, producing *Vertisols.* These soils typically occur on talus slopes and deeply dissected valley floors, such as those found in Wai'anae. The tendency of Vertisols to shrink and swell with wetting and drying can be hazardous to overlying construction. *Alfisols,* fertile soils with an accumulation of clay in the subsoil, occur in small areas on O'ahu and Lāna'i. Alfisols are similar to Ultisols, but are less weathered and contain higher concentrations of nutrients.

After extreme weathering, kaolinite (clay) and oxides of iron and aluminum dominate soils. If the soils contain a subsoil composed of clay translocated from higher in the profile, they are classified as *Ultisols.* Such soils occur on old geomorphic surfaces in areas such as windward O'ahu that have high rainfall but dry summers. Without a translocated clay subsoil, the soils are termed *Oxisols;* these too are found on old, stable surfaces and, being resistant to physical deterioration under intensive mechanized agriculture, are the state's most important agricultural soils. Examples are the red soils of Kaua'i and central O'ahu. Oxisols and Ultisols, which formed in both basalt and volcanic ash, span sizable areas on old landscapes of all islands except Hawai'i.

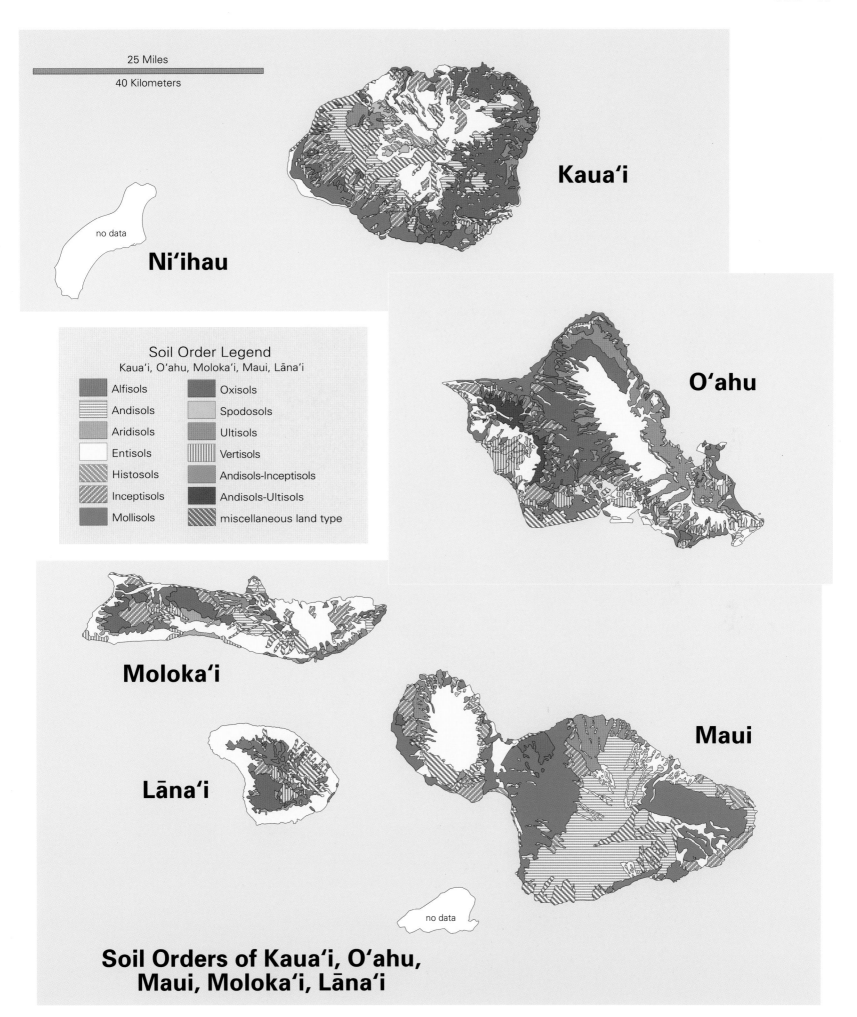

25 Miles
40 Kilometers

Ni'ihau

no data

Kaua'i

O'ahu

Soil Order Legend
Kaua'i, O'ahu, Moloka'i, Maui, Lāna'i

Alfisols
Andisols
Aridisols
Entisols
Histosols
Inceptisols
Mollisols

Oxisols
Spodosols
Ultisols
Vertisols
Andisols-Inceptisols
Andisols-Ultisols
miscellaneous land type

Moloka'i

Lāna'i

Maui

no data

Soil Orders of Kaua'i, O'ahu, Maui, Moloka'i, Lāna'i

Soil Orders of Hawai'i

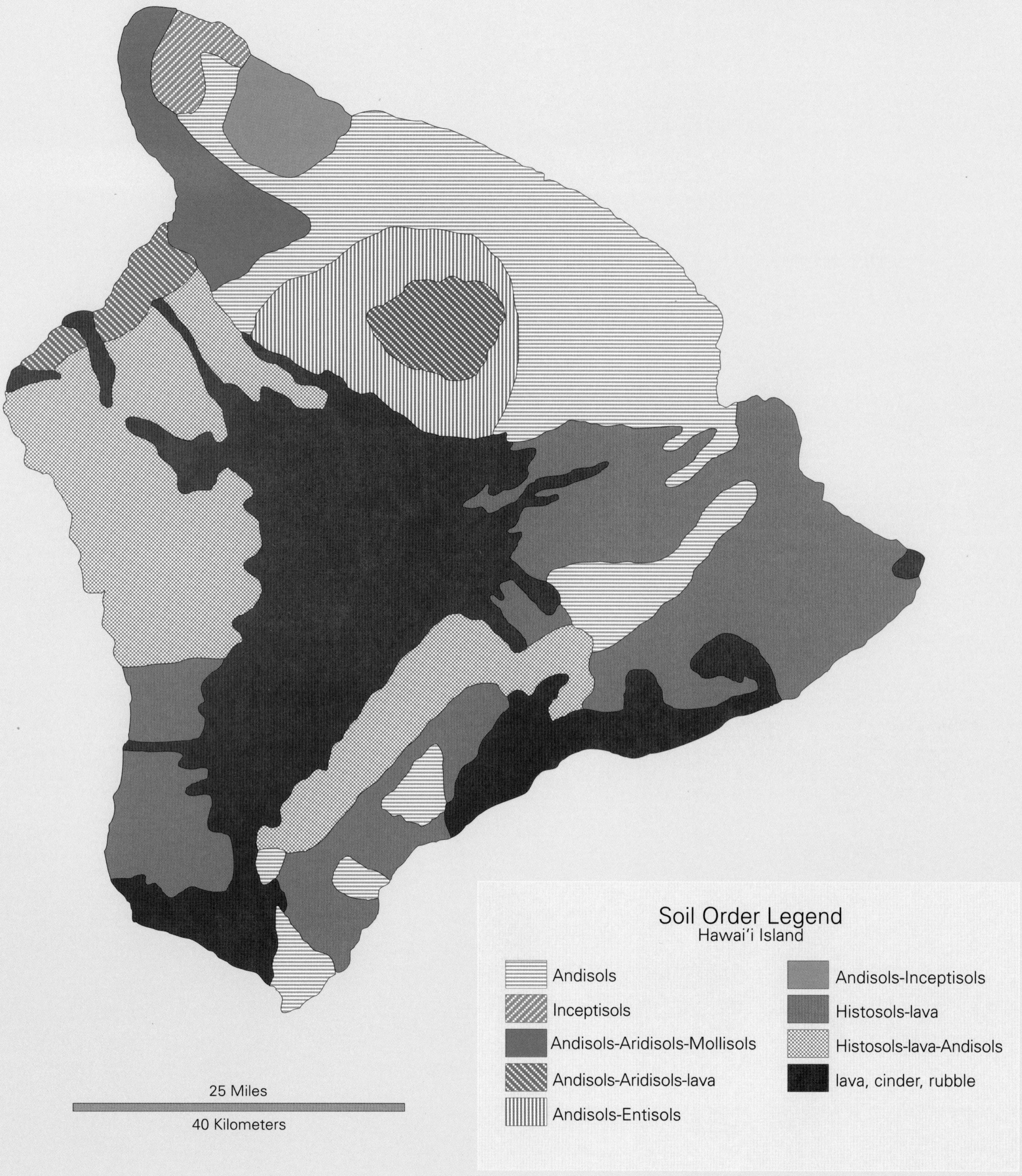

Soil Order Legend
Hawai'i Island

- Andisols
- Inceptisols
- Andisols-Aridisols-Mollisols
- Andisols-Aridisols-lava
- Andisols-Entisols
- Andisols-Inceptisols
- Histosols-lava
- Histosols-lava-Andisols
- lava, cinder, rubble

25 Miles

40 Kilometers

Erosion

Maintaining soil quality is essential to both sustainable agriculture and environmental protection. Erosion is one highly visible cause of declining soil quality. The loss of topsoil removes the most favorable layer for plant cultivation and diminishes nutrients and organic matter in the soil. In addition, eroded soil, carried by runoff into streams and coastal waters, degrades water quality and habitat for many freshwater and marine organisms.

Annual rates of sheet and rill erosion—defined as the removal of soil in fairly uniform layers or by numerous small, shallow channels, respectively—are shown in the graph. (The estimates do not include erosion due to wind, gullying, and the presence of plantation roads, or soil loss caused by sugarcane harvests, because the technology to quantify these types of erosion has been unavailable for conditions in Hawai'i.) In the past, soil loss due to sheet and rill erosion from intensively tilled croplands (including sugar and pineapple acreage) has fallen within traditionally acceptable levels for all islands except Hawai'i, where the cultivation of steeply sloping and rain-soaked soils, especially along the Hāmākua

(continued on next page)

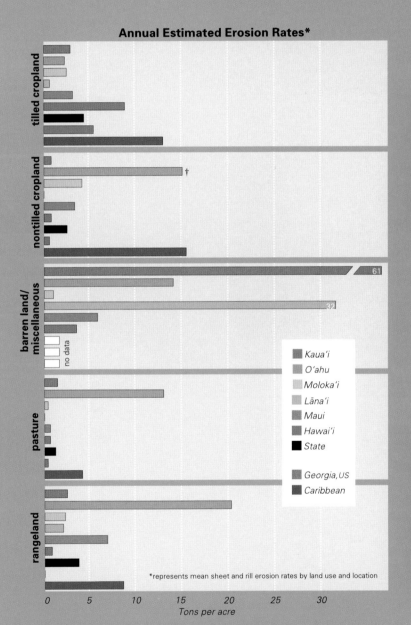

Annual Estimated Erosion Rates*

Legend:
- Kaua'i
- O'ahu
- Moloka'i
- Lāna'i
- Maui
- Hawai'i
- State
- Georgia, US
- Caribbean

*represents mean sheet and rill erosion rates by land use and location

x-axis: Tons per acre (0, 5, 10, 15, 20, 25, 30)

Categories (top to bottom): tilled cropland, nontilled cropland, barren land/miscellaneous, pasture, rangeland

† The abnormally high value probably reflects the fact that during the data collection period many plantings of bananas were underway, triggering levels of erosion that would be expected to taper off as the crop canopy closes.

By about 700,000 years ago, extensive erosion on the older islands had removed the upper soil layer. The erosion surface shown here in Wai'anae Range, O'ahu, alluvium is buried by two layers of weathered volcanic ash. The topsoil is formed partly from dust blown in from central Asian deserts. The depth of dust accumulation indicates that the landscape has remained stable for 100,000–200,000 years. [R. Gavenda]

On the island of Kaho'olawe, a history of deforestation and overgrazing by domestic and feral animals, combined with the forces of wind and water, have produced extreme sheet, rill, and gully erosion. Throughout the state, areas where pronounced wet and dry seasons occur and where careful soil management is lacking are likewise prone to severe erosion. [C. Smith]

(Erosion continued)

have long believed that if annual topsoil losses could be limited to less than 5 tons per acre, natural weathering and soil formation processes would be sufficient to replenish deep soils. This standard has been based on the goal of sustained agricultural productivity. It does not, however, address issues such as water quality and habitat conservation—concerns that are currently prompting soil scientists to reevaluate standards of acceptable erosion rates.

Nontilled cropland (acreage planted in crops such as coffee, papaya, and macadamia nuts) typically has some erosion-reducing ground cover or tree canopy. O'ahu's high rate for this erosion type may be due, in part, to the production of crops such as bananas on steep foothills, where data were collected at a point in time before a good ground cover could be established.

Kaua'i's erosion value of 61 tons per acre per year for "miscellaneous land types" is due primarily to natural, or geologic, erosion occurring in Waimea and Olokele Canyons. Lāna'i's high rate, however, is attributable to past heavy overgrazing by domestic and feral animals in the island's northern region. Studies are being conducted to understand better how to reduce this human-induced, or accelerated, erosion.

Changes underway in the state's agricultural economy could alter erosion levels in the future. With the decline of the sugar industry the concern exists, especially on Hawai'i Island, that, without diligent conservation measures, a large-scale shift to the cultivation of small plots of crops accompanied by intensive and frequent tilling and harvesting could increase soil loss rates. Intercropping and planting tree crops on long rotation schedules, on the other hand, could result in lower rates of erosion.

CHRISTOPHER SMITH

(continued from page 92)

which can transform minerals inherited from parent rocks into other, more stable minerals such as kaolinite (clay particles) and oxides of iron and aluminum. Furthermore, the products of weathering can be transported or rearranged, often in association with the effects of changing climates, such as fluctuations in sea level. During periods of rising sea level, low-lying areas become eroded and reefs form; and when sea levels fall new sediment is deposited on the now-emerged coralline limestone benches. (The 'Ewa coastal plain on O'ahu and the Waimea coastal plain on Kaua'i are examples of such formerly submerged areas.) Past changes in climate have also influenced local soil development on a broad scale. The wetter conditions of past glacial eras, for instance, probably produced more intense weathering and accelerated soil formation.

The modern system of soil classification used worldwide distinguishes soil orders, or major types, based on their measurable physical and chemical properties and the primary environmental factors that influenced their formation. These characteristics include fertility, climate zone, degree of weathering, composition and arrangement of horizons (soil layers), and the soil's developmental history. As shown in the soils dis-

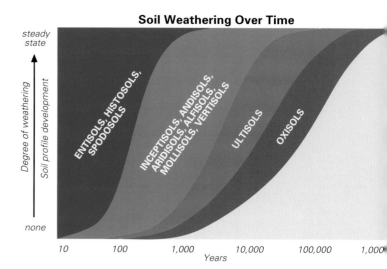

Soil Weathering Over Time

tribution maps, 11 of the 12 soil orders have been reported in Hawai'i. Soils from 9 orders are found on O'ahu alone, representing an impressive diversity for such a small area.

ROBERT GAVENDA,
CHRISTOPHER SMITH, AND
NICOLE VOLLRATH

ASTRONOMY

The Hawaiian Islands, situated in tropical latitudes with an equable climate, provide excellent opportunities to view the entire northern sky and nearly 80 percent of the southern sky. Since the early 1960s, astronomers from many countries have come to Hawai'i to establish observatories on the upper slopes of the state's three highest volcanoes: Mauna Kea at 13,796 feet (4,205 m), Mauna Loa at 13,677 feet (4,169 m), and Haleakalā at 10,023 feet (3,055 m). Because these mountains rise well above the tropical inversion layer into the dry upper atmosphere that has stabilized over thousands of miles of the Pacific, the images are clearer and more stable than at any other site in the world. The dry atmosphere is also ideal for infrared and submillimeter observations. The remoteness of Hawai'i's summits from major urban development, and on the island of Hawai'i a strong outdoor lighting ordinance, prevent light from polluting the night skies. These superb conditions have made Hawaiian astronomical sites, particularly Mauna Kea, the most sought after anywhere for optical, infrared, and submillimeter astronomy.

Astronomy in Hawai'i today continues a long tradition begun when Polynesians used celestial navigation to locate remote Pacific islands. A visit by King David Kalākaua to California's Lick Observatory in 1881 eventually led to the construction of a modest observatory on O'ahu in 1910. In the 1950s Walter Steiger led successful efforts to establish observatories on O'ahu and on Haleakalā, Maui. Since then, two facilities operated by the University of Hawai'i have been built on Haleakalā: the C. E. K. Mees Solar Observatory and the Lunar Ranging Facility, where laser signals are bounced off reflectors placed on the moon and on satellites to provide information about continental drift, polar motion, and the rotation and wobbling of Earth.

In the early 1960s the business community on the island of Hawai'i, led by Mr. Tetsuo Akiyama, promoted Mauna Kea as a site for future telescopes. In 1964, with the support of Governor John A. Burns, a road was constructed to the summit, where testing confirmed the superb astronomical conditions. In the

The Mauna Kea Observatories on Hawai'i as they appeared in early 1995. Eight telescopes were in operation and three were under construction. The summit of Haleakalā on the island of Maui appears on the northeast horizon. [R. J. Wainscoat]

A true-color image of the Crab Nebula taken with a digital camera on the University of Hawai'i 2.2-meter telescope. The Crab Nebula is the remnant of a star whose explosion as a supernova was recorded in A.D. 1054. [R. J. Wainscoat, J. Kormendy, © 1997, Astronomical Society of the Pacific]

Astronomical Facilities on Mauna Kea

name	telescope diameter	telescope type (wavelength)	operator-sponsor
University of Hawai'i Telescope (1968)	0.6m	optical	UH
University of Hawai'i Telescope (1970)	2.2m	optical/infrared	UH
NASA Infrared Telescope (IRTF) (1979)	3.0m	infrared	NASA
Canada-France-Hawai'i Telescope (CFHT) (1979)	3.6m	optical/infrared	Canada-France-UH
United Kingdom Infrared Telescope (UKIRT) (1979)	3.8m	infrared	UK
Caltech Submillimeter Observatory (CSO) (1987)	10.4m	millimeter/submillimeter	Caltech-NSF
James Clerk Maxwell Telescope (JCMT) (1987)	15m	millimeter/submillimeter	UK-Canada-Netherlands
W. M. Keck Observatory (Keck I) (1992)	10m	optical/infrared	Caltech-UC
Very Long Baseline Array (1992)	25m	centimeter	NRAO-AUI-NSF
W. M. Keck Observatory (Keck II) (1996)	10m	optical/infrared	Caltech-UC
Submillimeter Array (*1998)	8x6m	submillimeter	Smithsonian Taiwan
Subaru (Japan National Large Telescope) (*1999)	8m	optical/infrared	Japan
Gemini North Telescope (*1999)	8m	optical/infrared	USA-Canada-UK-Argentina-Brazil-Chile

year indicates beginning of operation, * under construction

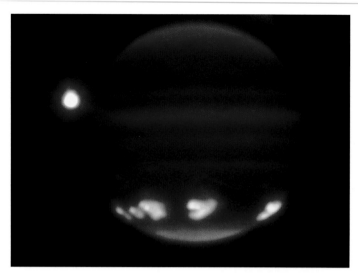

A digital image of Jupiter taken with the University of Hawai'i 2.2-meter telescope on Mauna Kea by University of Hawai'i astronomers. The image was recorded on July 21, 1994, approximately 75 minutes after the impact of fragment "R" from Comet Shoemaker-Levy 9. The impact site is the third bright spot from the left. The bright object to the left of the planet is Io, one of Jupiter's moons. [K. Hodapp, J. Hora, K. Jim, D. Jewitt, R. Wainscoat, L. Cowie]

The southern sky seen from Mauna Kea. At the left is the glow of lava from the erupting Kīlauea volcano. In the sky at the center is the Southern Cross. The snow-covered peak in the center is the true summit of Mauna Kea, the highest point in the Pacific. At the right, the dome of the 8-meter Gemini North telescope is under construction. [© 1997, R. J. Wainscoat]

words of astronomer Gerard Kuiper of the University of Arizona, Mauna Kea is "the best site in the world—I repeat—in the world, from which to study the moon, the planets, the stars." Since then, in only 30 years, the site has become home to the largest concentration of telescopes in the world, with observatories operated by astronomers from the U.S. mainland and Hawai'i, Argentina, Brazil, Canada, Chile, France, Japan, the Netherlands, the United Kingdom, and Taiwan.

Mauna Kea's telescopes fall into three categories: optical, infrared, and millimeter/submillimeter. To observe the universe, optical telescopes gather light at wavelengths from 0.3 to 1 micron; the human eye is sensitive to wavelengths from 0.4 microns—the violet—to nearly 0.7 microns—the red. The location of optical telescopes on Mauna Kea, where the stability of air minimizes atmospheric distortion, has made possible the clearest images ever obtained from Earth. Professional astronomers no longer look through telescopes or even use film cameras. Today, observations on Mauna Kea are made with advanced electronic cameras that use huge, high-performance silicon chips to capture digital images more detailed than those of the highest quality Imax movies. The images require huge amounts of digital mass storage; each image occupies the same amount of space as is required to hold several sets of the *Encyclopaedia Britannica.*

Infrared telescopes are used to study the universe at wavelengths we normally sense as heat. This waveband (1–35 microns) is particularly well suited to observing the birth and early evolution of stars, to determining the properties of cooler celestial bodies such as planets, and to capturing images of the most distant known objects, waves from which have been traveling through space to us for most of the age of the universe—over 10 billion years. These telescopes are located on Mauna Kea primarily because of the excel-lent images, the low stable temperature, and the extremely dry air, which transmits the infrared spectrum well.

At all but the highest, dry, cold sites, submillimeter waves are blocked by the earth's atmosphere. However, waves as short as one-third of a millimeter reach the summit of Mauna Kea during particularly dry conditions. Millimeter/submillimeter telescopes are particularly well suited for research on giant molecular clouds, vast concentrations of tenuous molecular gas where the earliest phases of star formation occur. Because such observations demand the lowest humidity, they must be made near the summit of Mauna Kea. As they do not require the same atmospheric stability as optical and infrared telescopes, submillimeter observatories are located in the valley just below Mauna Kea's summit ridge, where they are more protected from severe weather and interference from radar.

Located on the south flank of Mauna Kea, at the 12,200-ft (3,720 m) level, is a 25-meter (82-foot) antenna, one of ten identical structures spread across the U.S. from Hawai'i to the Virgin Islands that comprise the Very Long Baseline Array (VLBA). Under remote control via the Internet, the ten antennas simultaneously observe an identical area of the sky at the same radio frequency. Signals from the ten antennas produce a radio image with the same detail as a single radio telescope 5,000 miles (8,000 km) in diameter. The VLBA has produced the most detailed images ever obtained at any wavelength, shedding light on phenomena such as massive black holes at the centers of violently energetic galaxies. The Hawai'i antenna is critically important, since its distance from the mainland greatly enhances the detail of the images.

Some of the most important astronomical discoveries of the 1990s have been made from Mauna Kea. In 1992, astronomers first sighted a vast population—many tens of thousands—of small, primitive bodies, which have been orbiting the sun beyond Neptune since early in the formation of our solar system; these bodies make up the Kuiper Belt. In July 1991, nearly all Mauna Kea's telescopes observed the total solar eclipse. In 1994 the observatories captured images of the spectacular collision of the comet Shoemaker-Levy 9 with Jupiter. The two Keck 10-meter telescopes, the world's largest optical instruments, have detected galaxies in formation more than halfway across the known universe. Other Mauna Kea observatories have collected a wealth of other results, such as compelling evidence for black holes at galaxy centers and eruptions of active sulphur volcanoes on one of Jupiter's moons.

There are 13 telescopes on Mauna Kea either now in operation or under construction, with completion scheduled before the end of the decade. They are all sited within the Mauna Kea Science Reserve, developed and managed by the University of Hawai'i Institute for Astronomy. The University also operates the Onizuka Center for International Astronomy at 9,300 feet (2,800 m), which includes a visitor information center and accommodations for astronomers and technicians working on the summit. To preserve Mauna Kea's unique astronomical qualities, the institute has worked with county planners to limit light pollution and with state and federal agencies to minimize electromagnetic interference.

The telescopes on Mauna Kea are operated out of base facilities in Waimea and at University Park in Hilo. The completion in 1997 of a fiber-optic link between Waimea and Hilo, with a branch to the observatories on Mauna Kea, has provided advanced communication links between the telescopes and their sea level base facilities. Many observations on telescopes such as Keck are now made remotely, eliminating the need for astronomers and other personnel to travel to Mauna Kea and adapt to its extreme altitude.

Astronomy is already a major factor in the Big Island economy. It is projected that by the year 2000 the operation of the observatories on Mauna Kea will contribute $50 million annually to Hawai'i Island's economy and employ 350 people.

The new generation of large telescopes going into operation in the late 1990s on Mauna Kea ensures that Hawai'i will continue as a premier astronomical site well into the twenty-first century.

DONALD N. B. HALL

DUMAND

Another, one-of-a-kind astronomical instrument under construction in Hawai'i stretches the very definition of the term *telescope*. Located at submarine depths 18 miles (29 km) off the Kona coast of Hawai'i Island, the Deep Underwater Muon and Neutrino Detector (DUMAND) is poised to detect the most numerous elementary particles in the universe: neutrinos. Physicists estimate that every nuclear reaction creates one of these high-energy subatomic particles, and perhaps a third of those made since the birth of the universe still exist. They travel at almost the speed of light and interact so weakly with matter that they can penetrate any material, including the entire diameter of Earth. However, when neutrinos collide in a certain way with atomic nuclei, they spawn cascades of particles, some of which can be detected by their electrical charge. DUMAND's huge array of photodetectors—anchored to the seafloor and pointed downward to use Earth to filter out interference—is designed to register these signals, and its computer brain can pin down their sources. Astronomers believe the unsurpassed penetrative power of neutrinos will allow them to "see" past barriers such as interstellar dust clouds, which obscure the vision of optical telescopes, to unmapped realms of the cosmos. They hope to study the most energetic cosmic processes, such as quasars, black holes, and supernova explosions, and geoscientists may be able to use neutrinos to "map" Earth's interior. Scheduled for completion in the late 1990s, DUMAND may give the world a truly new window on the universe.

NOREEN M. PARKS

THE BIOTIC ENVIRONMENT

BIOGEOGRAPHY

The Land Biota

If we exclude the large number of plants and animals introduced into the Hawaiian Islands by humans over the past 1,500 years, we are left with an impressive array of native plants, invertebrates, and birds, whose ancestors reached these remote shores by natural means.

Biogeographers distinguish between "continental" and "oceanic" islands. Pacific islands such as New Zealand and Fiji are considered continental because their geology indicates past direct connections to larger nearby landmasses. These past continental connections provide a simple explanation for the presence of some plants and animals. For example, the native frogs of both Fiji and New Zealand are intolerant of salt water, which makes it very unlikely that these amphibians could have dispersed across even narrow ocean passages.

True oceanic islands like those of Hawai'i have been built by volcanic eruptions from the seafloor and, consequently, have never been connected to continents. Their native flora and fauna thus could only have arrived by long-distance dispersal. The resulting biota is typically "disharmonic"; that is, it lacks representatives of many of the plant and animal groups that populate surrounding continental source areas. In general, those groups with the best dispersal capabilities (such as birds), dominate the Islands' native biota, while other groups lacking mechanisms that would allow them to cross ocean waters (such as amphibians and mammals) may be largely or completely absent. The diversity of island-colonizing species is thus restricted to a relative few.

Geographically, the Hawaiian Islands are extremely isolated. More than 2,000 miles (3,200 km) separate Hawai'i from the nearest continent (North America), and the closest Pacific atolls lie 1,000 miles (1,610 km) to the south. Despite the various ways that plants and animals might have immigrated to Hawai'i and the millions of years during which chance colonizing events could have occurred, comparatively few immigrants succeeded, distance being the major deterrent. The modes of long-distance dispersal available to potential colonizers include:

Direct Dispersal Flying animals (birds, bats, and large insects) are best equipped for actively reaching remote locations and are usually well represented in the biota of oceanic islands.

Seeds of the native 'ōhelo are transported when the fleshy fruit in which they are enclosed is eaten by birds. [M. Merlin]

Windborne Dispersal Winds and air currents can passively disperse tiny seeds and invertebrates. The common native tree 'ōhi'a (*Metrosideros polymorpha*) bears very small, lightweight seeds that are easily carried long distances in the wind.

The ancestors of 'ōhi'a apparently evolved in New Zealand, where some species became well adapted to harsh volcanic terrain. As shown on the map, members of this group have colonized other remote Pacific islands with similar volcanic landscapes. Species of *Metrosideros* likely spread to Hawai'i via "stepping-

103

Distribution of the genus *Metrosideros*

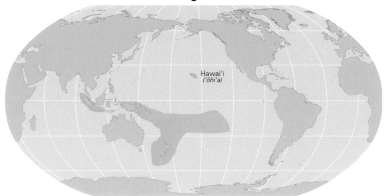

Distribution of the genus *Sophora* (series Tetrapterae)

Distribution of the genus *Vaccinium*

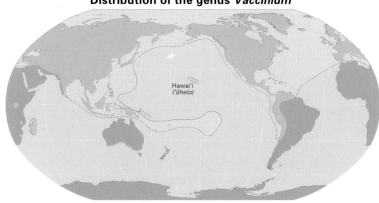

'Ōhi'a lehua flower and seed capsules. The native *Metrosideros* bears very small, lightweight seeds that are easily carried by the wind. [J. Juvik]

stone" islands between New Zealand and Hawai'i.

Waterborne Dispersal Large seeds capable of floating in seawater for extended periods can be transported great distances by ocean currents. For example, the native *māmane* tree (*Sophora chrysophylla*) is closely related to a South Pacific species whose seeds can survive in seawater for more than three years. *Sophora*'s successful colonization of remote islands in the Pacific, Indian, and Atlantic Oceans testifies to its adaptation to long-distance dispersal by ocean currents. Interestingly, some common plant species with large, buoyant seeds, such as coconut and mangroves, did not reach Hawai'i naturally but rather were introduced by humans.

Another means of waterborne dispersal is rafting. Plant seeds—or even small animals and their eggs—can lodge in the bark, branches, and root masses of trees and mats of vegetation washed into the ocean during floods, hurricanes, and landslides. Such floating debris rafts can ultimately transport their passengers to remote islands.

Dispersal by Birds Although birds are themselves active migrants or accidental wanderers to remote islands, they can also serve as inadvertent carriers of plant and animal "hitchhikers." Barbed or sticky fruits and seeds can adhere to a bird's feathers at one location only to be preened off at another distant site. The Hawaiian silverswords and their relatives, for instance, are descended from New World "tarweeds" equipped with small, barbed seeds.

Birds also disperse plants by ingesting fruits and later discharging undigested seeds at a new location. The tiny seeds of the native *'ōhelo* (*Vaccinium* species), embedded in its tasty fruit, are ideally suited for such distribution. 'Ōhelo belongs to the blueberry and cranberry family, which is widely distributed, particularly in northern temperate regions. This may explain why the 'ōhelo thrives best in cooler mountain habitats in Hawai'i.

Mud encrusted on the legs and feet of birds provides yet another method for the dissemination of plant seeds and the eggs and encysted larvae of small invertebrates.

Biogeographer Sherwin Carlquist has examined some 250 native flowering plants and suggested their most likely means of dispersal based on fruit and seed characteristics. As the diagram indicates, seeds carried in one way or another by birds account for almost three-fourths of the successful plant colonists. Flotation (including rafting) provided the dispersal means for another 23 percent, and wind-dispersed seeds (excluding ferns) contributed less than 2 percent of the flora.

How often were the Hawaiian Islands colonized by these various means? Researchers have estimated that the roughly 1,000 species of native flowering plants found in Hawai'i today evolved from perhaps 275 immigrants, while as many as 10,000 endemic insect species descended from about 350–400 original colonizers. (Native species occurring in only a limited area are termed *endemic*.) Assuming a time span of 27 million years (the approximate age of Midway, the oldest extant island in the Hawaiian chain), we can estimate the rate of colonization for plants as one species every 98,000 years, and for insects as one species every 68,000 years. For the native birds, which evolved from as few as 20 original immigrants, less than one successful colonizing event occurred every million years. These very low immigration rates underscore the biological significance of Hawai'i's extreme geographic isolation.

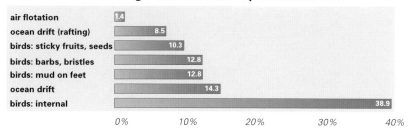

Modes of Long-Distance Plant Dispersal to Hawai'i

air flotation	1.4
ocean drift (rafting)	8.5
birds: sticky fruits, seeds	10.3
birds: barbs, bristles	12.8
birds: mud on feet	12.8
ocean drift	14.3
birds: internal	38.9

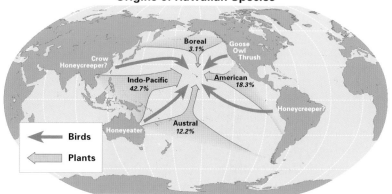

Origins of Hawaiian Species

Boreal 3.1%
Goose Owl Thrush
Crow Honeycreeper?
Indo-Pacific 42.7%
American 18.3%
Honeycreeper?
Austral 12.2%
Honeyeater

← Birds
← Plants

23.7% of plant species are of pan-tropical or unknown origin

These infrequent immigrants came to Hawai'i from all points of the compass. Almost 43 percent of the plant colonists originated in the tropical region spanning Southeast Asia, Indonesia, and the Pacific island stepping-stones scattered east and south of Hawai'i. Another 12 percent of the flora arrived from the temperate Austral region (Australia, New Zealand, and Patagonia), and about 18 percent immigrated from tropical and subtropical areas of North, Central, and South America. Native bird species also apparently arrived from several source areas. Although the origin of the honeycreepers, Hawai'i's best-known endemic birds, is not yet resolved, the group appears related to cardueline finches, which are widespread in both the Old and New World.

The Marine Biota

We might assume that, although oceanic isolation has limited the colonization of Hawai'i by land organisms, the sea surrounding the Islands would be advantageous for the dispersal of marine life. Even for marine organisms, however—and particularly those adapted to shallow coastal environments—the thousands of miles of deep, open ocean separating Hawai'i from the major source areas of marine species present a significant barrier.

Marine creatures capable of swimming can disperse actively. But nonswimmers can spread only passively, as tiny floating larvae (plankton). Alternatively, some marine organisms (such as coral larvae) can attach to floating debris and disperse by rafting. Studies have shown that some planktonic larvae can survive 3–6

Bidens seeds attached to bird feathers. The barbed seeds of many weedy species may "hitchhike" to islands on birds. [J. Jeffrey Photography]

Ocean Currents and Biodiversity

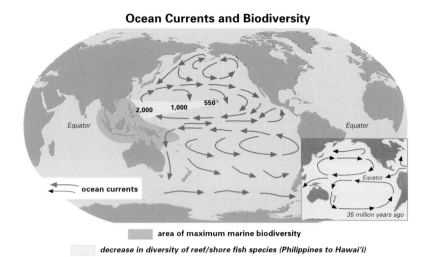

area of maximum marine biodiversity

decrease in diversity of reef/shore fish species (Philippines to Hawai‘i)

months in the open sea and are transported about 45 miles (72 km) a day by equatorial currents—potentially thousands of miles over their larval life stage.

The tropical waters surrounding Indonesia, the Philippines, Northern Australia, and the islands of Melanesia, which support the world's greatest diversity of marine organisms, have served as the source for the majority of marine plant and animal species now found in Hawai‘i.

Although this region is several thousand miles from Hawai‘i, central Pacific islands such as the Marshall Islands and Kiribati—as well as former islands now sunken to the depths west of Hawai‘i—have probably acted as stepping-stones (as they did for terrestrial organisms) in the spread of many shallow-water-dwelling marine creatures.

The limitations that distance imposed on many marine groups are clearly demonstrated by the progressively diminishing number of species found from west to east across the Pacific. For example, the Philippines, situated in the western Pacific, support more than 2,000 species of reef and shore fishes, while the Marshall Islands—2,500 miles (4,000 km) to the east—are home to only about 1,000 species; and in Hawai‘i—1,800 miles (2,900 km) farther to the east

—the number dwindles to 550. A similar pattern exists for reef-building corals, which are estimated at 500 species in the tropical western Pacific, but number only about 50 species in Hawai‘i. (Less-than-optimal ocean temperatures—several degrees lower than in the tropical western Pacific—probably depress coral diversity in Hawai‘i as well.)

As might be expected, Hawai‘i's isolation has led to the evolution of many endemic marine species. Roughly 20–30 percent of the fish and coral species, 20 percent of the mollusks, and 18 percent of the marine algae are endemic to Hawaiian waters. The percentage of endemism for Hawai‘i's marine biota, although not as high as that for the land biota, is higher than that reported from any other island group in the insular tropical Pacific.

Ancient changes in the geographic configuration of continents bordering the Pacific also influenced the timing and rates of colonization by certain marine organisms. For example, geologic sampling of submarine seamounts northwest of Midway Atoll has revealed that corals may not have arrived in Hawaiian waters until about 35 million years ago. One possible explanation for this earlier absence of corals lies in the significantly different ocean circulation patterns of the past. Thirty-five million years ago Panamanian and Indonesian seaways linked the Atlantic, Pacific, and Indian Oceans. This produced strong, westward-flowing, equatorial currents that reduced the likelihood of marine organisms dispersing from west to east. As the drifting continents later closed off these sea passages, ocean circulation gradually changed to assume the modern pattern, which includes equatorial and subtropical countercurrents. These eastward-flowing currents are more conducive to the dissemination of planktonic larvae from the species-rich western Pacific into Hawaiian waters. Likewise, the eastward-spiraling Kuroshio Current has facilitated the natural immigration of many Japanese marine organisms to Hawai‘i.

JAMES O. JUVIK

EVOLUTION

After returning from a trip to the Galápagos in the 1830s, Charles Darwin wrote:

> Seeing every height crowned with its crater, and the boundaries of most of the lava-streams still distinct, we are led to believe that within a period, geologically recent, the unbroken ocean was here spread out. Hence, both in space and time, we seem to be brought somewhat near to that great fact—that mystery of mysteries—the first appearance of new beings on this earth.

The extraordinary peculiarity of life found on isolated oceanic islands has long intrigued biologists. The H.M.S. *Beagle,* on which Darwin voyaged, did not stop in Hawai'i. If it had, he would have encountered evidence of evolution that surpassed in detail and diversity even that of the Galápagos. Scientific studies have revealed that many species are endemic, or unique to Hawai'i, having evolved on these islands and not merely having reached here from somewhere else. These endemic species include about 70 land birds, 1,000 flowering plants, 100 ferns and related plants, 5,000 insects, and 800 land and freshwater snails. Equally peculiar is what is missing from Hawai'i's flora and fauna. For example, except for one species of bat, one species of seal, and the Polynesian rat, mammals were absent when Polynesians discovered the Islands around 2,000 years ago.

Beyond the discovery and description of these species lie the questions that challenged Darwin: How and why have these forms of life evolved on these small, remote, and isolated islands? What were the ancestors of unique Hawaiian species? From where did they come and when did they arrive? How did they manage to reach the middle of the ocean? Why did some life forms change very little, while others produced something new?

To understand island biology, we must be familiar with geological and geographical settings. The Hawaiian Islands are the above-water peaks of huge mountains built from lava pushed up by volcanic activity at the "Hawaiian hotspot," a melting anomaly in Earth's mantle that is thought to be fixed in position. For the past 40 million years the tectonic plate that lies beneath the Pacific Ocean has been moving slowly northwestward over the hotspot, resulting in a line of islands increasingly younger at the southeast end of the archipelago.

From southeast Maui, one can look toward Hawai'i Island and easily imagine with Darwin that not long ago the "unbroken ocean was here spread out." Although the island has many large, nearly barren, and relatively recently cooled lava flows, its older weathered flows harbor dense tropical forests. Some of the plant and animal species are unique, and their formation must have been relatively recent. Others appear to be variants of species that have colonized from an older neighbor island. What an unparalleled natural laboratory for the study of the evolution of species!

All of the main islands lie south of the Tropic of Cancer and at sea level are characteristically tropical. Warm rains brought inland by the trade winds periodically drench the northeast slopes of the volcanoes but leave the leeward sides and high altitudes relatively dry. The temperature and rainfall patterns, plus occasional tropical storms from the south, have led to the development of diverse ecosystems, each composed of a complex group of interacting species.

Hawai'i's native plants and animals are an odd mixture whose ancestors have drifted in over millions of years from all points of the compass in a series of rare introductions that occurred by means of natural long-distance dispersal. Since humans arrived, and especially since the advent of cargo ships and airplanes, thousands of species have been accidentally or intentionally introduced. Some continental species have spread rapidly, unbalancing native ecosystems and crowding out native species. A prominent feature of native plants and birds is their conspicuous lack of adaptations enabling them to resist being eaten or captured. Native plants have few thistlelike spines, distasteful leaves, or other protective devices.

The mixture of native and introduced forms poses

puzzles for the naturalist: Which of the plants and animals seen today were recently introduced by humans, and which predate human arrival in the Islands? Precise tracing of the ancestry of living forms is now possible with new biological techniques using chromosomes and DNA molecules. Most of the more ancient natural introductions can be traced back through intermediates to forms that arrived when Kaua'i, or its severely eroded, northern neighbor Necker, were much higher islands with a broader diversity of environments that presumably supported greater biological richness. As each island has arisen southeast of an older one, descendants of the early founders from the continents have themselves put out colonists that have crossed the interisland channels separating them from the newer territory.

Genetic analysis of the silverswords, for example, illustrates well a common evolutionary pattern in Hawai'i. All 36 species of this plant group (the subfamily Madiinae of the Asteraceae) are so similar in the DNA of their chromosomes and chloroplasts (light-collecting organelles) that it is hard to escape the hypothesis that all evolved from a single founder population. Despite their genetic relatedness, the silverswords exhibit an impressive array of growth forms—from rosette shrubs and compact cushion plants to sprawling or erect shrubs, perennial vines, and large, woody trees. This is an example of adaptive radiation: over time, genetic recombination and natural selection have produced different forms to match different environments.

The magnificent silversword in Haleakalā Crater, Maui. The silversword has evolved into a form that allows it to prosper in the harsh alpine desert of Haleakalā. [B. Tipper]

Plants of the genus *Dubautia* have radiated into a wide range of growth forms. *D. reticulata* (top) is a large, woody tree occurring in wet forests, while *D. scabra* (bottom) is a sprawling shrub often seen on lava flows on Kīlauea, Hawai'i. [G. Carr]

Past studies to pin down the possible identity of the silverswords' ancestor had uncovered a similarity between silverswords and certain California tarweeds, small sunflower-like plants. Chloroplast-DNA studies have now confirmed this link, pinpointing an existing species of tarweed in the mountains of California that closely resembles the silverswords' probable ancestor, as inferred from its Hawaiian descendants. Likewise, the cholorplast-DNA of the very numerous and diverse lobelia-like plants of Hawai'i indicates they may also be descended from a single ancestor.

Biologists also use the accumulated differences in the DNA between island and continental forms to estimate the time since the founders arrived. Likewise, the extent of divergence between different island forms is the basis for estimates of the span of time for the group's sojourn in the Islands. These methods utilize what biologists call the "DNA clock." Calculations show the silversword founders arrived at least 6 million years ago, and the lobeliad founders about 10 million years ago. Both perhaps first colonized an island older than Kaua'i, such as Necker, which in its current eroded state is inhabited by neither silverswords nor lobeliads.

Similar evolutionary stories are found among Hawai'i's pomace or vinegar flies. These belong to two genera, *Drosophila* and *Scaptomyza*. Researchers have identified about 350 species of *Drosophila* flies; many more have not yet been scientifically described. The focus of considerable genetic research, these insect species appear to have descended from one or possibly two ancestors introduced at least 10 million years ago. The nearest living relatives appear to be in Asia.

About 100 species of *Drosophila* flies are quite large, with distinctive patterns of dark spots on their wings. These "picture-winged" flies have giant, banded

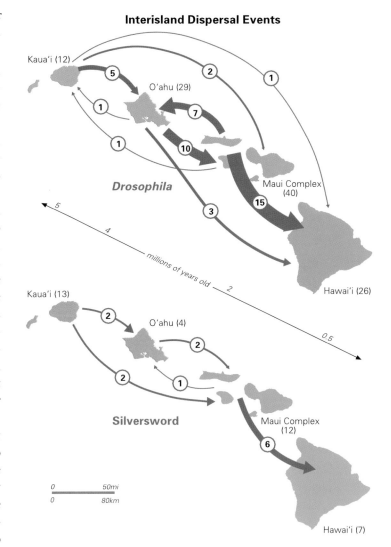

A geographical summary of the proposed founder events explaining the origin on each island of species of picture-winged *Drosophila* (above) and species in the silversword alliance (below). Numbers of species found on each island are given in parentheses.

The courtship behavior of native Hawaiian pomace flies is unique. The *Drosophila clavisetae* male uses visual, olfactory, tactile, and even acoustical stimuli to entice the female to mate with him. He curls his abdomen up over his head to waft his scent toward the female. [K. Kaneshiro]

Native Hawaiian "picture-winged" flies in combat stance. Two males of *Drosophila heteroneura* stand head-to-head, posturing in defense of a territory. [K. Kaneshiro]

chromosomes, the structure of which allows researchers to trace the history of migrations down the Island chain. Despite the fact that their population size was significantly reduced each time they colonized a younger volcano, the "picture-winged" *Drosophila* have retained substantial genetic variability, and thus natural selection has continually produced adaptations. Perhaps the most remarkable of these are inherited structures and behaviors that enhance male sexual behavior. These have arisen within each new drosophilid species. These varying sexual habits are not to be mistaken for adaptive radiation, which has occurred for other features, however. For instance, although most *Drosophila* breed on decaying twigs or leaves of different plants, 11 species have evolved a genetically determined parasitic habit in which they lay their eggs among the eggs of certain native spiders.

Large numbers of beetles, plant bugs, moths, and other insects have also evolved in the Islands. Many exhibit peculiar features as compared with continental forms. In dragonflies, for example, the larvae usually hatch from eggs laid in ponds, but in Hawai'i the larvae are found in rainwater held in the axils of the leaves of certain plants. Among the moths, a small cluster of "measuring-worm" species (Geometridae) has evolved a carnivorous habit in the larval stage. Instead of eating leaves as continental species do, the caterpillars feed on insects they capture with specially adapted legs, snapping them up when the potential prey triggers sensitive hairs at the posterior end of the caterpillar's body. Plant bugs of the family Miridae show extensive speciation in which each species is adapted to feed on a particular species of plant.

Among the land birds, the family of finches known as "honeycreepers" reveals patterns remarkably similar to the silverswords, lobelias, and drosophilids. This group of birds also probably traces its ancestry to a single colonizing event. Honeycreepers are basically similar in their genetics, but their radiation into diverse environments has entailed genetically determined adaptations such as bill forms specialized for different modes of feeding. Unlike the other cases discussed above, a few species of honeycreepers still occur in the eroded leeward islands.

Conventional wisdom has held that genetic variability is low in island life forms because the repeated reductions in population sizes each time they occupy newly emerging islands should cause a loss of genetic variability by chance. Yet the extraordinary capacity for evolutionary change in many island life forms seems to belie this idea. Genetic studies of populations have shown various island lineages retain a surprising amount of genetic variation. Clarifying this curious situation poses a challenge for future research.

HAMPTON L. CARSON

MARINE ECOSYSTEMS

Diverse marine ecosystems are found in Hawaiian waters, occurring to depths of 16,500 feet (5,000 m) and extending inland from the coasts to include marine ponds. Native species dominate all but two of the marine ecosystems described here. Several factors control the variety, distribution, and abundance of marine life.

Geographic Isolation Hawai'i is situated far from continents and other major islands and reef systems. Many species that colonized other Pacific island groups never reached Hawai'i. Those that did sometimes evolved into new species that filled previously unoccupied ecological niches.

Subtropical Climate Situated at latitudes ranging from 19 to 28 degrees north, the Hawaiian archipelago straddles the tropic of Cancer, the imaginary dividing line between tropical and temperate climates. The combination of cooler winter seawater temperatures and exposure to destructive waves has created a naturally harsh, mostly subtropical marine environment inhabited by fewer species than reported in the equatorial and tropical western Pacific.

Storm Waves Hawai'i's midocean exposure permits storm waves from both the Arctic and Antarctica to reach the Islands unimpeded, giving rise to repeated cycles of beach erosion, reef damage, and disruption of marine ecosystems. Periodically storm surges and waves from tropical cyclones also cause significant disturbance to coastal and nearshore environments.

Island subsidence, earthquakes, tsunamis, and freshwater flooding and coastal discharges also affect marine ecosystems. For example, at present and during most of Hawai'i Island's past existence, subsidence has been too rapid to allow the growth of extensive offshore reefs. However, recent deep-sea exploration of the island's northwest flank has revealed a series of drowned coral reefs hundreds to thousands of meters below the shallow depths at which they had to have grown. These reefs probably formed during periods of glaciation, when the associated falling sea levels canceled out the effect of sea level "rise" resulting from island subsidence. Today, reefs and many other marine

ecosystems are poorly developed along many northern, and some southern, coasts of the main islands. In some locations this may be due in part to recent, human-caused pollution and coastal development.

Zonation

The distribution of marine plants and animals in more or less distinct zones is best portrayed along the slopes of three types of volcanic islands in Hawai'i: large, young volcanic islands, mature volcanic islands, and drowned volcanic islands (atolls and seamounts). The primary factors governing the zonation of marine ecosystems are the island's age, amount of reef growth, exposure to waves, depth (which controls light and temperature), geographic orientation (which determines the degree of exposure to damaging waves), and latitude.

New volcanic islands are covered by numerous relatively recent lava flows and experience frequent earthquakes and rapid shoreline subsidence. Such islands support few, if any, living structural reefs. Instead, communities of algae, corals, and sand-dwelling species inhabit the island's underwater basaltic slopes. Anchialine ponds and tidepools lie along mostly rocky shorelines. Offshore islets are uncommon. Some beaches are present but are generally small and concentrated around bays and coves. Black, green, and pink sand beaches are found mostly off new volcanic islands, but white sand beaches are most common. Drowned reefs are sometimes found in deep offshore waters.

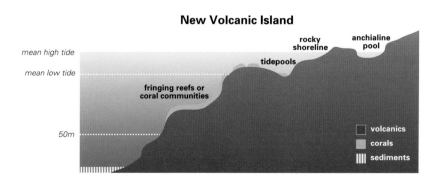

New Volcanic Island

111

Having undergone weathering and erosion for longer periods, *mature volcanic islands* typically have eroded slopes, broad, gently sloping coastal plains, numerous streams and estuaries, many white sandy beaches, abundant fringing reefs, and, occasionally, barrier reefs. Offshore islands of volcanic and carbonate (reef-associated) origins may be present, created by frequent cycles of erosion and accumulation of material. Subsidence on mature islands is relatively slow, allowing the outward growth of fringing and barrier reefs. Algae, coral, and sand-adapted biotic communities dominate reef surfaces. Lagoons within embayments or behind barrier reefs provide protected environments that permit the development of unique coral "patch" and "pinnacle" reefs. Rocky beaches are also present, especially along north and south coasts and where wave action and lack of reefs prevent sandy beaches from forming. The gentle slopes and shallow offshore waters of mature volcanic islands were conducive to the construction of Hawaiian fishponds, many of which still survive. While seagrasses (and mangroves introduced by humans) and coral reef flats are more common in the nearshore waters of mature islands than around younger islands, tidepools and anchialine ponds are comparatively less common.

Eventually all Hawaiian volcanoes erode and subside to the point that they disappear underwater, unless corals maintain sufficient growth along the island flanks to compensate for sinking and form an *atoll.* The atoll reef, which represents the coastal perimeter of a drowned volcanic island, encloses a lagoon, whose quiet, protected waters sometimes are connected to the open ocean by passes cut through the reef. One or more coral islets are normally found on the top of wider perimeter reefs of atolls. Freshwater flooding, streams, and estuaries typically are absent on atolls, although ponds and lakes of varying degrees of salinity may exist. Sometimes benches formed by wave action during higher or lower sea levels are present above or below the tidal zone, and reef flats are very common. Caves and terraces frequently exist along the steep submarine slopes of atolls. Guyots (sunken atolls that become flat-topped seamounts) and other seamounts that have never emerged above the sea's surface lie deep below the lighted zone of the ocean. Fisheries and precious corals may be concentrated near the tops of seamounts and guyots.

Evolution of Ecosystems

The oldest islands in the Hawaiian chain, Midway and Kure Atolls, are less than 28 million years old. Hawaiian marine ecosystems, however, have been evolving for 75–80 million years, as the Hawaiian hotspot created volcanic islands that were first rafted slowly northward across the ocean by movement of the Pacific Plate. The first truly Hawaiian marine ecosystems originated

An anchialine pool in Pueo Bay, Hawai'i. [M. Lee]

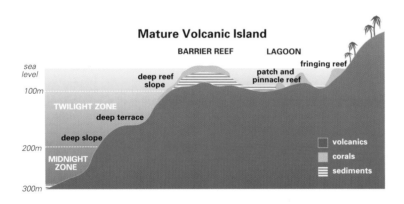

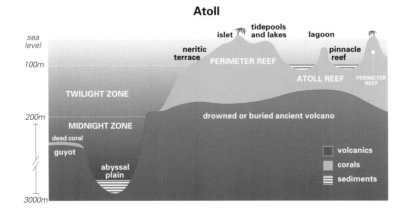

Marine tide pool off Kapoho, Hawai'i, showing luxuriant coral growth. [J. E. Maragos]

on the oldest islands, now seamounts sunken to great depths. As these ancient islands moved north, and later northwest, the spores of marine plants and the larvae of corals, fishes, and other marine animals drifted away to colonize younger islands. This process fostered the evolution of marine species over millions of years. As a result many marine species, including almost 25 percent of reef corals and fishes, are endemic, or found nowhere else. Although this is much lower than rates of endemism for many of Hawai'i's terrestrial plant and animal groups (1–2 species per genus in marine organisms and typically over 10 species per genus in terrestrial organisms), endemism (found only at the species level) ranks as the highest reported among marine ecosystems from any tropical archipelago in the Pacific and perhaps in the world.

Black sand beach off Wai'ānapanapa, Maui, in 1969. [J. E. Maragos]

CLASSIFICATION OF MARINE ECOSYSTEMS

Marine Pools (Tidepools and Anchialine Ponds)

DISTRIBUTION Found along rocky coasts up to several hundred meters inland. The porous rock walls of anchialine ponds allow them to maintain subsurface connections with the sea. Tidepools, which flood during rising tides, are continuous with the open ocean at the surface.

ENVIRONMENTAL CONDITIONS/SUBSTRATES Lava rock depressions subsiding to sea level become flooded with seawater, creating anchialine pools. Further subsidence and wave action break down surface barriers, forming tidepools. All pools show marine salinities except shallow surface layers, which may be brackish due to freshwater infiltration.

BIOTA Plants: marine algae (seaweeds), cyanobacteria (blue-green algae); where sediments accumulate along pond edges, widgeon grass (*Ruppia maritima*), rushes (*Juncus* species), or pickleweed (*Batis maritima*) may become established. Anchialine pond animals: shrimp (*Metabetaeus lohena* and *Halocaridina rubra*), eels (*Gymnothorax*), mullets (*Mugil*), other crustaceans and mollusks. A variety of reef animals and plants occupy tidepools.

THREATS Filling, pollution, soil erosion, sewage infiltration, alien species, and physical modification threaten anchialine ponds and resident species of shrimp and fish, some of which may be rare or endemic.

CULTURAL SIGNIFICANCE Used by Hawaiians for raising and harvesting fish and shrimp.

Sandy Beaches

DISTRIBUTION Island shorelines; most common on older islands and atolls.

ENVIRONMENTAL CONDITIONS/SUBSTRATES Hawaiian beaches come in a variety of colors. Pink sand beaches are derived from the breakdown of iron-rich coastal cinder cones; green sand beaches from olivine crystals eroded from lava; black sand

The *Metabetaeus* shrimp, a native inhabitant of anchialine pools in Hawai'i. [M. Lee]

A pink cinder beach off Hāna, Maui. [J. E. Maragos]

beaches from tiny tephra particles formed when molten lava flows into the sea; and white sand primarily from the breakdown of coralline algae and corals. Wave action and biological and chemical erosion determine composition and longevity of beaches. Offshore sand reservoirs connected to beaches often undergo seasonal cycles of erosion, accretion, and alongshore drift.

BIOTA Plants: beach morning glory (*Ipomoea*), beach heliotrope (*Tournefortia*), milo (*Thespesia*), and hau (*Hibiscus*). Animals: ghost crabs (*Ocypode*), mitre and auger shells (*Terebra*), clams, seabirds; threatened green sea turtle (*Chelonia mydas*), endangered monk seal (*Monachus schauinslandi*), and endangered hawksbill sea turtle (*Eretmochelys imbricata*) use beaches for resting and nesting.

THREATS Sand mining, harbor and channel construction, degradation by trash, beach erosion caused by seawalls and other shoreline fortifications,

CULTURAL SIGNIFICANCE Hawaiians used beaches for cemeteries, canoe launch sites, and recreational, subsistence, and ceremonial purposes. Beach sand and waterworn pebbles were used in the floors of Hawaiian houses.

A rocky beach and cliff off Kīlauea Point, Kaua'i.
[J. E. Maragos]

Rocky Beaches

DISTRIBUTION Shorelines of all islands where sand and other sediments are absent due to constant wave action, currents, steep submarine slopes, and lack of offshore sand reservoirs.

ENVIRONMENTAL CONDITIONS/SUBSTRATE Mostly consolidated basalts, but sometimes consolidated limestones (cemented beach rock or raised coral reefs).

BIOTA Plants: sea lettuce (*Ulva*), sargasso or *kala* (*Sargassum*), coralline red algae (*Hydrolithon*), red fleshy algae (*Melanamansia, Pterocladiella, Jania*), brown algae (*Padina, Turbinaria, Dictyota*), and fleshy green algae (*Neomeris, Halimeda,* and *Caulerpa*). Animals: keyhole limpet, or 'opihi (*Cellana*), periwinkles, littorine snails (*Littorina, Nerita*), rock crabs, or 'a'ama (*Metapograpsus*), gastropods (*Drupa, Morula, Cypraea, Strombus*), and rock urchin (*Colobocentrotus atratus*); adjacent offshore waters are possible feeding areas for the threatened green turtle.

THREATS Coastal, urban, resort, and harbor development.

CULTURAL SIGNIFICANCE Rocky beaches often were important fishing grounds and canoe-launching sites for Hawaiians.

Estuaries

DISTRIBUTION Places where fresh and marine waters meet at the coastline; three types in Hawai'i: large embayment at Pearl Harbor, O'ahu; stream mouths on all major islands; and locations where streams are absent, but coastal groundwater dis-

An aerial view of the Waiākea estuary, Hilo, Hawai'i.
[J. Juvik]

charges abundantly offshore, such as around Hawai'i Island.

ENVIRONMENTAL CONDITIONS/SUBSTRATES Freshwater flowing into the ocean floats on the sea surface because of its lower salt content and density. Eventual mixing of the waters and high levels of freshwater nutrients stimulate productivity, while tidal currents transport seawater in and out of estuaries. Floors of embayments and stream-mouth estuaries are sediment covered; groundwater estuaries are sometimes rocky.

BIOTA Plants: Marshes and mudflats dominated by introduced pickleweed (*Batis maritima*); *Panicum purpurascens* and *Schoenoplectus* species; some seaweeds (*Ulva, Enteromorpha*). Animals: crabs, shrimps, mollusks, mullets (*Mugil*), endemic flagtails, *āholehole* (*Kuhlia sandwichensis*), anchovies, small jacks, barracudas, eels; shorebirds, waterbirds, including endangered Hawaiian stilt, or *āe'o* (*Himantopus mexicanus knudseni*); endangered Hawaiian duck, or *koloa* (*Anas wyvilliana*), and Hawaiian coot (*Fulica americana alai*) are occasional visitors.

THREATS Modifications for harbors and settlements; pollution by sewage and industrial discharges.

CULTURAL SIGNIFICANCE Sources of freshwater and fish for Hawaiian communities in the past.

Fishponds and Harbors

DISTRIBUTION Fishponds still exist along many island shorelines; harbors are generally constructed in areas sheltered from heavy waves.

ENVIRONMENTAL CONDITIONS/SUBSTRATES Fishponds were typically built in embayments (naturally protected inlets), on reef flats, or over subma-

Sea Turtles

The green turtle (*Chelonia mydas*), called *honu* in Hawaiian, can frequently be seen feeding on marine plants in shallow coastal waters throughout the Islands. Following decades of overexploitation, the population has shown encouraging signs of recovery after receiving protection in 1978 under the U.S. Endangered Species Act. Elsewhere in the Pacific and worldwide, most green turtles continue to be threatened with extinction from excessive subsistence and commercial hunting.

Adult green turtles migrate every two to five years across hundreds of miles of open ocean to breed at French Frigate Shoals in the Northwestern Hawaiian Islands. During the summer months females come ashore at night on the sandy islets, where they excavate nests and deposit several clutches of a hundred or more eggs. During the day males and females bask peacefully in the sun along the shore.

After the eggs incubate for about 2 months, the hatchlings emerge and swim far out to sea, where they drift in the currents and feed on small invertebrates. When they have grown to dinner-plate size, juvenile turtles take up residence in the nearshore waters of all the Hawaiian Islands, grazing on algae and seagrass and

sleeping on the bottom under protective ledges. Green turtles are vegetarians that grow slowly and take more than two decades to reach an adult breeding size of 200 pounds (90 kg) or more.

Although the population has clearly increased, green turtles residing at certain sites in Hawai'i continue to be threatened by an often-fatal disease that forms fibrous growths on the eyes, neck, flippers, and mouth. A mysterious virus that affects only turtles is believed to be the cause, and research is underway to find a means to prevent or control the disease.

The hawksbill turtle (*Eretmochelys imbricata*) or *honu'ea,* also native to Hawai'i, is critically endangered, and very few of these turtles remain. They nest on several small, unprotected beaches on Hawai'i Island, Maui, Moloka'i, and O'ahu. Recent satellite tracking of hawksbills suggests that adults nesting at Kamehame in the Ka'ū District of Hawai'i Island live on the opposite side of the island along the rugged Hamākua coast. Hawksbills feed on sponges, which are toxic to most animals, and hawksbill meat can be poisonous to humans.

The leatherback turtle (*Dermochelys coriacea*) normally does not nest in Hawai'i but regularly visits offshore waters, probably from breeding sites in Mexico, Costa Rica, and Malaysia. The world's largest turtles, leatherbacks can weigh up to 2,000 pounds (900 kg).

Sea turtles have been a traditional part of Hawaiian and other Pacific cultures for millennia. Legend relates that a mystical turtle named Kauila, who could transform herself into a human and watch over children as they played, lived at Punalu'u Bay on Hawai'i Island. The people of the region are said to have loved Kauila. Even today, some people of Hawaiian heritage revere sea turtles as their *'aumakua,* or personal deity.

Turtle watching in Hawai'i has become an increasingly popular activity for both visitors and residents. Tour boat operators frequently promote sea turtles as a major underwater attraction, and enthusiasts spot turtles from high-rise hotels along Waikīkī and elsewhere, thereby assisting researchers.

GEORGE H. BALAZS

Honokōhau Small Boat Harbor, Kona Coast, Hawai'i, as it appeared in 1978. [J. E. Maragos]

Stands of the red mangrove *Rhizophora mangle,* south Moloka'i. [J. E. Maragos]

The historic Hawaiian fishpond, Kaloko'eli, Moloka'i. [J. E. Maragos]

rine springs. Fish were trapped and tidal flows replenished nutrients through gates in fishpond walls. Sands, clays, silts, and/or muds cover the floors of fishponds and harbors.

BIOTA Plants: rock-dwelling algae; *limu* (seaweeds) were cultivated in some fishponds; *Halophila* seagrass. Animals raised in fishponds: mullet, *moi,* anchovies, crabs, shrimps, clams, oysters; seabirds, shorebirds, and waterbirds (including endangered stilt, coot, gallinule, and duck) inhabit or feed in embayments and fishponds. Harbors attract fish, sediment-adapted biota, and fouling organisms.

THREATS Harbor construction, housing development, and natural catastrophes have destroyed many fishponds, resulting in significant loss of habitat for endemic waterbirds. Erosion, sewage contamination, and the spread of nonnative mangroves degrade fishponds and embayments; harbors often cause shoreline erosion and destroy coral reefs; oil and litter pollute harbors.

CULTURAL SIGNIFICANCE Fishponds were invaluable to Hawaiians for their readily available food sources.

Mangroves

DISTRIBUTION Intentionally introduced to south Moloka'i and Kāne'ohe Bay, O'ahu, in the early 1900s, mangroves have since spread to muddy reef flats and estuarine waters around most of the major islands and to some rocky coastal areas of Hawai'i Island.

ENVIRONMENTAL CONDITIONS/SUBSTRATES Elongate mangrove seeds float in seawater, then, after drifting into brackish water, sink and root in muds and sands of inner reef flats, fishponds, and stream mouths; tidal flows and leaf fall maintain mangrove tree productivity, as roots and lower trunks are submerged at high tide.

BIOTA Plants: mangrove trees (*Rhizophora mangle* and *Bruguiera gymnorhiza*); animals: mangrove or Samoan, crab (*Scylla serrata*) is heavily harvested; oysters, clams, and other crabs attach to mangrove roots; native black-crowned night heron, cattle egret, and endangered Hawaiian stilt nest and feed among the mangroves. Many animals that typically inhabit native mangroves elsewhere have not been introduced to Hawai'i.

THREATS Mangroves are often cut down or trimmed; mangroves may displace native species such as marine algae and seagrasses that occupy the same habitats.

CULTURAL SIGNIFICANCE No established cultural importance for these relative newcomers, but eventually they may prove useful for mariculture and fisheries.

Seagrasses

DISTRIBUTION Found close to shore below the tidal zone. Seagrass is common off the inner reef flats of south Moloka'i, 'Anini (Kaua'i), and a few other locations, but is generally not widespread.

ENVIRONMENTAL CONDITIONS/SUBSTRATE Typically seagrasses are completely submerged on shallow reef flats, regardless of tidal stage, surviving

The seagrass *Halophila hawaiiana* inhabiting Kūpeke Fishpond, south Moloka'i. [J. E. Maragos]

Shallow benthic marine community dominated by living stony corals off Moloka'i. [J. E. Maragos]

where wave action is not severe, such as the inner reaches of broad reef flats. Seagrasses root in soft sands and muds, either carbonate or terrigenous.

BIOTA Plants: a single endemic seagrass species, *Halophila hawaiiana* (small, often mistaken for green seaweeds) and wigeon grass (*Ruppia maritima*). Animals: sea cucumbers (*Holothuria*), sand-dwelling gastropods, clams, crabs, shrimps, flagtails (*Kuhlia*), mullets (*Mugil*), and rudderfish (*Kyphosus*).

THREATS Heavy beach and reef use (wading, trampling, outboard motors), seawall construction, and soil erosion leading to discharge of sediments into nearshore coastal waters.

CULTURAL SIGNIFICANCE None that can be identified, although seagrasses commonly grow in coastal fishponds.

Shallow Benthic Communities

DISTRIBUTION Found in depths to 160 feet (50 m) or more.

ENVIRONMENTAL CONDITIONS/SUBSTRATES Within the lighted zone of the ocean, all substrates, including basalts, consolidated limestones (reef carbonates, beach rock), and sediments (sands, gravels, pebbles, etc.) support benthic communities. Light penetration, temperature, wave action, availability of hard or soft substrates, and movement and accumulation of sediments affect the nature and distribution of benthic communities.

BIOTA Common communities: fleshy algae include brown algae *Sargassum, Turbinaria, Dictyota, Padina,* and *Dictyopteris;* green algae *Halimeda, Dictyosphaeria, Cladophora, Caulerpa,* and *Ulva;* red algae *Pterocladiella, Melanamansia, Asparagopsis,* and *Laurencia;* coralline algal communities include *Porolithon* species; coral communities include *Cyphastrea, Fungia, Psammocora, Porites, Pocillopora, Montipora, Pavona,* and *Leptastrea;* sand-dwelling communities include cone shells (*Conus*), tritons (*Charonia*), mitres and augers, pen shells (*Pinna*), garden eels. Reef and

Stands of the native finger coral, *Porites compressa,* south Moloka'i. [J. E. Maragos]

shore animals: parrotfishes, wrasses, damselfishes, surgeonfishes and other reef fishes, jacks; sea urchins, sea cucumbers; endangered Hawaiian monk seal feeds on offshore communities, mostly in the Northwestern Hawaiian Islands.

THREATS Sewage discharges, coastal construction, soil erosion and runoff, overfishing.

CULTURAL SIGNIFICANCE Benthic plants and animals provided and continue to provide food for traditional Hawaiian subsistence.

Fringing Reefs

DISTRIBUTION These reefs grow, terracelike, off island shores, with their outer slopes extending to depths of about 165 feet (50 m). Poorly developed or absent among small, volcanic northwestern islands and larger islands where shorelines are rapidly subsiding or exposed to heavy waves. Hawai'i's longest continuous fringing reef (30 miles [50 km] long) lies off south Moloka'i.

ENVIRONMENTAL CONDITIONS/SUBSTRATES Calcium carbonate skeletons and sediments produced by corals and coralline algae comprise bulk of reefs. Sand deposits and seaweeds common on shal-

Aerial view of the east end of the fringing reef off south
Moloka'i, the longest reef in the Hawaiian Islands.
[J. E. Maragos]

low inner reef flats; living corals and coralline algae
predominate at reef's outer edge; deeper slopes are
mostly dominated by live corals or old reef rock.
Beneath living outer layer of reef organisms, remains
of previous reef builders are compacted and
cemented into a hard, limestone, wave-resistant
structure, which in places may be cut through by
channels.
BIOTA Same as previous section on benthic communities. Threatened green sea turtle forages on reef
flats; endangered hawksbill turtle feeds where
sponges are common.
THREATS Coastal construction, erosion, sewage discharges, overharvesting of fish, freshwater flooding.
CULTURAL IMPORTANCE Fishpond development
and intensive fishing occurred on reef flats.

Barrier Reefs and Lagoons
DISTRIBUTION Two barrier reefs exist in Hawai'i:
Kāne'ohe Bay (O'ahu) and Mānā (off northwest
Kaua'i) to depths of about 165 feet (50 m).
ENVIRONMENTAL CONDITIONS/SUBSTRATES
Between barrier reefs and shores lie deep lagoons,
where waters are relatively calm, as the reef face

forms a natural breakwater. Lagoon and ocean waters
are connected by passes cut through the reefs. Barrier reefs consist of consolidated carbonate rock;
lagoon floors are covered with sediments varying
from gravel to muds. Kāne'ohe Bay reef grew on a
shallow platform as sea level rose at the end of the
last ice age, about 8,000–11,000 years ago. Pinnacle and patch reefs occur within the lagoons, and
fringing reefs line the lagoon shoreline of Kāne'ohe
Bay. Mānā reef is submerged 50 feet (15 m) and the
lagoon floor lies 100 feet (30 m) below sea level.
BIOTA Same as benthic communities. Threatened
green sea turtle and endangered hawksbill turtle
feed on barrier reefs and in lagoons.
THREATS Eutrophication, coastal construction, sedimentation, flooding, intensive recreational use,
heavy wave action.
CULTURAL SIGNIFICANCE Barrier reefs were
important fishing grounds for Hawaiians.

Atolls
DISTRIBUTION Six true atolls (Kure, Midway, Pearl
and Hermes, Lisianski, French Frigate Shoals, Maro
Reef) exist in the Northwestern Hawaiian Islands.
Laysan is probably a slightly raised atoll.
ENVIRONMENTAL CONDITIONS/SUBSTRATES
Atolls encompass at least one vegetated island, a
shallow, protected lagoon, and deep ocean waters
outside reefs. Wave-driven currents wash over reefs,
and strong tidal currents flow through reef passes.
Atoll surfaces to depths of about 3,300 feet (1,000
m) consist of reef carbonates; below this, basaltic
rock of the subsided volcano forms an atoll's foundation. Lagoon floors and inner reef flats covered
with fine sands or muds. Sandy beaches common on
lagoon sides of atoll islands, beaches of rubble and
rock typical on seaward sides. Steep, leeward ocean-
facing, upper reef slopes usually hard surfaced; shallow wave terraces on windward-facing slopes; sediments accumulate on terraces at greater depths.
BIOTA Beach vegetation on islands; seaweeds on shal-

The submerged Mānā barrier reef off Kaua'i's northwest
Nā Pali coast, showing the rare table coral *Acropora cytherea.*
[N. Konstantinou]

Laysan Island, Northwestern Hawaiian Islands, and its central
marine lake. [G. H. Balazs]

low slopes and reef flats. Corals, including rare species of *Acropora,* abundant in lagoons and on seaward reef slopes; invertebrates at greater depths; large variety of fishes. Breeding populations of endangered Hawaiian monk seal and threatened green turtle concentrated at French Frigate Shoals and nearby atolls. Numerous seabirds, including Laysan finch, rare species of albatross, and other nesting seabirds. Atoll fishes are similar to those found on other Hawaiian reefs.

THREATS Overfishing, human disturbance of seabirds and endangered species, dredge-and-fill operations for channels, docks, and airfields, bird collisions with radio antennas and moving aircraft.

Offshore Deep Reefs ("Twilight Zone")

DISTRIBUTION Found between depths of 165 and 660 feet (50–200 m), encircling all of the Hawaiian Islands.

ENVIRONMENTAL CONDITIONS/SUBSTRATES Although light penetrates to these depths, it is normally insufficient for much photosynthesis. The water column above these habitats is the neritic (shallow coastal) zone. Substrates vary from rocky bottom, especially on outcrops and steep slopes, to sediment deposits.

BIOTA Plants: depth-adapted algae are common. Animals: deep-dwelling fishes, corals (*Cycloseris, Leptoseris, Coscinaraea*), other invertebrates, and black corals, concentrated below normal scuba-diving depths. Endangered monk seal and threatened sea turtle forage in these habitats.

THREATS Black corals, although not listed as threatened or endangered species, are severely depleted due to excessive collection. Offshore deep ocean sewage discharges and postwar munitions dumping have degraded these habitats.

CULTURAL SIGNIFICANCE Hawaiians fished by handline and dropline for bottom fish, including snappers.

Offshore Islands

DISTRIBUTION Present around main islands; more abundant around larger and older islands, rare off Hawai‘i Island.

ENVIRONMENTAL CONDITIONS/SUBSTRATES Volcanic islets were probably connected to main islands before being eroded and/or subsiding; lime-

Marine life in an atoll lagoon. [D. R. and T. L. Schrichte]

Offshore basalt island, or sea stack (‘Ōkala Rock), northeast coast of Moloka‘i. [J. E. Maragos]

stone islets are lithified dunes or relict reefs. Typically, strong currents run in the open expanses of water separating main islands and islets. Islets generally have rocky beaches, seacliffs, and some pocket beaches of white sand; rocky submarine slopes, with occasional caves, and covered with live coral and coralline algae; sand substrates typically offshore from sandy beaches.

BIOTA Submerged species comparable to those of benthic communities, fringing reefs, and barrier reefs (all described above). Most islets uninhabited by humans but support native (some endangered) and sometimes alien plants and animals (such as rabbits and goats). Islets are important seabird rookeries; some may be used for hauling out by sea turtles and monk seals. Beach vegetation grows on islet shorelines.

THREATS Overuse and littering by picnickers and fishermen; harassment of seabirds; trampling and cutting of rare plants.

CULTURAL SIGNIFICANCE Most offshore islets retain cultural significance to Hawaiians.

Neritic Water

DISTRIBUTION Neritic zone consists of open ocean waters to depths of 660 feet (200 m) directly associated with coasts surrounding all of the Hawaiian Islands

ENVIRONMENTAL CONDITIONS/SUBSTRATES Neritic zone waters receive discharges and effluents from the land. Swells, waves, and surf are common. No substrates exist, as this habitat consists solely of water.

BIOTA Plants: phytoplankton and floating seaweeds (*Sargassum* and others). Animals: zooplankton, fish, marine mammals (seals, dolphins, porpoises, whales), marine turtles, and seabirds. Endangered hawksbill turtle, Hawaiian monk seal, humpback whale, and threatened green turtle all forage, rest, or otherwise use neritic waters around the Hawaiian Islands.

THREATS Overfishing, harassment of endangered and threatened species, and water pollution from sedimentation, soil runoff, and sewage discharges.

Pelagic Ocean and Deep Ocean Floor

DISTRIBUTION These ecosystems occur in the deep open waters beyond the neritic zone around all the islands and on and above the seafloor at depths greater than 660 feet (200 m, "midnight" zone).

ENVIRONMENTAL CONDITIONS/SUBSTRATES Pelagic ocean is exposed to swells, currents, and winds from all directions, generally beyond the sheltering effects of islands; deep currents and eddies also pass through this zone. Waters are usually pristine. Sunlight is absent on deep seafloor. Basalt and carbonate rock substrates are common on slopes, sediments prevalent on flatter surfaces.

BIOTA Phytoplankton are only common plants in pelagic zone; living plants rare or absent on deep seafloor. Pelagic animals: zooplankton, fishes, squids, sea turtles, marine mammals, including endangered humpback whale and monk seal; endangered seabirds (such as Newell's shearwater) may forage in neritic or pelagic waters. Deep seafloor supports many fish species, dark-adapted invertebrates, and rare, depleted precious corals, including gold coral and pink coral (*Corallium*).

THREATS Excessive fishing of migratory fish species and harvesting of precious corals; harassment and incidental catching of marine mammals and sea turtles during fishing operations.

JAMES E. MARAGOS

Marine Mammals Found in Hawaiian Waters

Minke whale	*Balaenoptera acutorostrata*
Bryde's whale	*Balaenoptera edeni*
Fin whale	*Balaenoptera physalus*
Humpback whale	*Megaptera novaeangliae*
Right whale	*Eubalaena glacialis*
Rough-toothed dolphin	*Steno bredanensis*
Spinner dolphin	*Stenella longirostris*
Bridled dolphin	*Stenella attenuata*
Striped dolphin	*Stenella coeruleoalba*
Risso's dolphin	*Grampus griseus*
Melon-headed whale	*Peponocephala electra*
Pygmy killer whale	*Feresa attenuata*
False killer whale	*Pseudora crassidens*
Shortfin pilot whale	*Globicephala electra*
Killer whale	*Orcinus orca*
Sperm whale	*Physeter macrocephalus*
Pygmy sperm whale	*Kogia breviceps*
Cuvier's beaked whale	*Ziphius cavirostris*

TERRESTRIAL ECOSYSTEMS

The Hawaiian Islands rival continents in their ecosystem richness. Unlike the sand and palm trees of popular vision, the tapestry of native vegetation in Hawai'i is in fact much more diverse. It includes not only coastal strand and tropical rain forests, but also dry woodlands, mesic forests, sparsely vegetated deserts, montane wet forests, bogs, and subalpine grasslands, among other vegetation types.

Climate, substrate, and elevation are important factors controlling the types of natural ecosystems that develop at different sites. The single most important factor influencing habitat conditions is the northeast trade winds. As they pass over the Islands the trades release moisture in clouds and precipitation on windward slopes and summits. Thus, while windward sides of the higher islands generally receive ample rainfall, lower islands and leeward slopes of high islands are almost invariably dry. The figure depicts two typical moisture settings, each governed by the height of the island.

Classification of Hawaiian Ecosystems An ecosystem is a community of organisms interacting with its physical environment. About 150 such communities have been identified in Hawai'i's aquatic, subterranean, and terrestrial environments. Aquatic ecosystems encompass streams, estuaries, freshwater lakes, and anchialine pools. Subterranean ecosystems include lava tubes, limestone caves, and other underground habitats. The classification of terrestrial ecosystems is based on the elevation at which they occur, moisture regime, and dominant life forms and vegetation structure. Five elevation zones are defined.

For each elevation zone three general moisture categories are recognized, based on prevailing soil moisture due to rainfall, fog, cloud drip, soil drainage, proximity to groundwater and exposure to wind and sun. *Dry* communities typically receive less than 50 inches (1,200 mm) of annual rainfall. *Mesic* (moist) communities receive 50–100 inches (1,200–2,500 mm) of annual rainfall. *Wet* communities get more than 100 inches (2,500 mm) of annual rainfall, and wet soil conditions typically prevail in all seasons.

A third level of ecosystem classification is based on dominant plant(s) and vegetative structure of the community. *Forests and woodlands* are dominated by trees; a forest canopy is dense (60–100 percent cover), while a woodland canopy is more open (10–60 percent cover). *Shrublands* are distinguished by multi-

Ecological Zone	Elevation Range	Key Environmental Factor
Alpine	>9,000 feet (~3,000 m)	Frost common
Subalpine	6,000–9,000 feet (~2,000–3,000 m)	Frost frequent
Montane	3,000–6,000 feet (~1,000–2,000 m)	Frost infrequent
Lowland	0–3,000 feet (0–1,000 m)	Frost-free
Coastal	0–100 feet (0–30 m)	Sea spray

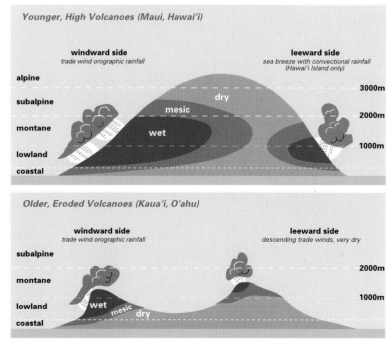

Generalized Moisture Conditions

121

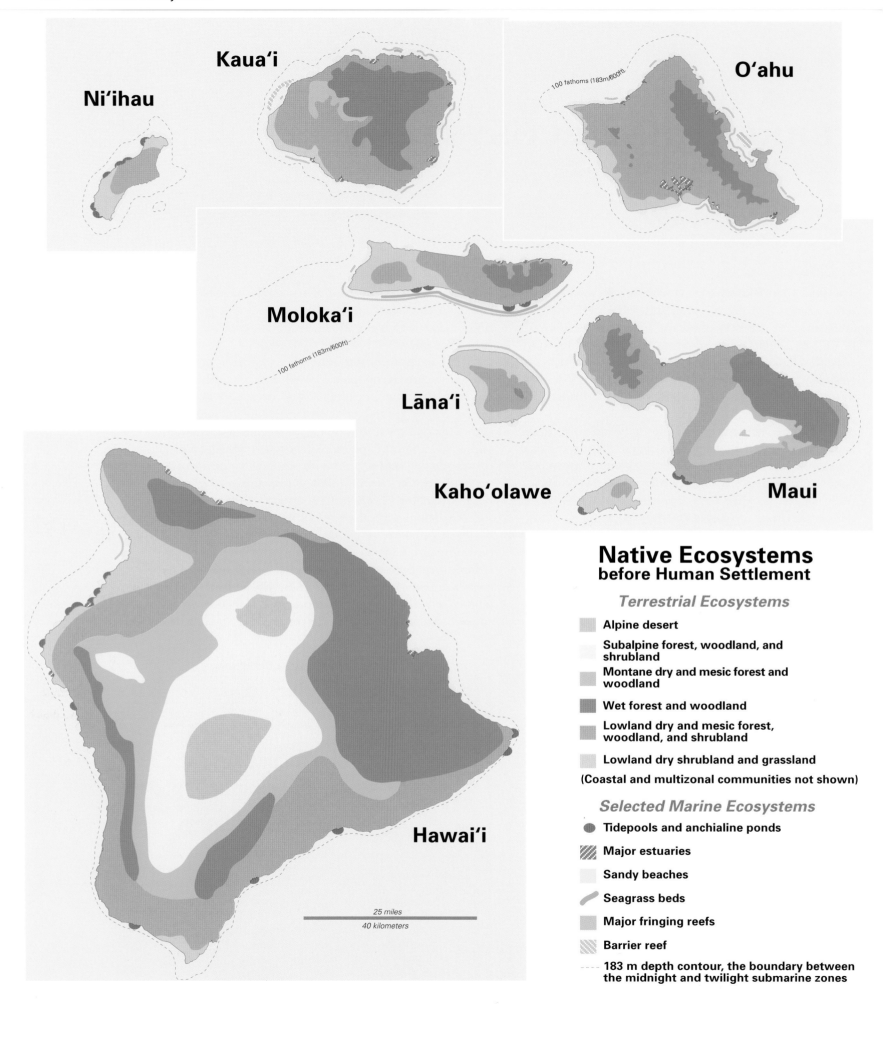

Native Ecosystems
before Human Settlement

Terrestrial Ecosystems

Alpine desert

Subalpine forest, woodland, and shrubland

Montane dry and mesic forest and woodland

Wet forest and woodland

Lowland dry and mesic forest, woodland, and shrubland

Lowland dry shrubland and grassland

(Coastal and multizonal communities not shown)

Selected Marine Ecosystems

Tidepools and anchialine ponds

Major estuaries

Sandy beaches

Seagrass beds

Major fringing reefs

Barrier reef

183 m depth contour, the boundary between the midnight and twilight submarine zones

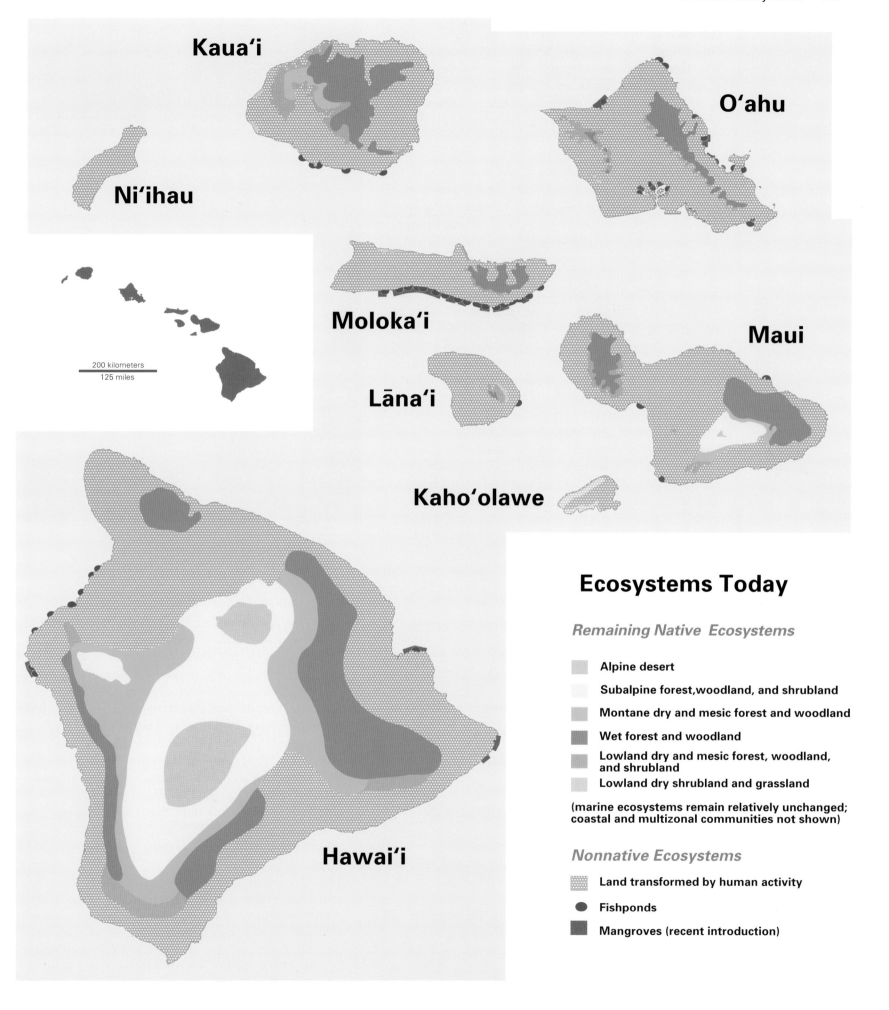

Kaua'i

Ni'ihau

O'ahu

200 kilometers
125 miles

Moloka'i

Lāna'i

Maui

Kaho'olawe

Hawai'i

Ecosystems Today

Remaining Native Ecosystems

Alpine desert

Subalpine forest, woodland, and shrubland

Montane dry and mesic forest and woodland

Wet forest and woodland

Lowland dry and mesic forest, woodland, and shrubland

Lowland dry shrubland and grassland

(marine ecosystems remain relatively unchanged; coastal and multizonal communities not shown)

Nonnative Ecosystems

Land transformed by human activity

Fishponds

Mangroves (recent introduction)

branched shrubs over 3.3 feet (1 m) in height. ***Dwarf shrublands*** have a canopy height of 3.3 feet (1 m) or less. ***Grasslands*** are covered by grasses or sedges, ***herblands*** are composed of small, nonwoody plants, and ***deserts*** are extremely arid (less than 20 inches [500 mm] of rainfall annually) and sparsely vegetated. Sometimes combinations of life forms characterize a community.

Terrestrial communities usually are named for their dominant or codominant species. For example, in a *Metrosideros* montane wet forest, *Metrosideros* (*'ōhi'a*) is dominant (the prevalent tree species in the canopy). The summary that follows highlights the diversity of habitats and species in Hawai'i's native ecosystems.

Prior to human presence in Hawai'i, native communities extended from coast to summit. In the past 1,500 years or so of human habitation, changes wrought by direct human land use, and also by the effects of hundreds of introduced plants and animals, have in many places completely displaced the original communities with human landscapes and alien-dominated ecosystems. Wet valley bottoms and mesic slopes became prime sites for agriculture and, later, preferred residential areas. Dry coasts became the focus of tourism, resort development, and the most recent expansions of island population. In nearly all elevation zones, alien animals such as feral pigs and goats damage native vegetation, and in their path alien plants take hold and spread, threatening what remains of native ecosystems.

Today, while there are still large areas of mostly intact montane and subalpine/alpine habitat remaining, most of the native coastal and lowland dry and mesic ecosystems have been lost. This makes the few small examples that remain all the more valuable to us as windows on the past and the last biological treasures to protect. It is no coincidence that the loss of these habitats is paralleled by extinction and/or endangerment of many of the plants and animals that once thrived there. The biological heritage of the Hawaiian Islands is by no means secure, and protection of species and habitat should be a high priority for private and government entities alike.

CLASSIFICATION OF TERRESTRIAL ECOSYSTEMS

Alpine Desert

DISTRIBUTION Summits of high volcanoes of Maui and Hawai'i Island above 9,000 feet (~3,000 m) elevation.

CLIMATE/SUBSTRATE Extremely dry, less than 20 inches (500 mm) annual precipitation; great daily variation in temperature with frost common at night. Substrates include recent and old, weathered lava flows on Mauna Loa; cinder and ash soils on Mauna Kea and Haleakalā.

Alpine Mauna Kea, Hawai'i, with Mauna Loa in the background. [J. Juvik]

BIOTA Vegetation: above treeline, sparsely vegetated with dwarf native shrubs, especially *pūkiawe* (*Styphelia tameiameiae*) and *'ōhelo* (*Vaccinium reticulatum*); on Maui, shrubland of *'āhinahina/na'ena'e* (*Argyroxiphium sandwicense/Dubautia menziesii*). Mountain summits are aeolian deserts populated by a few mosses, lichens, and grasses. Fauna: native spiders, centipedes, and insects, such as the Mauna Kea *wēkiu* bug (*Nysius wekiuicola*), which feeds on insects blown upslope by wind. Endangered species: dark-rumped petrel (*'ua'u, Pterodroma phaeopygia sandwichensis*), which nests in burrows at high elevation; Mauna Kea and Haleakalā silverswords (*'āhinahina, A. sandwicense* subsp. *sandwicense* and *macrocephalum*, respectively).

THREATS Nonnative ungulates, such as mouflon sheep and feral goats; alien insects, such as the Argentine ant; some nonnative plant species. Human impacts include construction of roads and buildings, particularly astronomical observatories.

CULTURAL SIGNIFICANCE Mauna Kea's summit is the traditional realm of Poli'ahu, the snow goddess, and the site of Keanakāko'i, an extensive

Unlike its flighted seed-eating relatives, the flightless *wēkiu* bug (*Nysius wekiuicola*) lives at the summit of Mauna Kea where it scavenges on dead and dying insects stunned by the cold. A different species lives on Mauna Loa. [W. P. Mull]

Treeline *māmane* (*Sophora*) forest, Mauna Kea, Hawai'i. [J. Juvik]

quarry used by Hawaiians for adze material. Haleakalā's alpine summit was the location where the demigod Māui snared the sun. Several *heiau* (religious sites) are present at alpine sites.

Subalpine Forest, Woodland, and Shrubland

DISTRIBUTION High islands of Maui and Hawai'i Island above 6,000 feet (~2,000 m) elevation.

CLIMATE/SUBSTRATE Relatively dry; annual precipitation 20–50 inches (500–1,300 mm); large diurnal variation in temperature; frequent frost. Substrates include lava flows (bare or with shallow soils) primarily on Mauna Loa and Hualālai; cinder and ash soils on Mauna Kea, Hualālai, and Haleakalā.

BIOTA Vegetation: dry forests and woodlands of *māmane* (*Sophora chrysophylla*) or *māmane* and *naio* (*Myoporum sandwicense*) on older cinder and *pāhoehoe* substrates; dry forests of 'ōhi'a (*Metrosideros polymorpha*) on young *pāhoehoe* and 'a'ā; dry shrublands of mixed native species, particularly *pūkiawe*, 'ōhelo, *na'ena'e* (*Dubautia* species), and 'a'ali'i (*Dodonaea viscosa*); dry shrublands of 'āweoweo (*Chenopodium oahuense*) on Mauna Kea; mesic dwarf shrublands of 'ōhelo and 'ama'u fern (*Sadleria cyatheoides*) on Maui; dry and mesic grasslands of endemic tussock grass *Deschampsia nubigena*; dry grasslands of lovegrass (*Eragrostis atropioides*) on Hawai'i Island. Fauna: native spiders and insects, such as native yellow-faced bees (*Hylaeus* species); many endemic forest birds, Hawai'i 'amakihi (*Hemignathus virens*) particularly abundant. Endangered species: a mint (*Stenogyne angustifolia*), a spleenwort found at lava-tube openings (*Asplenium fragile*), honeycreepers *palila* (*Loxioides bailleui*) and 'akiapōlā'au (*Hemignathus munroi*).

THREATS Alien species: ungulates (mouflon, feral goats, sheep, and pigs); mongoose, feral cats, rats; insects, such as Argentine ants and western yellow-

Māmane (*Sophora*) flower. [Nature Conservancy of Hawai'i]

jackets; grasses and plants such as mullein (*Verbascum thapsus*). Human impacts include cattle grazing, military training, fires, and roads.

CULTURAL SIGNIFICANCE The 'ua'u and other seabirds, which nested in subalpine areas, were hunted by Hawaiians for food. Rock shelters, habitation caves, *heiau*, and sections of cross-island trails are also present.

'I'iwi on native *Lobelia*. [R. A. Western]

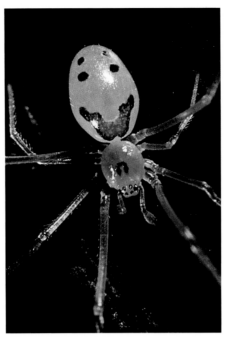

Happyface spider (*Theridion*), showing one of the many color patterns known among different species of this native spider. [W. Mull]

Kohala cloud forest, Hawai'i. [J. Juvik]

Montane Dry and Mesic Forest and Woodland

DISTRIBUTION Occurs on Hawai'i Island and Maui, primarily on leeward slopes, as transitional zone between subalpine forest/shrubland and wet forest or lowland dry vegetation; on leeward Kaua'i below wet forest.

CLIMATE/SUBSTRATE Annual precipitation less than 100 inches (2,500 mm), usually strongly seasonal (summer dry); temperate climate; frost uncommon. Substrates vary from lava flows with little soil to old, deep soils.

BIOTA Vegetation: closed- and open-canopy forests of 'ōhi'a, koa (*Acacia koa*), māmane, and sometimes 'ākoko (*Chamaesyce* species), mānele (*Sapindus saponaria*), and 'iliahi (*Santalum freycinetianum*); remnant woodland of diverse mesic tree species occurs on leeward Haleakalā; shrublands similar to those of subalpine zone; also, dry tussock grasslands of *Deschampsia nubigena*. Fauna: many native arthropods, including spiders, wood-boring beetles (*Plagithmysus* species), the Kamehameha butterfly (*Vanessa tameamea*), and Blackburn butterfly (*Udara blackburni*); common endemic forest birds include 'i'iwi (*Vestiaria coccinea*) and 'elepaio (*Chasiempis sandwichensis*). Endangered species: many tree species, such as a'e (*Zanthoxylum hawaiiense*) and ma'oloa (*Neraudia ovata*); forest birds, including Hawai'i 'ākepa (*Loxops coccineus*) and Hawai'i creeper (*Oreomystis mana*).

THREATS Alien species: ungulates (feral goats, sheep, pigs); rats; invasive, flammable grasses, such as fountain grass (*Pennisetum setaceum*) and kikuyu (*P. clandestinum*). Human impacts: severe disturbance by cattle grazing; logging, especially of *koa;* development associated with military training zones.

CULTURAL SIGNIFICANCE One of the traditional resource zones of *koa* trees for canoe construction, plants for medicinal practices, and birds for featherwork; not commonly visited except by *kāhuna* dedicated to these activites.

Wet Forest and Woodland

DISTRIBUTION Occurs on windward slopes of Maui and Hawai'i Island, summits of Kaua'i, O'ahu, Moloka'i, and Lāna'i and along a narrow band on leeward (Kona) slopes of Hawai'i Island; before human disturbance extended from sea level to 6,000 feet (~2,000 m) elevation.

CLIMATE/SUBSTRATE Annual rainfall 80– >400 inches (2,000– >10,000 mm), without regular dry periods; temperatures warm at low elevation, cool in montane areas. Substrates vary from very weathered soils on older islands to soils on more recent lava flows on younger islands. Ash-derived soils common on Hawai'i Island.

BIOTA Vegetation: closed-canopy forests of 'ōhi'a, sometimes with *koa* or 'ōlapa codominant; dense tree fern (*Cibotium* species) understory on Hawai'i Island; also, open-canopy forests or woodlands of '*ōhi'a* and *uluhe* (*Dicranopteris linearis*). Forests of *hala* (*Pandanus tectorius*) in coastal lowlands; lowland remnants of *loulu* (*Pritchardia* species) forest on O'ahu. Shrublands of '*ōhi'a* and ferns; also, '*ākala* (*Rubus hawaiensis*) shrublands. Rare bogs of mosses (*Racomitrium* species), sedges, grasses, and native shrubs. Fauna: primary habitat of most extant Hawaiian honeycreepers and other forest birds: '*apapane* (*Himatione sanguinea*) most common; great diversity of native invertebrates; Endangered species: more than 50 plant species, including lobelioids (genera *Clermontia* and *Cyanea*), *ha'iwale* (*Cyrtandra* species), endemic mints (*Phyllostegia* species), and ferns such as *kihi* (*Adenophorus* [*Oligadenus*] *periens*); birds include '*ō'ū* (*Psittirostra psittacea*), Maui parrotbill (*Pseudonestor xanthophrys*), and '*ākohekohe* (*Palmeria dolei*).

THREATS Feral pig, mongoose, feral cat; black and Polynesian rats; alien slugs; introduced plants, such as melastomes (*Clidemia hirta, Miconia calvescens*), banana poka (*Passiflora mollissima*), Hilo grass (*Paspalum conjugatum*), yellow raspberry (*Rubus ellipticus*), and strawberry guava (*Psidium cattleianum*). Clearing for agriculture and grazing, suburbanization.

CULTURAL SIGNIFICANCE Traditional realm of Hawaiian gods (*wao akua*); not for casual human visitation. Source of plants used for fiber ('*olonā,* *Touchardia latifolia*); weaving ('*ie'ie, Freycinetia arborea*), clothing (*kapa,* beaten-fiber cloth from *māmaki, Pipturus albidus*), medicines, and construction woods. Also was the primary zone for bird collection for featherwork.

Lowland Dry and Mesic Forest, Woodland, and Shrubland

DISTRIBUTION Lower leeward slopes of high islands; originally most extensive zone on mature low islands (for example, O'ahu).

Lowland dry forest. [S. Gon III]

CLIMATE/SUBSTRATE Annual rainfall 20–80 inches (500–2,000 mm); warm to hot, with seasonal drought. Soils less weathered than in wet forest; on Maui and Hawai'i these communities occur on old lava flows.

BIOTA Vegetation: plains, lower slopes, dry ridge tops, and cliffs support grasslands of *pili* (*Heteropogon contortus*) or *kāwelu* (*Eragrostis variabilis*). Dry or mesic shrublands of '*a'ali'i* (*Dodonaea viscosa*), '*ākia* (*Wikstroemia* species), *ko'oko'olau* (*Bidens* species), '*ūlei* (*Osteomeles anthyllidifolia*), and other shrubs. Dry forests of '*ōhi'a, koa, lama* (*Diospyros sandwicensis*), *wiliwili* (*Erythrina sandwicensis*), and rarer trees on ridges, rocky slopes, and leeward gulches. Mesic forests of '*ōhi'a, koa,* or *lama,* and rarely *olopua* (*Nestegis sandwicensis*) or *halapepe* (*Pleomele* species) occur in gulches, and on lower slopes and less-disturbed sites. More diverse mesic forests were once widespread, but are now rare. Fauna: native birds, particularly '*elepaio,* '*apapane* and '*amakihi;* native insects largely depleted. Endangered species: many trees and shrubs, including *koki'o* (*Kokia drynarioides*) and Kaua'i *hau kuahiwi* (*Hibiscadelphus distans*); Hawaiian goose (*nēnē, Branta sandvicensis*) on Hawai'i Island; Hawaiian hoary bat ('*ope'ape'a, Lasiurus cinereus semotus*) reaches its greatest abundance in this zone.

THREATS Feral goat, introduced game animals, cats, mongoose, rats; alien invertebrates, especially ants; invasive alien plants, particularly fire-adapted grasses and introduced shrubs such as Christmasberry (*Schinus terebinthifolius*); wildfire. Many lowland areas were burned and cleared in ancient Hawaiian times; today, cattle grazing, urbanization, and development continue.

CULTURAL SIGNIFICANCE Forested zone was the realm of Hawaiian gods, especially Kū. Sandalwood exploitation of the early 1800s occurred in lowland mesic forests. *Pili* grasslands, a source of thatch material, were maintained by fire; medicinal plants and hardwoods were gathered. Some mesic areas were converted from forest to dryland *kalo* (taro) and '*uala* (sweet potato) agriculture.

Lowland Dry Shrubland and Grassland

DISTRIBUTION Western Moloka'i, leeward Kaua'i, western plains of O'ahu, leeward lowlands of Hawai'i Island and Maui in mountain rain shadows, windward and leeward lowlands of Lāna'i, Kaho'olawe, and Ni'ihau.

CLIMATE/SUBSTRATE Very hot and dry; annual rainfall less than 20 inches (500 mm), seasonal. Dry, rocky soils, less weathered than those of wet areas.

BIOTA Vegetation: natural vegetation now rare, but *pili* grasslands and '*a'ali'i* shrublands, dry cliff vegetation, small patches of Hawaiian cotton (*ma'o, Gossypium tomentosum*), and dwarf shrublands of '*ākoko*

'Ene'ena (*Gnaphalium*) on coastal dunes at Mo'omomi, Moloka'i. [S. Gon III]

Beach *naupaka* (*Scaevola*). [Nature Conservancy of Hawai'i/ S. Gon III]

(*Chamaesyce* species) still exist. Open, dry woodlands of native trees once may have covered parts of this zone. Fauna: introduced animals such as rats, mongoose, and alien birds such as house finches (*Carpodacus mexicanus*) and Japanese white-eye (*Zosterops japonicus*) have largely replaced native animals. Endangered species: several, including remnant populations of the *ko'oloa'ula* (*Abutilon menziesii*), a showy, maroon-flowered shrub in the hibiscus family, and *Achyranthes splendens* var. *rotundata,* a shrub of the amaranth family.

THREATS Wildfire fueled by widespread alien grasses; alien shrubs also common. Feral goat, mongoose, and cats may be present. Much of this zone was altered in ancient Hawaiian times; cattle grazing, irrigated agriculture, and development, particularly resort hotel construction and expanding urbanization, are ongoing.

CULTURAL SIGNIFICANCE Except where springs allowed for habitation, this zone was sparsely occupied. The dry environment was ideal for burial and storage caves, as along leeward coasts of Hawai'i Island, Maui, O'ahu, and Kaua'i.

Coastal Communities

DISTRIBUTION Seashores of all Hawaiian islands.

CLIMATE/SUBSTRATE Warm; leeward shores dry with less than 30 inches (750 mm) annual rainfall; windward shores receive up to 120 inches (3,000 mm) annual rainfall; strong winds typical. Substrates include raised coral, basalt cliffs, sandy beaches, basalt and coral boulders, and littoral cones or tuff (consolidated ash).

BIOTA Vegetation: greatly influenced by proximity to ocean; many salt-tolerant species. Dwarf shrublands of *naupaka-kahakai* (*Scaevola sericea*) most common; those dominated by *'ilima* (*Sida fallax*), *naio* (*Myoporum sandwicense*), or *hinahina* (*Heliotropium anomalum*) uncommon. Simple communities of *'akulikuli* (*Sesuvium portulacastrum*), *'aki'aki* grass (*Sporobolus virgini-*

Nehe (*Lipochaeta*) on shrubland on coastal ash soil, Hawai'i. [S. Gon III]

cus), or the sedge *Fimbristylis cymosa* are widespread. Coastal forests of *hala* (*Pandanus tectorius*) in a few windward sites; wetlands of native sedges now rare. Fauna: threatened green sea turtle (*Chelonia mydas*) uses a few main island beaches and nests primarily in the Northwestern Hawaiian Islands. Shorebirds such as wandering tattler (*'ūlili, Heteroscelus incanus*) and ruddy turnstone (*'akekeke, Arenaria interpres*) common in winter. Several seabird species breed on offshore islets in good numbers; for example, wedge-tailed shearwaters (*Puffinus pacificus*) and sooty terns (*Sterna fuscata oahuensis*). Great frigatebird (*'iwa, Fregata minor palmerstoni*), brown booby (*'ā, Sula leucogaster plotus*), and brown and black noddies (*noio, Anous stolidus pileatus* and *A. minutus melanogenys*) can be seen along shores of main islands. Laysan finch (*Telespiza cantans*) is restricted to Laysan Island and has been introduced to Pearl and Hermes Reef. Also found are native, salt-tolerant coastal invertebrates, such as crickets (*Caconemobius* species). Endangered species: Hawaiian monk seal (*'īliohohoikauaua, Monachus schauinslandi*) now breeds only in North-western Hawaiian Islands; hawksbill turtle (*Eretmochelys imbricata*) very rare; black-necked stilt (*ae'o, Himantopus mexicanus knudseni*) and Hawaiian coot (*'alae ke'oke'o, Fulica americana alai*) depend on remaining wetlands. Plants include *'ōhai* (*Sesbania tomentosa*) and dwarf *naupaka* (*Scaevola coriacea*).

THREATS Most coastal areas, particularly where beaches occur, have been, and continue to be, used and altered by humans; many wetlands have been drained or modified; cattle grazing, development, and urbanization ongoing. Alien species: *kiawe* (*Prosopis pallida*); rats, cats, mongooses, and dogs, all of which harass nesting turtles, waterbirds, and seabirds.

CULTURAL SIGNIFICANCE Coastal areas, the most densely populated lands in ancient times, continue to be important in traditional Hawaiian culture, providing medicines, *lei* materials, and other resources.

Multizonal Communities

DISTRIBUTION These are examples of successional rather than climax communities, where the substrate age or conditions of disturbance influence vegetation development more than climate or elevation. Pioneer communities on lava flows occur only on Maui and Hawai'i Island; successional dwarf shrublands and herblands on steep sites on main islands; *'ōhi'a* dieback communities on O'ahu, Maui, and Hawai'i Island; fumarole communities only on Hawai'i.

CLIMATE/SUBSTRATE Climate variable, communities found across several elevational zones on leeward and windward sites. Recent lava flows, old weathered soils on steep slopes, variable soils in dieback areas.

BIOTA Vegetation: simple pioneer communities of *'ōhi'a,* native ferns, and lichens (especially *Stereocau-*

Kīlauea lava flow of 1790, Puna, Hawai'i. [J. Juvik]

lon vulcani) on young lava flows; *uluhe* (*Dicranopteris linearis*), with scattered *'ōhi'a* and shrubs on steep slopes; *'ōhi'a* dieback sites dominated by young *'ōhi'a* or *hāpu'u* (*Cibotium* species) where disruptive alien plants are absent; fumarole communities of native mosses, lichens, ferns, sedges, and heat-tolerant species. Fauna: native invertebrates of pioneer communities include lava flow crickets (*Caconemobius fori*) and wolf spiders (*Lycosa* species). Where fresh lava flows are very sparsely vegetated, native invertebrates may be the most important biological feature. Endangered species: the plant *'ihi mākole* (*Portulaca sclerocarpa*) has its largest known population near steam vents on Kīlauea volcano. Other endangered plant species found in *'ōhi'a* dieback areas.

THREATS Recently introduced two-spotted leafhopper (*Sophonia rufofasia*) appears to be decimating *uluhe* on several islands; feral pig and alien plants interfere with natural succession in *'ōhi'a* dieback areas. Past reforestation established alien tree species in *'ōhi'a* dieback areas; subdivision development and agriculture, particularly papaya and macadamia nut cultivation on recent lava flows.

CULTURAL SIGNIFCANCE Ancient trail systems took advantage of natural lava courses. Young *pāhoehoe* flows provided numerous cave systems for habitation, storage, and burial. Fumaroles on Kīlauea volcano are believed to be manifestations of Pele.

LINDA W. PRATT AND
SAMUEL M. GON III

BIRDS

When humans first arrived in Hawai'i, more than 140 species of native birds inhabited the Islands. Many of these, including all 80 species of landbirds present, were endemic, or found nowhere else in the world. Of the 24 varieties of seabirds, 2 species and 2 subspecies were endemic, while 29 of the 34 species (and 2 subspecies) of waterbirds were endemic. Today well over half of Hawai'i's original avifauna is extinct. Although only 2 or 3 seabird species are known to have gone extinct, only tiny scattered colonies of seabirds have survived—remnants of the once-large populations found on all the main islands. Of the 66 native bird species and subspecies still present, 30 are considered endangered. As of 1995, 12 of these were literally on the brink of extinction, and 6 may already be extinct. Ornithologists identified several other species that

Extinct Birds

Paleontologists speculate that numerous populations of seabirds and more than 2,000 species of landbirds—primarily flightless rails—became extinct after humans colonized Pacific islands. Of the roughly 9,600 bird species that have been described worldwide, about 20 percent have been lost through extinctions in the Pacific. Hawai'i's avifauna represents this situation well.

An exciting chapter in Hawaiian ornithology opened about two decades ago, when paleontologists began to uncover the remains of many fossil birds from sand dunes, lava tubes, caves, and limestone sinkholes (although a single fossil discovery was made in 1926). About half of Hawai'i's extinct birds are known only through fossils, or actually "subfossils," since the remains of these birds have not yet turned to stone because the extinctions occurred so recently. As on other Pacific islands, almost 20 percent, or 10, of these "fossil" species were flightless rails. Others included a small petrel, a shearwater, 4 flightless ducks, 6 flightless geese, 3 flightless ibises, 4 long-legged owls, a bald eagle, a harrier, 2 crows, a honeyeater related to the 'ō'ō, and at least 22 species of honeycreepers.

Most of the fossil bird species that have been discovered were extinct by the time continental settlers reached the Islands, but virtually all were still present at the time of Polynesian colonization. We will never know the exact causes of extinction for most of them, but throughout human history in Hawai'i the conversion of bird habitat to human uses and the introduction of alien predators have taken a heavy toll. The last 2 flightless rail species probably perished as the result of predation by introduced European roof rats. Although the collection of feathers for making capes and other adornments has been suggested as one cause of extinction, evidence to support this claim is scant. The native avifauna succumbed quickly to rapid ecological changes: between 1778 and 1995, at least two dozen endemic species and subspecies became extinct. More than 30 of the remaining varieties are now considered endangered, and ornithologists speculate that as many as 6 of these may actually be extinct.

The 'ō'ō'ā'ā, whose hauntingly beautiful song and bold presence among the 'ōhi'a canopy's red flowers long delighted naturalists, epitomizes Hawai'i's sad stories of extinction. Common in the late 1800s, this bird was said to be rare by 1928, and by 1960 a survey turned up only 12 birds. During the early 1970s, a single pair of birds made futile attempts to raise their young in nest cavities of large 'ōhi'a trees next to the headwaters of the Halehaha Stream deep in the Alaka'i Swamp. In the early 1980s biologists who periodically visited the site heard a single 'ō'ō'ā'ā singing alone, its partner having vanished. A newspaper article published in 1991 declared that the species was extinct. While it is impossible to prove that something no longer exists, the newspaper report may well have been correct, for no 'ō'ō'ā'ā have been recorded since 1987, in spite of numerous expeditions to its last haunts. Though the 'ō'ō'ā'ā, the Kaua'i 'akialoa, the 'ō'ū, the oloma'o, the kakawahie, and the Maui 'akēpa are all still listed as endangered, none of these species has been seen recently, some not for more than 30 years. Are they extinct? Perhaps, but we will never know why or when.

SHEILA CONANT

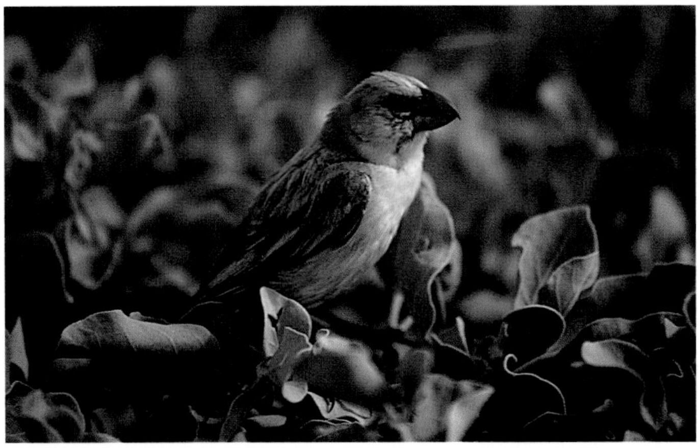

Laysan finch, Pearl and Hermes Reef. [S. Conant]

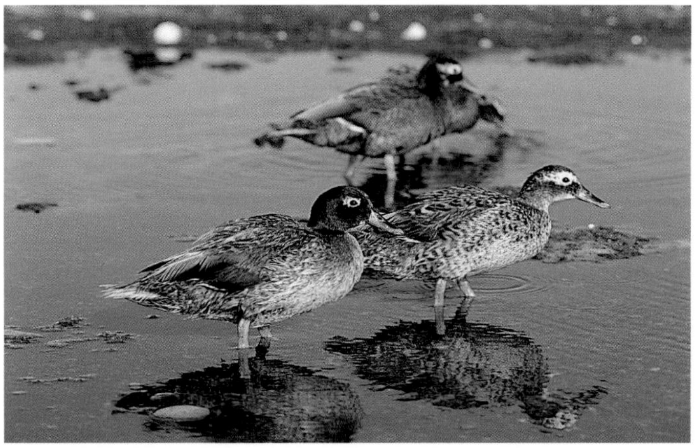

Laysan ducks (female left, male right) on Laysan Island. [S. Conant]

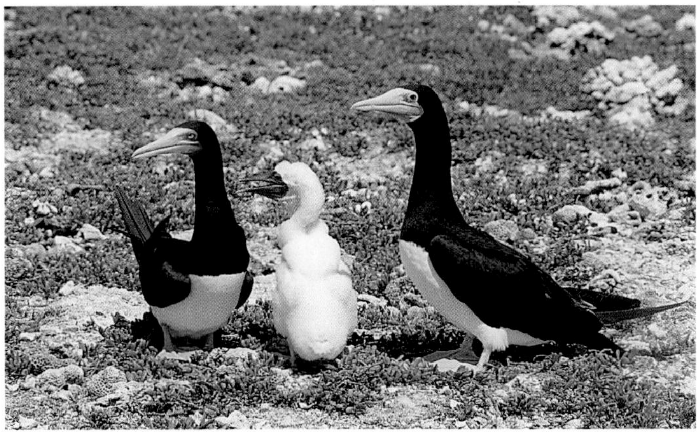

Brown boobies, *'ā* (male left, chick center, female right), on Pearl and Hermes Reef. [S. Conant]

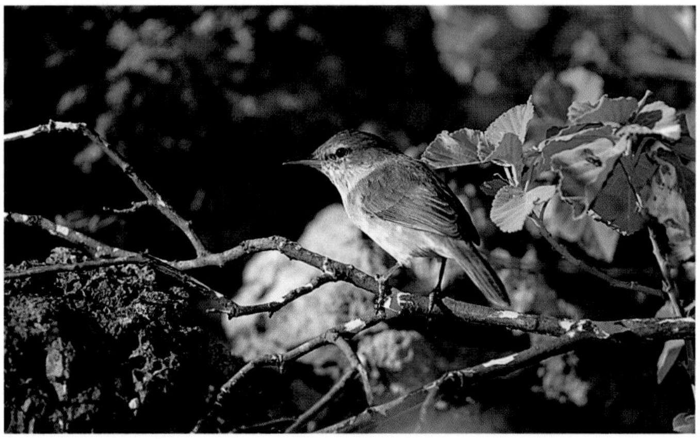

Nihoa millerbird (*Acrocephalus familiaris kingi*), Nihoa Island. [Jack Jeffrey Photography]

may need to be added to the endangered list in the near future.

Birds are the only terrestrial vertebrates, except for 2 species of bats, that successfully colonized the Hawaiian Islands without human assistance. Hawai'i's 113 described endemic bird species, believed to have descended from only about 20 original colonists, proliferated to occupy every conceivable habitat, from dry, treeless, leeward plains to wet rain forest, and from well above the tree line on the highest mountains to the remote shores of atolls hundreds of miles northwest of the main islands. Despite the fact that birds were such a conspicuous part of Hawai'i's biota, they did not represent a broad spectrum of the world's avian diversity. For example, only 6 of the 84 families of songbirds colonized the Islands, and altogether only 19 bird families (out of a world total of 144) include species native to Hawai'i.

Although the number of native bird families was low, species diversity among the groups was high. The native avifauna included seabirds (albatrosses, shearwaters, petrels, boobies, frigatebirds, tropicbirds, and terns), waterbirds (ducks, geese, rails, herons, and var-

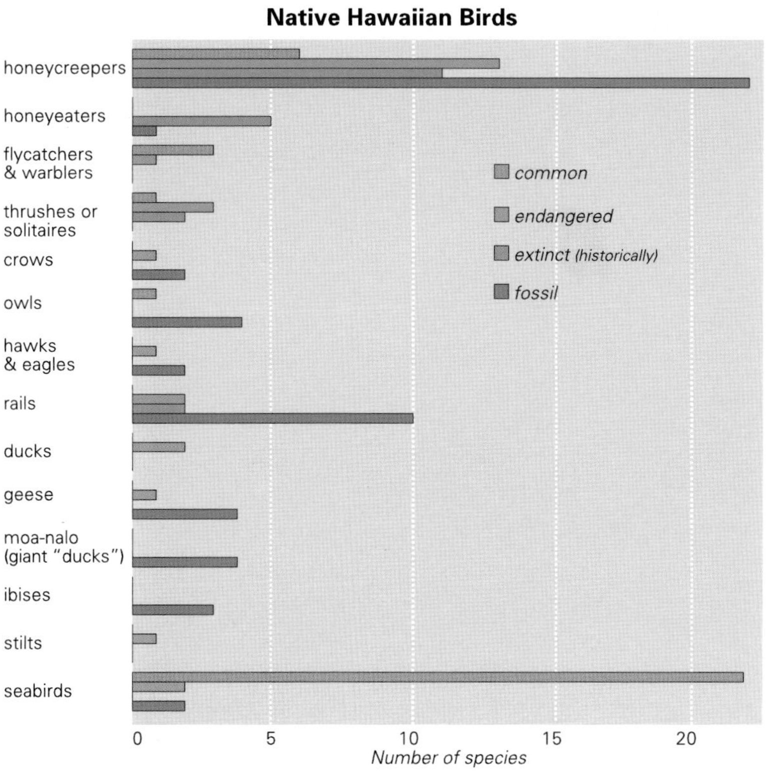
Native Hawaiian Birds
honeycreepers
honeyeaters
flycatchers & warblers
thrushes or solitaires
crows
owls
hawks & eagles
rails
ducks
geese
moa-nalo (giant "ducks")
ibises
stilts
seabirds
common
endangered
extinct (historically)
fossil
0
5
10
15
20
Number of species

Variation in color and bill shape among selected species of the endemic Hawaiian family of honeycreepers (*Drepanidinae*). Painting by H. Douglas Pratt.

Hawaiian stilt, *ae'o*. [Jack Jeffrey Photography]

Laysan albatross (*mōlī*, at top of photo) and black-footed albatross (below) on Nihoa Island. [S. Conant]

ious shorebirds), and landbirds (hawks, eagles, owls, and numerous songbirds). Moreover, the birds that survived in Hawai'i took some spectacular evolutionary paths. For example, flightlessness evolved repeatedly, leading to the development of at least 10 species of giant flightless ducks and geese and more than a dozen species of flightless rails.

Flightlessness is a common characteristic of island birds. Flight and the musculature required to fly are energetically costly. Thus flightlessness has often evolved on islands free of ground-dwelling mammalian predators, where flight would confer small advantage to birds. Most Pacific island groups had several species of endemic flightless rails, and Hawai'i was no exception. But flightlessness became a liability when humans arrived on the islands, and most of Hawai'i's flightless birds became extinct soon after human colonization—a pattern that has been repeated in every Pacific island group studied thus far. Paleontologists estimate that when all the fossil evidence is accounted for, several species of endemic flightless rails from each of the main Hawaiian islands will be recorded. Cur-

rently 10 fossil species of flightless ducks and geese and 12 species of flightless rails are known from Hawai'i, and others will likely be discovered.

The Hawaiian honeycreepers are undoubtedly the world's most spectacular avian example of the evolutionary phenomenon called adaptive radiation. From a single finchlike ancestor who colonized the Islands, more than 40 species have evolved (47 varieties altogether if subspecies are included). Current estimates based on genetic evidence place the age of the honeycreeper group at less than 3.5 million years. The radi-

Bird Species in the Hawaiian Islands, 1997

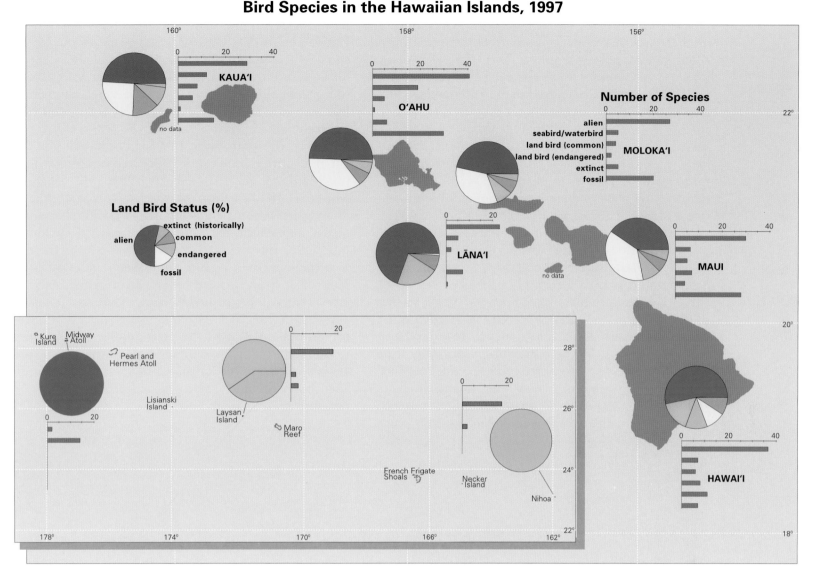

ation was thus spectacular in both its rapidity and diversity, and new fossils are being discovered every year.

Adaptation to a variety of diets was clearly a major factor driving the radiation of the honeycreepers. Their varied bills were used for an amazing array of foraging techniques: short, thick bills for crushing very hard seeds; thin, straight bills for gleaning insects from bark, twigs, and leaves; long, thin, decurved bills for probing flowers for nectar, or probing epiphytes for invertebrates; short, thick, decurved bills for crushing twigs to flush out wood-boring insects; and bills with crossed mandibles for twisting apical leaf buds to get at the insects inside. Bill forms ranged from the very stout bill of the now-extinct "King Kong" finch (which had the most massive bill of any known finch) to the elongate bill of the Kaua'i 'akialoa (whose bill is two-thirds the length of the rest of its body). Many of the honeycreepers are specialized feeders. For example, the 'akiapōlā'au uses its short, straight, lower mandible in woodpecker-like fashion to drill holes in branches, and its thin, flexible, curved, upper mandible to extract the

exposed beetle larvae. This species prefers *koa* forests, but as native forests have shrunk from grazing, logging, and other factors, so has the number of *'akiapōlā-'au*, until today fewer than 1,500 survive.

Many factors associated with human presence and civilization have negatively affected native birds, and biologists are far from completely understanding the role each factor plays. Loss of habitat and the introductions of alien species, however, are key causes of declining populations. Loss of habitat to plantation agriculture, cattle grazing, and urban and resort development is highly visible, but the effects of alien species are not always obvious. Alien species pose threats nearly as numerous as the aliens themselves. Predators—especially small mammals such as rats, mongooses, cats, and dogs—but also introduced birds, including cattle egrets and barn owls, take their toll on a variety of native birds, from the 3-foot (1 m) tall Laysan albatross to the diminutive 5.5-inch (14 cm) long O'ahu 'elepaio. Foreign diseases such as avian malaria and avian pox are spread by other aliens: mosquitoes. Also, native birds must compete for their insect and plant foods with rats, introduced birds, and predacious insects such as yellowjackets, which devour moth larvae that honeycreepers feed their nestlings. Alien plants have overgrown and displaced many forests, which native songbirds depended on for shelter and food, and have choked shallow wetland feeding areas favored by waterbirds such as *aeʻo, ʻalae keʻokeʻo,* and *ʻalae ʻula.* Although stringent laws have been passed to protect the state's endangered plants and animals, government agency budgets and personnel are inadequate to ensure implementation of numerous conservation plans and enforcement of wildlife protection and land use statutes.

Just as it has suffered the greatest number of avian extinctions, Hawaiʻi has experienced the introduction of more species of alien birds than any other geographic region on Earth. Humans have intentionally or accidentally introduced about 170 bird species to the Islands, although only about one-third (around 60 species) have become naturalized, or established wild populations. While conservationists deplore the presence of these species, they comprise the only bird life in most of lowland Hawaiʻi, and many residents and visitors enjoy the colorful birds and their songs. Others find the depredations to orchid and fruit crops more than annoying.

One of the most numerous alien birds, the familiar and entertaining common myna, was brought to Hawaiʻi in 1865 to control insect pests. In the 1920s and 1930s a number of colorful and melodious songbirds were introduced to enhance residential gardens shunned by the few remaining native songbirds, which had retreated to higher elevations where mosquitoes are scarce. Acclaimed as one of the world's virtuoso songsters, the white-rumped shama usually heads the list of favorite garden exotics, followed by the northern (red) cardinal, the red-crested cardinal, the Japanese white-eye, the Java sparrow, the leiothrix, and others. Many game birds (including turkeys, doves, pheasants, quails, and francolins) were also introduced for hunting. Today the major source of new species is the pet bird trade. Introduced birds in Hawaiʻi include a large number of escaped caged birds: parrots, small African weaver finches, cardueline finches, the ubiquitous Japanese white-eye, and the pesky fruit- and orchid-eating bulbuls. Although the pests among these species would be virtually impossible to eradicate, agriculturalists and environmentalists alike agree that no more alien birds should be released, accidentally or intentionally.

Sheila Conant

NATIVE PLANTS

The native plants of Hawaiʻi evolved from a relatively small number of original immigrants that were able to cross broad expanses of ocean and become successfully established in the Islands. Many have undergone considerable evolution, changing so much from their ancestors that they are now recognized as species unique to Hawaiʻi, and they are referred to as endemic species. Those species that are still considered identical to their relatives elsewhere are called indigenous native species. About 90 percent of the 1,000 or so native flowering plants and about 70 percent of the 150 or so native ferns are endemic. The degree of endemism in Hawaiʻi's terrestrial plants is the highest known for any major island group and is much greater than that of continental floras.

Native Hawaiian flora and fauna are disharmonic; that is, they lack entire families and orders of plants and animals usually found in continental biotas. Plants that are widespread in the tropics but not native to Hawaiʻi include figs and banyans (*Ficus*), gymnosperms, mangroves, and the family Araceae (taro, philodendron, anthurium, and others). In the case of some plants, their seeds may never have reached Hawaiʻi. In other instances seeds brought by birds probably germinated and grew to maturity but were unable to become established as a species because their required pollinators were absent. For example, each fig species is pollinated by a different species of wasp, and the likelihood is very small that the right wasp would have reached Hawaiʻi while the associated fig was flower-

Hawaiian Plants — Endemic, Indigenous, and Alien*

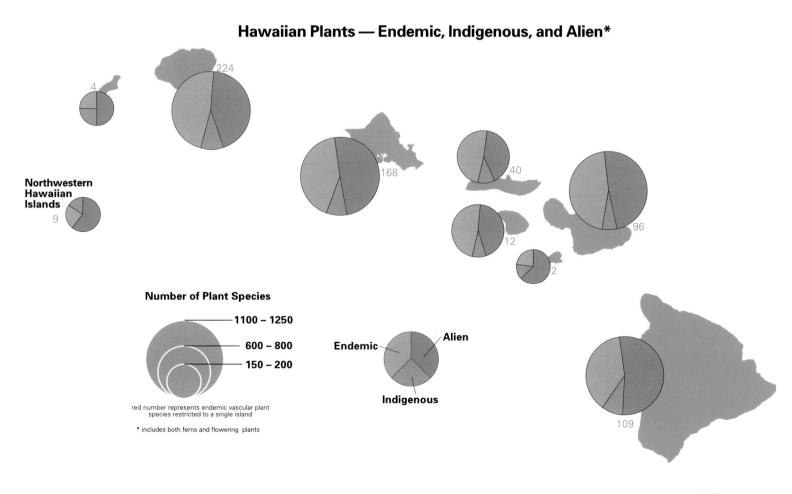

Northwestern Hawaiian Islands

Number of Plant Species

- 1100 – 1250
- 600 – 800
- 150 – 200

red number represents endemic vascular plant species restricted to a single island

* includes both ferns and flowering plants

Endemic

Alien

Indigenous

ing. Similarly, seeds of many orchid species, which are tiny and widely dispersed by wind, undoubtedly reached the Islands in the past, but their specialized insect pollinators apparently were not present at the right times. Thus Hawai'i has only three native orchids—far fewer than any other tropical area of comparable size.

In contrast, a greater proportion of species in the sunflower and lobelia families (Asteraceae and Campanulaceae) appear in Hawai'i than in other parts of the world, perhaps due simply to the chance arrival of colonizers from these families under auspicious conditions. In the absence of some biotic groups and the disproportionate presence of others, Hawaiian plants and animals evolved in very different ways than they might have on continents.

Evolution in Hawaiian Plants

The geographic and environmental conditions under which plants evolved in Hawai'i also differed from those of continental areas, and as a result native flora have reached some unique evolutionary forms. Three factors are of major importance. First, climate varies greatly over short distances in Hawai'i. Consequently, many microclimates and microhabitats are located within sufficiently short distances of one another that

propagules (seeds or spores) have a chance of being distributed to different ecosystems. This increases the survival chances of random genetic variants from the parent plant and makes it possible for offspring to become adapted to new environments.

Second is the factor of isolation, which restricts gene flow between segments of a population and permits them to evolve in quite different ways. Not only is the Hawaiian archipelago isolated from continents and other island groups, but each island in the chain is isolated from the others. Further isolation occurs

Native tree fern, *hapu'u* (*Cibotium hawaiense*), Pua 'Ākala, Hawai'i. [Jack Jeffrey Photography]

Top: Rare native lobelia (*Clermontia pyrularia*), Pīhā, Hawai'i. *Center: C. lindseyana*), Hakalau Forest, Hawai'i. *Bottom: C. tuberculata*, Hanawī, Maui. [Jack Jeffrey Photography]

between mountains on a single island, between valleys on a single mountain, and between *kīpuka* (older, vegetation-covered lava surfaces surrounded by a more recent flow) in single- or different-age lava flows.

The third factor is the disharmonic nature of the biota. Many plants that once produced chemical or mechanical defenses that discouraged grazing and browsing mammals have lost such defenses when they further evolved in places that lacked such herbivores. Likewise, plants that were adapted to coexist with animals that pollinated their flowers or dispersed their seeds have necessarily evolved different strategies in the absence of such pollinators and seed dispersers.

As a result of these factors, the native Hawaiian flora exhibits many different patterns and endpoints of evolutionary change that differ from ancestral species outside Hawai'i. Some examples are:

Hybridization In several groups of Hawaiian plants, naturally occurring hybrids between species with pronounced morphological differences have been discovered. The ability to produce natural hybrids may be a selective advantage in evolution, providing an important source of variation that could be retained as seeds are dispersed to nearby but totally different habitats. Examples of hybridization occur in the genus *Bidens* and among the Hawaiian silversword alliance.

Gigantism From ancestors that were herbaceous, the species of some widely distributed genera have developed into woody shrubs or small trees in Hawai'i. For instance, most of the world's 365 species of *Lobelia* are small herbs, but the 13 species in Hawai'i have woody stems to 13 feet (4 m) tall. Worldwide *Chenopodium* has 150 species, mostly native to temperate regions, that are weedy herbs. In contrast, the Hawaiian 'āweoweo (*Chenopodium oahuense*) can become a tree more than 16 feet (5 m) tall.

Adaptive Shifts Many Hawaiian plants have undergone adaptive shifts; that is, evolutionary changes from ancestral conditions that enable them to survive better under conditions encountered in Hawai'i. Examples are:
- **shifts from insect pollination to bird pollination.** The native species of *Hibiscus* were most likely pollinated by native insects such as moths. The endemic genus *Hibiscadelphus* (*hau kuahiwi*), with curved, tubular flowers adapted for bird pollination, appar-

The striking red flowers of the native 'Ōhi'a lehua (*Metrosideros polymorpha*). [Nature Conservancy of Hawai'i]

Sadleria fern, Saddle Road, Hawai'i. [Jack Jeffrey Photography]

Rare native hibiscus (*Hibiscus waimeae*), Kōke'e, Hawai'i. [Jack Jeffrey Photography]

Left: Hawaiian *Bidens* (*Bidens micrantha ctenophylla*), Kona, Hawai'i. *Right:* Hawaiian *Bidens* (*Bidens menziesii*), Pu'u Lā'au, Hawai'i. [Jack Jeffrey Photography]

Colorful *Sadleria* fern, Hāna Forest Reserve, Maui.
[Jack Jeffrey Photography]

Hawaiian raspberry (*Rubus hawaiensis*) flowers and fruits,
Pua ʻĀkala, Hawaiʻi. [Jack Jeffrey Photography]

Maʻo hau hele (*Hibiscus brackenridgei mokuleianus*), Puʻu Waʻawaʻa,
Hawaiʻi. [Jack Jeffrey Photography]

ently has evolved from *Hibiscus* in Hawaiʻi. A similar shift has occurred in the Hawaiian geraniums: *Geranium cuneatum* (*hinahina*) is insect-pollinated, while *G. arboreum* (*nohoanu*) is pollinated by birds.

- **shifts in fruit- or seed-dispersal mechanisms.** In most of the 230 species of *Bidens,* small, dry, one-seeded fruits are spindle shaped and topped with two long awns, or spines, covered with backward-pointing bristles. These fruits stick to the fur of mammals, which then disperse the seeds. In Hawaiʻi, where mammal dispersers were lacking, the fruits in native species of *Bidens* (*koʻokoʻolau*) have become adapted for wind dispersal. In some species the spines are shortened or even absent. The fruits are flattened, and in some cases have "wings."
- **loss of prickles, spines, and thorns.** Usually considered to be defenses against grazing and browsing mammals, these plant appendages were lost on islands free of grazers and browsers. The Hawaiian raspberry (*ʻākala, Rubus hawaiiensis*) is losing its

prickles through evolution. Some plants still have a few soft prickles, while others have lost them completely over thousands of years.

- **loss of stinging hairs.** Many plants in the nettle family have stinging hairs, which help discourage mammals from eating them. The endemic Hawaiian *olonā* (*Touchardia latifolia*) has lost these stinging hairs during its evolution in Hawaiʻi.
- **loss of chemical defenses against herbivores.** Most plants in the mint family (including peppermint, spearmint, basil, oregano, thyme, and sage) have aromatic oils. While humans use these scented plants to flavor foods, animals such as goats and sheep tend to avoid the plants. In Hawaiʻi the 52 species of native mints in the genera *Phyllostegia, Stenogyne,* and *Haplostachys* have all lost their essential oils during evolution.
- **adaptation to absence of ants.** Ants have symbiotic relationships with many plants around the world, including 38 of the 39 known species of cot-

ton (*Gossypium*), which have extrafloral nectaries—small glands on the undersides of their leaves that secrete a sugary liquid attractive to aphids. Ants move in to tend the aphids and to consume the "honeydew" liquid that the aphids produce. The ants also protect their host plant from other insects that feed on its leaves and stems. The endemic Hawaiian cotton (*ma'o, Gossypium tomentosum*) lost nectaries during evolution, as there were no ants in Hawai'i until humans introduced them. Since aphids transmit diseases, cotton breeders now use Hawaiian cotton to produce plants that lack nectaries.

Adaptive Radiation Over time the descendants of some plant colonizers went through several adaptive shifts, evolving into many new species, or even genera, that were able to occupy a range of habitats. More than 20 different plant groups in Hawai'i exhibit adaptive radiation. Examples include:

- **silversword alliance.** The best-documented example of adaptive radiation in plants is the Hawaiian silversword alliance, described in the section of this *Atlas* on Evolution.
- **mints.** About 52 species in 3 genera—*Haplostachys* (*honohono*), *Phyllostegia* (*kāpana*), *Stenogyne* (*mā'ohi'ohi*)—have been derived from a common ancestor and today vary greatly in appearance and in the habitats they occupy.
- **naupaka.** All derived from a single ancestor, 8 species of black-fruited, bird-dispersed *Scaevola* (*naupaka kuahiwi*) are found in diverse habitats, from dry coastal areas to montane rain forests.
- **spurges.** About 15 species of *Chamaesyce* (*'akoko*)—ranging from small subshrubs on sandy beaches, to trees in mesic and wet forests, to creeping shrubs in montane bogs—have been derived from one ancestor, which was probably a widespread subshrub that still grows on Pacific island beaches.

CHARLES H. LAMOUREUX

INSECTS AND THEIR KIN

Hawai'i has one of the most spectacularly evolved insect faunas on Earth, with an estimated 10,000 native species, some 95 percent of which are unique (endemic) to the Islands. Insects are arthropods ("jointed feet"), a division within the larger group invertebrates, animals without backbones. Arthropods possess stiff, external skeletons and segmented legs. In most ecosystems they are the dominant animals, both in variety and absolute numbers. They play especially important roles on isolated islands, where most larger animals are absent.

Hawai'i's endemic insect fauna evolved from 400 to 500 colonizing species. Over a span of 30 million years of evolution, successful colonizing events occurred every 50,000 to 75,000 years. Only 15 percent of Earth's insect families and 50 percent of insect orders are represented in the Hawaiian Islands. Absent for the most part are large species and forms not well equipped to disperse. For example, there are no native scarabs, leaf beetles, metallic wood-boring beetles, swallowtail butterflies, sawflies, or ants. Those species that did "win the dispersal sweepstakes" established populations and thrived in the Islands. The majority of these successful colonizers—small flies, beetles, wasps, moths, bugs, leafhoppers, and planthoppers—were swept in by storms and jet streams. Others flew to the Islands under their own power, and some were transported by birds or rafted by sea on floating debris. They came from every direction, often island-hopping from other Pacific landfalls.

Insects were significant in Hawaiian culture. The creation chant, *Kumulipo,* mentions many native insects. Some served as food for Native Hawaiians, dragonfly nymphs were used in indigenous rituals, and certain caterpillars and other insects were honored as *'aumākua* (guardian spirits).

The scientific study of Hawai'i's insects began

The predatory caterpillar, *Eupithecia staurophragma,* eating an endemic *Drosophila.* Resembling a brown twig, this caterpillar can wait days or weeks for prey to approach. The 18 closely related species that practice this stealth use different perch sites: green caterpillars sit on leaf margins; brown, wrinkled ones on twigs; and fuzzy ones on mossy tree trunks. One species even modifies its perch on ferns by chewing a gap between leaflets, enabling it to hide and capture prey walking along both the upper and lower surfaces. [W. P. Mull]

The delicate adult predatory moth (*Eupithecia staurophragma,* female pictured) feeds on nectar and belies the macabre lifestyle of its caterpillar. Carnivorous caterpillars that ambush active prey were discovered in 1972, and the behavior among the order Lepidoptera remains unique to Hawai'i. [W. P. Mull]

Insect Life in Caves

It has long been assumed that young oceanic islands had many empty ecological niches with food resources and habitats not fully exploited. For example, it was thought that specialized cave animals similar to those found in limestone caves of considerable age could not evolve on young volcanic islands, where lava tube caves usually persist for only a few thousand years. Moreover, the moisture-loving animals inhabiting continental caves did not

opment of different forms to match different environments by means of genetic recombination under the effects of natural selection. In 1971 scientists discovered communities of specialized cave animals in lava tubes. Many of these animals, including lycosid spiders, *Thaumatogryllus* and *Caconemobius* crickets, *Nesidiolestes* bugs, and *Oliarus* planthoppers, represent the epitome of rapid changes in body forms that are associated with adaptive

The marine littoral rock cricket (*Caconemobius sandwichensis*) scavenges at night on wave-splashed boulder beaches on the main Hawaiian islands. It probably disperses between islands on floating debris. On Kaua'i, Maui, and Hawai'i, related inland species have evolved to live in similar barren wet-rock habitats, such as cliffs, young lava flows, and caves. Compare with the cave species at right. [W. P. Mull]

This cave rock cricket (*Caconemobius howarthi*) lives in lava tubes on Maui; other cave species occur on Hawai'i Island. The pale, translucent color, vestigial eyes, and reduced jumping ability are adaptations for living in caves. [W. P. Mull]

disperse to Hawai'i, and important food resources for these animals are absent in local caves. The extreme physical changes displayed by cave species were assumed to require a long time to evolve. Evidence from Hawai'i Island contradicts these assumptions, however, and suggests that species may fill niches within a comparatively short time through adaptive radiation; that is, the devel-

shifts. Indeed, one could say the Hawaiian cave fauna contains examples of macroevolution on microcontinents in minitime. Many specialized cave animals are sensitive to human disturbance of their unique habitat, where visitors are liable to bring in pollutants, break plant roots, and trample animals, their food, and hiding places.

FRANCIS G. HOWARTH AND
STEVEN L. MONTGOMERY

with the Reverend Thomas Blackburn, who collected insect specimens in the Islands from 1877 to 1883. Human activity and introduced species, especially cattle and other ungulates, destroyed many natural communities at lower elevations in Hawai'i before insects were seriously collected. From 1892 to 1897 British scientists, in collaboration with Bishop Museum, conducted a survey (Fauna Hawaiiensis) that established a baseline for information on Hawai'i's arthropods. Today Bishop Museum's Hawaiian insect collection of nearly a million specimens contains three-quarters of all species described for the Islands.

Flightlessness

Flightlessness among insects is not unique to islands. It is common in every ecosystem, and nearly all insects spend the majority of their active lives in flightless stages. The evolution of flightlessness is especially prominent, however, among island insects. There are flightless moths, beetles, bugs, planthoppers, leafhoppers, crickets, katydids, wasps, beetle-like lacewings, and even flies. Of the 11 orders of winged insects that dispersed to the Islands, only the Odonata (damselflies and dragonflies) have not evolved flightless forms. As most continental flightless groups did not disperse to

With nearly 1,000 endemic species, the native Hawaiian pomace flies (Drosophilidae) are a showcase of evolution. Here, a male Big Island picture wing species, *Drosophila conspicua,* poses next to the cosmopolitan vinegar fly, *D. melanogaster,* which is widely used in genetic studies. [W. P. Mull].

One of 140 native wood-boring beetles, *Plagithmysus varians* is found only on the Big Island and bores in *koa* (*Acacia koa*). [W. P. Mull]

The flightless brown lacewing, *Micromus lobipennis,* lives in the rain forests on Haleakalā on Maui. These marvels of evolution have modified their characteristic delicate lacelike forewings into thickened protective body covers and now resemble beetles. [W. P. Mull]

Hawai'i, many winged species evolved to fill these roles. This process is particularly well demonstrated where closely related flighted and flightless species often live side-by-side, sometimes with intermediate forms. Thus the pieces to these evolutionary puzzles can be fitted together.

Introduced Species and Conservation

About 2,700 alien insect species, plus 560 other introduced terrestrial arthropods such as spiders and centipedes, are present in the Islands. Alien ants that form large, aggressive colonies, such as the big-headed ant (*Pheidole megacephala*), the Argentine ant (*Linepithema humile*), and the long-legged ant (*Anoplolepis longipes*), have been strongly implicated in the extinction of many native species. In 1977 an aggressive race of the yellowjacket (*Vespula pensylvanica*) became established in Hawai'i, most likely through the importation of unfumigated Christmas trees. The population explosion and spread of yellowjackets corresponded with an

The *koa* bug (*Coleotichus blackburniae*) is the largest and most conspicuous native true bug. Its hosts are *koa* and *'a'ali'i*. Once common on all main islands, it and its relatives have declined markedly since 1970 because of the impacts of introduced parasites. [W. P. Mull]

alarming decline of many native arthropods and possibly of certain native birds.

The insect fauna of Hawai'i is undergoing profound changes, with many native species declining from the combined impacts of invasive alien species and the alteration of habitats by human activities. These effects are exacerbated by a widespread lack of knowledge of the biology of both native and alien species.

Francis G. Howarth,
Steven L. Montgomery,
and William P. Mull

HAWAIIAN TREE SNAILS

During the last several million years, a few small land snails arrived by chance in the Islands and evolved through adaptive radiation into more than 750 uniquely Hawaiian terrestrial snail species. We will never know exactly how these pioneers got to Hawai'i —perhaps stuck on the feathers or in mud on the feet of far-traveling birds or on floating tree trunks. Neither can we expect to learn more about the way they lived, since most of these endemic snails are now extinct— victims of land clearing, habitat degradation, shell collecting, and introduced predators.

Tree-living species evolved in most of the terrestrial snail families in Hawai'i. Among them the achatinellids, known as *kāhuli* or *pūpū kanioe,* the "singing snails" of legends, are the best known. These large (up to 1 inch [2.5 cm] long), gaily banded and brightly colored tree snails once occurred abundantly in the forests of O'ahu, Moloka'i, Lāna'i, Maui, and Hawai'i Island, and the most widely known and studied were the little agate shells, the *Achatinella* species of O'ahu. Between 35 and 40 species occupied small ranges on ridges and valleys in the Wai'anae and Ko'olau Mountains, often exhibiting different color patterns in different parts of their ranges. Some of these unique color variants were restricted to only one or a few closely spaced trees.

The O'ahu tree snails had no known native predators, and the great variations in shape and color are attributed to evolutionary factors other than typical natural selection. Isolation of small populations, followed by genetic mutations and genetic drift (chance preservation or extinction of traits as a result of small population size), may account for the spectacular variations observed. Among the life-history traits that evolved in the achatinellids are many that left them ill prepared for the predators that were to arrive with human colonists, first Polynesians and later Europeans. Although live-born at relatively large sizes (about 0.2

Each of the O'ahu tree snail species lives on but a small part of the island. *Achatinella mustelina* occurs along the length of the Wai'anae Range, *A. livida* and *A. sowerbyana* have nonoverlapping ranges on the northern Ko'olau summit, and *A. fuscobasis* occupies peaks in the southern Ko'olau Range. [M. G. Hadfield]

O'ahu Tree Snails

inches [5 mm]), the baby snails grow very slowly, reaching reproductive maturity only after four to five years. Then they reproduce at a virtual snail's pace. While the tree snails are hermaphroditic (each functioning as both male and female), a typical snail has only four or five offspring per year, most of which are likely to die from a variety of natural causes during the first year of life.

The characteristics of long juvenile life and low birthrate have left small tree-snail populations vulnerable to sudden annihilation by alien threats such as human shell collectors, rats (the first rat species arrived on the Polynesian canoes, and two more came with the European sailing ships), or, worst of all, the predatory "cannibal snail," *Euglandina rosea.* The latter was brought to Hawai'i from the southwestern United States by the Hawai'i Department of Agriculture in an ill-conceived attempt at biological control of the giant African snail. These predators easily scaled the highest reaches of O'ahu where they are, even now, destroying the last of many tree-snail species. Sometime in the early 1990s another snail predator arrived in Hawai'i: the voracious New Guinea flatworm, *Platydemis manokwari.* Although not yet seen in upper-elevation habi-

tats, it may ultimately reach these last remaining refuges.

Endemic tree snails persist today only near the mountain summits of O'ahu, Lāna'i, and Moloka'i and in middle-elevation forests between 1,500 and 5,000 feet (450–1,500 m) on Maui and Hawai'i Island. For the even more vulnerable, mostly ground-dwelling snails of the family Amastridae, probably less than a dozen species survive of the more than 300 found in the Islands a century ago. The loss of these magnificent land- and tree-snail assemblages is an ecological, cultural, and scientific tragedy. These snails, which fed only on fungi growing on leaves of trees or leaf litter, must have played a significant role in forest ecology, a specialized role that no other organism now performs. It is another of the tragic losses that contributes to Hawai'i's reputation as the "extinction capital of the world." Efforts are underway to save some of the *Achatinella* species by propagating them in captivity, but it is too early to know whether this costly method will succeed.

MICHAEL G. HADFIELD

ALIEN SPECIES AND THREATS TO NATIVE ECOLOGY

Alien organisms are those that were brought to Hawai'i intentionally or accidentally by humans. Almost 6,000 species of the present terrestrial and freshwater biota have come from overseas in recent decades. The cumulative impacts of introduced organisms have resulted in the decline of the unique native biota. The overall consequences of alien species invasions can be appreciated by considering the rates of species introduction, the types of organisms introduced, and the resulting interactions between native and alien organisms.

Rates of Species Introductions

Prior to human colonization of Hawai'i, the natural rate of change in biological communities was extremely slow. New species additions from natural overseas dispersal and from island evolution were so infrequent that elements of the biota coevolved, adjusting to each other. Once humans arrived, species were introduced far more frequently than the natural immigration rate. The rapid accumulation of these new arrivals impacted the native biota progressively, extinguishing species and replacing complex native communities with simple alien associations.

During the first 1,500 years of Polynesian habitation in Hawai'i, 40–50 plant and animal species were intentionally brought in, effecting a thousandfold increase over previous natural rates of species arrival. Because most Polynesian introductions were domesticated species, the major impacts were generally confined to cultivated areas below 2,000 feet in elevation. In the first century following European contact, alien species introductions and their associated ecological impacts greatly accelerated as about 175 plants and scores of animals were added to the landscape. Some of these spread beyond agricultural areas, disturbing native habitats and depleting numerous native species. Feral cattle and goats became the most damaging of these early European introductions, opening up huge expanses of the upland native vegetation.

During the last century the numbers of alien spe-

Native and Naturalized Alien Organisms in Hawai'i

Group	Native*	Alien	Total	% Native
Lower plants	+/- 1,600	+/-1,200	+/- 2,800	55–60%
Vascular plants	1,300	1,100	2,400	54%
Arthropods	10,000–12,000**	3,178***	13,000–15,000	76–79%
Mollusks	788	108	896	88%
Other invertebrates	166	156	322	52%
Reptiles & amphibians	0	33	33	0
Birds	142	53	195	73%
Mammals	1	19	20	5%
Totals	+/- 14,000–16,000	+/- 5750	+/- 20,000–22,000	70–74%

* Totals of native species include those that have become extinct.
** 7,800 described of the estimated 10,000–12,000 native arthropods.
***This number of naturalized alien arthropods grows by 20–40 per year.

Many of the table numbers have been provided courtesy of the Hawaii Biological Survey, B. P. Bishop Museum, Honolulu; others have been collated by the author.

cies and their cumulative impacts have increased exponentially. Large ranches grew out of damaged forests and shrublands and they replaced some feral ungulates with pastured livestock. Cattlemen brought in numerous foreign grasses for forage, and in the process weeds were unintentionally introduced. The sugar industry imported seeds from thousands of tree and shrub species for trials to revegetate damaged watershed forests. Other alien organisms, such as ornamental plants and songbirds, were imported simply because they caught people's fancy. Unintentional imports slipped in as well, many becoming weeds and pests. More aliens were introduced to combat pests. As rural areas became more biologically cosmopolitan, suites of these introduced plants and animals spread into disturbed native communities. Interactions among the aliens enhanced their establishment and adverse impacts.

Alien species are still being introduced in large numbers, with and without official approval. Overall, the rate of species introductions has been about a million times the natural rate of species colonization prior to human settlement and a thousandfold more than during the Polynesian period.

Types of Organisms

Most native species are fine-tuned to their physical environments and associated biotic assemblages, and they have evolved defenses only against indigenous stresses. Stresses caused by certain life forms very alien to oceanic islands have proven very damaging to the Hawaiian biota. In addition to humans, some of the most damaging aliens are ungulates, rats, and certain social insects (ants and some wasps). When exposed to the cumulative stresses from these introduced animals, most native plants and animals succumb, as do their dependent associate organisms. Aliens that are natu-

rally resistant to these stresses tend to replace the natives. Fifty to a hundred alien organisms of the 5–6,000 introduced with humans have initiated the bulk of the ecosystem damage in Hawai'i, tearing up landscapes, eliminating suites of organisms, and facilitating the establishment of other aliens.

The successful establishment of so many alien species in Hawai'i can be partly explained by characteristics of the native biota that render it vulnerable to destabilization and displacement by introduced organisms. These features include slow growth rates, host specificity, restricted habitats, and small population sizes. Numerous alien species that reproduce prolifically, disperse widely, and tolerate the damage have gained elevated presence within stressed native ecosystems. Introduced species often possess an additional competitive edge because they arrive unaccompanied by their natural predators and parasites. In general native predators have fairly specific native prey and hosts, so they rarely threaten aliens. Correspondingly, few native animals forage on or benefit from foreign plants.

These old flightless goose bones and snail shells in a lava tube are all that remain of these species. This goose and over 20 other flightless birds could not survive the changes brought by humans and their imported animals. Other groups of birds (e.g., ground feeders and seed eaters) and invertebrates were similarly decimated. [R. Warshauer]

A comparison of these two areas flanking Wailau Valley on windward Molokai'i illustrates the devastating effects that ungulates can cause. Inaccessible Oloku'i (*top*) has remained free of ungulates, but equivalent forest to the east (*below*) was degraded in less than 40 years after deer and feral pigs spread into the area. [R. Warshauer]

Ungulates are large herbivores such as cattle, sheep, goats, pigs, and deer. Their voracious feeding habits ravage the relatively fragile foliage and branches of native plants, and their hooves destroy surface roots and cause extensive soil degradation and erosion. Ground-dwelling plants and animals are crushed or consumed. Ungulates have converted many diverse native forests and shrublands into pastures now dominated by alien organisms.

Rats are also highly adaptable and widely distributed in all ecological zones. They forage on the ground and in trees, feeding on major native animal groups—insects, snails, and birds—as well as on seeds of native plants. In Hawai'i, as on other Pacific islands, rats have been a major factor in the disappearance of native birds and invertebrates.

While ungulates and rats alone have caused great ecological damage, their negative impacts have been amplified through interactions with other introduced organisms, especially plants. Although some alien plants can directly invade intact native ecosystems, most become established in vegetation previously disturbed by ungulate or human activity. In the relative stability of the prehuman Hawaiian environment, few such disturbance-adapted plants evolved, but many have since been introduced.

Alien invertebrates have had adverse consequences similar in scale to ungulates and introduced plants. Ants and predatory yellowjacket wasps, for example, have caused the extinction of countless native arthropods. In most lowland areas native invertebrates were decimated and later replaced by opportunistic aliens such as cockroaches, sowbugs, slugs, millipedes, and centipedes—all better able to cope with predation by invading social insects. At higher elevations, many native insects are succumbing to adaptable generalist

South American banana poka (*Passiflora mollissima*) smothers forest canopy, understory, and ground cover. Pigs and birds spread the vine locally, but longer-distance dispersal is by humans and by the Nepal kalij pheasant, which carries the seeds in its gizzard to sites favorable for the vine's growth. [Jack Jeffrey Photography]

insect predators and parasites. Various alien arthropods consume native plants directly, spread diseases, and deplete native pollinators. Introduced mollusks feed on endemic land snails and seedlings of native plants.

Alien Species Interactions

Interaction among introduced species is often synergistic. Introduced animals disperse most invasive plants and open up native vegetation for colonization. Alien birds spread new fruit-bearing plants out from urban and agricultural areas. As more species of these plants become established in remote areas, they develop an expanding, year-round food supply that supports enlarged ranges for additional alien birds, mammals, and insects. The more extensive and diverse the alien biota, the greater is the chance for establishment of future introductions. Some widespread alien organisms serve as hosts to others. Such hosts and insect vectors (carriers of disease organisms) facilitate the spread of introduced plant and avian diseases from alien to native species. Until the appropriate alien mosquito species became well established, there was no potential for deadly introduced, mosquito-borne diseases to be carried from alien bird hosts to native birds. This process is enhanced by feral pigs and humans creating mosquito breeding sites in large areas where they might otherwise be lacking.

Some alien plants fundamentally alter the nature of ecosystems that they invade. Different grasses can alter the moisture status of an area, causing either excessive drying or saturating of the soil. Others increase the flammability of invaded vegetation to the point that recurrent fires permanently degrade it. Certain introduced trees that can "fix" atmospheric nitrogen (for example, *Myrica faya*) have a competitive advantage over native species normally living in nitrogen-limited conditions. Such nutrient enrichment then encourages the proliferation of other aliens requiring nitrogen enhancement.

Current Situation

Of the many thousands of alien species brought to Hawai'i, nearly 6,000 have escaped from captivity, but only a fraction of these have had major adverse impacts on native ecosystems. About half of the approximately 15,000–20,000 plants imported into Hawai'i became established in cultivation; fewer than a tenth have escaped to the wild. Fewer than 1 percent are creating serious adverse consequences for native ecosystems. Nonetheless, even minor consequences are cumulative and the mere presence of some aliens may enable later-arriving species to secure a foothold in the Islands.

Although this discussion emphasizes effects on native biota, many aliens also negatively affect economically important plants that are themselves introduced species. This has occurred so frequently that for over a century other organisms have been brought in

Alien mosquito feeding on the eye of an '*apapane* (a Hawaiian honeycreeper), potentially infecting it with avian malaria and bird pox that originated with imported birds. The mosquito vector is extending its range (and the deadly effects of disease) farther into forest areas. Volcano, Hawai'i. [Jack Jeffrey Photography]

for biological control. The predatory *Euglandina* snail was a particularly misguided intentional introduction. Brought in to control African snails, *Euglandina* became a wide-ranging predator of native snails, threatening 300 species with extinction. *Euglandina* is still promoted by agricultural people for introduction to other islands worldwide. About 650 organisms, mostly insects, have been introduced for biological control, and more than a third are known to have become established. Early biological control species were often generalists, and they depleted many native insects along with target noxious species. Nowadays, selec-

tions are more careful and specific. However, we continue to treat the problem of alien species by introducing still more alien species.

The human role in alien invasions continues to be central. Humans select species to be imported, create opportunities for accidental introductions, and provide much of the disturbance that enhances alien establishment. Despite quarantine regulations, about 5 plant and up to 20 to 40 new insect species a year continue to become established.

Where native communities have escaped ungulate disturbance, they are relatively free of other aliens. Some areas cleared of ungulates and extremely invasive alien plants have recovered from heavy damage. Many aliens are now inextricably a part of otherwise native ecosystems without posing a significant additional threat to their stability. Some native birds may be acquiring resistance to disease. These outcomes offer hope for future recovery of native ecosystems. At present the number and distributions of alien species capable of disrupting native ecosystems are still relatively limited, but effective measures must be taken soon to curtail the degradation of native habitats. The most essential protective steps are: permanently clearing ungulates from large areas of native habitats using fences or other effective measures; removing the next-most disruptive alien organisms from native ecosystems or controlling them to minimal impact levels; and carefully scrutinizing the importation of introduced organisms.

F. R. Warshauer

ENDANGERED AND THREATENED SPECIES

The vast majority of native Hawaiian plants and animals are found nowhere else on Earth. Many, unfortunately, are in grave danger of extinction. While Hawai'i represents less than 1 percent of the U.S. total land mass, it has 363 (over 30 percent) of the 1,104 species federally listed as threatened or endangered. Among the endangered Hawaiian species are the state flower, yellow hibiscus (*ma'o hau hele, Hibiscus brackenridgei*), and the state bird, the Hawaiian goose (*nēnē, Branta sandvicensis*).

The Federal Endangered Species Act (ESA) was passed in 1973 with the goal of conserving endangered species and their habitats. To this end, the ESA:

- defines a process for determining which species are endangered or threatened

- requires that federal agencies prepare recovery plans outlining the actions needed to restore species to the point that they no longer need special protection

- prohibits federal agencies from undertaking actions likely to increase a species' chances of becoming extinct

- prohibits individuals from killing, collecting, selling, or harassing endangered animals, without

The hibiscus, *Kokia drynarioides,* an endangered species very rare in dry forest on Hawai'i Island, now nearly extinct in the wild but surviving in cultivation. [L. A. Mehrhoff]

Terminology

Endangered species: Any species in danger of extinction throughout all, or a significant portion, of its range.

Threatened species: Any species likely to become endangered within the foreseeable future.

Proposed species: A species that has been officially recommended for listing as endangered or threatened, but listing has not yet been approved.

Candidate species: A species identified as qualifying for listing as endangered or threatened but has not yet been proposed for listing.

At-risk species: Any species, subspecies, or variety that is either endangered or may become endangered in the foreseeable future. (Includes listed, proposed, and candidate species of concern, and thought-to-be extinct species.)

Critical habitat: Areas officially deemed necessary to a species' conservation; given some legal protection under ESA.

Essential habitat: Areas that may be needed to recover an endangered species; used in species recovery efforts, but not given legal protection under ESA.

authorization, on both federal and nonfederal lands, although it specifically protects endangered plants only on federal lands

- enables agencies to designate "critical" habitat where it is determined to be necessary to the survival and recovery of an endangered species

- mandates that a violation of any state's endangered species law is likewise a violation of the federal statute.

The state's endangered species law is similar to the federal act, with two notable exceptions. First, state law

150

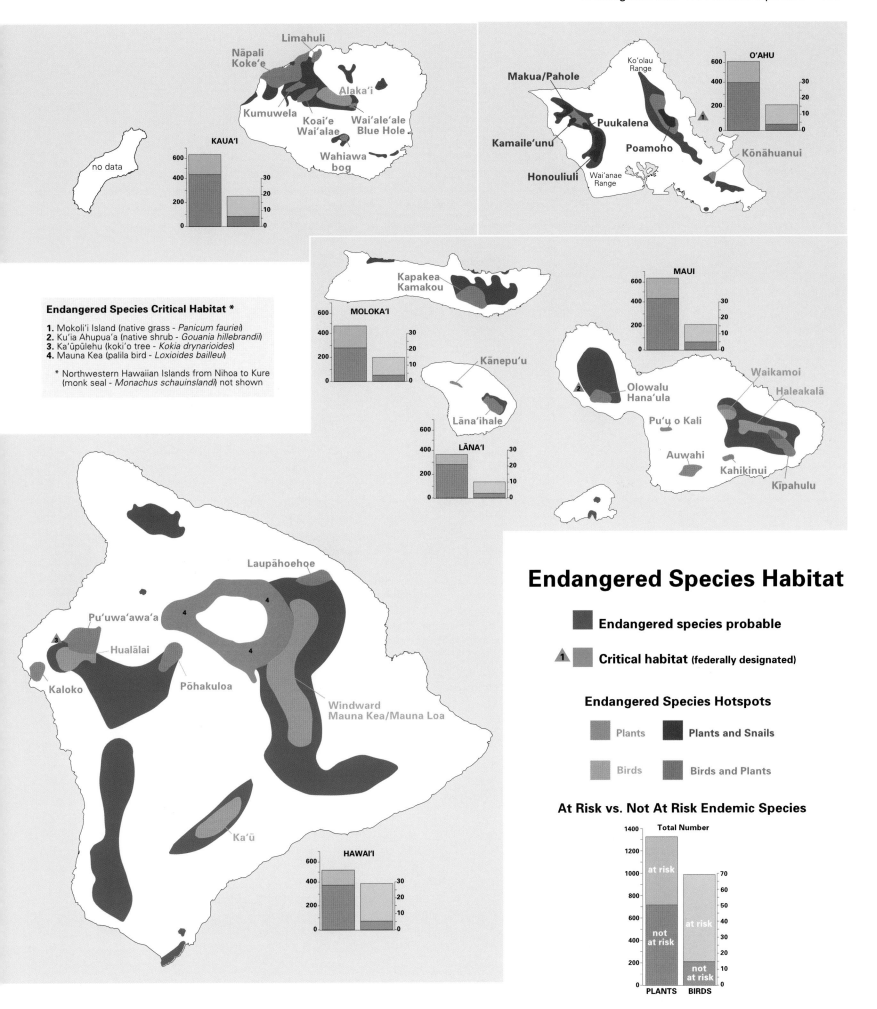

KAUA'I

no data

Limahuli
Nāpali
Koke'e
Alaka'i
Kumuwela
Koai'e
Wai'alae
Wai'ale'ale
Blue Hole
Wahiawa
bog

Endangered Species Critical Habitat *

1. Mokoli'i Island (native grass - *Panicum faurlei*)
2. Ku'ia Ahupua'a (native shrub - *Gouania hillebrandii*)
3. Ka'ūpūlehu (koki'o tree - *Kokia drynarioides*)
4. Mauna Kea (palila bird - *Loxioides bailleul*)

*** Northwestern Hawaiian Islands from Nihoa to Kure
(monk seal - *Monachus schauinslandi*) not shown

O'AHU

Ko'olau
Range
Makua/Pahole
Puukalena
Kamaile'unu
Poamoho
Honouliuli
Wai'anae
Range
Kōnāhuanui

Kapakea
Kamakou

MOLOKA'I

Kānepu'u

Lāna'ihale

LĀNA'I

MAUI

Olowalu
Hana'ula
Waikamoi
Pu'u o Kali
Haleakalā
Auwahi
Kahikinui
Kīpahulu

Laupāhoehoe

Pu'uwa'awa'a
Hualālai
Kaloko
Pōhakuloa

Windward
Mauna Kea/Mauna Loa

Ka'ū

HAWAI'I

Endangered Species Habitat

■ **Endangered species probable**

▲ ■ **Critical habitat** (federally designated)

Endangered Species Hotspots

Plants   Plants and Snails

Birds   Birds and Plants

At Risk vs. Not At Risk Endemic Species

Total Number

at risk

not
at risk

at risk

not
at risk

PLANTS   BIRDS

Status of Hawaiian Plants and Animals*
historically known species, subspecies, varieties

	native	endemic	extinct	status under U.S. Endangered Species Act				
				endangered	threatened	proposed	cs**	concern
Plants	1,304	1,160	106	272	10	10	2	293
Invertebrates								
Snails	1,267	1,263	800-900	41	0	1	0	597
Insects	~10,000	~10,000	>100	0	0	1	25	283
Fish	22	12	0	0	0	0	0	1
Turtles	5	0	0	2	3	0	0	0
Birds	93	71	33	30	1	0	2	6
Mammals								
Whales	2	0	0	2	0	0	0	0
Seals	1	1	0	1	0	0	0	0
Bats	1	1	0	1	0	0	0	0
Totals	~12,500	~12,000	>1,000	349	14	12	29	1,180

* status as of June 1997 **candidate species

protects plants and animals on both federal and non-federal lands. Second, state law does not specifically protect endangered species habitat. Species listed under the federal ESA are automatically covered by state law. However, Hawai'i can (and has) listed additional species not on the federal endangered species list.

The sweeping changes to landscapes wrought by direct human modification and the serious impacts on native ecosystems due to the introduction of hundreds of alien species have been discussed elsewhere in this *Atlas*. Almost all of Hawai'i's endangered species are significantly affected by alien species, which have

Hawaiian Monk Seal

The Hawaiian monk seal (*Monachus schauinslandi*), one of Hawai'i's two endemic mammals, although occasionally seen on beaches on the main Hawaiian islands, is found almost exclusively at small breeding sites in the Northwestern Hawaiian Islands, such as Laysan Island and Kure Atoll. Listed as endangered since 1976, the species has suffered more than a century of human exploitation and disturbance. As of 1995 the total population was approximately 1,300 animals, about 40 percent of the number observed in the late 1950s.

Monk seal births commonly occur from February to July, with a few pups born in other months. Following birth, the mother nurses and attends to her pup constantly until weaning, approximately 6 weeks later. During that time, the pup will grow from its 30-pound (14 kg) birth weight to 150–200 pounds (70–90 kg). Once they are weaned, the pups must learn to find and catch food for themselves. This may take 4 to 5 months, during which time they lose weight until their prey-catching skills are developed enough to sustain them. Pups that survive reach adult size in 5 to 8 years.

Hawaiian monk seals feed on octopus, lobster, and many species of reef fishes, including eels. A monk seal spends over half of its life in the water and regularly dives as deep as 300 feet (90 m) to feed, although dives to 1,600 feet (485 m) have been recorded. Most monk seals remain near the island of their birth for life; only about one in ten swims to another location to find a new home. Many monk seals live to more than 20 years of age; the oldest seals known were estimated to be about 30 years old. While shark predation on monk seals does occur, it is not believed to be a serious threat to recovery of the species.

The National Marine Fisheries Service manages an endangered species recovery program for the monk seal. Its primary goal, to reduce losses of female seals, has been accomplished by several means. Small female pups that would probably die if left unattended have been collected, rehabilitated at Sea Life Park on O'ahu, and then reintroduced to the wild. Adult male seals responsible for deaths of females have been captured and relocated away from the major breeding islands. Tons of marine debris that can entangle and kill seals are collected and destroyed every year at the breeding islands. Also, area restrictions on longline fishing for swordfish have been established to reduce seal interactions with longline equipment.

A catastrophic decline in monk seals has occurred during the 1990s at French Frigate Shoals, near the center of the Hawaiian archipelago. Most young seals there seem to be starving. This dramatic loss, appearing to include close to half of that population as of 1995, is thought to be caused by climate and oceanographic

A Hawaiian monk seal and pup. [V. McCormick]

changes that have reduced biological productivity. In response to the decline in the availability of food for the monk seals, some young females have been relocated to more productive sites.

The Hawaiian monk seal is a top predator in these small and fragile island ecosystems and, as evidenced by the recent population decline at French Frigate Shoals, a sensitive indicator of disturbance in the environment around the Islands. It faces tremendous obstacles, of both natural and human origins, in making a recovery.

WILLIAM G. GILMARTIN

probably been responsible for more extinctions than all other human activities combined. Alien ungulates (pigs, goats, and deer) destroy native forest and kill endangered plants. Introduced mosquitos transmit diseases to native birds, and introduced predatory snails wipe out endemic land snails. Numerous alien insects and diseases decimate remnant populations of native invertebrates and plants, and alien weeds invade native ecosystems, thereby drastically increasing the risk of wildfire. Analysis reveals that the most common threats to Hawai'i's endangered plants (and those proposed for offical listing) are alien weeds (92 percent), pigs and goats (82 percent), fire (45 percent), rats (33 percent), collecting (33 percent), and development projects (15 percent).

Habitat loss caused by the above factors is a major reason Hawai'i has so many endangered species. At present less than 10 percent of the state's dry forest remains, and most of the remaining forest has been significantly degraded. Mesic and wet forests have been less damaged, but degradation by alien species, particularly pigs and deer, continues. The fencing of large areas of native forest in Haleakalā and Hawai'i Volcanoes National Parks, and the removal of most of

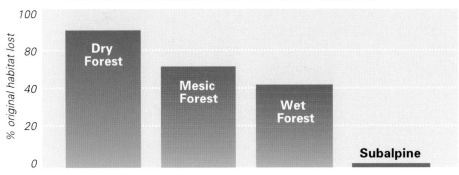

Habitat Destruction since Human Settlement

% original habitat lost

Dry Forest

Mesic Forest

Wet Forest

Subalpine

the alien goats and pigs from them, has slowed forest degradation there, resulting in substantial recovery of some endangered species. Likewise, intensive conservation management in some reserves and refuges, largely focused on alien species control, has benefited endangered species. Also, programs have been initiated to propagate selected endangered birds, plants, and snails for reintroduction efforts and to build up reserves of captive-bred individuals should wild populations be destroyed.

Nonetheless, Hawai'i's extinction crisis is far from over. Dozens of native species have been reduced to such low numbers that their wild populations will likely become extinct within a few years. Indeed, 109 species of native plants have fewer than 20 individual plants remaining in the wild, 10 of which have been reduced to a single surviving wild individual. Of these, 25 species have not yet been officially proposed for listing or listed as endangered or threatened.

To prevent the extinction of these vulnerable species, it will be necessary to develop effective and economical measures to control threats posed by alien mammals, weeds, and diseases. Similarly, effective techniques and facilities to propagate, grow, and reintroduce endangered plants and invertebrates must be found.

LOYAL A. MEHRHOFF

An endangered species restricted to Hawai'i Island, the *palila* (*Loxioides bailleui*) inhabits the *māmane-naio* forest on the slopes of Mauna Kea, from 6,000 to 9,000 feet. [Jack Jeffrey Photography]

PROTECTED AREAS

The term "protected areas" commonly refers to lands managed to preserve unique, endangered, or representative natural and cultural assets and to set them aside from conflicting uses. In the Hawaiian Islands the problems that necessitate aggressive protected area management of native biological systems arise from the comparatively small sizes of species populations and habitats, as well as the intrinsic vulnerability of an insular biota to human impacts. These factors limit the application of traditional multiple-use resource management strategies that are used successfully in continental settings. In Hawai'i proactive management of protected areas is essential to exclude or minimize negative influences such as those associated with harmful alien species. In addition to biological reserves, protected area designation may also apply to unique or important cultural assets, ranging from ancient Polynesian ceremonial sites to the USS *Arizona* Memorial.

Throughout the state more than 1 million acres (405,000 ha), over 25 percent of the state's land area, are under varying degrees of protected areas management. Relatively few areas meet the rigorous proactive management ideal desirable for oceanic islands. However, statewide management is gradually evolving toward that goal.

There are eight types of publicly owned protected areas. In addition there are privately owned sites dedicated to preservation. Forest reserves may only marginally meet criteria for protected areas but nevertheless are very important reservoirs of biological diversity.

Publicly owned protected areas are managed by either federal or state agencies. National parks and national wildlife refuges are managed by the U.S.

Greensword bog, Hāna rain forest, Haleakalā National Park. [B. Gagné]

Kīpahulu Valley, Haleakalā National Park. [B. Gagné]

Haleakalā Crater and silversword from White Hill, Haleakalā National Park. [B. Gagné]

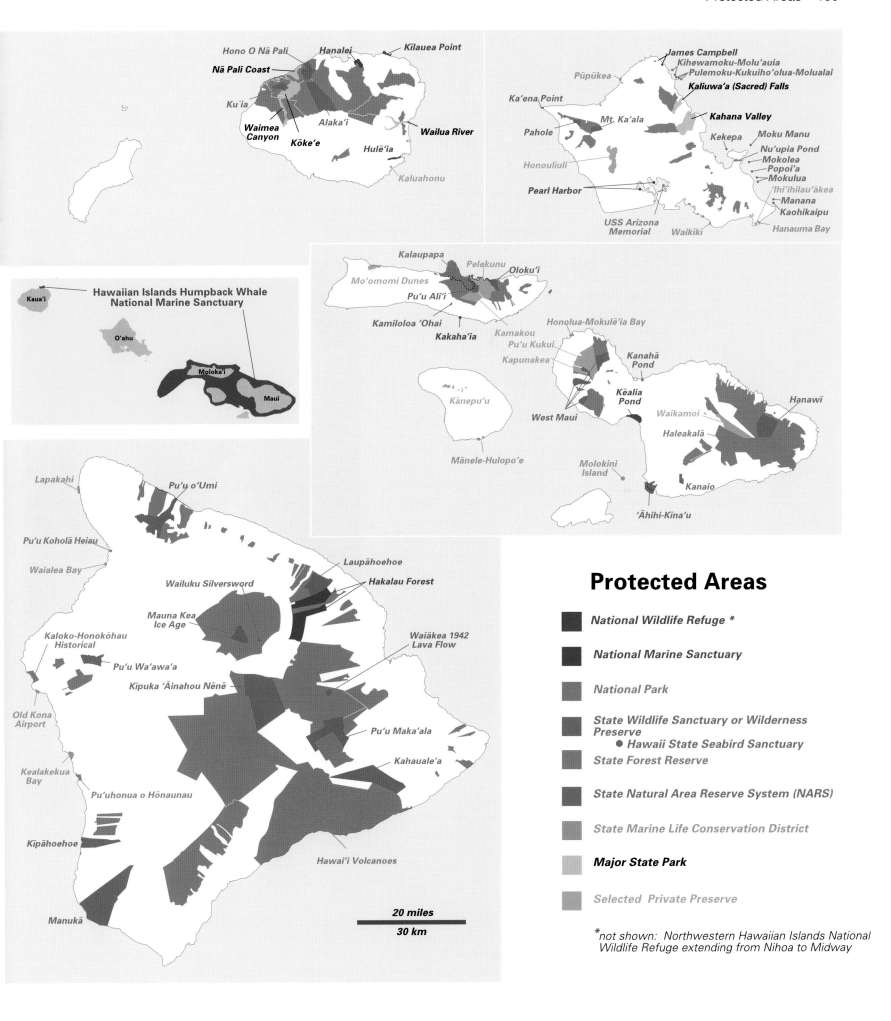

Hono O Nā Pali
Hanalei
Kīlauea Point
Nā Pali Coast
Ku'ia
Waimea Canyon
Alaka'i
Kōke'e
Wailua River
Hulē'ia
Kaluahonu

Pūpūkea
James Campbell
Kihewamoku-Molu'auia
Pulemoku-Kukuiho'olua-Molualai
Kaliuwa'a (Sacred) Falls
Ka'ena Point
Mt. Ka'ala
Kahana Valley
Pahole
Kekepa
Moku Manu
Nu'upia Pond
Mokolea
Popoi'a
Mokulua
Honouliuli
'Ihi'ihilau'ākea
Manana
Kaohikaipu
Pearl Harbor
USS Arizona Memorial
Waikīkī
Hanauma Bay

Hawaiian Islands Humpback Whale National Marine Sanctuary

Kaua'i

O'ahu

Moloka'i

Maui

Kalaupapa
Pelekunu
Oloku'i
Mo'omomi Dunes
Pu'u Ali'i
Kamiloloa 'Ohai
Kakaha'ia
Kamakou
Honolua-Mokulē'ia Bay
Pu'u Kukui
Kanahā Pond
Kapunakea
Kēalia Pond
Kānepu'u
West Maui
Waikamoi
Hanawī
Haleakalā
Mānele-Hulopo'e
Molokini Island
Kanaio
'Āhihi-Kīna'u

Lapakahi
Pu'u o'Umi
Pu'u Koholā Heiau
Laupāhoehoe
Waialea Bay
Wailuku Silversword
Hakalau Forest
Mauna Kea Ice Age
Waiākea 1942 Lava Flow
Kaloko-Honokōhau Historical
Pu'u Wa'awa'a
Kīpuka 'Āinahou Nēnē
Old Kona Airport
Pu'u Maka'ala
Kealakekua Bay
Kahauale'a
Pu'uhonua o Hōnaunau
Kīpāhoehoe
Hawai'i Volcanoes
Manukā

20 miles
30 km

Protected Areas

- **National Wildlife Refuge ***
- **National Marine Sanctuary**
- **National Park**
- **State Wildlife Sanctuary or Wilderness Preserve**
  - **● Hawaii State Seabird Sanctuary**
- **State Forest Reserve**
- **State Natural Area Reserve System (NARS)**
- **State Marine Life Conservation District**
- **Major State Park**
- **Selected Private Preserve**

*not shown: Northwestern Hawaiian Islands National Wildlife Refuge extending from Nihoa to Midway

Department of the Interior. The National Marine Wildlife Sanctuary is managed by the U.S. Department of Commerce. The State Department of Land and Natural Resources manages forest reserves, natural area reserves, wildlife (and plant) sanctuaries, marine life conservation districts, and state parks. The Nature Conservancy, a private, nonprofit organization, manages many private reserves, sometimes in cooperation with other landowners.

National Parks Hawai'i National Park was established by the U.S. Congress in 1916. In 1961, Congress separated the designated area into Hawai'i Volcanoes National Park (HAVO) on Hawai'i Island and Haleakalā National Park (HALE) on Maui. Extending from volcano summits to the sea, both parks are outstanding for the range of environments and biodiversity they protect. HAVO is by far the state's largest terrestrial protected area. It includes the summit areas of two active volcanoes, Kīlauea and Mauna Loa. These volcanoes have created a remarkable mosaic of lava flows of different ages and textures across altitudinal climatic zones for the establishment of plant and animal communities. HALE includes the relatively barren summit depression and high-elevation slopes of dormant Haleakalā volcano, as well as some of the most biologically rich rain forests in the state. Both national parks are internationally designated biosphere reserves—a status that implies proactive management in cooperation with adjacent landowners. Other areas in Hawai'i that have been designated national historical parks and sites primarily because of historic or archaeological importance may also contain significant natural areas.

National Wildlife Refuges (NWRs) These areas are extremely varied. Nationwide, they generally provide protection and management of exceptional concentrations of wildlife—most often waterfowl, shorebirds, and seabirds. Many refuges in Hawai'i protect crucial wetland habitat. Others include the low atolls of the Northwestern Hawaiian Islands, which harbor one of the world's largest concentrations of seabirds, and montane rain forests, such as Hakalau Forest NWR on Hawai'i Island, an important habitat for endangered forest birds.

National Marine Sanctuaries The U.S. Congress in 1972 authorized creation of sanctuaries to protect marine resources. Fourteen national marine sanctuaries have been established as of 1996. Designated in 1992, the Hawaiian Islands Humpback Whale Sanctuary encompasses approximately 1,300 square nautical miles (4,450 sq. km) of state and federal waters surrounding the four-island area of Maui County (including Penguin Bank) and a small segment of ocean adjacent to Kīlauea Point National Wildlife Refuge on Kaua'i. The purpose of the sanctuary is to provide enhanced protection for an important breeding, calving, and nursing area of the humpback whale.

State Forest Reserves These areas were originally set aside early in the twentieth century to protect important watersheds from destruction by domestic and feral cattle and other browsing animals. Forest reserves contain a large percentage of the state's remaining biological diversity, and effective management of these areas will be an important factor determining how much of Hawai'i's natural heritage survives into the middle of the twenty-first century.

Natural Area Reserves The Natural Area Reserves System (NARS) was established by Hawai'i statute in 1970 to "preserve in perpetuity specified

Sand dunes and native coastal vegetation at Ka'ena Point NARS, O'ahu. [M. G. Buck]

land and water areas which support communities, as relatively unmodified as possible, of the natural flora and fauna, as well as geological sites, of Hawai'i." Originally they were a network of largely neglected "paper preserves"; however, an excellent NARS management program is evolving, although it is constrained by limited funding and by opposition in some areas from local hunting groups.

State Wildlife Sanctuaries These include an array of areas set aside to protect individual species of rare or endangered animals or plants. (Many very small plant sanctuaries are not shown on the accompanying map.)

Marine Life Conservation Districts (MLCDs) These nearshore areas have been established to protect marine life to the greatest extent possible, allowing residents and visitors opportunities for viewing marine organisms in their natural habitat. The taking of any type of living or nonliving material is generally prohibited. The first MLCD was established in 1967 at Hanauma Bay, Oʻahu. By 1996 there were ten MLCDs statewide, with a combined total of 1,469 acres (595 ha).

State Parks Some of the most scenic areas in Hawaiʻi, as well as sites with important native ecosystems or cultural and historic features, are included in state parks. Unfortunately, because of their attractiveness, high accessibility, and relative lack of proactive management, the biological stability of some parks (for example, Kōkeʻe State Park) is severely threatened by invasions of alien species. The management of state parks must cope with the difficulty of balancing the competing objectives of satisfying recreational demands and protecting native ecosystems.

Privately Owned Protected Areas The Nature Conservancy of Hawaiʻi (TNCH) manages a superb network of nature preserves. TNCH was founded in 1980 as an affiliate of an international nonprofit conservation organization. The mission of the national and Hawaiʻi groups is "to preserve plants, animals, and natural communities that represent the diversity of life on Earth by protecting the lands and waters they need to survive." TNCH has acquired key natural areas through conventional real estate purchase and conservation easements, in addition to supporting the creation of public and private landowner partnerships for ecosystem conservation. TNCH has an active program of management, which makes extensive use of volunteers. Other private landowners, notably Bishop Estate on Hawaiʻi Island and Maui Land and Pineapple on Maui, have recently become actively involved in land management for conservation.

LLOYD L. LOOPE
AND SONIA P. JUVIK

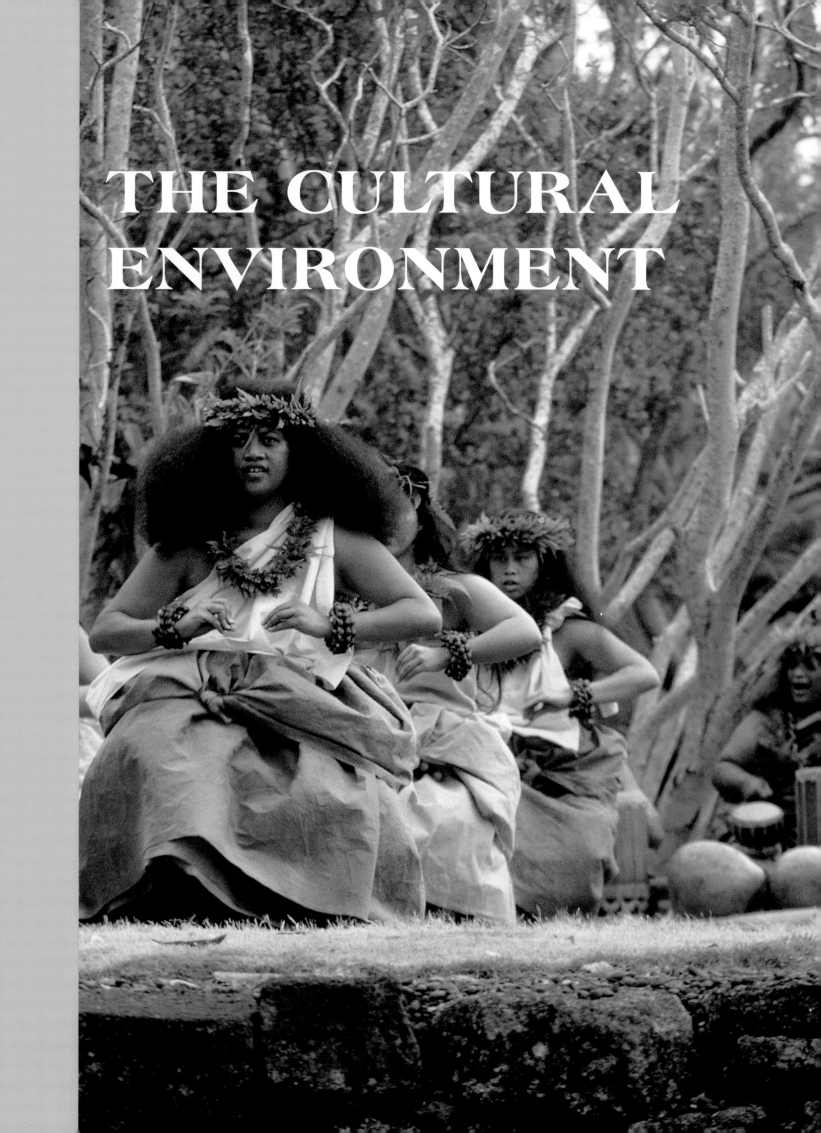

THE CULTURAL
ENVIRONMENT

Overleaf: Halau ‘O Kekui performing ancient hula (*kahiko*).
[P. J. Buklarewicz]

ARCHAEOLOGY

The discovery of the Hawaiian Islands was one of the most remarkable achievements of the Polynesian navigators, whose voyages through the vast expanses of the eastern Pacific have only recently been appreciated by Western scholars. Archaeological sites, and radiocarbon dates obtained from them, reveal the general sequence of Polynesian colonization, beginning about 1000 B.C. in the Tongan and Samoan archipelagoes and extending into central East Polynesia (the Cook, Society, and Marquesas Islands) by the beginning of the Christian era. The immediate homeland of the first Polynesian voyagers to Hawai'i may have been the Marquesas, as suggested by both archaeological and linguistic evidence. However, multiple, two-way voyages between the Hawaiian Islands and the archipelagoes of central East Polynesia apparently occurred for some time before Hawai'i became isolated from the rest of Polynesia, after about A.D. 1200.

Efforts to date the initial Polynesian discovery and settlement of the Hawaiian Islands have generated considerable scholarly controversy. Evidence from several habitation sites (for example, the Bellows Dune Site on O'ahu and the Hālawa Valley Dune Site on Moloka'i) indicates that permanent settlements were established by at least A.D. 600. Initial discovery and colonization of the Islands may have occurred, however, as much as three or four centuries earlier, although further research will be required to verify this.

Archaeological studies in Hawai'i began early in the twentieth century with the pioneering work of William T. Brigham and John F. G. Stokes. Islandwide surveys of *heiau* (temple sites) and other above-ground sites continued throughout the pre–World War II period, but the excavation of subsurface sites did not begin until 1950, with Kenneth P. Emory's work at Kuli'ou'ou Rockshelter (O'ahu). Since then, archaeologists from the Bernice P. Bishop Museum, University of Hawai'i, and other institutions (as well as private consultants performing extensive contract archaeology) have conducted excavations at several hundred archaeological sites. This work, together with thousands of radiocarbon dates from the sites, has yielded a rich record for constructing a detailed chronology of precontact history.

The Archaeological Landscape

The Hawaiian archaeological landscape includes a wide range of site types, most consisting of dry-laid stone constructions utilizing natural lava rock. The largest sites are typically the stone foundations of

Pu'ukoholā Heiau, Kawaihae, Hawai'i. [P. V. Kirch]

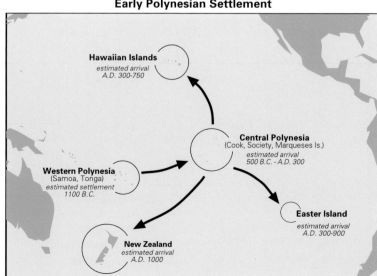

Early Polynesian Settlement

Hawaiian Islands
estimated arrival
A.D. 300-750

Central Polynesia
(Cook, Society, Marqueses Is.)
estimated arrival
500 B.C. - A.D. 300

Western Polynesia
(Samoa, Tonga)
estimated settlement
1100 B.C.

Easter Island
estimated arrival
A.D. 300-900

New Zealand
estimated arrival
A.D. 1000

Polynesian Navigation

The greatest wonder of the Pacific world began more than 40,000 years ago, when the ancestors of the Pacific Islanders ventured out from the shores of mainland Southeast Asia into the Pacific Ocean. In an eastward migration that spanned millenia and covered thousands of miles—including lengthy stretches of open ocean—these early voyagers discovered and settled hundreds of tiny islands scattered across Earth's largest ocean. All of this was accomplished without the use of navigational instruments, at least 2,000 years before the Vikings ventured beyond familiar waters and well before the explorations of Christopher Columbus.

This amazing maritime tradition reached its pinnacle with the settling of Polynesia, an ocean area about the size of the combined land masses of Europe and North America. By 1100 B.C. the ancient Polynesian mariners had colonized Tonga and Samoa. Over the next thousand years canoes pointed upwind and reached the Marquesas and the Society Islands. By A.D. 1200 these courageous seagoing people had settled the distant islands of the Polynesian Triangle: Hawai'i in the north, Aotearoa (New Zealand) in the southwest, and Rapa Nui (Easter Island) in the southeast, bringing to an end the long voyages of discovery.

While Polynesian oral traditions tell of long ocean voyages and distant homelands, it was explorer Captain James Cook who first recorded the Polynesians' navigational capabilities. Cook observed these skills in the Tahitian native Tupaia, who sailed aboard Cook's ship in the Pacific. Tupaia amazed the British with his ability to point out the direction of Tahiti with great accuracy and without using navigational charts or the ship's compass.

Cook and his crew also recognized that the natives of Hawai'i were of the same "nation" as the inhabitants of Tahiti and other Polynesian islands they had visited. In his journal Cook wrote, "How shall we account for this nation having spread itself to so many detached islands so widely disjoined from each other in every quarter of the Pacific Ocean?" A keen observer of people and places,

Cook further noted that this was "by far the most extensive nation on earth."

Cook must have been convinced that these far-flung Polynesians included people capable of building canoes that could be navigated and sailed over great distances between island groups. What he may not have recognized was that this great achievement by a people with limited natural resources resulted from the intimate relationship developed over centuries with their island-ocean environment. Their system of navigation relied not upon instruments, but upon the movements of stars, the moon, and the sun across the heavens. It required detailed knowledge of the winds, seas, ocean currents, clouds, and sea animals and birds. Survival and success on the open ocean also may have been due, in addition to seaworthy canoes, to favorable weather and, perhaps, good luck.

In the 1970s, a performance-accurate replica of a Polynesian voyaging double-hulled canoe was built in Hawai'i. This canoe, named *Hōkūle'a*, has sailed throughout Polynesia for more than two decades, reenacting the traditional practices of early Pacific voyagers. Its extensive expeditions have brought together people from distant lands and sparked interest in Pacific history and heritage. New Hawai'i voyaging canoes, *Makali'i* and *Hawai'iloa*, have joined the legacy of building a broader Polynesian identity. With the addition of canoes from Aotearoa, the Cook Islands, and Tahiti, the voyaging canoes have become the dominant cultural symbol of Polynesia and Pacific islanders.

GORDON PI'IANĀI'A

Polynesian voyaging double-hulled canoe. [M. A. Tongg]

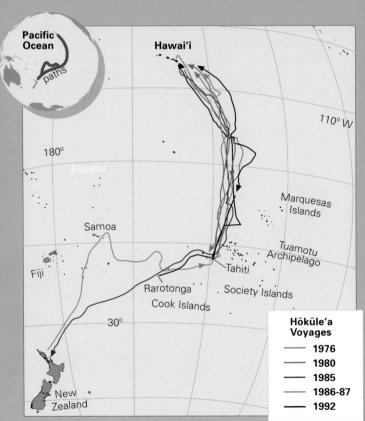

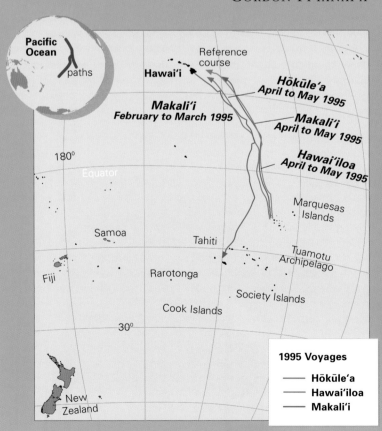

Ethnobotany

On their long-distance voyaging, the Polynesian settlers of remote Pacific islands carried with them an assortment of life-sustaining plants and animals. Of 29 plant species that were widely distributed throughout Oceania, 23 were brought to Hawai'i. It was fortunate that these early colonizers brought staple food plants—taro, sweet potatoes, breadfruit, bananas, and several species of yams—for none of these existed in Hawai'i, and no native Hawaiian plants could furnish sufficient carbohydrates in their stead. Most other plants useful to Polynesians, such as coconut, sugarcane, and *kī*, (ti) were not present in Hawai'i either, but it was possible to survive without them, as the endemic species *olonā* (*Touchardia latifolia*) could replace coconut for cordage, and sugarcane and *kī* were not essential. Certain species, including *kamani, kou,* and *milo,* were obviously brought for their hard wood, but here too, other native Hawaiian species such as *koa, olomea, lama,* and *olopua* could have taken their places.

The Polynesians found endemic fiber plants (*ma'aloa* and *māmaki*) in Hawai'i suitable for making cloth, or tapa (*kapa*), but they probably could never have turned out what is considered to be some of the finest tapa in the Pacific without the paper mulberry (*wauke*) they brought from Polynesia. Hawaiian tapa, with its intricate designs applied by bamboo stampers to thin, delicate, watermarked *wauke,* is unlike any other Polynesian tapa. The endemic *olonā* furnished strong but flexible cordage for fishing nets, as well as light netting onto which the colorful feathers of native forest birds could be tied to fashion unique and remarkable Hawaiian feather capes, helmets, and lei. Archeological excavations have revealed the remains of *wauke* tapa, *olonā,* and gourd fragments, some decorated with small geometric designs known as *pāwehe.* The gourd *Lagenaria siceraria,* used more extensively by Hawaiians than by any other Polynesians, was even made into musical instruments such as drums and whistles.

Hawaiians enriched their nutritionally adequate but bland diet of fish and poi with about 30 varieties of native *limu* (seaweeds), the largest diversity consumed in Polynesia. Possibly because of the many *kapu* (prohibitions) on foods from the land, women specialized in exploiting nearshore and brackish waters for food plants and animals.

The wet mountain forests became the province of the men, who sought woods for constructing canoes and houses, as well as herbs for medicines, although the most frequently used medicinal herbs grew close to lowland habitations. *Noni, kukui,* and *'ōhi'a 'ai,* introduced to Hawai'i, were the most important herbs, used to treat a large variety of ailments. Of the dozen most valuable medicinal plants, the only native is *ko'oko'olau* (*Bidens*). Other endemic species were used, but only for very specific ailments, which suggests that Hawaiians turned to the very rich endemic flora only after the efficacy of familiar plants had been tested. That they had no medicines for foreign diseases introduced through Western contact was not surprising, as the foreigners themselves had no cures either.

Important Plants Polynesians Brought to Hawai'i

Hawaiian/English Name	Scientific Name
kalo, taro	*Colocasia esculenta*
'uala, sweet potato	*Ipomoea batatas*
'ulu, breadfruit	*Artocarpus altilis*
'uhi, yams (3 main species)	*Dioscorea* species
mai'a, banana	*Musa acuminata* hybrids
niu, coconut	*Cocos nucifera*
kō, sugarcane	*Saccharum officinarum*
'awa (kava)	*Piper methysticum*
kī, ti	*Cordyline fruticosa*
wauke, paper mulberry	*Broussonetia papyrifera*
ipu, gourd	*Lagenaria siceraria*
hau	*Hibiscus tiliaceus*
kamani	*Calophyllum inophyllum*
kou	*Cordia subcordata*
kukui	*Aleurites moluccana*
milo	*Thespesia populnea*
noni	*Morinda citrifolia*
'ōhi'a 'ai	*Syzygium malaccense*
'ohe, bamboo	*Schizostachyum glaucifolium*

ISABELLA A. ABBOTT

---

major war temples (*luakini heiau*)—such as Pu'uomahuka (O'ahu), 'Ili'ili'ōpae (Moloka'i), Pi'ilanihale (Maui), and Pu'ukoholā (Hawai'i)—each of which may cover more than 100,000 square feet (9,300 sq m). Smaller *heiau* are found throughout the Islands in a variety of platformed, walled, and terraced structures. These varied in function, although many were agricultural temples (*heiau ho'oulu'ai*). Habitation sites typically were dispersed over the landscape rather than clustered, although some villagelike aggregations apparently did exist, such as the Kaunolū fishing settlement on Lāna'i and the Koai'e hamlet at Lapakahi (Hawai'i). Precontact Hawaiian habitations consisted of groups of functionally separated structures (the *kau-hale* group), which are represented archaeologically by C- and L-shaped walls, rectangular enclosures, platforms, terraces, and other forms. In some areas, the Hawaiians lived in rock shelters and lava tubes. Caves, lava tubes, and large sand dunes (such as at Mōkapu, on O'ahu), served as burial places, and caves were also used as refuges.

Hawaiian subsistence was based on intensive forms of agriculture and aquaculture, and these have left their marks on the archaeological landscape as well. In windward and some leeward valleys with permanent streams, the islanders constructed terraces on alluvial plains and hillslopes for the irrigated cultivation of taro (*Colocasia esculenta*). Stone-faced terrace

'Ulalapu'e Fishpond, Moloka'i. [J. E. Maragos]

Ancient Hawaiian trail, South Kona, Hawai'i. [J. Juvik]

complexes and stone-lined water ditches (*'auwai*) are major agricultural relics in these regions. On leeward slopes of Hawai'i Island (especially in the Kohala and Kona Districts), remains of the once-extensive "field systems" still stand: parallel stone-and-earth rows that separated intensively cultivated dryland gardens of taro, sweet potato (*Ipomoea batatas*), and bananas (*Musa* hybrids).

The Hawaiians practiced intensive aquaculture in large, stone-walled fishponds (*loko kuapā*) constructed on shallow reef flats. All together, 449 ponds have been recorded, the majority of them on O'ahu and Moloka'i, where the coastal geomorphology was highly conducive to pond construction. Some of the larger ponds incorporated more than 500 acres (200 ha) and are estimated to have yielded as much as 365 pounds (166 kg) per acre annually, primarily of mullet (*Mugil cephalus*) and milkfish (*Chanos chanos*).

With the Native Hawaiian population numbering in the hundreds of thousands (estimates have ranged widely, from 250,000 to more than 1 million) prior to Captain James Cook's arrival in 1778, lower-elevation regions (below about 3,000 feet [1,000 m]) were densely settled. Archaeological surveys have revealed more than 400 sites within the *ahupua'a* of Kawela on Moloka'i for instance, and more than 1,000 sites on the *ahupua'a* of Kīpapa and Nakaohu in southeast Maui. Unfortunately, extensive plantation agriculture, ranching, and urban developments during the late nineteenth and twentieth centuries have destroyed countless archaeological sites. The database of the Historic Preservation Division of the State of Hawai'i currently includes about 20,000 sites and site complexes, and these represent only a small fraction of the sites still in existence.

The Cultural Sequence

Culture and society in Hawai'i were continually changing during the 12 centuries or more between the discovery and settlement of the Islands by ancestral East Polynesians and the arrival of the British explorer Cook. This process of change led to the development of a Hawaiian culture and language distinct from those of other, related Polynesian peoples. The evolution of precontact Hawaiian culture can be traced in the archaeological record, and understanding this process of cultural development has been a major goal of archaeologists.

Hawaiian precontact history can be divided into four main periods: the Colonization Period (A.D. 300–600), the Developmental Period (600–1100), the Expansion Period (1100–1650), and the Proto-Historic Period (1650–1795).

The Colonization Period remains the least understood, simply because very few archaeological sites of this early time have been discovered or investigated. However, findings from sites such as Bellows Beach at Waimānalo, O'ahu, indicate that early Hawaiian settlers had a lifestyle similar in many respects to that on the Marquesas Islands during the same period. For example, at both the Hane Dune Site in the Marquesas and the Bellows Beach Dune Site, house floors were paved with waterworn gravel and had shallow burials beneath the paving. The occupants used fishhooks made of bone and pearl shell and adzes flaked from basalt in triangular and trapezoidal forms of early East Polynesian type.

Slightly more archeological evidence has been discovered from the Developmental Period, during which certain distinctly Hawaiian patterns began to emerge. At sites dating from this period in the Hālawa Valley on Moloka'i, and at Ka Lae (South Point) on Hawai'i Island, early forms of the Hawaiian two-piece bone fishhook, as well as new types of adzes, have been found.

The Expansion Period, beginning about A.D. 1100, was an era of sweeping transformation. The appearance of sites dating from this period along the leeward coasts (such as those at Lapakahi and 'Anaeho'omalu on Hawai'i Island) indicates an overflow of population from more ecologically favorable windward valleys into drier regions. The evidence strongly suggests that by the mid-to-late Expansion Period population levels had soared and most major agricultural production zones in both windward and leeward environments had been developed. Accompanying this population increase and economic development were significant social, political, and religious changes. During this time the classic *ahupua'a* system of land division seems to have evolved, in tandem with an increasingly hierarchical social stratification of chiefs (*ali'i*) and commoners (*maka'āinana*). Also, late in the Expansion Period Hawaiians began constructing large, stone temple foundations, which reflected the rise of new religious ideologies, especially the cult of the war god, Kū.

The Proto-Historic Period might be thought of as the "classic" phase of Hawaiian culture, as described in the writings of Hawaiian scholars such as Samuel Kamakau and David Malo. Politically, Hawai'i was divided into four great chiefdoms that were centered on Kaua'i, O'ahu, Maui, and Hawai'i. The smaller islands—Moloka'i, Lāna'i, and Kaho'olawe—became the spoils of interisland wars of conquest. Presiding over these major political entities were the great *ali'i*, whose daily lives were governed by strict protocol. An elaborate *kapu* (taboo) system likewise regulated the lesser chiefs (*ali'i 'ai ahupua'a*), who controlled individual land units (*ahupua'a*), and commoners whose labor provided the economic base of the chiefdoms. Among other restrictions, the *kapu* system required the separate cooking and eating of food by men and women, as reflected in the functionally separated structures of the *kauhale*, or dwelling cluster.

After European contact, the pace of change again accelerated. Introduced diseases—to which Native Hawaiians had little or no resistance—took a terrible toll on the population, while new social, political, and religious ideas radically reshaped the culture. The *kapu* system was formally abrogated by Ka'ahumanu and Liholiho after the death of Kamehameha I in 1819. Many of these postcontact changes are also represented in the archaeological record. In the Anahulu Valley of O'ahu, for example, studies of postcontact archaeological sites have revealed a sequence of architectural changes associated with the abolishment of the *kapu* system and the adoption of new lifestyles.

Major Sites

Many significant archaeological sites and site complexes have been preserved throughout the Islands and are accessible to those interested in learning more about precontact Hawaiian history. Most of these, along with information on major zones of prehistoric settlement and economic activity, are indicated on the map of major sites. On Kaua'i, sites of particular note include the *heiau* complex at Wailua, the Ke-ahu-a-Laka Hālau Hula (dance platform) at Hā'ena, and the postcontact Russian Fort Elizabeth at Waimea. On O'ahu, preserved and accessible *heiau* sites include Ulu Pō, Pu'uomahuka, Kāne'ākī, and Keaīwa. Several fishponds

Kāne'ākī *Heiau,* O'ahu. [P. V. Kirch]

Kūkaniloko, birthing stone, O'ahu. [P. V. Kirch]

(such as He'eia) are still visible around the margins of Kāne'ohe Bay. Two unique sites on O'ahu are the chiefly birthing stones at Kūkaniloko and the fortification notches at Nu'uanu Pali, scene of the battle in 1795 between Kamehameha and Kalanikupule, high chief of O'ahu.

Moloka'i is particularly noteworthy for the 73 stone-walled fishponds that line its southern coastline. Many of these ponds are readily visible from the coastal highway, and a few are still used. Several large *heiau* sites are located in the Kamalo-Mapulehu area, and Hālawa Valley is a virtually continuous archaeological complex of irrigated terraces and habitation sites. On Lāna'i is the Kaunolū fishing village, typical

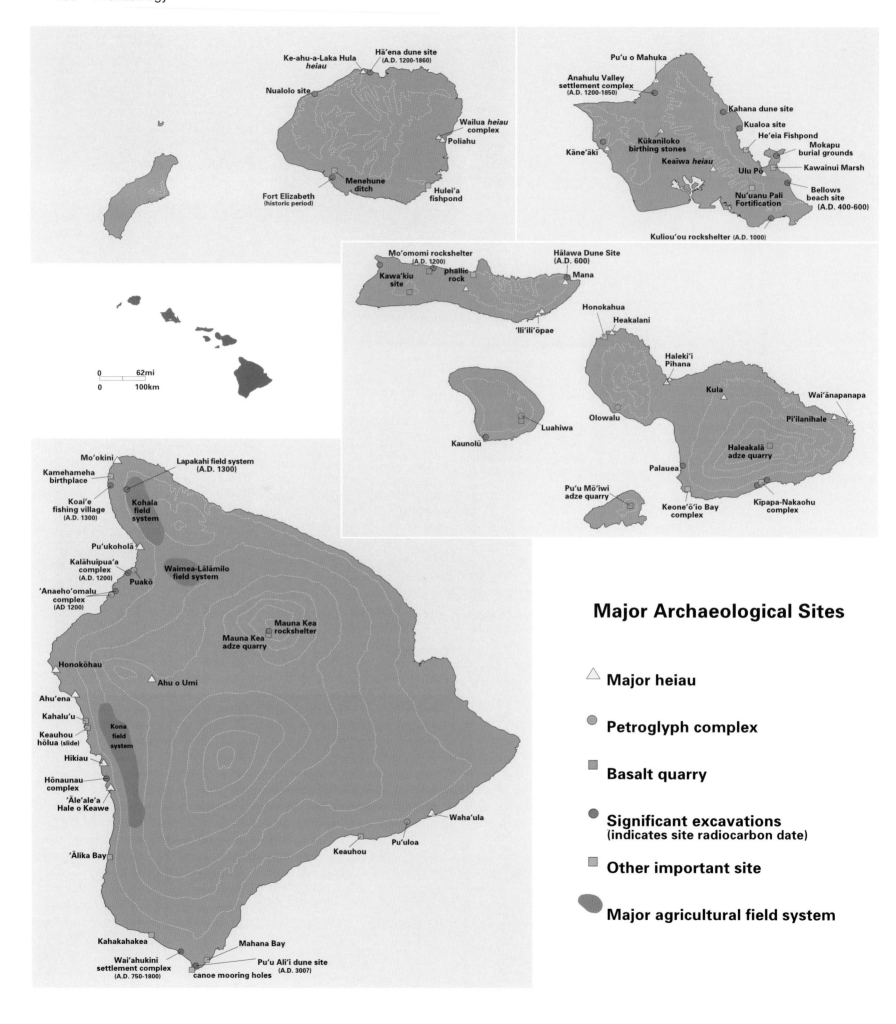

Ke-ahu-a-Laka Hula *heiau*
Hāʻena dune site (A.D. 1200-1860)
Nualolo site
Wailua *heiau* complex
Poliahu
Fort Elizabeth (historic period)
Menehune ditch
Huleiʻa fishpond

Puʻu o Mahuka
Anahulu Valley settlement complex (A.D. 1200-1850)
Kahana dune site
Kualoa site
Heʻeia Fishpond
Mokapu burial grounds
Kūkaniloko birthing stones
Kāneʻākī
Keaīwa *heiau*
Ulu Pō
Kawainui Marsh
Nuʻuanu Pali Fortification
Bellows beach site (A.D. 400-600)
Kuliouʻou rockshelter (A.D. 1000)

Moʻomomi rockshelter (A.D. 1200)
Hālawa Dune Site (A.D. 600)
Kawaʻkiu site
phallic rock
Mana
ʻIliʻiliʻōpae

Honokahua
Heakalani
Halekiʻi Pihana
Kula
Waiʻānapanapa
Olowalu
Piʻilanihale
Luahiwa
Haleakalā adze quarry
Kaunolū
Palauea
Puʻu Mōʻiwi adze quarry
Keoneʻōʻio Bay complex
Kīpapa-Nakaohu complex

Moʻokini
Lapakahi field system (A.D. 1300)
Kamehameha birthplace
Koaiʻe fishing village (A.D. 1300)
Kohala field system
Puʻukoholā
Kalāhuipuaʻa complex (A.D. 1200)
Puakō
Waimea-Lālāmilo field system
ʻAnaehoʻomalu complex (AD 1200)
Mauna Kea rockshelter
Mauna Kea adze quarry
Honokōhau
Ahu o Umi
Ahuʻena
Kahaluʻu
Keauhou hōlua (slide)
Kona field system
Hikiau
Hōnaunau complex
ʻĀleʻaleʻa Hale o Keawe
Wahaʻula
ʻĀlika Bay
Puʻuloa
Keauhou
Kahakahakea
Mahana Bay
Waiʻahukini settlement complex (A.D. 750-1800)
Puʻu Aliʻi dune site (A.D. 300?)
canoe mooring holes

0 — 62mi
0 — 100km

Major Archaeological Sites

△ **Major heiau**

● **Petroglyph complex**

■ **Basalt quarry**

● **Significant excavations** (indicates site radiocarbon date)

■ **Other important site**

⬬ **Major agricultural field system**

Traditional Land Tenure on Moloka'i

The Hawaiian people devised a complex system of land division, tenure, and patterns of use over the many centuries that they have inhabited the Islands. By the early contact period, this land system was characterized by the division of each island into several major districts (*moku*); these in turn were subdivided into territorial units called *ahupua'a* (literally, "pig altar"). In theory, each *ahupua'a* was a roughly pie-shaped area that originated on the central mountain range or peak of each island and expanded seaward, thus encompassing every major ecological resource zone: forest, agricultural area, coastal region, and reef and/or nearshore waters. In practice, *ahupua'a* varied greatly in size, shape, and the degree to which they incorporated various resource zones. Each *ahupua'a* was under the control of a chief (*ali'i 'ai ahupua'a*), who in turn appointed a land manager or steward (*konohiki*) who lived in the *ahupua'a*, oversaw the chief's interests, and was responsible for the daily management of the production systems.

Moloka'i provides an excellent example of the distribution of *ahupua'a* in relation to local environmental variables. The higher East Moloka'i Mountains (maximum elevation 4,970 feet [1,515 m]) capture most of the rainfall, and the island's windward coast is marked by dramatic, heavily eroded valleys and sea cliffs. The leeward side of East Moloka'i has been less eroded, and the old volcanic slopes there are incised by narrower valleys. The western portion of the island (Kaluako'i), which lies in the rain shadow created by East Moloka'i, is arid and has undergone only minimal stream erosion.

As can be seen on the map, the highest density of *ahupua'a* is along the southeastern shoreline; the many stone-walled fishponds (*loko kuapā*) and numerous *heiau* sites indicate that dense settlement occurred in this area. Because population density and agricultural and aquacultural production were high in this region, *ahupua'a* could be smaller in area, yet accommodate sufficient numbers of people. Along the northeast coast, each of the main valleys corresponds with a single *ahupua'a*. These were also densely populated, with an economy based on irrigated taro. The arid western part of the island was subdivided into just a few very large *ahupua'a*, reflecting low population density and a lack of rich agricultural resources. This region, however, was a valuable source of fine-grained basalt for manufacturing adzes and a major area for inshore and deep-sea fishing. The numerous fishing shrines (*ko'a*) that dot the coastline testify to the importance of fishing.

Archaeological excavations at the Hālawa Valley Dune Site suggest that initial settlement on Moloka'i occurred by at least A.D. 600 and was probably concentrated along the southeast shore and in the windward valleys. Evidence exists that dry, leeward areas (such as at Mo'omomi on the northwest coast) were first used during the early Expansion Period, around A.D. 1200. By the late Expansion Period (about A.D. 1600) the *ahupua'a* system was presumably well established, although additional subdivision of *ahupua'a* and redistribution of these to leading chiefs occurred as late as the reign of Kamehameha III.

PATRICK V. KIRCH

Archaeological Sites of Moloka'i

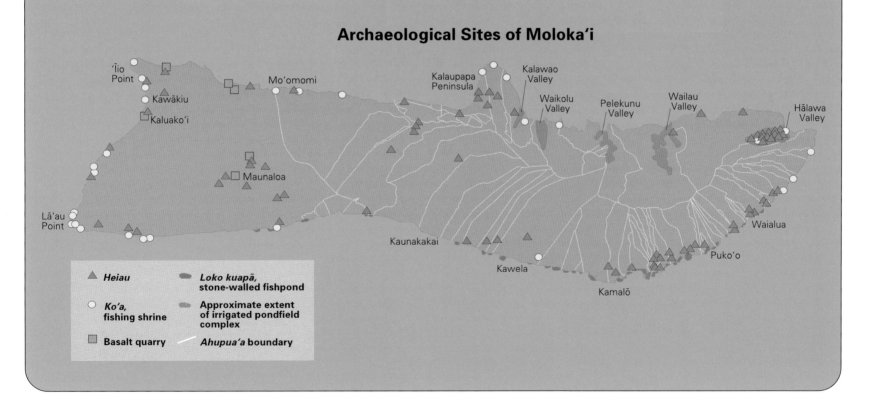

Pu'u Loa petroglyphs, Hawai'i. [P. V. Kirch]

of arid region settlement patterns, and including the Halulu Heiau.

Preserved and publicly accessible *heiau* sites on Maui include Pihana and Haleki'i, Pi'ilanihale, and Wai'ānapanapa. A well-preserved habitation complex can be found in the Keone'ō'io Archaeological District near La Pérouse Bay. The upland region of Kula was once a densely settled agricultural zone, and remnants of ancient Hawaiian dryland fields can still be seen in various places from the Kula Highway.

Hawai'i Island boasts a greater number of well-preserved and accessible sites—especially in the Kohala, Kona, and Ka'ū districts—than any other island. Among the major temple sites are Mo'okini and Pu'ukoholā in Kohala (both used by Kamehameha I), and Ahu'ena, Ke'ekū, Hikiau, Hale o Keawe, and 'Āle'ale'a in Kona. Waha'ula in Puna was covered by lava in 1997. The Koai'e fishing village site at Lapakahi, maintained as a state historical park, was the locus of major archaeological studies by the University of Hawai'i from 1968 to 1971. Large petroglyph complexes are found at Puakō, Kalāhuipua'a, 'Anaeho'omalu, and Pu'u Loa. Extensive dryland agricultural field systems are visible in the uplands of Kohala, and preserved remnants of such a system can be examined at the Amy Greenwell Botanical Garden in the town of Captain Cook. A truly unique archaeological site is the footprints of Keoua Kūahu'ula's army, preserved in volcanic ash in the Ka'ū Desert from an explosion on Kīlauea in 1790, within the present-day Hawai'i Volcanoes National Park.

PATRICK V. KIRCH

HISTORY

Native Hawaiians lived in Hawai'i 1,500 or more years before Western contact. They developed a large and complex society with a hierarchy of *ali'i* (chiefs), an elaborate religion that gave the *ali'i* authority, and a system of irrigated taro fields and constructed fishponds that supported the dense population and satisfied the demands of the chiefly hierarchy. In January 1778, Captain James Cook happened accidentally upon the Hawaiian Islands during his third voyage of Pacific exploration. Cook was on his way from Tahiti to North America, in search of a northwest passage that would provide a more direct route between England and the Orient. His visit set in train a series of momentous changes for the Hawaiian population.

Cook's ships, the *Discovery* and the *Resolution,* first landed at Kaua'i, where he and his men went ashore for several days, then anchored off Ni'ihau before leaving for North America. After a fruitless summer searching for the passage, Cook turned south to find a winter anchorage in Hawai'i where he could repair his ships, take on supplies, and allow his men some time on land. Cook found the sheltered bay of Kealakekua halfway up the west coast of Hawai'i Island on January 18, 1779. He and his men were welcomed by Kalani'ōpu'u, *ali'i nui* (paramount chief) of the island, given a place to

---

This reproduction of Captain James Cook's map of the Sandwich Islands—as he called them—is the earliest published map of the Hawaiian Islands. [Original map in Special Collections, University of Washington Libraries, Seattle. Photo by R. P. Campbell.]

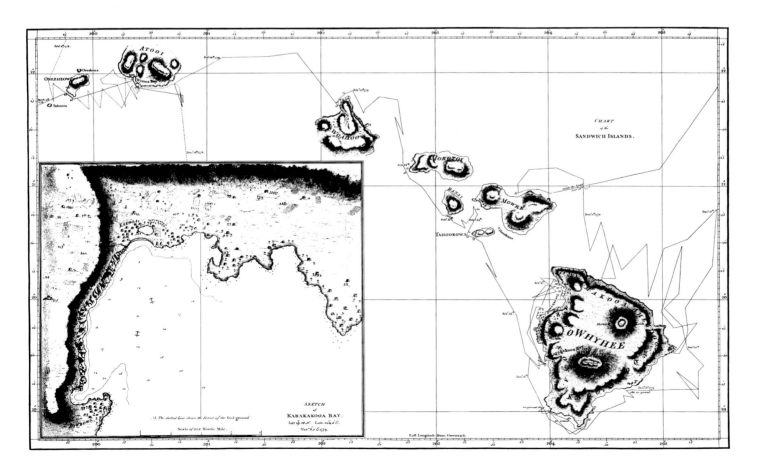

The Sandalwood Trade

Sandalwood, one of the world's most precious woods, is derived from a group of woody plants in the genus *Santalum*. Sixteen species of sandalwood are known; four are native to the Hawaiian Islands, and the others are found in India, East Malaysia, Australia, and several Pacific islands. Like all sandalwood plants, the four endemic Hawaiian species are partly parasitic, small shrubs or trees up to 50 feet (15 m) in height, bearing variously colored flowers with four or five petals and juicy, purplish fruits. Hawaiian sandalwoods, all known as *'iliahi*, occur in dry areas (*S. ellipticum*), moderately wet forests (*S. freycinetianum*), the subalpine zone on Haleakalā volcano, Maui (*S. haleakalae*), or only on Hawai'i Island (*S. paniculatum*). Although they were once abundant in many regions of the Islands, their distribution is now much more restricted, and even severely threatened in some areas.

Traditionally, the fragrant heartwood of *'iliahi* trees was used as a scent and a medicinal agent, but starting in the late eighteenth century the aromatic lower trunks and rootstock of the trees were harvested in great quantity, traded to aggressive foreign traders, and shipped to China for making incense, fine furniture, and other luxury items. The extensive, often exploitive sandalwood trade adversely affected both the natural environment and the human population, with far-reaching and long-

Chinese fan and soap made from sandalwood. [M. Merlin]

lasting effects in Hawai'i. For example, by 1827, heavy taxes, paid in sandalwood, were being levied on commoners; each year able-bodied males were required to deliver one-half picul (a picul is a Chinese measurement equal to 133.33 pounds (60 kg), the amount that a typical man could carry) of sandalwood to their local governing *ali'i* in order to retire a debt of $500,000 owed American merchants from spending by Kamehameha II. Large numbers of people were forced to abandon their subsistence activities to search for wood, and Western visitors reported seeing processions of 2,000–3,000 men carrying sandalwood down from the forests. By around 1840 forests on Hawai'i Island, O'ahu, Moloka'i, and Kaua'i were largely stripped of mountain sandalwoods, and the sandalwood trade may have been partly responsible for the precipitous decline in Hawaiian population in the early nineteenth century.

Sandalwood remains one of the world's most valuable natural products. In the Hawaiian Islands, with ecologically responsible management, natural or perhaps artificial regeneration could once again provide a sandalwood resource that might be harvested on a sustainable basis.

MARK MERLIN

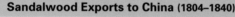

Sandalwood Exports to China (1804–1840)

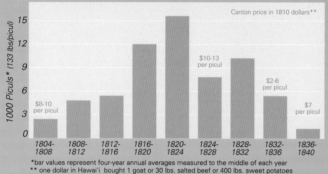

*bar values represent four-year annual averages measured to the middle of each year
** one dollar in Hawai'i bought 1 goat or 30 lbs. salted beef or 400 lbs. sweet potatoes

camp, and allowed to trade. Hawaiians were eager to barter vegetables and pigs for coveted iron nails.

After two and one-half weeks, the two ships set sail to resume their North Pacific exploration but were forced to return to Kealakekua by a storm that damaged the *Resolution*'s foremast. The people now seemed less friendly and stole one of the ship's boats for its iron. Cook went ashore with a small party, intending to take Kalani'ōpu'u hostage and force the return of the boat. The attempt to take the chief, together with the news that an *ali'i* had just been shot dead by another British officer, led to the gathering of a large group of Hawaiians that threatened Cook's party. Before Cook could escape to his ship, he was killed. So ended Cook's illustrious career as a Pacific explorer.

To the English, their stay in Hawai'i was merely a convenient stop for rest and provisions—until Cook's death gave it tragic significance for them. Their visit was more significant to the Hawaiians, however, since it introduced factors that would transform their world: previously unknown diseases, firearms, and trade. The venereal diseases gonorrhea and syphilis were introduced by Cook's sailors, who were eager to couple with the Hawaiian women who swam out to the ships to meet them. Although not an epidemic killer, gonorrhea significantly reduces population growth by causing female sterility. Other European diseases followed, notably the *ma'i 'ōku'u* ("squatting sickness," possibly cholera), which killed thousands in an epidemic in 1804. As a result of such contagious diseases, the

Hawaiian population declined precipitously throughout the first half of the nineteenth century and did not begin to rebound until about 1900.

No other ships arrived until 1786, but thereafter Hawai'i's midocean location made it a favored provisioning stop for the mostly New England traders who carried furs from the Pacific Coast of North America to China. About 1800, as the supply of furs dwindled, traders began to acquire Hawaiian sandalwood to sell to the Chinese. The Hawaiian sandalwood trade thrived from 1812 to 1830, then declined as the trees were depleted. The trade was monopolized by the *ali'i,* who forced their *maka'āinana* (commoner) tenants to provide both ship provisions and sandalwood as part of the tribute they owed for using the land. Early in the trade, the *ali'i* were mainly interested in obtaining firearms and ammunition to use in competitive warfare. As time went on, they acquired a taste for foreign status goods, such as costumes, china, and other exotic luxuries, which replaced feathered capes and helmets as marks of high rank.

Establishment of a Kingdom

After the death of Kalani'ōpu'u in 1781, Kamehameha fought to gain rule over Hawai'i Island and then to conquer the other islands. By 1795 he had taken Maui, Moloka'i, and O'ahu. Kaua'i and Ni'ihau were ceded to him in 1810. The introduction of firearms surely played a role in Kamehameha's success. He was favorably located to gain an advantage in firearms, since Kealakekua was the main harbor used by traders until 1794, when they learned of the harbor at Honolulu. However, Kamehameha's conquests were in fact the culmination of a centralization process that had begun before European contact and the introduction of guns. About 1775, *ali'i nui* Peleiholani of O'ahu had conquered Moloka'i. Then around 1783, *ali'i nui* Kahekili of Maui won control of both O'ahu and Moloka'i. Kamehameha's was the third and final conquest.

Having unified the Hawaiian islands, Kamehameha established a pattern of more centralized rule to

Woman of the Sandwich Islands (Kaahumanu), 1816, pen, ink, wash, and watercolor by Louis Choris. [Honolulu Academy of Arts]

overcome the Hawaiian tendency to rebel. He controlled the sandalwood trade to keep guns in his own hands and deny them to other *ali'i.* He appointed loyal governors on the outlying islands and kept the highest-ranking *ali'i* at court with him. He centralized the religious system as well, bringing the sorcery gods of Moloka'i to his capital (first in Honolulu and later in Kailua-Kona) to help control rebels. When Kamehameha died in 1819, he was *mō'ī* (king) of a strong, unified state. His last words, *"E na'i wale nō 'oukou i ku'u pono 'a'ole e pau,"* admonished his successors to maintain the strength and righteousness of his reign. But in this they failed.

The Kingdom under Kamehameha's Successors

After Kamehameha's death, his heir Liholiho succeeded him as Kamehameha II, but the monarchy was weakened. Liholiho lost control of power to the ambitious and politically astute Ka'ahumanu, Kamehameha's favorite wife. She announced that she was to rule along with Liholiho as *kuhina nui* (chief councilor) and gained effective power over the realm with the support of other great *ali'i* by giving them control over the sandalwood collected from their lands.

Following tradition, Liholiho's first act as ruler would have been to restore the *'aikapu*—the exclusive male eating of sacrificial meals to the gods—which was in abeyance during the mourning period for Kamehameha. Instead, Liholiho was persuaded by Ka'ahu-

Kamehameha, King of the Sandwich Islands, 1816 pen and watercolor by Louis Choris. [Honolulu Academy of Arts]

Monarchs	
Kamehameha I	1795–1819
Liholiho, Kamehameha II	1819–1824
Kauikeaouli, Kamehameha III	1825–1854
Alexander Liholiho, Kamehameha IV	1854–1863
Lot Kamehameha, Kamehameha V	1863–1872
William C. Lunalilo	1873–1874
David Kalākaua	1874–1891
Lili'uokalani	1891–1893

Whaling

For half a century, the Hawaiian Islands were the hub of the Pacific whaling industry. Although the bustling, boisterous ports of Honolulu and Lahaina were the most visible symbols of whaling, the industry transformed the economic and social life of the kingdom and was a potent force for political change.

From the late eighteenth century, right whales (so-called because they were the "right" whale to catch) were hunted on the margins of the Pacific Ocean, and in 1819 the existence of rich sperm-whaling grounds near Japan was confirmed. Right whales provided oil, used for heating, lamps, and industrial purposes; and "whalebone" (long, fibrous baleen strips suspended from the whale's upper jaw), used for corsets, skirt hoops, umbrellas, and buggy whips. The sperm whale had no whalebone, but its oil was of high quality and ideal for making candles.

Whalers probed north into the Japan grounds during the northern summer and returned to Hawai'i to repair their vessels and refresh the crews in October, before heading "along the line" to islands of the central Pacific or to the American coast. They visited Hawai'i again in March or April and then sailed north for another summer season. This pattern, repeated throughout a 3 to 5 year voyage, reflected the whales' migratory habits and the hostility of Japanese authorities to visits by foreign vessels. The discovery of the Arctic grounds in 1848 further enhanced the importance of Hawaiian ports.

Honolulu and Lahaina were the most popular ports, with the former offering the best ship services and the latter offering cheaper produce and, generally, a more sober society. A secondary interisland trade in livestock, vegetables, and firewood soon emerged. The whaling economy brought migrants to the ports and encouraged the growth of grog shops, prostitution, and public disorder. Missionaries and government authorities tried with fluctuating enthusiasm and success to control both visiting whalemen and the urbanized Hawaiian population.

Except for a short slump in the early 1850s following the discovery of gold in California, the heyday of Pacific whaling (1840–1860) brought as many as 500 ships, most with crews of 25 or 30, to Hawaiian ports each year. There were perhaps 500–600 Hawaiians working as crewmen on whalers by the mid-1840s and at least twice that number later in the decade. The average whaleship stayed about 15 days in port and spent heavily in the local economy—mostly on repairs and stores, but also in bars, brothels, and dancehalls.

Although local produce such as pigs, yams, and taro was sold in large quantities, introduced livestock and crops dominated trade. Cattle, pigs, and goats were sold "on the hoof" or salted, while chickens, turkeys, and ducks were caged and fed on board the ships until they were required. Firewood and water were also major purchases. The provision trade also encouraged local cultivation of potatoes, onions, pumpkins, melons, cucumbers, beans, cabbages, oranges, pineapples, and mangoes. The consequent changes to cultivation practices and land use, and the opportunities for individuals to profit, had a wider effect on relationships between landowners and tenants. Whereas in the 1820s trade had been under the control of the chiefs, by the 1850s independent farmers paid market fees to trade with visiting vessels. Later in the nineteenth century the initiative passed to the major (settler-owned) trading companies.

In the 1860s diminishing whale stocks, a shortage of ships due to the U.S. Civil War, and the growing use of petroleum-derived oils contributed to a decline in whaling. Some 30 whaling vessels were lost in Arctic pack ice in 1871 and, around the same time, new technology caused a shift in emphasis to rorqual (finback) whales and the newly discovered Antarctic grounds, which together became the major focus of commercial whaling. San Francisco eventually replaced Honolulu as the major port of call for Pacific whalers.

BARRIE MACDONALD

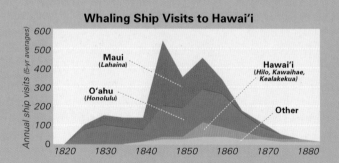

Whaling Ship Visits to Hawai'i

Annual ship visits (5-yr averages)

Maui (Lahaina)
O'ahu (Honolulu)
Hawai'i (Hilo, Kawaihae, Kealakekua)
Other

600 500 400 300 200 100 0

1820 1830 1840 1850 1860 1870 1880

---

manu and her supporters to abandon the 'aikapu and with it the great rituals that empowered Hawaiian rulers, demonstrating that the gods supported them. Temples were abandoned, images discarded, and the priesthood disbanded.

The overthrow of the religious system was probably an overdetermined event: there are several likely causes, each seemingly sufficient. Given that the Hawaiian state created by Kamehameha was now maintained by force of arms, the religious underpinning of the ruler was no longer essential. The rituals

and the priesthood might have been seen as an unnecessary drain on state resources that could better be spent on guns and ships. Apparently the religion was increasingly coming into question as well. The old gods seemed unable to prevent epidemic death or to rival Western military power. Both of those arguments may have moved Ka'ahumanu, but the overthrow of the *kapu* system was also a way for her to gain power, since the male-only ritual empowered Liholiho and excluded her.

The dual rulership of male *mō'ī* and female *kuhina*

The *Māhele* of 1848

The *Māhele* of 1848 was a legal event that changed the traditional system of Hawaiian land tenure from communal to private. Before the *Māhele* (which means to divide or share), land in Hawai'i was not privately owned. Instead, every Hawaiian had communal rights to use land for living on and growing food. Land was viewed as a source of food and, like water and air, a basic necessity for life. Hence, land should be shared and available for all.

Land was also viewed as an ancestor, because in Hawaiian mythology the islands and people of Hawai'i were born from the mating of Papahānaumoku, the earth mother, with Wākea, the sky father. The lands and extensive, sophisticated irrigation systems (*lo'i* and *'auwai*) were administered by the *ali'i nui,* or high chiefs, while farming was done by *maka'āinana,* or commoners.

According to Hawaiian cosmogony, the *ali'i nui* were the elder siblings or senior lineages, and the *maka'āinana,* the younger siblings or junior lineages, all descended from the same divine ancestor, Hāloa. The duty of the junior lineages was to *mālama 'āina,* or care for the land and for the *ali'i nui,* who represented the first born. It was the reciprocal duty of the elder lineage, both *ali'i nui* and the land, to *hānai,* or feed, and to *ho'omalu,* or protect, the junior lineages. Through their prayers and close relationship to the *akua,* or gods, the *ali'i nui* protected the people from natural disasters on the land.

When each portion of society behaved in a *pono,* or righteous, fashion toward the land, then there was harmony in the universe. Hence, in traditional times land was accorded the status of an ancestor and could not be privately owned. After all, how could one buy and sell one's grandmother?

By 1848, however, Hawaiians had suffered massive depopulation from epidemics of foreign diseases. The steep and swift population decline (from estimates of up to 1 million in 1778 to 88,000 in 1848) caused a collapse of the traditional religion called *'aikapu.* In 1820, Calvinist missionaries from New England arrived in Hawai'i and taught that *ola hou,* or the new life, could be obtained by conversion to Christianity and Western modes of life. Calvinist missionaries were most insistent that among the "many evils" of traditional Hawai'i, one of the worst was a lack of individual ownership of land, which they argued was a major cause of Hawaiian depopulation. Coupled with threats of a foreign takeover of the Hawaiian kingdom from British, French, and American warships, and a subsequent loss of land not held in fee simple ownership, the *ali'i nui* finally agreed to the privatization of lands in the 1848 *Māhele.* Under the direction of American Calvinist William Richards, a land commission was established that awarded all land titles, dividing various interests to the land.

The event is often called the "great" *Māhele* as it divided all the lands of Hawai'i, but it was a great disaster for Hawaiians because it swiftly led to ownership of land by foreigners. Foreigners had money to buy land, whereas most Hawaiians did not. Also foreigners understood the concept and value of private ownership of land, while such a notion was nonsensical to the vast majority of Hawaiians.

By 1850 missionary advisors had convinced the *ali'i nui* that foreigners should be allowed to own land, which would encourage foreign investment and the establishment of a capitalist economy. While commoners received about 3 acres (1.2 ha) of land apiece, Calvinist missionaries were allowed 560 acres (226 ha) of land each. The 10 *ali'i nui,* 24 *kaukau ali'i,* or lesser chiefs, and 218 *konohiki,* or land stewards, were all required to give up 50 percent of lands they administered to the government. The majority of the government land was sold to foreigners.

By 1893 foreigners owned, or controlled through the crown lands commission and the boards of large chiefly trusts, 90 percent of the lands of Hawai'i. The 1893 overthrow of the Hawaiian government began with the 1848 *Māhele,* for once American Calvinists could own Hawaiian land some wanted to control the government as well.

Lilikalā K. Kame'eleihiwa

---

nui lasted for 25 years, weakening the power of the *mō'ī* relative to the other *ali'i.* When Liholiho died in 1825, he was succeeded by his young brother Kauikeaouli, Kamehameha III. Kauikeaouli was dominated by a series of female *kuhina nui,* first Ka'ahumanu and then her successors Kīna'u and Kekāuluohi, until the death of the latter freed him in 1845.

In the 1820s two new forces for change entered Hawai'i: American Congregationalist missionaries of Calvinist ideology and whalers. The first missionaries arrived in 1820—an opportune time given that Hawaiians had just abandoned much of their religious system. The missionaries soon won over Ka'ahumanu and several *ali'i* as converts. The new religion was one that Ka'ahumanu could embrace because it did not exclude her as a woman from a leading role. With the missionary leader Hiram Bingham as her main adviser, she promoted reading the Bible (translated into Hawaiian), had churches built, and imposed rules upon the population that prohibited non-Christian practices such as *hula,* the drinking of alcohol, and sexual relations outside of marriage. At first the *maka'āinana* were grudging participants in the Christian project, but during 1836 and 1837 a mass conversion movement arose and thousands were baptized. Bingham and his fellow missionaries aimed to recreate Hawaiians in their own puritanical and capitalist image, but they were frustrated in this attempt. Hawaiians remained unreconstructed sexually as well as economically—a people who preferred to share rather than save. Missionaries did, however, shape the political fate of the nation. William Richards and Gerrit Judd left the mission to become political counselors with a decisive influence on Kauikeaouli. Other religious denominations came later—French Catholics in 1827, Mormons in 1850, and Anglicans in 1862—but none had the political impact of the Congregationalists. The Catholics and their converts were in fact persecuted by the Congregationalist *ali'i* and made little headway until 1839, when a French warship enforced religious freedom in Hawai'i.

While the missionaries brought new ideas, the whaling trade enlarged the White business community. As the sandalwood trade declined, the Pacific whaling industry developed with Hawai'i as its base. From the 1820s, whaling ships, primarily from New England, stopped at Honolulu and Lahaina in spring and fall, between the summer whaling season in the North Pacific and the winter season in the central Pacific. They depended on Hawai'i for supplies, women, and grog. Whaling boomed from 1840 to 1860, then declined as whales became scarcer and petroleum replaced whale oil in the United States. A substantial merchant community, mostly American and English, developed to supply the whalers as well as the continuing intercontinental trade across the Pacific. The merchants sold imported goods and acted as intermediaries in the sale of local produce. Up to 1850, the *ali'i* supplied this produce from the tribute of their tenants, and the *maka'āinana* were shut out, except in minor roles as peddlers, prostitutes, and servants. Nevertheless, commoners were drawn to the growing towns of Honolulu and Lahaina. By 1860, 22 percent of the Hawaiian population lived in Honolulu. With the decline of the whaling industry, Lahaina dwindled, but Honolulu continued to grow by attracting rural Hawaiians.

The White business community was opposed to missionary puritanism, because the businesses catered to whaler appetites for women and alcohol, which the missionaries attempted to suppress. Nonetheless, the businessmen allied with the missionaries in pressing Kauikeaouli and the *ali'i* for changes in landholding. Both groups were unhappy with the Hawaiian landholding system, which gave the king, and under him the *ali'i,* control over the land. They granted land to Hawaiian tenants and foreign businessmen on the condition that sufficient tribute or rent was paid. Missionaries argued that the *maka'āinana* would become thrifty and industrious farmers and give up their indolent and sinful habits if given their own land. Foreign businessmen agitated for the opportunity to own land outright, or at least to obtain firm lease agreements so they could invest in businesses with security. In this they were supported by their government representa-tives, the American, British, and French consuls at Honolulu, and the naval gunships of the three powers, which periodically appeared in port to enforce their demands. Between 1836 and 1851 the threat of foreign takeover was continual, and an annexation by British captain Lord Paulet in 1843 lasted six months until the British government learned of the event and repudiated it. The Hawaiian government maintained its independence during this period only by acceding to foreign demands and by using each of the three powers as a check on the others.

The last female *kuhina nui* died in 1845, but the power of the *mō'ī* was thereafter limited in a new way. From 1840 to 1855 the political economy of Hawai'i was transformed into a constitutional monarchy with private landownership. In 1840 William Richards convinced Kauikeaouli and his council of chiefs to accept a constitution that would gain the Hawaiian government the respect of Western powers. The constitution established a partly elected legislature and a set of ministers to carry out government business. The king still had considerable power under the constitution, but resident Whites (former missionaries, local businessmen, and lawyers) dominated the government as ministers under Kauikeaouli. Faced with continued Western pressure, the new government passed a series of laws that culminated in the 1848–1850 *Māhele,* which divided up the land interests of Hawaiians, establishing private landownership for the king, *ali'i,* and *maka'āinana* and setting aside another portion of land for the government. Crucially, the new laws also allowed landownership by foreigners and the sale of government lands. White businessmen rapidly purchased most of the prime government land as it was put up for sale, as well as much of the desirable land the *ali'i* sold to pay off debts they incurred by living above their incomes.

The Sugar Economy

As whaling declined in the 1860s, sugar became the mainstay of the cash economy, and it remained predominant well into the twentieth century. From 1860 to 1900, sugar production and exports increased steadily, sugarcane acreage expanded, and sugar profits grew. Cultivated on large landholdings with hand labor, sugar turned Hawai'i into a plantation society. It was dominated by a mostly American elite of plantation owners and their financial associates in Honolulu, tied culturally and economically to the United States. They sold Hawaiian sugar to California, and the bulk of their imports came from the United States. Periodically, elements of the planter elite sought political union with the United States to guarantee their economic tie. An annexation treaty was negotiated in 1853, but it was never concluded.

As the plantation society developed, Hawaiians lost economic and political importance. The great

Chinese sugar plantation laborers cutting cane. [Hawai'i State Archives]

mass of Hawaiians became a lower class of plantation workers—until they were replaced by Asian immigrants. Or, they lived on the economic margins of plantation society in Honolulu or in rural subsistence communities outside the sugar-growing areas. The missionary vision of Hawaiians as small commercial farmers never materialized. The group of great land-owning Hawaiian *ali'i* dwindled in number and political-economic importance. The bulk of the unsold *ali'i* lands passed to Bernice Pauahi Bishop, the last recognized heir of the Kamehameha line, who had married banker Charles Bishop. When she died in 1884, her will turned those lands into Bishop Estate, a trust for the education of Hawaiian youth at Kamehameha Schools. The estate was managed by trustees drawn from the planter elite, beginning with Charles Bishop, and its usable lands were leased to sugar plantations.

The first substantial sugar plantation was established in 1835 at Kōloa, Kaua'i, by Ladd & Company, using local Hawaiian labor and land leased from the government. By 1847, eleven sugar manufacturers were exporting about 300 tons, and by 1860 that production had more than doubled. The biggest spur to production came with the American Civil War (1861–1865), which created a boom market in California for Hawaiian sugar because it disrupted the supply of sugar from the American South. The *Māhele* had made land available, and as whaling faded in economic importance Honolulu merchants put their capital into sugar plantations. After the Civil War the sugar market became more competitive again. In 1876, the sugar planters improved their position in the American market by obtaining a reciprocity treaty between the United States and Hawai'i that gave them preferential access: Hawaiian sugar was allowed into the United States duty free, in return for accepting American manufactured goods without tariff.

Increased profitability under reciprocity triggered a long-lasting expansion of sugar production, inter-

rupted only during the years 1891–1894 when the U.S. McKinley Tariff Act went into effect. That act removed the tariff from all foreign sugar, so that Hawaiian sugar no longer had an advantage. Sugar expansion resulted in a closer economic tie to the United States, centralization of the sugar industry, and an upsurge in the importation of Asian labor for the industry. Expanded production required investment in irrigation and more efficient mills to press the cane, innovations that required heavy capital investment and favored larger plantations. Most of the needed capital came from the financially interlocked planter establishment, rather than from outside investors. The heaviest investors were the sugar factors, the Honolulu agents who shipped sugar for the plantations, loaned them money, and ultimately became the "Big Five" business corporations in Hawai'i.

Sugar industry expansion also required a bigger labor pool. Before 1876 the bulk of plantation labor had been Hawaiian, but as the native population continued to decline it could not satisfy the growing demand for labor. Nor could free Hawaiians be kept on the job and worked to the limit as indentured laborers were. The first Chinese contract laborers arrived in 1852, but the heavy importation of contract labor began after the reciprocity treaty in 1876. When the Chinese government forbade further migration in 1881, the Hawaiian government concluded an agreement with Japan and, from 1886 until after annexation, the large majority of laborers brought in were

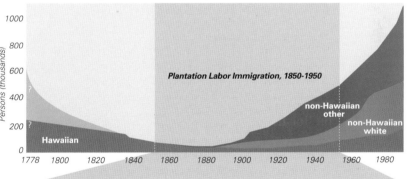

Population Change by Ethnicity, 1778-1990

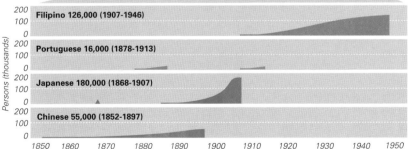

Other groups totalling less than 15,000 plantation-labor immigrants include South Pacific Islanders 2,500 (1859-1884); Norwegians 600 (1881); Germans 1,300 (1881-1897); Galicians 370 (1898); African-Americans 100 (1901); Puerto Ricans 6,000 (1900-1921); Koreans 7,900 (1903-1905); Russians 2,400 (1906-1912) and Spaniards 8,000 (1907-1913).

? indicates there is debate over the size of the Hawaiian population at the time of European contact. The lower estimate of 200,000–250,000 by Schmitt (1971) is based on the accounts of early European explorers. Based on Pacific-wide comparisons of island carrying capacity and post-contact population decline, Stannard (1989) has argued for a much larger Hawaiian population at contact of 800,000 or more (the Editors)

Japanese. Contract laborers often remained in Hawai'i after their contracts ended, and generally they moved to town. Some started enterprises that competed with White-owned businesses, to the Whites' dismay. Labor importation permanently altered the ethnic makeup of the population, making Hawaiians a minority in their homeland. Whereas in 1876 Asians made up only 4.5 percent of the population, by 1890 they were 33 percent and by 1900, 56 percent.

The economic dominance of the planters led first to their heightened political influence and then to political control. Kauikeaouli died in 1854, shortly after the *Māhele* was carried out. He was succeeded by his nephews Alexander Liholiho, as Kamehameha IV (1854–1863), and Lot Kamehameha, as Kamehameha V (1863–1872). Both sought to increase the power of the monarchy and limit missionary and business influence, but they still depended primarily on White ministers to run their governments.

When Lot died in 1872 without an heir, the legislature unanimously elected William Lunalilo (grand-nephew of Kamehameha) as the new king. Lunalilo died within the year and another election was held. There were two main candidates: *ali'i* David Kalākaua was backed by the planters because he had promised to work for a reciprocity treaty; Queen Emma, widow of Kamehameha IV, was favored by the Honolulu Hawaiians. When the legislators elected Kalākaua, a mob of Hawaiians attacked them. Kalākaua had to request troops from American and British warships in the harbor to quell the riot.

The king obtained the reciprocity treaty desired by the planters, but they were soon at odds with him because he paid little attention to their wishes otherwise. To control the legislature and to carry out his programs, Kalākaua mobilized the increasing anti-White sentiments of Hawaiians who had lost their land to White businessmen. Under him the government went into debt, taking out large loans to spend money on 'Iolani Palace, Kalākaua's world tour, and a belated

Kalākaua's coronation, performed on the ninth anniversary of his election to the throne. [Hawai'i State Archives]

coronation celebration in 1883. The planters saw these actions as improvident and worried that the government would raise taxes to pay for the expenditures. Half of the government debt was held by California millionaire Claus Spreckels, an "interloper" who was taking over the Hawaiian sugar industry and seemed to have the king in his pocket. Their alliance was another threat to the planters, until Spreckels offended Kalākaua and was eased out of Hawai'i in 1886. Most importantly, the reciprocity treaty was in danger of not being renewed. In 1887 the planters wanted to offer the use of Pearl Harbor to the United States to get a new treaty, but the king and his Hawaiian nationalists balked at the proposal.

From left to right:

Lydia Kamaka'eha Lili'uokalani, before she became queen. [Hawai'i State Archives]

David La'amea Kalākaua. [Hawai'i State Archives]

Robert W. Wilcox. [Hawai'i State Archives]

Lorrin Andrews Thurston [Hawai'i State Archives]

By 1887, the White business establishment was fed up with Kalākaua. When legislators Lorrin Thurston, Sanford Dole, and W. R. Castle failed to get the reforms desired by the planters during the 1886 legislative session, they staged a coup d'etat, using an all-White militia named the Honolulu Rifles to take over the government. The coup forced a new cabinet headed by Thurston on Kalākaua and established the "Bayonet Constitution," which turned the king into a figurehead monarch. The result was a legislature controlled by the largely White propertied class, rather than by the majority Hawaiians. Under the Thurston cabinet, Kalākaua was forced to sign a new reciprocity treaty that gave Pearl Harbor to the United States as a naval station. In 1889 part-Hawaiian Robert Wilcox led an ill-planned rebellion of Native Hawaiians against the new constitution, but they were defeated the day they began. Kalākaua died in 1891 and was succeeded by his sister Liliʻuokalani.

The nationalism that Kalākaua cultivated during his reign to enhance his political control was part of a wider Hawaiian cultural renaissance. In the 1860s Hawaiian writers such as Samuel Kamakau published articles in Hawaiian-language newspapers that recorded traditional culture and celebrated former rulers. Hawaiian composers, with Kalākaua and Liliʻuokalani at the forefront, created a new and sophisticated hybrid Hawaiian music. At Kalākaua's coronation, *hula* was once again performed publicly, after years of missionary prohibition. The revived Hawaiian culture was syncretic—European-style ʻIolani Palace and traditional Hawaiian *hula* were both used to glorify the monarchy. Strongest in urban Honolulu, the renaissance reawakened pride in Hawaiian culture for people who had lost their traditional life on the land. With the Bayonet Constitution, the Hawaiian revival lost its political force, but it renewed cultural forms that have lasted into the present.

Liliʻuokalani ruled for only 2 years. Sworn in on January 29, 1891, she was forced to abdicate on January 17, 1893, by a group of White business leaders under the leadership of Lorrin Thurston who viewed the overthrow of the monarchy and the annexation of Hawaiʻi to the United States as a solution to their economic and political difficulties. The economic problem was that sugar profits were down. The McKinley Tariff Act passed by the U.S. Congress in 1891 permitted Caribbean sugar to compete on equal terms with Hawaiian sugar. Annexation would return the competitive advantage to Hawaiian sugar by making it eligible for the price bounty given to domestic U.S. sugar growers, although it also posed the danger that the U.S. might prohibit immigration of Asian labor into Hawaiʻi.

The political situation appeared even worse to the planters than the economic one. The planters lost control of the legislature in the 1890 and 1892 elections, they found Liliʻuokalani even more difficult to work with than Kalākaua had been, and Wilcox was plotting another rebellion to overthrow the Bayonet Constitution. Thurston organized a secret Annexation Club in 1892 and sounded out the U.S. government. The Republican administration was encouraging. On January 14, 1893, Liliʻuokalani announced that she intended to promulgate a new constitution that would empower the monarch and give Native Hawaiians control over the legislature. In response, the annexationists went into action.

Thurston and his associates formed a Committee of Safety, which seized the government on January 17. The committee had taken steps to procure the cooperation of the U.S. Minister to Hawaiʻi, John Stevens, and Commander G. C. Wiltse of the USS *Boston,* a warship then in Honolulu harbor. Under the pretext of protecting American property, Wiltse sent ashore marines who camped near ʻIolani Palace. When the Committee of Safety announced its takeover, it was actually outgunned by the Queen's forces, but the U.S. marines took control of the situation. Minister Stevens immediately recognized the new provisional government and Liliʻuokalani capitulated to prevent bloodshed, surrendering to the "superior force of the United States." She expected the U.S. government in Washington to restore her to power once the details of the overthrow became known.

In fact, the U.S. government satisfied neither Liliʻuokalani nor the provisional government. The Republican administration that had encouraged the annexationists had been replaced by Grover Cleveland's Democratic administration which, when it learned that the overthrow had been imposed by U.S. military power and lacked popular support, refused to annex Hawaiʻi. The provisional government then formed the Republic of Hawaiʻi, with Sanford Dole as president. When it became clear that the United States was not going to act on the queen's behalf, a group of Royalist Hawaiians led by Wilcox planned a rebellion to restore her. Again poorly prepared and surprised into action before they were ready, they surrendered after only ten days. Wilcox and others were sentenced to death, but all were eventually pardoned.

Under the Republic the White establishment was firmly in power: few Hawaiians and no Asians, or Whites without property, were given the vote. The lands of the monarchy (crown land), designated as public property under the Republic, became part of the government land. In 1897 President Cleveland was replaced by the Republican William McKinley, who favored annexation, and in 1898 Congress passed a resolution to annex Hawaiʻi as a territory. The United States had just taken possession of the Philippines after the Spanish-American War, and Hawaiʻi would be a useful strategic base on the route to Asia.

Hawai'i as a U.S. Territory

As a U.S. territory, Hawai'i remained a plantation society until World War II. The dominant industry, sugar, stayed profitable because of the quota assigned to Hawai'i as a domestic producer. Production increased from a quarter-million tons in 1896 to more than a million tons in 1932, as acreage and efficiency of production increased. In 1900, James Dole began to develop pineapple as a secondary plantation crop for drier areas. The world market for canned pineapple was created and dominated by Hawai'i producers. Pineapple production increased until World War II, although both the sugar and pineapple industries slumped for a while in the early 1930s as a result of reduced markets during the Great Depression. When the U.S. Congress cut the quota for Hawaiian sugar in 1934, thus limiting its preferred access to the mainland market, the sugar-based business establishment began to see statehood as a means of increasing its political pull in Washington.

Plantation expansion required continued immigration of cheap labor, particularly as Japanese laborers tended to move away from the plantations into towns, just as the Chinese had done earlier. U.S. territorial status affected labor immigration in two ways: it ended the system of forced contract labor and it limited the immigration of Asians from China and Japan. Racist sentiments prompted Congress to pass legislation preventing further Chinese immigration in 1882, to limit Japanese immigration in 1907, and to stop it altogether in 1924. The planters then turned to the Philippines to recruit labor, since there were no bars to immigration from a U.S. territory. Between 1910 and 1931, about 100,000 Filipino laborers were brought to Hawai'i. The Filipinos were the last group recruited

in large numbers and have remained the largest ethnic group on the plantations. During World War II, a shortage of workers led to mechanization of the sugar industry. Mechanization continued after the war owing to unionization and increasing labor costs. Plantation work became scarce, well paid, and desirable. Like Chinese and Japanese immigrants before them, many Filipino immigrants eventually returned home. But enough stayed to become a major ethnic group in Hawai'i, making up about 12 percent of the population in 1950.

With the termination of forced labor contracts at annexation, laborers were free to leave the plantations. The plantation owners tried to maintain a submissive, unorganized, and low-paid workforce in other ways. They broke the 1909 Japanese strike, the 1920 Japanese and Filipino strike, and the 1924 Filipino strike without increasing wages by bringing in strike breakers, imprisoning strike leaders, and evicting strikers' families from plantation housing. But the owners also instituted changes to hold and motivate workers: they built better plantation housing, began to provide medical care, and gave laborers annual bonuses dependent on profit.

One reason for the failure of the 1920 strike was the inability of the Japanese and Filipino labor federations to act together, partly because workers had always been housed in separate ethnic camps to prevent them making common cause. After 1937 the U.S. government enforced the National Labor Relations Act in Hawai'i and labor was allowed to organize freely. The labor situation was frozen during the war, however, and the plantations were not effectively unionized until 1946, when the ILWU (International Longshoremen's and Warehousemen's Union) won industry-wide contracts for sugar and pineapple.

At annexation, Hawai'i's plantation economy was largely owned by a White *kama'āina* (longtime resident) elite of intermarried missionary and business families. Increasingly the economy came under the control of the Big Five Hawai'i business corporations —Castle & Cook, Theo H. Davies, C. Brewer, American Factors, and Alexander & Baldwin—controlled by *kama'āina* families through stock ownership and interlocking directorates. In 1910 the Big Five controlled 75 percent of the sugar crop; in 1933, 96 percent. The pineapple company started by newcomer James Dole in 1900 came under the control of Castle & Cook in 1932. Banks, utilities, railroad lines, wholesale and retail businesses, and steamship lines to the mainland all fell into the stranglehold of the Big Five. Chinese and Japanese entrepreneurs were able to set up small businesses such as restaurants, village stores, and poi factories, but outsiders found it difficult, if not impossible, to break in. Small-scale immigrant White farmers in Hilo were driven out of business and their land taken over by the plantation. Even Kress and Sears

Early Heads of State

President, Provisional Government
Sanford B. Dole — 1893–1894
President, Republic of Hawai'i
Sanford B. Dole — 1894–1900
Territorial Governors
Sanford B. Dole — 1900–1903
George R. Carter — 1903–1907
Walter F. Frear — 1907–1913
Lucius E. Pinkham — 1913–1918
Charles J. McCarthy — 1918–1921
Wallace R. Farrington — 1921–1929
Lawrence M. Judd — 1929–1934
Joseph B. Poindexter — 1934–1942
Ingram M. Stainback — 1942–1951
Oren E. Long — 1951–1953
Samuel W. King — 1953–1957
William F. Quinn — 1957–1959

found it difficult to penetrate Hawai'i because of the Big Five's control of real estate and transportation.

Until World War II, the *kama'āina* elite controlled both the governorship and the territorial legislature. The governor held the greater power. He was appointed by the U.S. president, but generally he came out of the local White business establishment. Even Democratic governors acted in the interests of the *kama'āina* oligarchy, which dominated the legislature through the Republican Party, a coalition of White businessmen and poorer White and Hawaiian voters. Hawaiians voted for the Republican Party in exchange for patronage jobs and the selection of Prince Jonah Kūhiō Kalaniana'ole, nephew of Lili'uokalani, as territorial representative to Congress. By controlling government, the business elite was able to achieve the passage of laws that held plantation labor in check, to obtain irrigation water projects, and to prevent land reform measures that would break their hold over desirable land. The number of Asian-American voters, especially Japanese, grew in the 1930s, but the White-led Democrats were unable to appeal to them and challenge Republican control until after World War II.

One outcome of the Republican coalition between the White elite and Hawaiian voters was passage of the Hawaiian Homes Act by Congress in 1920. The act was intended by Kūhiō as a means of getting Hawaiians living in poverty in Honolulu onto government land, so that they could make a living by farming. But the elite used their Washington connections to influence Congress, so that the act provided that the choice government lands would still be available for plantation leases. The 200,000 acres (80,800 ha) designated as Hawaiian Homelands were mostly unsuited for farming. Moreover, more than half of these lands were leased out to non-Hawaiians. The Hawaiian Homelands program did not provide a real route to upward socioeconomic mobility for Hawaiians. Neither did Kamehameha Schools during the territorial period, since it provided education only in manual arts and homemaking. In the 1920s and 1930s Hawaiians fell behind Chinese and Japanese, who were more successful as entrepreneurs and more likely to stay in school and become professionals.

Throughout the 1920s and 1930s, as Japan expanded by annexing Micronesia and invading China, it was apparent that conflict between the United States and Japan was imminent. The United States had begun building military bases at Pearl Harbor and Schofield soon after annexation. The impending Japanese threat led to more military construction and an increased military presence in the mid-1930s. By 1940 Honolulu had become a boomtown, attracting much of the rural population, as well as newcomers from the mainland, to work in Honolulu. Even women could get jobs formerly open only to men.

World War II came to Hawai'i on December 7,

1941, when the Japanese bombed the U.S. fleet at Pearl Harbor and U.S. air bases on O'ahu in a surprise attack inflicting tremendous damage. That same day U.S. Army General Walter Short declared martial law, placing Hawai'i under the rule of a military governor. Blackouts, censorship, military courts, and suspension of habeas corpus were imposed; employment and wages were frozen. Political and labor unrest were suspended for the duration of the war, a situation supported by the business elite. The military government did not give up its control until 1944—long after the threat of renewed Japanese invasion had passed.

A major reason for imposition of martial law was the suspicion that local Japanese residents were spies, or were at least of uncertain loyalty. Many local Japanese were questioned or arrested as suspected agents, but with 160,000 Japanese in Hawai'i they were too large a part of the population for mass internment like that carried out on the mainland. Only a few Japanese spies attached to the Japanese consulate were documented. The local Japanese reacted to the suspicion of their neighbors by diminishing their political activity, abandoning outward manifestations of their culture, and embracing American culture as Americans of Japanese Ancestry (AJAs). At first the AJAs were not allowed to enlist, but then the decision was made to form a special AJA regiment to fight in Europe, the 442nd Regimental Combat Team. Eager to prove their patriotism, the 442nd sustained unusually high casualty rates and won more medals than any other unit fighting in the war. When they returned, AJA veterans such as Daniel Inouye and Spark Matsunaga used the G.I. Bill to earn law degrees and enter politics. They became prime movers in the Democratic Party, which came to dominate postwar politics in Hawai'i.

With the end of World War II, labor unions gained a major role in the Democratic Party. Under Jack Hall the ILWU had already secured contracts for dockworkers in 1941. In 1946 the union organized not only the dockworkers throughout the territory but also

U.S.S. *Oklahoma* (*right*) hit by torpedoes and about to capsize as the U.S.S. *Maryland* (*left*) is trapped at her mooring after the bombing of Pearl Harbor. [Hawai'i State Archives]

the plantation workers, finally succeeding in uniting workers of varied ethnic groups on a class basis against their employers. In 1949 the ILWU called a 6-month dock strike, bringing on a recession in order to obtain a wage increase. The union attempted to take control of the Democratic Party between 1946 and 1954, but was defeated by the AJA politicians led by White policeman John Burns. Accusations that the union leaders were Communists hurt the ILWU. At the height of McCarthyism in 1951, Hall and six others were charged with conspiracy to overthrow the government but were eventually acquitted. After 1954 the ILWU shifted its role to that of pressure group, supporting the Democrats in return for favorable legislation.

Statehood

Beginning in the 1930s public opinion in Hawai'i increasingly favored statehood. With an appointed governor, Hawai'i's voters had limited political control, and with a nonvoting congressional delegate their leverage in Washington was limited. Hawai'i's successive congressional delegates advocated statehood, and the administrations of Franklin Roosevelt, Harry Truman, and Dwight Eisenhower supported the idea. Finally in 1959 Congress admitted Hawai'i to the Union, and a plebescite held in Hawai'i approved statehood by a margin of seventeen to one.

Since World War II the three pillars of Hawai'i's economy have been military spending, plantation agriculture, and tourism. In 1959, they ranked in that order of importance. By 1967 tourism had outgrown plantation agriculture; by 1976 it had overtaken military spending; and by 1979 tourism's economic contribution was larger than the other two combined. In the decades after statehood Hawai'i was transformed by mass tourism and in-migration from the mainland. Slow-moving, low-rise Honolulu became a high-rise city choked with cars. Rural resorts and luxury subdivisions were built on the neighbor islands at favored leeward locations.

Immediately following the war military spending in Hawai'i was cut back, but as the Cold War escalated spending was increased again to maintain U.S. strategic interest in the Pacific. It has remained high

Statehood, as reported in the *Honolulu Star Bulletin,* March 12, 1959. [Courtesy Hawai'i State Archives; photo by G. Bacon]

since. Hawai'i was a major staging area for both the Korean War in 1950–1953 and the Vietnam War in 1964–1975. Thousands of soldiers passed through the state, having a major impact on its economy and society.

The great expansion of tourism began in 1959 with the initiation of jet aircraft service to Honolulu from the West Coast. The number of visitors increased until the 1990s, and so did their expenditures in the state. Tourism fueled a long-term development boom as investors speculated in land and built resorts. Increased in-migration from the mainland also boosted development and by 1970 made Whites the largest ethnic group. In the 1970s and 1980s, Japanese tourism and investment contributed to expansion—until the Japanese economy hit a slump in the 1990s. Tourism revenues declined for the first time in 1991 as the number of tourists fell. In the mid-1990s there was some question as to whether tourism would rebound or whether visitors would find other destinations more attractive.

Profits began to decline in the sugar and pineapple industries during the 1950s and 1960s as unionization drove up the costs of labor and competition increased from other tropical producers with lower

State Seal. [Hawai'i State Archives]

State Governors	
William F. Quinn	(1959–1962)
John A. Burns	(1962–1974)
George R. Ariyoshi	(1974–1986)
John Waihee	(1986–1994)
Benjamin J. Cayetano	(1994–)

labor costs. Faced with diminishing profits, the Big Five plantation owners diversified in the 1960s. They built subdivisions such as Mililani Town on Oʻahu (Castle & Cook) and destination resorts such as Kāʻanapali on Maui (Amfac). The Big Five transformed themselves into multinational corporations with the bulk of their investments and stock owners outside of the state, and with lessened concern for Hawaiʻi as a society. In the 1980s the Big Five closed down many of their sugar and pineapple plantations, plunging former plantation communities into economic depression.

The economic development based on tourism, immigration, and military spending that occurred after statehood brought a general increase in living standards. Between 1960 and 1987, per capita disposable personal income rose about twice as fast as living costs. But Hawaiʻi also has paid a price for development in terms of negative social and environmental consequences. Local people have watched rural communities disintegrate, beaches become crowded with tourists, and Honolulu turn into a congested and difficult city. Since 1987 the rise in personal income has been offset by a comparable rise in the cost of living. In particular, housing costs have been driven upward by land speculation and concentration on the luxury market. Affordable housing became scarce in the 1970s and reached such critical levels by 1990 on Oʻahu that young middle-class couples could no longer count on buying a house, and some low-income families became homeless. Despite its negative effects, there has been no consensus to limit or effectively direct land development. The construction industry, which depends on continuous land development, employs many local people and is politically powerful.

The heavy reliance on tourism since the 1970s has also increased the vulnerability of the state's economy to outside business recession. Based on discretionary spending, tourism is affected to a greater degree by recession than are agriculture or military spending. In the absence of viable alternatives, Hawaiʻi remains dependent on tourism and related development to maintain its economic well-being.

Since statehood the control of Hawaiʻi's political economy has shifted from the White elite-based Republican Party to the multiethnic Democratic Party. In the early 1950s John Burns forged a coalition of AJA politicians, which took over the leadership of the Democrats. The Democrats won control of the territorial legislature in 1954, and Burns was elected governor in 1962, serving until 1974. With the AJAs comprising 40 percent of the electorate, it was not difficult for the Democrats to win sufficient support from other have-not ethnic groups to oust the Republican elite. Since the 1960s Hawaiʻi has been virtually a one-party state. Democratic nominees for governor and U.S. congressional representatives are generally assured of election, and the majority of the state legislature is

Democratic as well. The legacy of the Burns-led coalition of local ethnic groups can be seen in the varied ethnicity of the Democratic governors who succeeded him: Japanese George Ariyoshi (1974–1986), Hawaiian John Waihee (1986–1994), and Filipino Ben Cayetano (elected in 1994). This ethnic coalition has been paralleled since the 1970s by an emerging "local" identity. Transcending specific ethnic identities, local identity is the result of continuing intermarriage between ethnic groups, which produces an ever-larger mixed group, and of reaction to large-scale *haole* (White/stranger) immigration from the mainland.

The Democrats came to power just as mass tourism and land development began, and they bought into it both philosophically and personally. The Burns administration promoted development as a means to economic growth that would benefit everyone, but especially would give opportunities to non-White businessmen. Chinese, Japanese, and Portuguese entrepreneurs became land developers working with the Democrats. In 1961 the Democrat-dominated legislature passed a strong land use law to rationalize development, but it never acted to limit development or to break up the large holdings of the Big Five and Bishop Estate and reduce their economic power. Most Democratic politicians benefited personally by becoming involved in development as lawyers, corporate officers, and investors. The consensus government of John Burns won the support of all the major players: the ILWU, the unions for government workers that he encouraged, the new land developers, and even to a degree the Big Five. It was popular not only for the economic growth it fostered, but also because it generously supported education and welfare.

The Ariyoshi and Waihee administrations continued the aggressive prodevelopment stance Burns had taken. Reformist political challengers within the Democratic Party like Tom Gill and Jean King, who argued to limit development and spoke out against political corruption, were defeated. As the state economy continued to grow, the state government bureaucracy expanded under both Ariyoshi and Waihee, and government spending increased. As tourism and outside investment declined in the 1990s, so did state revenues. When Cayetano became governor he was faced with a large shortfall and the need to make painful cuts in spending.

The biggest challenge to the political-economic establishment of today is the Hawaiian sovereignty movement. Emerging in the 1980s to demand control over Hawaiian life and lands, the movement developed from the Hawaiian cultural renaissance that followed statehood, restoring a sense of pride in being Hawaiian. During the territorial years, Hawaiian culture and language were disvalued—as were other non-White cultures—and Hawaiian language was suppressed. White American culture was promoted as the

Ka Lāhui Hawaiʻi leads 10,000 people in a march for Hawaiian sovereignty on January 17, 1993. The march to ʻIolani Palace was part of *ʻOnipaʻa,* observing the overthrow of Queen Liliʻuokalani in 1893. [Courtesy *The Honolulu Advertiser*]

ideal, and many Hawaiians grew up ashamed of their heritage. While the Democratic political revolution brought economic success for Chinese and Japanese, Hawaiians stayed disproportionately at the bottom of the socioeconomic scale. In reaction, Hawaiians revived traditional music and *hula* in the 1960s and their native language in the 1980s. Increasingly, part-Hawaiians identify as Hawaiian and support Hawaiian causes. Ka Lāhui Hawaiʻi is the largest sovereignty organization, claiming a membership of 21,000 citizens in 1996. It is working to gain control of the Hawaiian lands ceded to the United States at annexa-

tion and is opposed to large-scale development by outsiders, favoring instead development based within the Hawaiian community.

Today the future for Hawaiʻi seems uncertain. Tourism and continued land development appear to be endangered both by market shifts and by Hawaiian activism. The negative consequences of unrestrained land development make it of dubious value; but if the alternative is a declining economy, that future is also difficult to embrace.

Charles M. Langlas

POPULATION

Hawai'i is one of the most cosmopolitan states. It surpasses most, if not all, of the other states in ethnic and national diversity, to the point that no single group makes up a majority of the population. Important minorities include Hawaiian and other Pacific Island peoples, Chinese, Japanese, Koreans, and Filipinos, along with Caucasians of mainland United States and European origins. This diversity is in large measure a result of Hawai'i's mid-Pacific location, its large military and naval presence, and its history of plantation agriculture employing contract laborers from many nations. In significant ways, the Islands form a natural demographic laboratory.

Historical Overview

The number of Hawaiians living in the Islands at the time of Captain James Cook's arrival in 1778 is unknown, but estimates by Cook's crew members and other early visitors to Hawai'i range from 200,000 to 400,000. Later authorities have approximated the native population during the era of European contact at around 250,000–300,000.

More recently, however, two researchers have challenged these estimates. Working from calculations of potential carrying capacities for the Hawaiian Islands and estimated population densities for other areas during the era of European contact, David E. Stannard has suggested that Hawai'i's precontact population may have reached between 800,000 and 1.5 million persons. A much more conservative opinion comes from Tom Dye, who has deduced from an analysis of radiocarbon evidence that the Hawaiian population peaked around the year 1450 at close to 200,000, then declined to about 150,000 by 1778. Without definitive archaeological evidence to resolve the conflicting estimates, precontact population levels are likely to remain a controversial subject.

Whatever the exact total was at the time of Cook's arrival, the population soon began a century-long period of decline. In 1823, newly arrived American missionaries reckoned the Islands' native population to be about 140,000. The missionaries' first census in 1831–1832 reported a population of about 130,000; their second census in 1835–1836 counted roughly 108,500, revealing a significant population decline. By 1850, the population had fallen to just above 84,000, as reported in the first complete census taken by the Hawaiian government, and the 1876 population stood at an all-time low of about 54,000.

There were many reasons for this sharp population decline. Late in the eighteenth century, Kamehameha's wars were responsible for local famines and a considerable number of battlefield deaths. In the same era European voyagers introduced gonorrhea and syphilis, which resulted in stillbirths and sterility. Throughout the nineteenth century, many Hawaiians died in epidemics of diseases previously unencountered in Hawai'i, including 'ōku'u (possibly cholera), influenza, mumps, measles, whooping cough, and smallpox. Fertility was remarkably low among Native Hawaiians, and infant mortality was exceptionally high. In addition, many Hawaiians, particularly young men recruited by captains of sandalwood and whaling ships, left the Islands.

Deeply concerned about this rapid depopulation, government and business leaders in the Kingdom took steps to improve public health. The Board of Health was established in 1850, and the first large general hospital, the Queen's Hospital (now the Queen's Medical Center), was built in 1860. Around the middle of the nineteenth century, plantation owners began indenturing large numbers of foreign laborers to supplement the diminished labor force. Chinese workers began

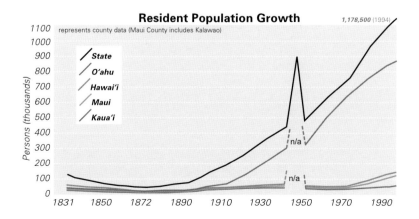

arriving in 1852, Japanese in 1868, Portuguese in 1878, Puerto Ricans in 1901, Koreans in 1904, and Filipinos in 1907. This organized immigration, together with foreigners arriving independently, counterbalanced the depopulation caused by reduced births and increased deaths. Hence, by the mid-1870s the population count began to rise.

Population growth accelerated from 1876 until the end of World War II as the birth rate of Hawaiians rebounded, mortality dropped, and immigrants continued to pour into the Islands. By 1940 the population had climbed to nearly 423,000. With the influx of armed forces and civilian defense workers during World War II, the number of people in what was then the U.S. Territory of Hawai'i more than doubled, to approximately 859,000.

After World War II thousands of residents left the Islands in response to military troop withdrawals, unemployment associated with an economic recession on the U.S. mainland, and extensive labor strikes in the local sugar, pineapple, and shipping industries. Population numbers dropped almost to the prewar level, but began increasing again after 1954, stimulated by the expansion of the tourism industry and renewed military spending. On the eve of statehood in 1959, the number of residents stood at 622,000. Since then, the population has approximately doubled. The 1995 estimate of 1.186 million by the U.S. Bureau of Census reflects a high rate of population growth—gains made despite the dampening economic effects of cutbacks in plantation agriculture and diminished vigor in the visitor industry during the late 1980s and 1990s.

The totals reported for 1990 are even greater if the de facto population, or the number of people actually present in the state, is considered. The 1990 census figure for the resident population includes the more than 55,000 members of the armed forces and their 60,000 civilian dependents, as well as almost 993,000 other residents, thousands of whom were temporarily absent from the state. However, the 1990 census figure does not account for the approximately 158,000 tourists and other visitors present in the state at the time of the census. If the number of visitors is added to the calculations, while excluding 18,000 absent residents, Hawai'i's de facto population climbs to approximately 1.25 million—about 12.6 percent more than the resident count.

Geographic Distribution

Historically the state's population has been unevenly distributed among the major islands. The great majority of residents live on O'ahu, which accounts for less than a tenth of the state's total land area. This concentration of inhabitants has been building up for more than a century. In 1831 O'ahu's population share was nearly 23 percent; in 1900, 38 percent; in 1940, 61 percent; and in 1970, about 82 percent. By 1990

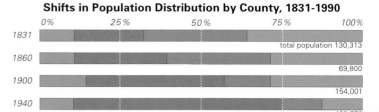

Shifts in Population Distribution by County, 1831-1990

O'ahu claimed more than 836,000 residents, or about three-fourths of the state's total.

From 1831 the population of the neighbor islands charted a steady decline, not only relative to O'ahu but also in absolute numbers. Their combined total population reached a modern peak in 1930 at about 165,400; then, with the mechanization of agriculture, it fell to approximately 132,300 by 1960. Resort development sparked a resurgence of growth in the ensuing decades, so that by 1990 the population of the neighbor islands rose to almost 272,000, or about one-fourth of the state's total.

As shown graphically, nearly 90 percent of Hawai'i's population resided in urban areas in 1990, as compared with 75 percent for the nation as a whole. About 45 percent of O'ahu's 1990 population lived in Honolulu proper, the urban cluster officially defined as the area from Red Hill to Makapu'u Point, between the crest of the Ko'olau Range and the island's southeastern shore. The population of Honolulu proper has climbed from more than 13,300 in 1831 to 39,300 in 1900, about 179,300 in 1940, and roughly 377,000 in 1990. The Honolulu Urbanized Area—defined for census purposes as the area encompassing Honolulu and the adjacent built-up areas as far as 'Ewa Beach, Schofield Barracks, and Whitmore Village—had a 1990 population of 632,600. A second urban cluster, the Kailua Urbanized Area, which encompasses Windward O'ahu from Kahalu'u to Waimānalo Beach, reported a population of about 114,500.

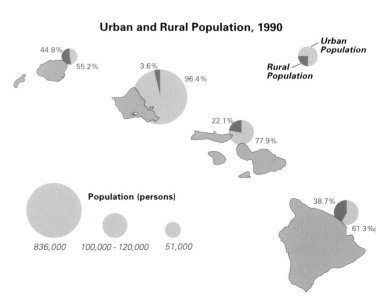

Urban and Rural Population, 1990

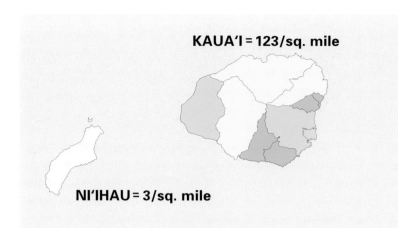

KAUA'I = 123/sq. mile

NI'IHAU = 3/sq. mile

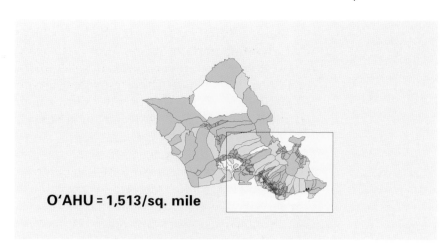

O'AHU = 1,513/sq. mile

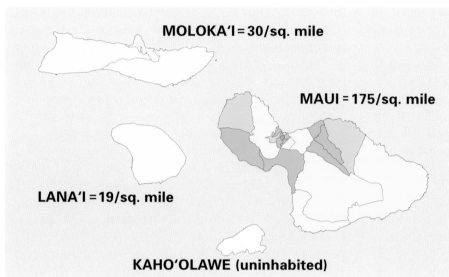

MOLOKA'I = 30/sq. mile

MAUI = 175/sq. mile

LANA'I = 19/sq. mile

KAHO'OLAWE (uninhabited)

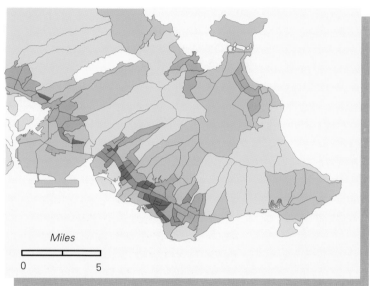

Miles

0   5

Population Density, 1990

per square mile by island and by census tract

- 1 to 10
- 11 to 50
- 51 to 150
- 151 to 500
- 501 to 1,500
- 1,501 to 5,000
- 5,001 to 15,000
- 15,001 to 25,000
- 25,001 and over

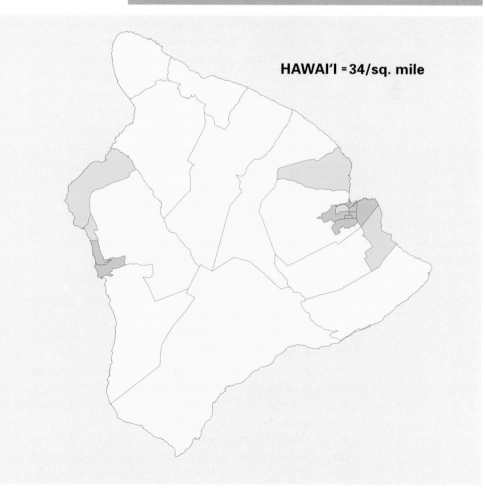

HAWAI'I = 34/sq. mile

As is generally true for the nation's older urban areas, the state's rate of urbanization has slowed over the last decade, and rural regions are now experiencing the fastest rates of population growth. Current rural population increases result largely from in-migration to locations where resort development is creating new jobs (such as North Kona and South Kohala on Hawai'i Island and Lahaina on Maui), or to places with relatively low land prices (such as Puna and Ka'ū on Hawai'i and, to a lesser degree, Makawao on Maui). Not surprisingly, these rural districts exhibit population characteristics (such as higher birth rates and a younger resident population) and socioeconomic features (such as lower rents) typical of rapidly growing areas. (For example, 28.4 percent of the state's rural population is under 18, compared with 24.9 percent for urban parts of the state.)

The population, however, has decreased in certain rural areas where the primary employer has been the pineapple or sugarcane industry. A case in point is the Hāmākua District on Hawai'i Island, which has lost approximately 10 percent of its population each decade since 1970 due to cutbacks in, and eventual closure of, sugarcane operations.

Population densities vary widely between islands and within urban areas. The state's 1990 de facto density was 194.3 persons per square mile, roughly equivalent to average densities in California or Illinois. As expected, the City and County of Honolulu has the highest number of persons per square mile—more than 1,500—while densities on the neighbor islands averaged only about 58 persons per square mile, ranging from zero on Kaho'olawe to around 174 on Maui.

O'ahu's 200 census tracts had 1990 resident densities ranging from 76,787 per square mile (Ala 'Ilima High Rise area) to around 25 (Hale'iwa-Kawailoa) and zero (Waipi'o Peninsula). If de facto densities are shown, in some cases these figures are far higher. For example, in 1990 about 19,800 residents lived within the 507-acre (205 ha) area of Waikīkī. However, this total does not account for the 30,000-plus workers employed in the area or the more than 76,500 visitors housed in Waikīkī hotels and condominiums on an average day in 1990. Thus the actual density of Waikīkī could be either 24,960 (based on resident population), 121,186 (the corresponding de facto number), or around 160,000 persons per square mile (adding workers).

Demographic Characteristics

The population of Hawai'i is rapidly aging. It still has a surplus of males—although much smaller than in the past—and includes a wide range of ethnic and national origins.

In the 1990 resident population, there were 104 males for every 100 females. The relative abundance of males was due partly to the state's sizable military population and partly to the large number of older plan-

tation workers who came to the Islands as single men many years ago and never married.

As shown in the population pyramids, in 1990 half of the residents were less than 32.6 years of age and slightly more than a quarter were younger than 18 years. Nearly two-thirds were between 18 and 64 and just over 11 percent were 65 or older.

For more than half a century the median age has maintained a mostly upward trend statewide, rising from 21.7 years in 1930 to 32.6 in 1990. The 1990 median age ranged from 32.2 years on O'ahu to 34.3 on Hawai'i, with the figures for Kaua'i and Maui counties falling between those values. By census tracts, median ages ranged from 15.6 years in part of Kaka'ako to 55.9 along Waikīkī Beach and 60.9 in Kalaupapa Settlement.

Hawai'i's major ethnic groups are Caucasian, Japanese, and part-Hawaiian, but, significantly, none of these groups is dominant in terms of population size. According to a survey conducted by the Hawai'i State Department of Health in 1990, approximately 24.1 percent of the population not living in institutions or military barracks was Caucasian (excluding Puerto Rican). The next largest group was Japanese (20.4 percent), followed by part-Hawaiians (18.0 percent), mixed ethnic background other than part-Hawaiian (17.5 percent), Filipinos (11.4 percent), Chinese (4.7 percent), Blacks (1.5 percent), Koreans (1.1 percent), Hawaiians (0.8 percent), and Samoans and Puerto Ricans (0.3 percent each). These figures differ considerably from 1990 census totals, which classified persons of mixed race (35.5 percent of the population and 59 percent of civilian births in 1990) either by the race of the mother or by "self-identification."

This ethnic breakdown has changed dramatically over the last 150 years. In 1853, nearly 96 percent of the population was Hawaiian, and the remainder was split between part-Hawaiians and foreigners. Within a half-century, the ethnic proportions of the population were nearly reversed. In 1910, only about 13 percent was Hawaiian and less than 7 percent was part-Hawaiian. Almost 80 percent was non-Hawaiian, chiefly Jap-

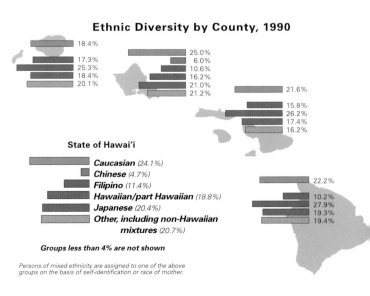

Ethnic Diversity by County, 1990

18.4%
17.3%
25.3%
18.4%
20.1%

25.0%
6.0%
10.6%
16.2%
21.0%
21.2%

21.6%

15.8%
26.2%
17.4%
16.2%

State of Hawai'i

Caucasian (24.1%)
Chinese (4.7%)
Filipino (11.4%)
Hawaiian/part Hawaiian (18.8%)
Japanese (20.4%)
Other, including non-Hawaiian mixtures (20.7%)

22.2%
10.2%
27.9%
19.3%
19.4%

Groups less than 4% are not shown

Persons of mixed ethnicity are assigned to one of the above groups on the basis of self-identification or race of mother.

Hawai'i Population by Gender and Age

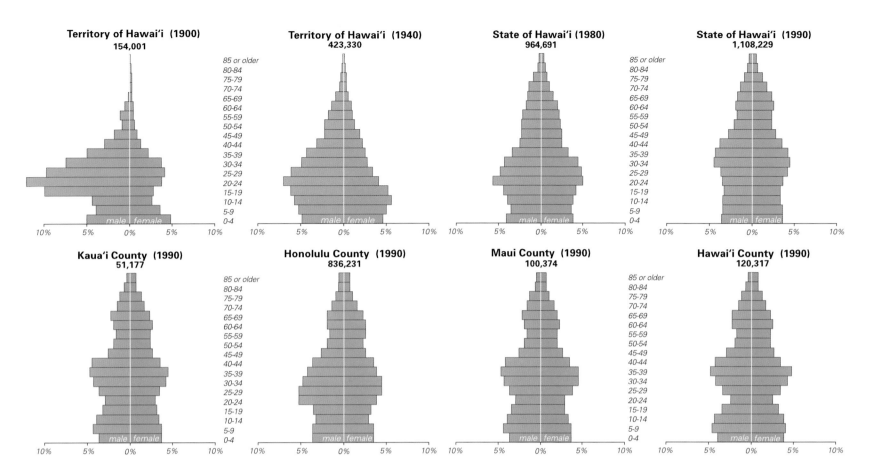

Territory of Hawai'i (1900)
154,001

Territory of Hawai'i (1940)
423,330

State of Hawai'i (1980)
964,691

State of Hawai'i (1990)
1,108,229

Kaua'i County (1990)
51,177

Honolulu County (1990)
836,231

Maui County (1990)
100,374

Hawai'i County (1990)
120,317

anese (41 percent) and Caucasian (23 percent). Since World War II population growth has been greatest for the Caucasians, Filipinos, Blacks, and persons of mixed race, although changing definitions for ethnic designations have made it very difficult to determine exact rates of change.

Few ethnic enclaves exist in Hawai'i. The best known are Ni'ihau—a totally rural, privately owned island inhabited almost entirely by Hawaiians and part-Hawaiians—and communities such as Nānākuli and Waimānalo on O'ahu, which are under the jurisdiction of the state's Department of Hawaiian Home Lands. Other distinctive ethnic concentrations are the O'ahu military bases, with their clusters of mainland Caucasians and Blacks. The plantation "camps," once populated by single ethnic groups, have largely disappeared.

Most Hawai'i residents were born in the Islands, although sizable fractions have mainland or foreign origins. The 1990 census reported that just over 56 per-

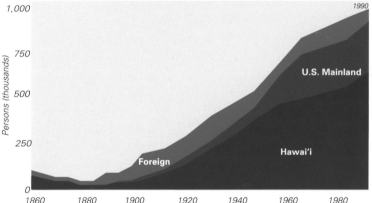

Resident Population Place of Birth

cent are Hawai'i-born, about 26 percent were born elsewhere in the United States, and roughly 17 percent were born in U.S. territories or other overseas locations.

Among persons 15 years of age and older, 54.8 percent of the males and 55.3 percent of the females were currently married, not separated, in 1990. These percentages have changed appreciably over the years with the changing balance of the sexes. In 1896, for example, only 34.4 percent of the males but 71.0 percent of the females were married. The number of unattached males per 100 unattached females rose from 191.9 in 1866 to 820.0 in 1900, then fell to 216.2 in 1940, 121.7 in 1970, and 104.9 in 1990.

The state had slightly fewer than 356,300 house-

Place of birth, 1872–1990

	1872	1900	1930	1960	1990
% Born in Hawai'i	92.1	38.3	58.2	66.6	56.1
% Born on U.S. mainland	1.6	2.8	8.2	22.6	26.4
% Foreign-born	6.4	58.9	32.9	10.9	17.5

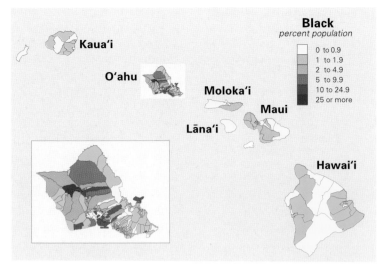

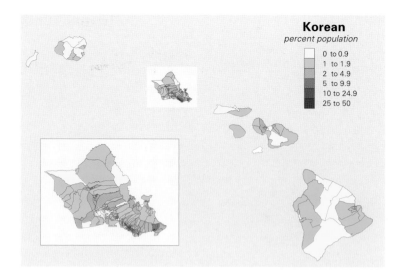

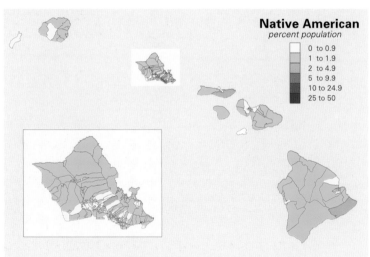

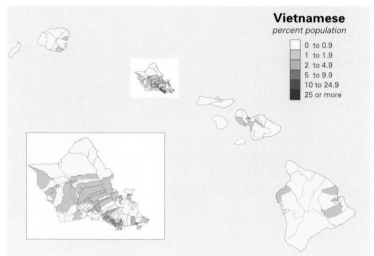

holds (defined as one or more persons occupying a housing unit) in 1990. Nearly three-fourths of these, about 263,500 households, were classified as families (two or more persons related by blood, marriage, or adoption). Statewide there were about 35,400 female heads of households, of which nearly half had one or more children under 18 years of age.

Hawai'i's average household size is steadily shrinking: in 1990 it was 3.01 persons, compared with 3.15 in 1980, 3.87 in 1960, and 4.46 in 1940. Within the state, household sizes ranged from 1.37 in Kalawao (Moloka'i) and 1.57 in downtown Honolulu to 5.48 on Ni'ihau. Persons living in group quarters (such as health care institutions and military barracks) accounted for 3.4 percent of the state's population.

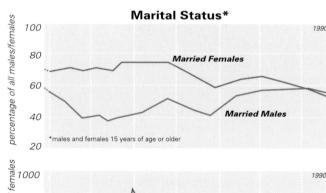

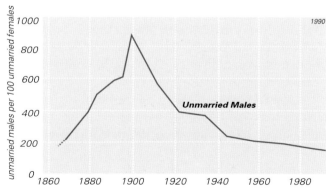

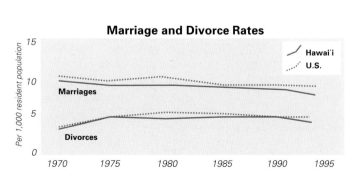

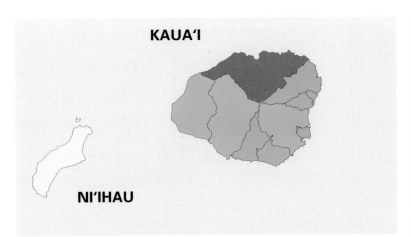

KAUA'I

NI'IHAU

O'AHU

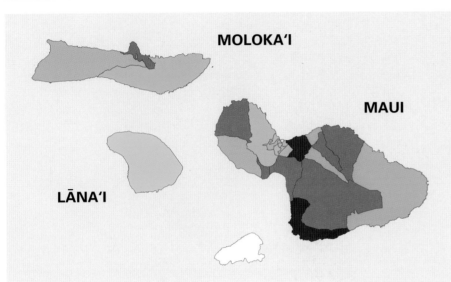

MOLOKA'I

MAUI

LĀNA'I

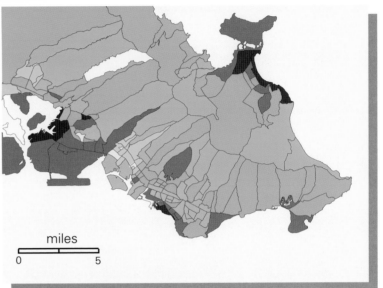

miles

0   5

Caucasian

Percent by Census Tract, 1990

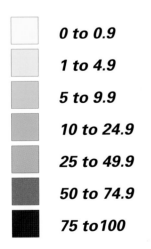

0 to 0.9

1 to 4.9

5 to 9.9

10 to 24.9

25 to 49.9

50 to 74.9

75 to 100

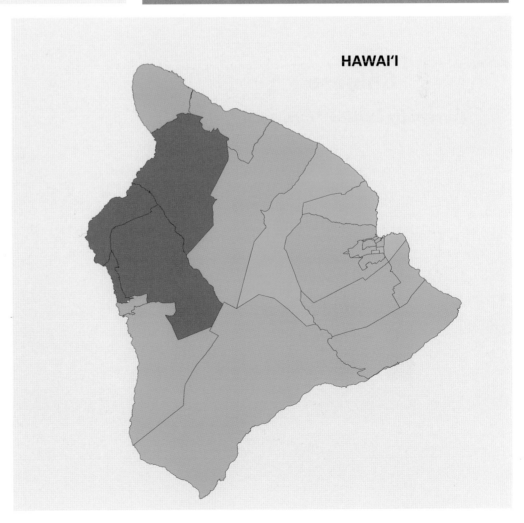

HAWAI'I

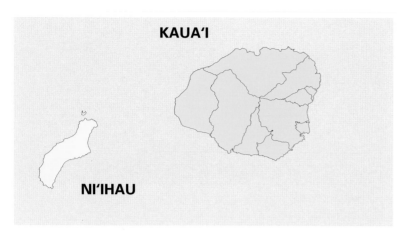

KAUA'I

NI'IHAU

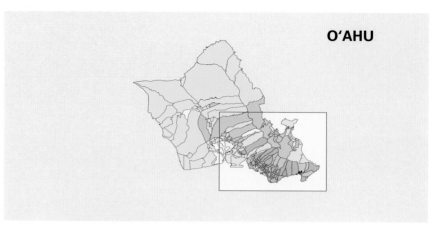

O'AHU

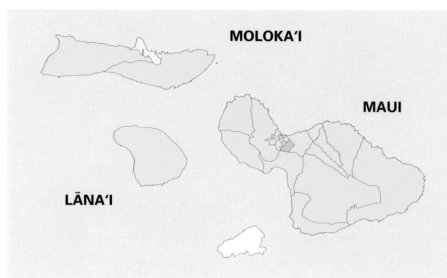

MOLOKA'I

MAUI

LĀNA'I

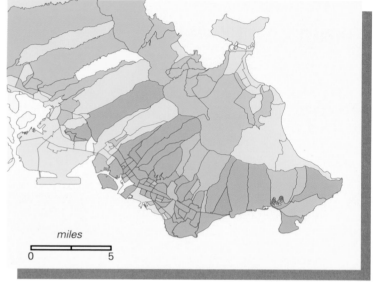

miles

0   5

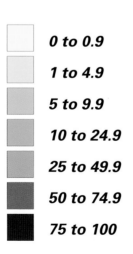

Chinese

Percent by Census Tract, 1990

	0 to 0.9
	1 to 4.9
	5 to 9.9
	10 to 24.9
	25 to 49.9
	50 to 74.9
	75 to 100

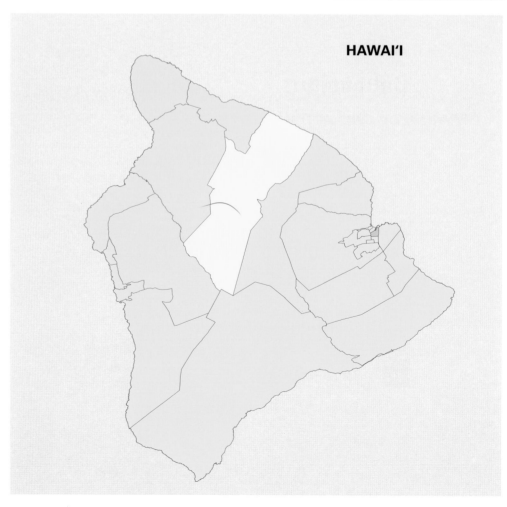

HAWAI'I

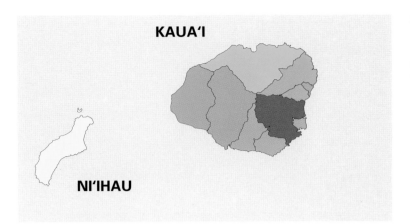

KAUA'I

NI'IHAU

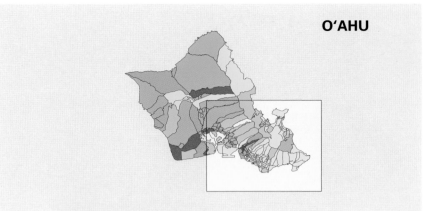

O'AHU

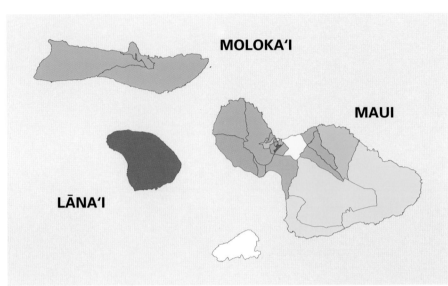

MOLOKA'I

LĀNA'I

MAUI

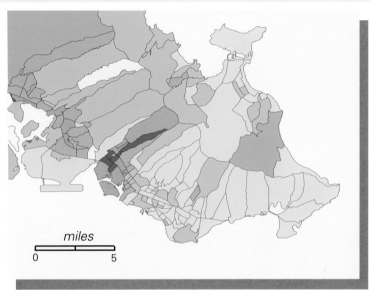

miles

0   5

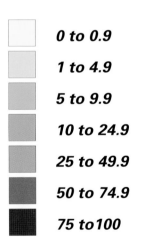

Filipino

Percent by Census Tract, 1990

0 to 0.9

1 to 4.9

5 to 9.9

10 to 24.9

25 to 49.9

50 to 74.9

75 to100

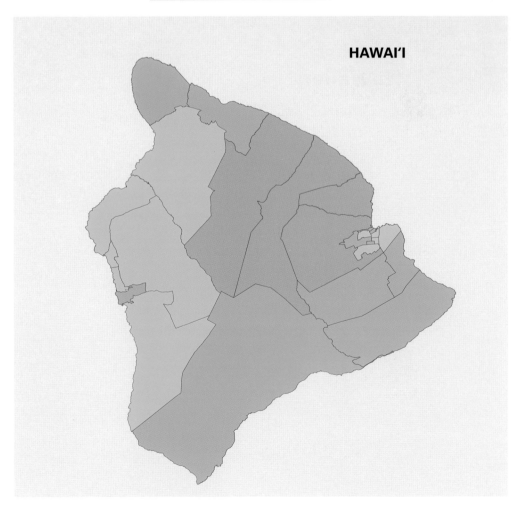

HAWAI'I

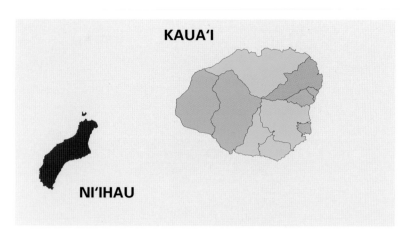

KAUA'I

NI'IHAU

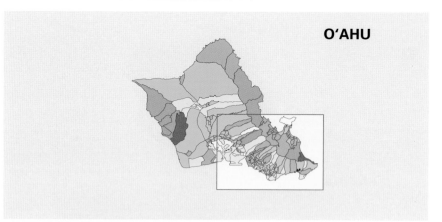

O'AHU

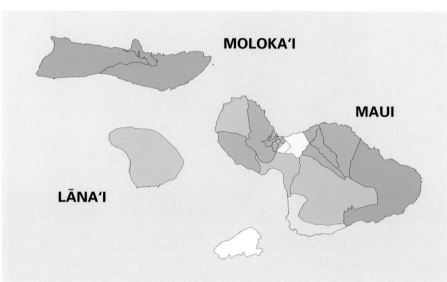

MOLOKA'I

MAUI

LĀNA'I

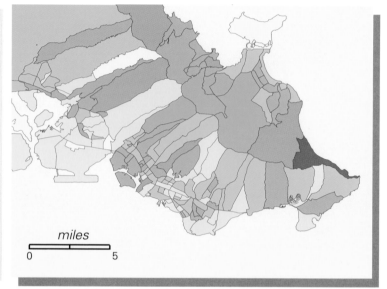

miles

0   5

Hawaiian

Percent by Census Tract, 1990

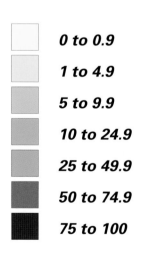

0 to 0.9

1 to 4.9

5 to 9.9

10 to 24.9

25 to 49.9

50 to 74.9

75 to 100

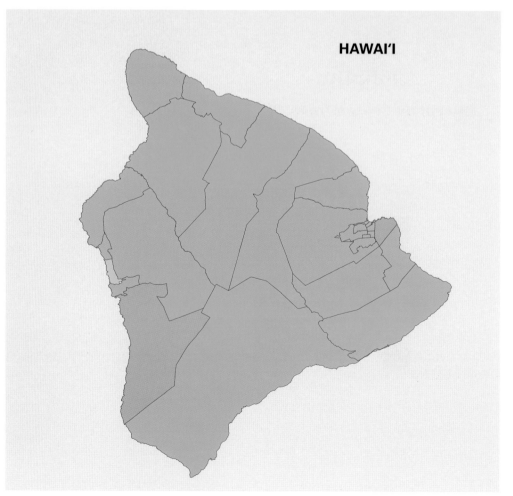

HAWAI'I

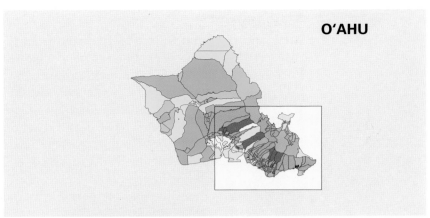

KAUA'I

NI'IHAU

O'AHU

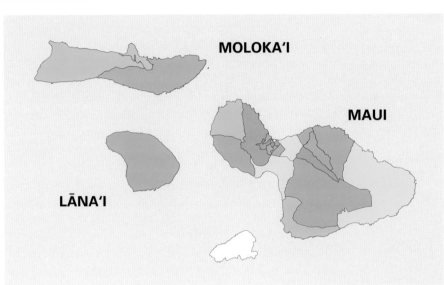

MOLOKA'I

MAUI

LĀNA'I

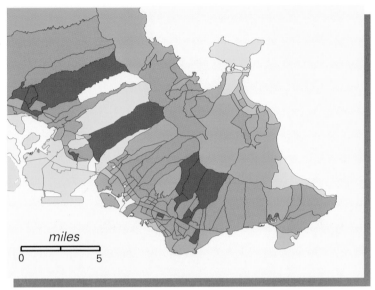

miles

0   5

Japanese

Percent by Census Tract, 1990

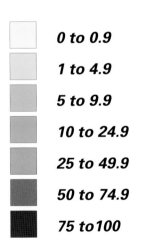

0 to 0.9

1 to 4.9

5 to 9.9

10 to 24.9

25 to 49.9

50 to 74.9

75 to 100

HAWAI'I

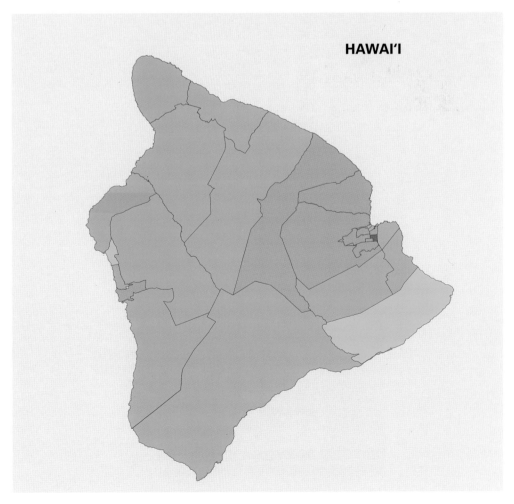

Vital Statistics

Birth and death rates have shifted significantly since the 1830s, when they were first calculated. Fertility has fluctuated in response to introduced diseases, immigration patterns, wars, economic conditions, and the availability of contraceptive methods. During the last hundred years, mortality rates have declined as medical discoveries have improved public health, and better living conditions have gradually overcome the effects of introduced diseases and epidemics, famine, high infant mortality, and other conditions responsible for the high death rates of earlier periods.

As discussed above, the balance between births and deaths dramatically altered nineteenth-century Hawai‘i. Epidemics killed an estimated 15,000 in 1804, 10,000 in 1848–1849, 6,800 in 1853, and 1,700 as late as 1918–1920. Venereal diseases spread by early visitors caused sterility and stillbirths. Some women resorted to known methods of abortion. Child-

hood diseases were prevalent, with severe effects among the previously unexposed Hawaiians. Missionary doctors in the 1830s and 1840s estimated that more than half of all infants died before the age of 2.

Before 1900, crude (unadjusted) birth rates ranged from 16 to 41 per 1,000 inhabitants; crude death rates varied from 19 to 105 per 1,000. (However, both births and deaths presumably were underreported.) The expected life span for babies born in Honolulu in 1878 was less than 22 years. The average length of stay at the Queen's Hospital in 1877–1879 was 59 days, at an average daily cost of 61 cents.

Crude birth rates have fluctuated considerably since 1900. During the first quarter of the century the birth rate rose. In 1924 there were 41.8 births per 1,000 inhabitants; the combined effects of urbanization, economic decline, and expanded knowledge of contraceptive techniques brought the birth rate down to 21.7 during the 1930s. It recovered rapidly during and after World War II, reaching a postwar high of 32.0 in 1954. Partly because of the introduction of contraceptive pills in 1960 and legalized abortion in 1970, the rate again dropped, and by 1975 fewer than 18 births per 1,000 persons were reported. Since then, birth rates have more or less stabilized; the figure for 1994 was 16.5 per 1,000.

Mortality rates in Hawai‘i declined sharply in the late 1800s and early 1900s, then began to level off. One of every four or five babies born during the early 1900s died before its first birthday. Thereafter the infant death rate (per 1,000 live births) plummeted from 43.7 in 1940 to 6.8 in 1994. Life expectancy at birth for males rose from 44.0 years in 1910 to 67.8 in 1950 and 75.9 in 1990; the corresponding estimates for females were 43.8, 71.7, and 82.1 years. The 1993 crude death rate (6.0 per 1,000 population) was well below the national average (8.5), reflecting in part the larger proportion of young people in Hawai‘i compared with most states.

The leading causes of death in 1993 were heart disease (30.5 percent), malignant neoplasms, or cancer (23.8), and cerebrovascular disease (7.6). These data differ greatly from those for earlier periods. In 1925, for example, heart disease accounted for only 7.9 percent of deaths in the territory, ranking below influenza and pneumonia (13.8 percent) and tuberculosis (9.5 percent). Malignant neoplasms were also less significant in 1925, causing only 5.0 percent of all deaths.

Migration

For much of Hawai‘i's history, migration has been a major factor in population growth and redistribution. As noted earlier, from 1852 until the early 1930s large numbers of workers were brought to Hawai‘i from China, Japan, Portugal, Korea, the Philippines, and other areas to labor on sugar and pineapple plantations. After 1931 the mainland United States became the chief source of new residents, as well as the major

Crude Annual Birth, Death, Infant Mortality Rates

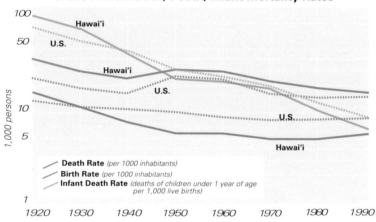

Death Rate *(per 1000 inhabitants)*
Birth Rate *(per 1000 inhabitants)*
Infant Death Rate *(deaths of children under 1 year of age per 1,000 live births)*

Births to Unmarried Mothers

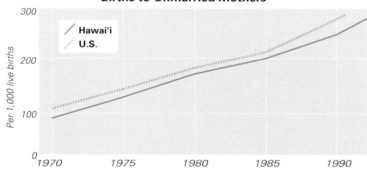

Hawai‘i
U.S.

Birth Rate in Hawai‘i by Ethnicity, 1992, Compared with State and National Rates

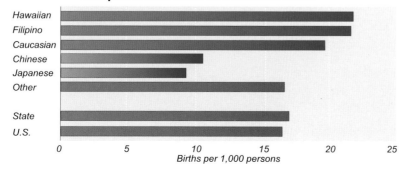

Hawaiian
Filipino
Caucasian
Chinese
Japanese
Other

State

U.S.

Births per 1,000 persons

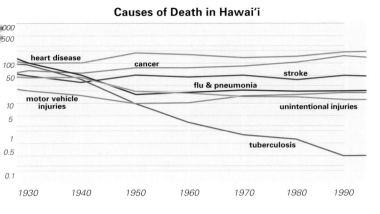

Causes of Death in Hawai'i

destination for those migrating from Hawai'i. The number of in-migrants has exceeded that of out-migrants in every intercensal period from 1853 to 1930, and again from 1950 to 1990.

Between 1980 and 1993 the resident population increased by 207,000 persons: there were 233,000 births, 79,000 deaths, and 52,000 more in-migrants than out-migrants. Migration was thus responsible for more than one-fourth of the net increase.

If, however, the armed forces and their dependents are excluded from these calculations, a very different picture emerges. Large numbers of young military families move to Hawai'i, but they usually remain only 2 or 3 years, significantly boosting the birth rate before moving on and taking their Hawai'i-born children with them. In 1993, military personnel and their dependents accounted for 9.8 percent of the resident population, 3.4 percent of deaths, and 18.1 percent of the babies born. From 1980 to 1993 they experienced a net out-migration of 51,000—mostly their locally born children. During this same period the civilian population recorded a net inflow of 104,000, which accounted for 48.6 percent of overall population growth, or double the share when military families are included in the calculations.

Most of the civilians moving to Hawai'i since World War II have been relatively young persons. Only a small number of retired and older persons have migrated to the state—possibly because of the high cost of living—and many older persons already living in the Islands have moved away upon reaching retirement age. New residents, many of them professional and technical workers, have come largely from Califor-

nia and other western states, the Philippines, Korea, and China.

During recent decades, the people moving from Hawai'i have included somewhat larger proportions of less skilled workers, along with young, Island-born residents who leave to seek work or pursue higher education on the mainland. The number of Hawai'i-born persons living on the mainland increased from 588 in 1850 to 1,307 in 1900, 51,955 in 1950, and 323,156 in 1990—again, many of them from military families. Census data reveal that Hawai'i's net out-migration to other states from 1985 to 1990 was more than matched by an influx of immigrants from foreign countries.

Social and Economic Characteristics

In general, Hawai'i residents report educational attainment, family incomes, and rates of participation in the labor force above the U.S. average. At the same time they face exceptionally high costs of living and suffer moderate levels of social problems. Nonetheless, the Islands score favorably in many of the standard indices that measure quality of life.

According to census reports, virtually all young people of elementary and secondary school age were enrolled in schools in 1990. Nearly 16 percent of them attended private schools—giving Hawai'i one of the highest levels of private school enrollment in the nation, which averages just under 10 percent.

Among persons 25 years or older, 80 percent have graduated from high school; however, if military personnel and dependents are excluded the proportion falls to just under 64 percent. Statewide in 1990 almost 23 percent of those 25 and older had attained at least a bachelor's degree—compared with a nationwide average of 20.3 percent—with the proportion ranging from 16.3 percent in Kaua'i County to 24.6 percent on O'ahu.

A 1988–1989 survey of literacy in English conducted for the Governor's Office found that 19 percent of persons 18 years or older were functionally illiterate, and only 53 percent are considered competent in English. These results may be related to the fact that in 1990 about one in four residents aged 5 or older spoke a language other than English at home, while 48,000 spoke English "not well" or "not at all."

The plantation economy that contributed largely to the state's ethnic diversity has clearly given way to today's retailing, service, and government-based economy. In 1900, agricultural workers outnumbered those in other civilian activities 1.7 to 1. The number of laborers in the agricultural sector peaked at approximately 63,600 in 1930, then dropped to about 16,000 in 1960; by 1990 the total stood at around 16,500. Meanwhile, nonagricultural employment soared from close to 74,300 in 1930 to about 193,400 in 1960, to 512,500 in 1990. By the latter year, 23 percent of all employed persons found occupations in wholesale or retail trade, while 26.4 percent had managerial or pro-

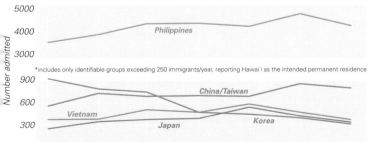

Foreign Immigrants to Hawai'i, by Country of Birth*

*includes only identifiable groups exceeding 250 immigrants/year, reporting Hawai'i as the intended permanent residence

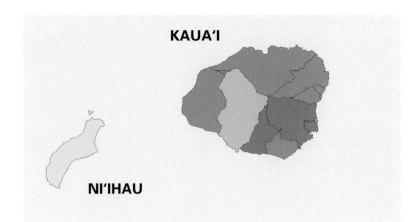

KAUA'I

NI'IHAU

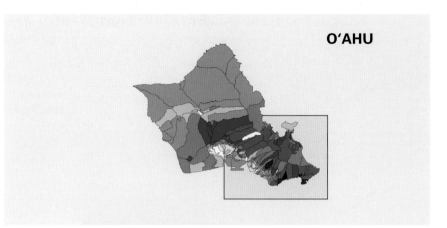

O'AHU

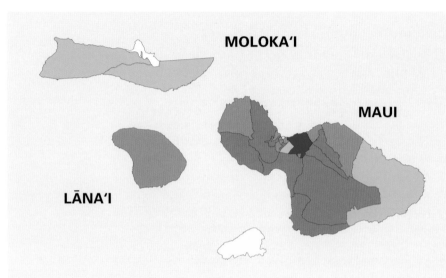

MOLOKA'I

LĀNA'I

MAUI

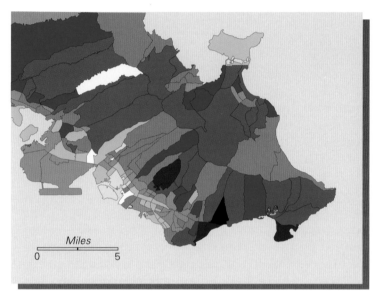

Miles

0   5

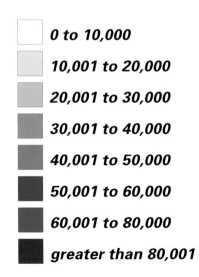

Median Household Income

Dollars by Census Tract, 1990

0 to 10,000

10,001 to 20,000

20,001 to 30,000

30,001 to 40,000

40,001 to 50,000

50,001 to 60,000

60,001 to 80,000

greater than 80,001

HAWAI'I

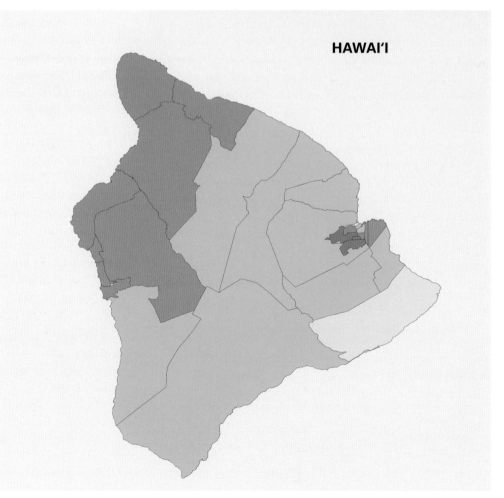

Employment Sector by County, 1991

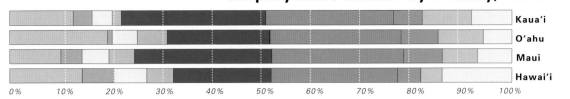

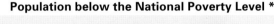

fessional positions, 17.6 percent were in service occupations, and 20.4 percent worked for the federal, state, or county governments.

Unemployment remained relatively low during the 1980s, and only 3.5 percent of the civilian labor force was unemployed at the time of the 1990 census. (However, state unemployment rates have climbed steadily since then.) About 63 percent of all females aged 16 years or older, including women with children under the age of 6, were employed in 1990—a significantly higher proportion than the national average of 56.8 percent. Among males 16 and older, close to 77 percent were in the labor force.

Family incomes were relatively high in 1989 (as reported in the 1990 census) compared with other states. The 1989 median family income of $43,176—more than 3.7 times higher than in 1969 and 12 times higher than in 1949—ranged from $33,186 on Hawai‘i Island to $45,313 on O‘ahu. By census tracts, median incomes ranged from $7,766 at Kūhiō Park Terrace to $113,028 in Wai‘alae Iki (O‘ahu) and around $144,000 (from a very small sample) at Spreckelsville, Maui. Although median household and family incomes in Hawai‘i exceeded those for most states, the average wage and salary income ($21,635 in 1989) was 4.2 percent below the national average.

Growth in median family or household income, interestingly, has far outstripped the gains in average earnings, largely because of the increased presence of women in the labor force and a rising trend of holding multiple jobs. Between 1969 and 1989, for example, the median family income rose 270 percent, but average wages and salaries increased by only 215 percent. Moreover, these seemingly impressive gains in median incomes fail to take inflation into account. During the same 20 years the Honolulu consumer price index recorded a 227 percent jump. Thus, in constant dollars, the median family income rose only 13 percent, and the average wage or salary actually declined by 4 percent.

The gap between the cost of living and family incomes has persisted through the 1990s, with wages and family incomes continuing to lag behind price levels. Indeed, living costs in Honolulu exceed those in mainland cities by ever-larger amounts. The annual intermediate budget for a four-person family on O‘ahu (calculated by the U.S. Bureau of Labor Statistics

through 1981 and unofficially since then by the Bank of Hawai‘i) exceeded the U.S urban average by 19.5 percent in 1971, 30.7 percent in 1989, and 39.6 percent in 1992.

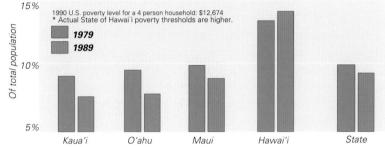

Population below the National Poverty Level *

Other measures of social well-being, or its lack, offer a mixed picture.

- A survey conducted for Homeless Aloha in 1992 indicated that there were at least 2,500 homeless persons and 17,000 other "hidden homeless" who unwillingly share housing with friends and relatives.
- The incidence of violent crimes in 1993 was 261 per 100,000 residents, only one-third the national average. But property crimes averaged 6,016 per 100,000 residents, the fourth-highest state rate in the country.
- The percentages of persons of voting age who actually registered and participated in recent general elections were among the lowest in the nation.
- About 14.5 percent of Hawai‘i's population is living in poverty, according to U.S. Census data. (However, this figure, based on a poverty standard calculated for mainland living costs, may seriously underestimate the number of poor in the Islands, where living costs are significantly higher.)
- In 1994, more than 6 percent of the population (75,000 persons) depended on the state's financial assistance programs.

Despite this less than ideal picture, six out of seven studies on the quality of life in U.S. states and metropolitan areas published in the early 1990s ranked Hawai‘i and Honolulu in the top 20 percent of the areas surveyed.

Robert C. Schmitt

LANGUAGES

Until Western contact in 1778, only one language was spoken in Hawai'i. It was not entirely uniform, but differed slightly in vocabulary and sound from island to island. This language, a member of the Polynesian family, had developed quite independently over time, changing to the extent that it became a separate language.

Within the Polynesian family, Hawaiian is more similar to some languages than to others. For example, its vocabulary is closest to that of Rarotongan, Marquesan, and Māori. Unfortunately, a comparison of these related languages by itself does not reveal the origin of the Hawaiian people. We may conclude, however, by adding other types of evidence, such as archeological, genetic, and oral-traditional, that Hawai'i was settled not at one specific time, but over a long period and by different waves of immigration.

The first written records of Hawaiian are the place names, personal names, and word lists gathered by Captain James Cook and his crew. Upon first hearing the Hawaiian language, these explorers were struck by its similarity to Tahitian (which they were familiar with), despite the great distance separating Hawai'i and Tahiti.

The influence of the English language on Hawaiian began soon after the first European contact. Beginning about 1790, a number of Hawaiians learned English as crew members aboard British and American ships. Moreover, a sizable English-speaking population

lived in the Islands, especially around the port of Honolulu. Even though some foreign residents wanted to maintain their power by withholding knowledge of written English from the Hawaiians, it was impossible to do so.

More significant developments in the Hawaiian language began with the arrival of American Protestant missionaries in 1820. The most important of these was the establishment of a writing system for Hawaiian. First, the missionaries discarded the awkward English convention for writing vowels in favor of the European (that is, Latin or Italian) system. Next, faced with an unusual amount of variation among consonant sounds, they came to realize the impossibility of continuing to write words exactly as they heard them. For example, some speakers referred to the paramount chief as *Tamehameha;* others called him *Kamehameha.* Since *t* and *k* did not function to keep words distinct, it was decided to use one letter instead of two. Other such pairs were *v-w* and *l-r.* Choosing one letter for each of these pairs of sounds did not affect pronunciation of the language, only its representation in print. And it allowed, for the first time, uniformity in spelling.

The only flaw in this otherwise ideal alphabet was the omission of symbols for vowel length (a *kahakō,* or macron over a vowel) and the glottal stop, or *'okina* ('). Used at first only in teaching materials, today these symbols are part of the regular writing system.

This highly efficient writing system resulted in relatively widespread literacy, achieved much more easily than that for English, with its inconsistent match between sound and symbol. Still, a shortage of books and other printed materials hampered Hawaiian literacy. And, as the foreign population with all its material goods increased, many Hawaiians equated English with power and prosperity.

Although the first English school for Hawaiians existed for only a few weeks in 1810, such schools grew in number, size, and longevity after the arrival of missionaries, who had to teach in English until they learned Hawaiian. From then on, most schools were conducted in Hawaiian. But even at the height of

Language Spoken at Home, 1990

English
Japanese
Tagalog
Ilocano
Chinese
Korean
Spanish
Samoan
Other

0%   2.5%   5%   7.5%   10%   60%   70%   80%

Hawaiian literacy, in 1839 a group of Hawaiian chiefs requested that the mission establish an English school for their children. Called the Royal School, it ensured that future Hawaiian leaders would be competent in the English language.

The merit of Hawaiian versus English as the medium of education for Hawaiian commoners was debated as early as the 1840s, with strong opinions expressed on both sides of the argument. The dynamics between these two languages were complicated by the large-scale importation of foreigners to work on plantations, beginning in 1852 with Chinese workers (who spoke mainly Hakka and varieties of Cantonese). In the following years, other immigrant groups added Portuguese, Japanese, Puerto Rican Spanish, Korean, and Filipino (especially Tagalog, Ilocano, and languages of the Bisayan family) to Hawai'i's linguistic mixture. Smaller groups of laborers also came from the Pacific Islands (chiefly Kiribati, the Gilbert Islands), Russia, Germany, Scandinavia, and other European countries, but their languages generally had little lasting effect on Hawai'i's linguistic mosaic.

Long after the importation of plantation laborers stopped, groups speaking other languages arrived, including Samoans, Vietnamese, Thais, Laotians, and speakers of a scattering of European languages.

More than 100 languages were listed as spoken by residents of Hawai'i participating in the 1990 census.

Hawaiian Language Renaissance

The Hawaiian language and culture contain a rich oral tradition tied to *nā akua* (the gods), *ka 'āina* (the land), and *ka 'ohana* (the family). This oral tradition was complemented with a broad literary tradition in the early nineteenth century, when missionaries developed a writing system and Hawaiian *ali'i* (chiefs) established hundreds of schools teaching the reading and writing of Hawaiian. By the mid-1800s, Hawaiian language publications dealing with a variety of subjects, including geography, geometry, anatomy, and zoology, had become part of the schools' curricula, and by 1890 more than 90 Hawaiian language newspapers had been in circulation.

By the late 1800s, more than 90 percent of the Hawaiian population could speak, read, and write in their native tongue. This accomplishment, however, was gradually reversed by the banning of Hawaiian as a medium of instruction in the public schools in 1896. Children caught speaking Hawaiian in the classroom were punished, and for generations a stigma remained attached to the Hawaiian language. Although no formal Hawaiian language survey has been conducted, by 1995 fewer than 600 native-speaking elders were estimated to remain in the general population. In addition, there is a native-speaking community of about 400 people living on, or with ties to, the island of Ni'ihau.

Beginning in the 1960s, the Hawaiian cultural renaissance has revived dance, music, and other native cultural traditions. Hawaiian gained status as a spoken language on University of Hawai'i campuses during the 1970s, and in 1978 the Hawai'i Constitutional Convention declared Hawaiian one of the state's two official languages. For a Hawaiian-speaking community to take root and blossom, however, children had to learn Hawaiian as their first language.

The revival of the Hawaiian language can be traced directly to the establishment of the Pūnana Leo and Kaiapuni Hawai'i programs. The first Pūnana Leo Hawaiian-medium preschool opened in 1984. Classes are conducted entirely in Hawaiian, and children become fluent within six months. As of 1995, the Pūnana Leo preschool system had expanded to nine sites, including every island except Lāna'i and Ni'ihau. Nearly every student who completes the Pūnana Leo preschool program continues into the public school K–12 Hawaiian-medium program called Papahana Kaiapuni Hawai'i. These programs were the first of their kind in any Native American language. Combined enrollment in 1995 was more than 1,000 students, and the number continues to increase as new Pūnana Leo and Kaiapuni Hawai'i schools open. Waiting lists for Pūnana Leo schools are consistently double their enrollment capacities.

Enrollment in Hawaiian language classes at the secondary and higher-education levels likewise attests to the demand for Hawaiian. Nearly 2,000 students were enrolled in such classes at the community colleges and the Mānoa and Hilo campuses of the University of Hawai'i in 1995. With the addition of students in elementary, high school, and community classes, about 4,000 people were studying the Hawaiian language in 1995.

This level of participation in Hawaiian language education is being accompanied by a high degree of advocacy and activism. For instance, in May 1995 several hundred university students successfully contested the reduction in the number of Hawaiian language classes in the University of Hawai'i system.

To the *malihini,* or newcomer, the Hawaiian language may appear secure in Hawai'i since it is seen on many street signs, heard in numerous place names, and commonly spoken in greeting (*aloha*) and appreciation (*mahalo*). Less than a generation ago the likelihood of hearing a radio newscast conducted in Hawaiian, a commencement speech delivered in Hawaiian, or young children conversing in Hawaiian was only a dream. Today, this dream is becoming reality as spoken Hawaiian regains ground that was lost after more than a century of erosion. Once again Hawaiian may be heard in these Islands.

ERIC M. KAPONO

The leading non-English languages were Japanese (70,000), Tagalog (55,000), and Ilocano (26,000). However, the figures may not reflect the subsequent immigration of growing numbers of Spanish-speaking workers.

The largest language categories are reflected in commercial enterprises, from video stores specializing in Asian films, to bus tours for Spanish speakers, to shops catering to tourists that provide Japanese-speaking employees and signs in Japanese.

Three important sociolinguistic patterns are rooted in the state's melange of languages. First, a significant number of speakers clung to their own languages through several generations, depending on private language schools (mainly Japanese, Chinese, and Korean) and the press to preserve their linguistic heritage. For instance, according to a survey in 1920, 98 percent of the Japanese students enrolled in public schools (more than 20,000) also attended private language schools. These groups, as well as the Portuguese, published newspapers in their respective languages. Some of the language schools and newspapers still exist today.

Next, many of the languages borrowed freely from each other as their speakers came into contact. Most of this exchange has occurred between English and Hawaiian. At first, because of the impact of foreign material culture and the need for terms for biblical and scholastic translation, the direction was mainly English to Hawaiian. On the other hand, English—both in Hawai'i and on the mainland—has borrowed many Hawaiian terms for flora, fauna, geographical features (such as the names for lava, *pāhoehoe* and *'a'ā*), and cultural terms (including *aloha, kapu, lei,* and *kuleana*).

Local English uses many more Hawaiian words even in formal conversation. Both Hawaiian and local English have borrowed words and phrases—most notably names of food and cultural activities—from later arrivals, resulting in a linguistic "mixed plate" for all involved.

Finally, from the interactions among speakers of widely different languages arose pidgins. There is evidence for a Hawaiian pidgin that may have developed between 1790 and 1820. By mid-century, the plantations gave rise to other forms. Whatever the origins, the pidgins then stabilized into a creole that included certain features (such as the intonation patterns and predicate-subject phrase order) reflecting Hawaiian influence. This language, Hawai'i Creole English (popularly known as Pidgin), is still the first dialect/language of many state residents.

Although mainstream education and the media exert pressure for Hawai'i Creole English to be replaced by Standard or General American English, other forces, including the needs to establish identity and to express values, pull in the opposite direction. After years of bad press, Hawai'i Creole English has gained wider acceptance. It now appears in print and is heard on stage and in many other venues in which it was once deemed inappropriate. Still, public opinion remains divided, and the topic rises regularly—phoenixlike—in local newspapers, where it is sure to elicit an emotional response from readers.

In summary, the state's complex linguistic past has produced a richly multilingual and multidialectal present.

ALBERT J. SCHÜTZ

RELIGION

Owing to the great diversity of religious organizations in the state and the dissimilar methods that groups use to calculate their membership, attaining precise religious data is extremely difficult. Nevertheless, the statistics presented here offer as accurate a picture as possible of the broad religious spectrum of the Islands.

The state's religious landscape is a multihued scene in which most of the major world religions play roles, exerting tangible influences on culture, economics, and politics. As of 1995 nearly 900 religious organizations, with combined property holdings in excess of 1 billion dollars, were registered statewide, and many other unregistered groups are known to exist. Active worship centers, including churches and temples, number well over 1,000, giving a statewide per capita ratio of at least one center for every 1,000 people. The religious affiliations of active groups range from the ancient traditions of the Pacific, Asia, and the Near East, to new religious movements gaining footholds around the world. Hawai'i encompasses a greater

diversity of religious traditions than any other state, with the possible exception of California. It also ranks among the most religiously diverse areas in the world.

The known introduction of foreign religions to Hawai'i began with the arrival of New England Prot-

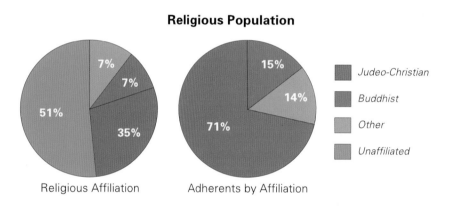

Religious Population

51% — 7% — 7% — 35%
Religious Affiliation

15% — 14% — 71%
Adherents by Affiliation

Judeo-Christian
Buddhist
Other
Unaffiliated

estant missionaries in 1820. Later in the nineteenth century, the influx of Asian immigrants with their religious traditions further broadened the religious panorama—a trend that has continued to the present day. The dating of the first Jewish arrival in the Islands is difficult, although there is evidence to suggest that Jews were present at the time of King Kalākaua. The first Jewish services in Hawai'i may have occurred about the beginning of the twentieth century. Currently there are between 10,000 and 15,000 Jews in the Islands.

Christianity presently ranks as the dominant religion, reflecting the historical nationwide pattern. Three-fourths of state residents who acknowledge specific sectarian affiliations are Christian, and half of these are Roman Catholic. Of the many Protestant denominations, Baptist and the Church of Jesus Christ of Latter-Day Saints (Mormons) have the largest memberships. However, the religious affiliations of a significant portion of the population are unknown, as newly arrived immigrants and non-Christians tend to be less likely to provide such information during censuses.

Buddhism is the largest non-Christian religion,

Makiki Christian Church (Honolulu) shows the influence of Japanese culture and philosophy. Completed in 1932, it was fashioned after an Edo period castle to represent the concepts of strength, peace, and order. [R. Lamb]

Hawaiian Religion

The Hawaiian religion was a highly structured institution characterized by hierarchy, traditions, and protocols. It evolved through many generations from the pragmatic worship of elemental gods to the highly complex and integrated political/ religious system of the late eighteenth and the early nineteenth centuries.

The foundation for this religion was the four major male gods: Kāne, Kanaloa, Kū, and Lono. All elemental male forms of the atmosphere, Earth, and the ocean were the body forms of these gods. The female elemental forms of the physical realms were associated with the four female gods: Haumea, Papa, Hina, and Pele. Hierarchy among the gods determined the sacredness of places belonging to these god forms. This sense of order among the gods extended to the *ali'i* class (the social elites or chiefs) and the *kahuna* (keepers of the religion and gods).

The *ali'i* and the *kahuna* acquired their status through genealogical connections. They were trained intensively from childhood until they earned their leadership role in the political or religious arenas. The growth of the population by 1778 demanded a more complicated structural order, resulting in more gods, more ceremonies, more offerings, and more *kapu* (laws of the gods). This population growth thus accelerated social stratification and the further development of the political/religious organization.

During the reign of Kamehameha I (1792–1819), Hawaiian religion was dominated by the god Kū and the *luakini heiau* milieu as the formal components of ceremonial worship. A secondary worship system of *makahiki* ceremonies was presided over by the god Lono. Both systems were seasonal and gave balance to the yearly activities concerning the sea, Earth, the sky, and humans. These systems, supported by the religious and political leaders, constituted the principal controlling mechanism in Hawaiian society.

The death of Kamehameha I was followed by war between supporters of the established religion and the aristocratic forces seeking to terminate the Kū-*luakini* and Lono worship systems. By deliberately breaking with the tradition of *kapu,* the new leaders ended religious unity and caused an irreversible chain of events that eliminated the state religion. The resulting upheaval crippled the political structure by rendering the order of the *kahuna* defunct. It abrogated land *kapu,* laws that regulated the balance of seasonal growth, and thereby gave rise to a disjointed economic system. The fall of formal Hawaiian religion ended many generations of developed traditions regarding the *ali'i,* the people, the deities, *kapu* for protection of the land, and *kānāwai,* earthly laws made by *ali'i* (who were considered living gods).

This chaos did not, however, leave the Native Hawaiian without spirituality. The *'aumākua,* or ancestral guardian, part of the basic system of spiritual guidance that belonged to each Hawaiian, was still in place, and this became the focus of religious observances. The nomenclature and form of *'aumākua* depended upon family genealogy, birthplace, tradition, and occupation.

The following are examples of family traditions and occupations that continued into the twentieth century and maintained a high level of connection to *'aumākua,* elemental forms, and the *wahi pana* (gathering places necessary to maintain *'aumākua*).

These are some of the more obvious practices that survived the tumultuous changes in lifestyle from 1778 to 1995.

Family Traditions & Occupations	Nā 'Aumākua	Forms: flora, fauna, elemental	Gathering places
Hula	Pele, Hi'iaka, Laka, Kapo, *kupuna, mākua*	volcanoes, clouds, steam, rising & setting sun, eruptions, earthquakes, magma, wind, *lehua, kī, palai*	vegetated areas
Fishing	Kū, Kanaloa, Ku'ula, *kupuna, mākua*	ocean currents, winds, rains, various sea creatures, birds	forests, ocean, shoals
Canoe making	Kū, Kāne, Laka, *kupuna, mākua*	rains, sun, trees (*koa, 'ōhi'a, hau,* etc.) birds	all forested areas
Medicinal	all male and female forms	water, most vegetation, some fauna	from the mountains to the deep oceans
Taro farming	Kū, Kāne, Lono, *kupuna, mākua*	fresh water, sun, rain	valleys, streams, forests

Today, there are common threads from earlier times throughout all categories of practices. As in the past, each practitioner has to know something about the land, the sea, and the sky. The knowledge of relationship with these realms has filtered down from the time of the god Kāne to the *mākua,* the present generation of parents. The coming of foreign peoples with their religions eroded the Hawaiian's relationship with the *'aumākua* religious system, and few retained their ancestral connections to it in the modern era. However, the current generation has revived the *'aumākua* practices.

The year 1976 was pivotal in the Native Hawaiian community because of political and religious developments regarding the island of Kaho'olawe. Practitioners who had maintained their *'aumākua* connections surfaced to aid the Hawaiian community in reawakening the *'aumākua* religion. Hawaiian spiritual roots literally were reestablished by using Lonomakua to bring life-giving water to reinvigorate Kaho'olawe. The opening and closing *makahiki* ceremonies there were performed by the *mo'o* (followers of) Lono, who asked for rain from the god. The *mo'o* Kanaloa reinstituted the practices associated with Kanaloa, invoking his assistance in cleansing the ocean waters surrounding Kaho'olawe. The *mo'o* Papa led the practices dedicated to Papahānaumoku, the deity responsible for propagating growth in the ocean and on the land.

In 1988 the spiritual insensitivity of exhuming the skeletal remains of more than a thousand Native Hawaiians from an ancient burial site slated for a hotel galvanized Hawaiian families to seek spiritual guidance from these ancestors to stop the desecration. The ancestral spirits guided the Hui Mālama I Nā Kūpuna O Hawai'i Nei, the concerned families, the Office of Hawaiian Affairs, and others who took responsibility to rectify the desecration. These groups regained the knowledge of burial rites, prayers, and funerary *kapa* making and *lauhala* weaving, and they received the direction needed to reinter Hawaiian remains.

Halau 'O Kekui performing ancient hula (*kahiko*).
[P. J. Buklarewicz]

(continued on next page)

(*Hawaiian Religion* continued)

Other modern practices associated with the religion of the 'aumākua lie in the realm of medicine. The practice of lā'au lapa'au (curing medicine), once again honorable, is being taught to people outside the families of practitioners. Young taro farmers are building ahu (altars) for offerings to 'aumākua forms of Kāne to ensure the continual flow of fresh water to lo'i (taro ponds). Traditional and nontraditional fishermen continue to use the old kū'ula (gods of fishing) along shoreline trails, leaving offerings of appreciation for fish caught in the area. (To leave an offering is to "use" the gods in Hawaiian thinking.) Pelehonuamea demands attention when erupting. The followers of the deity Pele compose new songs to describe volcanic eruptions and the extension of new land into the sea. The mo'o Pele also use fire names and incorporate the names of Pele's family in their genealogy.

As a formal institution, Hawaiian religion does not exist today. However, Hawaiian religion in association with the family 'aumākua practice is thriving. It is the birthright of all Native Hawaiians and remains a choice in spiritual life.

EDWARD KANAHELE AND PUALANI KANAHELE

The interior of the Honpa Hongwanji Mission (Honolulu), completed in 1918. The largest Buddhist temple in the Islands, it expresses the blending of religious elements: a traditional Buddhist altar coupled with Christian-style pews, hymnals, pulpit, and organ (not shown). [R. Lamb]

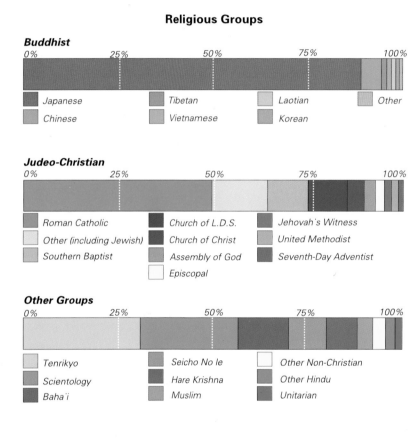

Religious Groups

Buddhist

Japanese, Chinese, Tibetan, Vietnamese, Laotian, Korean, Other

Judeo-Christian

Roman Catholic, Other (including Jewish), Southern Baptist, Church of L.D.S., Church of Christ, Assembly of God, Episcopal, Jehovah's Witness, United Methodist, Seventh-Day Adventist

Other Groups

Tenrikyo, Scientology, Baha'i, Seicho No Ie, Hare Krishna, Muslim, Other Non-Christian, Other Hindu, Unitarian

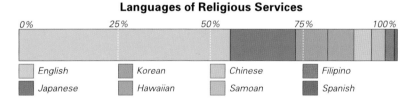

Languages of Religious Services

English, Japanese, Korean, Hawaiian, Chinese, Samoan, Filipino, Spanish

and the variety of Buddhist denominations has expanded greatly over the last several decades. Many immigrants from South, Southeast, and East Asia have brought their own forms of Buddhism with them. While first- and second-generation immigrants generally remain strongly attached to their ethnic religious forms, subsequent generations are more likely to abandon these ties, choosing either to become Christian or not to affiliate with any particular religion. The outcome of this trend is that while the variety of Buddhist sects has increased over the last two decades, the overall number of acknowledged Buddhists has dropped slightly.

Ethnic and cultural ties continue to be powerful factors influencing religious affiliation in the state, especially with respect to many of the Asian and Pacific Island residents involved in their native religious traditions. As a consequence, these groups are generally more ethnically monolithic than in the Christian denominations here. For example, it is rare to find Chinese Buddhists attending Japanese Buddhist services, and vice versa.

In addition, numerous Christian groups have arisen that have unique Asian or Pacific Island cultural forms and whose adherents tend to be of one ethnicity. Other Christian denominations have adapted to the

A contemporary Hawaiian *lele* ("sacrificial altar") associated with the 1994 occupation of Kaupō village, Makapuʻu, Oʻahu. The *lele* has become an important symbol of both Hawaiian religious identity and political protest. [R. Lamb]

prevalent ethnic diversity and patterns of ethnic preference by providing non-English-language services, most commonly in Japanese, Hawaiian, Korean, Samoan, Tagalog, and Ilocano. Several distinct expressions of Christianity have likewise evolved to assimilate elements of other religious cultures, reflecting the desires of their members to retain their cultural identity. For example, some Christian groups formally participate in the Obon and Lantern Festivals, which are Japanese Buddhist rites performed for departed ancestors.

Similarly, the dominance of Christianity in Hawaiʻi has also influenced some forms of Asian religious expression. The Buddhist Honpa Hongwanji Mission in Honolulu probably represents the most obvious outward expression of this influence. From its inception, the mission has sought to provide a religious atmosphere adapted to the dominant culture. Thus, the temple's interior, furnished with a pulpit, prayer pews, and hymnals, in many respects resembles a traditional Christian church. Sunday worship service includes a sermon and a choir. The temple acquired the first pipe organ in the state and was the setting for the first non-Christian service in English.

Because of the great diversity of religious expression, it is not uncommon to find adherents of two or three religious sects within one household, and even one person may be affiliated with more than one religion. Some first- and second-generation Asians, for example, consider themselves both Buddhist and Christian, and they feel comfortable attending services and rituals of both religions. The presence of so many diverse religious traditions tends to foster the acceptance of persons with differing religious and cultural practices and viewpoints. It is perhaps no exaggeration to say that the religious domain in Hawaiʻi reflects the overall social environment, which is characterized by a high degree of variety, accommodation, and adaptation—important aspects of what makes Hawaiʻi a special place.

RAMDAS LAMB

ARCHITECTURE

Prior to the nineteenth century Hawaiian architecture was based on thatch construction. Accounts from the late eighteenth and early nineteenth centuries describe these buildings as uniformly shaped, windowless, and having gable roofs that often extended to the ground with diminutive side entries, passable only by crawling. The size of a structure differentiated its function and the owner's social status.

The constancy of this building tradition over the previous two millennia is uncertain, although Hawaiian historian Samuel Kamakau described an evolution in native Hawaiian housing from caves to arched houses covered with tree bark, to thatched houses with post-and-ridgepole frames. Furthermore, archaeological evidence indicates that *heiau* construction became more elaborate from the twelfth century onward, which would coincide with the introduction of a new religion to Hawai'i by Pa'ao, a priest from Tahiti.

Contact with the world beyond Polynesia dramatically altered Hawai'i's built environment. By the opening decades of the twentieth century, the ubiquitous thatched *hale* disappeared from the landscape, having been supplanted by forms derived from Europe,

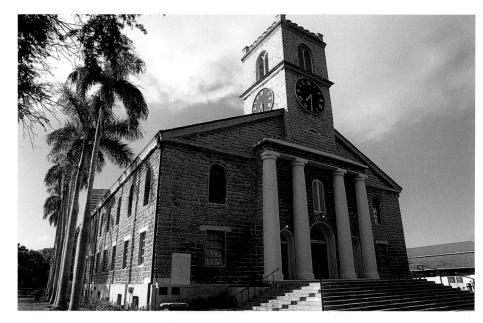

Built of coral blocks quarried from the reef and emulating New England church design, Kawaiaha'o Church (1842) is a representation of Hawai'i's early nineteenth century architecture. Its rugged simplicity, use of local materials, and architectural naiveté characterize the Islands' relative isolation from the world during this period. [J. Juvik]

The thatched *hale* underwent a variety of modifications following Western contact. The gable roof frequently gave way to a hip roof, the doorway was enlarged, windows and porches appeared with regularity, and interior spaces were partitioned. [Lyman House Museum]

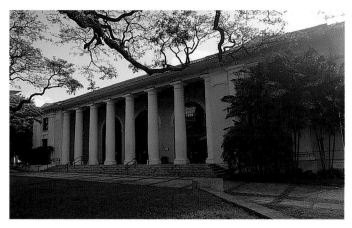

The two-story, colonnaded entry to the Hawai'i State Library (1910) asserted a grand, classical presence in Honolulu. Associated with the prevailing precepts of the City Beautiful movement, this Carnegie Library eloquently proclaimed Hawai'i to be a part of the United States of America. [J. Juvik]

Top left and right: A picturesque pile of majesty, 'Iolani Palace (1881), bearing a Mansard roof, round and segmental arches, and Corinthian columns, bespoke Hawai'i's attempt to take its place among the nations of the world. King Kalākaua, who commanded the Palace building, introduced Hawai'i to the telephone and electric light by installing them in his palace. [State Historic Preservation Office]

The Honolulu Academy of Arts (1927) sprang from the imagination and drafting table of New York architect Bertram Grovesnor Goodhue, an early advocate of a distinctive regional design for Hawai'i. Its deep *lānai,* interior courtyards, plastered lava rock walls, coral block pavers, and double-pitched hip, or Hawaiian, roof make it one of the quintessential statements on Hawaiian regional design. [State Historic Preservation Office]

Another masterpiece rendered in the Hawaiian style, the Alexander & Baldwin Building (1929) represented a design achievement for the Honolulu firm of Dickey & Wood. Its richly embellished terra cotta façade sets forth numerous Chinese motifs, a reflection of the conviction that Hawai'i had developed into a harmonious multicultural society. [State Historic Preservation Office]

Sensitively sited on the Punahou School campus, the Thurston Memorial Chapel (1966) integrates Hawai'i's architectural traditions with the precepts of the modern movement. With an enveloping spring, sunken entry, tiled hip roof, and plaster-covered lava rock walls, this distinguished ecclesiastical design for Hawai'i was created by architect Vladimir Ossipoff. [State Historic Preservation Office]

The Mantokuji Soto Zen Temple (1921) in Pā'ia, Maui, typifies the entwining of Buddhist traditions with plantation construction techniques. Ornamental motifs incorporated in the roof and portico are applied to the single-wall plantation building to make a distinctly Hawaiian architectural statement. [State Historic Preservation Office]

Echoing an architectural vocabulary established in the 1920s and 1930s by architects Goodhue and Dickey, the Hyatt Regency at Po'ipū (1993) perpetuates and expands upon an emerging sense of appropriate design for Hawai'i. Designed by Wimberly, Allison, Tong & Goo, the grounds and the hotel, with its masonry walls and green-tiled, double-pitched hip roof, enhance and celebrate a sense of place in Hawai'i. [Hyatt Regency Kaua'i Resort and Spa]

North America, and Asia. These new buildings were based on wood and masonry construction and provided not only more substantial shelter, but also security and privacy.

The initial foreign architectural transplants were simple versions of traditional Western forms. Many were prefabricated, while others were creations of people untrained in building design, who carried with them ideas of how a building should look. From the 1870s onward, more sophisticated architecture emerged, and Honolulu assumed a Victorian appearance, garbed in picturesque Gothic, Italianate, and Renaissance revival forms. The use of foreign styles continued into the twentieth century, as skillful designs following the beaux arts trends of North America announced the new colonial status of the Islands. Contemporaneous with these major architectural statements were vernacular designs derived from Asia and North America, which often utilized plantation-based building techniques, emphasizing a tradition of low-cost, single-wall construction.

A growing impetus toward a self-conscious regional design emerged during World War I and blossomed during the 1920s and 1930s, through the works of C.W. Dickey, Hart Wood, Claude Stiehl, Harry Sims Bent, and others. This tradition intermingled with the modern movement, as can be especially well seen in the 1940s and 1950s residential works of Val Osipoff, Johnson & Perkins, Pete Wimberly, Albert Ely Ives, and other architects. However, the post–World War II period eventually opened Hawai'i to the world in as dramatic a fashion as did Cook's earlier encounter with the Islands. The international style of design dominated the state's architecture from the mid-1960s onward, and by the late 1980s Hawai'i-based architectural firms (such as Wimberly, Allison, Tong & Goo) were recognized as world leaders in resort design.

DON J. HIBBARD

MUSEUMS AND LIBRARIES

Museums

Hawai'i's museums range from small, volunteer-staffed, specialized facilities to medium and large institutions with a full range of professionals providing a wide variety of exhibits, services, and research capabilities. Some are privately owned and funded, while four museums receive partial operating support from the state, and eight others are fully federally funded. From time to time, state and federal grants also support special programs and research activities. Considering the geographical remoteness and unique natural and cultural history of Hawai'i, the state's museums provide residents and visitors ample opportunities for a thorough acquaintance with the Islands in all their fascinating aspects.

Museums exist on five of the major islands. About 70 museums and related organizations make up the Hawai'i Museums Association, the purposes of which are to promote museum activities, to provide a forum for the exchange of information and ideas, and to stimulate research within the museum field. Four of the state's museums, which maintain professional standards established on a national basis, are fully accredited by the American Association of Museums.

Hawai'i's largest museum, Bernice Pauahi Bishop Museum on O'ahu is a major respository of Pacific and Polynesian archaeological research reports and artifacts. The museum's extensive natural history collections include the Herbarium Pacificum and an entomological collection of more than 13 million specimens. A broad range of exhibits and programs on early Hawaiian culture and history are popular with visiting school children, as are the museum's planetarium lectures and science programs. Museums depicting the early missionary influence in Hawai'i are found on Kaua'i, O'ahu, Maui, and Hawai'i. An example is the Lyman Museum in Hilo, which also showcases the natural history of the Islands and the state's multicultural past. Other museums offering an in-depth view of the once-predominant plantation economy in Hawai'i include the Alexander and Baldwin Sugar Museum on Maui, the Meyer Sugar Mill on Moloka'i, and the Waipahu Cultural Park Garden on O'ahu. The Honolulu Academy of Arts is well known for its collection of Japanese, Chinese, and Korean paintings, sculpture, and decorative arts. Another of Hawai'i's major art museums is O'ahu's Contemporary Museum. Recently, museums depicting the stories of specific immigrant groups have been established. The accompanying table provides information on the resources and special features of each museum.

LEON BRUNO

The first building of the Bishop Museum complex was begun in 1889 and the exhibits opened in 1891. The early buildings are of lava rock quarried nearby, and the interiors are of native *koa* wood. The architectural style is known as Richardsonian Romanesque. [Hawai'i State Archives]

Libraries

The Hawai'i State Public Library System (HSPLS) is the only statewide public library system in the nation. The HSPLS is composed of 49 libraries on six islands. On O'ahu there are 23, including the Hawai'i State

Museums, Libraries and Attractions, 1995

O'AHU	Agriculture	Archives	Art	Education	Gardens Aquariums	Hawaiian Culture-History	Historical Site
Bernice P. Bishop Museum		X	X	X		X	X
The Contemporary Museum			X	X			
Cultural Learning Center at Ka'ala	X			X	X	X	
Damien Museum & Archives		X					
Foster Botanical Garden					X		X
Harold L. Lyon Arboretum				X	X		
Hawai'i Maritime Center		X			X		X
Hawai'i Nature Center				X	X		
Hawai'i Okinawa Center		X				X	
Hawai'i State Archives		X					
Hawaiian Historical Society		X					
Hawaiian Railway Society					X		X
He'eia State Park			X	X	X	X	
Honolulu Academy of Arts		X	X	X		X	
Honolulu Zoo		X		X	X		
Ho'omaluhia Botanical Garden					X		
'Iolani Palace				X		X	X
Judiciary History Center		X				X	X
Mission Houses Museum		X		X		X	X
Moanalua Gardens Foundation		X		X	X		
Pacific Aerospace Museum		X	X	X			
Pacific Whaling Museum		X		X			
Queen Emma Summer Palace				X		X	X
Queen's Medical Center Historical Room		X		X			
Sea Life Park				X	X		
Senator Fong's Plantation Gallery	X			X	X		
Tennent Art Foundation Gallery		X	X	X			
U.S. Army Museum		X		X			X
U.S.S. Arizona Memorial Museum		X		X	X		X
U.S.S. Bowfin Submarine Museum & Park		X		X	X		X
Wahiawā Botanical Museum				X			
Waikīkī Aquarium		X		X	X		
Waipahu Cultural Garden Park	X	X		X	X	X	
Waimea Falls Park				X	X		

KAUA'I	Agriculture	Archives	Art	Education	Gardens Aquariums	Hawaiian Culture-History	Historical Site
Grove Farm Homestead	X	X		X	X		X
Ho'opulapula Haraguchi Rice Mill	X						X
Kaua'i Historical Society Museum	X	X	X			X	X
Kaua'i Museum		X	X	X		X	X
Koke'e Natural History Museum				X	X		
National Tropical Botanical Garden		X		X	X		X
Wai'oli Mission House	X				X		X
MOLOKA'I							
R. W. Meyer Sugar Mill	X						X
MAUI							
Alexander & Baldwin Sugar Museum	X	X					
Bailey House Museum		X	X	X		X	X
Hale Waiwai O Hanā		X					X
Haleakalā National Park		X		X			X
Lahaina Restoration Foundation		X	X	X		X	X
Whalers' Village Museum		X		X			
HAWAI'I							
Greenwell Botanical Garden				X			
Hawai'i Tropical Botanical Garden				X			
Hawai'i Volcanoes National Park		X	X	X			X
Hulihe'e Palace		X				X	X
Kamuela Museum		X				X	
Kona Historical Museum		X		X			X
Lapakahi State Historical Park				X			X
Lyman House Memorial Museum	X	X	X	X		X	X
Onizuka Space Center				X			
Pacific Tsunami Museum		X		X			
Parker Ranch Historic Home & Visitor Center	X	X	X	X	X		
Pu'uhonua O Hōnaunau National Historic Park		X		X	X		X
Pu'ukoholā Heiau National Historic Site				X			X
Thomas A. Jaggar Museum		X					
Volcano Art Center			X	X			X
Wailoa Center			X	X			

Major Museums, Libraries and Attractions in the Honolulu Area

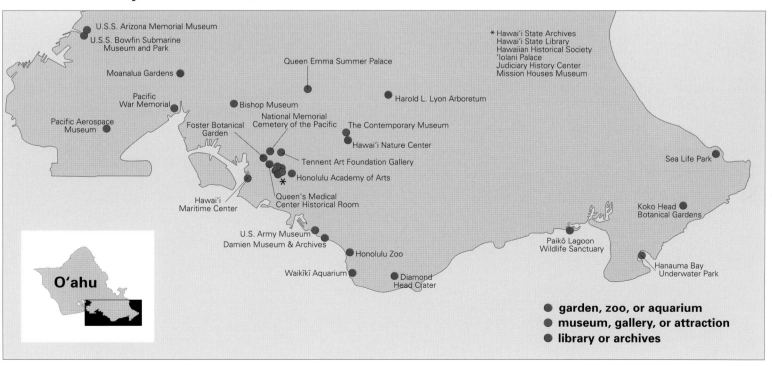

Library and the Library for the Blind and Physically Handicapped, both of which have statewide responsibilities and clienteles. Hawai'i Island has 13 libraries; Maui, 6; Kaua'i, 5; and Lāna'i and Moloka'i, 1 each. Since 1981 the public libraries have been administered by the State Board of Education.

An on-line computer Public Access Catalog lists the entire collection of the library system, making it available to everyone in the state with a personal computer and a modem. As of June 1995, the HSPLS holdings included 3.5 million books, videotapes, audio cassettes, and magazine subscriptions.

As a convenience, library patrons may return books and other library materials at any public library. In 1995, 7.4 million books and other library materials were borrowed from the libraries systemwide, and expenditures totaled $23.4 million.

The Hawai'i State Library's Hawai'i and Pacific Section is the only public library with the capacity to provide in-depth research and reference services in Hawaiiana and Pacificana. It holds 80,000 volumes in its book collection and serves patrons across the state and worldwide.

Free services offered by the HSPLS include telephone assistance for timely answers to quick reference questions and renewal of books and other materials by telephone.

The University of Hawai'i system is composed of ten campuses throughout the state, each with its own library. The largest research collection in the state is housed in Hamilton Library on the flagship campus at Mānoa on O'ahu. This collection contains more than 2.9 million volumes and nearly 27,000 currently received periodical and serial titles, 5.6 million micro-form units, 1,600 computer files, 33,000 audiovisual materials, 240,000 maps and aerial photographs, and 4,300 linear feet of manuscripts and archives. Noteworthy special components include the Asia Collections, Hawai'i and Pacific Collections, Rare Books, Maps, Government Documents, and the Charlot Collection. All of the system's libraries are linked through the on-line catalog, UHCARL, which provides access to each library's holdings, specialized databases and indexes, as well as access to other local and mainland library catalogs. Private colleges and universities within the state maintain their own campus libraries.

Hawai'i also has many special libraries dealing with such subjects as business, law, medicine, art, history, science, and genealogy. Important collections of Hawaiian and Pacific materials in addition to those maintained by the State Library and University of Hawai'i at Mānoa are at the Bernice Pauahi Bishop Museum, the State Archives, the Hawaiian Historical Society, the Hawaiian Mission Children's Society, and the Midkiff Learning Center at the Kamehameha Schools. Brigham Young University–Hawai'i, at its Lā'ie Campus, has an extensive Pacific collection as well as a large genealogical research library. Among the science libraries are the National Marine Fisheries Service, specializing in marine biology and oceanography, the Hawaiian Volcano Observatory with its volcanology collection, and the astronomy collection of the Hawai'i Institute for Astronomy. The military bases in Hawai'i maintain libraries for their personnel and dependents and for defense employees.

JUNKO IDA NOWAKI

CULTURE AND THE ARTS

The arts in Hawai'i reflect the varied cultural backgrounds of its citizens, who participate in activities that celebrate their own cultural heritage as well as practice art forms from other cultures. The delicate balance among cultures is always in flux as new immigrants arrive and converge with the existing cultural milieu. Strong infusions of American popular culture have periodically threatened the balance. The recent explosion of mass media television programming, compact discs, video, magazines, and computers has altered the lifestyle in Hawai'i and brought it closer to that of the U.S. mainland; however, vital cultural diversity persists.

Nearly displaced many times since foreign contact commenced in 1778, Hawaiian culture thrives today in both traditional and innovative contemporary forms. Ancient hula and chants are preserved, but the popular *hula hālau* (schools) are notable for inventive new dances set to recently composed chants. The Merrie Monarch Festival in Hilo features *hālau* from throughout Hawai'i and the U.S. mainland competing for prizes in *hula kahiko* (traditional) and *hula 'auwana* (modern). Hawaiian slack key guitar is experiencing a

Merrie Monarch Festival, *kahiko* style, Hawai'i. [T. Dawson]

Deborah Kakalia (right) stitches her Hawaiian quilt with members of her quilting club at Bernice P. Bishop Museum. [Lynn Martin/Folk Arts Program/SFCA]

Kanaka'ole Hālau o Kekuhi, chanting an *oli* at Mauna Loa. [S. Zane]

Koolau Mountains, 1983, oil on canvas, 60" x 70", by John Young. [Honolulu Academy of Arts, anonymous gift, 1983]

Ke Mau Nei Ke Ea O Kaua'i Puhi 'Aina Malu (The spirit of Kaua'i thrives in the peaceful land of Puhi), by Bumpei Akagi. Copper and bronze sculpture completed in 1977 and located at Kaua'i Community College. [D. Peebles/Art in Public Places Collection/SFCA]

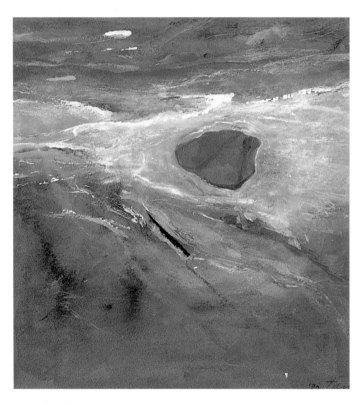

Islanding: Red Kauai, acrylic watercolor, 7" x 8", by Reuben Tam. [Honolulu Academy of Arts, gift of Geraldine King Tam, 1992]

Spirit Way, Sean Browne. Cast bronze sculpture completed in 1988, located at Kapi'olani Community College. [P. Kodama/Art in Public Places Collection/SFCA]

revival. Keola Beamer, Raymond Kane, and Leonard Kwan are three exponents of the older style, while Ledward Kaapana, George Kuo, and Cyril Pahinui represent a younger generation. The *'ukulele* and steel guitar are indispensable as instruments in Hawaiian ensembles. Tourists enjoy Hawaiian and Polynesian entertainment at hotels and at the Polynesian Cultural Center in Lā'ie. The Kamehameha Schools' Song Contest on O'ahu is an annual musical highlight. Festivals of

Hawaiian crafts on Maui have showcased local craftspeople who create feather leis, plaited and woven mats and containers, turned wooden bowls, and sculptured images.

Asian cultures are generously represented around the state. Hawai'i's tradition of Japanese *buyō* (Kabuki-derived) dance, begun by teacher Hanayagi Miharu of Hilo in 1941, is continued in various dance studios today. These schools occasionally bring master teachers from Japan to coach and perform locally. Each summer Japanese temples sponsor traditional *bon* dances, with musical accompaniment from Japanese recordings or the Fukushima or Iwakuni Bon Dance Clubs. The Hawai'i Gagaku Kenkyūkai preserves this court music

Contemporary Literature

Late-eighteenth and nineteenth century historical narratives, such as Queen Liliʻuokalani's *Hawaiʻi's Story by Hawaiʻi's Queen,* mark the beginning of what has emerged in the second half of the twentieth century as an ethnically inclusive, internationally significant body of work. Through poetry, drama, memoir, and fiction, Hawaiʻi's contemporary writers confront and explore the tension inherent in a highly complex social structure. In the process, they have created a literary language unique to their experiences and to Hawaiʻi.

Though the particulars of their experiences are dissimilar—and at times conflicting—many of Hawaiʻi's writers, including Native Hawaiian and Asian American writers, share similar histories of cultural dislocation and economic hardship. As they probe the complexities of cultural identity these writers must reconcile generational shifts in language, traditions, and values. For example, the young protagonist in John Dominis Holt's *Waimea Summer: A Novel* nearly succumbs to the seductions of a fragmented history before he ultimately rejects an unknowable and thus dangerous past, choosing instead the uncertainties of the future. Similarly, Milton Murayama's *All I Asking for Is My Body* explores the futility of clinging to dislocated traditions. Yet for Holt, Murayama, and a growing number of Hawaiʻi's writers, responses to cultural change are mediated not by a rejection of tradition and history, but by redefining their contexts and functions.

The power of language, as both a tool of domination and an instrument of self-definition, has been a significant social issue in Hawaiʻi for most of this century.

Following the overthrow of the Hawaiian monarchy in 1893, Standard English eventually supplanted the Hawaiian language in public education and government. At roughly the same time, Hawaiʻi's multiethnic plantation laborers, moved by necessity to create a means of intercommunication, developed a language that has evolved over time into Hawaiʻi Creole English (HCE), locally called "Pidgin." Hence, as a result of Hawaiʻi's complex political history its literary languages include three intertwined mother tongues: Hawaiian, HCE, and Standard English.

Hawaiʻi's writers struggle spiritually, politically, and intellectually to communicate their experiences through these three languages. The results are often stunning. In *Light in the Crevice Never Seen,* Hawaiian poet and activist Haunani-Kay Trask blends Hawaiian and English words in a process that fundamentally transforms the sound of "English" poetry. Several poems from *The Rain in the Trees* by W. S. Merwin explore the life, death, possibilities, and limitations of language. Written in various forms of HCE, works such as Darrell H. Y. Lum's *Pass On, No Pass Back!* and Lois-Ann Yamanaka's *Wild Meat and the Bully Burgers* destabilize the political privileging of Standard English and enhance the status of local identity and experience.

Through the competing languages of a complex social history, Hawaiʻi's contemporary literature reflects the inherent tension that inevitably accompanies cultural conflict and transformation.

Lydia Kualapai

House Pet, 1992, hand-built stoneware, oxides, commercial underglaze and glaze, 10" x 8" x 10", by Esther Shimazu. [D. Edmonds/The Contemporary Museum Collection]

and dance form. The Sawai Koto School of Tokyo has maintained a Hawaiʻi studio. Kenny Endo composes and performs new works for his *taiko* (drum) ensemble. Okinawan folk and classical music are taught in half a dozen studios. Seisho (Harry) Nakasone, honored in Okinawa, teaches and performs classical (*koten*) and ballad (*minyo*) traditions. *Paranku* drumming is a popular Okinawan music form.

Filipino dance ensembles have been active for more than 25 years. Pat and Orlando Valentin's Pearl of the Orient dance group entertained tourists for many years. Hana Trinidad, Wayne Mendoza, and Zack Labez lead groups that study and perform music and dance from many regions of the Philippines. Recently a BIBAK group was organized to perform dances and music of the Cordillera region of the central Philippines. Halla Pai Huhm's Korean Dance Studio has been honored in Korea and Hawaiʻi. The Tai Hsüan School of the Six Chinese Arts and the Phoenix Dance Company perform Chinese classical, folk, and martial art forms. Festive occasions are blessed with a Chinese lion dance. The ethnomusic program at the University of Hawai'i at Mānoa is well known and its two Indonesian gamelan (orchestras) perform regularly. Kabuki and Beijing Opera productions from the UH Mānoa Department of Theatre and Dance have been performed abroad and on the U.S. mainland.

Hawai'i's King David Kalākaua (1836–1891) loved the arts. In addition to encouraging renewed interest in Hawaiian hula and music, he introduced European music and opera to the Islands. He also invited Henry Berger to revitalize the Royal Hawaiian Band, a group still active today. Founded in 1902, the Honolulu Symphony acquired a new music director in 1996: Samuel Wong, former assistant conductor of the New York Philharmonic. The symphony plays an 18-

University of Hawai'i at Mānoa 1990 production of *Yu Tangchun: The Jade Hall of Spring,* directed and translated by Elizabeth Wichmann, University of Hawai'i at Mānoa, Department of Theatre and Dance. [Courtesy of Kennedy Theatre Archives]

University of Hawai'i production of a Balinese *topeng* dance performed by I. Wayan Dibia, Guest Director, accompanied by the UH Balinese Gamelan Ensemble, 1995. [Courtesy of Kennedy Theatre Archives]

week season and accompanies the Hawai'i Opera Theatre's three annual productions. The semiprofessional Maui Symphony, in existence since 1978, and the three ensembles of Chamber Music Hawai'i perform concerts throughout the year. The 22 members of the Hawai'i Association of Music Societies, the nation's oldest statewide consortium of presenters' groups, pool resources to sponsor seasons of music and, with their sister organization, dance and theater from around the world. European music and dance are also performed by a variety of ensembles, including the Royal Scottish Country Dancers, Pleasant Peasant Band, Scandia Dancers, and Portuguese and Puerto Rican groups.

Participation in modern dance and ballet continues to grow on all the main islands because of individual creativity and the support of the Hawai'i State Dance Council, which annually provides cash awards for six outstanding choreographies from all dance forms. Since the 1960s modern dance has been strong in Hawai'i thanks to important contributions from artists such as Carl Woltz, Jean Erdman, and Ernest Morgan. Morgan pioneered modern dance on Hawai'i Island, where the art form flourishes.

While an occasional professional Broadway musical is performed in Honolulu, most theater is produced by local companies. The Diamond Head Theatre of O'ahu is one of the oldest community theaters in the country. Kaua'i, Maui, and Hawai'i Island each has its own companies. Children's theater is ably represented by Honolulu Theatre For Youth and Maui Academy of Performing Arts. Repeated efforts to build a film industry in Hawai'i have been mostly unsuccessful; however, several feature films are produced in the state each year. No television series has replaced the once popular *Hawaiian Eye, Hawai'i Five-0,* and *Magnum P.I.* series. Since 1970 the Honolulu Academy of Arts has screened notable foreign, independent, and classic cinema. The annual Hawai'i International Film Festival is recognized as a leader in the introduction of Asian

Hawai'i Opera Theatre's 1992 production of *Andrea Chenier,* Act II, sets by Peter Dean Beck. [E. Yanagi]

Maui Academy of Performing Arts' 1994 production of *Fame: The Musical*. [Maui Academy of Performing Arts]

Lynne Yoshiko Nakasone, director and master teacher of the Jinpu Hoge Kai Nakasone Ryubu Kenkyusho in a pose from an Okinawan court dance staged in 1996 for the 40th anniversary of the studio. [Marimura Photo, Okinawa]

Hawai'i State Foundation on Culture and the Arts

The State Foundation on Culture and the Arts was established by the Hawai'i State Legislature in 1965 as the state arts agency of Hawai'i. Its mission is to promote, perpetuate, preserve, and encourage culture and the arts and history and the humanities as central to the quality of life of the people of Hawai'i. At the core of the SFCA is the public funding provided to support arts and culture projects that enhance the quality of life for the people of Hawai'i.

Acknowledging the importance of integrating the visual arts with architecture, the state legislature in 1967 created the Art in State Buildings Law, which set aside 1 percent of the appropriations for the construction of state buildings for the acquisitions of works of art, making Hawai'i the first state in the nation to establish a percent-for-art law. Currently, through the Works of Art Special Fund, the SFCA's Art in Public Places Program acquires, exhibits, and conserves artworks for permanent and temporary placement in state public locations.

Ethnic, cultural, and occupational folk traditions in Hawai'i are identified and documented by the SFCA's Folk Arts Program. Through the program's Folk Arts

Apprenticeships, experienced practitioners of a traditional art form have an opportunity to train under master traditional artists, thereby perpetuating their unique artforms and traditional values for future generations.

The SFCA's Individual Artist Fellowship Program recognizes and honors Hawai'i's exceptionally talented visual and performing artists for their outstanding work and commitment to the arts. The Individual Artist Fellowships are intended to help those artists further their artistic goals. Hawai'i writers are recognized for their outstanding achievements through the annual Hawai'i Award for Literature, the State's highest honor in the field of literature, given by the SFCA and the Hawaii Literary Arts Council.

Through its History & Humanities Program, the SFCA promotes and stimulates community history activities and encourages greater professional management of cultural resources.

Culture and arts and history and humanities projects that are supported by the State Foundation on Culture and the Arts each year reach approximately 2 million people in Hawai'i.

Onoe Kikunobu and Onoe Kikunobukazu in a 1981 production of the Nihon Buyu dance "Yoshiwara Suzume" staged by the Kikunobu Dance Company of Honolulu. [Courtesy of Kennedy Theatre Archives]

and Pacific films to the West. Screenings are scheduled throughout the state.

Most observers agree that while Hawaiian subject matter may appear in paintings, prints, and sculpture, a Hawai'i regional style does not exist. The visual arts in Hawai'i show another rich mix of ideas and influences that parallels the current wide range of representational-to-abstract styles seen in American and other international art centers. A Hawai'i style of furniture reworks the turn-of-the-century vernacular style, which included elements of the arts and crafts style. In crafts, most of the production is in mainstream Euro/American media but with an integration of various Asian aesthetics. Many ceramic artists favor *raku* methods, and an annual Raku Ho'olaulea (gathering) is sponsored by Hawai'i Craftsmen. Several other statewide or local island arts organizations sponsor workshops and exhibitions of painting, sculpture, photography, prints, and traditional and contemporary crafts. The largest statewide juried exhibition, the Artists of Hawai'i exhibition sponsored by the Honolulu Academy of Arts, features about 125 works in all media. Works by Hawai'i artists are regularly displayed at the Kaua'i Museum; the Maui Arts and Cultural Center, Hui No'eau Visual Arts Center, and Lahaina Arts Society on Maui; East Hawai'i Cultural Center, Hilo's Wailoa Center, and Volcano Art Center on Hawai'i Island; and the Contemporary Museum in Honolulu, Honolulu Hale, and the Tennent, Amfac, Ramsey, and Queen Emma art galleries on O'ahu. Concentrations of artists exist in several areas, especially on O'ahu's north shore and at Hōlualoa and Volcano on Hawai'i Island. Many of the galleries in Hawai'i cater to the tourists and are situated in areas like Lahaina and Waikīkī, where visitors are concentrated.

JAMES H. FURSTENBERG

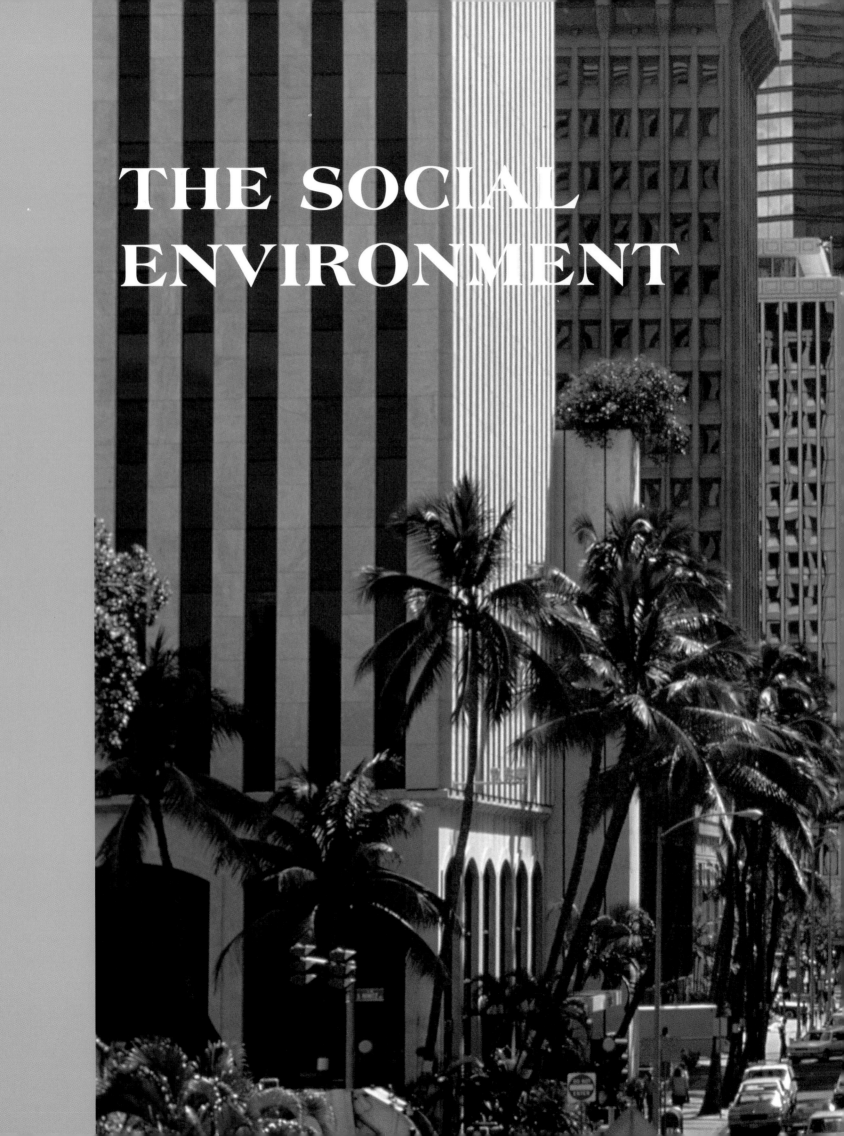

THE SOCIAL ENVIRONMENT

Overleaf: Central Business District, Honolulu. [Hawai'i Visitors Bureau]

GOVERNMENT AND POLITICS

Government

The structure and operations of Hawai'i's state government are similar to other state governments, but Hawai'i is unique in its centralization of power. Several factors that probably set the precedent for this concentration of power are the legacy of absolute rule by early Hawaiian monarchs, the authoritarian management style of plantation owners, the submissive attitude and respect for authority shown by Asian immigrants, and the centralization of power in the hands of Hawaiian territorial governors appointed by U.S. presidents under the Organic Act. Examples of the state government's unique powers are its direct responsibility for public education, health, and welfare. The resulting lack of home rule for the county governments has led to perennial complaints.

Yet Hawai'i's state constitution is considered one of the most progressive ever promulgated. For instance, Article XVII of the constitution states that amendments may be made either by the state legislature (by a two-thirds majority vote in both the senate and the house of representatives) or by a constitutional convention. To hold such a convention, the legislature must submit for voter approval the question: "Shall there be a convention to propose revision of, or amendment to, the constitution?" If the legislature has not submitted the question to voters within a ten-year period, the question is automatically placed on the ballot at the first general election following expiration of the ten-year interval. This innovative provision allows the voters periodically to initiate changes in the basic law for the state. It has been designed to ensure a responsive, as well as a more responsible, government. Since Hawai'i became a state in 1959, the voters called for constitutional conventions in 1968 and in 1978. There was no interest in holding a constitutional convention in 1988. In the 1996 election, voters again chose to convene a constitutional convention; the decision was subsequently invalidated by the state supreme court on technical grounds.

The state legislature consists of two chambers: a 25-member senate and a 51-member house of representatives. The state legislature is based on the single-member district system in accordance with the "one man, one vote" principle mandated by the U.S. Supreme Court. Beginning in 1981 state reapportionment on legislative boundaries was to be conducted every ten years to coincide with changing population trends as revealed by the U.S. Census. The district boundaries for the present legislature were approved in 1991 by the reapportionment commission. Under the 1991 reapportionment plan, each representative district has an average of 19,488 permanent residents and each senatorial district an average of 39,756.

The legislature meets annually for a 60-day session. In odd-numbered years, the session is devoted to the appropriation of a 2-year budget. The state budget was about $12 billion for the 1995–1997 biennial cycle. In even-numbered years, the legislature provides only a supplementary budget.

The constitution states that only a member of the legislature may introduce a bill. Standing committees, organized according to function, screen and review bills; the senate has 17 such committees, the house 19. While as many as 3,000 bills are introduced annually, only about 10 percent are enacted into law. To become law under the Hawai'i Revised Statutes, a bill must win the approval of both legislative chambers and be signed by the governor. The governor's veto of a bill can be overridden by a two-thirds majority vote in both the house and senate. A special legislative session can be convened either by the governor or by the written request of two-thirds of the members of both chambers.

The governor, the chief executive for the state government, is elected by the voters for a 4-year term and is limited to no more than two consecutive terms. As the central figure in Hawai'i's state politics, the governor is expected to deal with all of the state's major problems and attend to every aspect of state affairs. This heavy dependence on the governor arises from the power vested in the office by the state constitution. The executive powers include deciding on budgetary and fiscal matters, granting pardons and clemency, acting

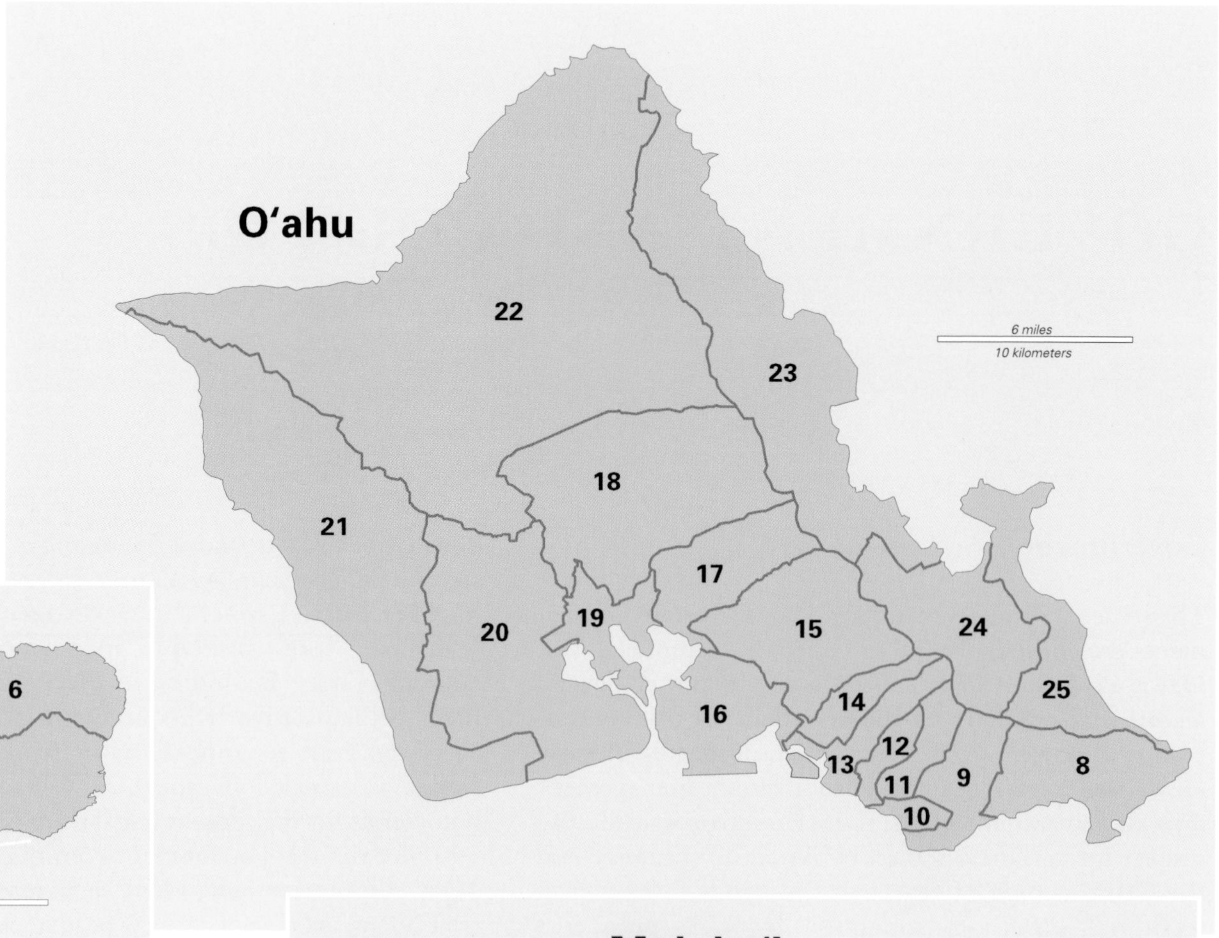

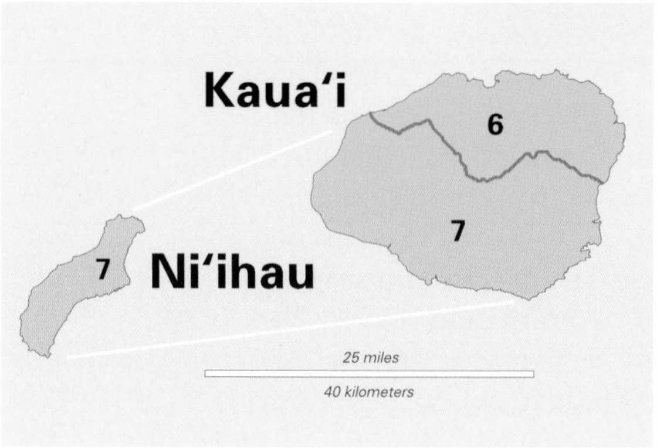

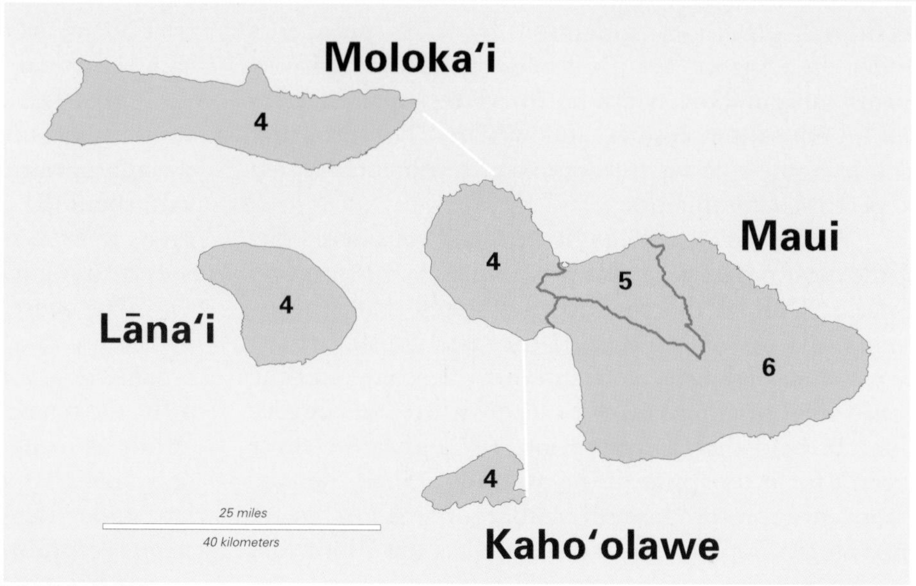

O'ahu

22

23

6 miles

10 kilometers

18

21

17

20

19

15

24

25

Kaua'i

6

7

14

16

7

Ni'ihau

12

13

9

11

8

25 miles

10

40 kilometers

Moloka'i

4

Maui

4

Lāna'i

4

Hawai'i

5

6

1

4

25 miles

2

40 kilometers

Kaho'olawe

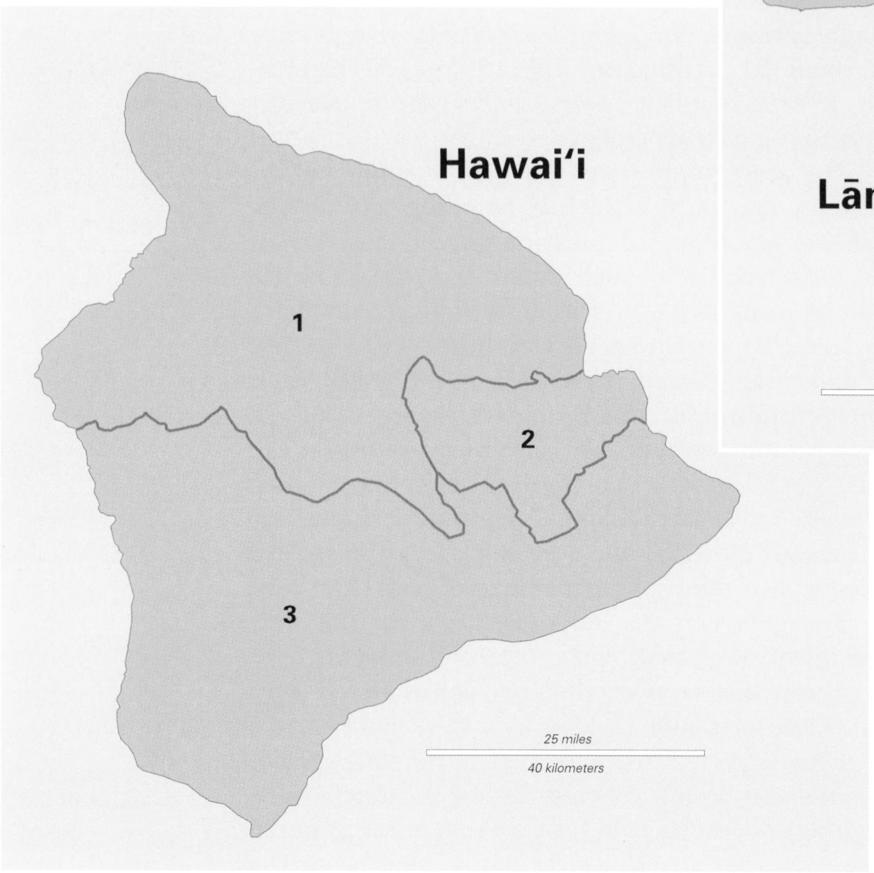

3

State Senatorial Districts, 1991

25 miles

40 kilometers

The split constituencies of *canoe districts* such as
district 4 (Moloka'i, Lāna'i, West Maui, Kaho'olawe),
district 6 (North Kaua'i, East Maui) and district 7 (Ni'ihau,
South Kaua'i) include portions of different islands.

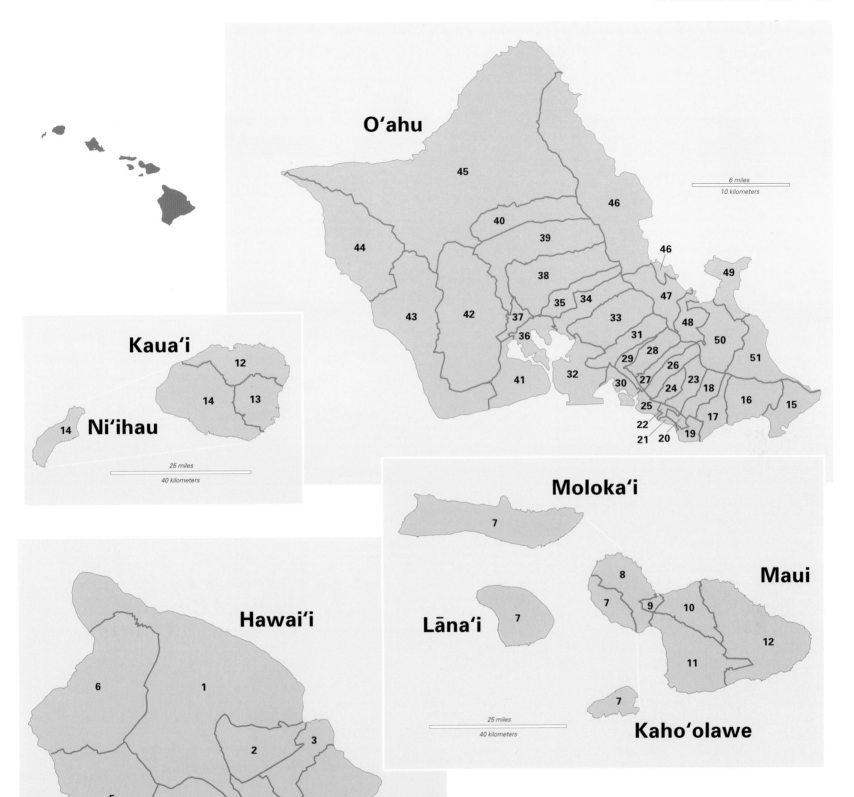

O'ahu

Kaua'i

Ni'ihau

Hawai'i

Moloka'i

Lāna'i

Maui

Kaho'olawe

State Representative Districts, 1991

The split constituencies of ***canoe districts*** such as district 7 (Moloka'i, Lāna'i, West Maui, Kaho'olawe) and district 14 (West Kaua'i, Ni'ihau) include portions of different islands.

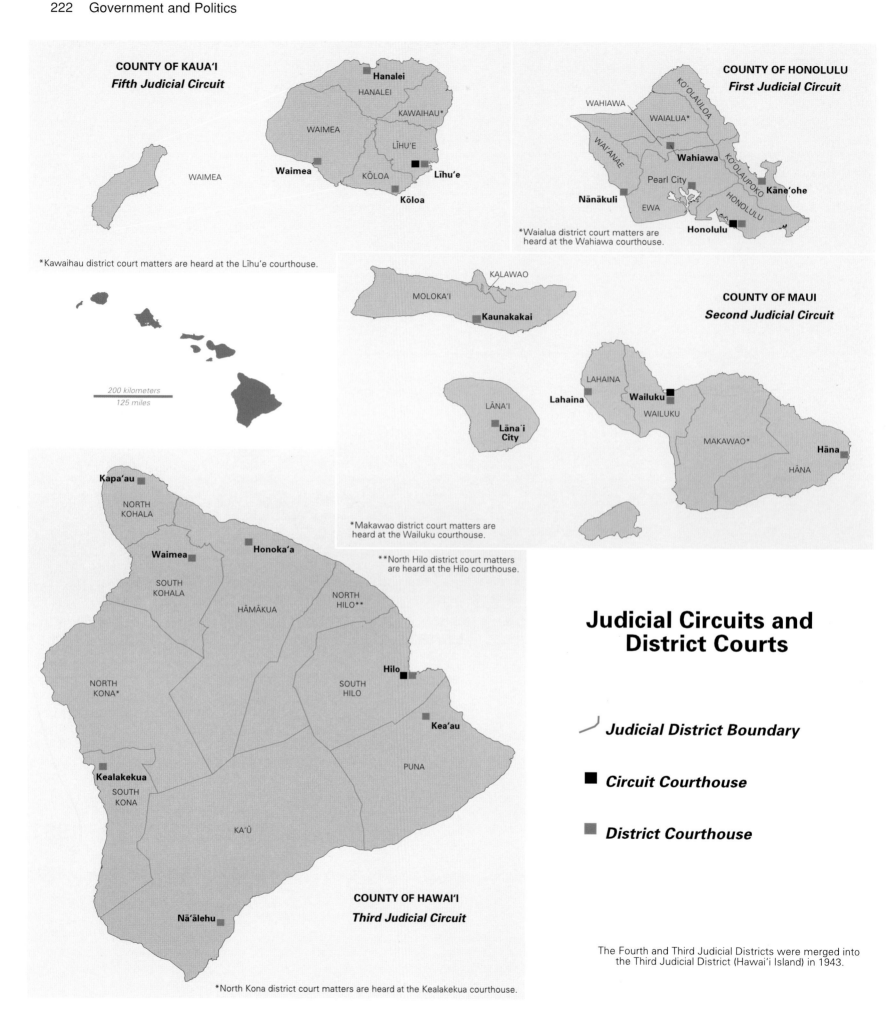

Judicial Circuits and District Courts

COUNTY OF KAUA'I
Fifth Judicial Circuit

HANALEI
Hanalei
KAWAIHAU*
WAIMEA
LĪHU'E
Waimea
KŌLOA
Līhu'e
Kōloa
WAIMEA

*Kawaihau district court matters are heard at the Līhu'e courthouse.

COUNTY OF HONOLULU
First Judicial Circuit

WAHIAWA
KO'OLAULOA
WAIALUA*
WAI'ANAE
Wahiawa
KO'OLAUPOKO
Pearl City
Kāne'ohe
Nānākuli
HONOLULU
EWA
Honolulu

*Waialua district court matters are heard at the Wahiawa courthouse.

KALAWAO
MOLOKA'I
Kaunakakai

COUNTY OF MAUI
Second Judicial Circuit

LĀNA'I
LAHAINA
Lahaina
Wailuku
WAILUKU
Lāna'i City
MAKAWAO*
Hāna
HĀNA

*Makawao district court matters are heard at the Wailuku courthouse.

200 kilometers
125 miles

Kapa'au
NORTH KOHALA
Waimea
Honoka'a
SOUTH KOHALA
HĀMĀKUA
NORTH HILO**
**North Hilo district court matters are heard at the Hilo courthouse.
Hilo
SOUTH HILO
NORTH KONA*
Kea'au
PUNA
Kealakekua
SOUTH KONA
KA'Ū
Nā'ālehu

COUNTY OF HAWAI'I
Third Judicial Circuit

*North Kona district court matters are heard at the Kealakekua courthouse.

⌐ **Judicial District Boundary**

■ **Circuit Courthouse**

■ **District Courthouse**

The Fourth and Third Judicial Districts were merged into the Third Judicial District (Hawai'i Island) in 1943.

The Law of the Sea Convention and Hawai'i's Waters

The 1982 Law of the Sea Convention (LOS) came into force on November 16, 1994. The LOS provides a comprehensive legal framework governing the uses of the oceans and the rights and obligations of nations thereto. A key provision of the LOS defines the nature and extent of the jurisdiction of nations over coastal waters adjacent to their boundaries. It limits a nation's territorial sea to 12 nautical miles (22 km) and sets up exclusive economic zones (EEZs) extending 200 nautical miles (370 km). The LOS, moreover, deals with the exploration and exploitation of deep seabed resources on the continental shelf beyond national jurisdiction.

The United States signed an agreement in July 1994 that removed most U.S. objections to the LOS. The convention, however, as of mid-1996 still must be ratified by the Senate. When the United States declared its 200-nautical-mile EEZ on March 3, 1983, it established a zone that covers about 2.2 million square nautical miles (7.5 million sq. km) of ocean, with nearly a quarter of the total surrounding the Hawaiian Islands. Later a proposal was introduced in the U.S. Congress that would allow Hawai'i to assume jurisdiction over the islands of Midway, Wake, Howland, Baker, Johnston, Jarvis, Palmyra, and the Kingman Reef. Under the LOS Convention, all inhabited Hawaiian islands have jurisdiction over a 12-nautical-mile territorial sea, a 12-nautical-mile contiguous zone, and a 200-nautical-mile EEZ. While those islets in the Northwestern Hawaiian chain that stand above water at high tide can claim a territorial sea and a contiguous zone, legal experts say it is uncertain whether the uninhabited islets can claim an EEZ. The LOS Convention does not consider the Hawaiian Islands an archipelagic state because they are part of the United States, a continental nation. Legal scholars believe that without recognition as an archipelagic state, Hawai'i has little or no control over the waters between the main islands—that is, the 'Alenuihāhā, Kaiwi, and Kaua'i Channels. While the United States has declared an EEZ for the Hawaiian Islands, the State of Hawai'i has jurisdiction over marine resources within the first 3 nautical miles (5.6 km) only; the remainder of the EEZ falls within federal jurisdiction.

Native Hawaiians have traditionally claimed jurisdiction over resources on submerged lands and, therefore, currently view submerged land under federal or state control as part of the ceded lands trust. In support of this position, an opinion issued in June 1982 by the state's attorney general proclaimed that the submerged lands surrounding the Hawaiian Islands (including Midway, Palmyra, and Johnston Islands) were ceded land in accordance with Section 5(b) of the Admissions Act of 1959, when Hawai'i became a state. In 1989 the Office of Hawaiian Affairs filed a similar claim over the submerged lands on behalf of itself and other Hawaiian groups against the state and federal governments. This case has not been resolved as of 1997.

JAMES C. F. WANG

Exclusive Economic Zone (EEZ) Boundary of the Hawaiian Islands

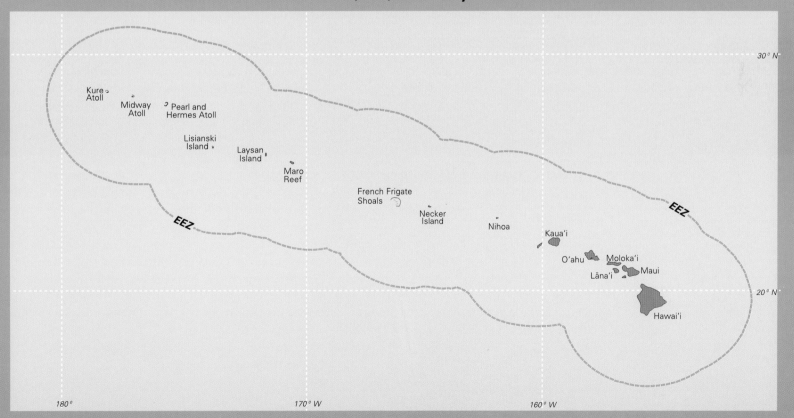

as chief initiator for bills or proposals for annual legislative sessions, and appointing (subject to senate confirmation) directors and deputies for some 17 executive departments as well as members to numerous boards and commissions. Although the governor also plays an important role in the area of education, policy decisions for the public schools are made by a voter-elected board of education, and for the ten campuses of the University of Hawai'i, by a board of regents appointed by the governor.

Hawai'i's judicial branch has a simple organizational structure with clearly delineated jurisdictions, or areas of power. Unlike that of many other states, it includes no municipal courts. The state constitution has provided for a four-tiered, unified system with district and circuit (appeals) courts on each of the main islands, an intermediate appellate court, and a state supreme court. The closest to the citizens, the district court has jurisdiction not only over all nonjury trials in both civil and criminal cases, but also over traffic violations and fines. Furthermore, it holds exclusive jurisdiction over misdemeanor cases. The circuit court is a general trial court. Circuit court judges are assigned to four judicial circuits; there are 15 judges for O'ahu, 3 for Hawai'i, 2 for Maui, and 1 for Kaua'i.

The intermediate court, established in 1979, serves as an appeals court to lessen the caseload of the state supreme court. All appeals go to the supreme court, but the chief justice determines which are referred to the intermediate court. The highest appellate authority resides in the supreme court, which holds the power to review the proceedings of all trial courts. The supreme court also administers the state court system and, in rendering decisions, clarifies laws and public policies, which sometimes leads to the development of new laws. The chief justice appoints district court judges, and other judicial vacancies are filled by the governor from a list of four to six nominees submitted by an impartial judicial selection commission. Appointments to all judgeships now must be confirmed by the senate.

County Government

The state's four counties (O'ahu, Hawai'i, Maui, and Kaua'i) have all adopted the mayor-council form of local government. County councils for O'ahu and Hawai'i are based on single-member district representation. Maui's council has a nine-member district system with specific residency requirements for Kahului, Wailuku, West Maui, South Maui, Up Country, Makawao, East Maui, Moloka'i, and Lāna'i. All nine council members are to be elected by voters of the county. Kaua'i's county council has seven at-large seats. The county councils are vested with the power to enact ordinances dealing with planning, zoning, land use, and the administration and collection of property taxes. The mayor is responsible for managing county affairs, submitting an annual budget requiring council approval, and implementing ordinances enacted by the council. Each year the counties lobby the legislature for state grants or subsidies to help run local government programs, particularly those programs mandated by the legislature without any appropriation for implementation. In recent years there have been suggestions for the legislature to grant the counties the power to levy excise taxes. A large proportion of the counties' revenues currently comes from property taxes.

Electoral Politics

Article II, section 8 of the state constitution specifies that general elections be held during November in even-numbered years to provide regular voter participation in the electoral process. All citizens who are at least 18 years old, legal residents of Hawai'i, and registered to vote may do so. Some 372,000 out of a total of 489,889 registered voters participated in the 1994 general elections for federal, state, and local offices. Although this turnout represented more than 77 percent of registered voters, it was only about 42 percent of the 890,000 eligible voters.

The Democratic Party has dominated politics in Hawai'i by its ability to win a majority of elective offices since 1962, when voters elected the state's first Democratic governor. Thus Hawai'i often has been described as a one-party state with very little party competition. A longstanding coalition in electoral politics exists between the Democratic Party and the labor unions, particularly the public employees unions. In the 1994 gubernatorial election, two newly formed parties—the Best Party and the Green Party—joined the Democrats and Republicans in the contest. The split in votes resulted in a Democratic governor being elected by a plurality of only 35.8 percent of the total votes cast.

Campaigning in Hawai'i has always been a lively affair on all islands, with rallies, door-to-door canvassing, coffee hours, and the ubiquitous roadside sign waving. Candidates employ the latest electronic techniques for advertising their candidacy and addressing issues through the press, radio, and television. Consequently, campaign spending has been on the rise to meet ever-higher costs. Fundraising activities must be closely monitored by the state campaign spending commission. Total campaign spending for the 1994 gubernatorial contest was about $9 million.

JAMES C. F. WANG

LAND USE AND TENURE

Since the early nineteenth century, land tenure and land use in Hawai'i—influenced by changing political and economic conditions—both local and international, have shifted through several important phases.

Traditional Ownership and Use

The traditional Hawaiian system of land ownership has been described as "communal," "feudal," or "autarkic," each term being an interpretation of the system of land use and ownership that existed in Hawai'i until the reign of Kamehameha III (1825–1854). In traditional Hawaiian society, all lands were held in trust by the high chief of an island or portion of an island (the *mō'ī* or *ali'i 'ai moku*), who then distributed land to his subchiefs (*ali'i 'ai ahupua'a* and *konohiki*). The latter were responsible for the allocation of *ahupua'a,* or portions thereof, for use by the *maka'āinana* (people of the land). (The *ahupua'a* is a generally wedge-shaped area of land that extends from ridgetop to its base at the coastline.) The *maka'āinana* were obliged to pay tribute to those above them in the social hierarchy in return for use rights, but they could move to another *ahupua'a* if the chiefly exactions became unacceptable. Likewise, the right to use land was not guaranteed but was subject to revocation at the will of the chief.

Important changes in this system occurred after Kamehameha I (whose reign extended from 1795 to 1819), by war and conquest, brought the several existing independent kingdoms under his single leadership and control. This centralization of control would prove to be a most consequential and enduring feature of the history of land use and tenure in Hawai'i. The earliest changes in the land tenure system reflected a tendency on the part of the ruling monarch to recognize hereditary rights to property held by the *ali'i,* thereby introducing a degree of security for traditional landholders. By the 1840s, when links with the outside world were well established, pressure grew from White immigrant entrepreneurs for changes in the control of land by the *ali'i.* It was under these circumstances that Hawaiian royalty were forced to initiate actions that led to the ownership of land in fee simple.

A series of policy changes adopted by Kameha- meha's successors led to the *Māhele*—a division and privitization of all lands in the archipelago. Under the *Māhele,* a process of awarding private title to lands took place between 1848 and 1855. Over this time, all lands in Hawai'i were distributed among the government (1,500,000 acres [600,000 ha]), the crown (approximately 1,000,000 acres [400,000 ha]), chiefs (1,500,000 acres [600,000 ha]), and commoners (28,700 acres [11,600 ha], also called *kuleana* lands). A consequence of this land tenure revolution was that a minority of adult male *maka'āinana* (perhaps 25–30 percent) secured title to less than 1 percent of the land area of Hawai'i.

Private Ownership

The *Māhele* opened the era of private property rights with its attendant economic and social costs and benefits. Legislation in 1850 permitted any resident of Hawai'i to own and exchange land regardless of citizenship. Hawaiians of means as well as other individuals could now purchase government lands, and, as a result, 44 percent was sold off by 1886 to provide government revenues. Hawaiian royalty and chiefs extinguished personal debts to westerners with payments of land; land leases were issued to residents by royalty, government, and chiefs alike. By 1890 nearly 800,000 acres (325,000 ha) of crown and government lands were in leases.

A fundamental outcome of the shift in land tenure was that it made possible the acquisition of large acreages of land for the full development of commercial agriculture. Consequently, by the late 1800s a small group of sugar planters, mostly White *kama'āina* entrepreneurs, was able to dominate land tenure and land use in the Islands. The major players among them became known collectively as the Big Five: Alexander & Baldwin, American Factors, Castle & Cooke, C. Brewer, and Theo H. Davies. The resulting concentration of land ownership by these and other individuals, groups, and trusts (e.g., Bernice P. Bishop Estate) remains with us to the present.

After Queen Lili'uokalani was overthrown in 1893, all of the then remaining crown lands were con-

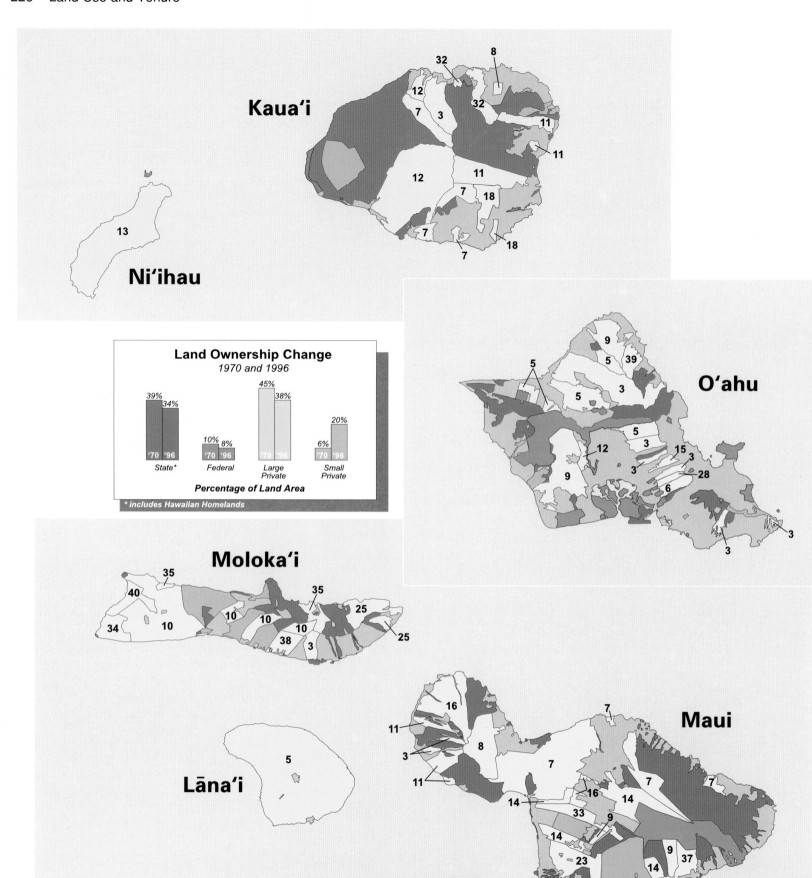

Kaua'i

Ni'ihau

13

32

8

12

7   3

32

11

11

12

11

7   18

7

7

18

Land Ownership Change
1970 and 1996

39%   34%

10%   8%

45%   38%

6%   20%

'70   '96   '70   '96   '70   '96   '70   '96

State *   *Federal*   *Large Private*   *Small Private*

Percentage of Land Area

* includes Hawaiian Homelands

O'ahu

9

5   39

5

5

3

5

3

5

3

12   15   3

9   3   28

6

3

3

Moloka'i

35

40   35

10

34   10

10   10

38   10   3

35

25

25

Lāna'i

5

Maui

16

7

11

8

3   7

11   7   7

14   16

14

33

9

14   9

23   14   37

Kaho'olawe

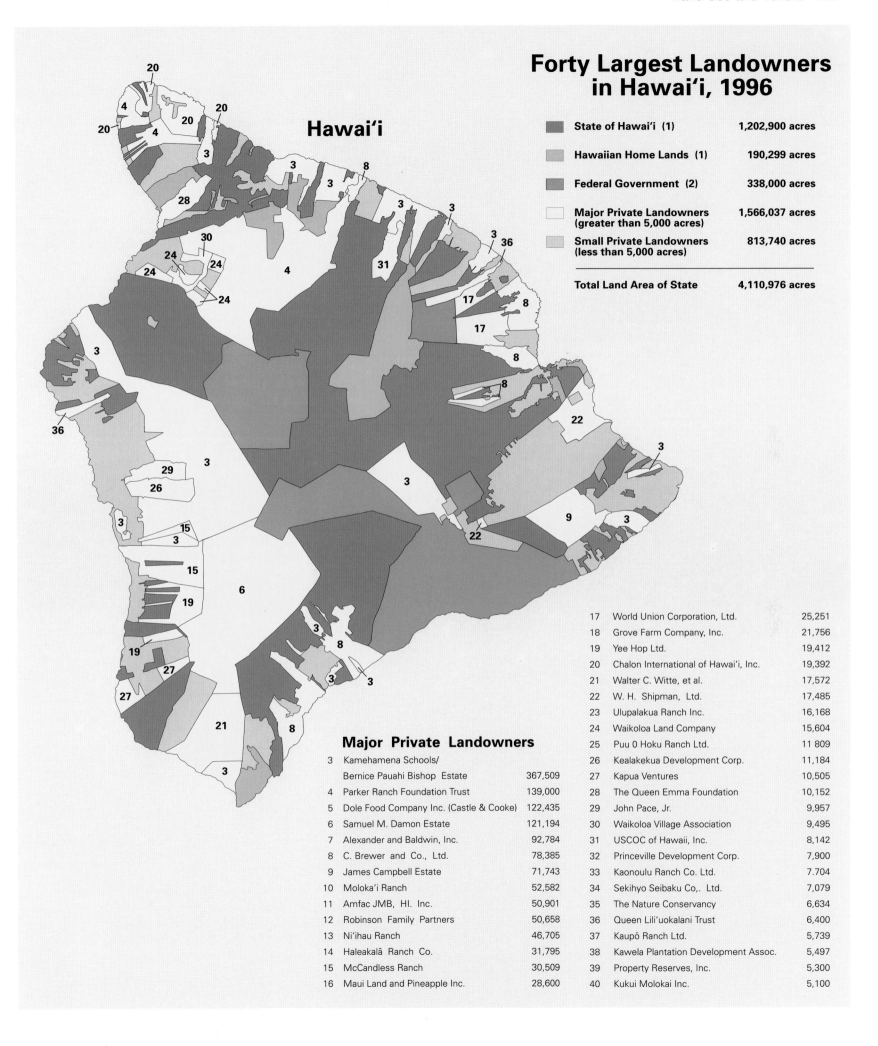

Forty Largest Landowners in Hawai'i, 1996

Hawai'i

▉	State of Hawai'i (1)	1,202,900 acres
▉	Hawaiian Home Lands (1)	190,299 acres
▉	Federal Government (2)	338,000 acres
☐	Major Private Landowners (greater than 5,000 acres)	1,566,037 acres
▉	Small Private Landowners (less than 5,000 acres)	813,740 acres
	Total Land Area of State	4,110,976 acres

Major Private Landowners

3	Kamehamena Schools/ Bernice Pauahi Bishop Estate	367,509
4	Parker Ranch Foundation Trust	139,000
5	Dole Food Company Inc. (Castle & Cooke)	122,435
6	Samuel M. Damon Estate	121,194
7	Alexander and Baldwin, Inc.	92,784
8	C. Brewer and Co., Ltd.	78,385
9	James Campbell Estate	71,743
10	Moloka'i Ranch	52,582
11	Amfac JMB, HI. Inc.	50,901
12	Robinson Family Partners	50,658
13	Ni'ihau Ranch	46,705
14	Haleakalā Ranch Co.	31,795
15	McCandless Ranch	30,509
16	Maui Land and Pineapple Inc.	28,600
17	World Union Corporation, Ltd.	25,251
18	Grove Farm Company, Inc.	21,756
19	Yee Hop Ltd.	19,412
20	Chalon International of Hawai'i, Inc.	19,392
21	Walter C. Witte, et al.	17,572
22	W. H. Shipman, Ltd.	17,485
23	Ulupalakua Ranch Inc.	16,168
24	Waikoloa Land Company	15,604
25	Puu 0 Hoku Ranch Ltd.	11,809
26	Kealakekua Development Corp.	11,184
27	Kapua Ventures	10,505
28	The Queen Emma Foundation	10,152
29	John Pace, Jr.	9,957
30	Waikoloa Village Association	9,495
31	USCOC of Hawaii, Inc.	8,142
32	Princeville Development Corp.	7,900
33	Kaonoulu Ranch Co. Ltd.	7.704
34	Sekihyo Seibaku Co,. Ltd.	7,079
35	The Nature Conservancy	6,634
36	Queen Lili'uokalani Trust	6,400
37	Kaupō Ranch Ltd.	5,739
38	Kawela Plantation Development Assoc.	5,497
39	Property Reserves, Inc.	5,300
40	Kukui Molokai Inc.	5,100

verted to government lands. These public lands (crown plus government lands), estimated at 1.8 million acres (725,000 ha), were ceded to the United States in 1898 when Hawai'i became a U.S. Territory. The vast majority of the remaining land (approximately 2 million acres [810,000 ha]) was already in the hands of large private owners.

Between 1898 and 1959 the Territory of Hawai'i owned only those lands it purchased from private land-owners or acquired through condemnations or other means. Although legal title to ceded public lands was transferred to the United States, the Territory of

Hawai'i retained administrative control and use of ceded lands through the Organic Act of 1900. The United States retained administrative control only of those lands officially set aside for its own use.

In 1920 the U.S. Congress passed the Hawaiian Homes Commission Act, by which the Hawaiian Homes Commission was established to manage roughly 188,000 acres (76,000 ha) of the ceded lands for the benefit of Native Hawaiians. Although Hawaiian Home Lands are scattered throughout the state, the bulk of them are either too dry or at too high an elevation for reasonable habitation or farming other than ranching. Recent land transfers by the state brought the amount of Hawaiian Home Lands to 190,299 acres (76,880 ha) in 1995.

Throughout the territorial years (1898–1959), large private landowners were able to retain control by restricting access to land except through leases. The small amounts of land released for fee simple purchase commanded high prices in the presence of rising demand from a growing population of workers who were leaving the plantations.

Hawaiian Home Lands Classification, 1995

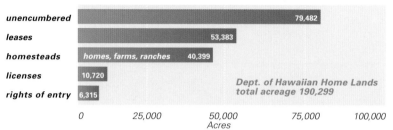

Land Use Districts

Hawai'i was the first state to approve a general plan and to enact a statewide land use zoning law. The State Land Use Law, passed in 1961, established the State Land Use Commission (SLUC), whose task it is to broadly classify all lands in the state into one of four land use districts: urban, rural, agricultural, and conservation. Particular attention is given to encouraging orderly and efficient development of land for urban use and minimum encroachment on prime agricultural land. Urban districts encompass lands already in urban use, with a reserve to accommodate foreseeable growth. Rural districts (found on Kaua'i, Maui, Moloka'i, Lāna'i, and Hawai'i) are land areas primarily in small farms mixed with low-density residential lots; the minimum lot size for one house is 0.5 acre (0.2 ha). Public facilities may also be placed in rural districts. Agricultural districts include lands with a high potential for intensive cultivation; the minimum lot size is 1 acre (0.4 ha). Conservation districts include open space, scenic and historic areas, wilderness and beach reserves, plant and wildlife habitat, and lands necessary for the protection of watersheds and water sources and for the prevention of floods and soil erosion.

Land uses within urban districts are administered solely by the counties. Agricultural and rural districts are jointly administered by the state and the counties. Permissible uses in the agricultural and rural districts are identified in the State Land Use Law and through SLUC rules. The counties may choose to adopt more stringent controls than those imposed by the state. Land uses in the conservation districts are governed solely by the State Department of Land and Natural Resources. District boundaries for lands in the conservation district and for all lands greater than 15 acres (6 ha) may be changed by the SLUC through a petition and quasijudicial hearing process. District boundaries for lands 15 acres or less except in conservation districts may be changed by the applicable county land use authority. During 1991–1992, the state conducted a review of land use district boundaries. By 1995, as a result of the boundary review, more than 6,900 acres (2,800 ha) had been reclassified by the SLUC as urban land, and about 16,000 acres (6,500 ha) had been reclassified as conservation land.

Land Use District Acreage by Island, 1995

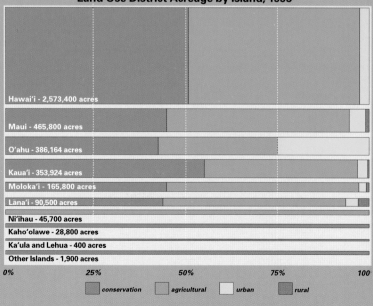

MARY LOU KOBAYASHI

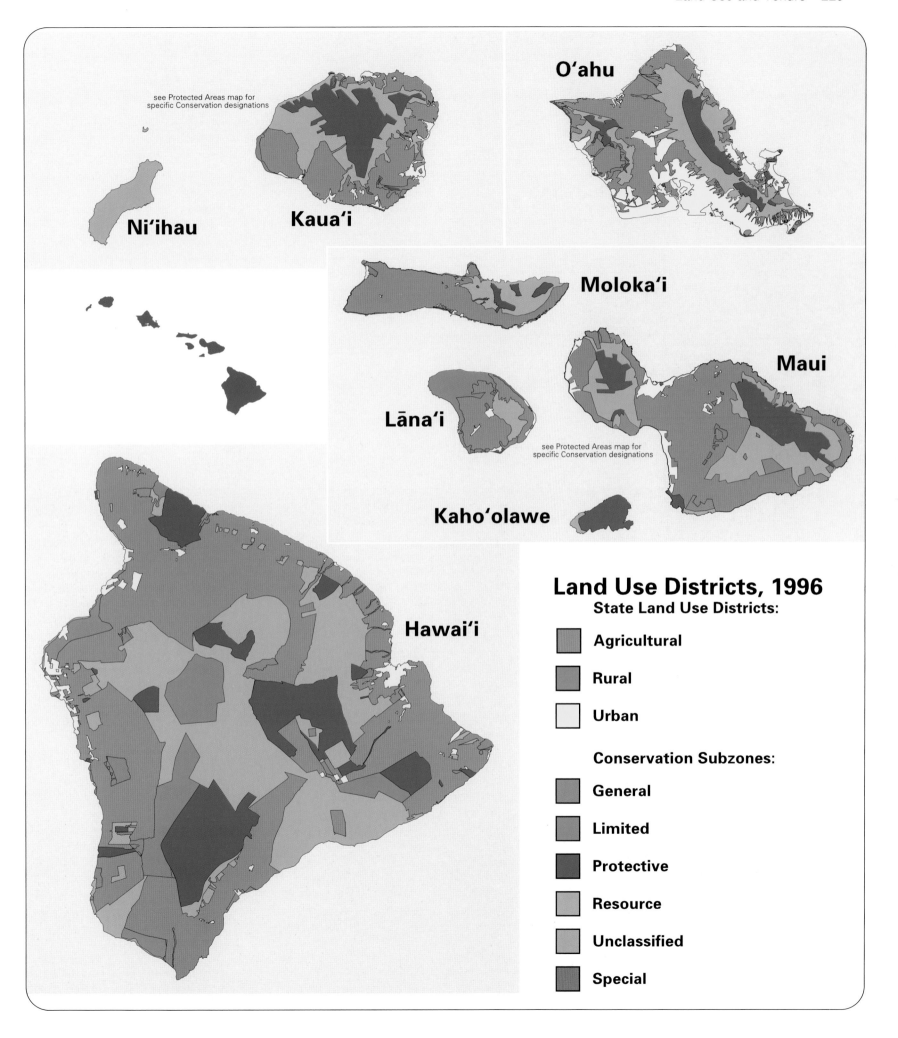

see Protected Areas map for
specific Conservation designations

Ni'ihau

Kaua'i

O'ahu

Moloka'i

Lāna'i

Maui

see Protected Areas map for
specific Conservation designations

Kaho'olawe

Hawai'i

Land Use Districts, 1996
State Land Use Districts:

- Agricultural
- Rural
- Urban

Conservation Subzones:

- General
- Limited
- Protective
- Resource
- Unclassified
- Special

Land Use and the Counties

Although the State Land Use Commission is responsible for broadly deciding whether land in Hawai'i is used for conservation, agriculture, or urban purposes, it is the four counties (Hawai'i has no legally incorporated cities, villages, or towns) that determine the manner of residential, commercial, and industrial development. This they do by means of zoning ordinances, comprehensive development plans, and development or subdivision codes. Each county classifies the land in its jurisdiction according to existing and prospective use on a zoning map. The regulations governing each zone are set out in the county zoning code or land use ordinance. Both the zoning map and zoning ordinances must conform to county comprehensive development plans that prospectively designate land for various uses, from agriculture and preservation/open space to industrial. The public infrastructure necessary to support such development (streets and roads, sewers, water, public parks) is provided by a combination of public funds, development permit conditions, and exactions levied on developers by county government in exchange for subdivision and building permits. Finally, land in the coastal zone is subjected to special review in each county under the Coastal Zone Management Act, which requires a shore-line management permit from the relevant county for any development in the coastal zone.

Further, all land development in Hawai'i—indeed, all land whether public or private, undeveloped or not "substantially" developed—is subject to the exercise of traditional Native Hawaiian rights guaranteed by the state constitution and affirmed by the state supreme court. These rights include, but are not necessarily limited to, gathering, access, and worship (but not exclusive occupancy), all exercisable by anyone with any Hawaiian ancestry, however remote.

In sum, the use of land in Hawai'i is the most regulated of the 50 states. The state broadly defines whether land may be used for the purpose of open space, agriculture, or urban development, after which the counties control the land development process through zoning and development codes. All is subject to the relatively undefined but constitutionally guaranteed traditional rights of the state's roughly 200,000 citizens of Hawaiian ancestry. It is not without reason that Hawai'i's complex and sophisticated land use systems have been collectively called the most stringent in the United States.

DAVID L. CALLIES

Hawaiian Sovereignty and the Ceded Lands

The Hawaiian sovereignty movement has its roots in the overthrow of the Hawaiian Kingdom on January 17, 1893—a conspiracy by sugar plantation owners and their financiers, with unauthorized participation by the resident American minister to Hawai'i. Despite U.S. President Grover Cleveland's condemnation of the unlawful overthrow and request for the restoration of the Hawaiian Kingdom, a republic was established after Queen Lili'uokalani was forced to abdicate her throne.

The heart of the sovereignty movement has been the controversy over the disposition of 1.8 million acres (727,000 ha) of crown and government lands that were ceded, or transferred, to the United States under the 1898 annexation. By tradition, all land in the kingdom was held in trust for the Hawaiian people by the monarch, who was responsible to the gods for its proper management. The 1898 Newlands Joint Resolution for Annexation stated clearly that all government and crown lands were to be ceded to the United States as trustee for the betterment of the conditions of Native Hawaiians. Section 5(b) and (c) in the Admissions Act of 1959 delineated categories within the total 1.8 million acres (727,000 ha) of land transferred from federal trusteeship to the new state of Hawai'i: Hawaiian homelands, 188,000 acres (76,000 ha); land retained by the federal government for national parks, 285,000 acres (115,000 ha); land expropriated by executive order, 87,000 acres (35,000 ha); and public trust land (now under the jurisdiction of the Office of Hawaiian Affairs in accordance with Article XII of the amended state constitution), 1.2 million acres (485,000 ha).

Following statehood, Native Hawaiians suppressed their feelings of economic injustice and deprivation until the national civil rights movement raised their consciousness in the mid-1960s. Then, as tourism boomed and real estate values soared, Hawaiian activists began to vocalize their grievances over having been dispossessed from use of the lands held in trust. Hawaiian political activism began in the 1970s with protests against the eviction of Hawaiian and other tenants to allow development at the Kalama, Waiāhole, and Waikāne Valleys on O'ahu. The movement came of age with the long-term struggle to reclaim Kaho'olawe, which was being used for bombing practice by the U.S. Navy. These protests provided strong impetus for Hawaiian claims to the ceded lands.

To some extent the sovereignty movement also was inspired by the 1971 Alaskan Native Claims Settlement Act, which set a precedent by making reparations for land claims to Native Alaskans and Eskimos. In reaction to the apparent plight of Hawaiians and demands for reparation for the loss of ceded lands, the 1978 Constitutional Convention framed an amendment, passed by the electorate, to establish the Office of Hawaiian Affairs (OHA). Funded by 20 percent of the income from ceded lands, OHA uses its funds to assist Hawaiians in various ways. With the 1980s housing crisis on O'ahu, conditions worsened for Hawaiians. In 1987 Hawaiian attorney Mililani Trask led the formation of Ka Lāhui Hawai'i (The Hawaiian Nation) as an alternative to OHA to solve Hawaiian problems. Subsequently, other sovereignty organizations have arisen. The settlement of Native Hawaiian claims to ceded lands has been a key objective of the sovereignty movement.

JAMES C. F. WANG

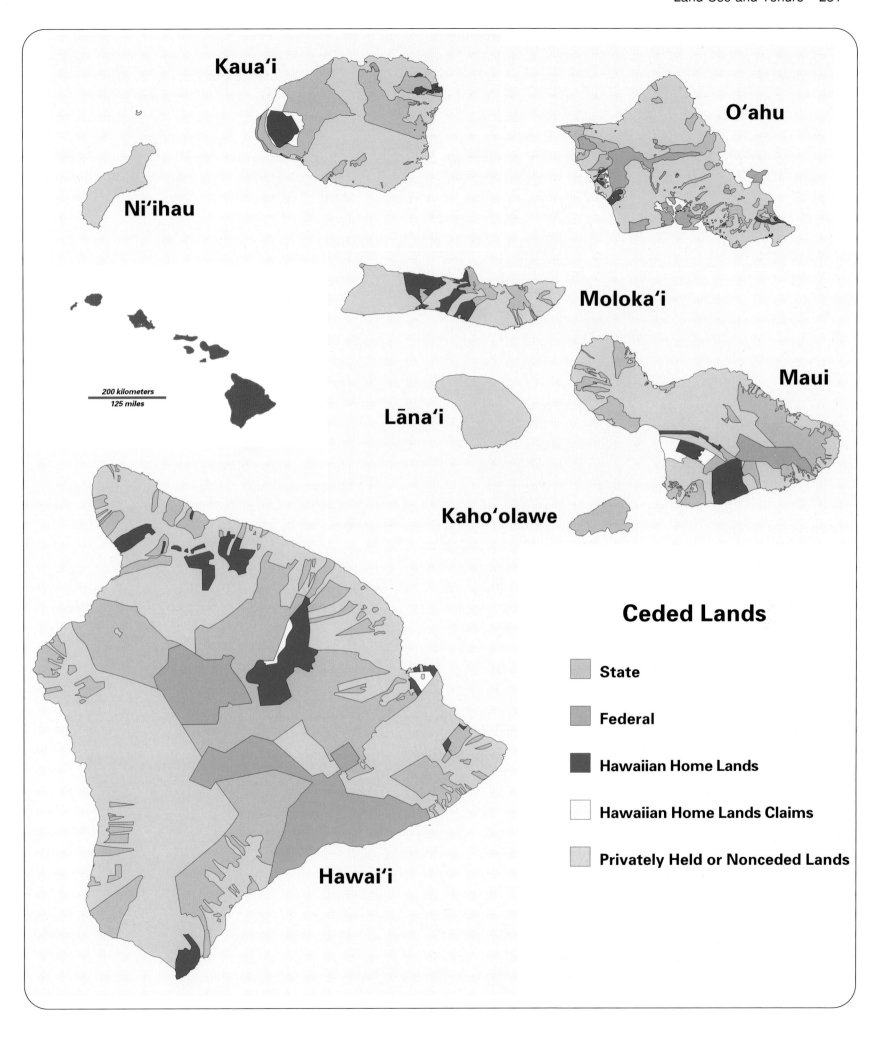

Kaua'i

Ni'ihau

O'ahu

Moloka'i

200 kilometers
125 miles

Lāna'i

Maui

Kaho'olawe

Ceded Lands

State

Federal

Hawaiian Home Lands

Hawaiian Home Lands Claims

Privately Held or Nonceded Lands

Hawai'i

Government Involvement after Statehood

The Admissions Act of 1959, by which Hawai'i was granted statehood, specifically addressed the fate of the lands previously ceded to the U.S. government. The act required that ceded lands should not be retained by the federal government if that government deemed such lands "surplus." Furthermore, the act specified that the public lands returned to the state should be held as "a public trust for the support of the public schools and other public educational institutions, for the betterment of the conditions of native Hawaiians . . . and for the provision of lands for public use."

It was not until 1963 that the Ceded Lands Act allowed the transfer to the state title to all but the 300,000 acres (121,000 ha) of ceded land that were excepted for use by the U.S. government. As a result of this transfer, the state became the largest landowner in Hawai'i with title to approximately 1.3 million acres (525,000 ha) or 31 percent of the land, the largest proportion of any state in the United States.

Land Ownership in Hawai'i, 1968-1988

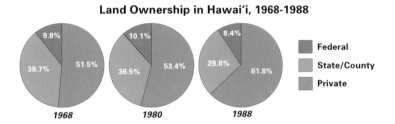

In the early 1960s, state land use policy was dramatically altered when the newly elected Democratic Party majority enacted the State Land Use Law (Act 187), which resulted in a high degree of state government control over the use of private land, a situation that remains unique in the United States. Despite the regulator-landowner tensions inherent in this strong government control of land use, serious pressure for overturn of the system did not mount until the 1980s.

The State Land Use Law authorized the creation of a State Land Use Commission responsible for classifying all lands into one of four land use districts: urban, agricultural, conservation, and rural. Management of land within these classifications was divided among the counties and the state. Each county has total jurisdiction over land designated for urban use (about 3.8 percent of the state), while the State Department of Land and Natural Resources approves all uses of conservation lands. Both state and county levels of government share in the management of land in the agricultural (about 48 percent) and rural (less than 1 percent) districts.

A significant challenge to landownership and landowners' preference for residential lease over residential fee sales was initiated in 1967 with the Land Reform Act. This act seeks to enable lessees holding long-term leases of single-family residential land to purchase the land in fee simple. Property owners challenged the act but the U.S. Supreme Court upheld it.

Several factors point to possible modifications of land use and tenure in the future. The present decline of plantation agriculture could make additional land available for purchase by the general public. Concerns about overregulation of land may result in legislation to ease the burden of compliance with government land use regulations. Such an outcome would reduce compliance costs, which ultimately would affect the price of land. In addition, the Hawaiian sovereignty movement, through which some Hawaiians seek to gain ownership and control of all ceded lands, has the potential to bring about significant impacts on land use and tenure.

Present patterns may persist, despite the possibility of change. Large areas in the hands of a few landowners will likely remain, as will a high degree of government involvement in land use. Limited buildable land area, especially on O'ahu, and the lack of public infrastructure (such as streets, roads, water, and sewers) will keep residential land prices among the highest in the United States.

SONIA P. JUVIK

URBAN CENTERS

Urbanization is the process by which cities are formed, and its most obvious manifestations are high population concentration, a densely built environment, nonagricultural employment, and an urban lifestyle. According to the 1990 census, 89 percent of the population of Hawai'i lives in urbanized areas covering about 10 percent of the land, which compares with national averages of 75.2 percent and 2.5 percent, respectively. The maps in this section provide several different views of the extent and location of the state's urbanization.

Hawai'i's urban growth has been concentrated on O'ahu, which encompasses 25 of the 36 Census Designated Places (CDPs) with more than 5,000 people. Honolulu, with a third of the state's population, is by far the largest city and is ranked forty-fourth in the United States as a whole. It is a classic "primate city," dominating the regional urban hierarchy through its central administrative and commercial functions. The next largest CDPs—Hilo on Hawai'i Island and Kailua, Kāne'ohe, Waipahu, Pearl City, Waimalu, and Mililani Town on O'ahu—are each roughly one-tenth the size of Honolulu.

The map shows the locations and relative populations of the state's principal Census Designated Places (CDPs) as defined by the state government and measured by the U.S. Bureau of the Census for statistical purposes.

Population of Principal Census Designated Places (CDPs), 1990

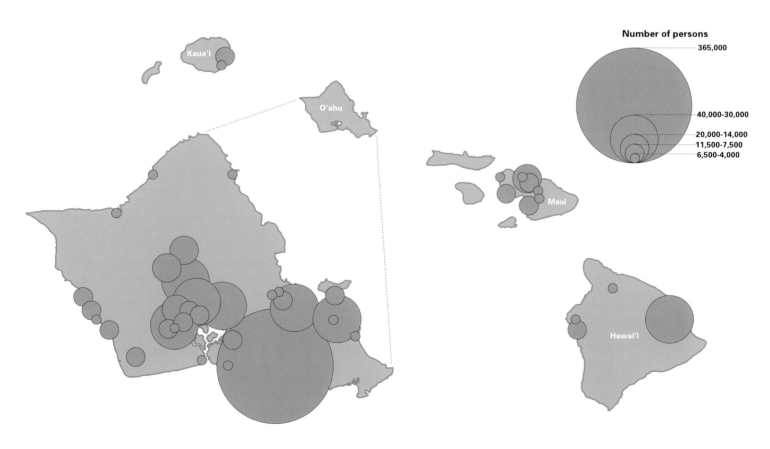

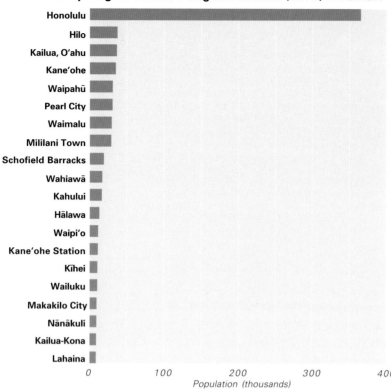

Twenty Largest Census Designated Places (CDPs) in Hawai'i

Honolulu
Hilo
Kailua, O'ahu
Kane'ohe
Waipahū
Pearl City
Waimalu
Mililani Town
Schofield Barracks
Wahiawā
Kahului
Hālawa
Waipi'o
Kane'ohe Station
Kīhei
Wailuku
Makakilo City
Nānākuli
Kailua-Kona
Lahaina

0   100   200   300   400
Population (thousands)

History of Urban Growth

Hawai'i's pattern of urbanization is closely tied to its economic and political history. Prior to European contact, most Hawaiians lived in scattered small settlements tied to subsistence resources of the islands. The *ali'i* (chiefs) moved regularly for various reasons, so there was no recognizable urban tradition. Postcontact trade for salt, ships' provisions, and sandalwood also depended on dispersed resources. Safe anchorages such as Kealakekua, Hilo, Waimea, Lahaina, and Honolulu competed as commercial centers and as bases for the Pacific whaling fleet. Royal policy intervened in Honolulu's favor, however, when King Kamehameha moved his court there in 1809 to consolidate and control foreign trade. By 1831, Honolulu had become a bustling settlement with several American and British merchant houses and more than 18,000 people.

The *Māhele* of 1848 and related acts replaced traditional land tenure with Western-style private ownership, thereby facilitating the sale and development of land. One outcome of these changes was the growth of plantation agriculture, with dispersed villages and mill towns. Financial and political institutions, however, were concentrated in Honolulu, which had been declared the capital of the Kingdom of Hawai'i in 1850. The plantation economy supported some industrial development, such as the iron works in Hilo and Honolulu and the pineapple canning and packing plants in Honolulu. The development of plantation-related transportation infrastructure such as railroads and harbor facilities also promoted urban growth at

favored locations. The plantations further contributed to urban population growth as some of the 350,000 workers brought to Hawai'i between 1852 and 1946 moved to cities to enter informal trade or to take up small-scale farming on the urban fringe. Honolulu grew rapidly, reaching 40,000 by annexation in 1898. Plantation workers and Hawaiians displaced from their traditional lands settled in urban ethnic enclaves. In Honolulu, for example, Chinese moved to Chinatown, Portuguese to Punchbowl, Japanese to Pālama, Hawaiians to Iwilei, and, later, Filipinos to Kalihi.

Real estate development had become big business in Honolulu even before 1900 as the growing, mostly Caucasian middle class sought to escape the crowded and somewhat insalubrious conditions of city living. The introduction of streetcars and trolleys in the early 1900s, together with speculative subdivision development, expanded opportunities for non-White populations, particularly Chinese and Japanese, to move out of downtown Honolulu into new suburbs such as Kaimukī and Kapahulu. The City and County of Honolulu, incorporated in 1907, passed laws to control development and regulate land use, but the city lacked a coherent plan, and developers drove urbanization. The business community encouraged urban growth, even recruiting immigrants from the U.S. mainland, and between 1920 and 1950 Honolulu was the second fastest growing city of its size in the nation.

Tourism also influenced Hawai'i's urbanization, and this new industry was supported by publicly funded projects such as the construction of the Ala Wai Canal and the improvement of facilities at Honolulu Harbor in the 1920s. Large luxury hotels were built, beginning with the Moana in 1901 and the Halekulani in 1917. These developments, together with promotional efforts, led to the transformation of Waikīkī

O'ahu Census Tracts with an Ethnic Majority, 1990

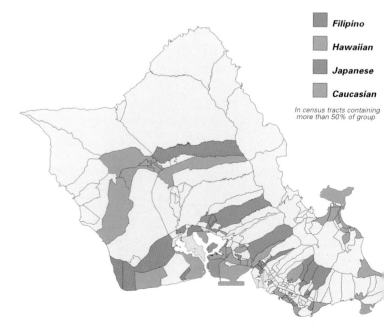

Filipino

Hawaiian

Japanese

Caucasian

In census tracts containing more than 50% of group

Central Business District, Honolulu. [Hawai'i Visitors Bureau]

Honolulu skyline. [W. Waterfall/Hawai'i Visitors Bureau]

into an urban resort area. The Great Depression and World War II slowed tourism's growth, but statehood and the advent of jet-airliner transportation to Hawai'i revitalized it in the 1960s. Waikīkī rapidly became one of the most densely populated urban areas in the world. Modern Waikīkī has become the high-rise urban engine that powers Hawai'i's tourism- and land development-based economy. Destination resorts, including Kā'anapali, Maui, and Princeville, Kaua'i, have also been built on neighbor islands. Although much smaller in scale, such resorts similarly drive up real estate values and encourage speculative urban development.

Postwar economic growth, together with expanded infrastructure such as highways and water and sewage facilities, spurred further suburbanization. For example, tunnels built through the Ko'olau Range for the Pali Highway in 1957 and the Likelike Highway in 1958–1960 increased the accessibility of the windward coast of O'ahu for residential development. Improved transportation infrastructure likewise facilitated development of former agricultural land in Hawai'i Kai, east of Honolulu, and Mililani, west of the city. Large landowners created leasehold arrangements that allowed families the security and economic benefits of home ownership, while the landowners were ensured revenues and ultimate control. This situation has created political controversy, however, as leaseholders resist increases in rents caused by the dramatic rise in the market value of urban land and demand conversion to fee simple ownership.

Future Growth Patterns

The trend for population to leave the neighbor islands for Honolulu that began after World War II reversed around 1970. Although neighbor island urban centers—Hilo, Lahaina, Wailuku, and Līhu'e—had been growing steadily, urbanization has since been more rapid on the neighbor islands than on O'ahu. Not surprisingly, growth rates are highest where absolute populations are small. Speculative subdivisions in rural and agricultural districts of neighbor islands have pro-

duced scattered, low-density tracts of vacation homes, vanity farms, and houselots for retirees and commuting workers. While such subdivisions do not seem to constitute urban settlement at present, they are perhaps pioneering future "sprawl" in these areas.

On O'ahu, the state's promotion of a second major city at Kapolei on the 'Ewa Plain defines one direction for contemporary urban growth. Originally planned by the Campbell Estate in the 1950s as a response to the impending demise of large-scale agriculture, urbanization of the 'Ewa Plain under public/private partnership had become part of government policy by the 1970s. The goal is to establish a growth center with its own harbor and diversified employment base on about 32,000 acres (12,900 ha), approximately 8 percent of O'ahu's land area. As of early 1996, a number of industries had invested in Barbers Point Harbor and the James Campbell Industrial Park, and a tourist resort had opened at Ko'olina, but relatively few jobs had materialized for new residents. In contrast, residential development in Kapolei has been nothing short of dramatic: between 1990 and 1994, nearly 5,000 new housing units were built—almost twice as many as on the rest of O'ahu. There are plans for 40,000 additional units to be constructed by 2012.

The present rate of growth will continue to put enormous strain on infrastructure. The state has modified existing road connections and plans a new highway on the 'Ewa Plain, but development there has already increased road traffic. Moreover, rapid rail transit has been rejected by the city council, commuter ferries have proved unpopular, and experiments to relieve congestion by encouraging telecommuting have not produced promising results. Perhaps more serious is the problem of water supply, the solution for which depends upon continued diversion of massive amounts of water from Windward O'ahu and public funding of costly new distribution facilities. Recognizing the problem, the state has jointly invested in a desalination plant, but the small amount of water it produces is said to be the most expensive in the nation.

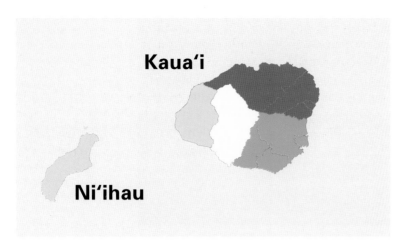

Kaua'i

Ni'ihau

O'ahu

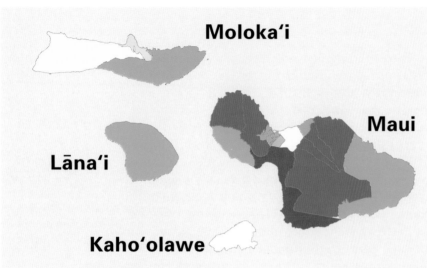

Moloka'i

Lāna'i

Maui

Kaho'olawe

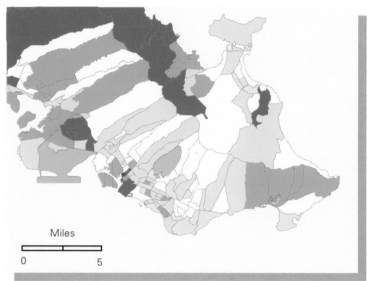

Miles

0   5

Population Change
1980-1990

Percent by Census Tract

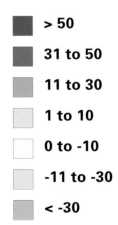

> 50

31 to 50

11 to 30

1 to 10

0 to -10

-11 to -30

< -30

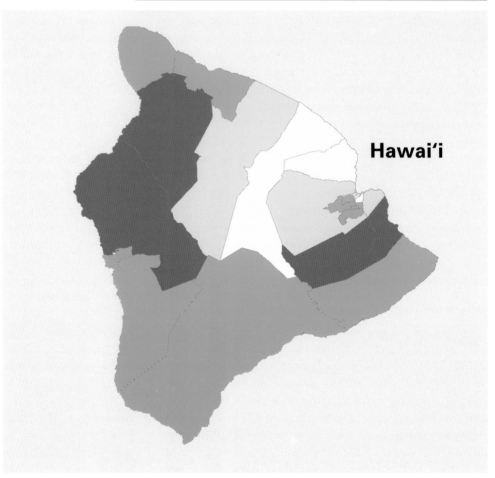

Hawai'i

A persistent theme in the urbanization of Hawai'i, which Kapolei exemplifies well, has been the combination of economic and political interests in land development. Rather than being a product of broader economic growth, urbanization is conceived as the engine of growth. In the absence of any real alternative to tourism, which is closely connected to real estate development, the state and private capital promote urbanization and, implicitly, population growth as a solution to the state's economic problems. While development of land produces substantial profits, the question remains whether it can be a sustainable, long-term program for economic development of the Islands.

MATTHEW MCGRANAGHAN
AND JON GOSS

ECONOMY

The contemporary economy of Hawai'i is structured around the state's dominant source of export earnings, tourism. It also encompasses a variety of highly specialized "niche" sectors that capitalize on Hawai'i's unique natural and multicultural assets and on the technical and professional skills pool centered on O'ahu. The neighbor islands each possess distinctive economic attributes but in general have proportionately more prominent agricultural and tourism sectors than are found on O'ahu. Once predominant, plantation agriculture and defense have diminished in both absolute and relative importance during recent decades—due in part to stagnation in agricultural output and prices, Cold War détente, and the growth of tourism.

Geography and the Economy

The Hawaiian Islands are the most geographically isolated archipelago in the world. The Polynesians who settled Hawai'i many centuries ago are thought to have carried on a modest sea trade with Marquesans and Tahitians. Indigenous Hawaiian society gradually became independent and self-sufficient until European explorers, beginning with British Captain James Cook, reopened the Islands to foreign trade late in the eighteenth century.

Today Hawai'i's trade consists of the export of tourism-related services and the reexport of merchandise, primarily to tourists, in exchange for imported goods for local consumption. A substantial volume of imported building materials varies with local construction and investment cycles. Small volumes of agricultural and manufactured goods are produced in the state for both consumption and export, but this output is limited by the disadvantages of small market size and scope. Nonetheless, the "made-in-Hawai'i" identity, which capitalizes on casual island lifestyle and draws from a diverse cultural milieu, confers a unique attribute on a variety of products (Kona coffee, aloha wear and "surf" wear, and chocolate macadamia nut candy, for example) that have found a worldwide market. The export of nontourism services, such as engineering, financial, and medical, throughout the Pacific

and Asia is increasingly redefining Hawai'i's comparative advantage in the region.

Since the 1800s, Hawai'i's industries have depended on the development of transportation to unite the islands into a single internal market and connect them as a group to external markets. Sandalwood traders and whalers initiated this process and established the most important commercial ties between Hawai'i and the outside world during the first half of the nineteenth century. Following the 1848 gold rush in California, new markets on North America's west coast opened up. Ultimately, commerce in nonperishable, processed foods such as sugar and canned pineapple forged the most enduring trade link between Hawai'i and the United States. This, combined with America's growing strategic interests in the Pacific during the twentieth century, gave rise to Hawai'i's importance as a military outpost.

As crucial as sea links were to the early development and integration of the Islands' economy, air transportation has played an essential role in tying Hawai'i to overseas markets in the twentieth century. Commercial interisland air transport began in the 1920s, the

Foreign Merchandise Trade Flow, 1990

same decade in which aviation pioneers proved that Hawai'i could be reached from North America. These developments gave new impetus to tourism, which previously had relied solely on ocean liners. The introduction of jet aircraft service to Honolulu in 1959 and wide-bodied jet airplanes in 1967 brought modern, mass-market tourism to Hawai'i, and expanded mobility for state residents. Air transportation also has been crucial to the successful marketing of floral products and other local goods dependent on rapid delivery to overseas destinations.

Modern telecommunications and microprocessing technologies are providing fresh opportunities by which Hawai'i can integrate local and global economies. The rapid development of the Internet and the "information superhighway" also bodes well for Hawai'i in making available new channels for the export of information; management, technical, and professional services; and access to the global marketplace of the future. Like transportation and telecommunications, this increased connectivity will continue to allow Hawai'i to transcend its geographic remoteness in the future.

The Rise and Fall of Industries

Hawai'i's natural resources, historically the foundation of its capacity to export, have in recent decades been complemented by the emergence of a pool of exportable skills in the local labor force. This long-standing dependence on the extraction of a natural-resource base has not been without negative environmental consequences.

The first export industry was the sandalwood trade, which flourished during the reign of King Kamehameha I. A thriving market for sandalwood in China, combined with an emerging fur trade in the Pacific Northwest, created an advantageous position for the Hawaiian Kingdom as both supplier of raw material and provisioner of trading ships early in the nineteenth century. Within a few decades, however, the bountiful sandalwood forests were destroyed and the sandalwood trade vanished.

Successor exports were also natural-resource based. The whaling trade, which thrived after sandal-

wood's demise, followed the seasonal migrations of large populations of whales. Hawai'i played an important role in whaling, first as a seasonal hunting ground and later as a provisioning center for whalers. The trade peaked in the 1840s and 1850s, and it was during this era that a merchant community became established that later provided the commercial infrastructure for agricultural export industries.

As a result of the whaling trade's collapse, for much of the latter half of the nineteenth century Hawai'i's economy was threatened by instability. Desperate to secure new export markets, the largely foreigner-dominated business community sought to obtain access to the United States market, which by midcentury had begun to expand rapidly. However, such access was intermittent (during the California Gold Rush and the U.S. Civil War) until the late 1800s, when plantation agriculture blossomed under the Reciprocity Treaty of 1876 and brought economic stability based on sustained exports. Capitalizing on the year-round growing season and gaining permanent access to North American markets through annexation in 1898, Hawai'i's agricultural pioneers made sugar, canned pineapple, and later pineapple juice into mainstays of the economy for nearly a century. Unlike whaling and sandalwood before them, plantation agriculture did not rely on the extraction of resources but rather on the sustained use of land and water in large-scale cultivation. Financial and merchant services arose in response to the needs of plantation agriculture and related manufacturing.

Hawai'i's strategic location and geopolitical history further strengthened economic ties with the United States. As America looked westward, it required an outpost from which to project its military and diplomatic influence in the region. However, it was not until after annexation, and particularly after World War II, that U.S. military spending in the Islands grew to rival agriculture in economic importance.

Tourism, another export activity dependent on Hawai'i's natural environment, tapped into American consumers' emerging demand for exotic travel experiences in the 1950s and 1960s. In subsequent decades Hawai'i, with its well-developed tourism infrastruc-

Industrial Dominance in Hawai'i, 1800-1995

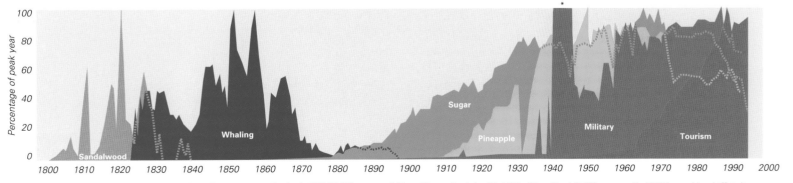

* In this graph the peak year (100 percent) for military sector contribution is 1988 (69,891 personnel). The military spike during World War II (reaching 442,160 personnel in 1944) is considered off-scale.

ture, has met with great success in attracting visitors from Asia, especially from Japan.

Hawai'i's Economy in the 1990s

Gross Product Gross product is a measure of aggregate income and output. Using the U.S. Standard Industrial Classification, this output can be measured by the summation of values added by industry. Industry and industry groups include goods production (manufacturing, construction, and agriculture), distribution services (retailing, wholesaling, transportation, utilities, and communication), financial services (finance, insurance, and real estate), nonfinancial services (hotels, health, and business), and public services. Tourism is not an industry under this classification—it is instead an export that comprises the output of a variety of industries.

In 1995 Hawai'i's Gross State Product (GSP), the market value of all goods and services produced, was $33 billion. Adjusted for inflation, annual growth of GSP averaged 4.4 percent between 1960 and 1990, the years after statehood and the approximate peak of the state's most recent economic boom, respectively. Although economic growth averaged less than 1 percent annually between 1990 and 1995, it is expected

to rise gradually to an annual rate of 2.5 percent. The transition from 4.4 percent growth (averaged over expansions and recessions) to 2.5 percent growth as a sustainable pace of future expansion is expected to prove the most significant economic shift for Hawai'i since statehood.

Local Variations The distribution of output by industry provides the most revealing picture of the composition of each island's economy. Tourism, agriculture, and state and local government are proportionately more important on the neighbor islands than on O'ahu. The relative importance of tourism for the neighbor islands is clear from the large shares of gross product represented by hotel services and retail trade. Though half of the state's hotel inventory is located on O'ahu, nontourism industries are economically more prominent there. Although manufacturing's share of output is small overall, the continued importance of agriculture on the neighbor islands makes value-added activities such as food processing relatively more significant there than on O'ahu.

As the state's metropolitan center, O'ahu is dominated by nontourism industries, including financial, health, and other services. Federal defense and civilian employment is also concentrated on O'ahu.

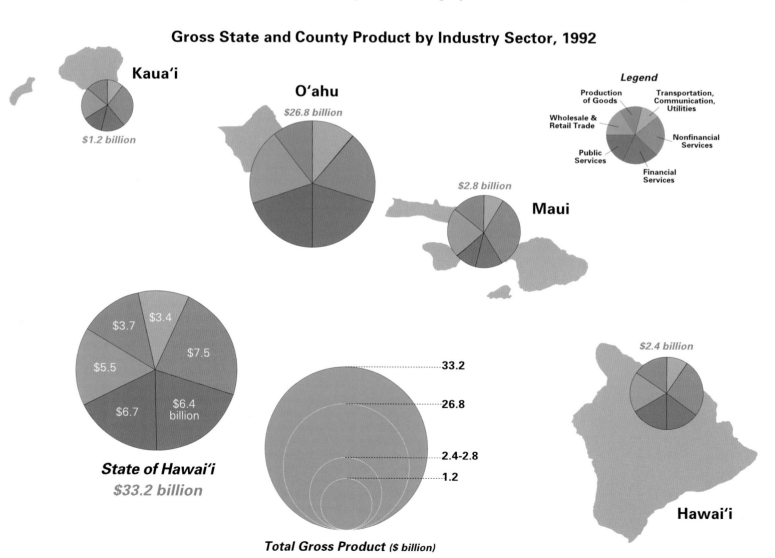

Gross State and County Product by Industry Sector, 1992

Kaua'i — $1.2 billion

O'ahu — $26.8 billion

Maui — $2.8 billion

Legend
Production of Goods
Transportation, Communication, Utilities
Wholesale & Retail Trade
Nonfinancial Services
Public Services
Financial Services

State of Hawai'i $33.2 billion
$3.4 $3.7 $7.5 $5.5 $6.7 $6.4 billion

Total Gross Product *($ billion)*
33.2
26.8
2.4-2.8
1.2

Hawai'i — $2.4 billion

Employment Civilian employment (including the self-employed) decreased from a peak of almost 600,000 in 1991 to 570,000 in the first quarter of 1996, a by-product of economic stagnation of the early 1990s. Much of the adjustment to the state's economic stagnation in the 1990s came through corporate and public-sector downsizing. Unfortunately, this diminished opportunities for secondary (part-time) employment, which is crucial to many households given the comparatively high costs of living in Hawai'i. In 1995, following slight changes in unemployment definitions (which added 0.5–1.0 percent to prior estimates), the unemployment rate hovered at around 5.5 percent. This rate falls between the relatively high unemployment levels experienced during the 1970s, when the labor force was growing rapidly, and the 2 percent rate that was the norm during the economic boom of the late 1980s.

For almost three decades, from the Vietnam War until 1988, the number of military personnel in the Hawaiian Islands reached upward of 60,000, but as a result of post–Cold War demilitarization the number fell to around 45,000 in 1995. The U.S. military's increasing reliance on rapid deployment to smaller military conflicts in an array of geopolitical hotspots has made the number of military personnel stationed in the Islands considerably more variable. Approximately 10 percent of the resident population is employed by the military in either civilian or armed forces capacities.

Despite Hawai'i's economic stagnation in the early 1990s, per capita personal income remained among the highest in the U.S. Per capita personal income in 1996 was $25,404 (compared to the national average of $24,426); this produced a drop in rank from sixth to twelfth highest among the 50 states. Personal income is a broad measure of incomes received by residents from all sources, including wages and salaries,

dividends, interest, rents, transfer payments, and proprietors' income. Because of the state's high individual income taxes, Hawai'i's disposable (after-tax) per capita personal income ranked tenth in the U.S. in 1996 at $22,065, while the national average was $21,087.

Prices and Living Costs Since the end of World War II, average inflation in Hawai'i has closely followed national levels—an expected outcome given economic mechanisms that tend to keep interest rates and, in turn, inflation consistent within the United States.

However, the state's inflation rate has shown a tendency to exceed the national average in periods of economic expansion and to fall below the national average during recessions. For example in 1991, at the end of the 1980s economic expansion, the state's inflation rate reached nearly 8 percent, compared to a nationwide average of around 5 percent. In contrast, during recessions of the late 1950s, the early 1980s, and early 1990s Hawai'i's inflation measured around 2 percent, falling to near 0 percent in 1997.

The inflation accompanying economic expansion in the late 1980s pushed the state's prices well above the nation's as a whole, producing a consumer price index for Honolulu that exceeded the U.S. urban aver-

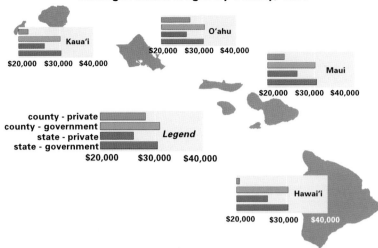

Average Annual Wages by County, 1994

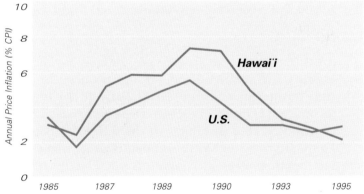

Consumer Price Inflation

Civilian Employment, 1985-1995

Civilian Unemployment, 1985-1995

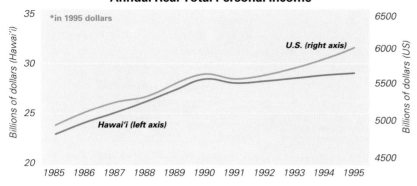

Annual Real Total Personal Income*

*in 1995 dollars

U.S. (right axis)

Hawai'i (left axis)

Billions of dollars (Hawai'i)

Billions of dollars (US)

1985 1986 1987 1988 1989 1990 1991 1992 1993 1994 1995

age by 12 percentage points, as measured on the 1982–1984 base. Higher inflation in Hawai'i contributed to raising the estimated cost of living for a four-person family from around 25 percent higher than the average U.S. city in the early 1980s to more than 35 percent higher than average in the early 1990s. This characteristic should be qualified, however, as Honolulu's cost of living is comparable to that of large cities such as San Francisco, New York, and Boston.

A major contributor to Hawai'i's living costs is the price of housing, which has consistently ranked the highest in the country for both renters and homeowners. Median resale prices for a single-family home on O'ahu hovered around $300,000 by the late 1990s, while condominium resale prices averaged $150,000. The advantages of slightly lower housing costs on the neighbor islands have typically been offset by the relative lack of economic opportunities and lower average incomes there.

High housing costs, which top the list of items contributing to the living cost differential between Hawai'i and the mainland, are compounded by high state income tax rates applied at relatively low levels of income in Hawai'i. Together these two factors have contributed to a widening in the difference between Honolulu's cost of living and that of other major U.S. metropolitan areas, although this trend has been mitigated somewhat by the state's economic stagnation during the 1990s.

The high cost of living differential between Hawai'i and the mainland is often cited as a motivation for out-migration by residents, and it is doubtless a critical factor, along with employment opportunities elsewhere, in explaining these migration choices. The cost-of-living premium acts also as an equilibrating mechanism, which, by serving as a disincentive to in-migration, has balanced the net migration flows in recent years. Hawai'i's attractiveness as a place to live from a variety of environmental and cultural perspectives might otherwise lead to an influx of migrants creating pressures for further urbanization and growth. That the overwhelming majority of residents stay in Hawai'i is a testimony to the value of the many non-economic amenities that accompany life in the Islands.

Outlook for the Economy At the beginning of the 1990s, the state's economy reached a crossroads when the pace of economic growth slowed. While the structure of the economy is not expected to change significantly during the remainder of the 1990s, the rate of growth is likely to be modest. Tourism will continue to dominate exports and support Hawai'i's high standard of living. The Islands' maturation as a tourist destination should lead to more gradual expansion of the visitor industry than in recent decades as Asia markets are developed to match the North American tourist market. Moreover, disincentives to in-migration, changes in demography following the "baby boom," and the achievement of high rates of female employment will slacken expansion of the state's labor force in coming years and further restrain economic growth potential. Technological progress and improved productivity likely will become more important than tourism and population increase in maintaining economic growth.

Economic Sectors

Agriculture The state's agriculture in the 1990s has been shifting decisively away from plantation crops and toward diversified crops and agricultural concepts new to Hawai'i, such as agroforestry. Throughout the 1980s sugar and pineapple continued to dominate agricultural output, but beginning in the 1990s foreign competition, uncertainties in federal farm policy and price supports, and the termination of long-term land leases precipitated a wave of plantation closures that freed up more than 100,000 acres (40,000 ha) of prime agricultural lands across the state. These changes created opportunities for the establishment or expansion of diversified crops in closer proximity to local consumer markets. The export of tropical fruits, vegetables, flowers and nursery products, and specialty crops such as coffee and macadamia nuts also has steadily grown, and specialized products such as winter corn seed have flourished. Other replacements for the plantations will be longer in coming. Agroforestry appears to be one alternative, with some landowners committed to wood chip and fiber production on Hawai'i Island. Whether the production of tropical hardwoods has a future in the Islands remains to be seen, but global deforestation may create such market opportunities by early in the twenty-first century. Hawai'i's cattle industry in the mid-1990s, struggling to maintain profitability against high production costs, depended primarily on the export of feeder cattle to Canadian markets.

Manufacturing Once dominated by sugar milling and refining and pineapple canning, manufacturing also has suffered from plantation closures of the 1990s, and consequently the relative importance of other industries has been enhanced. The state's next most significant manufacturing sectors are garment manufacturing, printing and publishing, and petroleum refining. The garment industry has long benefited from Hawaiian fashion design and the increasing popularity of casual wear on the U.S. mainland.

Printing and publishing thrive partly on the basis of a lively, home-grown demand for Hawaiiana fiction and nonfiction—a market not entirely driven by tourism. Music and other performing and fine arts have defined a thriving market for recordings, paintings, Native Hawaiian crafts, and other products reflecting the state's unique cultural mix.

With the only petroleum refinery in the Pacific Island region, Hawai'i is a net exporter of refined petroleum products. Serving the refueling needs of transpacific aircraft, aviation fuel dominates the market for exportable petroleum derivatives. Nonetheless, Hawai'i's small market size inhibits the exploitation of manufacturing economies of scale, resulting in an overall dependence on imported merchandise.

Construction Construction and real estate investment are the state's most cyclical industries, and their fortunes have been particularly sensitive to waves of offshore investment enveloping the economy in recent decades. Construction is cyclical in nature because large structures cannot be built incrementally over time to match the gradual increases in demand. Instead, construction of hotels, resorts, and other large structures tends to cluster around periods of favorable economic conditions, which are followed by lulls as the excess capacity constructed is absorbed by growing demand. Upswings and downturns are exacerbated by changing monetary policies and interest rates. At the peak of the construction cycle in 1991, total construction spending in Hawai'i reached $4.5 billion, nearly triple the level of 7 years earlier, while in 1997 contracting receipts declined to $2.8 billion. Employment in the industry likewise declined from 33,000 to 21,000 over the same period (although in the mid-1980s construction employment had fallen briefly below 20,000). Hotel and resort construction have been highly cyclical components of the construction industry, while real estate speculation from both local and overseas sources also has made condominium development volatile. Offshore investors have typically fueled repeated cycles of boom and bust in the construction of resort-related properties.

Value of Construction in Hawai'i

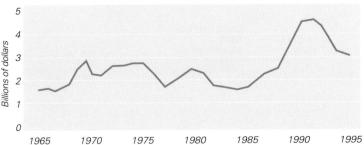

Transportation, Communications, and Utilities Hawai'i's popularity as a travel destination, along with interisland transit requirements, have allowed the transportation industry to flourish, although an increasing amount of transpacific merchandise shipping and passenger travel bypasses the Islands. Communications and utilities industries stagnated somewhat in the early 1990s, primarily because rapid technological change, consolidations within the industries, and mergers with national corporations inhibited employment growth. As semiregulated industries, communication and utility sectors have offered comparatively high wages and held relatively insulated positions in the economy. Recent deregulation, however, has diminished these conditions, subjecting these industries to threats of entry from U.S. mainland service providers but also creating new opportunities for local entrepreneurs.

Wholesale and Retail Trades Wholesale distribution, headquartered on O'ahu, is about a $5 billion dollar industry statewide. The retail trade serves about 1.2 million resident consumers and a daily average of about 150,000 visitors with a high propensity to consume. Statewide, retail sales totaled around $15 billion during 1995, but the wholesale and retail trades continued to experience intense competition and restructuring begun early in the decade as new trends swept into the state from the U.S. mainland. Current retail concepts range from "big box discounters" to "category killers" and "eclectic niche" retailers. In addition, the influx of generally high-spending Japanese tourists has made Hawai'i a haven for designer boutiques and high-end retailers, while also supporting new factory outlet malls. These changes in retailing have generally benefited resident consumers by lowering prices and expanding product choices, but they also have generated upheaval among incumbent retailers and forced some of them to exit local markets.

Finance, Insurance, and Real Estate Hawai'i's role as a regional provider of financial services has expanded in recent decades. Unlike many sectors that experienced employment declines during the early 1990s, job levels in finance and insurance have remained generally stable, despite industry contraction. Hawai'i's banking and insurance industries have been challenged by new technologies, the U.S. savings and loan crisis of the 1980s, and Japan's banking crisis of the 1990s. Meanwhile, consumer investments have increasingly shifted from conventional deposits to stock mutual funds and other securities, as financial securities have proliferated. Moreover, deregulation, financial innovation, mergers and acquisitions, interstate banking and branching, and the emergence of the Internet are likely to keep the financial services industry in a fluid state for the near future.

In tandem with the state's construction activity, the real estate industry has experienced cycles of boom

Small Business

The term *small business,* as used by the U.S. Small Business Administration (SBA), varies by industry, with the defining characteristic being either annual sales (less than $5 million) or number of employees (fewer than 500). By these criteria, small businesses represent 99.7 percent of all businesses nationwide and employ 65 percent of the U.S. labor force. In Hawai'i 92.3 percent of all firms are considered small businesses if the annual sales limit is applied, and 99.4 percent fall into the category if the employee limit is used.

Those who identify themselves as small business operators, however, typically work in enterprises of much more modest size than the legal category suggests. In Hawai'i 65 percent of all firms generate sales under $500,000 annually, and 91.3 percent have fewer than 40 employees. Indeed, 63.7 percent of the state's businesses have fewer than 5 employees. In some contexts, those in the latter group are more accurately referred to as microbusinesses.

The nature of small business differs from large business more than size alone would indicate. For instance, small businesses—and especially microbusinesses—are underwritten by the personal assets of the owners, and these enterprises tend to have little or no financial reserves. As a result, owners are not only personally at risk, but consequences are experienced as immediate. Decision making is personal, quick, and focused on operations, with a concern for protecting markets. The owners of small entrepreneurial businesses have somewhat different priorities: they vigorously seek new opportunities with less regard for existing resources. Entrepreneurial companies are characterized by rapid growth and, arguably, experience lower risk due to a more fundamental understanding of competitiveness.

As with most business in Hawai'i, small businesses are relatively new, although disproportionately so: 10.5 percent of all businesses are no more than 5 years old, and 46.9 percent are no more than 15 years old.

The state had 48,876 registered businesses in 1995, of which 65.7 percent were on O'ahu. The services sector included the greatest number of microbusinesses (49.6 percent), while only 2.5 percent were in the manufacturing sector. Retail trade predominated among firms with 20 or more employees.

The total number of businesses with fewer than 5 employees increased during the period 1989–1993 from 14,736 to 15,456, an average increase of 1.2 percent per year. Anecdotal evidence indicates that the lack of jobs, especially career jobs with growth potential, is driving the formation of new businesses in Hawai'i. At the same time, difficulty in accessing capital by those without significant collateral is limiting the formation of new businesses. Interestingly, the number of businesses owned by women in Hawai'i increased from about 21,700 in 1987 to roughly 29,750 in 1992. The 1992 total of female-owned firms represented 37.6 percent of all businesses in the state, as compared to the nationwide average of 34 percent.

Small business figures prominently in the national economy. In the 1970s small businesses—particularly microbusinesses—became the principal generators of new jobs. By the late 1980s firms with more than 20 employees began losing jobs through layoffs, and smaller firms became the only job generators. This is not entirely the case in Hawai'i, where in 1980 half of all jobs existed in small companies with 50 or fewer employees, and by 1990 the share had declined to 46 percent. Hawai'i's anomaly in this regard is thought to be caused by a pervasive and debilitating regulatory environment, which is increasingly under attack by small business owners.

DARRYL MLEYNEK

and bust driven by sporadically high levels of foreign investment in the Islands. During the late 1980s foreign investors acquired existing properties and developed new projects such as hotels, luxury condominiums, and downtown Honolulu office buildings. In the 1990s real estate activity slowed and property values plummeted, particularly at the high end. Since statehood, real estate cycles have lasted, on average, 8–10 years, and with each cycle housing prices have tended to double.

Nonfinancial Services As with postindustrial economies elsewhere, Hawai'i's nonfinancial services sector has grown since statehood, in part assisted by the expansion of tourism. Hotel services comprise approximately 5 percent of Gross State Product but represent significantly larger shares on neighbor islands. Health services, enhanced by the state's role as a regional pro-

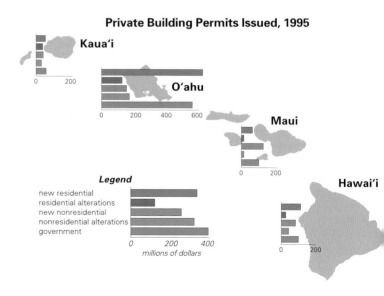

Private Building Permits Issued, 1995

Kaua'i

O'ahu

Maui

Hawai'i

Legend
new residential
residential alterations
new nonresidential
nonresidential alterations
government

millions of dollars

O'ahu Home Resale Values, 1960-1995

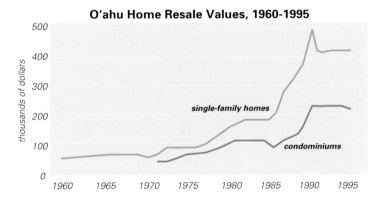

Japanese Investment in Hawai'i

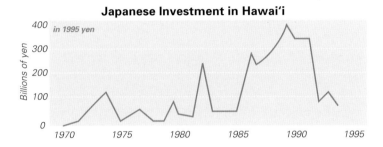

vider, are equally important and comprise one of the few sectors that experienced job growth during the early 1990s, when 25,000 jobs were lost statewide. Other business and professional services, such as architectural, engineering, and construction management companies, also have capitalized on Hawai'i's role as a regional center by marketing their skills throughout the Pacific and Asia. Excluding the hotel sector, nonfinancial services comprise more than 15 percent of the Gross State Product and provide nearly 25 percent of total employment.

Government Collectively, federal (civilian and military), state, and county government contributes just over 20 percent of the Gross State Product, a considerable decline from the early 1960s when defense alone accounted for 20 percent of the economy. The decline in government's relative importance is a reflection of the increasing economic contribution of the private sector and, particularly, the growth of tourism. Continued military reduction following the end of the Cold War had an especially significant impact on the defense sector.

Hawai'i State Government General Fund, 1985-1995

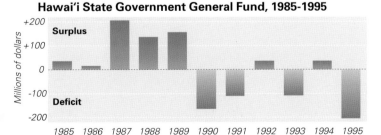

State and local governments combined produce about 8.5 percent of the GSP and employ nearly 12 percent of the total workforce. Annually state government expenditures amount to more than $5 billion, and county governments spend more than $1 billion. In recent years the stagnant economy has forced state and county governments into fiscal austerity, which has been implemented through program cuts and restrained growth in spending. Hawai'i's taxes are collected from three primary sources: individual and corporate (net) incomes, gross business receipts, and real property, along with a variety of fees from public enterprises, such as receipts from airport operations.

The federal government figures prominently in the state's economy on several levels. Hawai'i serves as a management center for federal expenditures throughout the region, including former U.S. territories in the western Pacific. Federal military expenditures to support the large number of military personnel present in the Islands exceed $3 billion annually, while federal civilian expenditures exceed $4 billion. The military's 7 percent of Gross State Product remains, after tourism and civilian government, one of the largest sectors in the economy.

Since European contact in the late eighteenth century, Hawai'i's economy has grown more and more dependent on trade, first in goods, but increasingly in services, and as a result has become more interlinked with other economies in the region. Many lament the loss of isolation and self-sufficiency that trade required, but Hawai'i's relatively high incomes and living standards are a direct result of its open economy and the political and economic stability conferred by its status as a U.S. state. Industries have always been founded on the Islands' natural endowments. The sandalwood and whaling trades harvested renewable resources that were ultimately depleted. Plantation agriculture sustained itself for a century and a half before its drastic curtailment in the face of international competition. Strategic location has made Hawai'i a prime military outpost, and climate and geographical features are the basis for the state's now dominant tourism industry. Hawai'i's future will continue to depend on sustaining renewable resources—agricultural lands, marine resources, and the biodiversity of unique natural environments—and on the growth of service exports from knowledge-based industries. The state's economic future will be one in which electronic pathways complement the sea and air transportation routes that first made it possible for Hawai'i to participate in the global economy.

PAUL H. BREWBAKER

AGRICULTURE

During the first half of the twentieth century, agriculture dominated the economy of Hawaiʻi. At the same time, sugarcane and pineapple production dominated agriculture. Since midcentury, however, agriculture has diminished in economic importance, as the tourist and defense industries have risen to prominence. In 1994 less than 1 percent of the Gross State Product was derived directly from agriculture. The number of agricultural workers has likewise declined; by 1993 agriculture claimed only 2 percent of the total workforce. Although sugarcane and pineapple are still important, the closing of several plantations has allowed diversified agriculture to overtake these traditional crops in total sales.

In spite of its reduced contribution to the state's economy, agriculture is still of special concern. Many industries and jobs depend on agricultural commodities. Agriculture continues to occupy a large land area and is closely associated with the people's cultural heritage and attitudes. The protection of agricultural land by zoning offers one of the principal ways to control urban sprawl. And producing crops for local markets keeps the state from being overly dependent on outside sources of food supplies.

The state's agriculture can be divided into three categories: traditional plantation crops (sugarcane and pineapple) produced for export; commodities such as vegetables, eggs, and milk, produced for the local market; and the newer export crops, such as macadamia nuts, flowers, and nursery products.

Statewide, the amount of land devoted to agriculture continues to diminish. In recent years the decrease in acreage of traditional plantation crops has been offset partly by an increase in the acreage of new export crops. However, because many of these crops, as well as commodities produced for the local market, are more labor- and capital-intensive, they occupy much less land area than do sugarcane and pineapple. Vegetables and melons, for example, account for only 4 percent of the crop acreage, and coffee for another 4 percent. Flowers and nursery products likewise require very little land. Moreover, while plantation croplands have included marginal areas, to maximize profits the growers of higher-value diversified crops typically utilize only the most productive land available. In addition, because these crops have a limited market, they are cultivated in much smaller quantities than sugar or pineapple.

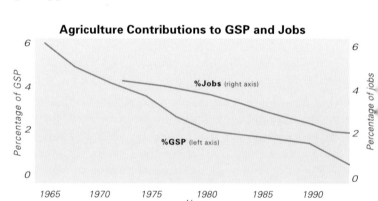

Agriculture Contributions to GSP and Jobs

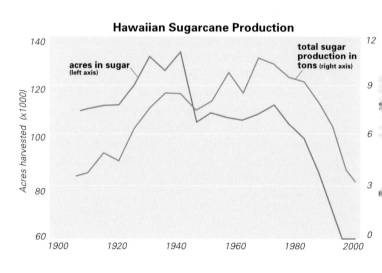

Hawaiian Sugarcane Production

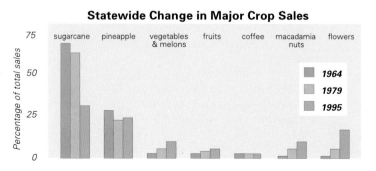

Statewide Change in Major Crop Sales

The graph for crop acreage indicates a nominal, but definite, decline in traditional plantation crop acreage and a corresponding increase in diversified crops. In 1995, sugarcane still predominated, occupying 55 percent of the state's cropland. In crop sales, however, the shift from plantation crops to diversified ones is readily apparent. Overall, agricultural exports (including traditional as well as newer ones) continue to be extremely important, accounting for 68 percent of sales income in agriculture.

With the shift from large plantations to smaller agricultural operations, the average farm size in Hawai'i has continued to shrink. This trend is not surprising, but it contrasts with the situation of most other states and most industrialized countries, where farm size is generally on the rise.

Geographic Specialization

The state's agricultural operations tend to be concentrated in relatively level areas at lower elevations, near the coasts of the mountainous major islands. Growing conditions, influenced by elevation, temperature, rain-

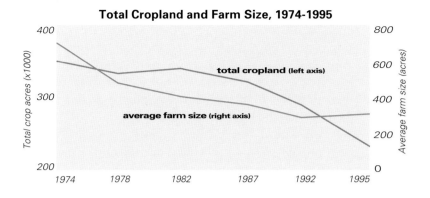

Total Cropland and Farm Size, 1974-1995

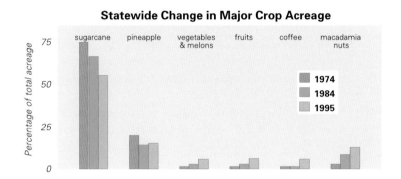

Statewide Change in Major Crop Acreage

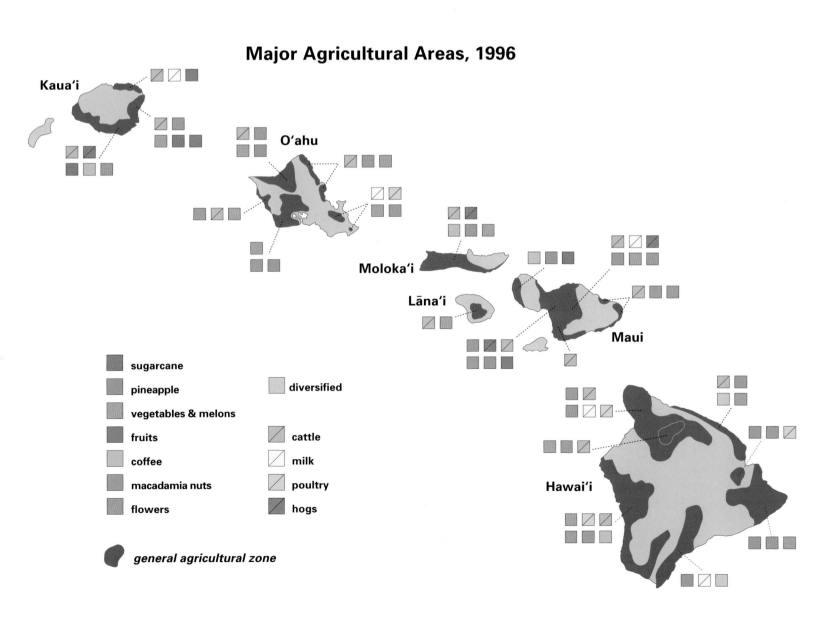

Major Agricultural Areas, 1996

fall, and soil type, can vary considerably over short distances. And, as mentioned above, market and production factors encourage the cultivation of diversified crops on the best land. It is not unusual, therefore, for certain crops to occupy relatively small areas. For example, virtually all of the ginger root is grown along Hawai'i Island's Hāmākua coast, where rainfall is high and soils well drained. Most papayas are cultivated in the Puna District of Hawai'i Island, and almost all onions are produced in the Kula area on Maui.

Regional specialization of agricultural products is a definite statewide trend. One-half of the acres devoted to flower and nursery products are located on Hawai'i Island. With its extensive grasslands, Hawai'i also leads in beef cattle production. Likewise, the island predominates in fruit production and accounts for 94 percent of papaya acreage and over 50 percent of banana acreage.

O'ahu, because of its large urban population and its demand for fresh dairy products, leads in production of milk and eggs and is second only to Hawai'i Island in production of flowers and nursery products. It is the state's top producer of hogs.

Maui accounts for 36 percent of the total sales in vegetables and melons and leads in the production of many individual vegetables, including green peppers, sweet potatoes, tomatoes, and onions. Maui accounts for one-fourth of the state's total crop and livestock sales, about one-half of sugarcane acreage, and slightly less than one-half of pineapple acreage.

As might be expected, Hawai'i Island has more acres of farmland and more agricultural workers than the other islands. But in value of agricultural sales, Hawai'i, O'ahu, and Maui are fairly close. Kaua'i, on the other hand, accounts for only 11 percent of the state's farm workers and 11 percent of agricultural sales.

Food Supply

People in Hawai'i consume a rich variety of foods. Although more than two-thirds of the food supply is imported, some items, such as milk, eggs, and certain fruits and vegetables, are produced in the Islands in

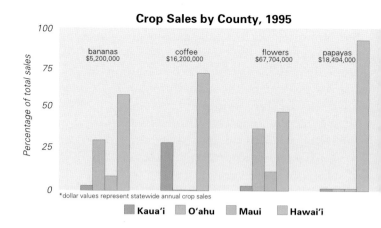

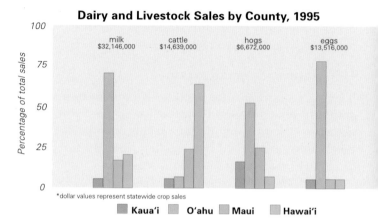

abundance. All of the papayas and pineapples consumed in Hawai'i are grown in Hawai'i, as are most of the head cabbage, Chinese cabbage, green onions, and watermelons. But only 10 percent or less of the demand for broccoli, carrots, and lettuce is met by Hawai'i producers. Farmers boosted their contribution of fresh fruits for the local market from 41 percent in 1984 to 49 percent in 1995, but the proportion of locally grown vegetables during that period declined from 41 percent to 30 percent. Ninety-three percent of the locally consumed beef and veal were imported into the state in 1995, up considerably from 31 percent in 1984. (In recent years, because of the high cost of livestock feed in Hawai'i, beef cattle producers have found it more profitable to export young cattle to the mainland rather than feed them locally.) Fourteen percent of

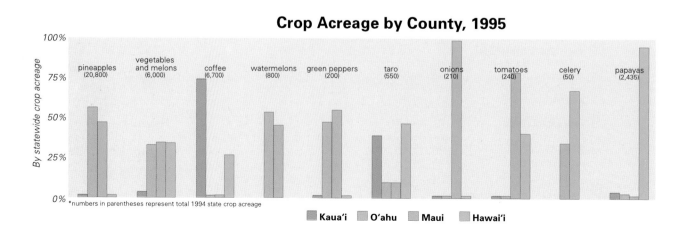

Forest Industry

Forests cover about 1.7 million acres (690,000 ha) in Hawai'i, approximately 41 percent of the state's total land area. About 40 percent of forested land is classified as commercial—that is, suitable for commercial forestry operations. Most is located on Hawai'i Island, which contains some of the most productive forest lands in the world as measured by volume production per acre per year.

Hawai'i's climate and soils are ideal for growing timber, and yet forestry today is not a major industry, largely because to import most forest products is more economical than to produce them locally. In 1993, the forest industry generated an estimated $28.9 million, employed 802 workers, and paid out $23.2 million in wages and salaries. Commercial forestry jobs represent

Forest Product Sales from State Forest Reserves

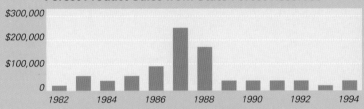

Koa Seedling Production by Hawai'i State Nursery

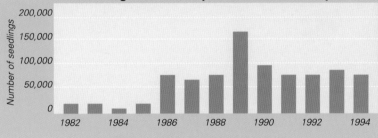

0.1 percent of the total nongovernment jobs for that year. The value of forest product sales from state forest reserves has generally been less than $50,000 annually, except for a brief period in the mid-1980s when chipwood operations significantly boosted the sales volume. However, the state's forests are invaluable for other purposes, such as providing watershed protection, recreational opportunities, and habitat for Hawai'i's unique plants and animals. Nearly all state-owned lands under forest cover are in the Forest Reserve System (643,134 acres [259,826 ha]) and the Natural Area Reserves System (122,703 acres [49,572 ha]). Approximately half of forested lands are privately owned.

Deforestation on the major islands during the 1800s resulted in a loss of watershed protection that brought on serious flooding and soil erosion by the late nineteenth century. To address the problem, in 1901 the territorial government initiated a system of forest reserves, which was completed by World War II. During the 1930s Depression, public work projects (the Civilian Conservation Corps) launched large-scale planting of

eucalyptus, sugi pine, Norfolk Island pine, and many other mostly nonnative species on public and private lands throughout Hawai'i. Although a large-scale commercial forest industry based on plantation timber never materialized, a small but thriving hardwood industry did develop. Today the commercial forest industry includes the hardwood industry, the cultivation of short-rotation tree crops, agroforestry, and the processing of specialty forest products. The most important of these, in economic terms, is the harvest and processing of hardwoods, which take 25–40 years to mature. In highest demand is the native _koa_ tree (_Acacia koa_), a beautifully grained, dense wood that is especially valued for its cultural significance. _Koa_ is fashioned into a range of products from paneling and furniture to bowls and art objects. As of 1996 there were 30 small sawmills processing hardwoods statewide, mostly for use in the local economy. Between 1990 and 1994 the State of Hawai'i Nursery produced an average of 78,000 _koa_ seedlings for outplanting annually.

Short-rotation production utilizes fast-growing tree species that are harvestable in 6 to 12 years for producing chips and wood pulp. These products can serve as fuel for electrical power production or as raw material for the manufacture of paper and composite wood products such as chipboard, particleboard, and plywood. Many species are suitable for short-rotation production, but several species of eucalyptus have been preferred in Hawai'i.

Agroforestry integrates agricultural and timber crops into systems that can be sustained for long periods with minimum inputs of pesticides and synthetic fertilizers. Still relatively new to the Islands, agroforestry is becoming more widespread.

Although locally important, the processing of specialty forest products is generally a small-scale, family-based activity. Such products include greenery for floral arrangements; culturally significant plants for traditional uses, such as _maile_ for leis; and the _hāpu'u_ tree fern (_Cibotium_ species), used for producing laundry starch, orchid planting medium, and fiber filling.

The future for commercial forestry will likely reflect increasing demand for _koa_ and other locally produced hardwood products. Many private landowners are growing high-value hardwoods such as _koa_. While the planting and harvesting of eucalyptus for biomass has all but ceased, the downsizing of Hawai'i's sugar industry has created new opportunities for commercial forestry. Former plantation lands on the Hāmākua coast of Hawai'i Island, for example, are suitable for agroforestry, as well as for the production of both high-quality hardwoods and short-rotation tree species. One international timber company began planting short-rotation timber crops on Hawai'i Island in late 1996, and others have expressed interest in setting up operations.

RONALD CANNARELLA

Sustainable Agriculture

The impressive levels of agricultural production in Hawai'i are often the result of an enormous consumption of nonrenewable, fossil-fuel-based materials such as synthetic fertilizers, herbicides, and insecticides. Sustainable agriculture embraces ecological principles to achieve elimination of dependence on synthetic chemicals, preservation of soil and water resources, and support of rural communities. Sustainable farming relies on farm resources and practices that minimize environmental degradation and hazards to human health. It uses fewer energy resources in raising a wider range of crops and livestock compared to conventional farming. The key ecological principle on sustainable farms is the pursuit of biodiversity, since monoculture (single-crop) systems may invite rapid spread of insects and diseases by providing continuously available host plants. The aim of diversification is to stabilize farm production by spreading the risk associated with growing crops in monoculture.

Throughout history traditional farmers have practiced ecological principles of recycling nutrients and utilizing natural pest controls. Organic farmers also use these farming practices. The increasing number of organic farmers in Hawai'i demonstrates a growing awareness for farming in an environmentally sound, sustainable, and economically viable manner. By 1996, 89 commercial farmers had been certified organic by the Hawai'i Organic Farmers Association (HOFA), and 40 other farmers had received organic certification through other agencies. Many other farmers practice sustainable methods without becoming certified. The economic viability of sustainable farming therefore can only be measured when benefits to human health and the environment are included in the analysis.

Sustainable agriculture practices include:

- interplanting of crops and noncrops, such as trees for fodder and timber (agroforestry), to increase the biodiversity of the farm site
- utilization of on-farm products, such as animal manures, compost, and green manures (cover crops), as soil amendments
- use of crop residues to improve soil fertility, organic matter, and texture
- rotation of crops to enhance soil quality and to interrupt insect, disease, and weed cycles
- maintenance of livestock systems that mitigate soil and water pollution by incorporating animal wastes in a composting system for fertilizing farm crops
- use of biological insect controls, or least-toxic pest management controls when biological agents prove inadequate
- nontoxic weed control methods, such as mechanical cultivation and propane-powered weed burning
- pursuit of measures that bridge the gap between farmers and consumers, including direct marketing, farmers' markets, farmer-chef associations, and community-supported agriculture.

In a National Research Council study of 12 sustainable agriculture systems in the United States, farm yields were found to equal those on conventional farms, and energy consumption levels were less than those of conventional farms. With sugar and pineapple production on the decline throughout Hawai'i, sustainable agriculture systems present a viable new approach for the state's agricultural economy.

KATHLEEN DELATE

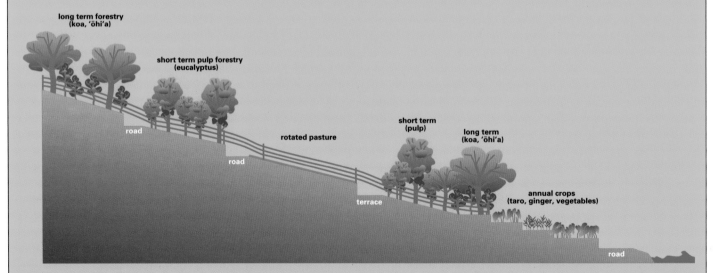

Profile of an Agroforestry System. The diagram illustrates how forestry, grazing, and cropping systems can be linked to produce food and fiber, recycle by-products, decrease use of pesticides and herbicides, and minimize soil erosion for a more sustainable agriculture. Tree plantations that are contour-planted and block-harvested to eliminate large clear-cut areas can be grazed to control grasses and reduce chemical usage. Blocks of long-term forest, planted downhill of short-rotation trees, serve as filter strips that check erosion and runoff. Open pastures maintained between blocks of trees buffer the effects of upslope logging. The flatter lowland areas can be intensively farmed, fallowed, and grazed in cycles to allow organic matter to accumulate in the soil and prevent farmland degradation.

Irrigated *kalo* (taro), Hanalei Valley, Kaua'i. [J. Juvik]

Macadamia orchard, South Kona, Hawai'i. [J. Juvik]

the Islands' supply of pork in 1995 was also imported, down from 21 percent in 1984. The share of eggs produced locally, however, was 78 percent in 1984 and in 1995.

Although this lack of self-sufficiency in food supply has been cause for concern, it is understandable given the physical, social, and economic conditions in Hawai'i. When plantations dominated the state's land use, the cultivation and exportation of sugar and pineapple for a large market were more profitable than producing crops for a small local market. Therefore, emphasis was placed on using as much land as possible

for a single cash crop. As a result, small farming and marketing systems for locally grown crops were never highly developed.

In addition, although the climate and soils in Hawai'i are suitable for sugarcane and pineapple production, yields for many other crops are relatively low. In contrast, yields for many crops in California, as well as production and marketing efficiency there, rank among the highest in the nation. Consequently, Hawai'i-grown crops, especially vegetables, have not been able to compete with produce imported from the mainland. Moreover, given the state's mix of ethnic groups and the large numbers of visitors from abroad, the state could hardly be self-sufficient in the wide variety of foods demanded in the Hawai'i market.

Market Share of Foods Produced in Hawai'i

Commodity	%	Commodity	%
Papayas	100	Avocados	42
Pineapples	100	Tomatoes	31
Watercress	100	Celery	17
Daikon	95	Pork	14
Head Cabbage	92	Onions	12
Chinese Cabbage	92	Cauliflower	11
Watermelons	89	Lettuce	8
Green Onions	88	Beef and Veal	7
Eggs	78	Tangerines	5
Cucumbers	70	Broccoli	4
Bananas	44	Carrots	>1

Diversity of Food

The many ethnic groups that have populated the state—including Hawaiian, American, Japanese, Chinese, Portuguese, Filipino, and others—have contributed to the diversity of foods consumed. The large numbers of people in each of these ethnic groups have created a substantial and continuous market for ethnic foods. Upon arriving in Hawai'i, most immigrants continued to follow the food traditions of their home country, eating the same foods prepared in the same ways.

Today, as during the last several decades, most state residents eat a combination of foods borrowed from several ethnic groups. For instance, most markets carry Portuguese sausage, and sashimi is often served as a party snack and holiday fare in many homes, regardless of ethnic background. Spam is commonly used in musubi, teriyaki steak appears widely in restaurants, and McDonald's restaurants serve saimin noodles. Rice has replaced potatoes in many Western meals, while sandwiches have become common fare for people of Asian ancestry. In short, the people of Hawai'i typically enjoy a diet that reflects the state's ethnic diversity and the bounty of its tropical climate.

JAMES L. KELLY

FISHERIES

Polynesian settlers in Hawai'i adapted a variety of off-shore and nearshore fishing strategies to local waters and invented new fishing techniques. Asians and other immigrants brought additional fishing methods to the Islands. Fishing is an important activity in the local lifestyle and consumption of fresh seafood is important to many cultural traditions in Hawai'i. The charter-boat industry and the state's reputation for sportfishing opportunities contribute significantly to tourism revenues.

Large pelagic fish, including tunas and billfish, range close enough to the Islands to be captured by small recreational and commercial boats. Hawai'i's commercial fishery reached a low point in 1969, when landings totaled less than 10 million pounds. Since then landings have risen, and the 1994 catch reached almost 30 million pounds, worth more than $50 million. The primary source of this growth is the offshore longline fishery, which targets tunas and swordfish. Longline fishing was brought to Hawai'i by early Japanese and Okinawan immigrants who used wooden sampans. Longliners use baited branch lines attached to a single mainline (traditionally of cotton, more recently of monofilament) suspended by surface floats across many miles of ocean. Sampans used to patrol their catch by attaching flags to surface floats, hence the name "flagline" fishing. The mainline is set and hauled in daily, either at night or during the day, depending on the target species. Today's longliners are modern steel-hulled vessels up to 110 feet (34 m) long. Federal regulations prohibit longline fishing within 25–75 nautical miles (46–193 km) from shore to avoid catch and gear competition with smaller troll and handline vessels. Nonetheless, most longline tuna is caught within the 200-mile (320 km) Exclusive Economic Zone, while swordfish is caught as far as 1,500 miles (2,730 km) offshore. The state's commercial longline fleet, which in the mid-1990s consisted of approximately 125 active vessels, produces three-quarters of Hawai'i's commercial fishing revenue, with approximately half coming from traditional tuna species and half from the newly developed swordfish fishery.

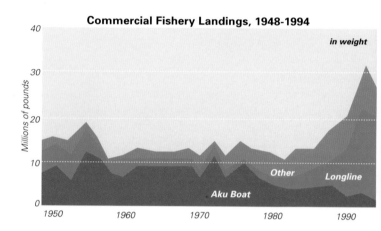

Commercial Fishery Landings, 1948-1994

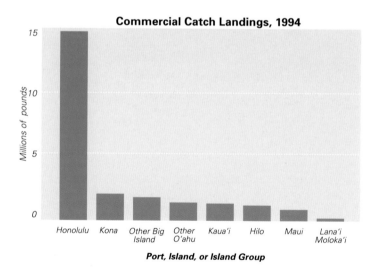

Commercial Catch Landings, 1994

Although longline fishing has been considered environmentally benign, the growth of the swordfish component has raised important questions about by-catch of nontarget species. Longliners setting for swordfish take sharks, many of which are harvested for their fins, and a much smaller by-catch of turtles and seabirds. Swordfish and shallow-set yellowfin tuna longliners also take an incidental catch such as blue marlin, which has concerned small-scale commercial and sports fishermen who place a higher relative value on these species. This concern led to longline area closures around the main Hawaiian islands to reduce conflict in the early 1990s.

Nearshore trolling and handlining for tunas and other species such as mahimahi and ono are common. In Hawai'i these fishermen tend to use smaller vessels (16–40 feet [5–12 m]) than for the longline fishery, with lower per vessel catches, but with many more participants. Some are full-time commercial fishers, but more are part-time commercial or entirely recreational. Tournaments are an important part of the recreational sector and range from small local competitions to large and prestigious international competitions. A number of world record fish for various line classes have been caught in Hawaiian waters.

Trolling is the technique of dragging one or several baited lines behind a boat to lure fish. Many

trollers operate around Fish Aggregating Devices (FADS). Handline fishing for tunas consists of two techniques: *palu ahi* and *ika shibi,* the former being a traditional Hawaiian technique. Anchored or drifting boats drop individual weighted lines over the side, with single baited hooks and sometimes a "chum" sack of bait released at the desired depth. Nighttime *ika shibi,* an Okinawan fishing technique, is important on Hawai'i Island, particularly off Hilo, while daytime *palu ahi* handlining is frequently practiced off Kona. *Palu ahi* is done on established *ko'a* (grounds) and around FADS.

In the early 1980s the Northwestern Hawaiian Islands were rediscovered as a major fishing location, and landings rose to over 3 million pounds (1.35 million kg) of bottomfish (snappers, groupers, and jacks)

Aquaculture

Global fish catches have leveled off and some stocks are drastically declining, so cultured sources must be developed to satisfy growing demand for aquatic foods. The potential of aquaculture to fill the projected 60 million metric ton gap in world aquatic protein supplies in the next century is gaining attention in Hawai'i.

The Islands claim the oldest tradition of aquaculture in the United States, based on the coastal, stone-walled fishponds constructed by early Hawaiians 800 to 1,000 years ago. At present Hawai'i enjoys a growing reputation as a pro-aquaculture development state that encourages private investment and is striving to become a world center for research and technology transfer.

From 1979 to 1995 the number of aquaculture farms increased from 25 to 107; the number of species grown jumped from 7 to 35, and total sales volume went from less than $500,000 a year to more than $13 million a year. Farms have been developed on each of the main islands, with Hawai'i Island and O'ahu having the major concentrations. Technologies employed range from the traditional operation of ancient coastal fishponds to high-technology, intensive culture of microalgae in shallow ponds carved into lava. Major species produced include microalgae, seaweed, freshwater prawns, marine shrimp, Asian catfish, and tilapia.

Hawai'i has pioneered new approaches in aquaculture development by fostering research and technology transfer that creates jobs and brings revenues into the state through the sale of expertise to national and international clients. Revenue from this sector has increased from less than $1 million a year in 1979 to more than $15 million in 1995, largely from federal and private sources.

The trend for aquaculture expansion is expected to continue, as there is no other way to supply the world's need for aquatic foods. Hawai'i's aquaculture industry is successfully growing products in environmentally sound

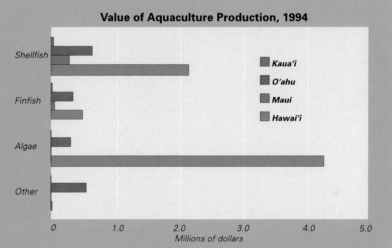

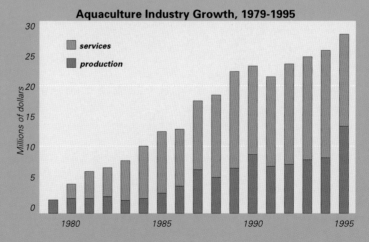

ways for local consumption and export and is sharing innovative technical expertise with Asian and Pacific countries.

JOHN S. CORBIN

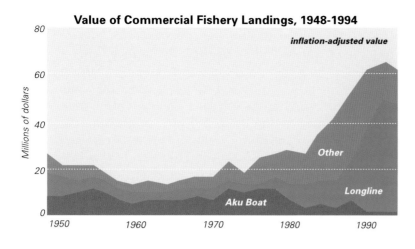

Value of Commercial Fishery Landings, 1948-1994

inflation-adjusted value

Millions of dollars

Other

Aku Boat

Longline

1950   1960   1970   1980   1990

Ahi fishing with handline, South Kona, Hawai'i. [C. Severance]

and spiny and slipper lobster. However, the combination of high operating costs and unsustainable yield levels have led to a stabilization of catch at lower levels, as well as the imposition of limited entry that restricts participation in the fishery to a reduced number of permittees. Today less than 1 million pounds (450,000 kg) of fish are landed from the Northwestern Hawaiian Islands, but these landings still are an important component of the Hawai'i commercial fishery.

The home port of most of the longline and Northwestern Hawaiian Islands fishing fleets is Honolulu, making it one of the top ten commercial fishing ports in the United States. The other commercial, recreational, and subsistence fisheries in Hawai'i operate from smaller harbors, slips, and launching ramps around the state. Hauling small boats by trailer from one launch site to another is a common practice.

Hawai'i's nearshore fisheries, which include the handline fishery for bottomfish and various shoreline reef fisheries, including spearfishing and pole-and-line fishing, face increasing pressure from growing numbers of recreational and commercial participants, as well as nearshore habitat degradation from various sources of pollution. Important species within the nearshore areas include desirable deepwater snappers, *ulua,* and smaller reef fish. Most of their habitat lies in state waters (0–3 nautical miles [0–5.5 km] from shore), so they are currently subject to state rather than federal management. Two important deepwater snappers— *onaga* (*Etelis coruscans*) and *'ehu* (*E. carbunculus*)—appear to be seriously overfished, and the state is implementing management restrictions to protect these bottomfish stocks.

In the immediate future, any further growth in commercial fishing is likely to occur in relatively distant waters. Such growth may reduce commercial/

Suisan fish auction, Hilo, Hawai'i. [J. Juvik]

recreational competition and increase economic and social values for all participants. Meanwhile, both state and federal government regulatory agencies continue to explore methods for maintaining healthy nearshore fisheries and maximizing value-added fisheries, while not overly restricting participation by residents and visitors.

SAMUEL G. POOLEY

THE MILITARY

The military is an important component of the population and economy of Hawai'i. The nearly 100,000 military personnel and dependents make up 8 percent of Hawai'i's population, the highest proportion of any state in the country. Military expenditures of $3.2 billion in 1994 accounted for 9 percent of the Gross State Product (GSP), placing Hawai'i second only to Virginia in proportion of GSP contribution from the military, and almost three times the national mean. Military payroll contributed $2.4 billion to the state's economy in 1994, and major military contracts for construction and services added $803 million. The 17,000 civilian employees of the military, with an annual payroll of $670 million, account for almost 3 percent of Hawai'i's workforce, the highest percentage in any state.

Hawai'i is the headquarters for the commander in chief, U.S. Pacific Command, and all five services are represented. Army personnel make up 44 percent of the total, navy 25 percent, Marine Corps 16 percent, air force 12 percent, and Coast Guard 3 percent. In addition, in 1995 almost 5,000 residents were members of the Hawai'i National Guard. In 1994, 116,000 residents were veterans, and 13,000 (in 1993) were retired from one of the military services.

Military personnel in Hawai'i are almost wholly concentrated on O'ahu: of the 44,000 active duty personnel in 1994, fewer than 200 were assigned to other islands. Although there are about 100 military installations, 78 percent of personnel are stationed at just four of them: Schofield Barracks, Pearl Harbor, Kāne'ohe Marine Base, and Hickam Air Force Base. Most civilian personnel (77 percent) work at Pearl Harbor, Hickam Air Force Base, Tripler Army Hospital, and Fort Shafter Army Base. Pearl Harbor and Schofield Barracks account for 53 percent of military expenditures in Hawai'i, with 38 percent of the spending for prime contracts at Pearl Harbor.

Military activities and facilities such as housing, weapons warehouses, and airstrips require large areas of land. The military owns or controls more than 200,000 acres (80,000 ha), about 5 percent of the state's total land area. The army has the largest landholdings: approximately 150,000 acres (60,000 ha). Although Hawai'i Island has the largest acreage devoted to the military (102,000 acres [41,000 ha]), much more significant are the roughly 80,000 acres (32,000 ha) the military controls on O'ahu—a staggering 21 percent of the island's limited land area. The military also has a distinct influence on O'ahu's population composition. In 1990, 71 percent of military personnel were Whites, 17 percent Blacks, and only 8 percent Asian/Pacific Islanders. This contrasts markedly to the state's overall population, of which 33 percent are Whites, 2.4 percent are Blacks, and 62 percent are Asian/Pacific Islanders. Most active duty military personnel are men (88 percent). Their median age is 27, compared to the state's median age of 35.

Hawai'i's central Pacific location has had a strategic military importance for more than half a century, and it is the key to explaining the large military presence. Hawai'i played a major role as a base of operations during the three major wars in Asia during the twentieth century—WWII, Korean, and Vietnam. Moreover, Pearl Harbor was the site of one of the most

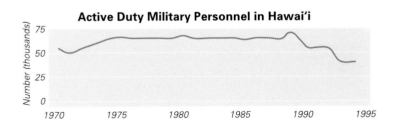

Active Duty Military Personnel in Hawai'i

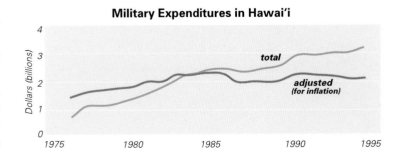

Military Expenditures in Hawai'i

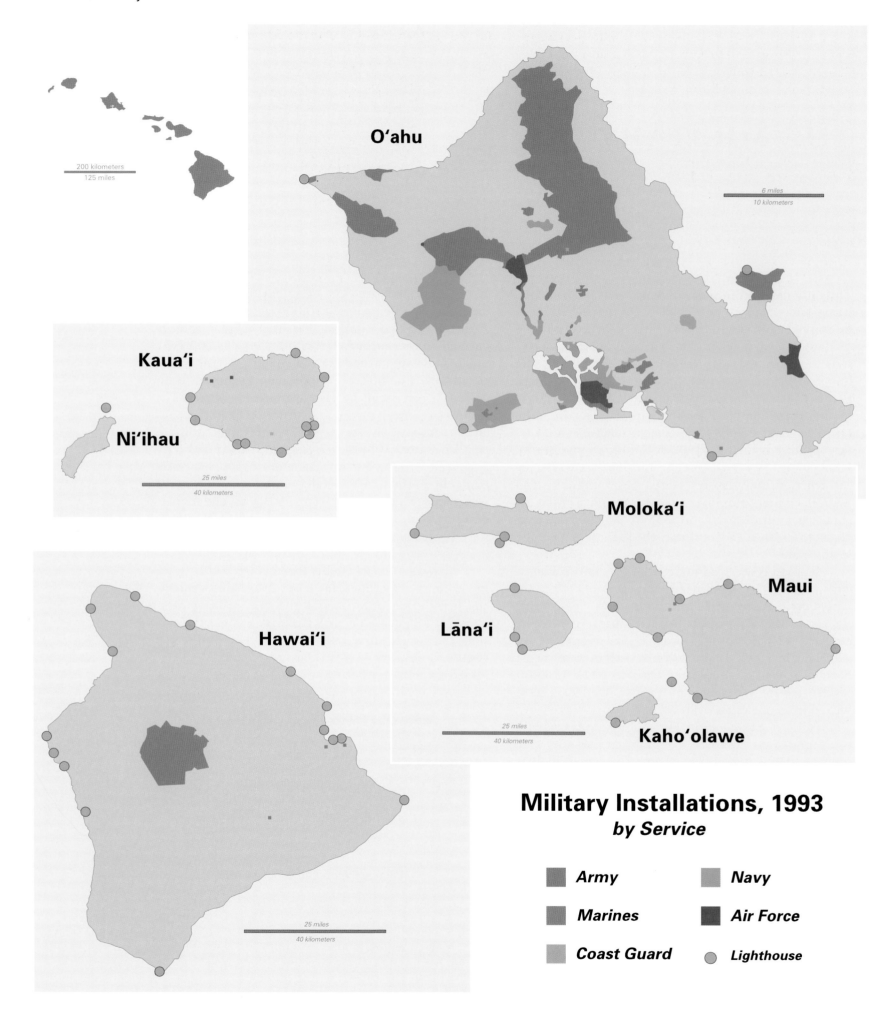

O'ahu

200 kilometers
125 miles

6 miles
10 kilometers

Kaua'i

Ni'ihau

25 miles
40 kilometers

Moloka'i

Lāna'i

Maui

Kaho'olawe

25 miles
40 kilometers

Hawai'i

25 miles
40 kilometers

Military Installations, 1993
by Service

Army   Navy

Marines   Air Force

Coast Guard   Lighthouse

significant events of the twentieth century—the surprise bombing in December 1941 that thrust the United States into World War II. Pearl Harbor came to symbolize the need for military preparedness, which will likely assure a continuing military presence in Hawai'i.

In a decade and a half, the number of active duty personnel in Hawai'i has decreased 28 percent, from 61,019 in 1980 to 44,193 in 1994. During this same period the number of dependents decreased only 15 percent, indicating a change toward more personnel having dependents accompany them to the state. Several reasons may account for the decrease in numbers of active duty personnel. The United States has not been involved in a major war in Asia; therefore, reduced levels of operation have been possible at Hawai'i bases. Likewise, the end of the Cold War has resulted in a decline in number of military personnel as part of national defense cutbacks. Despite the decline in personnel numbers, expenditures for the military in Hawai'i increased from $862 million in 1977 to $3.2 billion in 1994. In constant dollars (adjusted for inflation), however, this increase was less dramatic: from $1.4 billion in 1977 to $2.2 billion in 1994.

The future presence of the military in Hawai'i will probably be shaped by U.S. withdrawal from bases

Military Personnel in Active Service, 1994

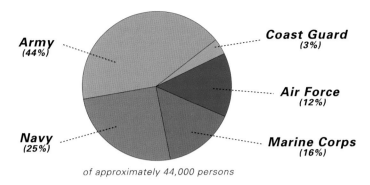

of approximately 44,000 persons

in Asia. The reduction of the U.S. military presence in Okinawa or in South Korea, for instance, may prompt the transfer of some military personnel to Hawai'i. Alternatively, continuing reductions in defense spending could further reduce military expenditures in Hawai'i. While the state possesses the advantage of a mid-Pacific location, training and maintaining military personnel and their dependents in Hawai'i are significantly more expensive compared with other states.

JAMES L. KELLY

TOURISM

Every year Hawai'i draws more than 6 million visitors from the U.S. mainland, Canada, Japan, and many other countries. These visitors come to enjoy a variety of attractions—the balmy climate, a wide offering of recreational opportunities, the varied cultures and famed hospitality of the state's residents, and scenic landscapes ranging from active volcanoes to verdant tropical flora and blue green seas washing onto sandy beaches.

In the late 19th century, small numbers of travelers visited the Islands, lured by romantic tales of the Pacific by writers such as Mark Twain and Robert Louis Stevenson. These mostly wealthy visitors arrived by steamship and headed for the beaches of Waikīkī, with the more adventurous ones making the long overland trek to view Kīlauea Volcano on Hawai'i Island. Hawai'i's exposure during World War II as a strategic military post in the Pacific, the development of wide-body jet transportation, and, more recently, the rising prosperity of the U.S. and Japanese economies transformed the scale of tourism to new heights in the

1990s. From 1959, when less than a quarter of a million tourists visited Hawai'i, to 1990, the visitor industry grew steadily except for brief periods associated with recessions of the U.S. economy and a major airline strike. But events including the Persian Gulf War, the 1992 Hurricane 'Iniki, the reduction in U.S. commercial airline seating capacity to Hawai'i, and Asian financial instability in the late 1990s have been responsible in part for a decline in visitor arrivals. Whether this means that Hawai'i's tourism industry has peaked in terms of growth remains to be seen, but increasingly sophisticated travelers and growing competition from other vacation destinations are presenting fresh challenges to the industry.

Tourism is Hawai'i's economic lifeline. As a small regional economy, Hawai'i has historically been dependent on its export sector for economic growth; today tourism dominates that export sector. In 1994, 6.4 million visitors spent a total of $10.6 billion statewide, while the next largest source of outside dollars, military defense spending, was $3.2 billion. Among the 50

Visitors to Hawai'i, 1993 — Places of Origin

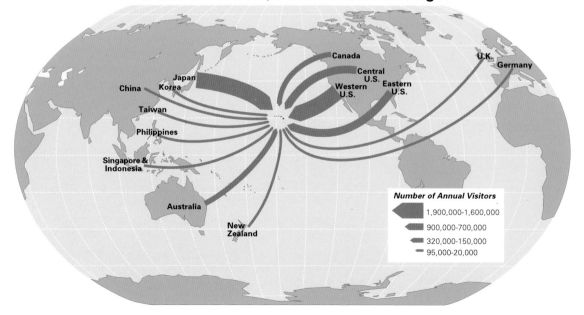

Asia	
Japan	1,592,000
Korea	93,000
Taiwan	76,000
Philippines	27,000
Indonesia/Singapore	25,000
China	21,000
Other Countries	19,000

Europe	
Germany	91,000
United Kingdom	87,000
Other Countries	103,000

Oceania	
Australia	157,000
New Zealand	47,000
Other Countries	14,000

North America	
Western U.S.	1,900,000
Central U.S.	928,000
Eastern U.S.	670,000
Canada	312,000

Number of Annual Visitors
1,900,000–1,600,000
900,000–700,000
320,000–150,000
95,000–20,000

states, Hawai'i is second only to Nevada in its dependence on tourism, although other states (New York, Florida, and California, for example) have larger tourism receipts. The visitor industry directly contributes about 23 percent to Hawai'i's Gross State Product according to World Travel and Tourism Council estimates for 1993. Tourism employs 23 percent of the workforce, accounts for 28 percent of jobs, and generates 23 percent of state and local tax revenues.

Trends

The state's visitors come primarily from the U.S. mainland, Japan, and increasingly from other parts of Asia —a significant change from the mostly U.S. makeup of the tourist population at the time of statehood. By the mid-1980s, economic prosperity in Japan, a strong currency and the relaxation of travel restrictions there, and the introduction of wide-body jumbo jet airliners encouraged millions of Japanese tourists to visit Hawai'i. Coupled with stagnating numbers of U.S. mainland travelers, the surge in Japanese visitors has altered the state's mix of tourists. Notably, the number

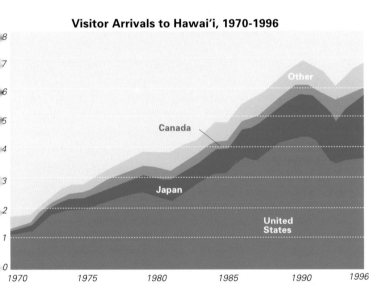

Visitor Arrivals to Hawai'i, 1970-1996

of non-Japanese Asian tourists, particularly from Korea and Taiwan, is growing faster than the number of Japanese tourists, signaling a growing internationalization of Hawai'i as a tourist destination. In 1994, U.S. arrivals accounted for 56 percent of all visitors, compared to 70 percent in 1984. Arrivals from the major West Coast markets of California, Washington, and Oregon tied the Japanese count at 27 percent. Asians (mostly East Asians) represented 32 percent of all visitors. China, with a population of over 1 billion and the fastest growing economy in Asia, is expected to boost the significance of future Asian travel to Hawai'i.

Almost two-thirds of U.S. tourists in 1994 had visited the state previously. Mostly independent travelers rather than participants in planned tours, repeat visitors view Hawai'i as a set of competitive island des-

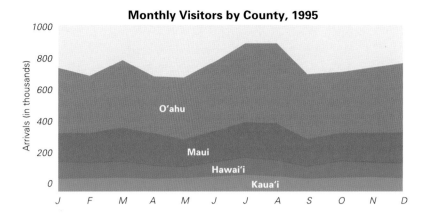

Monthly Visitors by County, 1995

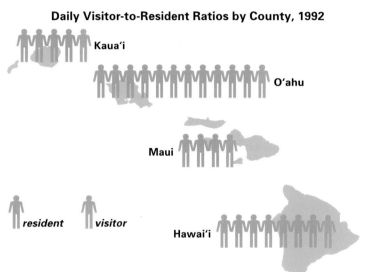

Daily Visitor-to-Resident Ratios by County, 1992

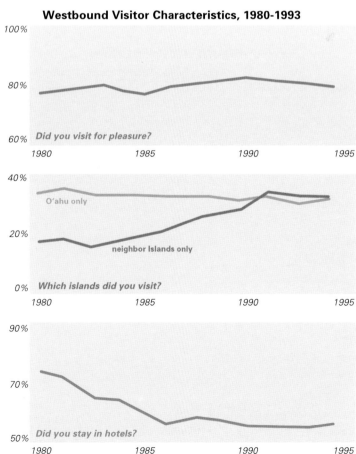

Westbound Visitor Characteristics, 1980-1993

tinations, rather than a single destination. About two-thirds of all U.S. visitors in 1994 planned to visit only one island. Half of them chose urban Waikīkī, on Oʻahu, but the other half chose destinations other than Oʻahu, continuing a trend started in the 1960s toward preference for travel to the less populated and less developed neighbor islands.

Since 1970 the average length of a U.S. visitor's stay in Hawaiʻi has remained relatively stable at 10 days, with differential island stays ranging from 4 days in the Hilo area of Hawaiʻi Island to 7 days on Maui. However, the proportion of U.S. visitors staying in hotels has declined from more than 70 percent in 1980 to 55 percent in 1994, which indicates that more are opting for alternative accommodations.

In contrast to U.S. travelers, the Japanese are

Waikīkī at night. [Hawaiʻi Visitors and Convention Bureau]

largely first-time visitors who depend on group or package tours. On average they outspend U.S. visitors by a 2.5-to-1 margin on a daily basis (less, 1.5 to 1, on spending for trips), with larger shares of their travel dollar going toward the purchase of clothing and souvenirs. For the most part, Japanese tourists stay on Oʻahu and make day trips to other islands, although this is expected to change with direct flights from Tokyo to Kona, Hawaiʻi Island, which began in mid-1996. The 44 percent of Japanese visitors who were repeat visitors in 1994, like U.S. travelers, are increasingly choosing independent travel. More Japanese visitors are renting cars and developing their own daily itineraries, and it is likely that more of them will choose specific neighbor island destinations as time goes by. Reflecting traditional vacation periods in their home country, Japanese visitors stay an average of 6 days in Hawaiʻi, ranging from 2 days on Kauaʻi to 5 days on Oʻahu.

Local Attractions

Environmental quality, scenic landscape, unique natural resources, and recreational opportunities are primary visitor attractions. The state has many accessible beach parks and ocean sites where tourists can swim, sunbathe, and snorkel or scuba dive. Hawaiʻi's dramatic volcanoes are also a major tourist stop. The active volcano Kīlauea attracts about 2.5 million people to Hawaiʻi Volcanoes National Park each year, while Haleakalā National Park on Maui draws approximately 1.4 million visitors annually.

Hawaiʻi's Top 20 Visitor Attractions, 1993

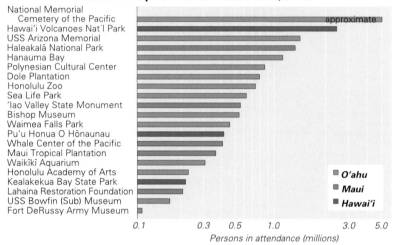

National Memorial Cemetery of the Pacific
Hawaiʻi Volcanoes Natʻl Park
USS Arizona Memorial
Haleakalā National Park
Hanauma Bay
Polynesian Cultural Center
Dole Plantation
Honolulu Zoo
Sea Life Park
ʻIao Valley State Monument
Bishop Museum
Waimea Falls Park
Puʻu Honua O Hōnaunau
Whale Center of the Pacific
Maui Tropical Plantation
Waikīkī Aquarium
Honolulu Academy of Arts
Kealakekua Bay State Park
Lahaina Restoration Foundation
USS Bowfin (Sub) Museum
Fort DeRussy Army Museum

approximate

■ Oʻahu
■ Maui
■ Hawaiʻi

0.1   0.3   0.5   1.0   3.0   5.0
Persons in attendance (millions)

Commerical Recreational Activities

	Kauaʻi	Oʻahu	Molokaʻi	Lānaʻi	Maui	Hawaiʻi
Dinner and Sunset Cruises	2	9			5	5
Lūʻau	2	6			9	3
Polynesian Shows		4			5	4
Tours: Air	11	13	1		21	20
Tours: Ground	13	24	5		10	17
Tours: Ocean	16	27	1	1	34	16
Windsurfing	1	4			12	1
Parasailing		4			5	2
Sailing	3	5			13	4
Kayak and Rafting	4	2			8	5
Scuba and Snorkeling	9	22	1		50	31
Sportfishing	14	24			21	69
Hiking and Climbing					3	3
Bicycling	2				8	5
Walking						5
Horseback Riding	2	3			12	8
Firearm Shooting		5			5	5
Golfing (resort courses only)	4	4	1	2	11	8
Whale Watching	3	5			14	6
Natural Site Visits		1				3

Calendar of Statewide Events

JANUARY

- World Bodyboard Championships - O'ahu
- Criminal Justice Walk - Maui
- Hawaiian Open Golf Tournament - O'ahu
- Quicksilver Longboard Invitiational - O'ahu
- Ala Wai Challenge - O'ahu
- Hale 'Aina Awards - O'ahu
- Hawai'i Special Oympics Winter Classic - O'ahu
- Annual Moloka'i Makahiki - Moloka'i
- Mountain Bike Classic - Hawai'i
- Hula Bowl Football Game - Maui
- Narcissus Festival Night in Chinatown - O'ahu
- Rusty Pro Surf Meet - Maui
- Senior Skins Golf Tournament - Hawai'i
- Maui Marine Art Expo - Maui

FEBRUARY

- Humpback Whale Awareness Month - O'ahu
- Shaun Gayle Pro-Bowl Billiard Invitational - O'ahu
- Punahou School Carnival - O'ahu
- Annual Family Expo - O'ahu
- U.H. Annual Dance Concert - O'ahu
- Waimea Cherry Blossom Festival - Hawai'i
- NFL Pro Bowl Football Game - O'ahu
- Chinese New Year - All Islands
- Makaha World Surfing Championship - O'ahu
- Big Board Surfing Classic - O'ahu
- Annual Richard Mamiya Golf Tournament - O'ahu
- Heart Ball and Silent Auction - O'ahu
- Lei Queen Contest - O'ahu
- Hilo Mardi Gras Festival - Hawai'i
- Great Aloha Run and Walk - O'ahu

MARCH

- Maui Marathon - Maui
- Scottish Heritage Week - O'ahu
- Honolulu Kite Festival - O'ahu
- Annual International Sportkite Championship - O'ahu
- Lahaina Whalefest - Maui
- Cherry Blossom Festival and Pageant - O'ahu
- Annual Mauna Kea Ski Meet - Hawai'i
- Cemiesee Windsurfing Championship - Maui
- Saint Patrick's Day Parade and Party - O'ahu
- Great Hawaiian Rubber Duckie Race/Benefit - O'ahu
- Annual Honolulu Festival - O'ahu
- Prince Kūhiō Festival - Kaua'i
- East Maui Taro Festival - Maui
- Annual Holokū Ball - O'ahu
- Kamehameha Schools' Song Contest - O'ahu
- Miss Hawai'i Teenager Scholarship Pageant - O'ahu

January - April
event locations

APRIL

- Scottish Games - O'ahu
- Honolulu International Bedrace/Parade - O'ahu
- 'Iao Valley 10K Run - Maui
- Kapalua Celebration of the Arts - Maui
- Tin Man Biathlon - O'ahu
- Merrie Monarch Festival and Parade - Hawai'i
- Annual Pro Board Association Competition - Maui
- Big Brothers/Big Sisters 10K Run and Walk - Maui
- Hula Heritage Festival - Hawai'i
- Annual Hula Pākahi and Lei Festival - Maui
- Whale Day - Maui
- Annual Easter Sunrise Service - O'ahu
- May Day by the Bay - Kaua'i

MAY

- Lei Day Celebration - O'ahu
- Nā Holo Wahine 5K Run - Maui
- Spring Arts Festival - O'ahu
- Police Fun Run - Kaua'i
- Cultural Festival - Volcanoes National Park, Hawai'i
- Asian/Pacific Heritage Day - All Islands
- Memorial Day Special Services - All Islands
- Cinco de Mayo Celebration - O'ahu
- Pineapple Festival - Lāna'i
- Ultra Marathon and Relay - Hawai'i
- Annual Kayak Challenge - Moloka'i to O'ahu
- Mauna Lani Big Island Bounty Festival - Hawai'i
- Hawai'i State Fair - O'ahu
- Da Kine Windsurfing Classic - Maui
- Ho'omana'o Canoe Challenge - Maui to O'ahu
- Annual Keauhou-Kona Triathlon - Hawai'i

May - August
event locations

JUNE

- Kapalua Music Festival - Maui
- Aloha State Games - O'ahu
- Office Olympics - All Islands
- Celebration of Hawaiian Trails - All Islands
- Conservation Day Fair at Sea Life Park - O'ahu
- Town & Country Pro-Am Surfing Contest - O'ahu
- Waiki'i Music Festival - Hawai'i
- King Kamehameha Hula Competition/Parade - O'ahu
- Annual Fancy Fair - O'ahu
- Art Night Celebration - Maui
- Hawai'i State Fair - O'ahu
- Taste of Honolulu - O'ahu
- Annual Wailea Tennis Open - Maui
- Annual Historic Park Cultural Festival - Hawai'i
- 10K Run for the Homeless - O'ahu

JULY

- Fourth of July Celebration and Fireworks - All Islands
- Nā Wāhine O Hawai'i Music Festival - O'ahu
- International Festival of the Pacific - All Islands
- Hawaiian Invitational Billfish Tournament - Hawai'i
- Kīlauea Volcano Marathon and Rim Runs - Hawai'i
- Hawaiian Flag Day Celebration - All Islands
- Mauna Kea Hotel Pro-Am Golf Tournament - Hawai'i
- Hilo Orchid Show and Sale - Hawai'i
- Pacific Island Taro Festival - O'ahu
- Annual Makawao Rodeo - Maui
- Parker Ranch Rodeo and Horse Races - Hawai'i
- Nā Hula O Ka'ohikūkapulani - Kaua'i
- Quicksilver Windsurfing Cup - Maui
- Big Island Slack Key Festival - Hawai'i
- Koloa Plantation Days - Kaua'i

AUGUST

- Nā Hula O Hawai'i Festival - O'ahu
- Hilo Junior Open - Hawai'i
- Summer Kite Festival - O'ahu
- Hawaiian Cultural Festival at Pu'ukoholā - Hawai'i
- Hawai'i State Junior Open - O'ahu
- Kī Ho'alu Hawaiian Slack Key Guitar Festival - O'ahu
- Annual Ka Hīmeni 'Ana - O'ahu
- Queen Lili'uokalani Keiki Hula Competition - O'ahu
- Ka Ho'ola'a 'Ana Ceremony - Hawai'i
- State Canoe Racing Championships - various Islands
- Floating Lantern Ceremony - O'ahu
- Hawaiian Professional Championship Rodeo - O'ahu
- Annual Kaua'i County Fair - Kaua'i
- Hawaiian International Billfish Tournament - Hawai'i
- Maui Onion Festival - Maui
- Windward Triathlon - O'ahu

SEPTEMBER

- Kapalua Open Golf Classic - Maui
- Parker Ranch Round-Up Rodeo - Hawai'i
- Adventure Bicycle Trek - Kaua'i
- Terry Fox 10K Race - Kaua'i
- Aloha Festivals - All Islands
- Annual Makahiki Festival - O'ahu
- Moloka'i Music Festival - Moloka'i
- Hawai'i County Fair - Hawai'i
- Annual Nā Wāhine O Ke Kai - O'ahu
- Waikīkī Roughwater Swim - O'ahu
- Maui Channel Relay Swim - Maui
- Haleakalā Run-to-the-Sea - Maui
- Polynesian Festival - O'ahu
- Try-a-Papaya Festival - Hawai'i
- Annual Honolulu Oceanfest - O'ahu

OCTOBER

- Aloha Festivals - All Islands
- Ironman Triathlon - Hawai'i
- Maui County Fair - Maui
- Waikoloa Open Golf Classic - Hawai'i
- Kona Coffee Cultural Festival - Hawai'i
- Ka'anapali Senior Golf Classic - Maui
- Lahaina Historic 5K Fun Run - Maui
- Hilo Macadamia Nut Festival - Hawai'i
- Pearl Harbor Hydrofest - O'ahu
- Honolulu Orchid Society Show - O'ahu
- Annual Taro Festival - Kaua'i
- Hawaiian International Rugby Tournament - O'ahu
- Annual Moloka'i Hoe - Moloka'i
- Discoverer's Day Celebrations - All Islands

NOVEMBER

- Kapalua Invitational Golf Tournament - Maui
- Harbor-to-Harbor Ten Mile Run - Maui
- Annual Turkey Trot - O'ahu
- Ho'omaika Thanksgiving Celebration - Maui
- Mauna Kea Hotel Golf Tournament - Hawai'i
- World Invitational Hula Festival - O'ahu
- Kamehameha School Ho'olaule'a - O'ahu
- Kapalua Invitational Tennis Tournament - Maui
- King's Cup Invitational Golf Classic - Hawai'i
- Kona Coffee Cultural Festival - Hawai'i
- Hawaiian Lacrosse Invitational Games - O'ahu
- Triple Crown of Surfing - O'ahu
- Annual Christmas Crafts Fair - O'ahu, Hawai'i
- Hawaiian International Film Festival - All Islands

September - December
event locations

DECEMBER

- Kapalua Music Festival - Maui
- Long Distance Invitational Roughwater Swim - O'ahu
- Aloha Bowl Football Classic - O'ahu
- Aloha Airlines Tennis Tournament - O'ahu
- Christmas at Hulihe'e Palace - Hawai'i
- Jingle Bell Run - O'ahu
- Honolulu Marathon - O'ahu
- First Night Honolulu - O'ahu
- U.H. Rainbow Basketball Classic - O'ahu
- Holiday Dance Festival - Hawai'i
- Nā Mele O Maui Song and Hula Festival - Maui
- Mākaha Longboard Pro-Am Competition - O'ahu

Numerous resort golf courses, especially on the neighbor islands, garner high ratings from visitors. Sports events are popular with visitors and residents alike. Many are publicized nationally and internationally, especially the Hawaiian Open golf tournament and the Ironman Triathlon. Watersport competitions—surfing, windsurfing, outrigger canoe racing, speedboat racing, and offshore fishing—are also well attended. Other favorite activities include sightseeing, whale watching, hiking, and reef viewing.

Shopping is a major draw in itself, with opportunities ranging from upscale shops in Waikīkī and nearby Ala Moana Center and resort boutiques to the colorful theme shops of Lahaina, Kailua-Kona, and the International Market Place in Waikīkī, to large outlet stores in Waikele on Oʻahu.

Cultural attractions such as the Polynesian Cultural Center, the Bishop Museum, and the Aloha Week Festival are popular must-sees. Festivals and events that celebrate the ethnic diversity of Hawaiʻi's population occur year-round throughout the state and are well attended by both residents and visitors. Of these, the Merrie Monarch Hula Festival is the most widely known. More U.S. visitors rate culture as an important reason to visit Hawaiʻi than do Japanese visitors.

The National Memorial Cemetery of the Pacific and the USS *Arizona* Memorial at Pearl Harbor are major historical attractions where over 1.5 million and 1.4 million visitors, respectively, honor the past each year. Puʻuhonua o Hōnaunau National Historical Park on Hawaiʻi Island, which depicts life before westerners arrived, and ʻIolani Palace on Oʻahu also draw many visitors.

Infrastructure

Hawaiʻi's extensive network of visitor accommodations includes more than 70,000 hotel rooms, condominiums, and other lodgings that are generally located on the sunnier leeward coast of each island. Oʻahu's famous Waikīkī Beach ranks as the oldest, best-known, and most densely developed of the state's resort areas.

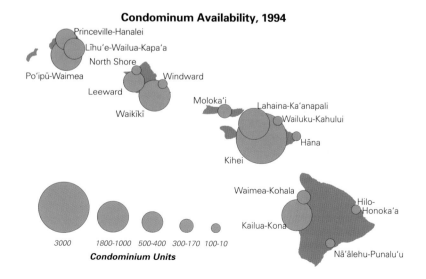

Condominum Availability, 1994

A land area of less than 1 square mile contains 85 percent of Oʻahu's 36,000 hotel rooms. On the islands of Maui, Kauaʻi, and Hawaiʻi, resort development has been rapid, although not as concentrated. In 1965 Oʻahu had 80 percent of all rooms in the state, but that share fell to 50 percent by 1990 because of the increasing popularity of the new neighbor island destinations and a moratorium on room construction in Waikīkī.

While hotel rooms still make up the vast majority of accommodations on Oʻahu, a mix of condominiums and hotel rooms and a scattering of bed-and-breakfast lodgings (particularly in rural areas) are available on the neighbor islands. The prices for accommodations range widely, from luxury resort to budget. Much of the recent luxury property development has occurred on the neighbor islands, where close to 60 percent of the luxury and first-class rooms are located. Oʻahu, by contrast, has 60 percent of the budget-class rooms.

Since 1985 hotel room occupancy rates have been the most stable on Oʻahu and Hawaiʻi Island, with Oʻahu enjoying strong demand for Waikīkī accommodations and the highest occupancy rates, while Hawaiʻi Island has experienced the lowest rates (improving somewhat with the initiation of direct flights from Asia). Occupancy rates on Maui and Kauaʻi have been more variable.

Impacts and the Future of Tourism

Tourism impacts are uneven across the islands. Oʻahu, whose popularity is driven by the familiarity of Waikīkī and its major share of lower-priced hotel accom-

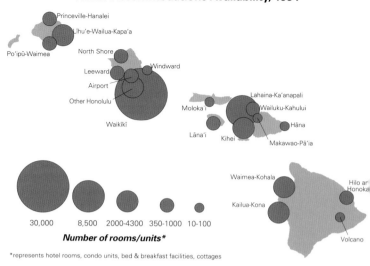

Visitor Accommodations Availability, 1994

*represents hotel rooms, condo units, bed & breakfast facilities, cottages

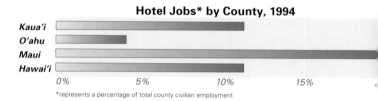

Hotel Jobs* by County, 1994

*represents a percentage of total county civilian employment

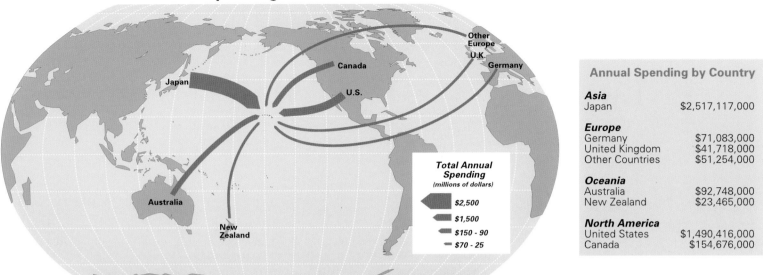

Visitor Spending in Hawaiʻi, 1993

Annual Spending by Country	
Asia	
Japan	$2,517,117,000
Europe	
Germany	$71,083,000
United Kingdom	$41,718,000
Other Countries	$51,254,000
Oceania	
Australia	$92,748,000
New Zealand	$23,465,000
North America	
United States	$1,490,416,000
Canada	$154,676,000

Total Annual Spending (millions of dollars): $2,500; $1,500; $150 - 90; $70 - 25

modations, has the largest number of tourists present on any given day and receives more than half of tourist expenditures in the state yearly. However, the share of tourist dollars spent per resident is lowest on Oʻahu. Its visitor-to-resident ratio—1 per 11 residents—also ranks the lowest, and only 4.4 percent of Oʻahu's labor force is employed in hotels. As the financial and mercantile center and the seat of state government, Oʻahu is home to more than 80 percent of the state's population, so despite tourism's larger presence there, its relative impact is less significant than on Hawaiʻi, Maui, and Kauaʻi.

By contrast, on Maui, the state's second most popular island destination, tourists account for a much bigger part of the population on any given day. With one visitor for every three residents, Maui's hotel industry employs 17 percent of the island's labor force. Visitor patterns on Kauaʻi were comparable to Maui's until the devastating occurrence of Hurricane Iniki in 1992. Since then Kauaʻi's experience has been more similar to that of Hawaiʻi Island in terms of tourist spending per resident, visitor-to-resident ratio, and the proportion of the workforce employed in hotels—all falling between the values for Oʻahu and Maui.

The future direction of tourism will be governed by competition, market changes, and the response of the state's visitor industry. U.S. and Japanese travelers are educated, sophisticated, and aware of the many destination options. The level of competition for tourists is likely to increase as locations with similar vacation offerings in the Caribbean, Mexico, the South Pacific, and Southeast Asia develop and as alternative forms of vacationing, such as cruising, expand. The experience of declining visitor counts due to economic slowdowns in the U.S. and Japan shows that the absence of diversification in tourist markets can be a threat to a healthy tourism sector. But many opportunities exist for increased travel from new markets. Despite the economic slowdown in Japan, and Asia in general, travel in the Asia-Pacific region has been growing more rapidly than anywhere else in the world. Strong Asian economic fundamentals mean that in the long term Hawaiʻi's proximity will be an asset.

The unique natural qualities of the Islands continue to provide the "dream of Hawaiʻi" for many tourists. The Hawaiʻi Visitors and Convention Bureau, which is funded by state taxes and contributions from travel-related businesses, provides information to visitors and works with travel and advertising agencies to promote the state as a destination. The state's travel-related enterprises are working hard to develop activities consistent with Hawaiʻi's image. A convention center in Honolulu was completed in 1998. Eco- or nature-oriented tourism is expanding, and hotels and other lodging facilities are altering their accommodation packages to encourage family travel. In recognition of the significance of air transportation, tourism-related businesses are working more closely with airline companies to provide greater capacity to the Islands.

Hawaiʻi has always offered something special for visitors to what Mark Twain described as "the most beautiful fleet of islands anchored in any ocean." Hawaiʻi should continue to provide something special if it adapts to changes in the marketplace and continues to recognize the importance of preserving and sustaining those unique assets that attracted visitors in the first place.

MARCIA SAKAI

ENERGY

For decades the energy supply in Hawai'i has been much less diversified than that of the United States as a whole. In 1995, 87 percent of Hawai'i's total energy came from oil, 5 percent from biomass and municipal waste, 5 percent from coal, and 3 percent from other sources. By way of comparison, in 1995 the nation relied on petroleum for only 38 percent of its energy, while natural gas supplied 25 percent, coal provided 22 percent, and nuclear power generated 8 percent. Hydroelectricity and other sources provided 7 percent of the nation's energy.

Formal recognition of the economic and security problems caused by Hawai'i's overdependence on a single energy source began in the mid-1970s, soon after the "energy crisis" caused by the sharp rise in world petroleum prices. Since then state government programs have focused on improving energy efficiency, conserving energy, shifting to locally available energy resources, planning for emergencies, and developing long-term planning capabilities.

Nonrenewable Energy Resources

Hawai'i's residents paid almost $1.7 billion for energy in 1995, or 5 percent of the Gross State Product. On a per capita basis, energy bills are fairly low—forty-fourth in the nation for 1994—because less energy is used per person, but proportionately more is paid for the energy used. Overall, state energy prices were the seventh highest in the country in 1994.

Both the public and private sectors have made significant progress in reducing energy demand. Between 1980 and 1995, the resident population in Hawai'i grew by 22 percent, the number of visitors by 63 percent, and the number of registered vehicles by 42 percent. During that same period, energy consumption rose only 12 percent, the result of improved technologies that allow for more efficient use of energy.

By far the most oil-dependent of the 50 states, Hawai'i imported 34 percent of its crude petroleum from Alaska in 1996 and the remainder from the Asia-Pacific region, primarily Indonesia. Oil exports from both areas are projected to decrease significantly by the year 2000, and thus reliance on other sources will increase. In recent years, use of oil for electrical power generation has dropped. About one-third of the total energy consumed statewide is used for electricity. Through 1991 oil fueled about 90 percent of electrical power generation, but by 1995 the share had fallen to 74 percent, despite strong growth in demand.

In some places new demand is being met by locally available, renewable energy resources. However, the most significant diversification in power generation has been the addition of a coal-fired plant on O'ahu. Rated at 180 megawatts, the AES Barbers Point plant is one of the state's two largest power plants. It began full-scale operation in 1992 and in 1995 provided approximately 13 percent of O'ahu's generating capacity and 19 percent of that island's electricity. Using low-sulfur Indonesian coal and modern fluidized-bed-combustion technology, the plant's emissions amount to less than one-half those permitted under the standards of the federal Clean Air Act. The cement and sugar industries also burn coal for internal power and process heat, in some cases, for export to the local utility. In 1995 coal contributed nearly 1.7 billion kilowatt-hours to the Islands' electrical grids.

Transportation is a major use of energy resources,

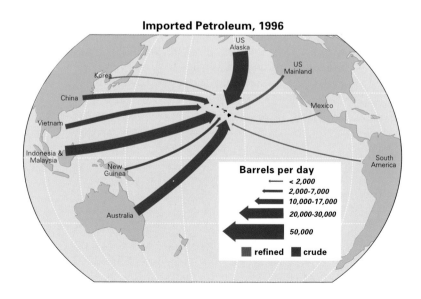

Imported Petroleum, 1996

US Alaska
US Mainland
Korea
China
Mexico
Vietnam
Indonesia & Malaysia
New Guinea
South America
Australia

Barrels per day
< 2,000
2,000–7,000
10,000–17,000
20,000–30,000
50,000

■ refined ■ crude

Energy Production and Consumption in Hawai'i, 1994

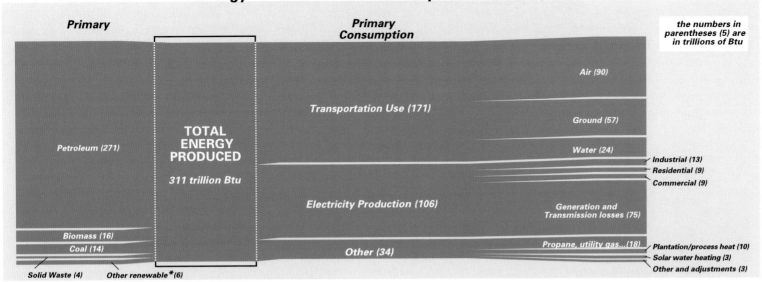

Primary

Primary Consumption

the numbers in parentheses (5) are in trillions of Btu

Petroleum (271)

TOTAL ENERGY PRODUCED

311 trillion Btu

Biomass (16)

Coal (14)

Solid Waste (4)   Other renewable *(6)

Transportation Use (171)

Air (90)

Ground (57)

Water (24)

Industrial (13)

Residential (9)

Commercial (9)

Electricity Production (106)

Generation and Transmission losses (75)

Other (34)

Propane, utility gas...(18)

Plantation/process heat (10)

Solar water heating (3)

Other and adjustments (3)

*represents hydroelectric (1.5), geothermal (1.8), wind (0.2), and solar water heating (2.8)

Oil-fired Kahe electrical generation plant, O'ahu. [J. Juvik]

Puna Geothermal Venture geothermal power plant, Puna District, Hawai'i. [Hawai'i Department of Business, Economic Development and Tourism]

H-POWER, garbage-to-energy plant, Barbers Point, O'ahu. [Hawai'i Department of Business, Economic Development and Tourism]

Kamao'o Wind Farm, South Point, Hawai'i. [J. Juvik]

consuming nearly two-thirds of the petroleum supply in Hawai'i and more than three-quarters of it in the nation as a whole. Because of Hawai'i's geographical location, 36 percent of the oil was used for air transportation in 1995 compared to only 13 percent for the United States as a whole. Ground and marine trans-

portation account for over 31 percent of the oil used. Reducing the use of oil for transportation in Hawai'i has proven more difficult than supplanting oil-fired electricity. Conservation efforts by state and county governments have included the promotion of ride sharing, mass transportation, and telecommuting.

Natural gas is unavailable in Hawai'i, but synthetic natural gas (SNG) and propane are used, primarily by the commercial, industrial, and residential sectors. The output of the state's single SNG plant on O'ahu could be significantly expanded without additional imports of petroleum, from which synthetic natural gas is manufactured, but to date the level of demand has not warranted such an expansion.

The state's Public Utilities Commission requires all energy utilities to develop integrated resource plans in an effort to balance traditional "supply-side" responses—such as the construction of additional power plants—with "demand-side management" measures, including conservation and the shifting of power loads from peak-use periods to times of lower demand. The commission has also mandated that supply-side plans include alternative energy resources and address the social, cultural, and environmental impacts of various energy options. The state and county governments also participate in this integrated resource planning.

Sources of Renewable Energy

Efforts to increase the share of energy supplied by locally available, renewable resources continue. It is estimated that in 1995 renewable resources displaced 3.4 million barrels of oil and reduced carbon dioxide emissions by nearly 1.7 million tons. Some renewable sources, such as wind, hydroelectricity, geothermal power, solar thermal for water heating, photovoltaics, and certain applications of biomass are already cost-effective in Hawai'i.

Historically, the largest local energy source has been biomass, which in 1980 provided 13 percent of the state's electricity. By 1995, that share had shrunk to 6.4 percent of the state's total electricity—or about 674 million kilowatt-hours—and about 57 percent of this power production came from the combustion of municipal solid waste at O'ahu's H-POWER plant,

which began operating in 1989. This decline in biomass-fueled energy production resulted from the dwindling of the primary fuel supply, bagasse, as sugarcane acreage decreased during the 1970s and 1980s. Biomass remains a critically important resource, since it can serve both as a fuel for electricity generation and as a feedstock for liquid and gaseous fuels. The development of new production technologies that could make biofuels competitive in Hawai'i has sparked a resurgence of interest in ethanol and methanol fuels. Other projects that could boost biomass use include the construction of a demonstration bagasse gasifier on Maui and statewide research into species of grasses and trees suitable for biomass plantations.

The second most significant renewable source of electricity in the state is geothermal energy. Exploration into this resource began in the 1960s on the flank of Kīlauea volcano. In 1976, a 6,450-foot-deep (1,966 m) well was completed and flashed. The HGP-A demonstration geothermal power plant was constructed in Puna, on Hawai'i Island, with support from both public and private sector agencies. Operating from 1982 to 1989, the 2.5-megawatt facility proved the commercial viability of the geothermal resource, which at 676°F (358°C) ranks among the hottest in the world. Between 1985 and 1989, experiments in the direct use of geothermal heat for food drying, plant propagation, and other purposes were conducted at the site.

Some 24,300 acres (9,800 ha) of land on Hawai'i and Maui are now designated as "subzones" where geothermal development is authorized. Currently there is only one commercial geothermal power plant—the 25-megawatt Puna Geothermal Venture facility—which contributed 228 million kilowatt-hours, or roughly 24 percent of the electricity used on Hawai'i Island in 1996. State monitoring of air quality surrounding the geothermal plant site is ongoing, and research continues on geologic history, groundwater chemistry, seismic events, and geothermal reservoir pressure. However, the current use and further development of this resource remains controversial, given the concerns raised by some members of the community over safety, the health effects of geothermal emissions, Native Hawaiian rights, and land use conflicts.

The most common renewable energy technology in Hawai'i—and one most residents can utilize—is solar water heating. With more than 60,000 household systems installed, Hawai'i boasts the highest per capita use of solar water heating in the nation. These systems provide approximately 733 billion Btu of heat energy annually and contribute more energy than any other renewable energy resource statewide except for biomass and solid waste. Most systems were installed in the late 1970s and early 1980s, encouraged by generous federal tax credits. When these credits expired, installations declined rapidly from several thousand

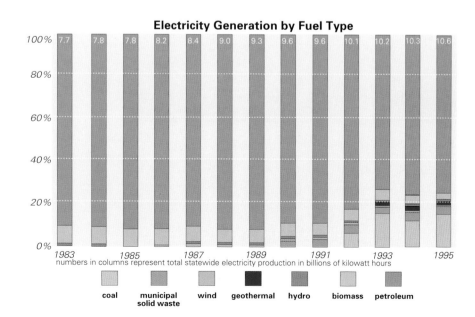

Electricity Generation by Fuel Type

numbers in columns represent total statewide electricity production in billions of kilowatt hours

coal   municipal   wind   geothermal   hydro   biomass   petroleum
        solid waste

per year to a few hundred per year statewide. In 1989, the state increased its own tax credit to 35 percent; since that time installations have averaged over 1,000 systems a year. In 1994, 2,127 residents claimed the credit for solar devices.

Another popular solar option, especially for residences in rural areas not served by the electric utility grid, is photovoltaics. The earliest known residential solar-electric systems date back to the early 1970s; today, estimates of the number of homes powered by photovoltaics range in the thousands. There are also a few grid-connected demonstration residences and two large grid-connected systems—a 20-kilowatt photovoltaic installation at Kīhei, Maui, and a 15-kilowatt rooftop system on a county gymnasium in Kailua-Kona. Photovoltaic modules are commonly used by various agencies for emergency highway telephones, remote seismic-monitoring equipment, and navigational beacons. To date, larger-scale solar technologies have not enjoyed similar success, although the use of solar-thermal electric technologies for utility power generation has been studied.

Hawai'i also has excellent wind resources, which provided 23 million kilowatt-hours of electricity in 1995. Wind power plants with capacities of several megawatts each were installed at Kahuku on O'ahu and at Kahuā Ranch, Lālāmilo, and South Point on Hawai'i Island. The Kahuku development included the world's largest wind turbine, with a generating capacity of 3.2 megawatts. Equipment failures and high maintenance costs, however, have affected the commercial success of wind power; some machines—for instance, at the Kahuku and Kahuā sites—have since been removed from service, while repairs and renovations have temporarily reduced the output of others. Modern, state-of-the-art wind turbines could provide electricity less expensively than the models currently installed.

Hydroelectricity is among the oldest electricity resources in the Islands, with some plants dating back to the late 1800s. Hydroelectric plants in Hawai'i use no dams; they rely on the natural flow of water at their stream sites and, as such, are intermittent electricity providers like wind and solar facilities. Statewide there are 20 hydro plants with capacities of 0.2 megawatt or greater; most are owned and operated by sugar companies. The only utility-owned hydro plants are on Hawai'i Island, as is the newest and largest plant, a 12-megawatt system operated since 1993 by the Wailuku River Hydroelectric Company. Hydroelectricity contributed 103 million kilowatt-hours to the state energy supply in 1995.

The world's premier research site for the development of ocean thermal energy conversion (OTEC) technologies is the Natural Energy Laboratory of Hawai'i Authority facility at Keāhole Point on Hawai'i Island.

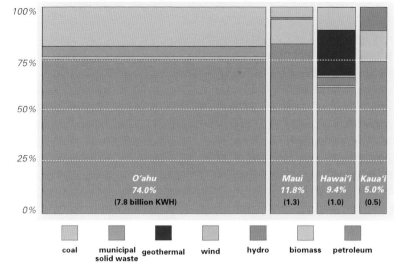

County Electricity Generation by Fuel Type, 1995

O'ahu 74.0% (7.8 billion KWH) — Maui 11.8% (1.3) — Hawai'i 9.4% (1.0) — Kaua'i 5.0% (0.5)

coal — municipal solid waste — geothermal — wind — hydro — biomass — petroleum

OTEC utilizes the temperature differences, which can range up to 40°F (22°C), between water pumped in from the warm ocean surface and the cold depths (2,000 feet [610 m] or greater) to generate electricity. The deep, cold water is also rich in nutrients and nearly pathogen-free, making it valuable for a broad range of aquaculture and agriculture enterprises. The cold water is suitable for chilled-water air conditioning systems as well.

Closed-cycle OTEC was first demonstrated in Hawai'i in 1979 by the Mini-OTEC barge, which had a gross electrical output of 52 kilowatts. Experimentation continued through the 1980s, and ground was broken in 1993 at Keāhole Point for a new plant to test improved components. An experimental open-cycle OTEC plant, rated at 210 kilowatts gross output, began intermittent operation in 1994. Open-cycle OTEC can produce desalinated water as well as electricity.

As part of an effort to diversify transportation fuels, a major electric vehicle demonstration program, partially funded by the federal government, began in 1993. Some electric vehicles are being converted from internal combustion engines, while others are initially designed as electric vehicles. The program will include more than 60 sedans, trucks, vans, buses, and boats statewide. Electric vehicles have also been demonstrated by the university and private enthusiasts.

Other alternative fuel initiatives have included ethanol- and methanol-powered vehicle fleets at public agencies and the University of Hawai'i. Propane, the most widely used and only commercially available alternative fuel in the state, powers more than 3,000 vehicles.

ANDREA GILL BECK

TRANSPORTATION

Hawai'i's transportation network differs from that of the other 49 states in several ways. First, and most obviously, Hawai'i is the only state that must rely entirely upon air and sea transport for exports and imports. Its archipelagic geography also rules out any statewide system of land transportation. Furthermore, the state's lack of self-sufficiency in agriculture and industry creates an imbalance between westward and eastward trade, causing a major backhaul problem for both air and sea carriers. This imbalance is reflected in freight rates, which in turn boost the cost of living.

Hawai'i's highly centralized administration of transportation infrastructure also differs from that of other states. When Hawai'i became a state in 1959, the Department of Transportation was established to administer major ports, airports, and highways. The Harbors and Airports Divisions of the Department of Transportation owns and operates all major ports and airports, while the responsibility for state roadways rests with the Highways Division.

Ground Transportation

Private vehicles are by far the major form of transportation for residents commuting to work and general activities. All major indicators of road transportation use are rising. A sample of the trends follows.

- The number of registered passenger vehicles (automobiles, pickup trucks, and vans) rose from around 600,000 in 1984 to more than 691,000—or 586 motor vehicles per 1,000 population—in 1994.
- In 1994 the total of freight trucks, tractor-trailers, and other motor carriers was about 31,500. There also were 3,772 buses statewide, most of them used as tour buses for visitors.
- From 1984 to 1994 the annual total of miles logged by all vehicles jumped from about 6.5 billion to

H-1 Freeway, O'ahu. [J. Juvik]

Registered Motor Vehicles by County, 1950-1994

Total Vehicles Registered by County, 1994

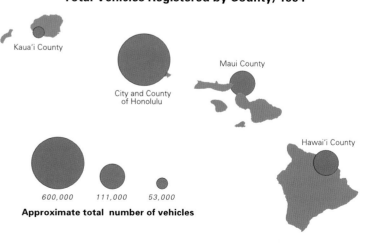

more than 7.9 billion—in excess of 9,000 miles (14,400 km) per vehicle.

- In 1994 close to 745,400 licensed drivers (compared to around 657,000 in 1989) had access to more than 4,100 miles (6,500 km) of roads throughout the state.

- Streets and highways have become more crowded as motor vehicle density has increased from 280 vehicles per mile (175/km) of road in 1985 to 314 vehicles per mile (196/km) in 1994.

The state's urban road networks contrast with those of most other U.S. cities because Hawai'i's mountainous topography makes it difficult to lay out streets on a north-south/east-west grid, as is common on the mainland. Instead, streets run *mauka* (toward the mountains), *makai* (toward the sea), and between major physical features (such as Diamond Head and the Wai-'anae Mountains). Three interstate highways, H-1, H-2, and H-3 serve O'ahu. H-3 was under construction for 25 years; it finally opened at the end of 1997, at a total cost of about $1.6 billion.

Honolulu is the only city in the state with a major mass-transit system. In 1994 the system used 495 buses to carry more than 79 million passengers a total distance of more than 19 million miles, collecting $24.8 million in revenues—an increase of $4.1 million over the previous year. Kaua'i and Hawai'i Island also have islandwide public bus systems, but Maui does not. Kaua'i's system officially opened in 1995, following the phase-out of the highly popular, federally financed transit program that operated after Hurricane Iniki. Kaua'i's 28 buses and vans serve 18 routes daily and provide door-to-door transportation for disabled and senior citizens. Hawai'i Island's "Hele-On" bus system, in operation since 1975, maintains 12 daily routes. In 1994 the system accommodated about 310,000 passenger trips, generating around $570,000 in revenues.

Although Hawai'i is the only state in the country without a common-carrier railroad, seven such railroads

operated in the past—two each on O'ahu, Hawai'i, and Kaua'i, and one on Maui. The last of these went out of business in 1947. Small, private railroads continue to provide a few train rides for tourists and railroad hobbyists.

Overseas Shipping

Inevitably, the history of Hawai'i and the development of overseas (mainland and foreign) shipping in the Islands have been linked. The arrival of the first Polynesians by canoe, the exploration of the Hawaiian Islands by Captain Cook in 1778, and the birth of the

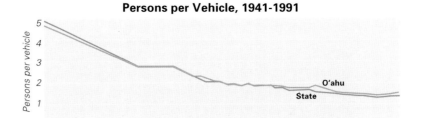

Persons per Vehicle, 1941-1991

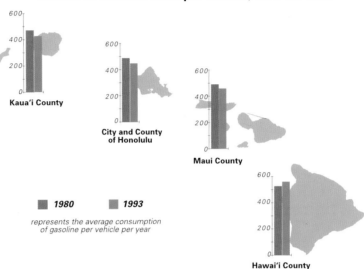

Gallons of Gasoline Used per Vehicle, 1980 vs. 1993

Kaua'i County

City and County of Honolulu

Maui County

■ 1980 ■ 1993

represents the average consumption of gasoline per vehicle per year

Hawai'i County

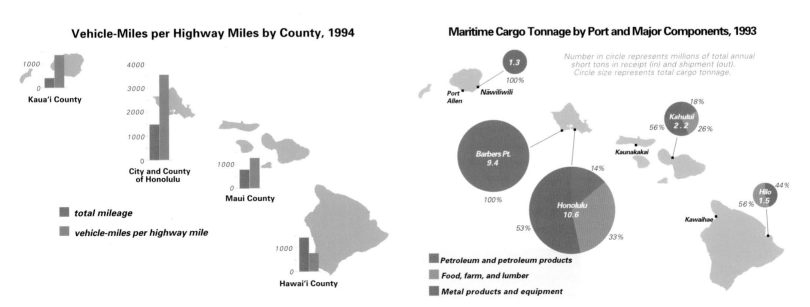

Vehicle-Miles per Highway Miles by County, 1994

Kaua'i County

City and County of Honolulu

Maui County

■ total mileage
■ vehicle-miles per highway mile

Hawai'i County

Maritime Cargo Tonnage by Port and Major Components, 1993

Number in circle represents millions of total annual short tons in receipt (in) and shipment (out). Circle size represents total cargo tonnage.

Port Allen • Nāwiliwili 1.3 100%

Barbers Pt. 9.4 100%

Honolulu 10.6 53% 33% 14%

Kahului 2.2 18% 26% 56%

Kaunakakai

Hilo 1.5 44% 56%

Kawaihae

■ Petroleum and petroleum products
■ Food, farm, and lumber
■ Metal products and equipment

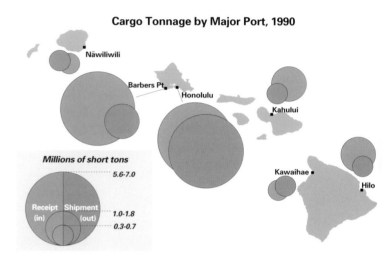

A Sea-Land container yard and cranes. A container ship is being assisted into Honolulu Harbor by a tug. [G. Hofheimer/courtesy of Sea-Land]

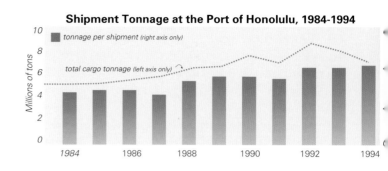

predominant domestic shipping company, Matson Lines, in 1882 all attest to this relationship. However, there have been cost disadvantages in Hawai'i's dependence on ocean transportation. The Merchant Marine Act of 1920, commonly called the Jones Act, requires that passengers and cargo moving from one port to another within the United States must be carried on vessels built and registered in the United States, as well as owned and operated by U.S. citizens. Traffic between Hawai'i and the mainland is covered by this legislation; therefore marine transportation costs are higher than if this trade were open to lower-cost foreign competition. U.S. congressional support for the Jones Act argues that any additional cost to Hawaiian consumers (and others) is outweighed by the national economic and security benefits resulting from the Jones Act.

Eight regular shipping services currently operate between Honolulu and the mainland, most of these being tug-and-barge operations. The amount of cargo shipped between Hawai'i and the mainland in fiscal year 1995 was almost 6.3 million tons, declining from around 6.9 million tons in fiscal year 1994. Twelve shipping lines also provide regular freight transportation between Honolulu and major ports in Asia, Australia, New Zealand, and the Pacific Islands, with connections to Europe as well.

No passenger liners have served the state on a regular basis since service by the Pacific Far East Lines was terminated in early 1978. However, 23 overseas cruise ships docked in Honolulu in 1995.

Interisland Shipping

Although many small operators provided interisland (within the state) shipping service in the past, the first major carrier was the Inter-Island Steam Navigation Company, which commenced operations in 1883. After this firm merged with the Wilder Steamship Company in 1905, it was the only interisland operator until 1935, when Young Brothers began its tug-and-barge

service. Inter-Island ceased operations in 1950. Since then Young Brothers has been the only exclusively interisland water common carrier. The only other significant carrier in the interisland trade is Matson Lines, which transships—that is, transfers cargo previously shipped from elsewhere—between the islands.

No significant interisland water passenger service has existed since 1949, except for a service using hydrofoils that operated from 1975 to 1978. In 1980 the passenger liner USS *Independence* began weekly cruises among the islands, carrying an average of 750 passengers per week. In 1982 she was joined by her sister ship, the USS *Constitution,* which went out of service in mid-1995.

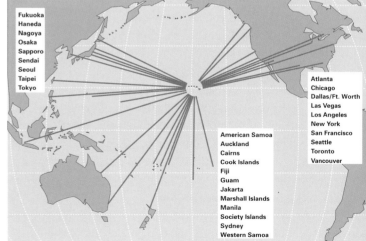

Major Interisland Flights and Airports, 1994

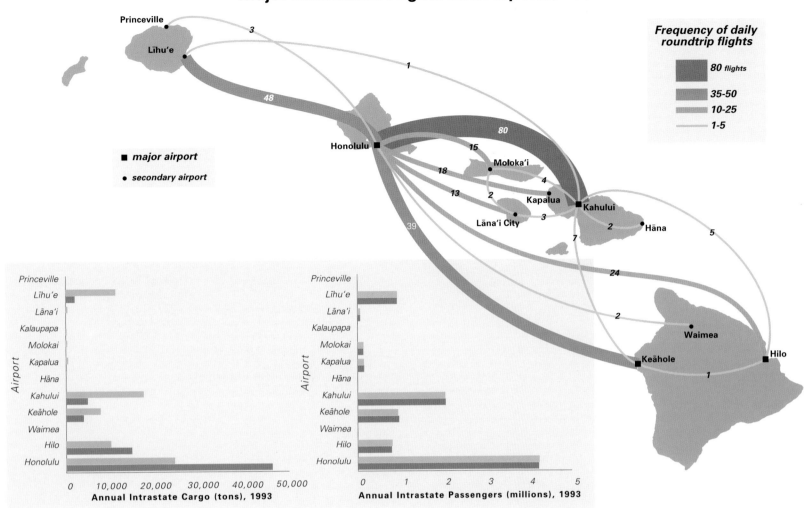

Frequency of daily roundtrip flights

- 80 flights
- 35-50
- 10-25
- 1-5

■ major airport
● secondary airport

Annual Intrastate Cargo (tons), 1993

Airport: Princeville, Līhuʻe, Lānaʻi, Kalaupapa, Molokai, Kapalua, Hāna, Kahului, Keāhole, Waimea, Hilo, Honolulu

x-axis: 0, 10,000, 20,000, 30,000, 40,000, 50,000

Annual Intrastate Passengers (millions), 1993

Airport: Princeville, Līhuʻe, Lānaʻi, Kalaupapa, Molokai, Kapalua, Hāna, Kahului, Keāhole, Waimea, Hilo, Honolulu

x-axis: 0, 1, 2, 3, 4, 5

Overseas Air Carriers

The first commercial flights to Hawaiʻi began in 1936, and until 1969 the air trade between the Islands and the mainland was plied by only three carriers: Pan-American World Airways, United Airlines, and Northwest Orient Airlines. The Pacific air route awards of 1969 added five additional airlines to this list. Federal decontrol of the airline industry, starting in 1977, led to a number of carriers entering and leaving the Hawaiʻi-mainland market. In 1994 there were 33 overseas air carriers linking Hawaiʻi with the major cities of the world.

Honolulu International Airport ranked as the fifteenth busiest airport in the country in 1994, handling 22.9 million passengers (both overseas and interisland). Statewide, approximately 35.6 million passengers arrived and departed from the Islands' 13 commercial airports, an increase of 5.2 percent over 1993. About 473,000 tons of cargo were enplaned or deplaned, up 10.4 percent over 1993. The total amount of airmail loaded and unloaded rose 3.5 percent from the previous year, to 113,000 tons.

Honolulu International Airport. [Hawaiʻi Department of Transportation]

Interisland Air Transportation

Hawaiian Airlines inaugurated scheduled air carrier service between the major islands in 1929, and it remained the only approved scheduled carrier until Trans-Pacific Airlines (now Aloha Airlines) was

Major Weekly Outbound Flights from Honolulu, January 1993

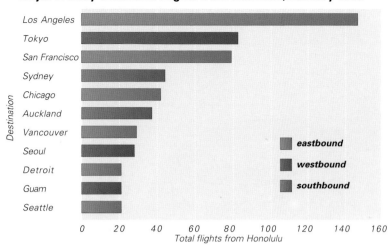

granted an operations permit in 1949. While these two airlines remain the dominant interisland carriers, others have started service, and some of these have subsequently terminated flight operations. The state's airline network claimed 4 of the 25 busiest city-pair markets (in terms of inbound and outbound passengers) in the United States during 1994: Honolulu-Kahului (number 5), Honolulu-Līhu'e (number 16), Honolulu-Keāhole, Kona (number 21), and Honolulu-Hilo (number 24). In 1994 more than 9.9 million passengers (up 30 percent from 1984), 74,000 tons of cargo, and nearly 14,000 tons of mail were transported intrastate.

DAVID BESS
AND HENRY MARCUS

COMMUNICATIONS

As an isolated archipelago in the middle of the world's largest ocean, Hawai'i has always faced tremendous obstacles to communication within the state and with the outside world. Hawai'i's multi-ethnic population likewise gives a distinctive character to some forms of communication such as newspapers and local radio and television programming. This discussion focuses on the historical roots, technological evolution, and developmental trends of various forms of communication in Hawai'i.

Postal Services in Hawai'i

From the arrival of Protestant missionaries in 1820 until the establishment of the postal service in 1850, outgoing mail was usually dispatched by arrangement with the captain or crew of sailing vessels. In these pre-postal days, letters were frequently sent collect, and incoming mail was often unreliable. Regular postal service in Hawai'i began in 1850, when foreign businessmen and missionaries persuaded King Kamehameha III's Privy Council and the Hawaiian legislature to establish a mail link with the rest of the world. The first stamps were hand-printed by the king's press in Honolulu.

Today, Hawai'i is part of the Pacific Area of the U.S. Postal Service. Reporting to the Pacific Area is the Honolulu Performance Cluster (HPC), consisting of Hawai'i, Guam, American Samoa, and the Commonwealth of the Northern Mariana Islands. The 127 post offices and stations and 49 contract stations in the HPC handle an average daily volume of nearly 2.4 million pieces of mail. They employ more than 3,000 permanent and temporary workers, and in fiscal year 1995 accounted for over $184 million in postal receipts. The HPC is served by the Honolulu Processing and Distribution Center (P&DC), located next to Honolulu International Airport, which acts as an international exchange office for air and surface mail. All overseas mail including military mail in the Pacific is processed at the Honolulu P&DC.

Newspapers

Missionaries in Hawai'i who ran the schools in the mid-1800s introduced newspapers as a tool to help increase literacy. The first newspaper printed in Hawai'i was *Ka Lama Hawaii* (The Hawaiian Luminary), a student newspaper, written in Hawaiian and first published on February 14, 1834, in Lahainaluna, Maui. That same year saw the start of the first regulary published newspaper, *Ke Kumu Hawaii* (The Hawaiian Teacher), also written in Hawaiian (as were many of the early Island newspapers). The Kingdom of Hawai'i also produced its own English/Hawaiian newspaper, *The Polynesian,* first in 1841 and then for a 20-year run from 1844 to 1864.

In 1856 Hawai'i's first regular English-language paper, *The Pacific Commercial Advertiser,* was established as a weekly publication. *The Advertiser* has published continuously since it became a daily in 1882 and was renamed *The Honolulu Advertiser* in 1921. The earlier *Advertiser* boasted such writers as Mark Twain, Jack London, and Robert Louis Stevenson. Today, *The Honolulu Advertiser,* owned by the Gannett Corporation, has a statewide circulation of approximately 150,000.

Hawai'i's other major English-language newspaper, the *Honolulu Star-Bulletin,* got its start in the 1880s as a posted "daily bulletin" of news items and shipping schedules in the window of a prominent Honolulu shopkeeper. When the small store was purchased a few years later, the new owner converted the posted bulletins into a newspaper called the *Daily Bulletin.* In 1912 the *Bulletin* was merged with the *Hawaii Star* to become today's *Honolulu Star-Bulletin,* which is owned by Liberty Newspapers and has a statewide circulation of approximately 80,000.

Since 1912, and throughout its more than eight decades of history, *Hawaii Hochi* (Hawai'i News) has been the voice of the Japanese community in Hawai'i. *Hawaii Hochi* outlived three major competitors and numerous weekly and occasional publications to survive as Hawai'i's only remaining Japanese-language daily newspaper. This was not the first foreign-language newspaper, however. Hawai'i's "ethnic press"

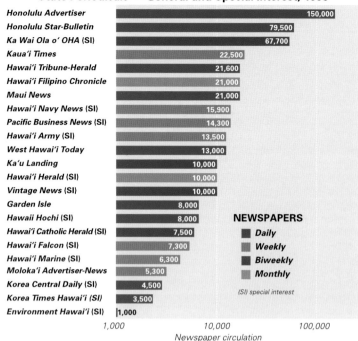

State Periodicals — General and Special Interest, 1995

Publication	Circulation
Honolulu Advertiser	150,000
Honolulu Star-Bulletin	79,500
Ka Wai Ola o' OHA (SI)	67,700
Kaua'i Times	22,500
Hawai'i Tribune-Herald	21,600
Hawai'i Filipino Chronicle	21,000
Maui News	21,000
Hawai'i Navy News (SI)	15,900
Pacific Business News (SI)	14,300
Hawai'i Army (SI)	13,500
West Hawai'i Today	13,000
Ka'u Landing	10,000
Hawai'i Herald (SI)	10,000
Vintage News (SI)	10,000
Garden Isle	8,000
Hawaii Hochi (SI)	8,000
Hawai'i Catholic Herald (SI)	7,500
Hawai'i Falcon (SI)	7,300
Hawai'i Marine (SI)	6,300
Moloka'i Advertiser-News	5,300
Korea Central Daily (SI)	4,500
Korea Times Hawai'i (SI)	3,500
Environment Hawai'i (SI)	1,000

NEWSPAPERS
- Daily
- Weekly
- Biweekly
- Monthly

(SI) special interest

Newspaper circulation

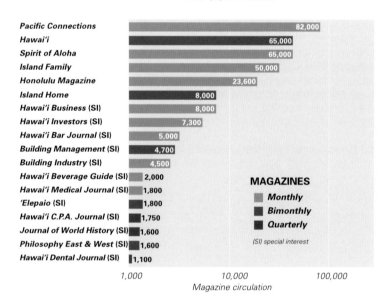

Publication	Circulation
Pacific Connections	82,000
Hawai'i	65,000
Spirit of Aloha	65,000
Island Family	50,000
Honolulu Magazine	23,600
Island Home	8,000
Hawai'i Business (SI)	8,000
Hawai'i Investors (SI)	7,300
Hawai'i Bar Journal (SI)	5,000
Building Management (SI)	4,700
Building Industry (SI)	4,500
Hawai'i Beverage Guide (SI)	2,000
Hawai'i Medical Journal (SI)	1,800
'Elepaio (SI)	1,800
Hawai'i C.P.A. Journal (SI)	1,750
Journal of World History (SI)	1,600
Philosophy East & West (SI)	1,600
Hawai'i Dental Journal (SI)	1,100

MAGAZINES
- Monthly
- Bimonthly
- Quarterly

(SI) special interest

Magazine circulation

had its beginning in the 1880s with the publication of the *Tan Shan Hsin Pao* (Hawai'i-Chinese News). Today, Hawai'i's "ethnic press" reflects the diversity of the state's population with a variety of daily, weekly, biweekly, and monthly publications in a number of Asian and Pacific Island languages. In addition, a vigorous alternative press contributes a number of free weeklies that expand the range of local newspapers available.

Telephone

The telephone came to Hawai'i in 1878, just 2 years after Alexander Graham Bell introduced his new invention. The first phones were installed on Maui and connected shopkeeper C. H. Dickey's store with his residence. For a while there were two independent telephone systems in Hawai'i, requiring different types of phones. However, in 1894 Mutual Telephone bought out Hawaiian Bell and became the sole telephone ser-

vice provider. In 1954, Mutual Telephone changed its name to Hawaiian Telephone and in 1967 Hawaiian Telephone merged with General Telephone & Electronics (GTE) to become GTE Hawaiian Telephone Company. By 1996 GTE Hawaiian Telephone Company was providing more than 755,606 access lines statewide, approximately two-thirds of which were in residences and one-fourth in businesses; the remainder were pay phones.

Many, though not all, transpacific cables pass through Hawai'i, making the state an important communications hub. The first undersea telephone cable between Hawai'i and the U.S. mainland was installed in 1957. The British Commonwealth completed a cable connecting Canada, New Zealand, and Australia via Hawai'i in 1963. In 1964, the first undersea cable between Hawai'i and Japan and the second Hawai'i–U.S. mainland cable were added. The third and fourth undersea cables went into service in 1974 and 1989.

Hawai'i's mid-Pacific location, likewise, places the state within the coverage area of many satellites, making it an ideal site for a satellite communications complex serving Asia, the Pacific Islands, and the U.S. mainland. The first complex was brought into service by ComSat in 1966 at Paumalū, O'ahu.

One of the first communications systems to use fiber optics was installed at Camp Smith on O'ahu in 1977. Within 2 years, the first working public-switched optical fiber trunkline was operating between the Alakea and Kalihi telephone exchanges in Honolulu. The nation's first long-wavelength optical fiber system was placed in service on a 22-mile (35 km) route between Honolulu and Wahiawā. By 1992 a total of 13,000 miles (21,000 km) of fiber-optic cable was installed statewide, and GTE Hawaiian Telephone Company's trunking network was over 95 percent digital, with 70 percent of the lines served by digital switching centers (the other 30 percent was served by analog switches).

Cellular telephone service began in Hawai'i in 1986, 3 years after the first licenses were granted on the U.S. mainland. By 1992 approximately 10 percent of residents were using cellular phones, the highest

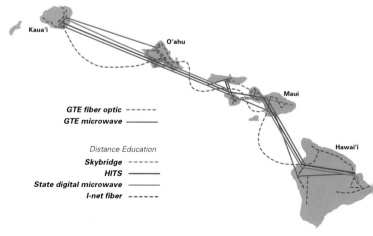

Communication Networks, January 1996

GTE fiber optic -----
GTE microwave ———

Distance Education
Skybridge -----
HITS ———
State digital microwave ———
I-net fiber -----

Kaua'i   O'ahu   Maui   Hawai'i

Pacific Cable and Satellite Network, 1995

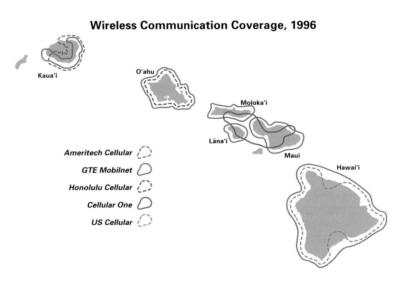

Russia
Japan (Ibaraki)
China
Japan (Yamaguchi)
Okinawa
Hong Kong
Taiwan
Saipan
Philippines
Guam
Yap FSM
Palau
Chuuk FSM
Ponape FSM
Ebeye
Kosrae FSM
Majuro
Singapore
Brunei
Jakarta
Port Moresby
Solomon Islands
Bariki
Nauru
Vanuatu
Cairns
Fiji
New Caledonia
Tonga
Norfolk Island
Ceduna
Moree
New Zealand

Lake Cowichan
Brewster
Pacific City
Jamesburg
Point Arena
San Francisco
San Luis Obispo
Santa Paula

Midway Island
Wake Island
Hawai'i (Paumalū)
Kiribati
American Samoa
French Polynesia

/ **Fiber-optic/cable network**

Satellite facilities

rate among the 50 states. While mainland cellular telephone users seem to prefer mobile units installed in vehicles, about 90–95 percent of Hawai'i users take advantage of handheld portables. This may be a result of Hawai'i's relatively limited road system and the large number of young adults (the fastest growing market segment) whose primary mode of transportation is a bicycle, moped, motorcycle, or TheBus rather than a car.

Radio

Hawai'i's first commercial radio station, KGU, began broadcasting in Honolulu in 1922. Few radio stations existed in Hawai'i prior to World War II, but postwar radio broadcasting grew rapidly. In 1995 there were 62 commercial stations and 6 noncommercial public radio stations statewide. The state's multi-ethnic population has supported over 15 radio stations broadcasting ethnic programming in Hawaiian and many Asian and Pacific Island languages. Four public radio stations are operated by Hawai'i Public Radio, a private nonprofit corporation. The University of Hawai'i operates KTUH, a low-power, student-run FM station on the Mānoa campus.

Wireless Communication Coverage, 1996

Kaua'i
O'ahu
Moloka'i
Lāna'i
Maui
Hawai'i

Ameritech Cellular
GTE Mobilnet
Honolulu Cellular
Cellular One
US Cellular

Film

The first Hollywood production in Hawai'i took place in 1913 with the shooting of two one-reel films (*Hawaiian Love* and *The Shark God*), both staring Virginia Brissac and James Dillon. Since then 169 movies have been filmed in Hawai'i, including *From Here to Eternity* (1953), *South Pacific* (1958), *The Old Man and the Sea* (1958), *Raiders of the Lost Ark* (1980), *Jurassic*

Radio Stations in Hawai'i by County, 1995

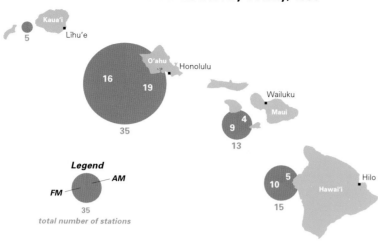

Park (1992), and Waterworld (1994). In addition, more than 88 television programs were made in Hawai'i between 1959 and 1995, including *Hawaiian Eye* (1959–1963), *Hawaii Five-0* (1968–1980), and *Magnum P.I.* (1980–1988). Activities by the film and television industry in Hawai'i have been accompanied by an increase in local directors and producers. The number of production companies grew from 2 in the early 1960s to more than 90 in 1995. The Film and Video Association of Hawai'i (FAVAH) has a membership list of more than 200 professional film and videomakers based in Hawai'i.

The Hawai'i Film Office was established in 1978 within the Department of Business, Economic Development, & Tourism to encourage the motion picture and television industries to use Hawai'i as a production site for films and TV programs. It also provides assistance to producers in obtaining film locations, equipment, facilities, and permits. The Hawai'i Film Office also operates the Hawai'i Film Studio, a multisound-stage facility for television and film productions located adjacent to the Diamond Head campus of Kapi'olani Community College.

Hawai'i has developed a reputation as a showcase for international films, mainly from Asia and the Pacific. The best-known film festival is the Hawai'i International Film Festival (HIFF). Inaugurated in November 1981, HIFF provides the state's film viewing audience an opportunity to see Asian and Pacific productions (many of them U.S. premieres) and to discuss their cultural significance and artistic and technical merits, often with the filmmakers themselves.

Educational and informational films in 16mm or videotape formats are distributed by three major public film libraries: the State Department of Education, the State Public Library, and Wong Audio-Visual Center at the University of Hawai'i Library.

Television

The first commercial television station in Hawai'i, KGMB-TV, began broadcasting in Honolulu on

December 2, 1952. It was followed in the same year by KHON and in 1954 by KHVH-TV (now KITV). By 1955 all three major national networks were established in Hawai'i. In 1996 there were 5 major broadcast stations affiliated with national television networks: KGMB (CBS), KITV (ABC), KHNL (NBC), KHON (FOX), and KFVE (UPN). There were also 4 independent stations: KWHE, KOBN, KBFD, and KIKU (mostly Japanese-language programming). Twenty-two licensed television stations were broadcasting in Hawai'i as of June 1995. Of these, 13 were on O'ahu, 7 on Hawai'i Island, and 8 on Maui. Neighbor island stations are relays of stations on O'ahu. In addition, numerous low-power translators and cable systems make television programming available to virtually all homes in Hawai'i.

After years of broadcasting programs from kinescope, film, and videotape (usually a week after U.S. mainland release dates), the advent of geosynchronous satellites made same-day and, in some cases, simultaneous broadcasts possible. Satellite television service to Hawai'i was inaugurated with the first earth station built by ComSat on O'ahu's north shore in 1966. Hawai'i's first live television program from the U.S. mainland was the broadcast of the Notre Dame vs. Michigan State football game on November 19, 1966. When the GTE Hawaiian Telephone/AT&T domestic satellite system went into service in 1976, the result was a substantial cost reduction in live TV transmissions to the Islands and an increase in satellite-delivered TV programming.

Educational broadcasting got its start in 1966 when the University of Hawai'i's Education Television Network (KHET) went on the air. In 1973 the switch was made to public programming when the license and station management were transferred from the university to the Hawai'i Public Broadcasting Authority. In 1978, the stations of the Hawai'i Public Television Authority, KHET Honolulu and KMEB Wailuku, were the first to achieve full-time satellite interconnec-

Major Television Stations in Hawai'i, May 1998

Cable Television Subscribers, 1995

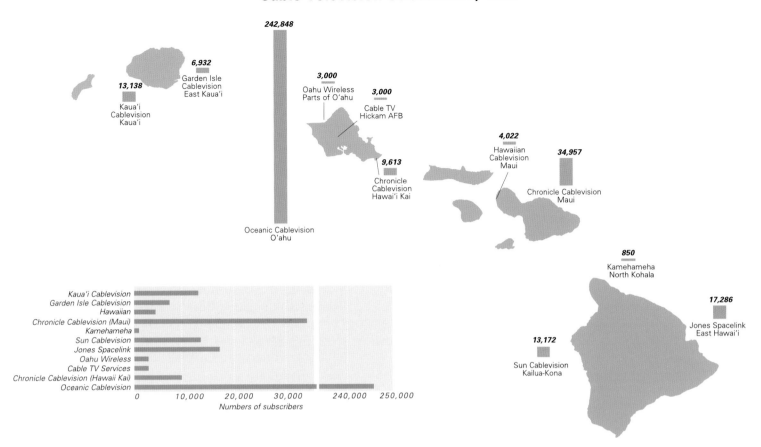

tion with mainland program sources. Commercial stations followed suit shortly thereafter.

The establishment of Hawai'i Interactive Television Service (HITS) in 1990 made long-distance instruction possible. During the 1995–1996 academic year the University of Hawai'i offered 69 courses via HITS, serving over 2,000 students statewide using two-way interactive video classrooms, cable programming, and the Internet. In addition, other video systems (e.g., SkyBridge and I-Net) assist in meeting the increased demand for distance education and videoconferencing.

The mountainous terrain of Hawai'i makes cable television especially important. The state ranks second in the nation in cable penetration; 84 percent of residences are connected to cable.

Cable television was introduced in Hawai'i in 1961 in the Kahala and Hawai'i Kai districts of O'ahu, initially to serve residences where TV antennas were banned for aesthetic reasons, or to improve reception from local broadcast television stations. In 1995, 11 cable television companies were in operation, providing about 65 channels. The installation of fiber-optic cable, however, will greatly increase the potential of program services and make interactive channels possible, and in the near future cable subscribers will be able to access the Internet. Furthermore, federal legislation (the Telecommunications Act of 1996) will allow telephone companies and cable services to com-

pete in all areas of wired communications including telephone, cable television, and Internet services.

The Internet

In the late 1980s and early 1990s, the Internet seemed suddenly to burst upon the scene and into popular culture. In actuality, the Internet evolved into its present form over several decades from its earliest incarnation as a computer network for military, scientific, and educational research (ARPAnet). As of early 1996, there were 20 Internet Service Providers (ISPs) with dial-up access in Hawai'i, not including CompuServe, America Online, and Prodigy. All of Hawai'i's ISPs provide Internet access via four national providers of Internet "backbone" connections. Some local ISPs resell a portion of their Internet access to other, smaller ISPs in Hawai'i. Some estimates place the number of Hawai'i computer users accessing the Internet through local ISPs at around 90,000 as of early 1996. An important development was the startup of Hawai'i Information Exchange (HIX), a network of local lines between a number of ISPs and the University of Hawai'i. This system was designed to facilitate the exchange of inter-ISP and inter-UH data over local links, making reliance on Hawai'i–U.S. mainland connections no longer necessary.

MICHAEL OGDEN
WITH CLIFF EBLEN

EDUCATION

State law requires that all children in Hawaiʻi between the ages of 6 and 18 attend school. During the 1994–1995 school year, enrollment in the state's elementary, intermediate, and secondary schools was at an all-time high, with 219,224 students. Of this total, 83.8 percent (183,795 students) attended the 242 public schools and received instruction from 11,602 teachers. With an annual growth in enrollment of at least 1.5 percent since 1991, approximately 3,000 additional students enter the public schools each year. This growth has created classroom shortages on Hawaiʻi Island, Maui, and Kauaʻi. According to the 1994 Superintendent's Annual Report, more than half of the state's public schools need additional classrooms, and all dis-

tricts have insufficient support facilities such as libraries, cafeterias, and administrative offices.

State expenditures for K–12 public education have generally been close to the national average. In 1996, Hawaiʻi placed eighteenth among the 50 states, spending $6,335 per student. This level of funding, however, contrasts markedly with Hawaiʻi's 1995 national rankings of ninth in per capita income and third in per capita state revenues. In student-teacher ratio, Hawaiʻi ranked thirty-ninth.

Private schools have long played an important role in shaping education in Hawaiʻi and continue to do so today. In 1994–1995, 132 private schools served 35,429 students, under the instruction of 2,443 teachers. Although enrollments have dropped slightly, from 17.5 percent of K–12 students in 1987 to 16.2 percent in 1995, Hawaiʻi continues to rank among the states having the highest proportion of students in private schools. More than 24,000 of these students attend the 44 member schools of the Hawaiʻi Association of Independent Schools (HAIS).

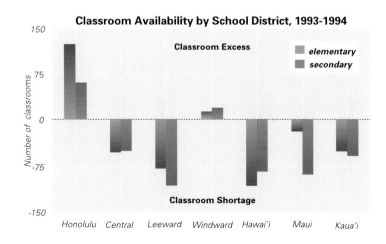

School Enrollment by District, 1986-1992

Classroom Availability by School District, 1993-1994

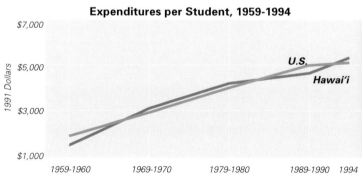

Expenditures per Student, 1959-1994

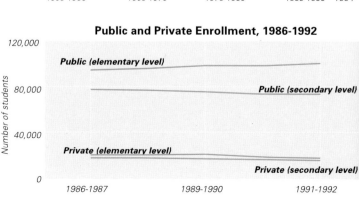

Public and Private Enrollment, 1986-1992

Adult Education Enrollment

Kaua'i

Central

Windward

Leeward

Honolulu

Maui

Number of Enrolled Adults

- 3,500
- 6,000-10,000
- 19,000-22,000
- 45,000

Hawai'i

Classroom Teacher Ethnicity, 1945 and 1995

Caucasian
Chinese
Filipino
Hawaiian
Japanese
Korean
Other

1944-1945   1994-1995

50%   25%   0%   0%   25%   50%

A major problem that has plagued K–12 public education in Hawai'i in recent years is a shortage of locally trained teachers. The state's four institutions that prepare teachers have been unable to meet the growing demand for them. During the 1993–1994 school year, for example, of a total of 1,099 new teachers, the Department of Education (DOE) had to hire 555 from the U.S. mainland. Projections through the year 2003 indicate a continuing shortage of locally trained teachers, particularly in special education, school counseling, science, mathematics, industrial arts, and home economics. Rural areas are most affected by the shortage.

Schools in Hawai'i exhibit a broad range of student performance levels—particularly in language skills—within schools, between schools, and between public and private schools. Student mean scores on the 1994 Student Achievement Test (SAT) were close to the national average for mathematics, while mean scores for verbal skills placed Hawai'i forty-eighth among the 50 states. Hawai'i's students spend less time in the classroom than those of any other state and have comparatively high rates of absenteeism. How to respond to the range of student abilities and differences between schools, while at the same time facilitating comparable levels of achievement in an ethnically diverse society in which immigration rates remain high, has long been a challenge in Hawai'i.

Structure of Public Education

Missionaries set the pattern for public education in Hawai'i. In 1820, they began transcribing the Hawaiian language, writing textbooks, and teaching the majority of adult Hawaiians the rudiments of reading and writing. From 1831 through 1840, missionaries shifted their educational focus from adults to children, trained teachers, and organized schools that used the Hawaiian language as the primary medium of instruction. When Hawai'i's system of education was formally established in 1840, missionaries began relinquishing their control of educational affairs. Concurrently, secular influence from business and commerce made English the language of choice. Common schools

changed gradually to the use of English, so that by 1894 only 2.8 percent of the students in public schools attended schools taught in Hawaiian. Beginning in 1854, the legislature authorized the establishment of schools with English as the medium of instruction. These were sometimes referred to as "select" or English-standard schools.

Common schools emphasized basic skills and vocational training, leading many observers to believe they were organized primarily to produce a labor class to serve the needs of the plantations and the wealthy. These schools were located mostly in rural areas and taught by teachers whose first language was not English. They served a diverse population of laborers' children—Hawaiian, Japanese, Portuguese, and other ethnic/linguistic groups—who often used Pidgin (now referred to as Hawaiian Creole English) as their primary language at school.

English-standard schools, on the other hand, selected students on the basis of oral and written communication in English, resulting in the overrepresentation of children of missionaries, merchants, and military personnel. Teachers spoke English as their first language, and the schools were capable of preparing students to attend college and enter professions. Although this divided school system contributed to strong differences in student achievement, especially in language learning, it was not completely abandoned until 1961.

The Department of Education

The public school system in Hawai'i has the most centralized administration of public education in the United States. The Department of Education is overseen by an elected Board of Education (BOE) which, in conjunction with the state legislature, sets educational policy and provides funds for the public schools. The BOE appoints a superintendent of education, who is the state's chief school officer. At the local level, seven district offices (four on O'ahu and one each on Hawai'i Island, Maui, and Kaua'i) carry out state mandates under the supervision of an appointed district superintendent.

Student Ethnicity by School District, 1993-1994

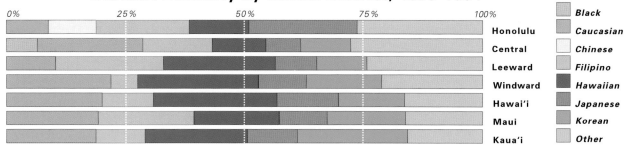

This centralized administrative structure would seem to have the potential to ensure equal distribution of benefits among the public schools. Improvement in schools and students' educational attainment, however, seems impossible without involving parents and local communities and giving more autonomy to local schools. However, local autonomy may create even greater disparity between schools and students.

The DOE has declared improvement in literacy and language learning its most urgent priorities. Schools are being encouraged to adopt the Success Compact Program, a curriculum focused on developing literacy. A publication of the DOE, "Restructuring of the Curriculum," reflects an effort to restore public confidence in the schools by empowering communities, including students, to take a more active role in the governance of their local schools. Another publication, the "Hawai'i State Performance Standards," designed by an appointed group of community leaders and school personnel, lists general goals and objectives, while leaving specific instructional decisions to individual teachers and schools. School/Community-Based Management (SCBM), another reform strategy, shifts a significant degree of decision-making authority from the centralized system to local schools. At the conclusion of the 1995 school year, more than 80 percent of the schools in Hawai'i had committed to the SCBM process. Even if a school has not adopted SCBM, the legislature has authorized school-based budgeting, which provides for flexibility and control of expenditures at the local school level.

Special Programs

The DOE receives a number of federal grants designed to support and supplement state initiatives aligned with the National Goals for Education. In addition to providing opportunities for students seeking vocational education, for gifted and talented youth, and for children with disabilities, the department administers programs that offer:

- educational opportunities for students in high-poverty schools to meet statewide performance standards
- support for teen parents and extended services and learning time for neglected and delinquent youth

- professional development programs for educators to upgrade their teaching skills
- comprehensive guidelines for school- and community-wide approaches for making schools free from drugs and violence
- assistance to schools and community organizations for delivering bilingual education and alternative instruction for children with limited English proficiency
- support for elementary and secondary foreign language studies
- special assistance to schools that experience large student population increases due to immigration, and help for immigrant students in making their transition into American society
- educational services for homeless children
- programs that match students with employers and provide work-based learning

Native Hawaiian Education

For many years Native Hawaiian students tended to be overrepresented in compensatory and remedial programs and underrepresented in gifted and talented programs. Several special programs, however, exist to improve achievement and enrich educational experiences for Native Hawaiian children. Kamehameha Schools/Bishop Estate (KSBE), founded in 1884 by Ke Ali'i Bernice Pauahi Bishop, great-granddaughter of Kamehameha I, offers numerous opportunities, including programs in early education and elementary and secondary schooling. KSBE's community education includes summer programs, the Hawaiian Studies Institute, and post–high school scholarship and counseling.

More recently, Nā Pua No'eau, the Center for Gifted and Talented Native Hawaiian Children, was established with federal funds in 1989 to raise the educational aspirations and achievement of Native Hawaiian youth and to provide them with educational experiences more compatible with native ways of learning than those used in traditional classrooms. The center also aims to integrate Hawaiian culture and values into instruction and to recognize and enrich Native Hawaiian academic, social, and artistic strengths. Nā Pua No'eau offers a variety of programs on the University of Hawai'i Hilo and Mānoa campuses, at Kaua'i and Maui Community Colleges, and, through outreach, to public and private schools statewide. In 1995–1996 more than 3,000 K–12 students attended these programs. The center also offers workshops for teachers, parents, and preservice education students. As of the 1995–1996 school year, Na Pua No'eau had received about $6.4 million in federal funds and about $500,000 in state grants. During the 1995–1996 school year, nine programs at the center provided instruction for approximately 1,000 students.

In addition, Native Hawaiian speakers have been successful in establishing Hawaiian language medium schools. The first, the preschool 'Aha Pūnana Leo (language nest), opened in 1984. In 1986, the state legislature approved the expansion of Hawaiian immersion instruction to the elementary grades, and in 1990 it established the Hale Kuamo'o Hawaiian Language Center at the University of Hawai'i at Hilo for the development of Hawaiian curricular materials that are distributed to immersion schools throughout the state.

Higher Education

The University of Hawai'i (UH) began as the College of Agriculture and Mechanical Arts, established at Mānoa in 1907 under the Morrill Act. Today, the university system includes University of Hawai'i at Mānoa, University of Hawai'i at Hilo, West O'ahu College, and seven community colleges. Systemwide, enrollment has grown steadily since 1985. In fall 1995 a total of 73,038 students were enrolled in regular credit programs and continuing education classes, and the UH system employed 7,953 faculty, staff, and administrative personnel. The state's three major independent universities and colleges (Chaminade University, Brigham Young University–Hawai'i Campus, and Hawai'i Pacific University) served about 12,400 students during 1994. The state's high school graduates

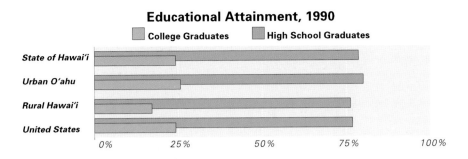

Educational Attainment, 1990

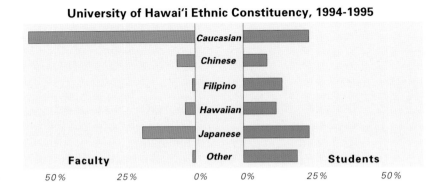

University of Hawai'i Ethnic Constituency, 1994-1995

Accredited Universities and Colleges, 1992-1993

University	Enrollment	Degrees				
		Certificate	Associate	Bachelors	Masters	Doctorate
Community Colleges	26,100	X	X			
U.H. Mānoa	20,037	X	X	X	X	X
Hawai'i Pacific	7,526	X		X	X	
U.H. Hilo	2,953	X		X		
Chaminade	2,284		X	X	X	
Brigham Young	2,064	X		X		
U.H. West O'ahu	676	X		X		

U.H. Mānoa Schools: Architecture; Hawaiian, Asian & Pacific Studies; Law; Library & Information Studies; Medicine; Nursing; Ocean, Earth Science & Technology; Public Health; Social Work; Travel Industry Management

account for nearly two-thirds of first-time enrollees in the UH system. Historically, however, the university has suffered from a perception that to receive a good college education a student should enroll in a U.S. mainland college. As a result, many of the state's best high school graduates pursue higher education on the U.S. mainland.

Support for the UH system comes primarily from appropriations of the state legislature (88 percent), with supplementary funds from federal, state, and private grants. Public higher education in Hawai'i has long been a bargain, with resident undergraduate tuition well below the national average for state universities. Disciplines including tropical agriculture, marine studies, astronomy, and volcanology utilize the unique physical attributes of the Islands as a laboratory for research and discovery. The university also offers instruction in more languages than any U.S. institution outside of the Department of State and provides special programs in Hawaiian, Pacific Island, and Asian Studies.

NINA BUCHANAN

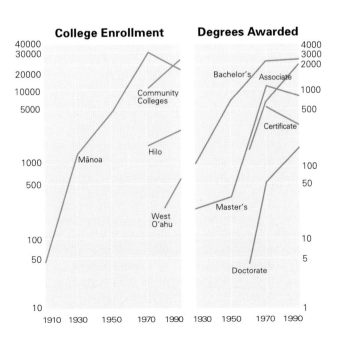

College Enrollment **Degrees Awarded**

HEALTH AND WELLNESS

Residents of Hawai'i enjoy very good health by national standards. Life expectancy at birth (82.1 years for females and 75.9 years for males) is the highest in the United States. Death rates from major causes (such as cardiovascular diseases, cancer, cerebrovascular diseases, and accidents) are well below the national averages. In addition, in the early 1990s when the federal government was considering health care reform, Hawai'i's health care system was often cited as a model of what could be accomplished.

The state's good health record reflects both patterns of behavior in the population and the quality and extent of health care provided. A 1992 national study of health risk factors shows patterns of healthier behavior in Hawai'i than are typical nationwide. In a few areas, Hawai'i really stood out: no other state had higher automobile seat belt usage or a lower percentage of overweight women. The prevalence of smoking and sedentary leisure-time behavior among state residents was also below the national median, while the proportion of the population whose leisure-time pursuits included regular and vigorous or sustained physical activity exceeded the national median.

One real problem area apparent in Hawai'i's health behavior data relates to the use of alcohol. For both men and women, the percent who had driven after drinking excessively exceeded the national median. Likewise, the percentages of those who engaged in binge drinking (the consumption of at least 5 drinks on one or more occasions during the previous month) and chronic drinking (the consumption of 60 drinks or more over the previous month) were also above the national median.

In terms of access to the health care system, the percentage of residents lacking health insurance in Hawai'i in 1993 was the lowest among the 50 states. Indicators of health services actually delivered were somewhat less striking but still added up to a good performance. For instance, the percent of residents who had had their cholesterol level checked within the past 5 years (66 percent), and the percent of women aged 50 or more who had undergone a breast exam and a mammogram within the past 2 years (60 percent), were both above the national median.

Health across Ethnic Groups

A State Department of Health (DOH) survey of health risk behaviors conducted in 1992 shows some differences between ethnic groups. In general, poor health plagues the state's indigenous people. One striking example is revealed by the variation in the percentage of individuals who reported they were overweight, which ranged from more than 40 percent for the Hawaiian/part-Hawaiian population to less than 20 percent for Japanese. The percentages of overweight persons who were trying to lose weight exhibited just the opposite pattern, being highest for Japanese and lowest for Hawaiians/part-Hawaiians. Given the significance of obesity as a risk factor for many diseases, these findings indicate that being overweight may rep-

Health Risk Behavior, 1993

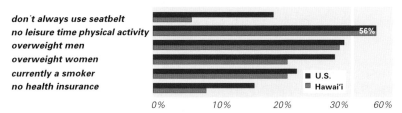

Alcohol Consumption, 1993

	Hawai'i median	U.S. median
driving after having too much to drink one or more times - men	4.4%	3.93%
driving after having too much to drink one or more times - women	1.4%	0.9%
60 or more drinks during the past month	5.7%	2.9%
5 or more drinks at least once during the past month	17.7%	14.3%

Alcohol Consumption by Ethnicity, 1993

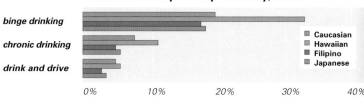

Comparative Health Risk Behavior by Ethnicity, 1993

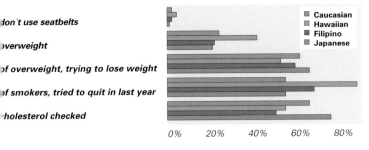

resent a serious health problem for the Hawaiian/part-Hawaiian population.

Ethnic differences in the prevalence of alcohol-related problems are also marked in the 1992 DOH survey results. About one-third of Hawaiian and part-Hawaiian respondents indicated they were binge drinkers, followed by 19.2 percent of Caucasians, and decreasing to a low of 15.4 percent for Filipinos. The proportion of smokers in the population did not vary significantly between major ethnic groups (20–22 percent), and more than half of smokers of all ethnicities had tried to quit during the previous year (ranging from 89 percent of Hawaiians/part-Hawaiians to 57 percent of Japanese smokers).

The adequacy of health care received by members of different ethnic groups also varied somewhat. For example, although Filipinos, Japanese, and Hawaiians/part-Hawaiians participating in the 1992 DOH survey were about equally likely to have undergone a checkup within the past year, Japanese were more likely than the other groups to have had their cholesterol level checked; they are also most conscientious about seat belt use.

Life Expectancy at Birth by Ethnicity, 1990

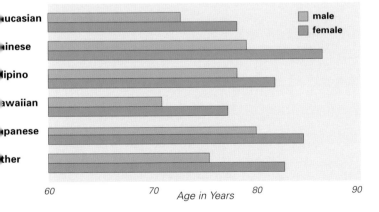

Contrasts across Islands

Although most residents of the state have health insurance, a significant minority lack it. The 1992 DOH survey indicates that the population with health insurance ranged from 95 percent on Moloka'i and Lāna'i to nearly 85 percent on Hawai'i Island. The extent of health insurance coverage (for physician visits, hospi-

talization, and preventive care) also varied. For those who had insurance, the comprehensiveness of coverage was greatest on O'ahu and least on Maui.

Despite a majority of the population having health insurance, the variation in incomes across the state (being highest on O'ahu and lowest on Hawai'i Island) likely affects accessibility to health care in other ways. The limited availability of public transportation outside O'ahu, for example, restricts the accessibility of health care, which is reflected in an increased concern on the part of neighbor islanders about getting to medical services.

Sara Millman

Social Welfare

A significant number of state residents experience difficulty in providing food, shelter, medical care, and other essentials for themselves and their families. The state Department of Human Services (DHS) administers the following programs to assist those in need:

Aid to Families with Dependent Children (AFDC) Families receiving temporary cash assistance under this program have little or no income and include children under 18 years of age. From 1994 to 1996 the number of families receiving monthly benefits increased from 19,900 to about 23,900—5.4 percent of the state's estimated population. Nearly two-thirds of those served by AFDC are children, and in 95 percent of the cases females head the households. AFDC funds, supplied in equal part by the state and federal governments, increased from $151 million in 1994 to approximately $177 million in 1996.

JOBS Program Many adults of families who receive benefits from AFDC also participate in the JOBS (Job Opportunities and Basic Skills) program, which provides basic education, training, and job-search skills to assist them in moving off welfare and into the workforce. The number of clients served by JOBS increased from 930 in 1992 to more than 4,200 in 1995. Nearly half of them were between the ages of 25 and 34; three-fourths were O'ahu residents. A total of 279 JOBS participants were able to terminate AFDC assistance by finding employment in 1995. The annual program budget averaged $14.1 million from 1994 through 1996, with roughly 45 percent supplied by federal funds and the remainder by the state.

General Financial Assistance This state-funded program serves single individuals and families who do not qualify for other, federal financial assistance. The numbers of recipients grew from about 7,000 single individuals and 1,160 families in 1994 to approximately 9,910 single individuals and 1,590 families in 1996.

Department of Health

The Department of Health (DOH) is responsible for the administration of community hospitals, district health resources, mental health services, an office of epidemiological research, and environmental monitoring programs. It also fulfills general health administrative functions, including support services such as planning, program and policy development, and personnel and fiscal management. The agency is the third largest in the state in terms of number of employees. Its budget of about $621.4 million (1995–1996) amounts to 10.9 percent of the state's budget, the fourth largest (after the Departments of Budget and Finance, Human Services, and Education).

The administration of community hospitals involves oversight for 13 health-care facilities statewide. For the most part, the community hospitals are the only care providers on the neighbor islands and are currently operating on their revenues alone, with no general-fund subsidy. The DOH is in the process of establishing a public benefit corporation, which will provide some autonomy for the operation of community hospitals.

The health resources administration has responsibility for family health services (with particular emphasis on primary and preventive

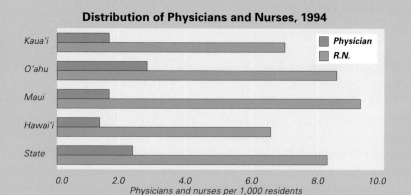

Distribution of Physicians and Nurses, 1994

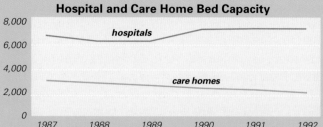

Hospital and Care Home Bed Capacity

care in maternal and child health) and community health services (including public health and school health nursing). Programs for alcohol and drug abuse prevention and treatment also fall under the DOH's aegis. It also has oversight over emergency medical services (primarily ambulance services), communicable disease prevention and tracking, institutional care for the developmentally disabled and Hansen's disease patients, dental health, and health education.

Environmental health administration includes environmental management and planning, as well as traditional health services such as sanitation, vector control, and the inspection and monitoring of foods and drugs. The DOH's environmental protection and regulation duties include the monitoring and enforcement of state and federal laws pertaining to clean air, clean water and safe drinking water, wastewater, and the management of solid and hazardous wastes.

To carry out its responsibilities, the DOH regularly collects and analyzes statistics on the health of the community and makes such information available statewide. The DOH promotes the use of scientific knowledge in public health decision making and in establishing assessment data and appropriate health policies. To ensure that public health services are provided for state residents, the department encourages or requires, through appropriate regulations, that other private or public entities provide such services directly, so that the DOH becomes the service provider of last resort for uninsurable populations or when no other satisfactory alternative exists. The department is obligated to make sure that federal government mandates are satisfied and that resources are dispersed geographically and are directed at problems that pose the greatest risk to public health or the environment.

ATLAS STAFF

Diagnosed AIDS Cases by County, March 31, 1996

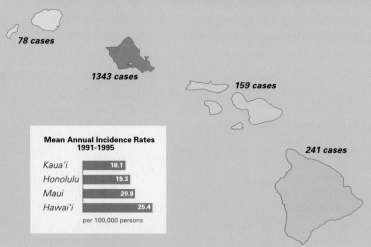

78 cases

1343 cases

159 cases

241 cases

Mean Annual Incidence Rates 1991-1995

Kaua'i	18.1
Honolulu	19.3
Maui	20.8
Hawai'i	25.4

per 100,000 persons

Communicable Diseases, 1991

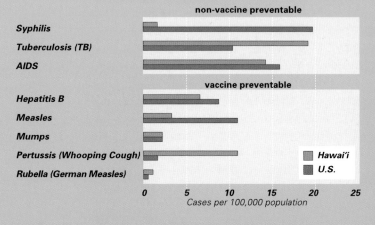

Self-Reported Chronic Conditions, 1992

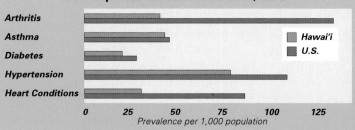

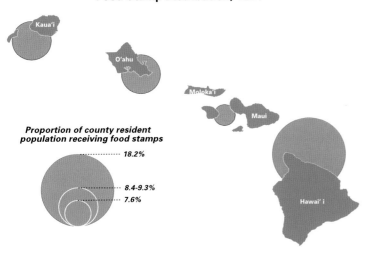

Food Stamp Distribution, 1994

Proportion of county resident population receiving food stamps

18.2%

8.4-9.3%

7.6%

Aid to the Aged, Blind, and Disabled DHS dispenses about $1.5 million each month in state funds under the Aid to the Aged, Blind, and Disabled Program, which supported approximately 2,600 needy persons monthly from 1994 through 1996.

Food Stamp Program Federally funded through the U.S. Department of Agriculture, this program assists households of low income and limited resources in supplementing their food budgets. The number of persons receiving food coupons monthly rose from almost 110,000 in 1994 to 133,350 in 1996—an increase of 21 percent. In 1996 more than 11 percent of the state's population received food stamps.

Medical Assistance (Medicaid) Programs For eligible individuals who are blind, disabled, or more than 65 years of age, medical and dental providers are reimbursed on a fee-for-service basis by DHS. For other individuals and family members in need, medical assistance is available through the QUEST program. QUEST participants are enrolled in managed care health plans, and DHS pays the plan premiums for those who qualify financially. Medicaid programs are jointly funded by the state and federal governments, and expenditures for 1996 were about $593,000. The Medicaid caseload grew from 126,400 in 1993–1994 to 154,250 in September 1995—a 22 percent increase statewide.

In response to the nationwide demand for welfare reform, in 1996 numerous changes regarding funding, eligibility requirements, benefit limits, and other features of public assistance programs were considered by the DHS and the 1996 state legislature.

ATLAS STAFF

Family Violence

Violence within intimate relationships and between family members has surfaced as a major social problem since the 1970s. Maltreatment of children, abuse of domestic partners, and suicide have been the most visible categories of family violence, with elder abuse, sibling violence, and child-to-parent violence receiving less attention.

Assembling accurate statistics on the incidence of family violence in the state is difficult due to the variations in reporting and law enforcement policies from island to island. According to the individual county police departments in Hawai'i, there was a total of 7,853 incidents of abuse of family and household members during 1994. Of these, a little more than one-half resulted in arrests.

Child Maltreatment State law defines child abuse as "an act by any person related to, residing with, or caring for a child under 18 which injures the child physically or psychologically." Child neglect is defined as failing to provide for a child "adequate food, clothing, shelter, psychological care, physical care, medical care or supervision." The state Department of Human Services (DHS), which investigates allegations of child abuse and neglect, received 88 reports of maltreatment in 1967. By 1994 that total had risen to 5,186. In 1996, 4,775 cases were reported, of which 44 percent involved general abuse, 26 percent neglect, 20 percent both abuse and neglect, and 10 percent sexual abuse.

DHS investigates all reports of child abuse or neglect to determine if there is sufficient evidence to substantiate the allegations. In 1994, only 45 percent of such reports were confirmed—the first time since

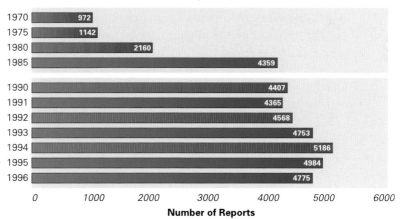

State Child Abuse Reports, 1970-1996

Year	Number of Reports
1970	972
1975	1142
1980	2160
1985	4359
1990	4407
1991	4365
1992	4568
1993	4753
1994	5186
1995	4984
1996	4775

Number of Reports

1983 that the number of confirmed child abuse/neglect reports fell below 50 percent. The confirmation rate for sexual abuse reports fell from almost 49 percent in 1992 to 37 percent in 1994, then rebounded to 44 percent in 1996. The fact that a report is not confirmed does not signify the absence of maltreatment but denotes that investigations did not find sufficient evidence to confirm that a child was harmed. For confirmed reports in 1996, 40 percent of the children were under the age of 6, 13 percent were less than 1 year old, and about 56 percent of the victims were female. Confirmed perpetrators were evenly divided by gender. Almost 88 percent were relatives of the victims, with 77 percent being biological parents.

During the first 3 months following the Hurricane 'Iniki disaster on Kaua'i in 1992, there was a 70 percent increase in child abuse reports as compared to previous years for the same calendar months. This increase in the incidence of abuse mirrored those following disasters in other parts of the country.

Violence between Domestic Partners The incidence of violence between spouses and other domestic partners is more difficult to tabulate than that for child maltreatment. Hawai'i law defines domestic abuse as "physical harm, bodily injury, assault, or the threat of imminent physical harm, bodily harm, or assault, extreme psychological abuse or malicious property damage between family or household members." The definition of family and household members includes current spouses, former spouses, and persons jointly residing or formerly residing in the same dwelling unit. Because the same law also applies to acts of abuse toward parents, children, and other family members, it is not possible to accurately segregate reports involving only domestic partnerships from other types of domestic abuse.

Statewide aggregate data on violence between domestic partners are not available. A 1995 study prepared by the Maui Police Department found that 81 percent of that county's reports of domestic abuse during 1994 involved married and unmarried couples. Physical confrontations were reported in 27 percent of the cases and injuries were reported in 26 percent of the cases. Verbal abuse alone was alleged in 73 percent of the reports. If these percentages were projected to the statewide total of 7,853 domestic abuse reports during 1994, the result would be an estimated 6,360 cases of violence between domestic partners.

A 1992 survey on Kaua'i disclosed that 14 percent of women on the island reported that they had been hit, kicked, or beaten in their home, and 4 percent claimed injuries that required hospital treatment. The survey indicated that the incidence of domestic violence was higher among unmarried mothers, those under 35, and those in low-income households.

Elder Abuse Prior to 1991, only cases of abuse or neglect involving victims over 60 years of age were investigated, but subsequent legal changes resulted in the tracking of all reports of abuse to dependent adults, regardless of age. During 1994 there were 481 cases of abuse or neglect of dependent adults reported, compared with 380 cases in 1991. Of these, about half were confirmed following investigation, and more than 60 percent involved female victims.

Suicide Hawai'i has consistently had one of the lowest suicide rates in the nation. However, between 1988 and 1992 Hawai'i's ranking among the states climbed from forty-eighth to thirty-ninth, with 11.2 suicides per 100,000 population. In 1993 the rate fell slightly, to 10.6 suicides per 100,000. Individual county rates ranged from 7.3 on Kaua'i to 14.3 on Hawai'i Island. Of the 104 people who committed suicide in 1993, 85 were male and 19 were female.

Family violence imposes great costs on society by undermining the family unit and shattering youth trust in adult caregivers. Considerable resources are being expended in Hawai'i to prevent child maltreatment, spouse battering, elder abuse, and suicide.

THOM CURTIS
WITH SHEILA HOLLOWELL

CRIME

Crime in Hawai'i decreased 9.1 percent from 1995 to 1996, the first drop in the crime rate since 1991, but Hawai'i still ranked fourth among the states in the total FBI crime index. What distinguishes Hawai'i from other states, however, is the ratio of violent crime to property crime: Hawai'i ranked third in the rate of property crime and forty-second in violent crime. Nationally, 13 percent of all crime is violent crime, while in Hawai'i only 4 percent is classified as violent. Three of the four crimes classified as violent—murder, forcible rape, and aggravated assault—dropped from 1995 to 1996, and the fourth, robbery, showed only a

slight increase, for an overall violent crime rate decrease of 5 percent. There was a 9 percent decrease for property offenses: burglary, larceny-theft, and motor vehicle theft.

Honolulu, with 73.6 percent of the state's population, accounted for 82.7 percent and 76.8 percent of the state's violent and property crimes, respectively, but like the state as a whole, showed a decrease from 1995 to 1996. If we compare crime rates by county, however, we find that Honolulu does not have the highest rate in all classifications (see graph). In 1996, for example, Honolulu had the lowest rate of forcible

Reported Offenses by County, 1996

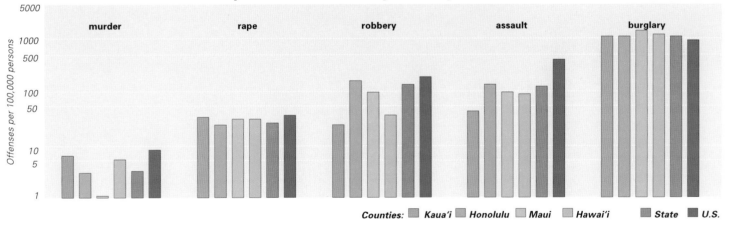

Major Offenses Reported in Hawai'i, 1982-1996

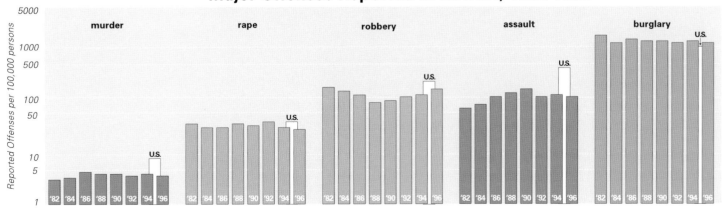

rape and Kaua'i the highest, while Maui had the highest burglary rate and Honolulu again the lowest. Murder rates in Hawai'i, Kaua'i, and Maui counties are quite variable due to the low numbers (Maui had only 1 and Kaua'i 4 in 1996), so it is not appropriate to compare rates for this crime except over time. From 1982 through 1996, Hawai'i County had the highest rate of 5.6 per 100,000, followed by Honolulu with 4.1, Maui with 3.6, and Kaua'i with 3.4. Very few drug offenses are reported, so it is more useful to use arrest data to compare drug offenses by county. Hawai'i County led the way with a rate of 4,963.1 per 100,000 population, while Maui had a rate of 4,397.9, Kaua'i 2,533.9, and Honolulu 983.1.

With respect to drug-related offenses, the efforts of federal, state, and county law enforcement personnel have significantly reduced the local cultivation and availability of marijuana. In 1990 Hawai'i, ranking forty-seventh in land area among the 50 states, ranked eleventh in eradication of cultivated marijuana plants and seventh in the value of assets seized, according to the Drug Enforcement Administration. While overall drug arrests have declined since the 1980s, arrests for crack cocaine, crystal methamphetamine, and heroin have increased, and law enforcement authorities are facing increasing difficulty in stemming the flow of these illegal substances into the state.

"Abuse of a family household member," the classification for domestic abuse cases that are not serious enough to constitute a felony, is not an FBI Part I ("serious") crime, but it is nevertheless an offense of growing concern that is frequently in the news as more attention is now being given to this "hidden" crime. Statewide, arrests for domestic abuse rose significantly, from 17 in 1982 to 3,021 in 1992, then declined to 1,890 in 1996 (most of this decline occurred on O'ahu). The increase in arrests likely can be attributed to heightened public awareness of the problem, greater willingness to report such offenses, and altered policies on the handling of such cases within police departments, rather than an absolute increase in the incidence of domestic violence.

Police and Prisons

Each county is responsible for recruiting and training personnel for its own police department. Statewide in 1996, there was a total of 2,591 sworn, active police officers, or roughly 2.12 per 1,000 resident population, ranging from 3.3 on Maui to 2.08 on O'ahu. The number of officers per square mile in 1993 ranged from 2.86 on O'ahu to 0.08 on Hawai'i Island. Maui and Hawai'i Island have many isolated settlements, some accessible only by four-wheel drive vehicles, which poses difficulties for effective law enforcement

by making response time to crimes in progress in some areas quite long. The 1992 combined state and county expenditures for criminal justice activities, including police protection, jails and prisons, and judicial and legal services, was $407 million, or $352 per capita, the ninth highest in the nation.

The state operates a jail in each county for detaining persons awaiting trial who have not been released on bail and for those serving sentences for misdemeanor offenses. In addition, there are minimum-security prisons on Hawai'i Island (Kūlani) and O'ahu (Waiawa and Hālawa). A high-security prison (Hālawa Special Needs Facility), a Women's Community Correctional Center, and the Hawai'i Youth Correctional Facility are all located on O'ahu, the last two in Kailua. All correctional facilities are seriously overcrowded, and state officials have begun transferring some inmates to underutilized prisons on the U.S. mainland. In 1993 the incarceration rate in Hawai'i was approximately 148 per 100,000 population, less than one-third the 1993 national average of 525 per 100,000 population.

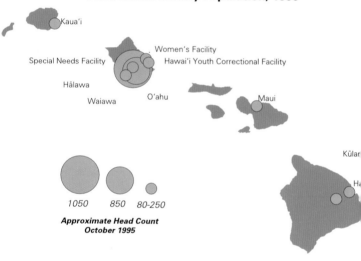

Correctional Facility Population, 1995

1050   850   80-250

Approximate Head Count October 1995

Honolulu, with a population of 871,000 in 1995, had a total crime rate of 6,889.3 per 100,000 in 1996, compared to the national average for cities between 500,000 and 999,000 population of 9,027.8. Many, if not most, crimes against the person (murder, rape, and assault) occur between friends, acquaintances, or family members, and thus largely do not involve strangers. In general, Hawai'i may be considered a safe place where, because of the island setting, most criminals are eventually apprehended. Yet it is clear that Hawai'i has earned its reputation as a paradise not because of the absence of crime.

A. DIDRICK CASTBERG

RECREATION

Hawai'i's topography, warm ocean waters, and diverse climate offer a wide variety of recreational opportunities within a small geographic area. Moreover, most outdoor recreational activities are available year-round, and an extensive public and private recreation infrastructure is in place for both tourists and residents.

The legacy of traditional Hawaiian lifestyles in some instances blends elements of recreation with work, so that activities such as fishing, hunting, and gathering may be recreational as well as economic. This is particularly true where traditional lifestyles remain relatively intact, such as at Kaimū on Hawai'i Island, Waimānalo and Wai'anae on O'ahu, much of East Maui, Moloka'i, and Waimea on Kaua'i.

The range of recreational opportunities reflects the geography of the traditional Hawaiian land division, the *ahupua'a,* proceeding from offshore and coastal activities to upland ones. Many ocean-based activities, such as surfing, outrigger canoeing, swimming, fishing, and gathering of marine resources, have a long history in Hawai'i. Surfing, which originated in Oceania, was first observed in the Islands by westerners in the late 1700s. Today surfers ride the waters off six islands at some 1,600 surfing sites with colorful names such as Banzai Pipeline, Avalanche, Leftovers, Suicides, Rice Bowl, and Gas Chambers. Hawai'i has won acclaim as a venue for surfing competitions, outrigger canoe races, sportfishing, windsurfing, triathalons, and transpacific yacht racing. Meanwhile new technology has given ocean sports enthusiasts broader opportunities for scuba diving, snorkeling, windsurfing, jetskiing, kayaking, and board surfing. The skies above Hawai'i have also been transformed into recreational space as hang gliding and parasailing have gained popularity.

The *mauka* (inland) regions of the islands are the setting for other recreational pursuits, including hiking, camping, hunting, horseback riding and rodeo participation, and snowboarding and skiing on the summit cinder cones of Mauna Kea. Hikers are rewarded with spectacular scenery on trails such as the 11-mile-long Kalalau Trail above Kaua'i's Nā Pali Coast, the networks of tracks through Hawai'i Vol-

canoes and Haleakalā National Parks, and trails in the Ko'olau Range immediately adjacent to urban Honolulu. Camping facilities are found on nearly every island. Hunting, for both sport and sustenance, is common, with wild pigs, mountain goats, axis deer, mouflon sheep, and game birds as typical quarry.

Public recreational sites and facilities in Hawai'i are administered by agencies at each level of govern-

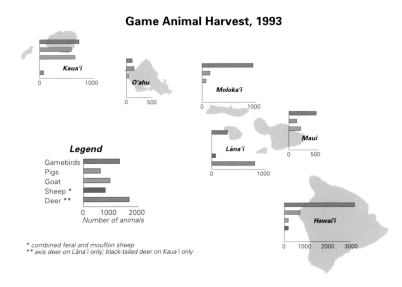

Game Animal Harvest, 1993

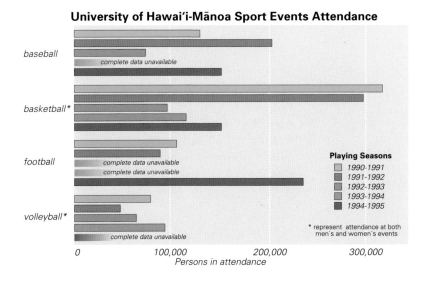

University of Hawai'i-Mānoa Sport Events Attendance

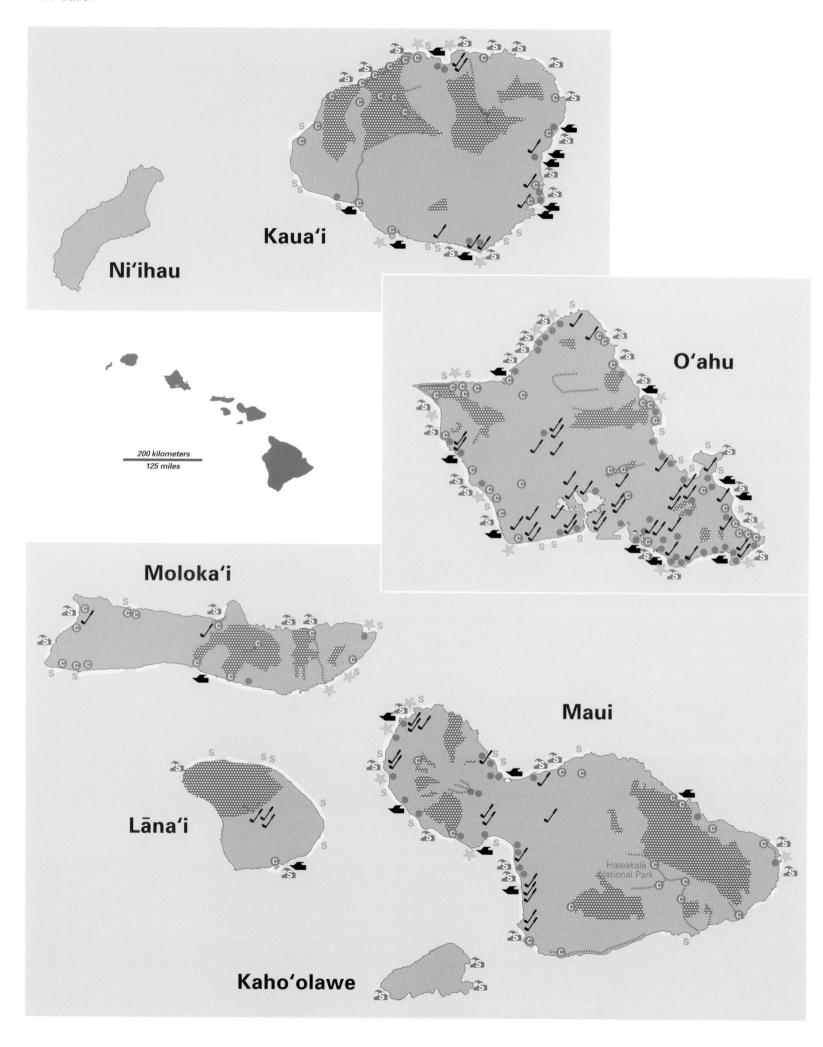

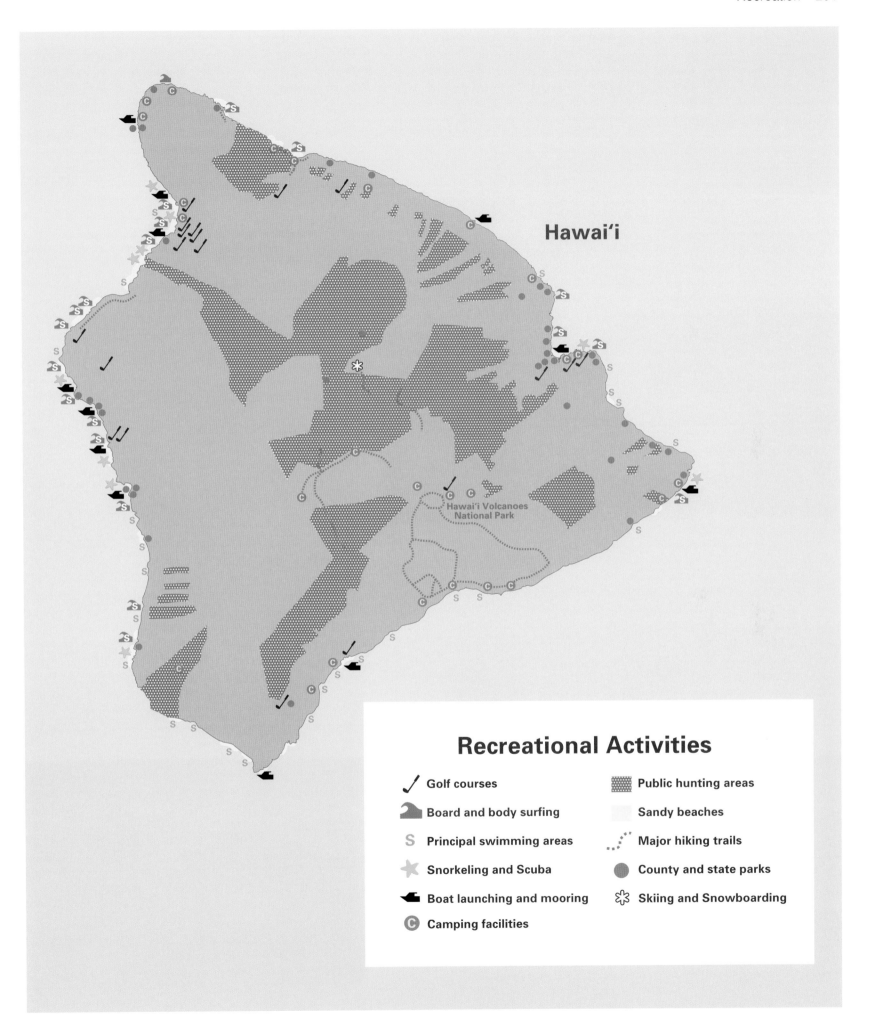

Hawai'i

Hawai'i Volcanoes
National Park

Recreational Activities

Golf courses		Public hunting areas
Board and body surfing		Sandy beaches
S Principal swimming areas		Major hiking trails
Snorkeling and Scuba		County and state parks
Boat launching and mooring		Skiing and Snowboarding
C Camping facilities		

ment. At the federal level, the National Park Service manages seven parks encompassing more than 260,000 acres (105,000 ha) on Hawai'i Island, Maui, Moloka'i, and O'ahu. In 1995 more than 6 million visitors to Hawai'i's national parks were recorded. Not surprisingly, the natural and cultural attractions in these parks are often a motivation for overseas visitors to come to the Islands. Hawai'i Volcanoes National Park, for instance, offers landscapes that incorporate the active volcanoes of Kīlauea and Mauna Loa with Hawai'i Island's austere coastal zone, while in Haleakalā National Park the Manhattan-sized core of Haleakalā is bordered by the rain forest–cloaked coast of Maui. The parks embody strong cultural value as well. For example, Kīlauea, long held to be the home of the goddess Pele, retains vital importance for Hawaiians.

Hawai'i Island also has three national historical parks in Kona and Kohala. On Moloka'i, Kalaupapa National Historical Park, centered around the settlement for people afflicted with Hansen's disease (leprosy), remains undeveloped in terms of visitor infrastructure. One of Hawai'i's most famous historical sites, the USS *Arizona* Memorial at Pearl Harbor on O'ahu, draws nearly 1.4 million visitors each year.

At the state level, the Department of Land and Natural Resources manages state parks; boat ramps and small boat harbors; hiking and mountain biking trails; camping, hunting, and picnic areas; and lands of cultural and historical interest. There are 80 state parks on five islands, including 31 on O'ahu; their combined acreage amounts to one-tenth of that contained in Hawai'i's national parks. O'ahu's largest state park is Kahana Valley, where local residents of Hawaiian ancestry act as cultural interpreters for visitors. Kaua'i offers the most acreage in state parks, with the contiguous Nā Pali Coast and Kōke'e parks totaling more than 10,000 acres (4,000 ha) of swampland, cliffs, canyons, and rain forest.

The state also provides sports facilities and sponsors athletic programs and events through the public schools and the University of Hawai'i. Volleyball, football, basketball, and baseball enjoy strong local support. Soccer, played year-round, surged in popularity during the 1990s. Organized youth soccer grew from about 300 players in 1974 to more than 22,000 in 1996. Adult clubs had more than 3,500 players in the mid-1990s, and nearly all the universities and colleges in the state have soccer teams. The infrastructure for

Hanauma Bay, O'ahu. [D. R. and T. L. Schrichte]

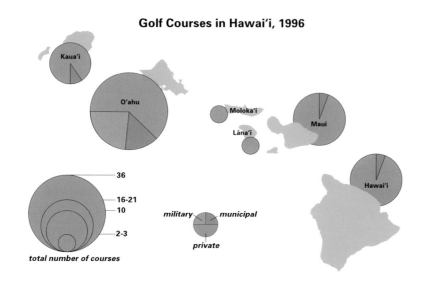

Golf Courses in Hawai'i, 1996

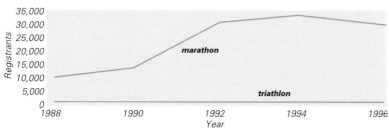

Registration in Honolulu Marathon and Ironman Triathlon

Surfer, O'ahu. [B. Romerhaus/Hawai'i Visitors Bureau]

sports has improved substantially under increased state funding, particularly at the University of Hawai'i at Mānoa.

The four county governments also offer an array of recreational services and facilities, including inland and beach parks, golf courses, zoos, botanical gardens, camping and picnicking areas, and lifeguard services at selected pools and public beaches. The counties maintain more than 600 parks on six islands, totaling approximately 9,000 acres (3,600 ha). Nearly half of the county parks are located on O'ahu. Local community organizations, families, and individuals make good use of county facilities.

Many commercial enterprises are also involved in the recreation business, providing a variety of opportunities for residents and especially tourists. Whale watching, snorkeling and diving tours, horseback riding, and surfing competitions are conducted almost exclusively by the private sector.

The number of park visits and participation in many recreational activities vary from year to year, as a result of fluctuations in the national and international economies and, occasionally, because of local natural disasters. The severe damage wrought upon Kaua'i in 1992 by Hurricane 'Iniki, for example, reduced the number of visitors for several years. Some county park facilities remained in disrepair for months after the disaster, and many trails were rendered unusable for a time. Volcanic eruptions, on the other hand, have served as a lure for visitors to Hawai'i Volcanoes National Park, though on occasion park facilities and recreational and cultural sites have been subject to closure and even destruction. From 1987 to 1990, a series of lava flows erased some of Hawai'i Island's finest recreational sites, including a historic surfing spot, the much-loved black sand beach at Kaimū, and the natural pool known as Queen's Bath near Kalapana.

Decreased public funding in the 1990s has reduced the parks and recreation workforce and has inhibited the capabilities of agencies to maintain previous levels of service. The expansion and renovation of facilities has been limited and parkland acquisition curtailed, and in some cases federal and state requirements for improved access and stricter environmental standards have not been met. In response to diminished funding, public agencies have in some instances imposed or increased user fees for some sites, sparking

Heavy recreational use of the Hanauma Bay Nature Park, a marine life conservation district created in 1967, has resulted in continual revision of management plans (fees and controlled access) to promote sustainable use. [D. R. and T. L. Schrichte]

public controversy among those who believe access to coastal and *mauka* public recreational areas should remain free of charge.

At the same time, rising levels of recreational use and the introduction of new activities such as windsurfing and jetskiing have led to community concern and conflicts among users in some locales. For example, activities that generate considerable noise and degrade the environment have proven controversial. The decreasing availability of surfing space has created tensions between surfers. Motorized recreational vehicles have encroached on bird sanctuaries; recreational overuse has compromised the pristine quality of some marine environments; and hunting and Native Hawaiian landuse claims have at times clashed with park policies and development programs. The representation of Hawai'i as a playground for the world is being challenged by Hawaiian activists and environmentalists who question whether the rate of growth in the use of outdoor recreational facilities is sustainable.

SONIA P. JUVIK,
JEAN NISHIDA SOUZA,
AND DREW KAPP

ENVIRONMENTAL QUALITY

Humans have left their imprint on Hawai'i's natural environment in a myriad of ways for centuries. In recent decades, the impact of human society on the natural environment has intensified and changed in character, reflecting population growth and the state's transition from a predominantly agricultural economy to a modern service-based one. The state's resident population doubled between 1960 and 1995, to about 1.2 million, and the annual number of visitors to Hawai'i since 1982 has doubled to more than 6 million. This increased human presence has created pressures on Hawai'i's limited land, water, and other natural resources. In the absence of major industrial sources of air pollution, much of the environmental management carried out by state agencies is concerned with maintaining the quality of surface waters (nearshore ocean and streams), groundwater, and solid and hazardous waste disposal.

Surface Water Quality

Water quality in Hawai'i is generally excellent. But the steeply sloping terrain, porous substrates, and proximity of the land to the ocean make coastal and stream waters especially vulnerable to both point-source and nonpoint-source pollution.

As the accompanying map shows, the state has designated nearshore waters in some areas as Class AA, with restrictions to maintain pristine quality for marine sanctuaries, oceanographic research, shellfish propagation, and other uses. The remaining waters surrounding the main islands are designated as Class A. Areas that do not meet current state or federal water quality standards because of heavy use and high pollution loads—and that may have adverse effects on public health, aquatic ecosystems, and fisheries—are designated as Water Quality Limited Segments by the state Department of Health (DOH).

Water quality sampling is conducted at least monthly at some 200 high-priority coastal sites around the state. However, only total nitrogen and phosphorus (nutrients), coliform bacteria, and turbidity are routinely monitored. The state's standard for microbial

contamination of water is the strictest in the nation, and violations are infrequent except at harbors and artificial drainage areas such as the Ala Wai Canal.

The parasite that causes leptospirosis, carried in the urine of introduced animals such as rats, is common in many Hawai'i streams, rendering water from them nonpotable. Another threat to human health, ciguatera poisoning, is suspected of occurring more frequently in coastal waters disturbed by human activities such as dredging and construction.

The metal arsenic, widely used in the past as a termite deterrent for lumber and in sugar and pineapple herbicides until World War II, has been detected in groundwater, seawater, and edible algae. In 1991 arsenic concentrations in waters off some O'ahu beaches were reported to be ten times greater than the maximum allowable contamination level set by the Environmental Protection Agency (EPA).

Point-Source Pollution With relatively little manufacturing in Hawai'i, there are only a small number of point (discrete) sources of industrial wastewater. The major wastewater producers are the U.S. Navy's industrial complex at Pearl Harbor, Hickam Air Force Base, Oahu's other military installations, Oahu's ten petroleum terminals and refineries, and the state's 25-plus electric power plants. Industrial discharges may contain ammonia, solvents, oil and grease, heated water, suspended solids, bacteria, and pesticides. Nutrients that support algal growth—metals such as iron, copper, and chromium, and organic wastes that reduce oxygen in receiving waters—may also be present in industrial wastewater. Under pollution control laws, two options exist for wastewater disposal: underground injection control (UIC) wells under permit from the DOH; or discharge into surface waters by permit under the National Pollution Discharge Elimination System (NPDES). In 1992, 79 facilities in Hawai'i held NPDES permits administered under the federal Clean Water Act. Of these, 24 (12 municipal, 8 industrial, and 4 agricultural) discharged more than a half-million gallons of effluent per day. In general, water quality monitoring and standards are more stringent under

NPDES permits than under injection well permits.

In 1995 there were about 500 injection wells registered for disposal of untreated sewage and wastes from industry, aquaculture, and septic systems. An additional 1,860 wells were used for stormwater drainage. The DOH initiated limited monitoring to determine pollutant levels in industrial wells in 1990. Discharges presumably filter into underground waters of limited use. However, information is scarce regarding the fate of well-injected wastes, and the human and ecological risks resulting from possible migration of contaminants to surface waters have not been evaluated conclusively.

The effects on water quality from effluent discharge into ocean waters are a matter of controversy. On Oʻahu, for example, where 1995 levels of sewage discharge totaled about 118 million gallons per day (mgd), studies have produced conflicting results. Some experts contend that coastal outfalls disperse effluent far enough from shore for tides, currents, and prevailing winds to minimize the return of effluents to coastal areas. But others estimate that effluent plumes reach the ocean surface 20 to 50 percent of the time, depending on the season, and can return to shore, posing health and environmental risks. While this controversy remains unsettled, the amount of sewage generated by the state's growing population continues to rise, and uncontrolled discharges of untreated sewage have increased. On Oʻahu there were 12 such spills in 1987, 75 in 1991, and 132 in 1995.

Many of the state's 150 or so private sewage treatment plants discharge wastewater into UIC wells. As with industrial wastewater, the use of injection wells for sewage wastewater disposal has not been studied sufficiently to determine its influence on coastal water quality. Studies on Maui have suggested a link between injection well fluids leaking into nearshore waters and an explosive growth of algae that continues to affect water quality and the health of coral reefs off the western shores of the island.

Finally, more than 100,000 cesspools are used statewide for domestic sewage disposal; these have the potential to pollute groundwater, depending on the geology of individual sites.

Nonpoint-Source Pollution Nonpoint-source pollution poses a widespread and significant hazard, the severity of which varies with land use, topography, vegetative cover, and soil erodability. Nonpoint sources are diffuse: rainfall moving over and through ground picks up and carries pollutants into streams, wetlands, and coastal waters. Such pollutants include chemicals from industrial, agricultural, urban, and residential areas, military installations, and golf courses; and sediments from construction sites, agriculture, and degraded natural areas. The decline of plantation agriculture has reduced the inputs of its associated soil erosion, pesticides, and fertilizers. For example, the state's total commercial fertilizer consumption decreased from 131,000 tons in 1989 to about 113,000 tons in 1993.

Drinking Water Quality

Groundwater is the source of most of Hawaiʻi's drinking water. In 1996 there were about 150 regulated public water systems utilizing approximately 450 wells for drinking water. In 1995 there were between one and five violations of coliform bacterial standards per month statewide. In addition to microbial contamination, other chemical contaminants of concern in Hawaiʻi are nitrates; trihalomethanes; the pesticides EDB, DBCP, atrazine, TCP, and DCP; and the industrial chemicals TCE, EDB (used as a fuel additive), and carbon tetrachloride.

Well sampling data and soil studies show that pesticides, solvents, and other persistent chemicals used in the past on plants, buildings, and soils are moving laterally downhill over much of Oʻahu, Maui, Kauaʻi, and Hawaiʻi Island. Statewide, there were some 40 contaminated drinking water wells in 1989, 57 in 1993, and 64 as of April 1996. Pesticides are the most frequently detected contaminants. The pollutant levels detected are generally well below the existing standards for public health protection. However, the speed at which these toxins move through the soils, how long they persist, or what happens when they reach aquifers is not well understood. The state does not routinely require treatment for toxic chemicals. If chemical pollutants are detected in a drinking water well, quarterly monitoring is conducted, and, if contamination approaches the maximum allowable level, the well is either shut down or treatment is required.

Solid and Hazardous Waste

The volume of solid waste generated in the state has increased much more rapidly than the population. On Oʻahu, for example, the volume nearly doubled between 1990 and 1994 from 825,000 tons to 1.5 million tons.

The state legislature set a goal in 1991 to divert 25 percent of the solid waste stream through recycling and greenwaste composting by 1995. In 1994 the state achieved a waste diversion rate of about 17 percent, with Maui diverting 24 percent, Oʻahu 18 percent, Kauaʻi 15 percent, and Hawaiʻi Island 10 percent.

To foster development of local businesses that utilize recyclable materials, the Clean Hawaiʻi Center was established in 1994 within the state Department of Business, Economic Development & Tourism. In addition, the Hawaiʻi Material Exchange (HIMEX) facilitates the statewide exchange of a wide variety of materials from industrial chemicals to used consumer goods. In 1994 more than $150 million was spent on solid waste collection and disposal; however, less than one-tenth that amount went to diversion programs.

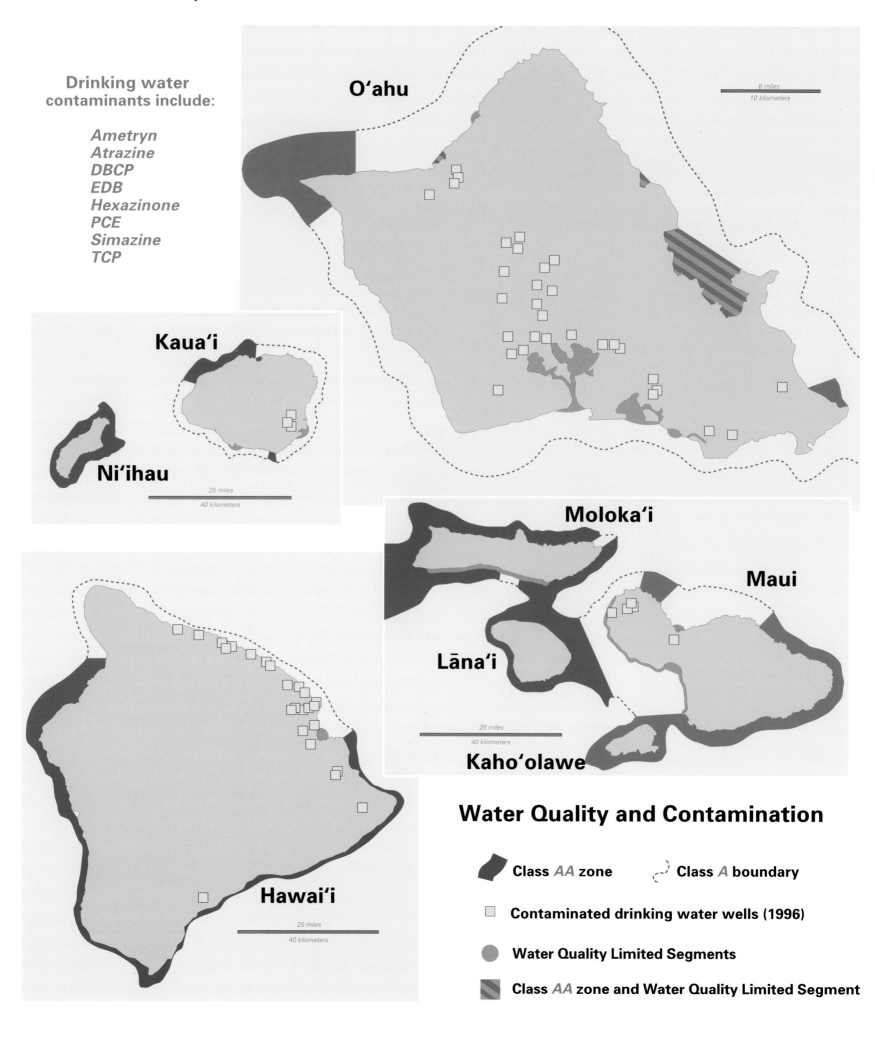

Drinking water contaminants include:

Ametryn
Atrazine
DBCP
EDB
Hexazinone
PCE
Simazine
TCP

O'ahu

6 miles
10 kilometers

Kaua'i

Ni'ihau

25 miles
40 kilometers

Moloka'i

Maui

Lāna'i

Kaho'olawe

25 miles
40 kilometers

Hawai'i

25 miles
40 kilometers

Water Quality and Contamination

Class *AA* zone   Class *A* boundary

Contaminated drinking water wells (1996)

Water Quality Limited Segments

Class *AA* zone and Water Quality Limited Segment

Highly Stressed Ecosystems, 1992

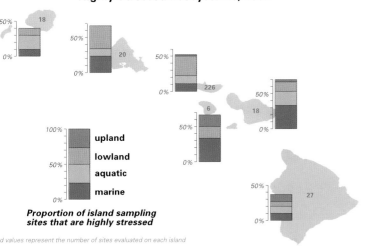

upland

lowland

aquatic

marine

*Proportion of island sampling
sites that are highly stressed*

...ed values represent the number of sites evaluated on each island

As they have in the past, human-induced ecosystem stressors continue to damage many valuable land and water resources. The 1992 Hawai'i Environmental Risk Ranking study analyzed 100 sites around the main islands (and 226 sites on Moloka'i) for 12 environmental stressors. Of the stressors considered, alien species rated in the top three for 70 percent of the sites; erosion and sedimentation for 63 percent; human crowding for 45 percent; and earthmoving and development for 30 percent. Other stressors, ranked in order of importance, were toxic chemicals, water diversion and channelization, nutrient load and biological oxygen demand, fire, noise and light, explosives, global warming, and heat.

In general, toxic chemicals and hazardous wastes are managed effectively in Hawai'i. A sizable portion of the state's hazardous waste is treated and reused locally; the remainder is sent to the U.S. mainland for disposal. The amount of hazardous waste generated statewide declined from 1,500 tons in 1987 to 1,365 in 1993, about half of it from military sources.

About 130 sites potentially contaminated by hazardous waste are being evaluated for inclusion on the EPA National Priorities List for federal remediation.

As of 1996, 4 sites were on the "Superfund" list, including the Pearl Harbor Naval Complex, Schofield Barracks, and the Del Monte Kunia facility.

Of the roughly 5,500 underground storage tanks statewide, about three-fourths are on O'ahu. Half of these tanks contain gasoline. The number of known leaking tanks rose from 100 in 1990 to nearly 1,000 in 1996. Fortunately, many underground storage tanks are located above caprock, which prevents transport of contaminants to aquifers. Stricter federal regulations to prevent corrosion and overfilling of underground tanks were in effect as of 1998.

Air Quality

Outdoor air quality in Hawai'i consistently meets federal and state environmental health standards. The reliable northeast trade winds and lack of significant industrial development mitigate the buildup of airborne pollutants over the Islands.

Volcanic emissions, called vog, often seriously affect populated areas on Hawai'i Island, where twice as many medical insurance claims for respiratory complaints have been reported in vog-impacted areas than in nonvog areas. Sulfate concentrations in West Hawai'i have sometimes reached levels comparable to areas with sulfate haze problems on the U.S. mainland.

Hawai'i's residents benefit from an environment of generally high quality with few risks to human health, despite relatively low levels of spending on environmental management. Funding for environmental management has generally remained stable in Hawai'i during recent years. The 1996–1997 DOH budget for environmental management programs was approximately $43.4 million, including nearly $31 million for construction, such as improvements on sewage treatment facilities. Of this total, $28.7 came from federal funds, $8.6 from the state, and $6 million from special funds (such as landfill tipping fees).

NOREEN M. PARKS

GOVERNMENT SERVICES

Government functions for protecting public health and safety that are not covered elsewhere in this *Atlas* include civil defense, solid waste management, sewage treatment, fire protection, and emergency medical (ambulance) services. (See Health and Wellness for information on health and social services, Crime for the police, and Government and Politics for judicial courts.)

Civil Defense The role of civil defense is to avert or minimize the impacts on the population of a wide range of natural and technological hazards. Civil defense plans for disaster response and assistance are prepared at the county level and approved by the director of State Civil Defense (SCD) within the State Department of Defense. These plans are coordinated with the Federal Emergency Management Agency (FEMA) and other federal agencies. In addition, all state departments have a designated civil defense coordinator, who is responsible for developing departmental plans to implement the provisions of the overall state plans.

The governor, as head of SCD, appoints a state director of civil defense, who in turn designates the mayor of each county as deputy director. Each county has a civil defense agency headed by an administrator who is appointed by the mayor. The county mayors are directly responsible for safeguarding public safety and for providing appropriate support to the county civil defense agency. Each county civil defense agency has an emergency operating center and a small full-time staff, which is partially supported by federal funds.

With county support, the SCD maintains a statewide communications and warning system made up of outdoor sirens and the emergency alert system (EAS). The EAS is operated over radio and cable television networks, which voluntarily supply broadcast time. It is linked with the National Weather Service, Pacific Tsunami Warning Center, and all county police and civil defense agencies. The SCD system also employs a computerized database that provides information for mapping, modeling, risk analysis, and alternatives for hazard response.

Municipal Solid Waste In 1995 approximately 2.1 million tons of solid waste were disposed of by local governments. Not surprisingly, 75 percent of the total volume of solid waste is produced on Oʻahu, the state's center of population, commerce, and industry.

Local government assumes responsibility for the safe disposal of all (residential and nonresidential) solid wastes. Municipal curbside collection of residential solid waste occurs in all counties except Hawaiʻi. On Hawaiʻi Island residents must pay for service by private waste-disposal companies or haul their solid waste to regional transfer stations for municipal disposal. The hauling of nonresidential and some multifamily residential solid waste, however, is not a local government responsibility on any of the islands.

There are three established modes of disposal for residential solid wastes: recycling, waste-to-energy conversion, and landfill. Only on Oʻahu are mechanisms for all three methods fully established. Except for diverted recyclable materials, all residential solid waste on Oʻahu is taken to the H-Power plant at Campbell Industrial Park, where combustibles are converted to approximately 50 megawats of electricity (6 percent of Oʻahu's electrical energy need). Noncombustible waste is disposed of in landfills. Throughout the state recycling and composting divert only 17 percent of the total solid waste stream, falling far short of the goal set

Hawaiʻi Civil Defense System Organization

Governor

Director of Hawaiʻi Civil Defense

The Civil Defense Director appoints the mayor as Deputy Director who in turn appoints the county Civil Defense Agency Administrator

Vice Director State Civil Defense

State Departments and Agencies

Federal Agencies and Private Organizations

County Mayor (Deputy Director)

Administrator of County Civil Defense Emergency Operating Centers Kauaʻi - Oʻahu - Maui - Hawaiʻi

County Agencies

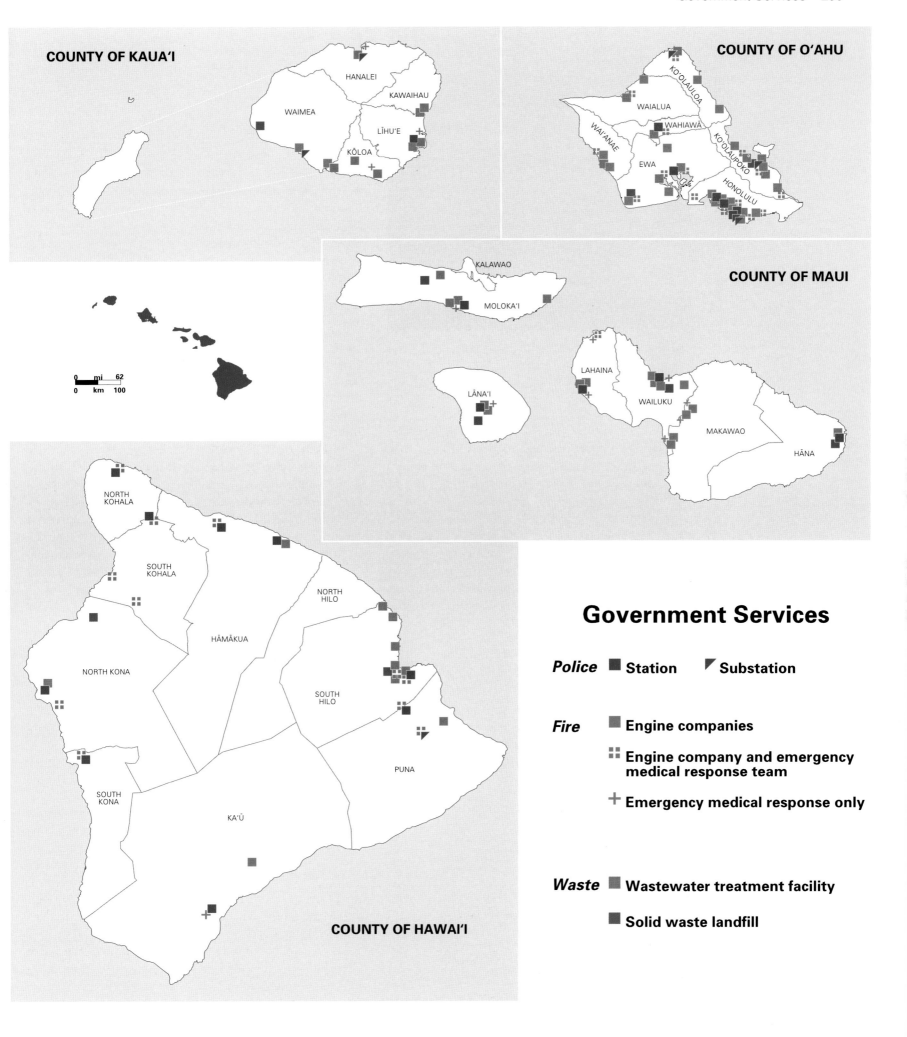

COUNTY OF KAUA'I

COUNTY OF O'AHU

HANALEI

KAWAIHAU

WAIMEA

LĪHU'E

KŌLOA

KO'OLAULOA

WAIALUA

WAHIAWĀ

WAI'ANAE

EWA

KO'OLAUPOKO

HONOLULU

KALAWAO

COUNTY OF MAUI

MOLOKA'I

LĀNA'I

LAHAINA

WAILUKU

MAKAWAO

HĀNA

NORTH
KOHALA

SOUTH
KOHALA

NORTH
HILO

HĀMĀKUA

NORTH KONA

SOUTH
HILO

SOUTH
KONA

PUNA

KA'Ū

COUNTY OF HAWAI'I

0   mi   62
0   km   100

Government Services

Police ■ Station   ◤ Substation

Fire ■ Engine companies

⚏ Engine company and emergency
medical response team

✚ Emergency medical response only

Waste ■ Wastewater treatment facility

■ Solid waste landfill

County of Hawai'i solid waste landfill at Pu'u Anahulu, North Kona. This new facility complies with stringent federal environmental standards and has been designed to handle all solid waste generated on the island. [Air Survey Hawai'i]

out in State Act 324-91 to achieve waste diversion of 25 percent by 1995 and 50 percent by 2000. This failure has been attributed to geographic isolation, limited volumes of recyclable materials, the absence of strong local markets for recoverable solid waste, and a general lack of commitment to alternative waste management.

Sewage Treatment Primary treatment, the most elementary level of treatment, involves the settling of solids and addition of chemical disinfectants to the sewage. In secondary treatment the sewage is subjected to further treatment by biological processes utilizing microorganisms. The most advanced sewage processing is tertiary treatment, in which varieties of physical and chemical processes are used to lower pollutant levels further.

Sewage treatment levels vary throughout the state, although most collected sewage is subjected to secondary treatment. On Maui tertiary treatment levels are achieved, while at two major facilities on O'ahu sewage receives only primary treatment before being discharged via outfalls into the ocean. Large areas of most islands remain without sewerage systems, and wastes are discharged into cesspools or septic tanks.

Maui County utilizes the most sophisticated system for disposing of treated sewage components, wastewater effluent, and sludge. Sewage treatment plant effluent either is injected into deep wells or reclaimed for irrigation of agricultural areas or golf courses. Sludge is combined with green waste in a process called co-composting to produce landscaping fertilizer. O'ahu has plans to begin recycling sludge to produce soil conditioner. Four of O'ahu's sewage treatment plants discharge treated effluent into the ocean via outfalls, one to a freshwater lake, and three to injection wells.

Fire and Ambulance Each county has a fire department that serves as the local counterpart for the State Emergency Management System. While ambulance service is the responsibility of the State Department of Health, it is managed by the fire departments of the individual counties, except on Maui where the county contracts ambulance service with private firms.

SONIA P. JUVIK

APPENDICES

Conversion Factors

1 foot = 0.3048 meter
1 meter = 39.37 inches = 3.2808 feet
1 statute mile = 0.8684 nautical mile = 1.6093 kilometers = 5,280 feet
1 nautical mile = 1.152 statute miles = 1.852 kilometers
1 kilometer = 0.6214 statute mile = 0.5396 nautical mile

1 acre = 43,560 square feet = 0.4047 hectare
1 hectare = 2.4710 acres
1 square mile = 640 acres = 258.998 hectares = 2.5900 square kilometers
1 square kilometer = 247.106 acres = 100 hectares = 0.386103 square mile

1 fathom = 6 feet = 1.8288 meters
1 nautical mile = 1,000 fathoms

1 mile per hour = 1.467 feet per second = 0.447 meter per second = 1.6093
   kilometers per hour = 0.868 knot
1 meter per second = 3.600 kilometers per hour = 1.940 knots
1 knot = 1.152 miles per hour = 1.854 kilometers per hour = 0.515 meter
   per second

1 pound (avoirdupois) = 0.4536 kilogram = 453.5924 grams
1 kilogram = 2.2046 pounds (avoirdupois)
1 ton (short) = 2,000 pounds = 907.1847 kilograms = 0.9072 tonne
1 tonne = 1,000 kilograms = 2,204.623 pounds

1 gallon (U.S. liquid) = 3.7853 liters = 231 cubic inches = 0.0038 cubic
   meter
1 liter = 0.2642 gallon (U.S. liquid)
1 cubic yard = 0.7646 cubic meter

1 inch mercury = 25.4 millimeters = 33.8640 millibars
1 millimeter mercury = 0.0394 inch = 1.3332 millibars
1 millibar = 0.0295 inch = 0.7501 millimeter

$°F = (°C \times 9/5) + 32$
$°C = (°F - 32) \times 5/9$

STATISTICAL TABLES

Airline Distances (Great Circle Distances between Honolulu International Airport and Specified Places)

Place	Distance from Honolulu	
	Statute miles	*Km*
Hawaiian Islands		
Cape Kumukahi, Hawaiʻi[1]	236	380
Hilo, Hawaiʻi	214	344
Ka Lae (South Point), Hawaiʻi	221	356
Kailua-Kona, Hawaiʻi	168	270
Kahului, Maui	98	158
Lānaʻi, Airport	72	116
Molokaʻi, Airport	54	87
Līhuʻe, Kauai	103	166
Puʻuwai, Niʻihau	152	245
Nihoa	283	455
Necker I	520	837
French Frigate Shoals	556	895
Gardner Pinnacles	688	1,107
Maro Reef	851	1,369
Laysan I	936	1,506
Lisianski I	1,065	1,714
Pearl and Hermes Atoll	1,208	1,944
Midway Atoll	1,309	2,106
Kure Atoll	1,367	2,200
Other Pacific locations		
Apra Harbor, Guam	3,806	6,124
Auckland, N.Z.	4,393	7,068
Avarua, Rarotonga	2,950	4,750
Brisbane, Australia	4,743	7,633
Funafuti, Tuvalu	2,550	4,106
Hong Kong	5,541	8,915
Jakarta, Indonesia	6,807	10,955
Johnston Atoll	820	1,319
Kingman Reef	1,073	1,726
Kolonia, Ponape	3,087	4,967
Koror, Belau	4,593	7,390
Kwajelein, Marshall Is	2,443	3,931
Majuro, Marshall Is	2,271	3,654
Manila, Philippines	5,293	8,516
Nukuʻalofa, Tongatapu	3,165	5,096
Nuku Hiva, Marquesas Is	2,400	3,864
Pago Pago, American Samoa	2,606	4,193
Palmyra Atoll	1,101	1,772
Papeete, Tahiti	2,741	4,410
Saipan, Mariana Is	3,704	5,960
Shanghai, China	4,934	7,940
Singapore	6,710	10,799

Place	Distance from Honolulu	
	Statute miles	*Km*
Suva, Fiji	3,159	5,083
Sydney, Australia	5,070	8,158
Taipei, Taiwan	5,046	8,120
Tokyo, Japan	3,847	6,190
Vladivostok, Russia	4,291	6,906
Wake Island	2,294	3,691
Wellington, N.Z.	4,738	7,625
North/South America		
Anchorage, Alaska	2,781	4,475
Cape Horn, Chile	7,457	11,998
Chicago, Illinois	4,179	6,724
Cristobal, Canal Zone	5,214	8,389
Lima, Peru	5,950	9,580
Los Angeles, California	2,557	4,114
Mexico City, Mexico	3,781	6,085
Miami, Florida	4,856	7,813
Montreal, Quebec	4,910	7,902
New York, New York	4,959	7,979
Portland, Oregon	2,595	4,175
Rio de Janeiro, Brazil	8,190	13,180
San Diego, California	2,610	4,199
San Francisco, California	2,397	3,857
Santiago, Chile	6,861	11,042
Seattle, Washington	2,679	4,311
Vancouver, B.C.	2,709	4,359
Washington, D.C.	4,829	7,770
Other world cities		
Athens, Greece	8,277	13,320
Bangkok, Thailand	6,585	10,597
Beijing, China	5,067	8,154
Bombay, India	8,010	12,890
Cairo, Egypt	8,840	14,226
Calcutta, India	7,037	11,325
Cape Town, South Africa	11,532	18,559
Colombo, Sri Lanka	7,981	12,844
London, England	7,226	11,627
Moscow, Russia	7,033	11,318
Paris, France	7,434	11,964
Rome, Italy	8,022	12,910
Vienna, Austria	7,626	12,273

1. The great circle distance from Kure Atoll to Cape Kumukahi, Hawaiʻi, is 1,523 statute miles. This distance represents the total length of the Hawaiian Archipelago.

Areas: State, Counties, and Islands

Place	Total Area		Inland Water
	Square km	Square miles	Square miles
State:	16,636.5	6,423.4	25.0
Counties			
Hawai'i	10,433.1	4,028.2	4.4
Honolulu	1,554.5	600.2	19.0
Kaua'i	1,612.2	622.5	8.9
Maui	3,002.5	1,159.3	3.6
Islands			
Hawai'i	10,433.1	4,028.2	4.4
Maui	1,883.7	727.3	3.4
O'ahu	1,546.5	597.1	18.8
Kaua'i	1,430.5	552.3	4.6
Moloka'i	673.5	260.0	0.2
Lāna'i	364.0	140.6	
Ni'ihau	179.9	69.5	3.4
Kaho'olawe	115.5	44.6	—
Lehua	1.0	0.4	—
Ka'ula	0.6	0.2	—
Molokini	0.1	0.04	—
Northwestern Hawaiian			
Islands:	8.0	3.1	0.2
Laysan I	4.1	1.6	0.2
Lisianski I	1.5	0.6	—
Kure Atoll	1.0	0.4	—
Nihoa	0.7	0.3	—
Pearl and Hermes Atoll			
(7 islets)	0.3	0.1	—
Necker I	0.2	0.07	—
French Frigate Shoals			
(12 islets)	0.2	0.1	—
Gardner Pinnacles	0.02	0.01	—
Maro Reef	Awash	Awash	—
Other nearby islands			
(not in the State)			
Palmyra Atoll	11.9	4.6	3.0
Midway Atoll	6.4	2.5	—
Johnston Atoll	0.8	0.3	—
Kingman Reef	1.0	0.4	—

Major Streams

Island Feature or Stream		Length or Avg. Discharge
Longest water feature (miles)		
Hawai'i	Wailuku River	32.0
Maui	Kalialinui–Wai'ale Gulch	18.0
Kaho'olawe	Ahupū Gulch	4.0
Lāna'i	Maunalei–Wai'alalā Gulch	12.9
Moloka'i	Wailau–Pūlena Stream	6.5
O'ahu	Kaukonahua Stream (So. Fork)	33.0
Kaua'i	Waimea River–Po'omau Stream	19.5
Ni'ihau	Keanauli'i–Puniopo Valley	5.9
Largest perennial stream (miles)[1]		
Hawai'i	Wailuku River	22.7
Maui	Palikea Stream	7.8
Moloka'i	Wailau–Pūlena Stream	6.5
O'ahu	Kaukonahua Stream	30.0
Kaua'i	Waimea River	19.7
Streams with greatest avg discharge (mill gal/day)[2]		
Hawai'i	Wailuku River	250
Maui	'Īao Stream	43
Moloka'i	Wailau Stream	27
O'ahu	Waikele Stream[3]	27
Kaua'i	Hanalei River	140

1. Estimated on basis of drainage area rather than stream runoff. Other major streams include Wailoa River, Hawai'i (1/2-mile long); Honokohau Stream (9.4 miles) and 'Īao Stream (5 miles) on Maui; Hālawa Stream (6.4 miles), Waikolu Stream (4.7 miles), and Pelekunu Stream (2.3 miles) on Moloka'i; Waikele Stream (15.3 miles), Kīpapa Stream (12.8 miles), Waiakakalaua Stream (11.8 miles), Nu'uanu Stream (4 miles), and Ala Wai Canal (1.9 miles) on O'ahu; Makaweli River (15.1 miles), Wainiha River (13.8 miles), Hanapēpē River (13.3 miles), and Wailua River (11.8 miles) on Kaua'i.

2. Most recent available year.

3. Most of discharge is from nearby groundwater outflow.

Highway Distances

Places	Statute Miles[1]	Km[1]
Kaua'i		
Līhu'e—Hā'ena	38.0	61.2
Līhu'e—Wailua	5.9	9.5
Līhu'e—Līhu'e Airport	2.0	3.2
Līhu'e—Po'ipū	11.9	19.2
Līhu'e—Mānā	32.9	53.0
Līhu'e—Kalalau Lookout	44.6	71.8
Po'ipū—Kalalau Lookout	36.8	59.2
Po'ipū—Princeville	40.7	65.5
O'ahu		
Honolulu—Ala Moana Center	1.6	2.6
Honolulu—UH, via King St	3.2	5.2
Honolulu—Waikīkī (Kalakaua and Lewers)	3.2	5.2
Honolulu—Waimānalo, via Koko Head	21.8	35.1
Honolulu—Waimānalo, via Nu'uanu	13.3	21.4
Honolulu—Kailua, via Nu'uanu	11.6	18.7
Honolulu—Kāne'ohe, via Kalihi	10.8	17.4
Honolulu—Kahuku, via Kahalu'u	36.2	58.3
Honolulu—Kahuku, via Kāne'ohe	39.0	62.8
Honolulu—Kahuku, via Wahiawā	46.2	74.4
Honolulu—Ka'ena, via Wahiawā	42.2	68.3
Honolulu—Ka'ena Point, via Wai'anae	44.3	71.3
Honolulu—Wahiawā	20.5	33.0
Honolulu—Pearl Harbor Shipyard	6.5	10.5
Honolulu—Honolulu Airport	4.8	7.7
Waikīkī—UH via Kapahulu	3.2	5.2
Waikīkī—Honolulu Airport	8.0	12.9
Waimānalo—Kahuku	36.2	58.2
Circle island, via Makapu'u	99.1	159.6
Circle island, via Nu'uanu Pali	81.1	130.6
Moloka'i		
Kaunakakai—Sheraton Hotel	19.5	31.4
Kaunakakai—Maunaloa	16.5	26.6
Kaunakakai—Ho'olehua Airport	7.0	11.3
Kaunakakai—Hālawa	27.6	44.4
Ho'olehua Airport—Sheraton Hotel	11.5	18.5

Places	Statute Miles[1]	Km[1]
Lāna'i		
Lāna'i City—Lāna'i Airport	2.7	4.3
Lāna'i City—Hulopo'e	8.0	12.9
Maui		
Wailuku—Kahului	2.3	3.7
Wailuku—Kahului Airport	4.2	6.8
Wailuku—Hāna, via Kaupō	59.8	96.3
Wailuku—Hāna, via Ke'anae	53.7	86.5
Wailuku—Haleakalā Summit	38.2	61.5
Wailuku—Lahaina, via Kahakuloa	38.0	61.2
Wailuku—Lahaina, via Olowalu	20.9	33.6
Wailuku—Mākena	17.6	28.3
Kahului—Kīhei	7.9	12.7
Lahaina—Wailea	32.4	52.2
Lahaina—Nāpili	8.9	14.3
Lahaina—Kā'anapali	3.7	6.0
Hawai'i		
Hilo—Hilo International Airport	2.0	3.2
Hilo—Kalapana	26.1	42.0
Hilo—Mauna Kea Summit	39.3	63.3
Hilo—Mauna Loa Observatory	52.4	84.4
Hilo—Volcano House	30.7	49.4
Hilo—Kailua, via Nā'ālehu	125.2	201.6
Hilo—Kailua, via Saddle Rd	84.3	135.7
Hilo—Kailua, via Hāmākua	91.2	146.8
Hilo—Waimea, via Saddle Rd	57.9	93.2
Hilo—Waimea, via Hāmākua	55.3	89.0
Hilo—Kawaihae, via Hāmākua	69.5	111.9
Hilo—'Upolu Point, via Hāmākua	83.7	134.8
Kailua—Keāhole-Kona Airport	6.8	11.0
Kailua—Keauhou	6.9	11.1
Kawaihae—Hāwī	18.0	29.0
Kawaihae—Kailua	48.4	77.9
Waimea—Hāwī	21.4	34.5
Waimea—Kawaihae	11.5	18.5

1. Mileages between towns represent distances between post office buildings. For Honolulu, the Downtown Station is the reference point.

U.S. Census designated cities, towns, and villages with populations of 1,000 or more (not entire neighborhoods). None of these places is an independent municipality: their boundaries are statistical rather than political.

Town (by island)	Land Area (acres)	Population 1980	Population 1990
Kaua'i			
Anahola	NA	915	1,181
'Ele'ele	NA	580	1,489
Hanamā'ulu	508	3,227	3,611
Hanapēpē	580	1,417	1,395
Kalāheo	1,152	2,500	3,592
Kapa'a	2,415	4,467	8,149
Kekaha	646	3,260	3,506
Kīlauea	NA	895	1,685
Kōloa	722	1,457	1,791
Lāwa'i	NA	NA	1,787
Līhu'e	3,959	4,000	5,536
'Ōma'o	NA	NA	1,142
Princeville	NA	500	1,244
Puhi	NA	991	1,210
Wailua	763	1,587	2,018
Wailua Homesteads	NA	NA	3,870
Waimea	624	1,569	1,840
O'ahu			
'Āhuimanu	1,646	6,238	8,387
'Aiea	3,716	32,879	8,906
Barbers Point Housing	149	1,373	2,218
'Ewa Beach	882	14,369	14,315
'Ewa Gentry	NA	NA	1,992
'Ewa Villages	NA	NA	3,780
Hālawa	NA	NA	13,408
Hale'iwa	1,207	2,412	2,442
Hau'ula	1,006	2,997	3,479
He'eia	931	5,432	5,010
Hickam Housing	776	4,425	6,553
Honolulu[1]	53,723	365,048	377,059
Iroquois Point	403	3,915	4,188
Ka'a'awa	NA	959	1,138
Kahalu'u	841	2,925	3,068
Kahuku	NA	935	2,063
Kailua	4,470	35,812	36,818
Kāne'ohe	3,886	29,919	35,448
Lā'ie	781	4,643	5,577
Mā'ili	573	5,026	6,059
Mākaha	1,600	6,582	7,990
Mākaha Valley	NA	NA	1,012
Makakilo City	1,791	7,691	9,828
Maunawili	2,230	5,239	4,847
Mililani Town	2,354	21,365	29,359
Mōkapu	2,718	11,615	11,662
Mokulē'ia	NA	NA	1,776
Nānākuli	1,602	8,185	9,575
Pūpūkea	NA	NA	4,111
Pearl City	5,449	42,575	30,993
Schofield Barracks	1,849	18,851	19,597
Village Park	NA	NA	7,407
Wahiawā	1,492	16,911	17,386
Waialua	784	4,051	3,943
Wai'anae	2,194	7,941	8,758

Town (by island)	Land Area (acres)	Population 1980	Population 1990
Waimalu	NA	NA	29,967
Waimānalo	255	3,562	3,508
Waimānalo Beach	973	4,161	4,185
Waipahu	1,815	29,139	31,435
Waipi'o	NA	NA	11,812
Waipi'o Acres	447	4,091	5,304
Wheeler AFB	NA	NA	2,600
Whitmore Village	470	2,318	3,373
Moloka'i			
Kaunakakai	1,289	2,231	2,658
Kualapu'u	NA	502	1,661
Lāna'i			
Lāna'i City	154	2,092	2,400
Maui			
Hā'ikū-Pā'uwela	NA	NA	4,509
Kahului	2,888	12,978	16,889
Kīhei	2,099	5,644	11,107
Lahaina	1,150	6,095	9,073
Makawao	1,111	2,900	5,405
Nāpili-Honokōwai	482	2,446	4,332
Pā'ia	626	193	2,091
Pukalani	1,478	3,950	5,879
Waihe'e-Waiehu	NA	NA	4,004
Wailea-Mākena	1,348	1,124	3,799
Wailuku	2,283	10,260	10,688
Hawai'i			
Captain Cook	4,800	2,008	2,595
Hawaiian Beaches[2]	NA	NA	2,846
Hawaiian Paradise Park[2]	NA	NA	3,389
Hilo	35,929	35,269	37,808
Hōlualoa	2767	1,243	3,834
Honalo	NA	NA	1,926
Honaunau-Nāpō'opo'o	NA	NA	2,373
Honoka'a	882	1,936	2,186
Kahalu'u-Keauhou	NA	NA	1,990
Kailua	4,988	4,751	9,126
Kalaoa	NA	NA	4,490
Kapa'au	NA	612	1,083
Kea'au	NA	775	1,584
Kealakekua	1,327	1,033	1,453
Mountain View	NA	540	3,075
Nā'ālehu	2,541	1,168	1,027
Pāhala	637	1,619	1,520
Pāhoa	NA	923	1,027
Pāpa'ikou	921	1,567	1,634
Pepe'ekeo	NA	NA	1,813
Volcano	NA	NA	1,516
Waikoloa Village	NA	NA	2,248
Waimea (Kamuela)	652	1,179	5,972
Wainaku	275	1,045	1,243

1. Estimated population of Honolulu in 1996 was 423,475.
2. Subdivisions

Largest Lakes

Island	Largest Lake[1]	Category	Max. Depth (feet)	Altitude (feet)	Area (acres)	Shoreline (miles)
Hawai'i	Waiākea Pond	natural	7	sea level	27	2
Maui	Kanahā Pond	natural	3	sea level	41	2
Kaho'olawe	None	—	—	—	—	—
Lāna'i	None	—	—	—	—	—
Moloka'i	Kualapu'u Reservoir	artificial	50	821	100	4
O'ahu	Wahiawā Reservoir	artificial	85	842	302	11
Kaua'i	Waitā Reservoir	artificial	23	241	424	3
Ni'ihau	Halulu Lake	natural	NA[2]	sea level	182	3

1. Excludes shoreline fishponds and areas filled only during floods. The largest intermittent lake is Halāli'i Lake, Ni'ihau (840.7 acres). Other important lakes include Lake Waiau, Hawai'i (1.28 acres), and Violet Lake, Maui (3.0 acres). Lake Waiau (elevation 13,020 feet) is the highest lake in the State and the third highest in the United States.

2. NA—Not available.

Channels

Channel	Approximate depth below sea level		Width		Adjacent Islands
	feet	m	statute miles	km	
Kaulakahi	3,570	1,088	17.2	27.7	Ni'ihau/Kaua'i
Kaua'i	10,890	3,319	72.1	116.0	Kaua'i/O'ahu
Kaiwi	2,202	671	25.8	41.5	O'ahu/Moloka'i
Kalohi	540	165	9.2	14.8	Moloka'i/Lāna'i
Pailolo	846	258	8.8	14.2	Moloka'i/Maui
Kealaikahiki	1,086	331	17.8	28.6	Lāna'i/Kaho'olawe
'Alalākeiki	822	251	6.7	10.8	Maui/Kaho'olawe
'Alenuihāhā	6,810	2,076	29.6	47.6	Maui/Hawai'i

Major Mountains

Island and Mountain	Elevation	
	feet	*m*
Hawai'i		
Mauna Kea[1]	13,796	4,205
Mauna Loa	13,679	4,169
Hualālai	8,271	2,521
Kohala (Kaunu o Kaleiho'ohie)	5,480	1,670
Kīlauea Caldera (Uwēkahuna)	4,093	1,248
Kīlauea (Halema'uma'u Rim)	3,660	1,116
Kaho'olawe		
Pu'u Mo'a'ulanui	1,483	452
Pu'u Mo'a'ulaiki	1,434	437
Maui		
Haleakalā(Red Hill)	10,023	3,055
Haleakalā (Kaupō Gap)	8,201	2,500
Pu'u Kukui	5,788	1,764
'Īao Needle	2,250	686
Lāna'i		
Lāna'ihale	3,366	1,026
Moloka'i		
Kamakou	4,970	1,514
Oloku'i	4,606	1,404
O'ahu		
Ka'ala	4,003	1,220
Kōnāhuanui[2]	3,150	960
Tantalus	2,013	614
Olomana	1,643	501
Diamond Head	760	232
Koko Crater (Pu'u Ma'i)	1,208	368
Nu'uanu Pali Lookout	1,186	361
Punchbowl (Pūowaina)	500	152
Kaua'i		
Kalalau Lookout	4,120	1,256
Kawaikini	5,243	1,598
Nounou (Sleeping Giant)	1,241	378
Wai'ale'ale	5,148	1,569
Ni'ihau		
Paniau	1,281	390
Other islands		
Lehua	699	213
Ka'ula	548	167
Nihoa (Millers Peak)	903	275
Necker I (Summit Hill)	276	84
French Frigate Shoals (La Pérouse Pinnacle)	120	37
Gardner Pinnacles	190	58
Maro Reef	Awash	Awash
Laysan I	40	12
Lisianski I	40	12
Pearl & Hermes Atoll	10	3
Midway Atoll[3]	12	4
Kure Atoll	20	6
Kingman Reef[3]	6	2

1. Includes 19 cones over 11,000 feet, 5 of them over 13,000. The summit of Mauna Kea is between 29,400 and 30,600 feet above the ocean floor at the base of the Hawaiian chain.

2. Two distinct peaks. The lower has an elevation of 3,105 feet.

3. Not part of the State of Hawai'i.

Major Named Waterfalls

Waterfall[1]	Height (feet)		Horizontal distance (feet)	Average Discharge (million gal./day)
	Sheer drop	Cascade		
Hawai'i				
Kaluahine	—	620	400	—
'Akaka	442	—	—	—
Wai'ilikahi	320	—	—	6.6
Hi'ilawe (3 falls)[2]	—	1,000	200	—
Rainbow	80	—	—	303.5
Maui				
Honokōhau	—	1,120	500	25.2
Waihi'umalu	—	400	150	—
Waimoku	—	400	50	37.1
Moloka'i				
Kahiwa	—	1,750	1,000	—
Pāpalaua	—	1,200	500	—
Wailele	—	500	150	—
Hāloku	—	500	200	—
Hīpuapua	—	500	300	—
'Olo'upena	—	300	150	—
Moa'ula	—	250	200	19.7
O'ahu				
Kaliuwa'a (Sacred)	80[3]	1,520	3,000	—
Waihe'e (Waimea)	40	—	—	6.8
Mānoa	—	200	250	2.4
Kaua'i				
Waipo'o (2 falls)	—	800	600	—
'Āwini	—	480	500	—
Hinalele	280	—	—	—
Kapaka Nui	280	—	—	—
Manawaiopuna	280	—	—	—
Wailua	80	—	—	—
'Ōpaeka'a	—	40	—	—
Pūwainui	20	—	—	90.9

1. Includes the largest named waterfall on each major island, either in height or average discharge; all other named falls 250 feet high or higher; and well-known smaller falls. Many unnamed falls have sheer drops of 200 feet or more.

2. No figure available for sheer drop, but Hi'ilawe is often referred to as the highest free-fall waterfall in Hawai'i.

3. Sheer drop refers to northernmost fall of a cascade of 6 falls.

Coastline

County or Island	General Coastline		Tidal Shoreline	
	miles	km	(miles)	km
The State[1]	750	1,206	1,052	1,693
Counties				
Hawai'i	266	428	313	504
Maui	210	338	343	552
Honolulu	137	220	234	377
Kaua'i	137	220	162	261
Islands				
Hawai'i	266	428	313	504
Maui	120	193	149	240
Kaho'olawe	29	47	36	58
Lāna'i	47	76	52	84
Moloka'i	88	142	106	171
O'ahu	112	180	209	336
Kaua'i	90	145	110	177
Ni'ihau	45	72	50	80
Ka'ula	2	3	2	3
Northwestern Hawaiian Islands[2]	25	40	25	40

1. Among the states and territories, Hawai'i ranks fourth in general coastline and seventeenth in tidal shoreline.

2. Excludes Midway Atoll, which is part of the Hawaiian Archipelago but not legally part of the State of Hawai'i.

Other Geographic Statistics

	Extreme length (miles)	Extreme width (miles)	Miles from Coast of Most Remote Point
The State	—	—	28.5
Hawai'i	93	76	28.5
Maui	48	26	10.6
Kaho'olawe	11	6	2.4
Lāna'i	18	13	5.2
Moloka'i	38	10	3.9
O'ahu	44	30	10.6
Kaua'i	33	25	10.8
Ni'ihau	18	6	2.4

	Percentage of Area with Elevation:		Percentage of Area with Slope:		
	Less than 500 feet	2,000 feet or more	Less than 10%	10 to 19%	20% or more
The State	20.8	50.9	63.5	19.5	17.0
Hawai'i	12.0	68.4	76.0	20.0	4.0
Maui	24.9	41.4	38.5	25.5	36.0
Kaho'olawe	38.9	0	60.0	31.0	9.0
Lāna'i	24.8	6.3	61.0	23.0	16.0
Moloka'i	37.3	17.8	5.0	21.0	26.0
O'ahu	45.3	4.6	42.5	12.0	45.5
Kaua'i	35.6	24.0	33.5	16.0	50.5
Ni'ihau	78.2	0	68.0	19.5	12.5

	Miles of Sea Cliffs with Heights of:	
	100 – 999 feet	1,000+ feet
The State	145	33
Hawai'i	50	4
Maui	29	0
Kaho'olawe	14	0
Lāna'i	13	1
Moloka'i	15	14
O'ahu	3	0
Kaua'i	14	11
Ni'ihau	7	3

REFERENCES

The references are listed by topic and arranged in the order they appear in the *Atlas*. The list is by no means exhaustive, but each group of references can be extended by use of the bibliography included with each publication.

HAWAIIAN PLACE NAMES

Pukui, M. K., S. H. Elbert, and E. T. Mookini. 1974. *Place Names of Hawaii.* Honolulu: University of Hawai'i Press.

MAPPING AND GEODESY

Chinen, J. J. 1958. *The Great Mahele: Hawaii's Land Division of 1848.* Honolulu: University of Hawai'i Press.

Fitzpatrick, G. L. 1986. *The Early Mapping of Hawaii,* Vol. 1. Honolulu: Editions Limited.

GEOLOGY

Decker, R. W., T. L. Wright, and P. H. Stauffer, eds. 1987. *Volcanism in Hawaii,* 2 Vols. U.S. Geological Survey Professional Paper No. 1350.

Moore, J. G., and D. A. Clague. 1992. Volcano growth and evolution of the island of Hawaii. *Bulletin of the Geological Society of America* 104: 1471–1484.

Moore, J. G., D. A. Clague, R. T. Holcomb, P. W. Lipman, W. R. Normark, and M. E. Torresan. 1989. Prodigious submarine landslides on the Hawaiian ridge. *Journal of Geophysical Research* 94(B12): 17,465–17,484.

Moore, J. G., W. R. Normark, and R. T. Holcomb. 1994. Giant Hawaiian underwater landslides. *Science* 264: 46–47.

Stearns, H. T. 1985. *Geology of the State of Hawaii.* 2nd ed. Palo Alto, CA: Pacific Books.

Wright, T. L., and T. J. Takahashi. 1989. *Observations and Interpretation of Hawaiian Volcanism and Seismicity 1779–1955.* Honolulu: University of Hawai'i Press.

GEOTHERMAL RESOURCES

Thomas, D. M. 1986. Geothermal resources assessment in Hawaii. *Geothermics* 15(4): 435–514.

Kauahikaua, J. P. 1993. Geophysical characteristics of the hydrothermal systems of Kilauea Volcano, Hawaii. *Geothermics* 22(4): 243–254.

Ingebritson, S. E., and M. A. Scholl. 1993. The hydrology of Kiluaea volcano. *Geothermics* 22(4): 255–270.

CLIMATE

Giambelluca, T. W., Nullet, D., and T. A. Schroeder. 1996. *Rainfall Atlas of Hawaii.* Honolulu: Water Resources Research Center, University of Hawai'i, Report No. R76.

Noguchi, Y. 1979. Deformation of trees in Hawaii and its relation to wind. *Journal of Ecology* 67: 611–628.

Sanderson, M., ed. 1993. *Prevailing Trade Winds: Climate and Weather in Hawai'i.* Honolulu: University of Hawai'i Press.

HAWAI'I AND ATMOSPHERIC CHANGE

Hofman, D. J., S. J. Oltmans, B. J. Johnson, J. A. Lathop, J. M. Harris, and H. Vomel. 1995. Recovery of ozone in the lower stratosphere at the South Pole during the spring of 1994. *Geophysical Research Letters* 22(18): 2493–2496.

Novelli, P. C., T. J Conway, E. J. Dlugokency, and P. P. Tans. 1995. Recent changes in atmospheric carbon dioxide, methane and carbon monoxide, and the implications of these changes on the global climate processes. *World Meteorological Bulletin* 44: 32–37.

Ryan, S. 1995. Quiescent outgassing of Mauna Loa Volcano 1958–1994. In *Mauna Loa Revealed: Structure, Composition, History, and Hazards.* Geophysical Monograph No. 92. Washington, D.C.: American Geophysical Union.

PALEOCLIMATE AND GEOGRAPHY

Dorn, R. I., F. M. Phillips, et al. 1991. Glacial chronology. *National Geographic Research and Exploration* 7(4): 456–471.

Fletcher, C. H. 1994. Sea-level change in Hawaii. *SOEST Report 1993–94.* School of Ocean and Earth Science and Technology, University of Hawai'i.

Gavenda, R. T. 1992. Hawaiian Quaternary paleoenvironments: A review of geological, pedological, and botanical evidence. *Pacific Science* 46: 295–307.

Porter, S. C. 1979. Hawaiian glacial ages. *Quaternary Research* 12: 161–187.

Selling, O. H. 1946–1948. *Studies in Hawaiian Pollen Statistics.* 3 Vols. Honolulu: B. P. Bishop Museum Special Publications 37, 38, 39.

NATURAL HAZARDS

Cutter, S. L. 1993. *Living with Risk: The Geography of Technological Hazards.* London: Edward Arnold.

Palm, R. I. 1990. *Natural Hazards: An Integrative Framework for Research and Planning.* Baltimore: Johns Hopkins University Press.

Saarinen, T. F. 1969. Perception of environment. Association of American Geographers, Commission on College Geography. Washington, D.C.

EARTHQUAKES

Bolt, B. A. 1993. *Earthquakes.* New York: W. H. Freeman.

Heliker, C. C. 1990. *Volcanic and Seismic Hazards on the Island of Hawaii.* U.S. Geologic Survey.

Wyss, M., and R. Y. Koyanagi. 1992. Isoseismal maps, macroseismic epicenters, and estimated magnitudes of historical earthquakes in the Hawaiian Islands. U.S. Geologic Survey Bulletin No. 2006.

Wyss, M., R. Y. Koyanagi, and D. C. Cox. 1992. The Lyman Hawaiian earthquake diary. U.S. Geologic Survey Bulletin No. 2027.

VOLCANIC HAZARDS ON THE ISLAND OF HAWAI'I

Sutton, J., and T. Elias. 1993. Volcanic gases create air pollution on the Island of Hawaii. *Earthquakes and Volcanoes* 24(4): 178–196. U.S. Geologic Survey.

Trusdell, F. A. 1995. Lava flow hazards and risk assessment on Mauna Loa Volcano, Hawaii. In *Mauna Loa Revealed*, eds. J. M. Rhodes and J. P. Lockwood. AGU Geophysical Monograph 92: 327–336.

Wright, T. L., J. Y. F. Chun, J. Esposo, C. Heliker, J. Hodge, J. P. Lockwood, and S. Vogt. 1992. *Map Showing Lava-Flow Hazard Zones, Island of Hawaii*. State of Hawai'i, Office of State Planning.

HURRICANES

Anthes, R. A. 1982. Tropical cyclones: Their evolution, structure, and effects. *Meteorologic Monographs* 19: 41. American Meteorological Society.

Fletcher, C. H., B. M. Richmond, G. M. Barnes, and T. A. Schroeder. 1995. Marine flooding on the coast of Kaua'i during Hurricane 'Iniki: Hindcasting inundation components and delineating washover. *Journal of Coastal Research* 11: 188–204.

Schroeder, T. A. 1993. Climate controls. In *Prevailing Trade Winds: Climate and Weather in Hawai'i*, ed. M. Sanderson. Honolulu: University of Hawai'i Press.

Simpson, R. H. 1950. Hiki—Hawaii's first hurricane of record. *Weatherwise* 3: 127–134.

TSUNAMIS

Curtis, G. 1992. Tsunamis—Seismic sea waves. In *Natural and Technological Disasters: Causes, Effects, and Preventative Measures*, ed. S. K. Majumdar. Easton, PA: Pennsylvania Academy of Science Press.

Dudley, W., and M. Lee. 1988. *Tsunami!* Honolulu: University of Hawai'i Press.

Lander, J. F., and P. A. Lockridge. 1989. *United States Tsunamis 1690–1988*. National Geophysical Data Center Publication 41-2. Boulder, CO.

Loomis, H. G. 1976. *Tsunami Wave Heights in Hawaii*. University of Hawai'i Institute of Geophysics Report HIG-76-5.

Walker, D. 1994. *Tsunami Facts*. School of Ocean and Earth Science and Technology, Technical Report 94-03. University of Hawai'i.

COASTAL HAZARDS

Hawaii Coastal Zone News, periodical. Honolulu Sea Grant Marine Advisory Program, University of Hawai'i.

Social Science Research Institute. 1993. *Hawaii Coastal Hazard Mitigation Planning Project*. Honolulu: Hawai'i Coastal Zone Management Program.

State of Hawai'i. Annual. *Hawaii Coastal Zone Management Program Annual Report*. Department of Business, Economic Development and Tourism.

THE OCEAN

A Collection. 1989. 4 Volumes: *Seawater: Its Composition, Properties and Behavior; Ocean Circulation; Waves, Tides and Shallow Water Processes; Ocean Chemistry, and Deep Sea Sediments*. Oxford: Pergamon Press.

Tomczak, M., and J. S. Godfrey. 1994. *Regional Oceanography, an Introduction*. Oxford: Pergamon Press.

WATER

A voluminous literature has been generated over the last century relating to the water resources of the Hawaiian Islands, especially the island of O'ahu. Much of it is credited to the Board of Water Supply, City and County of Honolulu; the U.S. Geological Survey; and the Water Resources Research Center of the University of Hawai'i. A substantial portion was written for other government agencies and as consultant reports.

Hawaii Division of Hydrography Bulletins. 1935–1960 for geology and groundwater resources of individual islands.

Mink, J. F., and L. S. Lau. *Aquifer Identification and Classification* (various islands). Water Resources and Research Center Technical Reports, University of Hawai'i.

Mink, J. F., and S. T. Sumida. 1984. *Aquifer Classification, State of Hawaii*. Technical Memorandum Report No. 75. Water Resources and Research Center, University of Hawai'i.

State of Hawai'i. 1990. *Hawaii Stream Assessment: A Preliminary Appraisal of Hawaii's Stream Resources*. Report No. R84. Prepared for the Commission on Water Resource Management by the National Park Service.

Stearns, H. T. 1985. *Geology of the State of Hawaii*, 2nd ed. Palo Alto: Pacific Books.

Takasaki, K. J., and J. F. Mink. 1985. *Evaluation of Major Dike-Impounded Groundwater Reservoirs, Island of O'ahu*. U.S. Geological Survey Water Supply Paper No. 2217. Government Printing Office.

SOILS

Foote, D. E., et al. 1972. *Soil Survey of the Islands of Kauai, Oahu, Maui, Molokai, and Lanai, State of Hawaii*. U.S. Department of Agriculture, Soil Conservation Service.

Sanchez, P. A. 1976. *Properties and Management of Soils in the Tropics*. New York: Wiley and Sons.

Sato, H. H., et al. 1973. *Soil Survey of the Island of Hawaii, State of Hawaii*. U.S. Department of Agriculture, Soil Conservation Service.

ASTRONOMY

Cruikshank, D. P. 1986. *Mauna Kea: A Guide to the Upper Slopes and Observatories*. Honolulu: Institute for Astronomy.

Parker, B. R. 1994. *Stairway to the Stars: The Story of the World's Largest Observatory*. New York: Plenum Press.

Rhoads, S. E. 1993. *The Sky Tonight: A Guided Tour of the Stars Over Hawaii*. Honolulu: Bishop Museum Press.

Robinson, J. 1991. *Solar Eclipse 1991: A Once in a Lifetime Event*, videorecording. Honolulu: Kamehameha Schools and Bishop Museum.

The Institute for Astronomy at the University of Hawai'i is on-line at http://www.ifa.hawaii.edu/

BIOGEOGRAPHY

Carlquist, S. 1980. *Hawaii, A Natural History: Geology, Climate, Native Flora and Fauna above the Shoreline*. Kaua'i: Pacific Tropical Botanical Gardens.

Carlquist, S. 1981. Chance dispersal. *American Scientist* 69: 509–516.

Gressitt, J. L., ed. 1963. *Pacific Basin Biogeography: A Symposium*. Honolulu: Bishop Museum Press.

Mueller-Dombois, D., K. W. Bridges, and H. L. Carson. 1981. *Island Ecosystems: Biological Organization in Selected Hawaiian Communities*. Stroudsburg, PA: Hutchinson Ross.

EVOLUTION

Carlquist, S. 1980. *Hawaii, A Natural History: Geology, Climate, Native Flora and Fauna above the Shoreline*. Kaua'i: Pacific Tropical Botanical Garden.

Carson, H. L. 1987. The genetic system, the deme, and the origin of species. *Annual Review of Genetics* 21: 405–423.

Carson, H. L., D. E. Hardy, H. T. Spieth, and W. S. Stone. 1970. The evolutionary biology of the Hawaiian *Drosophilidae*. In *Essays in Evolution and Genetics in Honor of Theodosius Dobzhansky*, eds. M. K. Hecht and W. C. Steere. New York: Appleton-Century-Crofts.

Giddings, L. V., K. Y. Kaneshiro, and W. W. Anderson. 1989. *Genetics, Speciation and the Founder Principle*. London: Oxford University Press.

Kay, E. A., ed. 1994. *A Natural History of the Hawaiian Islands: Selected Readings II*. Honolulu: University of Hawai'i Press.

Wagner, W. L., and V. A. Funk, ed. 1995. *Hawaiian Biogeography*. Washington, D.C.: Smithsonian Institution Press.

Wagner, W. L., D. R. Herbst, and S. H. Sohmer. 1990. *Manual of the Flowering Plants of Hawai'i*. Honolulu: University of Hawai'i Press.

Williamson, M. 1981. *Island Populations*. London: Oxford University Press.

Zimmerman, E. C. 1948. *Insects of Hawaii*, Vol. 1: Introduction. Honolulu: University of Hawai'i Press.

MARINE ECOSYSTEMS

Balazs, G. H. 1983. *Status Review Document for Pacific Sea Turtles*. Honolulu: National Marine Fisheries Service.

Devaney, D. M., and L. G. Eldredge., eds. 1977. *Reef and Shore Fauna of Hawaii: Section 1: Protozoa through Ctenophora*. Honolulu: Bishop Museum Press.

Fielding, A., and E. Robinson. 1990. *An Underwater Guide to Hawai'i*. Honolulu: University of Hawai'i Press.

Gosline, W. A., and V. E. Brock. 1960. *Handbook of Hawaiian Fishes*. Honolulu: University of Hawai'i Press.

Hobson, E. S., and E. H. Chave. 1972. *Hawaiian Reef Animals.* Honolulu: University of Hawai'i Press.

Kay, E. A. 1979. *Hawaiian Marine Shells: Reef and Shore Fauna of Hawaii: Section 4: Mollusca.* Honolulu: Bishop Museum Press.

Kay, E. A., ed. 1994. *A Natural History of the Hawaiian Islands. Selected Readings II.* Honolulu: University of Hawai'i Press.

Kay, E. A., and E. H. Chave. 1983. Reef and shore communities. In *Atlas of Hawaii, 2d ed.* Dept. of Geography, University of Hawai'i. Honolulu: University of Hawai'i Press.

Magruder, W. H., and J. W. Hunt. 1979. *Seaweeds of Hawaii: A Photographic Identification Guide.* Honolulu: Oriental Publishing Co.

Randall, J. E. 1996. *Shore Fishes of Hawaii.* Vida, Oregon: Natural World Press.

Russo, R. 1994. *Hawaiian Reefs: A Natural History Guide.* San Leandro, California: Wavecrest Publications.

TERRESTRIAL ECOSYSTEMS

Gagné, W. C., and L. W. Cuddihy. 1990. Vegetation. In W. L. Wagner, D. R. Herbst, and S. H. Sohmer. *Manual of the Flowering Plants of Hawai'i.* Honolulu: University of Hawai'i Press.

Stone, C. P., and J. M. Scott, eds. 1985. *Hawaii's Terrestrial Ecosystems: Preservation and Management.* Honolulu: University of Hawai'i Press for University of Hawai'i Cooperative National Park Resources Studies Unit.

Stone, C. P., and D. B. Stone, eds. 1989. *Conservation Biology in Hawaii.* Honolulu: University of Hawai'i Press for University of Hawai'i Cooperative National Park Resources Studies Unit.

BIRDS

Hawai'i Audubon Society. 1993. *Hawaii's Birds.* 4th ed. Honolulu: The Society.

Olson, S. L., and H. F. James. 1991. Descriptions of thirty-two new species of birds from the Hawaiian Islands. *Ornithological Monographs,* 45 and 46.

Pratt, H. D. 1994. Avifaunal change in the Hawaiian Islands, 1893–1993. *Studies in Avian Biology* (15): 103–118.

Scott, J. M. et al. 1986. *Forest Bird Communities of the Hawaiian Islands: Their Dynamics, Ecology and Conservation.* Columbus, OH: Cooper Ornithological Society.

NATIVE PLANTS

Kepler, A. K. 1990. *Trees of Hawai'i.* Honolulu: University of Hawai'i Press

Lamoureux, C. H. 1976. *Trailside Plants of Hawaii's National Parks.* Hawai'i Volcanoes National Park: Hawai'i Natural History Association.

Merlin, M. D. 1995. *Hawaiian Forest Plants.* Honolulu: University of Hawai'i Press.

Neal, M. 1965. *In Gardens of Hawaii.* Honolulu: Bishop Museum Press.

Rock, J. F. 1913–1974. *The Indigenous Trees of the Hawaiian Islands.* Tokyo and Rutland, VT: Tuttle.

Sohmer, S. H., and R. Gustafson. 1987. *Plants and Flowers of Hawai'i.* Honolulu: University of Hawai'i Press.

INSECTS AND THEIR KIN

Howarth, F. G., and W. P. Mull. 1992. *Hawaiian Insects and Their Kin.* Honolulu: University of Hawai'i Press.

Nishida, G. M. (ed.) 1994. *Hawaiian Terrestrial Arthropod Checklist.* 2nd ed. Bishop Museum Technical Report No. 4.

Tenorio, J. M., and G. M. Nishida. 1995. *What's Bugging Me?* Honolulu: University of Hawai'i Press.

Zimmerman, E. C., et al. 1948–1992. *Insects of Hawaii,* 15 vols. Honolulu: University of Hawai'i Press.

A complete list of insects found in Hawai'i is available on-line at http://www.bishop.hawaii.org/bishop.HBS/hbsdb.html

HAWAIIAN TREE SNAILS

Hadfield, Michael G. 1986. Extinction in Hawaiian achatinelline snails. *Malacologia* 27(1): 67–81.

Hadfield, M. G., S. E. Miller, and A. H. Carwile. 1993. The decimation of endemic Hawaiian tree snails by alien predators. *American Zoologist* 33: 610–622.

ALIEN SPECIES AND THREATS TO NATIVE ECOLOGY

Cuddihy, L. W., and C. P. Stone. 1990. *Alteration of Native Hawaiian Vegetation: Effects of Humans, Their Activities and Introductions.* Honolulu: University of Hawai'i Press for University of Hawai'i Cooperative National Park Resources Studies Unit.

Haselwood, E. L., and G. G. Motter. 1983. *Handbook of Hawaiian Weeds.* 2nd ed., revised and expanded by R. T. Hirano. Honolulu: University of Hawai'i Press for Harold L. Lyon Arboretum.

Stone, C. P., and C. W. Smith, eds. 1992. *Alien Plant Invasions in Native Ecosystems of Hawai'i.* Honolulu: University of Hawai'i Press for University of Hawai'i Cooperative National Park Resources Studies Unit.

Tomich, P. Q. 1986. *Mammals in Hawaii.* Honolulu: Bishop Museum Press.

ENDANGERED AND THREATENED SPECIES

Cuddihy, L. W., and C. P. Stone. 1990. *Alteration of Native Hawaiian Vegetation: Effects of Humans, Their Activities and Introductions.* Honolulu: University of Hawai'i Press for University of Hawai'i Cooperative National Park Resources Studies Unit.

Holing, D. 1987. Hawaii: the Eden of endemism. *The Nature Conservancy News* 37(1): 6–13.

Peters, R. L., and T.E. Lovejoy. 1990. Terrestrial fauna. In *Earth as Transformed by Human Action,* eds. B. L. Turner et al. New York: Cambridge University Press.

Stone, C. P., and J. M. Scott. 1985. *Hawai'i's Terrestrial Ecosystems: Preservation and Management.* University of Hawai'i Press for University of Hawai'i Cooperative National Park Resources Studies Unit.

PROTECTED AREAS

The Nature Conservancy of Hawai'i. 1987. *Biological Overview of Hawaii's Natural Area Reserves System.* State of Hawai'i, Department of Land and Natural Resources.

Natural Resources Defense Council. 1989. *Extinction in Paradise: Protecting Our Hawaiian Species.* New York: Natural Resources Defense Council.

ARCHAEOLOGY

Green, R. C. 1980. Makaha before 1880 A.D. *Pacific Anthropological Records* No. 31.

Kirch, P. V. 1985. *Feathered Gods and Fishhooks: An Introduction to Hawaiian Archaeology and Prehistory.* Honolulu: University of Hawai'i Press.

Kirch, P. V., and T. Babineau. 1996. *Legacy of the Landscape: An Illustrated Guide to Hawaiian Archaeologic Sites.* Honolulu: University of Hawai'i Press.

Kirch, P. V., and M. Sahlins. 1992. *Anahulu: The Anthropology of History in the Kingdom of Hawaii.* Vol. 1, *Historical Ethnography.* Vol. 2, *The Archaeology of History.* Chicago: University of Chicago Press.

Tuggle, H. D. 1979. Hawaii. In *The Prehistory of Polynesia,* ed. J. D. Jennings. Cambridge: Harvard University Press.

POLYNESIAN NAVIGATION

Finney, B. R. 1994. *Voyage of Rediscovery: A Cultural Odyssey through Polynesia.* Berkeley: University of California Press.

Gladwin, T. 1970. *East is a Big Bird.* Cambridge: Harvard University Press.

Kyselka, W. 1987. *An Ocean in Mind.* Honolulu: University of Hawai'i Press.

Lewis, D. 1994. *We, the Navigators:The Ancient Art of Landfinding in the Pacific.* 2d ed. Honolulu: University of Hawai'i Press.

ETHNOBOTANY

Abbott, I. A. 1992. *Lā'au Hawai'i: Traditional Hawaiian Uses of Plants.* Honolulu: Bishop Museum Press.

Buck, P. H. 1957. *Arts and Crafts of Hawaii.* Bishop Museum Special Publication 45. Honolulu: Bishop Museum Press.

Handy, E. S. C., and E. G. Handy. 1972. *Native Planters in Old Hawaii: Their Life, Lore and Environment.* Bishop Museum Bulletin 233.

HISTORY

Cooper, G., and G. Daws. 1990. *Land and Power in Hawaii: The Democratic Years.* Honolulu: University of Hawai'i Press.

Daws, G. 1974. *Shoal of Time: A History of the Hawaiian Islands.* Honolulu: University of Hawai'i Press.

Fuchs, L. H. 1997. *Hawaii Pono: An Ethnic and Political History.* Honolulu: Island Book Shelf.
Kamakau, S. M. 1961. *Ruling Chiefs of Hawaii.* Honolulu: Kamehameha Schools.
Kameʻeleihiwa, L. 1992. *Native Land and Foreign Desires.* Honolulu: Bishop Museum Press.
Kent, N. 1993. *Hawaii: Islands Under the Influence.* Honolulu: University of Hawaiʻi Press.
Kuykendall, R. S. 1938–1967. Th*e Hawaiian Kingdom,* 3 Vols. Honolulu: University of Hawaiʻi Press.

THE SANDALWOOD TRADE

Merlin, M. D., and D. VanRavenswaay. 1990. *The History of Human Impact on the Genus* Santalum *in Hawaiʻi.* USDA Forest Service General Technical Report PSW-122.

WHALING

Simpson, M. 1986. *WhaleSong: A Pictorial History of Whaling and Hawaii.* Honolulu: Beyond Words Publishing Company.

POPULATION

Nordyke, E. C. 1989. *The Peopling of Hawaii.* Honolulu: University of Hawaiʻi Press.
Schmitt, R. C. 1968. *Demographic Statistics of Hawaii: 1778–1965.* Honolulu: University of Hawaiʻi Press.

LANGUAGES

Carr, E. B. 1972. *Da Kine Talk: From Pidgin to Standard English in Hawaii.* Honolulu: University of Hawaiʻi Press.
Reinecke, J. E. 1969. *Language and Dialect in Hawaii: A Sociological History to 1935,* ed. S. M. Tsuzaki. Honolulu: University of Hawaiʻi Press.
Schütz, A. J. 1994. *The Voices of Eden: A History of Hawaiian Language Studies.* Honolulu: University of Hawaiʻi Press.
Tsuzaki, S. M., and J. E. Reinecke. 1966. *English in Hawaii: An Annotated Bibliography.* Honolulu: Pacific and Asian Linguistics Institute, University of Hawaiʻi.

RELIGION

Cunningham, S. 1995. *Hawaiian Religion and Myths.* St. Paul: Llewellyn Publications.
Fuchs, L. H. 1997. *Hawaii Pono: An Ethnic and Political History.* Honolulu: Island Book Shelf.
Gutmanis, J. 1983. *Na Pule Kahiki.* Honolulu: Editions Ltd.
Mulholland, J. 1970. *Hawaii's Religions.* Tokyo: Charles E. Tuttle and Co.
Pierce, L. W. 1992. *Hawaii's Missionary Saga.* Honolulu: Mutual Publishing.

ARCHITECTURE

Jay, R. 1992. *The Architecture of Charles W. Dickey.* Honolulu: University of Hawaiʻi Press.
Neil, J. M. 1972. *Paradise Improved: Environmental Design in Hawaii.* Charlottesville, VA: University Press of Virginia.

MUSEUMS AND LIBRARIES

Bernice P. Bishop Museum. Annual. *Bishop Museum Annual Report.* Honolulu: The Bishop Museum.
Hawaiʻi Museums Association. Biennial. *Hawaii Museums and Related Organizations.* Honolulu: Hawaiʻi Museums Association with the Hawaiian Historical Society.
Hawaii State Library News, a bimonthly periodical. Honolulu.
Marsh, C. 1991. *The Hawaii Library Book: A Surprising Guide to the Unusual Special Collections in Libraries across Our State.* Decatur, GA: Gallopade Publishing Group.

CULTURE AND THE ARTS

Kamae, E., and M. Kamae. 1993. *The Hawaiian Way.* Video recording of the art and tradition of slack key guitar.
McDonald, M. A. 1989. *Ka Lei: The Leis of Hawaii.* Kailua, HI: Press Pacifica.
Morrison, B. 1983. *Images of the Hula.* Volcano, HI: Summit Press.

Schmitt, R. C. 1988. *Hawaii in the Movies: 1898–1959.* Honolulu: Hawaiian Historical Society.
Vogelsberger, F., and L. T. Church. 1994. *Artists in Hawaii: The Book.* Honolulu: Printech Hawaiʻi.
Yano, C. R. 1984. *Japanese Bon Dance Music in Hawaii: Continuity, Change and Variability.* M.A. thesis, University of Hawaiʻi.

CONTEMPORARY LITERATURE

Lum, D. H. Y. 1990. *Pass on, No Pass Back!* Honolulu: Bamboo Ridge Press.
Merwin, W. S. 1988. *The Rain in the Trees.* New York: Alfred A. Knopf.
Trask, H. K. 1994. *Light in the Crevice Never Seen.* Corvallis, OR: Calyx Books.
Yamanaka, L. A. 1996. *Wild Meat and the Bully Burgers.* New York: Farrar, Straus, and Giroux.

GOVERNMENT AND POLITICS

Cooper, G. and G. Daws, 1990. *Land and Power in Hawaii: The Democratic Years.* Honolulu: University of Hawaiʻi Press.
Roth, R. W., ed. 1993. *The Price of Paradise,* 2 vols. Honolulu: Mutual Publishing.
Smith, Z. A., and R. C. Pratt, eds. 1992. *Politics and Public Policy in Hawaii.* Albany: State University of New York Press.
Wang, J. C. F. 1982. *Hawaii State and Local Politics.* Hilo: Wang Associates.
Wang, J. C. F. 1992. *Handbook on Ocean Politics and the Law.* New York: Greenwood Press.

LAND USE AND TENURE

Callies, D. L. 1994. *Preserving Paradise.* Honolulu: University of Hawaiʻi Press.
Cooper, G. and G. Daws, 1990. *Land and Power in Hawaii: The Democratic Years.* Honolulu: University of Hawaiʻi Press.
Creighton, T. H. 1978. *The Lands of Hawaii: Their Use and Misuse.* Honolulu: University of Hawaiʻi Press.
Kameʻeleihiwa, L. 1992. *Native Land and Foreign Desires.* Honolulu: Bishop Museum Press.
Legislative Auditor of the State of Hawaiʻi. 1983. *Progress Report on the Public Land Trust.* A Report to the Legislature of the State of Hawaiʻi.

URBAN CENTERS

Beechert, E. D. 1991. *Honolulu: Crossroads of the Pacific.* Columbia, S.C.: University of South Carolina Press.
Goss, J. D., and M. McGranaghan. 1995. Urbanization. In *Hawaii: A Unique Geography,* ed. J. Morgan. Honolulu: Bess Press.
Johnson, D. D. 1991. *The City and County of Honolulu: A Government Chronicle.* Honolulu: University of Hawaiʻi Press.
Keith, K. M. 1993. Land regulation: Is Hawaii being overdeveloped? In *The Price of Paradise: Lucky We Live in Hawaii?,* ed. R. W. Roth. Honolulu: Mutual Publishing.
Kim, K. E. 1992. Planning for rapid transit on Oahu: Another great planning disaster? In *Politics and Public Policy in Hawaii,* eds. Z. A. Smith and R. C. Pratt. Albany: State University of New York Press.
La Croix, S., J. Mak, and L. A. Rose. 1995. The political economy of urban land reform in Hawaii. *Urban Studies* (32) 6: 999–1015.

ECONOMY

Aoude, I. G., ed. 1994. *The Political Economy of Hawaii.* Honolulu: University of Hawaiʻi Press.
Bank of Hawaiʻi. 1997. *Hawaii's Economy.* Economic Report Vol. 45.
Bank of Hawaiʻi, Economics Division on-line at http://www.boh.com/econ/
Kondo, D. 1993. *Business Basics in Hawaii: Secrets of Starting Your Own Small Business in Our State.* Honolulu: Chamber of Commerce of Hawaiʻi.
State of Hawaiʻi, annual. *The Economy of Hawaii: Annual Economic Report.* Department of Business, Economic Development and Tourism.

AGRICULTURE

Garrod, P. et al. 1987. *The Hawaii Beef Industry: Situation and Outlook.* College of Tropical Agriculture and Human Resources, University of Hawaiʻi.
Hawaiian Sugar Planters' Association. 1995. *Hawaiian Sugar Manual.* Honolulu: Hawaiian Sugar Planters' Association.

Kirkendall, J. M. 1985. *Hawaiian Ethnogastronomy: The Development of a Pidgin-Creole Cuisine.* Ph.D. dissertation, University of Hawai'i.

State of Hawai'i. *State Data Book 1993–94. A Statistical Abstract.* Department of Business, Economic Development and Tourism.

State of Hawai'i. 1995. *Statistics of Hawaiian Agriculture.* Department of Agriculture.

Yokoyama, K. M. 1990. *Estimated Impact on Hawaii's Economy of Replacing Selected Fresh Vegetable and Fruit Imports.* College of Tropical Agriculture and Human Resource. University of Hawai'i.

FOREST INDUSTRY

Hawai'i State Forestry Symposium. 1993. *Hawaii's Forests—A Bridge to the Future.* Forestry Symposium Proceedings. Honolulu: Institute of Pacific Islands Forestry.

Yanagida, J. F., J. M. Halloran, U. Chakravorty, and D. J. Lee. 1993. *Hawaii's Forests: An Inventory and Analysis of Economic Potential.* University of Hawai'i, Department of Agriculture and Resource Economics.

SUSTAINABLE AGRICULTURE

Delate, K. 1997. Sustainable agriculture in the Pacific Islands. In *Sustainable Development in the Pacific Islands Conference Proceedings,* eds. M. M. Piazza and P. Young. U.S.–EPA, San Francisco.

Ferentinos, L. 1995. *Ho'olaulima (To Get Together) for Hawai'i's Sustainable Agriculture,* videorecording. College of Tropical Agriculture and Human Resources, University of Hawai'i.

Ferentinos, L., ed. 1993. *Proceedings of the Sustainable Taro Culture for the Pacific Conference.* College of Agriculture and Human Resources, University of Hawai'i.

International Conference on Agriculture for the 21st Century. 1991. *Toward a Sustainable Agriculture for the Pacific Rim Nations.* New York: MOA Foundation.

FISHERIES

Fisheries of Hawaii and U.S.–associated Pacific Islands. 1993. *Marine Fisheries Review* 55(2).

Titcomb, M. 1977. *Native Use of Fish in Hawaii.* Honolulu: University of Hawai'i Press.

AQUACULTURE

Corbin, J. S. 1996. Big Island is epicenter of aquaculture expansion. *Hawaii Ocean Industry and Shipping News,* September: 12–13.

Corbin J. S. 1996. Hawaii aquaculture 1996, an industry finding its niche. *Aquaculture Magazine,* September/October: 16–18.

State of Hawaii. 1993. *Hawaii's Future In Aquaculture, Strategy for the Blue Revolution.* Department of Land and Natural Resources.

THE MILITARY

State of Hawai'i. 1995. *Department of Defense Annual Report, Fiscal Year 1995.* Department of Defense.

State of Hawai'i. *State Data Book 1993–94. A Statistical Abstract.* Department of Business, Economic Development and Tourism.

U.S. Department of Defense. 1995. *Atlas/Data Abstract for the United States and Selected Areas, Fiscal Year 1994.* Washington, D.C.

Your Military in Hawaii: The Complete Military Guide to Hawaii. 1996. Honolulu: Hart Publishers, Inc.

TOURISM

Brown, D. 1982. *Hawaii Recalls.* Honolulu: Editions Limited.

Brown, D. 1985. *Aloha Waikiki.* Honolulu: Editions Limited.

Hawai'i Visitors and Convention Bureau. 1970–1996. *Annual Research Report.*

Mak, J., and M. Sakai. 1992. Tourism in Hawaii: Economic issues for the 1990's and beyond. In *Politics and Public Policy in Hawaii,* eds. Z. A. Smith and R. Pratt. Albany: State University of New York Press.

ENERGY

The East-West Center Program on Resources: Energy and Minerals. 1993. *World and Regional Fossil Energy Dynamics, Hawaii Energy Strategy Project 2: Fossil Energy Review, Tasks I and II.* State of Hawai'i, Department of Business, Economic Development, and Tourism.

Greer, L. S. 1997. *Hawai'i Renewable Energy Data Report.* State of Hawai'i, Department of Business, Economic Development and Tourism.

Greer, L. S., H. M. Hubbard, and C. N. Bloyd. 1995. Renewable energy in Hawaii—Lessons learned. In *Advances in Solar Energy,* Vol. 10. New York: American Solar Energy Society.

Hubbard, H. M., L. Totto, and D. Harvison. 1993. Renewable energy in Hawaii—Lessons learned. In *Advances in Solar Energy,* Vol. 8. New York: American Solar Energy Society.

TRANSPORTATION

State of Hawai'i. 1978. *The Statewide Transportation Plan.* Department of Transportation, Statewide Transportation Council.

COMMUNICATIONS

Bendix, B. 1983. *Serving Hawaii: The First 100 Years.* Honolulu: Hawaiian Telephone Company.

Cahill, E. 1987. *Hawaiian Stamps: An Illustrated History.* Volcano, HI: Orchid Isle Publishers.

Davis, D. 1993. Social impact of cellular telephone usage in Hawaii. In *PTC '93 Proceedings,* Vol. 2, eds. D. J. Wedemeyer and J. G. Savage. Honolulu: Pacific Telecommunications Council.

Hoelscher, A. 1996. *Hawaii Internet Service Provider (ISP) Rate List.* Updated monthly. Or on-line at http://www2.hawaii.edu/-hoelsche.

Ogden, M., and M. Jussawalla. 1994. Telecommunications and IT in Pacific Islands development. *Asian Journal of Communication* 4(2): 1–32.

Proceedings of the Pacific Telecommunications Council's Annual Conference. Honolulu: PTC.

EDUCATION

Dotts, C. K., and M. Sikkema. 1994. *Challenging the Status Quo: Public Education in Hawaii 1840–1980.* Honolulu: Hawai'i Education Association.

Jennings, H. 1978. *Chronology and Documentary Handbook of the State of Hawaii.* New York: Oceana Publications, Inc.

Wist, B. O. 1940. *A Century of Public Education in Hawaii.* Honolulu: Honolulu Star-Bulletin.

HEALTH AND WELLNESS

Hawai'i Medical Service Association. 1994. *Health Trends in Hawaii: A Statistical Chartbook for Policy Makers and Planners.* Honolulu: Hawai'i Medical Service Association.

Grossman, B. and J. Shon, eds. 1994. *The Unfinished Health Agenda—Lessons from Hawaii.* Honolulu: Hawai'i State Primary Care Association.

U.S. General Accounting Office. 1994. *Health Care in Hawaii: Implications for National Reform.* Report to the Chairman, Subcommittee on Oversight and Investigations, Committee on Energy and Commerce, House of Representatives.

CRIME

Castberg, A. D. 1992. Crime and justice in Hawaii. In *Politics and Public Policy in Hawaii,* eds. Z. A. Smith and R. C. Pratt. Albany: State University of New York Press.

Jardine, J. 1984. *Detective Jardine: Crimes in Honolulu.* Honolulu: University of Hawai'i Press.

Richmond, J. B. Larceny and theft in the State of Hawaii, 1979–1993. *Crime Trend Series* 2(4) Office of the Attorney General of Hawai'i.

Wright, T. 1990. *Rape in Paradise.* Honolulu: Mutual Publishing.

RECREATION

Clark, J. R. K. 1985. *Beaches of the Big Island.* Honolulu: University of Hawai'i Press.

Clark, J. R. K. 1987. *Statewide Recreation Resources Inventory: Principal Bodysurfing Sites.* State Department of Land and Natural Resources. Division of State Parks, Outdoor Recreation and Historic Sites.

Clark, J. R. K., and W. H. Souza. 1987. *Statewide Recreation Resources Inventory: Principal Swimming Areas.* State Department of Land and Natural

Resources. Division of State Parks, Outdoor Recreation and Historic Sites.

Hawai'i Visitors Bureau. 1993. *The Islands of Aloha: The Official Travel Guide of the Hawaii Visitors Bureau.* Honolulu: Davick Publications, Inc.

Pager, S. 1995. *Hawaii: Off the Beaten Path.* Old Saybrook, CT: Globe Pequot Press.

State of Hawai'i. 1990. *State Recreational Plan.* Department of Land and Natural Resources.

ENVIRONMENTAL QUALITY

Environment Hawaii, a monthly newsletter, Hilo, Hawai'i.

State of Hawai'i. 1992. *Environmental Risks to Hawaii's Public Health and Ecosystems.* A Report to the Hawai'i Environmental Risk Ranking Study by the East-West Center and Department of Health.

State of Hawai'i. 1995. *Hawaii's Coastal Non-Point Pollution Control Program, Draft Management Plan.* Office of State Planning, Hawai'i Coastal Zone Management Program.

GOVERNMENT SERVICES

Johnson, D. D. 1991. *The City and County of Honolulu: A Government Chronicle.* Honolulu: University of Hawai'i Press.

Smith, Z. A. 1992. *Hawaii State and Local Government: The Aloha County Simulation.* Lanham, MD: University Press of America.

State of Hawai'i. 1994. *Transportation, Communication, Utilities, Trade, Educational Services, and Government: State of Hawaii and Counties, 1991.* Department of Labor and Industrial Relations, Research and Statistics Office.

SOURCES

Data sources for maps, graphs, and tables are listed following the boldface title of the individual graphic. Sources are given where data were obtained from an individual or published material. Any figure without a source listed is from original data compiled by the *Atlas of Hawai'i* staff from a variety of sources.

Frontispiece: Duennebier, T. 1996. Bathymetric map of Hawaiian Island chain from Kure to Hawai'i. School of Ocean and Earth Science and Technology, University of Hawai'i.

MAPPING AND GEODESY

Geodetic Horizontal Control and Compass Variation: Coast and Geodetic Survey, 1930. Triangulation in Hawaii, Special Publication No. 156; National Ocean Survey, 1982 (unpublished).

U.S. Geological Survey Topographic Maps of Hawai'i: U.S. Geological Survey, 1993. Hawaii Index to Topographic and Other Map Coverage.

LANDSAT Image of Hawai'i Island: State of Hawai'i. *LANDSAT TM Image Mosaic.* Office of State Planning; Department of Land and Natural Resources, Division of Forestry and Wildlife; University of Hawai'i; Geographic Decision Systems International; Hogan Co.

GEOLOGY

Age Progression of Hawaiian Islands: D. A. Clague and G. B. Dalrymple. 1987. The Hawaiian-Emperor Volcanic Chain, part I. In Decker, R. W., T. L. Wright, and P. H. Stauffer, eds. *Volcanism in Hawaii,* Vol. 1. U.S. Geological Survey Professional Paper No. 1350.

General Geology Maps: V. A. M. Langenheim and D. A. Clague. 1987. The Hawaiian-Emperor Volcanic Chain, part II. In Decker, R. W., T. L. Wright, and P. H. Stauffer, eds. *Volcanism in Hawaii,* Vol. 1. U.S. Geological Survey Professional Paper No. 1350. Government Printing Office.

Submarine Landslides of Hawai'i: Moore, J. G., D. A. Clague, R. T. Holcomb, P. W. Lipman, W. R. Normark, and M. E. Torresan. 1989. Prodigious submarine landslides on the Hawaiian ridge. *Journal of Geophysical Research* 94: 17,465–17,484.

Flexure of the Lithosphere below Hawai'i: modified after Bays, B. 1994. *SOEST 1993–94 Report.* School of Ocean and Earth Science and Technology, University of Hawai'i.

GEOTHERMAL RESOURCES

Hawai'i Island Geothermal Resources: Thomas, D. M. 1986. Geothermal resources assessment in Hawaii. *Geothermics* 15(4): 435–514.

Hawai'i Island Geothermal Power Plant Diagram: Puna Geothermal Venture. 1992. *Geothermal Energy in Hawai'i.*

CLIMATE

Airflow and Orographic Rainfall: Schroeder, T. A. 1993. Climate controls. In *Prevailing Trade Winds: Climate and Weather in Hawai'i,* ed. M. Sanderson. Honolulu: University of Hawai'i Press.

Average Annual and Monthly Rainfall: Giambelluca, T. W., D. Nullet, and T. A. Schroeder. 1986. *Rainfall Atlas of Hawai'i.* State of Hawai'i, Department of Land and Natural Resources.

Global Atmospheric Circulation: Schroeder, T. A. 1993. Climate controls. In *Prevailing Trade Winds: Climate and Weather in Hawai'i,* ed. M. Sanderson. Honolulu: University of Hawai'i Press.

Seasonal High Pressure Systems and Wind Patterns: Schroeder, T. A. 1993. Climate controls. In *Prevailing Trade Winds: Climate and Weather in Hawai'i,* ed. M. Sanderson. Honolulu: University of Hawai'i Press.

Average Annual Solar Radiation Intensity: Nullet, D., and M. Sanderson. 1993. Radiation and energy balances and air temperatures. In *Prevailing Trade Winds: Climate and Weather in Hawai'i,* ed. M. Sanderson. Honolulu: University of Hawai'i Press.

Temperature Change with Elevation in Hawai'i: Nullet, D., and M. Sanderson. 1993. Radiation and energy balances and air temperatures, In *Prevailing Trade Winds: Climate and Weather in Hawai'i,* ed. M. Sanderson. Honolulu: University of Hawai'i Press.

Annual Temperature Cycle at Different Elevations: Nullet, D., and M. Sanderson. 1993. Radiation and energy balances and air temperatures. In *Prevailing Trade Winds: Climate and Weather in Hawai'i,* ed. M. Sanderson. Honolulu: University of Hawai'i Press.

Kona Storms and Cold Fronts: Armstong, R. W., ed. 1983. *Atlas of Hawaii,* 2nd ed. Honolulu: University of Hawai'i Press.

Prevailing Wind Patterns: Noguchi, Y. 1979. Deformation of trees in Hawaii and its relation to wind. *Journal of Ecology* 67(2): 611–628.

Diurnal Variation in Wind Direction and Speeds on Hawai'i Island: Nash, A. J. In *SOEST Report 1991–1992,* ed. B. Bays, School of Ocean and Earth Science and Technology, University of Hawai'i.

El Niño Influence on Honolulu Winter Rainfall: Schroeder, T. A. 1993. Climate controls. In *Prevailing Trade Winds: Climate and Weather in Hawai'i,* ed. M. Sanderson. Honolulu: University of Hawai'i Press.

Diurnal Variation in Rainfall on Hawai'i Island: Schroeder, T. A. 1993. Climate controls. In *Prevailing Trade Winds: Climate and Weather in Hawai'i,* ed. M. Sanderson. Honolulu: University of Hawai'i Press

Diurnal Variation in Relative Humidity on Hawai'i Island: Nullet, D., J. O. Juvik, and A. Wall. 1995. A Hawaiian mountain climate cross-section. *Climate Research.* 5: 131–137

HAWAI'I AND ATMOSPHERIC CHANGE

Global Atmospheric Climate Monitoring Sites, 1997: U.S. Department of Commerce, National Oceanic and Atmospheric Administration, Climate Monitoring and Diagnostics Laboratory. Boulder, Colorado.

Carbon Dioxide in the Atmosphere: U.S. Department of Commerce, National Oceanic and Atmospheric Administration, Climate Monitoring and Diagnostics Laboratory. Carbon Cycle Group. Boulder, Colorado.

Chlorofluorocarbons in the Atmosphere: U.S. Department of Commerce, National Oceanic and Atmospheric Administration, Climate Monitoring and Diagnostics Laboratory. Halocarbon Group Boulder, Colorado.

Mauna Loa Atmospheric Stratospheric Transparency: U.S. Department of Commerce, National Oceanic and Atmospheric Administration, Climate Monitoring and Diagnostics Laboratory. Mauna Loa Observatory, Hilo, Hawai'i.

Mauna Loa: Dust and Pollution from Asia: U.S. Department of Commerce, National Oceanic and Atmospheric Administration, Climate Monitoring and Diagnostics Laboratory. Mauna Loa Observatory, Hilo, Hawai'i.

PALEOCLIMATE AND GEOGRAPHY

Global Sea Level Change: modified after Fletcher, C. H. 1994. Sea-level change in Hawaii. *SOEST Report 1993–94.* School of Ocean and Earth Science and Technology, University of Hawai'i.

History of Mauna Kea Glaciation: Porter, S. 1979. Hawaiian glacial ages. *Quarternary Research* 12: 161–187.

Mountain Ecozone Response to Climatic Change: Juvik, J. O., University of Hawai'i, Department of Geography and S. Hotchkiss, University of Minnesota, Department of Ecology, Evolution and Behavior.

Reemergence of Maui Nui 21,000 Years Ago: Smith, J. R., and T. Duennebier. 1994. Maui Nui Shoreline at -125 meters. In *Hawaii Seafloor Atlas.* School of Ocean and Earth Science and Technology, University of Hawai'i.

EARTHQUAKES

Major Earthquakes on Hawai'i Island: Catalog of earthquake activity 1929–present. U.S. Geological Survey, Hawaiian Volcano Observatory.

VOLCANIC HAZARDS ON THE ISLAND OF HAWAI'I

Hazard Maps: Heliker, C. C. 1990. *Volcanic and Seismic Hazards on the Island of Hawaii.* U.S. Geological Survey.

Lava Flow Hazard Zones: Wright, T. L., et al. 1992. *Map Showing Lava-Flow Hazard Zones, Island of Hawaii.* State of Hawai'i, Office of State Planning.

HURRICANES

Vertical Cross Section of a Hurricane: after Fernald, E. A., and E. D. Purdum. 1992. *Atlas of Florida.* Gainesville: University of Florida Press.

Hurricane and Tropical Storm Tracks, 1950–1992: Schroeder, T. A. 1993. Hawaiian hurricanes: Their history, causes and the future. In *Hawaii Coastal Hazard Mitigation Planning Project.* State of Hawai'i, Office of State Planning, Coastal Zone Management Program.

Pacific Hurricane Origins: Bergeron, T., 1954. The problem of tropical hurricanes. *Quarterly Journal of the Royal Meteorological Society* 80:131–164.

Major Historic Hurricanes: Schroeder, T. A., University of Hawai'i, Department of Meteorology.

TSUNAMIS

Tsunami Movement across the State on May 22–23, 1960: Mader, C. L., Joint Institute for Marine and Atmospheric Research. University of Hawai'i.

Observed Major Tsunami Run-ups in Hawai'i, 1819–1994: Walker, D., 1994. Tsunami Facts. Hawai'i Institute of Geophysics, University of Hawai'i.

Tsunami Travel Time to Hawai'i: Pacific Tsunami Warning Center, National Oceanic and Atmospheric Administration.

1946 Tsunami Wave Run-ups in Hawai'i: Pacific Tsunami Warning Center, National Oceanic and Atmospheric Administration.

COASTAL HAZARDS

Potential Coastal Flooding and High Surf: Fletcher, C. H., University of Hawai'i, School of Ocean and Earth Science and Technology.

Potential Coastal Erosion and Collapse: Fletcher, C. H., University of Hawai'i, School of Ocean and Earth Science and Technology.

THE OCEAN

Data for the following graphics were compiled from a variety of sources by K. Bigelow, P. Caldwell, J. Firing, B. Kilonsky, C. Motell, J. Potemra, F. Santiago-Mandujano, and M. Seki. Specific sources listed as follows:

Surface Water Temperature: Pathfinder Sea Surface Temperature Project, Jet Propulsion Laboratory, National Aeronautic and Space Administration.

Surface Water Salinity: World Ocean Atlas, Ocean Climate Laboratory, National Oceanic and Atmospheric Administration.

Vertical Profiles of Water Properties: World Ocean Circulation Experiment, Hawai'i Ocean Time Series Project, University of Hawai'i.

Depth of the Thermocline: World Ocean Atlas, Ocean Climate Laboratory, National Oceanic and Atmospheric Administration.

Average Surface Currents and Variability: Atlantic Oceanographic and Meteorological Laboratory, National Oceanic and Atmospheric Administration; and Pelagic Fisheries Research Project, University of Hawai'i.

Effect of Wind and Islands on Currents: after Bays, B., University of Hawai'i, School of Ocean and Earth Science and Technology.

Tidal Sea Level Change at Hilo: Sea Level Center, University of Hawai'i and National Oceanic and Atmospheric Administration.

K-1 Tidal Range and Phase: TOPEX Project, Jet Propulsion Laboratory, National Aeronautic and Space Administration.

Observed Tidal Currents and Ranges: National Ocean Data Center, National Oceanic and Atmospheric Administration; University of Hawai'i, Hawai'i Institute of Geophysics; Ed Noda Associates, Honolulu.

Significant Wave Height: GEOSAT Altimeter Mission, United States Navy and National Oceanic and Atmospheric Administration; and TOPEX Altimeter Mission, National Aeronautic and Space Administration and CNES.

Seasonal Variation of Wave Height: National Buoy Center, National Oceanic and Atmospheric Administration.

WATER

Aquifer Sectors and Water Demand: State of Hawai'i. 1992. *Hawaii Water Plan: Water Resources Protection Plan,* 2 vols. Department of Land and Natural Resources, Commission on Water Resources.

O'ahu Water Resources: Mink, J., Mink and Yuen, Inc., Honolulu.

Water Budget of Hawai'i, 1995: State of Hawai'i. 1992. *Hawaii Water Plan: Water Resources Protection Plan,* 2 Vols. Department of Land and Natural Resources. Commission on Water Resources.

Freshwater Use in Hawai'i, 1990: State of Hawai'i. 1994. *State Data Book 1993–94.* A Statistical Abstract. Department of Business, Economic Development and Tourism.

SOILS

Soil Orders: Vollrath, N. and R. Gavenda. U.S. Department of Agriculture, Natural Resources Conservation Service, Honolulu and Kealakekua.

Annual Estimated Erosion Rates: National Resources Inventory Data, 1992. U.S. Department of Agriculture, Natural Resources Conservation Service, Honolulu.

Soil Weathering Over Time: Birkeland, P. W. 1984. *Soils and Geomorphology.* New York: Oxford University Press.

ASTRONOMY

Astronomical Facilities on Mauna Kea: Hall, D., University of Hawai'i, Institute for Astronomy.

BIOGEOGRAPHY

**Distributions of *Vaccinium, Metrosideros, and Sophora:* after Good, R. 1974. *The Geography of Flowering Plants,* 4th ed. London: Longmans.

Ocean Currents and Biodiversity: Grigg, R. W. 1994. Paleooceanography of coral reefs in the Hawaiian-Emperor chain. In *A Natural History of the Hawaiian Islands: Selected Readings II,* ed. E. A. Kay. Honolulu: University of Hawai'i Press.

Origins of Hawaiian Species: Fosberg, F. R. 1948. Derivation of the flora of the Hawaiian Islands. In *Insects of Hawaii* Vol. 1., ed. E. C. Zimmerman. Honolulu: University of Hawai'i Press.

EVOLUTION

Interisland Dispersal Events: 1. ***Drosophila,*** Carson, H. L. 1983. Chromosomal sequences and interisland colonizations in Hawaiian *Drosophila. Genetics* 103:465–482; 2. **Silversword,** Carr, G. D. et al. 1989. Speciation and the Founder Principle. In *Genetics, Speciation and the Founder Principle,* eds. L. V. Giddings et al. New York: Oxford University Press.

MARINE ECOSYSTEMS

New and Mature Volcanic Island and Atoll Profiles: Maragos, J. E., East-West Center Program on the Environment, Honolulu.

TERRESTRIAL ECOSYSTEMS

Native Ecosystems before Human Settlement: The Nature Conservancy, Honolulu.
Ecosystems Today: The Nature Conservancy, Honolulu.
Generalized Moisture Conditions: Gon, S., The Nature Conservancy, Honolulu.

BIRDS

Bird Species in the Hawaiian Islands, 1997 and Native Hawaiian Birds: Conant, S., University of Hawai'i, Department of Zoology.

NATIVE PLANTS

Hawaiian Plants—Endemic, Indigenous, and Alien: Lamoureux, C. H., University of Hawai'i, Lyon Arboretum

HAWAIIAN TREE SNAILS

O'ahu Tree Snails: Hadfield, M. G., University of Hawai'i, Kewalo Marine Laboratory.

ENDANGERED AND THREATENED SPECIES

Endangered Species Habitat: Mehrhoff, L. A., U.S. Fish and Wildlife Service, Portland, Oregon.
Status of Hawaiian Plants and Animals: Mehrhoff, L. A., U.S. Fish and Wildlife Service, Portland, Oregon.
Habitat Destruction since Human Settlement: The Nature Conservancy: Hawai'i Heritage Program. 1990.

PROTECTED AREAS

All maps: compiled from a variety of sources with the assistance of Hawai'i Office of State Planning, Nature Conservancy of Hawai'i, and State Department of Land and Natural Resources.

ARCHAEOLOGY

Major Archaeological Sites: Kirch, P. V., University of California, Department of Anthropology; Kirkendall, M. L., University of Hawai'i, Department of Anthropology.
Archaeological Sites of Moloka'i: Komori, E., State of Hawai'i, Department of Land and Natural Resources, State Historic Preservation Division.
Early Polynesian Settlement: Kirch, P. V., University of California, Department of Anthropology.

POLYNESIAN NAVIGATION

Hōkūle'a Voyages 1976–1992: Finney, B. 1980. In *Polynesian Seafaring Heritage,* eds. Lindo, C. K., and N. A. Mower. Honolulu: Kamehameha Schools; Kyselka, W. 1987. *An Ocean in Mind.* Honolulu: University of Hawai'i Press; Kilonsky, B., School of Ocean and Earth Sciences, University of Hawai'i; D. Kawaharada, Polynesian Voyaging Society.
1995 Voyages of Hōkūle'a, Hawai'iloa, and Makali'i: Kawaharada, D., Polynesian Voyaging Society.

ETHNOBOTANY

Important Plants Polynesians Brought to Hawai'i: Abbott, I., University of Hawai'i, Department of Botany. Compiled for classroom use by I. Abbott.

HISTORY

Sandalwood Exports to China: Bradley, H. W. 1968. *The American Frontier in Hawaii: The Pioneers 1789–1843.* Glouster, MA: Peter Smith; Gutzlaff, C. 1834. *A Sketch of Chinese History, Ancient and Modern,* Vol. 2. London: Smith, Elder, and Co.
Whaling Ship Visits to Hawai'i: Macdonald, B., Massey University, Palmerston North, New Zealand.
Population Change by Ethnicity, 1778–1990: State of Hawai'i. *State Data Book 1993–94. A Statistical Abstract.* Department of Business, Economic Development and Tourism; Lind, A. W. 1982. Immigration to Hawaii. *Social Processes in Hawaii, 29.*

POPULATION

Resident Population Growth: State of Hawai'i. *State Data Book 1993–94. A Statistical Abstract.* Department of Business, Economic Development and Tourism.
Shifts in Population Distribution by County: State of Hawai'i. *State Data Book 1993–94. A Statistical Abstract.* Department of Business, Economic Development and Tourism.
Crude Birth, Death, Infant Mortality Rates: State of Hawai'i. *State Data Book 1993–94. A Statistical Abstract.* Department of Business, Economic Development and Tourism.
Births to Unmarried Mothers: State of Hawai'i. *State Data Book 1993–94. A Statistical Abstract.* Department of Business, Economic Development and Tourism; U.S. National Center for Health Statistics, *Vital Statistics of the United States.*
Urban and Rural Population, 1990: State of Hawai'i. *State Data Book 1993–94. A Statistical Abstract.* Department of Business, Economic Development and Tourism.
Causes of Death in Hawai'i: State of Hawai'i. *State Data Book 1993–94. A Statistical Abstract.* Department of Business, Economic Development and Tourism.
Marriage and Divorce Rates: State of Hawai'i. *State Data Book 1993–94. A Statistical Abstract.* Department of Business, Economic Development and Tourism.
Population by Gender and Age: State of Hawai'i. *State Data Book 1993–94. A Statistical Abstract.* Department of Business, Economic Development and Tourism, for 1980–1993. Pre-1980, *Historical Statistics of Hawai'i.*
Ethnic Diversity by County, 1990: State of Hawai'i. *State Data Book 1993–94. A Statistical Abstract.* Department of Business, Economic Development and Tourism.
Population Density: State of Hawai'i. *State Data Book 1993–94. A Statistical Abstract.* Department of Business, Economic Development and Tourism.
Resident Population Place of Birth: *State Data Book 1993–94. A Statistical Abstract.* Department of Business, Economic Development and Tourism.
Marital Status: *State Data Book 1993–94. A Statistical Abstract.* Department of Business, Economic Development and Tourism.
Employment by County, 1991: State of Hawai'i. *State Data Book 1993–94. A Statistical Abstract.* Department of Business, Economic Development and Tourism.
Median Household Income: State of Hawai'i. *State Data Book 1993–94. A Statistical Abstract.* Department of Business, Economic Development and Tourism.
Population below the National Poverty Level: State of Hawai'i. *State Data Book 1993–94. A Statistical Abstract.* Department of Business, Economic Development and Tourism.
Foreign Immigrants to Hawai'i by Country of Birth: State of Hawai'i. *State Data Book 1993–94. A Statistical Abstract.* Department of Business, Economic Development and Tourism.
Birth Rate in Hawai'i by Ethnicity, 1992: State of Hawai'i, Department of Health.

LANGUAGES

Language Spoken at Home, 1990: State of Hawai'i. *State Data Book 1993–94. A Statistical Abstract.* Department of Business, Economic Development and Tourism.

RELIGION

All data compiled by Ramdas Lamb and Andrew Hartnett. Please note: all data here are a compilation of statistics and responses from state records, religious organizations, and individual members of religious organizations. Because some organizations declined to provide membership data and others are not registered as a religious organization, the data are based on available results.

Hawaiian Religion: Kanehele, E., and P. Kanehele, Hawai'i Community College.

MUSEUMS AND LIBRARIES

Hawai'i Museums and Related Organizations, 1995: Hawai'i Museums Association.

GOVERNMENT AND POLITICS

State Senatorial and Representative Districts: State of Hawai'i, 1991 Reapportionment Commission final report submitted to the 16th Legislature.

Exclusive Economic Zone Boundary of the Hawaiian Islands: *Proposed Marine Mineral Lease Sale in the Hawaiian Archipelago and Johnston Island:* U.S. Department of the Interior, 1987. Exclusive Economic Zone, and State of Hawai'i, Department of Planning and Economic Development.

LAND USE AND TENURE

Land Use Districts, 1995: State of Hawai'i, Office of State Planning.

Ceded Lands: *Office of Hawaiian Affairs Inventory and Acquisitions of Public Land Trusts.* Prepared for the Committee on Land and Sovereignty by PBR and the State Of Hawai'i. December 1, 1993.

Land Ownership in Hawai'i, 1968–1988: State of Hawai'i. *State Data Book 1993–94. A Statistical Abstract.* Department of Business, Economic Development and Tourism.

Hawaiian Home Lands Classification, 1995: State of Hawai'i, Department of Hawaiian Home Lands.

Land Use District Acreage by Island, 1995: State of Hawai'i. *State Data Book 1993–94. A Statistical Abstract.* Department of Business, Economic Development and Tourism.

URBAN CENTERS

All maps and graphs: U.S. Department of Commerce. *Census of Population, 1990.* Bureau of the Census.

ECONOMY

Foreign Merchandise Trade Flow, 1990: Bank of Hawai'i, Economics Department report, June 1995.

Consumer Price Inflation: U.S. Department of Labor, Bureau of Labor Statistics.

Average Annual Wages by County, 1994: Bank of Hawai'i, Economics Department report, June 1995.

Construction in Hawai'i: Bank of Hawai'i, Economics Department report June 1995.

Gross State and County Product by Industry Sector, 1992: Bank of Hawai'i, Economics Department report.

Industrial Dominance in Hawai'i, 1800–1995: Brewbaker, P., Bank of Hawai'i.

Annual Real Total Personal Income: U.S. Department of Commerce, Bureau of Economic Analysis.

Civilian Employment, 1985–1995: State of Hawai'i, Department of Labor and Industrial Relations.

Civilian Unemployment, 1985–1995: State of Hawai'i, Department of Labor and Industrial Relations.

Japanese Investment in Hawai'i: State of Hawai'i, Department of Business, Economic Development and Tourism; inflation and currency—adjusted by Bank of Hawai'i, Economics Department.

O'ahu Home Resale Values, 1960–1995: Honolulu Board of Realtors, Locations Research.

Hawai'i State Government General Fund, 1985–1995: State of Hawai'i, Department of Budget and Finance.

Private Building Permits Issued, 1995: Brewbaker, P., Bank of Hawai'i, Honolulu.

AGRICULTURE

Total Cropland and Farm Size: U.S. Department of Commerce. *Census of Agriculture, 1995.* Bureau of the Census.

Statewide Change in Major Crop Sales: U.S. Department of Agriculture. 1994. *Statistics of Hawaiian Agriculture.* Prepared by Hawaiian Agriculture Statistical Service. Honolulu.

Agricultural Contributions to GSP and Jobs: U.S. Department of Commerce. *Survey of Current Business.* July 1995.

Crop Sales by County, 1995: U. S. Department of Agriculture. 1995. *Statistics of Hawaiian Agriculture.* Hawaiian Agriculture Statistical Service. Honolulu.

Dairy and Livestock Sales by County, 1995: U.S. Department of Agriculture. 1995. *Statistics of Hawaiian Agriculture.* Hawaiian Agriculture Statistical Service. Honolulu.

Crop Acreage by County, 1995: U. S. Department of Agriculture. 1995. *Statistics of Hawaiian Agriculture.* Hawaiian Agriculture Statistical Service. Honolulu.

Statewide Change in Major Crop Acreage: U.S. Department of Agriculture. 1995. *Statistics of Hawaiian Agriculture.* Hawaiian Agriculture Statistical Service. Honolulu; U.S. Department of Commerce. *Census of Agriculture, 1990.* Bureau of the Census.

Hawaiian Sugarcane Production: Hawaiian Sugar Planters Association, *Hawaiian Sugar Manual.*

Major Agricultural Areas, 1996: U.S. Department of Agriculture. 1996. *Statistics of Hawaiian Agriculture.* Hawaiian Agriculture Statistical Service. Honolulu.

FOREST INDUSTRY

Koa Seedling Production by Hawai'i State Nursery: State of Hawai'i, Department of Land and Natural Resources. *Report to the Governor, 1981–92* and *1993–94.*

Forest Product Sales from State Forest Reserves: State of Hawai'i, Department of Land and Natural Resources. *Report to the Governor, 1981–92* and *1993–94.*

SUSTAINABLE AGRICULTURE

Sustainable Agriculture in Hawai'i: Johnson-Gary, M., U.S. Department of Agriculture, Natural Resources Conservation Service. Concept by S. Skipper.

FISHERIES

Commercial Fishery Landings, 1948–1994: Pooley, S., using National Marine Fisheries Service 1995 compilation, and Hawai'i Division of Aquatic Resources commercial catch reports.

Value of Commercial Fishery Landings, 1948–1994: Hawai'i Division of Aquatic Resources, 1994 commercial catch reports, compiled at port of landing by the National Marine Fisheries Service. Honolulu Laboratory.

Commercial Catch Landings, 1994: Pooley, S., using National Marine Fisheries Service 1995 compilation.

AQUACULTURE

Value of Aquaculture Production, 1994: State of Hawai'i, Department of Land and Natural Resources Aquaculture Development Program.

Aquaculture Industry Growth, 1979–1995: State of Hawai'i, Department of Land and Natural Resources Aquaculture Development Program.

THE MILITARY

Active Duty Military Personnel in Hawai'i: State of Hawai'i, Department of Business, Economic Development and Tourism.

Military Expenditures in Hawai'i: U.S. Bureau of the Census, *Statistical Abstract of the United States: 1993,* 113th ed, Washington, D.C.

Military Personnel in Active Service, 1994: State of Hawai'i, Department of Business, Economic Development and Tourism.

Military Installations, 1993: *Hawaii Military Installations and Facilities.* 1983 map prepared by the 29th Engineer Battalion, Fort Shafter, Hawai'i.

TOURISM

Condominium Availability, 1994: Hawai'i Visitors Bureau, Visitor Plant Inventory. 1994.

Visitors to Hawai'i, 1993—Places of Origin: Hawai'i Visitors Bureau. 1994. Annual Report of Visitor Statistics.

Visitor Arrivals to Hawai'i, 1970–1996: Hawai'i Visitors Bureau. 1996. *Annual Research Report.*

Daily Visitor-to-Resident Ratios by County, 1992: State of Hawai'i. *State Data Book 1993–94. A Statistical Abstract.* Department of Business, Economic Development and Tourism.

Hawai'i's Top 20 Visitor Attractions, 1993: State of Hawai'i. *State Data Book 1993–94. A Statistical Abstract.* Department of Business, Economic Development and Tourism.

Commercial Recreational Activities: GTE Hawaiian Telephone. 1995. Yellow Pages.

Calendar of Statewide Events: Hawai'i Visitors Bureau Event Calendar; GTE Hawaiian Telephone. 1995. Aloha Pages.

Visitor Accommodations Availability, 1994: Hawai'i Visitors Bureau. Visitor Plant Inventory. 1994.

Hotel Jobs by County, 1994: State of Hawai'i. 1995. *Labor Force Data Book.* Department of Labor and Industrial Relations.

Monthly Visitors by County, 1995: Hawai'i Visitors Bureau 1995: various monthly reports.

Westbound Visitor Characteristics, 1980–1993: Hawai'i Visitors Bureau. 1996. *Annual Research Report.*

Visitor Spending in Hawai'i, 1993: Hawai'i Visitors Bureau. 1994. *Hawaii Visitor Expenditures: An Annual Report.*

ENERGY

Imported Petroleum, 1996: State of Hawai'i, Department of Business, Economic Development and Tourism. Energy, Resources, and Technology Division.

County Electricity Generation by Fuel Type, 1995: State of Hawai'i, Department of Business, Economic Development and Tourism. Energy, Resources, and Technology Division.

Electricity Generation by Fuel Type: State of Hawai'i, Department of Business, Economic Development and Tourism. Energy, Resources, and Technology Division.

Energy Production and Consumption in Hawai'i, 1994: State of Hawai'i, Department of Business, Economic Development and Tourism. Energy, Resources, and Technology Division.

TRANSPORTATION

Total Vehicles Registered by County, 1994: State of Hawai'i. *State Data Book 1993–94. A Statistical Abstract.* Department of Business, Economic Development and Tourism.

Registered Motor Vehicles by County, 1950–1994: State of Hawai'i. *State Data Book 1993–94. A Statistical Abstract.* Department of Business, Economic Development and Tourism.

Persons per Vehicle, 1941–1991: State of Hawai'i. *State Data Book 1993–94. A Statistical Abstract.* Department of Business, Economic Development and Tourism.

Gallons of Gasoline Used per Vehicle, 1980 vs. 1993: State of Hawai'i. *State Data Book 1993–94. A Statistical Abstract.* Department of Business, Economic Development and Tourism.

Vehicle-Miles per Highway Miles, 1994: State of Hawai'i. *State Data Book 1993–94. A Statistical Abstract.* A Statistical Abstract. Department of Business, Economic Development and Tourism.

Major Weekly Outbound Flights, Jan. 1993: State of Hawai'i. *State Data Book 1993–94. A Statistical Abstract.* Department of Business, Economic Development and Tourism.

Major Interisland Flights and Airports, 1994: State of Hawai'i, Department of Transportation, Airports Division.

Maritime Cargo Tonnage by Port and Major Components, 1993: State of Hawai'i. *State Data Book 1993–94. A Statistical Abstract.* Department of Business, Economic Development and Tourism.

Shipment Tonnage at Port of Honolulu: State of Hawai'i. *State Data Book 1993–94. A Statistical Abstract.* Department of Business, Economic Development and Tourism.

Cargo Tonnage by Major Port, 1990: State of Hawai'i. 1994. *State Data Book 1993–94. A Statistical Abstract.* Department of Business, Economic Development and Tourism.

Direct Nonstop Flights from Hawai'i, 1995: State of Hawai'i. Department of Transportation, Airports Division; *State Data Book 1993–94. A Statistical Abstract.* Department of Business, Economic Development and Tourism.

COMMUNICATIONS

Pacific Cable and Satellite Network, 1995: Ogden, M., University of Hawai'i, Department of Communication.

State Periodicals—General and Special Interest, 1995: Individual publishers provided circulation data.

Communication Networks, January 1996: Information Technology Service, University of Hawai'i.

Major Television Stations in Hawaii, June 1995: *Broadcasting and Cable Yearbook 1996.* Washington: Broadcasting Publications.

Radio Stations of Hawai'i by County, 1995: *Broadcasting Yearbook 1996.* Washington: Broadcasting Publications.

Cable Television Subscribers, 1995: *Broadcasting Yearbook 1996.* Washington: Broadcasting Publications.

Wireless Communication Coverage, 1996: Information Technology Service, University of Hawai'i.

EDUCATION

School Enrollment by District, 1986–1992: State of Hawai'i, Department of Education, Office of the Superintendent, Planning and Evaluation Branch: *The Superintendent's Fourth Annual Report on School Performance in Hawai'i.* Oct. 1993.

Public and Private Enrollment, 1986–1992: State of Hawai'i, Department of Education, Office of the Superintendent, Planning and Evaluation Branch: *The Superintendent's Fourth Annual Report on School Performance in Hawai'i.* Oct. 1993.

Classroom Availability by School District, 1993–1994: State of Hawai'i, Department of Education, Office of Business Services, Facilities and Support Services Branch: *State Classroom Utilization Report, 1994–95.*

Adult Education Enrollment: State of Hawai'i, Department of Education, Community Services Section: *Semester Summary of Classes and Enrollment, Community School for Adults, 1993–94.*

Expenditures per Student, 1959–1994: U.S. Bureau of the Census, *Statistical Abstract of the United States: 1993,* 113th ed, Washington, D.C.

Student Ethnicity by School District, 1993–1994: State of Hawai'i, Department of Education, Office of the Superintendent, Evaluation Section, 1994: *School Improvement Data Base.*

University of Hawai'i Ethnic Constituency, 1994–1995: University of Hawai'i, Institutional Research Office, Fall 1994, *Faculty and Staff Report.* Spring 1994, *Spring Enrollment Report.*

College Enrollment: University of Hawai'i, Institutional Research Office. Spring 1994, *Spring Enrollment Report.*

Degrees Awarded: University of Hawai'i, Institutional Research Office.

Accredited Universities and Colleges, 1992–93: individual institutions provided data.

Educational Attainment, 1990: State of Hawai'i, Department of Business, Economic Development and Tourism. *Profile of Rural Hawai'i.* May 1994.

Classroom Teacher Ethnicity, 1945 and 1995: Hawai'i State Teachers Association: *Summary—Certified Personnel by Ethnic Category and Sex,* Nov. 1994.

HEALTH AND WELLNESS

Health Risk Behavior, 1993: State of Hawai'i. 1995. *Hawaii's Health Risk Behaviors 1992.* Department of Health; U.S. Centers for Disease Control, 1993. *BRFSS Summary Prevalence Report.*

Alcohol Consumption, 1993: State of Hawai'i. 1995. *Hawaii's Health Risk Behaviors 1992.* Department of Health; U.S. Centers for Disease Control, 1993. *BRFSS Summary Prevalence Report.*

Health Risk Behavior by Ethnicity, 1993: State of Hawai'i. 1995. *Hawaii's Health Risk Behaviors 1992.* Department of Health; U.S. Centers for Disease Control, 1993. *BRFSS Summary Prevalence Report.*

Alcohol Consumption by Ethnicity, 1993: State of Hawai'i. 1995. *Hawaii's Health Risk Behaviors 1992.* Department of Health; U.S. Centers for Disease Control, 1993. *BRFSS Summary Prevalence Report.*

Diagnosed AIDS Cases by County, 1996: State of Hawai'i. 1996. *AIDS Surveillance Quarterly Report.* Office of State Planning and Department of Health.

Communicable Diseases, 1991: State of Hawai‘i, Department of Health; U.S. Public Health Service.

Self-Reported Chronic Conditions, 1992: State of Hawai‘i, Department of Health; U.S. Public Health Service.

Distribution of Physicians and Nurses, 1994: State of Hawai‘i. *State Data Book 1993–94. A Statistical Abstract.* Department of Business, Economic Development and Tourism.

Hospital and Care Home Bed Capacity: State of Hawai‘i. *State Data Book 1993–94. A Statistical Abstract.* Department of Business, Economic Development and Tourism.

Physical Abuse and Neglect: State of Hawai‘i, Department of Human Services.

Food Stamp Distribution, 1994: State of Hawai‘i. Food Stamp Program Monthly Summary, Department of Human Services.

CRIME

Reported Offenses by County, 1996: State of Hawai‘i, Attorney General's Office.

Major Offenses Reported in Hawai‘i, 1984–1992: Federal Bureau of Investigation. 1995. *Uniform Crime Report.* U.S. Department of Justice, Washington, D.C.

Correctional Facility Population, 1995: Facility counts provided by each facility to State of Hawai‘i, Department of Public Safety.

RECREATION

Game Animal Harvest, 1993: State of Hawai‘i, Department of Land and Natural Resources. *Report to the Governor 1993–94.*

University of Hawai‘i–Mānoa Sports Events Attendance: State of Hawai‘i. *State Data Book 1993–94. A Statistical Abstract.* Department of Business, Economic Development and Tourism.

Registration in Honolulu Marathon and Ironman Triathlon: State of Hawai‘i. *State Data Book 1993–94. A Statistical Abstract.* Department of Business, Economic Development and Tourism.

Golf Courses in Hawai‘i: Professional Golfer's Association. *Hawaii Golf Guide 1996–97.*

Recreational Activities: Professional Golfer's Association *Hawaii Golf Guide 1996–97;* Chisholm, C. 1991. *Hawaiian Hiking Trails.* Lake Oswego, OR: The Fernglen Press; Clark, John R. K. 1987. *Statewide Recreation Resources Inventory: Principal Bodysurfing Sites.* State Department of Land and Natural Resources. Division of State Parks, Outdoor Recreation and Historic Sites.

ENVIRONMENTAL QUALITY

Highly Stressed Ecosystems, 1992: State of Hawai‘i. 1992. *Environmental Risks to Hawaii's Public Health and Ecosystems.* A report to the Hawai‘i Environmental Risk Ranking Study by the East-West Center and Department of Health.

Water Quality and Contamination: State of Hawai‘i, Groundwater Protection Program and Office of Environmental Planning, Department of Health; Hawai‘i Coastal Zone Management Program, Office of State Planning.

GOVERNMENT SERVICES

Government Services: County police and fire departments of individual counties; State of Hawai‘i, Department of Health.

Hawai‘i Civil Defense System Organization: State of Hawai‘i, Department of Defense, Office of the Director of Civil Defense.

GAZETTEER

Alphabetical listing of place names on the reference maps, pages 1 through 25.

The first number to the right of each entry identifies the map page on which the entry appears. The letter and number combination refers to the approximate coordinates for that site on the map. Coordinates usually refer to the full-size maps, rather than the inset maps, unless the place name is shown only on the inset map.

Island abbreviations following each entry are as follows: Ha = Hawai‘i, Kah = Kaho‘olawe, Ka = Kaua‘i, La = Lāna‘i, Ma = Maui, Mo = Moloka‘i, Ni = Ni‘ihau, NWHI = Northwestern Hawaiian Islands, and Oa = O‘ahu.

A place name in parentheses is an alternative for the preceding name; it is not necessarily a less-preferred name. Thus, "Chinaman's Hat (Mokoli‘i I.)" are both names for the small island off windward O‘ahu and are cross-referenced as "Mokoli‘i I. (Chinaman's Hat)."

Repeated entries with different coordinates refer to distinct geographical entities that share the same name. The spelling of place names in most cases follows Pukui, Elbert, and Mookini's *Place Names of Hawaii* and Pukui and Elbert's *Hawaiian Dictionary.*

A

‘A‘ahoaka, Ka . . . 5 . . . E6
‘A‘ahuwela, Ha . . . 19 . . . E1
‘A‘akaki‘i Gul., Oa . . . 8 . . . D4
A‘akukui Ridge, Ka . . . 5 . . . F3
A‘akukui Val., Ka . . . 5 . . . F3
‘A‘āwela, Ka . . . 5 . . . E4
Adams Bay, NWHI . . . 24 . . . H7
‘Āhihi Bay, Ma . . . 15 . . . G3
‘Āhihi Pt., Ka . . . 5 . . . D6
Āhole Rock, Ma . . . 15 . . . G7
‘Āhua‘elikū, Ka . . . 5 . . . F4
Āhualoa, Ha . . . 18 . . . C7
Āhualoa Gul., Ha . . . 18 . . . C7
‘Āhuimanu, Oa . . . 8 . . . E5
‘Āhuimanu Str., Oa . . . 8 . . . E5
Ahukini Pt., Ka . . . 5 . . . E6
Ahuloa, Ha . . . 20 . . . G3
Ahumoa, Ha . . . 18 . . . B4
Ahumoa, Ha . . . 18 . . . E6
Ahu o Laka I., Oa . . . 8 . . . E5
Ahupū, Kah . . . 15 . . . G1
Ahupū Bay, Kah . . . 15 . . . G1
Ahupū Gul., Kah . . . 15 . . . G1
Ahupūiki Gul., Kah . . . 15 . . . G1
‘Aiea, Oa . . . 8 . . . F4
‘Aiea Bay, Oa . . . 9 . . . E1
‘Aiea Hts., Oa . . . 8 . . . F4
‘Aiea Str., Oa . . . 8 . . . F5
‘Aikahi Park, Oa . . . 9 . . . D6
‘Āina Haina, Oa . . . 8 . . . G6
‘Āinahou, Ha . . . 18 . . . B6
‘Āinahou, Ha . . . 19 . . . G1
‘Āinakoa, Oa . . . 9 . . . G5
‘Āinaloa, Ha . . . 21 . . . C5
‘Āina Moana (Magic I.), Oa . . . 9 . . . H3
‘Āinapō, Ha . . . 20 . . . D7
‘Āinapō, Ha . . . 21 . . . D1
‘Āinapō Trail, Ha . . . 20 . . . D7
‘Āinapō Trail, Ha . . . 21 . . . D1
‘Akahipu‘u, Ha . . . 18 . . . F3
‘Akahukaimu, Ha . . . 18 . . . D3
‘Akaka Falls, Ha . . . 19 . . . E3
Akasaki Camp, Ha . . . 19 . . . C2
‘Akihi, Ha . . . 20 . . . G5
Āko‘ako‘a Pt., Ha . . . 18 . . . A5
‘Alaeloa Pt., Ma . . . 15 . . . C1
Alahaka Bay, Ha . . . 20 . . . D3
Alakaha, Ha . . . 20 . . . G6
Alakaha Pt., Ha . . . 19 . . . C2
Alakahi Str., Ha . . . 18 . . . C5
Alaka‘i Swamp, Ka . . . 5 . . . D4
Alakukui Pt., Ka . . . 5 . . . E6
‘Alalā (lava flow), Ha . . . 20 . . . D6
‘Alalākeiki Channel . . . 15 . . . G2
Alāla Pt., Oa . . . 8 . . . F6
Ala Moana Beach, Oa . . . 9 . . . G3
Alanahihi Pt., Ha . . . 18 . . . A4
Alapi‘i Pt., Ka . . . 5 . . . D2
‘Ālau I., Ma . . . 15 . . . F7
‘Ale‘ale, Kah . . . 15 . . . H2
‘Āle‘ale‘a Pt., Ha . . . 19 . . . F4
Alekoko (Menehune Fishpond), Ka . . . 5 . . . F6
‘Ālelele Str., Ma . . . 15 . . . F6
‘Alenaio Str., Ha . . . 19 . . . F4
‘Alenuihāhā Channel, Ma . . . 15 . . . G6
‘Ālewa Hts., Oa . . . 9 . . . F3
Alexander Res., Ka . . . 5 . . . F4
Āliaiki Lake, Ni . . . 4 . . . G5
‘Āliamanu Crater, Oa . . . 8 . . . F5
Āliapa‘akai (Salt Lake), Oa . . . 8 . . . F4
Ālia Pt., Ha . . . 19 . . . E4
Ālia Str., Ha . . . 19 . . . E4
Ali‘i Fishpond, Mo . . . 12 . . . C4
‘Ālika (lava flow), Ha . . . 20 . . . E4
‘Ālika Bay, Ha . . . 20 . . . E3
‘Ālika Cone, Ha . . . 20 . . . E5
Aluea Rocks, Ma . . . 15 . . . E6
‘Amikopala, Mo . . . 12 . . . B3
‘Anaeho‘omalu, Ha . . . 18 . . . D3
‘Anaeho‘omalu Bay, Ha . . . 18 . . . D3
‘Anaeho‘omalu Pt., Ha . . . 18 . . . D3
Anahaki Gul., Mo . . . 12 . . . B3
Anahola, Ka . . . 5 . . . D6
Anahola Bay, Ka . . . 5 . . . D6
Anahola Str., Ka . . . 5 . . . D6
Anahulu Str., Oa . . . 8 . . . D3
Anakaluahine Gul., Ma . . . 15 . . . C2
Ana Noio (cave), Mo . . . 12 . . . B5
Anapālau Pt., Ka . . . 5 . . . D6
Ana Puka (cave), Ha . . . 19 . . . F5
Ana Puka (cave), Ma . . . 15 . . . E7
Anapuka (cave), Mo . . . 12 . . . A2
Andrade Camp, Ha . . . 19 . . . E4
Anianikeha, Mo . . . 12 . . . B4
‘Anini Beach, Ka . . . 5 . . . C5
Anipe‘ahi, Ha . . . 20 . . . D7
Annexation Hill, NWHI . . . 24 . . . D6
Apakuie, Ha . . . 19 . . . D1
Āpana Val., Ni . . . 4 . . . F5
Apole Pt., Ma . . . 15 . . . G6
‘Āpua, Ha . . . 18 . . . B5
‘Āpua Pt., Ha . . . 21 . . . E3
‘Au‘au Channel, La . . . 12 . . . E6
‘Au‘au Pt., Ha . . . 20 . . . E3
‘Auwae, Ha . . . 21 . . . B5
‘Auwaiakeakua Gul., Ha . . . 18 . . . D4, E5
Awaawaloa (Mt. Olympus), Oa . . . 8 . . . F6
Awa‘awapuhi Val., Ka . . . 5 . . . D3
Awake‘e Bay, Ha . . . 18 . . . E2
Awalua Beach, Ma . . . 15 . . . E1
Awāwakāhao (str.), Ha . . . 20 . . . G5
‘Āwehi, La . . . 12 . . . E6
‘Āwehi Gul., La . . . 12 . . . E6
‘Āwehi Str., Ha . . . 19 . . . F3
‘Āwili Pt., Ha . . . 20 . . . G4
‘Āwīni Falls, Ka . . . 5 . . . D3

B

Barbers Pt. (Kalaeloa), Oa . . . 8 . . . G3
Barbers Pt. Housing, Oa . . . 8 . . . F3
Barbers Pt. NAS, Oa . . . 8 . . . G3
Bare I., NWHI . . . 24 . . . B6
Barking Sands Beach (Keonekani o Nohili), Ka . . . 5 . . . D2
Barking Sands Pacific Missile Range, Ka . . . 5 . . . E2
Beck Cove, Kah . . . 15 . . . H2
Bellows Air Force Station, Oa . . . 8 . . . F6
Big Hill Camp, Ha . . . 20 . . . D4
Bird I., NWHI . . . 24 . . . H2
Black Pt. (Kūpikipiki‘ō Pt.), Oa . . . 8 . . . G6
Blonde Reef, Ha . . . 19 . . . A6

C

Captain Cook, Ha . . . 20 . . . C3
Carter Pt., Ka . . . 5 . . . F6
Chain of Craters, Ha . . . 21 . . . D3
Chinaman's Hat (Mokoli‘i I.), Oa . . . 8 . . . E5
Coconut I. (Mokuola), Ha . . . 19 . . . A5
Coconut I. (Moku o Lo‘e), Oa . . . 8 . . . E6
Cook Pt., Ha . . . 20 . . . C3
Crater Hill (Kīlauea), Ka . . . 5 . . . C5
Crater Res., Ma . . . 15 . . . D1
Crestview, Oa . . . 8 . . . F3
Crouching Lion (Kauhi‘īmakaokalani), Oa . . . 8 . . . D5

D

De Mello Reservoir, Ka . . . 5 . . . A2
Devil Country, Ha . . . 18 . . . G4
Dewey Cone, Ha . . . 18 . . . H7
Diamond Head (Lē‘ahi), Oa . . . 8 . . . G5
Diamond Head Beach, Oa . . . 9 . . . H5
Dillingham Airfield, Oa . . . 8 . . . D1
Disappearing I., NWHI . . . 24 . . . C6
Disappearing Sands Beach, Ha . . . 18 . . . G2
Dowsett Highlands, Oa . . . 9 . . . F4
Dowsett Reef, NWHI . . . 24 . . . H5

E

Eastern I., NWHI . . . 24 . . . E2
East I., NWHI . . . 24 . . . B6
East Loch, Oa . . . 8 . . . F4
East Rift Zone, Ha . . . 21 . . . D4
‘Eke, Ha . . . 18 . . . C5
‘Eke Crater, Ma . . . 15 . . . D2
‘Ele‘ele, Ka . . . 5 . . . F4
‘Elehāhā Str., Oa . . . 8 . . . C3
‘Eleuweuwe, Mo . . . 12 . . . B4
Elevenmile Homestead, Ha . . . 21 . . . B4
Enchanted Lake, Oa . . . 9 . . . E6
‘Enuhe Ridge, Ha . . . 20 . . . F6
‘Ewa Beach, Oa . . . 8 . . . F4
‘Ewa Gentry, Oa . . . 8 . . . F3
‘Ewa Vil., Oa . . . 8 . . . F3

F

Farrington Hwy., Oa . . . 8 . . . E1
Fernandez Vil., Oa . . . 8 . . . F3
Fern Forest Vacation Estates, Ha . . . 21 . . . C3
Fern Grotto, Ka . . . 5 . . . E6
Flat I. (Popoi‘a I.), Oa . . . 8 . . . F6
Fleming's (Kapalua) Beach, Ma . . . 15 . . . C1
Ford I. (Moku‘ume‘ume), Oa . . . 8 . . . F4
Fort DeRussy Military Res., Oa . . . 9 . . . H4
Fort Kamehameha Military Res., Oa . . . 9 . . . F1
Fort Ruger Military Res., Oa . . . 9 . . . H5
Fort Shafter, Oa . . . 9 . . . F2
French Frigate Shoals, NWHI . . . 24 . . . E4
Frigate Pt., NWHI . . . 24 . . . F1

G

Garden of the Gods, La . . . 12 . . . D4
Gardner Pinnales, NWHI . . . 24 . . . D3
Gin I., NWHI . . . 24 . . . B6
Glenwood (Kapu‘euhi), Ha . . . 21 . . . C3
Goat I. (Moku‘auia), Oa . . . 8 . . . C4
Gooney Spit I., NWHI . . . 24 . . . F2
Grass I., NWHI . . . 24 . . . H1
Great Crack, Ha . . . 21 . . . E1
Great Wall of Kuakini, Ha . . . 20 . . . D2
Green I., NWHI . . . 24 . . . B2
Green Lake (Wai a Pele), Ha . . . 21 . . . C6
Green Sand Beach (Papakōlea), Ha . . . 20 . . . H6
Greenwell Ranch (Pu‘u Lehua Ranch), Ha . . . 18 . . . H4

H

H1, Oa . . . 8 . . . F3, F4
H2, Oa . . . 8 . . . B7, E4
H3, Oa . . . 8 . . . F5
Ha‘akoa Str., Ha . . . 19 . . . D2
Hā‘ao Val., Ni . . . 4 . . . F5
Hā‘ele‘ele Ridge, Ka . . . 5 . . . D2
Hā‘ele‘ele Val., Ka . . . 5 . . . D2
Hā‘ena, Ha . . . 18 . . . A3
Hā‘ena, Ha . . . 21 . . . A5
Hā‘ena, Ka . . . 5 . . . C4